CCNA SECURITY

Implementing Cisco Network Security Exam (210-260)

Technology Workbook

www.ipspecialist.net

Document Control

Proposal Name	:	CCNA Security
Document Version	:	Version 2
Document Release Date	:	10th-Feb-2019
Reference	:	210-260

Feedback:

If you have any comments regarding the quality of this book, or otherwise alter it to better suit your needs, you can contact us through email at info@ipspecialist.net

Please make sure to include the book's title and ISBN in your message.

About IPSpecialist

IPSPECIALIST LTD. IS COMMITTED TO EXCELLENCE AND DEDICATED TO YOUR SUCCESS.

Our philosophy is to treat our customers like family. We want you to succeed, and we are willing to do everything possible to help you make it happen. We have the proof to back up our claims. We strive to accelerate billions of careers with great courses, accessibility, and affordability. We believe that continuous learning and knowledge evolution are the most important things to keep re-skilling and up-skilling the world.

Planning and creating a specific goal is where IPSpecialist helps. We can create a career track that suits your visions as well as develop the competencies you need to become a professional Network Engineer. We can also assist you with the execution and evaluation of your proficiency level, based on the career track you choose, as they are customized to fit your specific goals.

We help you STAND OUT from the crowd through our detailed IP training content packages.

Course Features:

- Self-Paced Learning
    - Learn at your own pace and in your own time
- Covers Complete Exam Blueprint
    - Prep-up for the exam with confidence
- Case Study Based Learning
    - Relate the content with real life scenarios
- Subscriptions that Suits You
    - Get more and pay less with IPS subscriptions
- Career Advisory Services
    - Let the industry experts plan your career journey
- Virtual Labs to test your skills
    - With IPS vRacks, you can evaluate your exam preparations
- Practice Questions
    - Practice questions to measure your preparation standards
- On Request Digital Certification
    - On request digital certification from IPSpecialist LTD

About the Authors:

This book has been compiled with the help of multiple professional engineers. These engineers specialize in different fields e.g. Networking, Security, Cloud, Big Data, IoT etc. Each engineer develops content in his/her own specialized field that is compiled to form a comprehensive certification guide.

About the Technical Reviewers:

Nouman Ahmed Khan

AWS-Architect, CCDE, CCIEX5 (R&S, SP, Security, DC, Wireless), CISSP, CISA, CISM, Nouman Ahmed Khan is a Solution Architect working with a major telecommunication provider in Qatar. He works with enterprises, mega-projects, and service providers to help them select the best-fit technology solutions. He also works as a consultant to understand customer business processes and helps select an appropriate technology strategy to support business goals. He has more than 14 years of experience working in Pakistan/Middle-East & UK. He holds a Bachelor of Engineering Degree from NED University, Pakistan, and M.Sc. in Computer Networks from the UK.

Abubakar Saeed

Abubakar Saeed has more than twenty-five years of experience, managing, consulting, designing, and implementing large-scale technology projects, extensive experience heading ISP operations, solutions integration, heading Product Development, Pre-sales, and Solution Design. Emphasizing on adhering to Project timelines and delivering as per customer expectations, he always leads the project in the right direction with his innovative ideas and excellent management skills.

Muhammad Yousuf

Muhammad Yousuf is a professional technical content writer. He is Cisco Certified Network Associate in Routing and Switching, holding bachelor's degree in Telecommunication Engineering from Sir Syed University of Engineering and Technology. He has both technical knowledge and industry sounding information, which he uses perfectly in his career.

Free Resources:

With each workbook bought from Amazon, IPSpecialist offers free resources to our valuable customers. Once you buy this book, you will have to contact us at support@ipspecialist.net or tweet @ipspecialistnet to get this limited time offer without any extra charges.

Free Resources Include:

Exam Practice Questions in Quiz Simulation:

IP Specialists' Practice Questions have been developed keeping in mind the certification exam perspective. The collection of these questions from our technology workbooks is prepared keeping the exam blueprint in mind, covering not only important but necessary topics as well. It is an ideal document to practice and revise your certification.

Career Report:

This report is a step-by-step guide for a novice who wants to develop his/her career in the field of computer networks. It answers the following queries:

- Current scenarios and future prospects
- Is this industry moving towards saturation or are new opportunities knocking at the door?
- What will the monetary benefits be?
- Why to get certified?
- How to plan and when will I complete the certifications if I start today?
- Is there any career track that I can follow to accomplish specialization level?

Furthermore, this guide provides a comprehensive career path towards being a specialist in the field of networking and highlights the tracks needed to obtain certification.

IPS Personalized Technical Support for Customers:

Good customer service means helping customers efficiently, in a friendly manner. It is essential to be able to handle issues for customers and do your best to ensure that they are satisfied. Providing good service is one of the most important things that can set your business apart from the others of its kind.

Great customer service will result in attracting more customers and attain the maximum customer retention.

IPS is offering personalized TECH support to its customers to provide better value for money. If you have any queries related to technology and labs, you can simply ask our technical team for assistance via Live Chat or Email.

Become an Author & Earn with Us:

If you are interested in becoming an author and start earning passive income, IPSpecialist offers "Earn with us" program. We all consume, develop and create content during our learning process, certification exam preparations, and during searching, developing and refining our professional careers. That content, notes, guides, worksheets and flip cards among other material is normally for our own reference without any defined structure or special considerations required for formal publishing. IPSpecialist can help you craft this 'draft' content into a fine product with the help of our global team of experts. We sell your content via different channels as:

1. Amazon – Kindle
2. eBay
3. LuLu
4. Kobo
5. Google Books
6. Udemy and many 3rd party publishers and resellers

Our Products

Technology Workbooks

IPSpecialist Technology workbooks are the ideal guides to developing the hands-on skills necessary to pass the exam. Our workbook covers official exam blueprint and explains the technology with real life case study based labs. The content covered in each workbook consists of individually focused technology topics presented in an easy-to-follow, goal-oriented, systematic approach. Every scenario features detailed breakdowns and thorough verifications to help you completely understand the task and associated technology.

We extensively used mind maps in our workbooks to explain visually the technology. Our workbooks have become a widely used tool to learn and remember the information effectively.

vRacks

Our highly scalable and innovative virtualized lab platforms let you practice the IP Specialist Technology Workbook at your own time and your own place as per your convenience.

Quick Reference Sheets

Our quick reference sheets are a concise bundling of condensed notes of the complete exam blueprint. It is an ideal and handy document to help you remember the most important technology concepts related to the certification exam.

Practice Questions

IP Specialists' Practice Questions are dedicatedly designed from a certification exam perspective. The collection of these questions from our technology workbooks is prepared keeping the exam blueprint in mind covering not only important but necessary topics as well. It is an ideal document to practice and revise your certification.

Content at a glance

Table of Contents

About this Workbook

This workbook covers all the information you need to pass the Cisco CCNA 210-260 exam. The workbook is designed to take a practical approach of learning with real life examples and case studies.

- Covers complete CCNA blueprint
- Summarized content
- Case Study based approach
- Ready to practice labs on Virtualized Environment
- 100% pass guarantee
- Mind maps
- Free resources

About the CCNA Exam

- Exam Number: 210-260 CCNA
- Associated Certifications: CCNA Security
- **Duration:** 90 minutes (60-70 questions)
- Exam Registration: Pearson VUE

The Cisco Certified Network Associate (CCNA) Security composite exam (210-260) is a 90-minute, 60–70 question assessment that is associated with the CCNA Security certification. This exam tests a candidate's knowledge and skills related to the secured network infrastructure, understanding core security concepts, managing secured access, VPN encryption, firewalls, intrusion prevention, web and email content security, and endpoint security. The following topics are general guidelines for the content likely to be included on the exam

➢ Security Concepts	12%
➢ Secure Access	14%
➢ VPN	17%
➢ Secure Routing and Switching	18%
➢ Cisco Firewall Technologies	18%
➢ IPS	9%
➢ Content and Endpoint Security	12%

Note: Complete list of topics covered in the CCNA Security 210-260 exam can be downloaded from here.

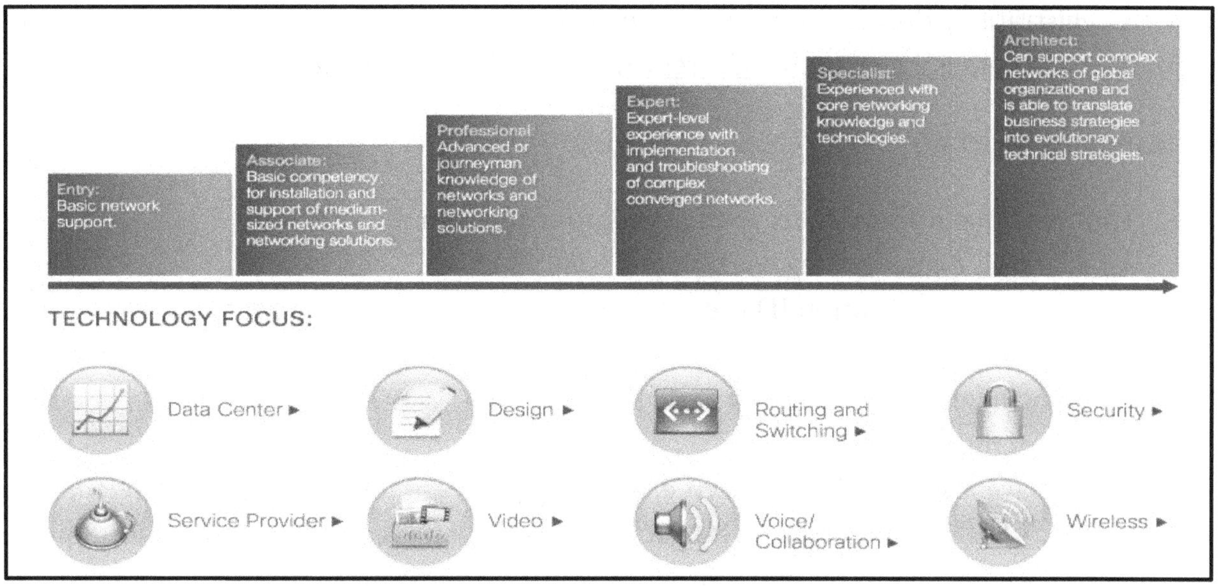

Figure 1: Cisco Certifications Skill Matrix

How to become CCNA Security?

Step 1: Pre-requisites

Any valid Cisco CCENT, CCNA Routing and Switching, or any CCIE certification can act as a pre-requisite.

Step2: Preparation for the CCNA Exam

Exam preparation can be accomplished through self-study with textbooks, practice exams, and on-site classroom programs. This workbook provides you all the information and knowledge to help you pass the CCNA Exam. Your study will be divided into two distinct parts:

- Understanding the technologies as per exam blueprint
- Implementing and practicing the technologies on Cisco hardware

IPSpecialist provides full support to the candidates in order for them to pass the exam.

Step 3: Register for the exam

Certification exams are offered at locations throughout the world. To register for an exam, contact the authorized test delivery partner of Cisco, *Pearson VUE*, who will administer the exam in a secured, proctored environment.

Prior to registration, decide which exam to take, note the exam name and number. For complete exam details, refer to the "Current Exam List" from the Cisco website.

Other important details to note are the following:

1. Your personal information are required prior to exam registration:
   a. Legal name (from government issued ID)
   b. Cisco Certification ID (i.e. CSCO00000001) or Test ID number
   c. Company name
   d. Valid e-mail address
   e. Method of payment
2. If you have already taken a Cisco exam before, please locate your Cisco Certification ID (i.e. CSCO00000001) before continuing with your registration to avoid duplicate records and delays in receiving proper credit for your exams.
3. A valid e-mail is required during exam registration. Cisco requires this in order to send e-mail reminders when a candidate's certification is about to expire, confirm the mailing address before shipping out the certificate, and to inform candidates if their certificate was returned due to an incorrect address.
4. Pearson VUE is the authorized test delivery partner of Cisco. You may register online, by telephone, or by walk in (where available).

How much does an exam cost?

Computer-based certification exam prices (written exam) depend on the scope and the exam length. You may refer to the "Exam Pricing" page on the Cisco website for complete details.

Step 4: Getting the Results

After you complete an exam at an authorized testing center, you will get immediate, online notification of your passed or failed status, a printed examination score report that indicates your pass or fail status, and your exam results by section.

Congratulations! You are now CCNA Security Certified.

Cisco Certifications

Cisco Systems, Inc. specializes in networking and communication products and services. A leader in global technology, the company is best known for its business routing and switching products that direct data, voice, and video traffic across networks worldwide.

Cisco also offers one of the most comprehensive vendor-specific certification programs in the world, the *Cisco Career Certification Program.* The program has six (6) levels, which begins at the Entry level and then advances to Associate, Professional, and Expert levels. For some certifications, the program closes at the Architect level.

Cisco Certification Tracks

Certification Tracks	Entry	Associate	Professional	Expert	Architect
Collaboration				CCIE Collaboration	
Data Center		CCNA Data Center	CCNP Data Center	CCIE Data Center	
Design	CCENT	CCDA	CCDP	CCDE	CCAr
Routing & Switching	CCENT	CCNA Routing and Switching	CCNP	CCIE Routing & Switching	
Security	CCENT	CCNA Security	CCNP Security	CCIE Security	
Service Provider		CCNA Service Provider	CCNP Service Provider	CCIE Service Provider	
Service Provider Operations	CCENT	CCNA Service Provider Operations	CCNP Service Provider Operations	CCIE Service Provider Operations	
Video		CCNA Video			
Voice	CCENT	CCNA Voice	CCNP Voice	CCIE Voice	
Wireless	CCENT	CCNA Wireless	CCNP Wireless	CCIE Wireless	

Figure 2: Cisco Certification Track

How does Cisco certifications help?

Cisco certifications are a de facto standard in networking industry, which helps you boost your career in the following ways:

1. Gets your foot in the door by launching your IT career
2. Boosts your confidence level

3. Proves knowledge, which helps improve employment opportunities

As for companies, Cisco certifications are a way to:

1. Screen job applicants
2. Validate the technical skills of the candidate
3. Ensure quality, competency, and relevancy
4. Improve organization credibility and customer's loyalty
5. Meet the requirement in maintaining organization partnership level with OEMs
6. Help in job retention and promotion

Chapter 01: Security Concepts

Security Principles

These days one of the most prominent topics in the news is network security or network attack. One after another, network has been compromising due to insufficient network security policies. But the question is; why network security is so important? Network security is directly related to the continuity of any organization's business. These attacks can cause:

- Loss of business data in any organization
- Interrupt and misuse of people's privacy
- Threaten and compromise the integrity of organization's data
- Loss of organization's reputation and more

Now days, however, people are becoming more aware about securing their devices connected to the public internet because of occurred events of data leakage, it's alteration and misuse in a past few years. Network vulnerability and new methods of attack are growing day by day, hence the evolving techniques of making network more secured is growing.

Security is a broad topic that should be discussed in everything we design related to computer networking. Network security has been considered important for quite some time, especially for those of us whose entire career has been around the field of network security. There has been a massive increase in public awareness about securing their devices connected to public internet because of events of data stealth and leakage in a past few years.

As new vulnerabilities and new methods of attack exist, even the least technical users have the potential to create a devastating attack against an unprotected network. As we strive to empower employees around the world with ubiquitous access to important data, it is increasingly important to take measures for the protection of data and the entities using it.

We begin this chapter with the description of challenges of current security landscape as well as the primary goals of security.

CIA Triad

Our *security objectives* are surrounding around these three basic concepts:

Confidentiality

We want to make sure that our secret and sensitive data are secured. Confidentiality means that only authorized persons can discover our infrastructure's digital resources. It also implies that unauthorized persons should not have any access or disclosure of the data. There are two types of data in general: data in motion as it moves across the network and data at rest, when data is in any media storage (such as servers, local hard drives, cloud). For data in motion, we need to make sure that the data is encrypted before sending it over the network. Another option we can use along with encryption is to use a separate network for sensitive data. For data at rest, we can apply encryption at storage media drive so that no one can read it in case of theft.

Integrity

We do not want our data to be accessible or manipulated by some unauthorized persons. Data integrity ensures that only authorized parties can modify data. Integrity ensures the information received at the recipient's end is exactly the information sent originally by the sender. This is the process to validate the message or communication between two end-users. If anyone alters the message by sniffing the packets, the integrity check value will notify that the communication has been modified. By the way, only authorized users are allowed to alter the message. Hash and Message authentication codes are used to validate the integrity of a message. Comparison of the received and calculated hash value determines if the communication has been altered or not.

Availability

Availability applies to systems, applications, services and data. If authorized persons are unable to access the data due to general network failure or denial-of-service (DOS) attack, it becomes a serious concern for the organization's reputation, which leads to financial loss and recording of some important data.

We can use the term **"CIA"** to remember these basic yet most important security concepts.

CIA	Risk	Control
Confidentiality	Loss of privacy. Unauthorized access to information. Identity theft.	Encryption. Authentication. Access Control
Integrity	Information is no longer reliable or accurate. Fraud.	Maker/Checker. Quality Assurance. Audit Logs
Availability	Business disruption. Loss of customer's confidence. Loss of revenue.	Business continuity. Plans and test. Backup storage. Sufficient capacity.

Table 1-01: Risk and Its Protection by Implementing CIA

Security Information and Event Management (SIEM)

Security Information Management (SIM) and Security Event Management (SEM) are evolved to form a by-product by the name of Security Information and Event Management (SIEM). In Network Security, SIEM technology allows you to get real-time visibility of all activities, threats and risks in your system, network, database and application.

- It provides a comprehensive and centralized view of an IT infrastructure.
- It provides real-time analysis of logs and security alerts generated by network hardware or application.
- It saves data for the long time, so the organizations can have a detailed report of the incident.
- SIEM provides details on the Cause of suspicious activity, which leads you to know "How that event occurred", "Who is associated with that event", "Was the user authorized for doing this", etc.

SIEM products are either sold as software, as appliances or as managed services. The following diagram shows the basic features of SIEM products generally available in the market.

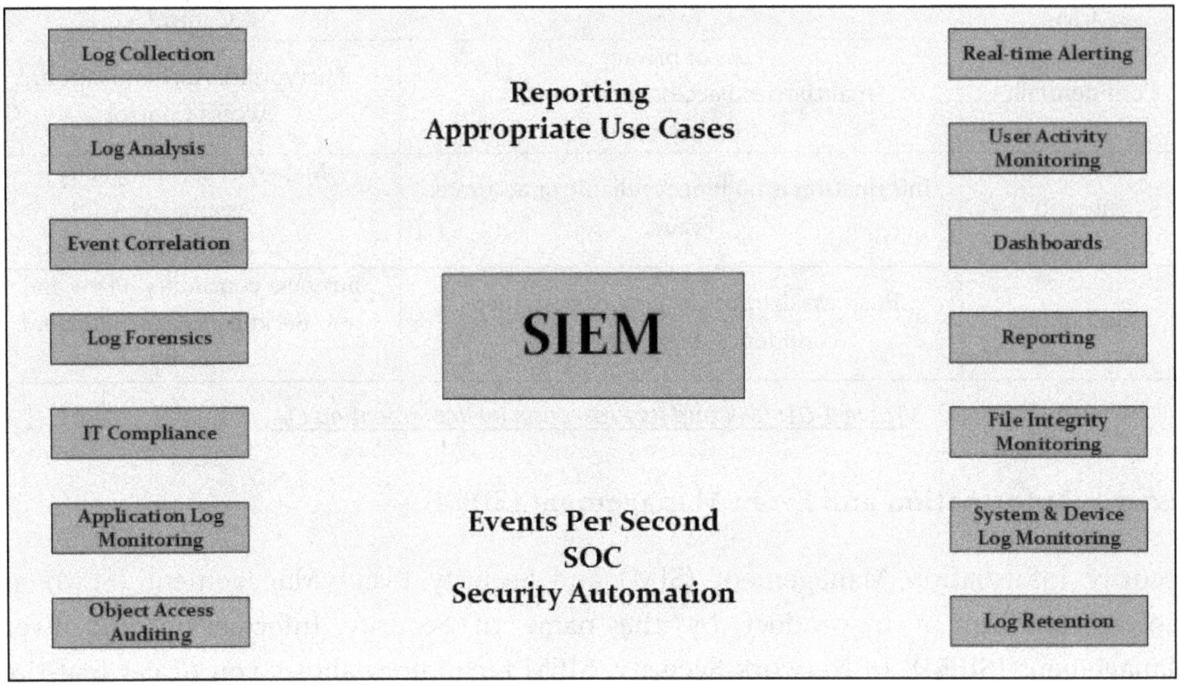

Figure 1-01: SIEM Components

Security Terminologies

Anything valuable to an organization is an **Asset** and it needs to be protected. It may vary from tangible items (people, computers etc.) to intangible items (some database information etc.). Required security level for a particular asset depends upon its value and nature. Information that should be publically accessible does not require enough security implementations as compared to the personal records of customers or employees of an organization that should be kept secured and private. Definitely, the required level of security of secret and confidential information is always higher.

Asset is something, which is directly or indirectly related to the revenue of an organization. Classification of *assets* helps to determine the precautions as per company's policy. For example, any confidential and sensitive data needs to be sent over VPN (Virtual Private Network) tunnel instead of directly communicating on a public network. Classifying data not only saves time but efficiently identify how to deal with that type of an asset.

For example, purchasing an asset for $400 and then spending $3,000 for its security does not make any sense. At the same time, accepting the full risk is also not a good idea. Hence, we can reduce the risk by spending money on security measures that seems important to specific environment. We can never claim to have eliminated the risk, thus we need to find the balance.

Vulnerability is a weakness in a system or its design that can be exploited by an attacker. Vulnerability can be present at any level of system architecture.

Classifying vulnerabilities that how threatening it is or how it would impact the system helps in identifying its impact on system. Cisco and other security vendors have created databases known as ***The Common Vulnerabilities and Exposures (CVE)*** that categorizes the threats over the internet. It can be searched via any search engine available today. The following are few of the important reasons, through which vulnerability can exist in the system:

- Policy flaws
- Design errors
- Protocol weaknesses
- Misconfiguration
- Software vulnerabilities
- Human factors
- Malicious software
- Hardware vulnerabilities
- Physical access to network resources

A "**threat**" indicates the involvement of an attacker with potentially harmful intentions. A **threat** is any danger from an attacker to an asset. The presence of vulnerability in a system results in a threat. The entity that uses the vulnerability to attack a system is known as **malicious actor** and a path used by this entity to launch attack is known as **threat vector.** Some of major threat classifications include:

User Identity Spoofing includes multiple techniques used to represent legitimate user information like GPS spoofing, email-address spoofing and Caller-ID spoofing, which is used in Voice-over-IP.

Information Tampering includes threats that are related to the changing of information rather than stealing it. Like changing the financial records and transactions used in banks, criminal records, etc.

Data leakage involves stealing of critical data like organization's patents etc.

Denial of Service (DoS) is a type of attack in which service offered by a system or a network is denied. Services may either be denied, reduce the functionality or prevent the access to the resources even to the legitimate users. There are several techniques to perform DoS attack such as generating a large number of requests to the targeted system for service. These large numbers of incoming requests overload the system capacity, which results in denial of service. Botnets and Zombies are the compromised systems, which are used for generating huge traffic for DDoS attack.

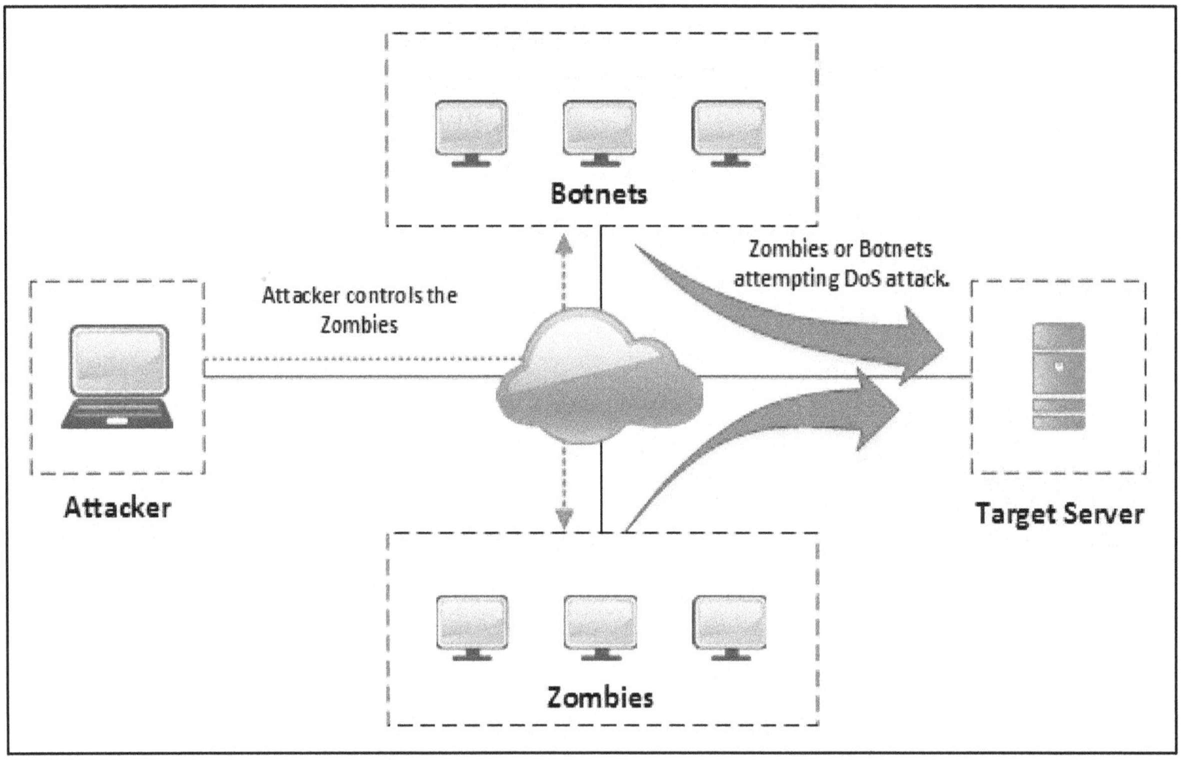

Figure 1-02: Denial-of-Service Attack

Common Symptoms of DoS attack are:

- Slow performance
- Increase in spam emails
- Unavailability of a resource
- Loss of access to a website
- Disconnection of a wireless or wired internet connection
- Denial of access to any internet service
- Elevation of privilege

This category contains threats of someone getting access to the organization's digital records higher than its current security level. Like a user with user mode access on router may get Level 15 access by doing some kind of hit and trials with being noticed.

A **countermeasure** is an action that somehow mitigates or compensates a potential risk. It may completely remove the vulnerability or prevent the threat agent to exploit the risk.

As we have discussed some of the security terms above, now here are some more terminologies to mitigate or countermeasure these security threats. *Classifying countermeasures* helps in implementing the various methods used to mitigate the attack because of vulnerability in the system.

Countermeasures can be:

- ***Administrative:*** This may include written policies and procedures for users on the network. It may also include items like background checks of specific users.
- ***Physical:*** As name suggests, it involves the physical security of server rooms, network equipment, etc.
- ***Logical:*** It includes strong password schemes for end users accounts, using firewall, Access lists, VPN tunnels, etc.
- By applying all or some defined control sets may help detect, prevent or correct any vulnerability present in the system.

Mitigating Risk: We can deal with the risk in many ways. One way is to eliminate it. For example, by disconnecting a web server from the internet makes it completely safe from being attacked, but this solution may not work for business depending heavily on its servers over the internet.

If we continue searching the solution for the example above, another way is to transfer the risk to someone else. For example, instead of running our own web server, we can use the outsourcing facility provided by many service providers. In this case, it is the service provider's responsibility to implement sufficient schemes to mitigate the attacks.

Risk	Threats	Vulnerabilities
Business disruption Financial losses Loss of privacy Damage to reputation Loss of confidence Legal penalties Impaired growth Loss of life	Angry employees Dishonest employees Criminals Governments Terrorists The press Competitors Hackers Nature	Software bugs Broken processes Ineffective controls Hardware flaws Business change Legacy systems Inadequate BCP Human error

Table 1-02: Risks and Corresponding Threat

Network Security Zones

Security zone is a group of interfaces and are created to control the flow of traffic. Each zone is associated with a security level. The security level represents the level of trust, from low (0) to high (100). Usually, all traffic from the LAN zone (with a Trusted security level) to the WAN zone or internet (with an Untrusted security level) is allowed but traffic from the WAN or internet (Untrusted) zone to the LAN (Trusted) zone is blocked. Firewalls have features by which we can specify the permit or block action for specified services. Here are some security levels and pre-defined zones:

Security Level	Description	Predefined Zones
Trusted (100)	Highest level of trust. By default, the DEFAULT VLAN is mapped to the pre-defined LAN zone. You can group one or more VLANs into a Trusted zone. Outbound traffic from LAN (Trusted) to Wan (Untrusted) is allowed, but inbound traffic from untrusted to trusted zone is blocked by default.	LAN
VPN (75)	Higher level of trust than a public zone (untrusted), but a lower level of trust than a trusted zone. This security level is used exclusively for VPN connections. All traffic is encrypted.	VPN SSLVPN
Public (50)	Higher level of trust than a guest zone, but a lower level of trust than a VPN zone	DMZ
Guest (25)	Higher level of trust than an untrusted zone, but a lower level of trust than a public zone.	GUEST
Untrusted (0)	Lowest level of trust. By default, the WAN1 interface is mapped to the WAN zone. If you are using the secondary WAN (WAN2), you can map it to the WAN zone or any other untrusted zone.	WAN
Voice	Designed exclusively for voice traffic. Incoming and outgoing traffic is optimized for voice operations. For example, assign Cisco IP Phones to the VOICE zone.	VOICE

Table 1-03: Network Security Zones

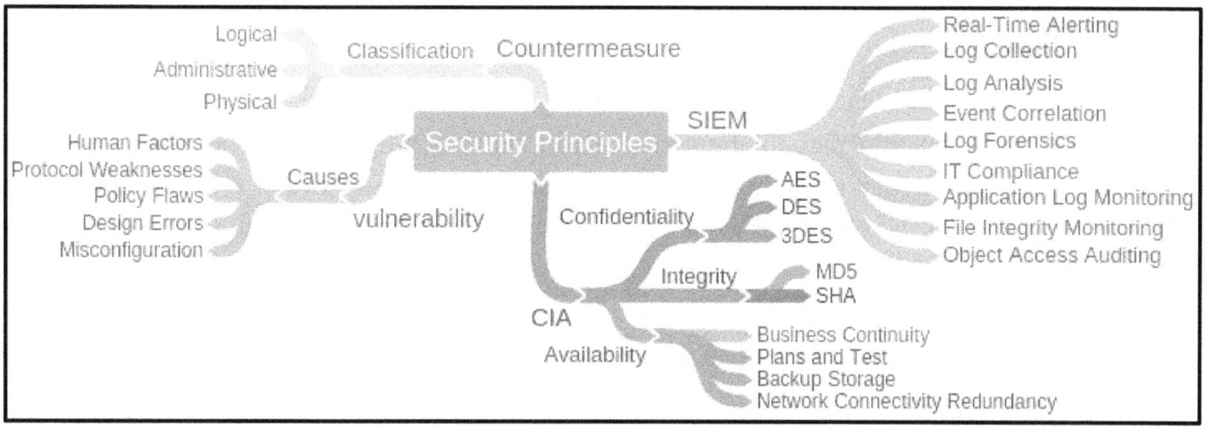

Figure 1-03: Common Security Principles Mind Map

Common Security Threats

Reconnaissance

Reconnaissance is an initial preparing phase for the attacker to get ready for an attack by gathering the information about the target before launching an attack using different tools and techniques. Gathering of information about the target makes it easier for an attacker, even on a large scale. Similarly, in a large scale, it helps to identify the target range.

In ***Passive Reconnaissance***, the hacker acquires the information about target without interacting with the target directly. An example of passive reconnaissance is public or social media searching for gaining information about the target.

Active Reconnaissance is gaining information by acquiring the target directly. Examples of active reconnaissance are via calls, emails, help desk or technical departments.

We can also call it as the *discovery process*. In this step, attacker tries to find out the exact IP addresses alive on a network and corresponding to opened TCP and UDP ports with these IP addresses.

Ping Sweep

A ping sweep is a tool, which can be used to mitigate reconnaissance attack. Reconnaissance attack is used to gather information about a network; network administrator can run ping sweep to identify if there is any unknown host is live in the network. A ping sweep is also referred to as an ICMP sweep, and it is a basic network monitoring and scanning technique used to determine live hosts within the range of IP addresses. Whereas, a pinging a particular host shows if the host is live and accessible. Basically, ping sweep analyses the response of the command i.e. an ICMP echo, from a series of live addresses to discover unauthorized or suspected hosts added to the network.

If ping sweep is being executed by a malicious host, it will easily get the view of all the live hosts running in a network and he can exploit this information.

Social Engineering Attack

Information gathering includes a collection of information about target using different platforms either by social engineering, internet surfing, etc. An attacker may use different tools, networking commands for extract information. An attacker may navigate to robot.txt file to extract information about internal files.

Here are some of the methods used worldwide while generating an attack:

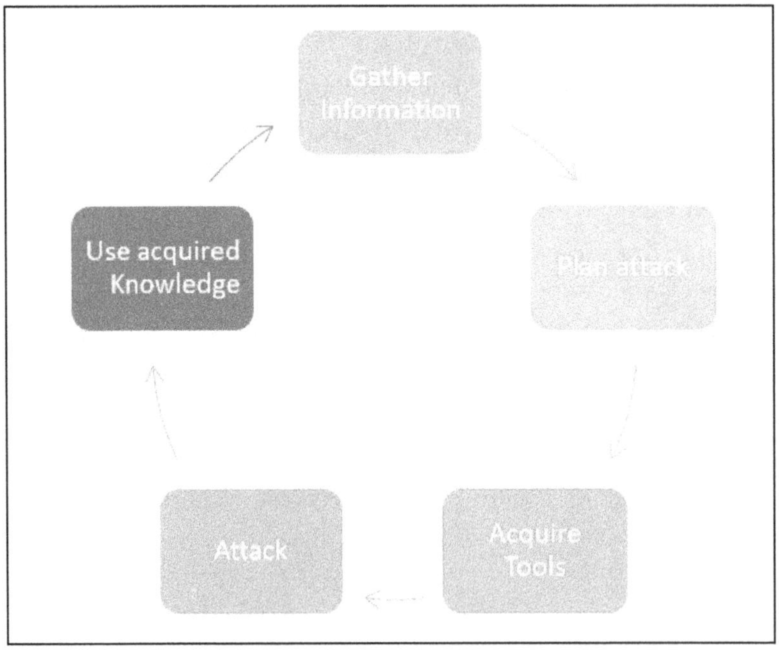

Figure 1-04: Phases of Launching an Attack

Social Engineering

Social Engineering in Information Security refers to the technique of psychological manipulation. This trick is used to gather information from different social networking and other platforms from people for fraud, hacking and getting information for being close to the target.

Social Networking is one of the best information sources among other sources. Different popular and most widely used social networking site has made quite easy to find someone, get to know about someone, including its basic personal information as well as some sensitive information. Advanced features on these social networking sites also provide up-to-date information. An example of footprinting through social networking sites can be finding someone on Facebook, Twitter, LinkedIn, Instagram and much more.

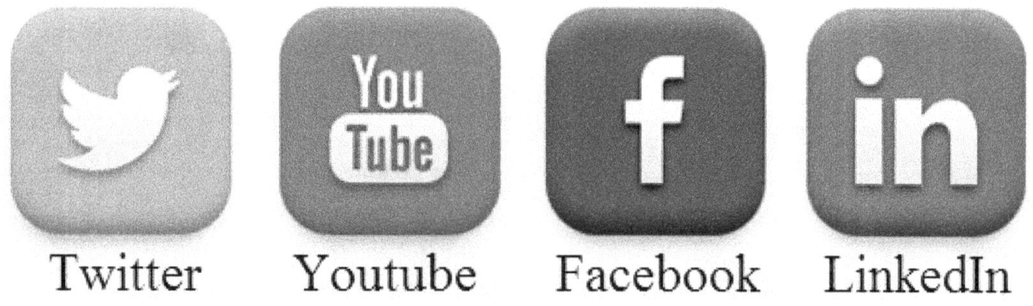

Figure 1-05: Social Networking Sites

Social Networking is not only a source of joy, but it also connects people personally, professionally and traditionally. Social Networking platforms can provide sufficient information of an individual by searching the target. Searching Social Networking for a person or an organization brings much information such as photo of the target, personal information and contact details, etc.

What Users Do	Information	What attacker gets
People maintain their profile	• Photo of the target • Contact numbers • Email Addresses • Date of birth • Location • Work details	• Personal Information about a target including personal information, photo, etc. • Social engineering
People update their status	• Most recent personal information • Most recent location	• Platform & Technology related information

	• Family & Friends information • Activities & Interests • Technology related information • Upcoming events information	• Target Location • List of Employees/Friends/Family • Nature of business

Table 1-04: Social Engineering

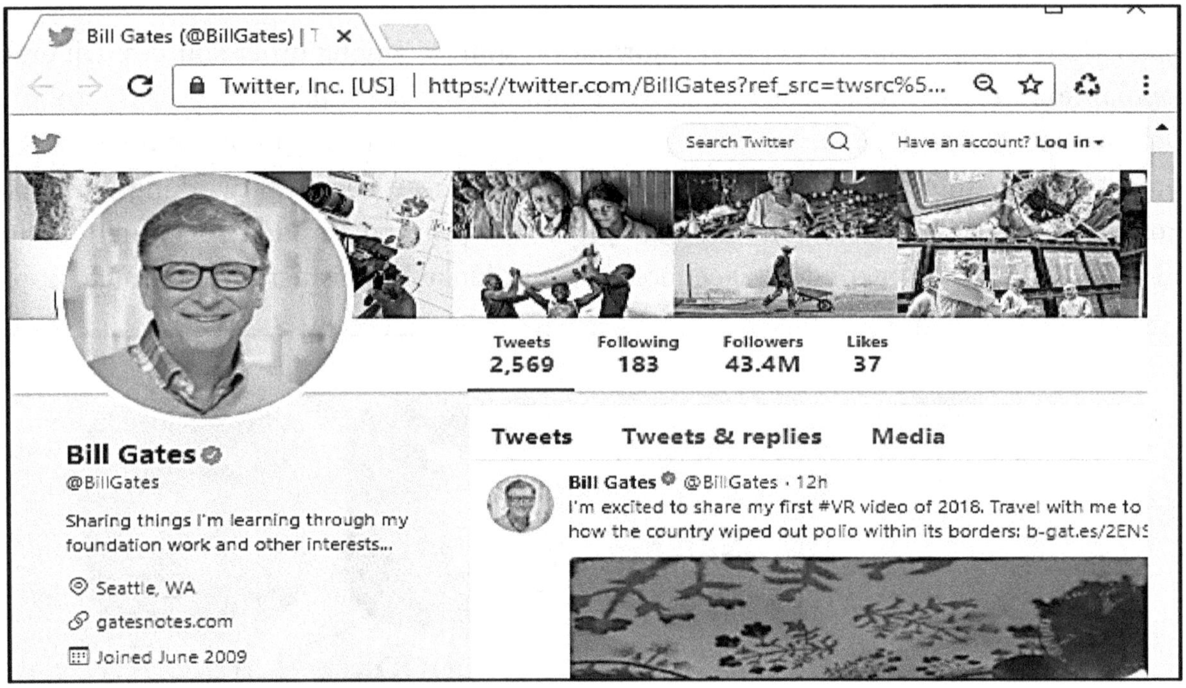

Figure 1-06: Collection of Information from Social Networking

Profile picture can identify the target; the profile can gather personal information. By using this personal information, an attacker can create a fake profile with the same information. Posts that have location links, pictures and other location information help to identify target location. Timelines and stories can also reveal sensitive information. By gathering information of interest and activities, an attacker can join several groups and forums for more footprinting. Furthermore, skills, employment history, current employment (and much more) are the information that can be gathered easily and used for determining the type of business, technology, and platforms used by an organization. Usually, in the posts, people posting on these platforms never think twice of that what they are posting. Their posts may contain enough information for an attacker, or a piece of required information for an attacker to gain access to their system.

There, the hacker's main focus is on the end user's sensitive data and this can be achieved via some bogus e-mail, forcing end users to input corporate username and password or some kind of webpage misdirection.

Types of Social Engineering

Two major types of social engineering are *Phishing* and *Pharming*.

In the **Phishing** process, e-mails are sent to a targeted group containing an e-mail message body, which looks legitimate. The recipient clicks the link mentioned in the e-mail assuming it as a legitimate link. Once the reader clicks the link, he/she is enticed for providing information. It redirects users to the fake webpage that looks like an official website. For example, the recipient is redirected to a fake bank webpage, asking for sensitive information like username/password or some confidential information in that link.

Similarly, the redirected link may download any malicious script onto the recipient's system to fetch information.

In **Pharming,** the user is directed from a valid URL to a malicious one, which looks exactly like a valid resource. It is then used to extract sensitive information from the user. Another type of social engineer attack is *phone scams*, although it is not very popular. Attackers try to call up an employee and use tricks to get as much corporate information as possible. An example of this type would be a fake recruiter asking for names, e-mail accounts, and phone numbers. Attacker can then use this information for future attacks and so forth.

The best way to protect employees from this type of attack is through consistent training. Employees must know the importance of the data they are dealing with regarding the company. Employees who already know about social engineering attacks and their role on corporate health can help employees to better deal with such situations. Standard Operation Procedures (SOP) regarding data and information security can also play an important role in this regard. Such SOPs may include, but not limited to, *Strong Password Policy* that include multiple character types and declaration to not to tell passwords to anyone, *Classification of Data* to make sure employees know which information is sensitive, *Physical Security* such as premises monitoring and background checks of employees. Use of Antivirus suites can also minimize phishing attacks to some extent. In order to have better protection, additional methods such as DNS protection and web browser protection must be implemented.

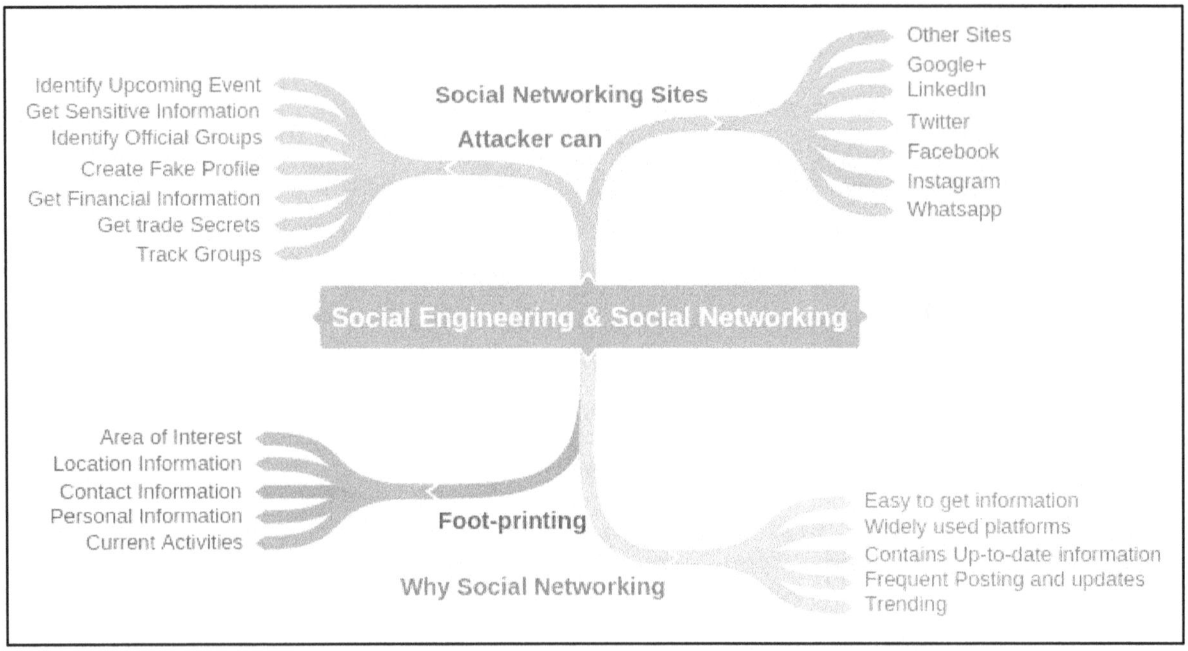

Figure 1-07: Social Engineering Mind Map

Privilege Escalation:

Privilege Escalation involves the process of what to do after gaining access to the target. There are still a lot of tasks to perform in Privilege Escalation. You may not always hack an admin account; sometimes, you have to compromise the user account, which has lower privileges. Using the compromised account with limited privilege will not help you to achieve your goals. Prior to anything after gaining access, you have to perform privilege escalation to complete your high-level access with no or limited restrictions.

Each Operating System comes with some default setting and user accounts such as administrator account, root account and guest account, etc. with default passwords. It is easy for an attacker to find vulnerabilities of pre-configured account in an operating system to exploit and gain access. These default settings and account must be secured and modified to prevent unauthorized access.

This is the process of gaining some level of access and then using different methods like brute-force attack to gain some high level of access. For example, a person with user mode access of router can use brute-force attack to gain level 15 access by cracking the enabled secret password.

Backdoors: When attackers successfully gain access to some system, they want to make future access as easy as possible. A backdoor application will be installed by using different techniques defined above to store confidential information, which can be retrieved by attacker when required.

Code Execution: This method is usually related with the activity of attacker after gaining access to the system and its impact on the system. It may have an impact on confidentiality, integrity or availability of the system and it depends on the level of access the attacker has gained and the code or piece of software he has used on the system.

Man-in-the-Middle Attacks: This happen when attackers break the normal link of communication between two nodes and act as a bridge between them. With the purpose of eavesdropping, it can occur at both TCP/IP Layer 2 and at Layer 3.

Attackers can use the concept of Address Resolution Protocol (ARP) Poisoning so that devices on LAN consider attacker's MAC address to be the MAC address of the default gateway. Attackers send the traffic to correct destination so that the sender and receiver do not feel anything unusual happening between their sessions. In order to mitigate this attack, we need to enable Dynamic Address Resolution Protocol (ARP) Inspection (DAI) on switches.

To implement man-in-the-middle attack at Layer 3, attackers introduce a rouge router in network and make sure that other routers see this router as preferred path for destination routes. To stop such kind of attacks, we can use authentication for routing protocols used in network, use Access Lists to permit only required traffic etc.

To make our data more secure, we must use HTTPS instead of HTTP, which sends traffic in plain text. For accessing devices, we can use SSH instead of TELNET for a secured connection. Similarly, we must use VPNs for traffic to be sent between end-to-end nodes.

Sometimes, the intention of attackers can be to affect the availability of data or resource. Major types of such attacks include *Denial of Service (DoS)* and *Botnet*. **Botnet**, attackers can generate TCP SYN or ICMP echo requests to a particular destination from a group of already infected computers by using the concept of backdoors defined earlier. In Client/Server communication, every device has some limitation for incoming requests. When this limit is crossed, application running on that specific device will be unavailable to clients.

Denial of Service (DoS) and **DDoS** have three distinct categories. In **Direct DDoS,** source of attack generates the traffic for victim computer/device. It does not use any indirect way to keep itself hidden. In **reflected DDoS**, attackers use some third node in a way that it receives spoofed packets that appear to be from a victim. Now the victim's device is affected when it receives response from this third node. In this type, original source of attack is actually hidden, in case the victim notices some strange activity on its network.

Amplification, which is the third distinct type of DDoS attack, is actually a sub category of reflected DDoS. In this type, attacker tries to increase the response traffic sent to the victim to be more that actual packets sent by an attacker. For example, when DNS queries are sent and packet size of response is much higher than initial queries, victim node gets flooded with unwanted traffic, which may affect its *availability*.

The following table summarizes the different types of attacks as previously discussed.

Type of attack	Description
Reconnaissance	Stealing network information
Social Engineering	Using employees for attack generation
Phishing	Fake links are presented to end user to launch an attack
Pharming	Rough web pages are presented to misguide the clients and steal information
Privilege Escalation	Getting high-level access of networking device
Backdoors	Installing application on victim devices for future access
Code execution	Presenting user a link with some executable code embedded in it
Man-in-the-middle attacks	Used for eavesdropping and stealing information exchange between two or more peers
Botnet	Attack generated by group of affected devices
Denial of Service	Attacks to effect the availability of devices or some services
Amplification	Increasing response or action of attack with less number of commands

Table 1-05: Types of Attacks

Network Threats

A network threat can be classified into three categories:

1. **Administrative**: It is usually policy and procedure based, administrative treat involves the change in configuration, policies, access controls and rules.
2. **Logical**: It involves threats for hardware and software.
3. **Physical**: It involves threats for physical infrastructure.

Potential Attackers

In the world of evolving technology, technology and threats of cyber-attacks are growing side by side. Understanding the nature of existing threats can help in dealing with new threats. It is more important to understand the type of adversaries behind these attacks rather than studying every single attack regarding some proprietary information or network infrastructure. Some of the types of adversaries are *Hackers, Criminals, Disgruntled Employees, Intelligence and Government Agencies*.

Some attackers do it for financial profit. Some do it just for fun. Sometimes, an attack can be at state level where you have to understand the geo political scenario to understand the overall payload of the attack. One perfect example would be the Sutxnet virus attack. Back in early 2000s, viruses were not as sophisticated as they are now. Most of the time, people did it just for fame. As computer literacy and sudden surge in technology has changed the whole landscape, there are many examples where the payload of the attack is stealth of information and damage of critical infrastructure.

Malware

The term **Malware** refers to a variety of hostile or intrusive software including computer viruses, worms, Trojan horses, ransomware, spyware, adware, scareware, and other malicious programs. It can take the form of executable code, scripts, active content, and other software.

Identifying malware as it attempts to enter the network or being already residing in network infrastructure is one the most tedious job of security-concerned persons. There are several factors, which make its identification a little bit difficult. Any new malware created is undetectable from signature based detection tools. Normally malwares are embedded in trusted applications and sent over the protocols that are traditionally permitted in firewalls and Access Lists of network devices like HTTP and HTTPS traffic. A dedicated human resources would be required if every single piece of data, which traverse across the network, needs to be monitored. Increasing use of encryption also adds another layer of complexity for an organization to classify malicious traffic.

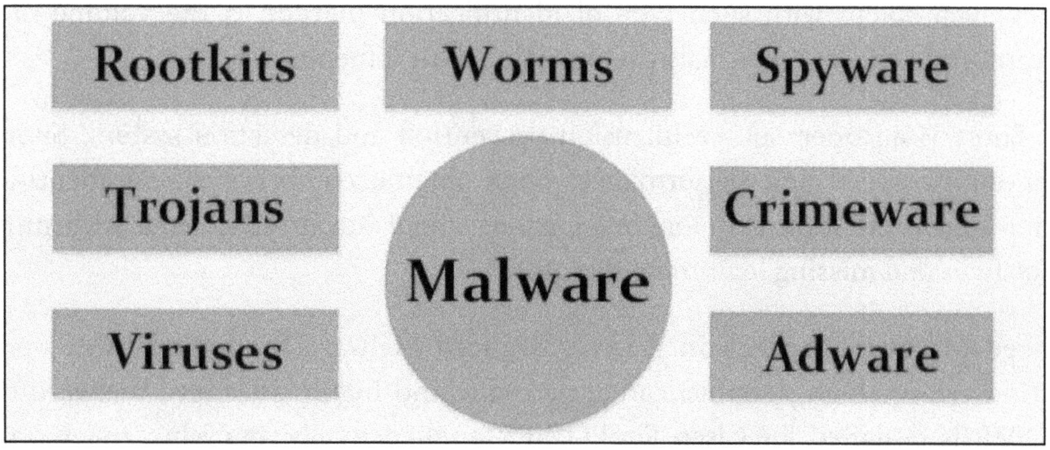

Figure 1-08: Malware Components

Malware	Description
Virus	It is a malicious program. It executes by itself and infects other files and programs in your system.
Worm	A worm is a self-replicating malware, which infects system, files or programs.
Spyware	Spyware is a malicious program that is designed to gather information and data from the system, without disturbing the system's user.
Adware	An adware is a malicious software application, which delivers ads through pop-up windows on any program's interface.
Scareware	Scareware is any malicious program that pretends to be legitimate antivirus software, it involves convincing users that their system is infected and they should purchase their fake antivirus. Once the user installs this software, it leads to the stealth of sensitive data.
Trojan horses	Trojan is malicious software, which disguises itself in some legitimate application like free screen saver, free antivirus cracker, etc. Once it is downloaded it will attack end users.
Ransomware	Ransomware is malicious software, which is designed to encrypt user's data, and then hackers demand ransom payment to decrypt the respective data.

Table 1-06: Malware Components

Malware Identification Methods

These are the tools and techniques used to identify malware existence over the network:

Packet Captures: Packet captures like Wireshark provide minute-to-minute detail related to traffic being sent or received over the network. Packet captures of malicious traffic can be separately taken under observation to find out its payload or purpose of attack. One problem with such type of identification method is the volume of traffic being captured, which makes malware detection a bit difficult.

Snort: Snort is an open source intrusion prevention and detection system. Snort is so popular for its speed and performance. Snort engine comprises threat identification, detection and prevention components, outputs about advanced threats with minimum false positives and missing legitimate threats.

Advanced Malware Protection: Cisco Advanced Malware Protection (AMP) provides protection against highly sophisticated, zero-day and highly advanced malware threats. Cisco AMP is designed for Cisco FirePOWER appliances. By analysing and monitoring files that have entered the network, AMP helps network administrators to take action during and after an attack by using security alerts. It also helps administrators to correlate discrete events for better detection by providing multi source indications of compromise.

NGIPS: Cisco's next-generation intrusion prevention system (NGIPS) provides multilayer threat protection at high throughput rates. It is centrally managed through Cisco FireSight Management Center and can be expanded to include extra features like URL Filtering, AMP, etc.

Data loss / Exfiltration

Data exfiltration or Data extrusion involves an unauthorized alteration like copying, retrieval or transfer of someone's data from his system or server. This alteration can be done by using software or can be done manually with physical access to the system.

Considering the current scenario of cyber-crime where well-funded and highly equipped teams are hired to penetrate through corporate security measures like firewall to steal digital information from corporates all around the world, security practices and measures are normally good for filtering and classifying inbound traffic. However, most of the practices implemented in different organizations lack visibility into traffic that is leaving the local network. This outbound traffic being stolen by malicious actors may include intellectual property like organization patents, customer's data and trade secrets. Having this type of outbound data leakage may place organization at huge risk for losing financial data, promising customers and much more.

The few data types considered important to malicious actors in this regard are:

Intellectual Property (IP): It consists of any kind of data or documentation, produced by employee of an organization. It may include patents, designs, layouts or documents supporting the overall business of an organization.

Personally identifiable information (PII): After some data breach, this kind of information is shared in press to support the cause. Normally it consists of usernames, date of birth, addresses and social security numbers (SSN).

Credit/Debit Card: Both credit and debit cards have user information embedded either on the chip inside the card or on a magnetic strip. Normally, malicious actors trying to get financial gain tries to steal such kind of information.

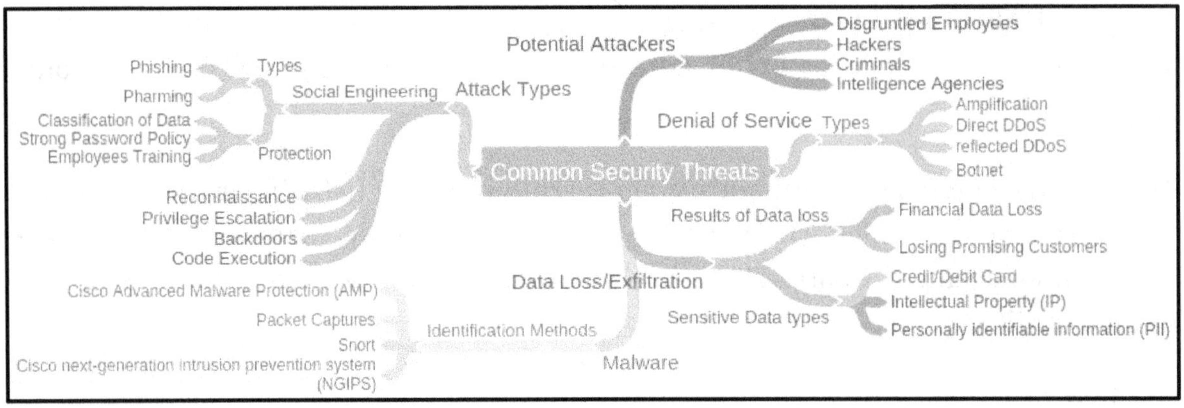

Figure 1-09: Common Security Principle Mind Map

Cryptography Concepts

As we have studied earlier, confidentiality, integrity, and availability are the three basic components around which we should build and maintain our security model. We must know different methods by which we can implement each one of these features. For example, by using encryption, we can make sure that only the sender and the receiver have the ability to read clear text data. Anybody between the two nodes needs to know the key to decrypt the data. Similarly, hashing is used to make sure of the integrity of data. This section explains the concepts and different methods by which we can implement encryption and hashing in our network. Several terminologies need to be explained before moving to the main agenda of this section.

Cryptography

Cryptography is a technique of encrypting the clear text data into a scrambled code. This encrypted data is sent over public or private network toward a destination to ensure the confidentiality. This encrypted data known as "Ciphertext" and is decrypted at the destination for processing. Strong encryption keys are used to avoid key cracking. The objective of cryptography is not all about confidentiality; it also concerns integrity, authentication, and non-repudiation.

Cipher

A cipher is a set of rules by which we implement encryption. Thousands of cypher algorithms are available on the internet. Some of them are proprietary while others are an open source. Common methods by which cyphers replace original data with encrypted data are:

- **Substitution:** In this method, every single character of data is substituted with another character. A very simple example in this regard would be to replace the character (let's say "**A**") by shifting three characters ahead of it. Therefore, "D" would replace "**A**" and so on. To make it more complex, we can select certain letters to be replaced in whole text. In this example, value of key is three and both nodes should know it otherwise, they would not be able to decrypt the data.
- **Polyalphabetic:** This method makes substitution even more difficult to break by using multiple character substitution.
- **Keys:** In the above example of substitution, we used a key of "three". Key plays the main role in every cypher algorithm. Without knowing the key, data cannot be decrypted.

The following are the major categories of symmetric and asymmetric ciphers:

Block Ciphers: In block cyphers, a block or specific chunk of data is encrypted at a time. For example, block size of 1,024 bits will encrypt 1,024 bits of data into cypher text at a time. In this type of encryption, the same key is used for decryption. This type is also known as symmetrical block cyphers. Some of the main symmetrical block cyphers are: Advanced Encryption Standard (AES), Digital Encryption Standard (DES), Triple Digital Encryption Standard (3DES), and Blowfish. If the size of available data block is less that decided block size, then block cypher will use padding techniques to make full block size.

Stream Ciphers: In this type, data is encrypted one bit at a time resulting in cypher text stream. This is also a symmetrical cypher i.e. same key will be used for decryption. Because data is encrypted one bit at time, it makes overhead lesser than block cyphers because no padding technique is used in this case.

Key Exchange

A "key" is a set of information that specifies the particular transformation of plain text into cypher text or vice versa.

In cryptography, the method of Key exchange or key establishment is basically the exchange of keys between source and destination to allow cryptographic algorithm to be implemented between them.

Government Access to Keys (GAK)

Government Access to Keys (GAK) refers to the agreement between government and software companies. All or necessary keys are delivered to a governmental organization, which keeps it securely and only uses them when the court issues a warrant to do so.

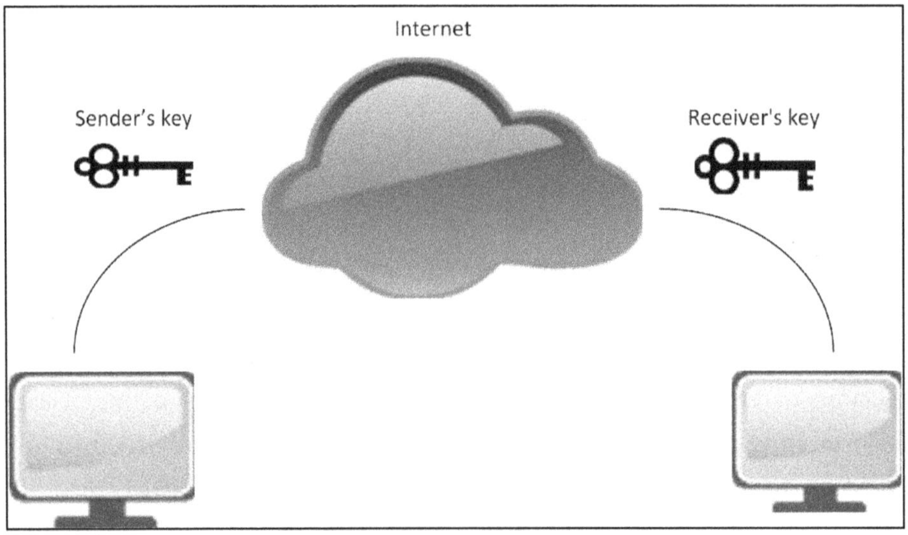

Figure 1-10: Common Security Principle Mind Map

Types of Cryptography

There are two basic types of cryptographic keys exchange that are listed below:

1. Symmetric Key Cryptography
2. Asymmetric Key Cryptography

Symmetric key Cryptography

Symmetric Key Cryptography is the oldest and most widely used cryptography technique in the domain of cryptography; symmetric cipher uses the same secret key for the encryption and decryption of data. Most widely used symmetric ciphers are AES and DES.

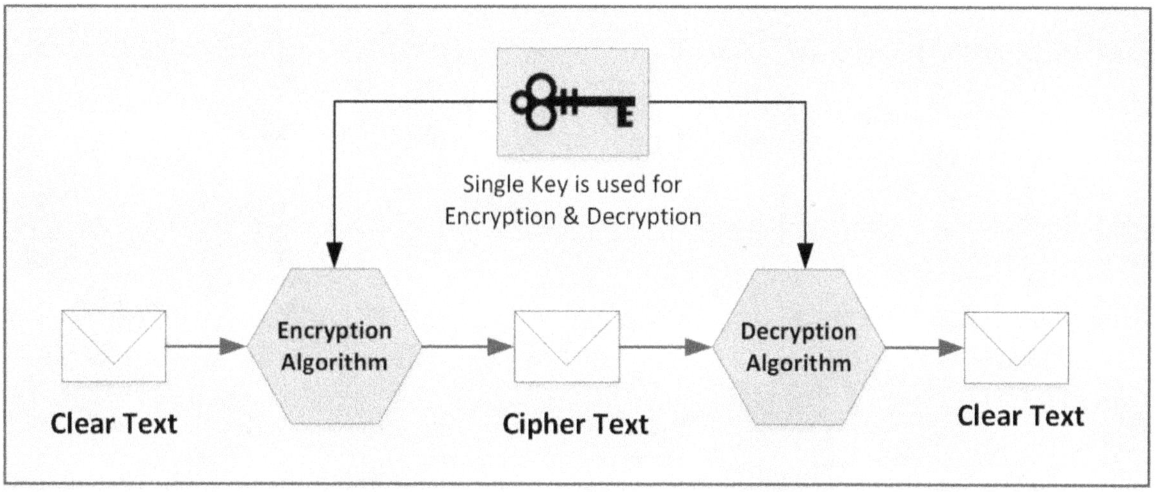

Figure 1-11: Symmetric Cryptography

Asymmetric key Cryptography / Public Key Cryptography

Unlike Symmetric Ciphers, two keys are used. One key is publically known to everyone while one key is kept secret and is used to encrypt the data by the sender hence, it is also called Public Key cryptography. Each sender uses its own secret key (also known as private key) for encrypting its data before sending. The receiver uses the respective public key of the sender to decrypt the data. RSA, DSA and Diffie-Hellman Algorithm are popular examples of asymmetric ciphers.

Asymmetric Key Cryptography delivers confidentiality, integrity, authenticity and non-repudiation by using Public and Private Key concept. The private key is only known by the owner itself. Whereas, the public key is issued by using Public Key Infrastructure (PKI), where a trusted Certification Authority (CA) certifies the ownership of key pairs.

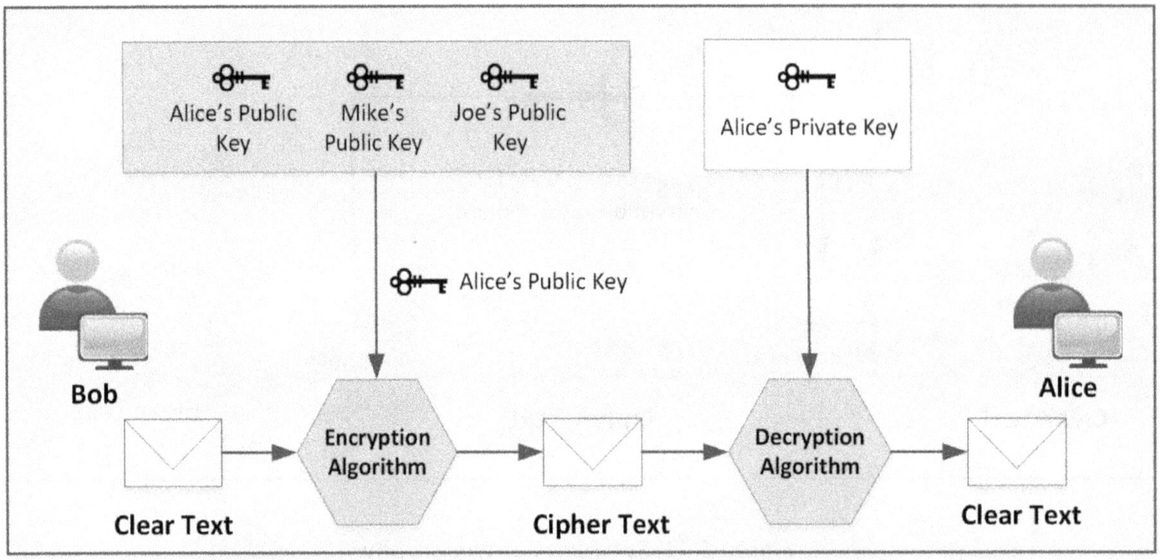

Figure 1-12: Asymmetric Cryptography

Symmetrical encryption algorithms are used in most of the VPNs we use today for data encryption. One of the reason symmetrical algorithms are preferred is their ability to encrypt data in bulk which is less CPU intensive as compared to bit by bit encryption. A longer key is generally preferred because the longer the key is, the more difficult it is to intercept the key by using methods like brute-force etc.

There is a type of symmetric key cipher that encrypts the plain text one by one. There are various types of stream ciphers such as synchronous, asynchronous. RC4 is the most common type of stream cipher design. The transformation of encrypted output varies during the encryption cycle.

Asymmetric Algorithms: In asymmetric algorithms, a pair of public and private key is used for encryption and decryption respectively. A private key is only known to the owner of the device's public/private key pair. A public key will be published online to be used by everyone to make a secured connection with that device. As encryption and decryption is a very CPU intensive process, this type of algorithms are used only for things like VPN peer authentication, which may be required at the start of making a connection.

Here are some of the examples of ***asymmetric algorithms***:

RSA (Rivest Shamir Adleman)

This algorithm is named after its creators, namely *Rivest, Shamir, and Adleman*. Also known as public key cryptography standard (PKCS) #1, the main purpose for its usage today is authentication. The key length varies from 512 to 2,048 with 1,024 being preferred one.

The RSA Signature Scheme

1. Two very large prime numbers "p" and "q" are required.
2. Multiply the above two primes to find n, the modulus for encryption and decryption. In other words, n = p * q.
3. Calculate $\phi = (p - 1) * (q - 1)$.
4. Choose a random integer "e" i.e. Encryption Key and calculate "d" Decryption Key so that $d \times e = 1 \mod \phi$.
5. Announce "e" and "n" to the public; keep "ϕ" and "d" secret.

Diffie-Hellman

Diffie-Hellman key exchange protocol is asymmetrical algorithm, which allows you to share a pair of keys over untrusted network. DH is asymmetrical in nature but the keys generated by DH are symmetric in nature, which in return are used by symmetrical cyphers like AES, DES etc.

Diffie-Hellman key agreement requires that both the sender and receiver of a message contain a pair of keys, one public and one private. By combining one's private key and the other party's public key, both parties share the same secret number. This secret number is then converted into cryptographic keying material. That keying material is typically used as a Key-Encryption Key (KEK) to encrypt (wrap) a Content-Encryption Key (CEK), which is in turn used to encrypt the message data and then the reverse procedure will be followed for decrypting the material.

Asymmetric vs Symmetric Algorithms

	Symmetric Cryptography	Asymmetric Cryptography
Key	Same pair of keys on both sides	Unique private and public key pair
Hardware	Performs simple algorithms, requires less expensive hardware	Requires complex and time consuming algorithms and need more powerful hardware
Digital signature	no	Yes
Key length	128 bits	2,049-4,096 bits
Security	Confidentiality and integrity	Confidentiality, integrity, authentication and non-repudiation
Advantages	Fast performance Easy to understand(if you know the key you can easily get the access to	Private keys are never exposed Exposure of information is limited Provides authenticity to the source

	the information)	
Disadvantages	Shared keys-the private key is exposed Does not provide authenticity of source(if shared key is compromised sensitive information can be leaked)	Public key management Computation intensive
Examples	AES, DES	RSA, ECDSA, Diffie-Hellman

Table 1-07: Symmetric Vs Asymmetric Cryptography

Hash algorithm

Hashes: Hashes are used to check the integrity of data. A hash function takes a small block of data and creates a fixed value known as hash value or message digest. If two computers take same block of data and use the same hash function on it, they should get the same hash value. A typical example of hash value is whenever we download some piece of software from the internet; an md5 hash is given along with the downloaded link to verify the authenticity of software. Three most popular hash functions are:

- **Message digest 5 (MD5):** MD5 creates a hash of 128 bits.
- **Secure Hash Algorithm 1 (SHA-1):** SHA1 creates a 160-bit hash or digest.
- **Secure Hash Algorithm 2 (SHA-2):** SHA2 has option to vary digest between 224 bits to 512 bits.

Message Digest (One-Way Hash) Functions

The message digest is a cryptographic hashing technique that is used to ensure the integrity of a message. Message and message digest can be sent together or separately through a communication channel. Receiver recalculates the hash of the message and compares it with the Message digest to ensure if any changes have been made. One-Way-Hash of message digest means the hashing function must be a one-way operation. The original message must not be able to be recreated. The message digest is a unique fixed-size bit string that is calculated in a way that if a single bit is modified, it changes 50% of the message digest value.

Message Digest Function: MD5

The MD5 algorithm is one from the message digest series. MD5 produces a 128-bit hash value that is used as a checksum to verify the integrity. Hashing is the technique to ensure the integrity. The hash value is calculated by computing specific algorithms to verify the integrity that the data was not modified. Hash values play an important role in proving the integrity of not only documents and images but also used in protocols to ensures the integrity of transporting payload.

Secure Hashing Algorithm (SHA)

As Message Digest 5 (MD5) is a cryptographic hashing algorithm. Another most popular, more secured and widely used hashing algorithm is Secure Hashing Algorithm (SHA). SHA-1 is a secure hashing algorithm producing 160-bit hashing value as compared to MD5 producing 128-bit value. However, SHA-2 is even more secure, robust and safer hashing algorithm as of now.

SHA-1

```
Syntax: The password is 12345

SHA-1: 567c552b6b559eb6373ce55a43326ba3db92dcbf
```

Secure Hash Algorithm 2 (SHA-2)

SHA2 has the option to vary digest between 224 bits to 512 bits. SHA-2 is a group of different hashes including SHA-256, SHA-384 and SHA 512. The stronger cryptographic algorithm minimizes the chances of compromise.

SHA-2

```
Syntax: The password is 12345

SHA-256: 5da923a6598f034d91f375f73143b2b2f58be8a1c9417886d5966968b7f79674
```

Hashed Message Authentication Code (HMAC)

HMAC uses the mechanism of hashing, and it adds another feature of using secret key in its operation. Both peers only know this secret key. Therefore, in this case, only parties with secret keys can calculate and verify the hash. By using HMAC, an attacker, who is eavesdropping, will not be able to inject or modify the data and re-calculate the correct hash because he will not know the correct key used by HMAC.

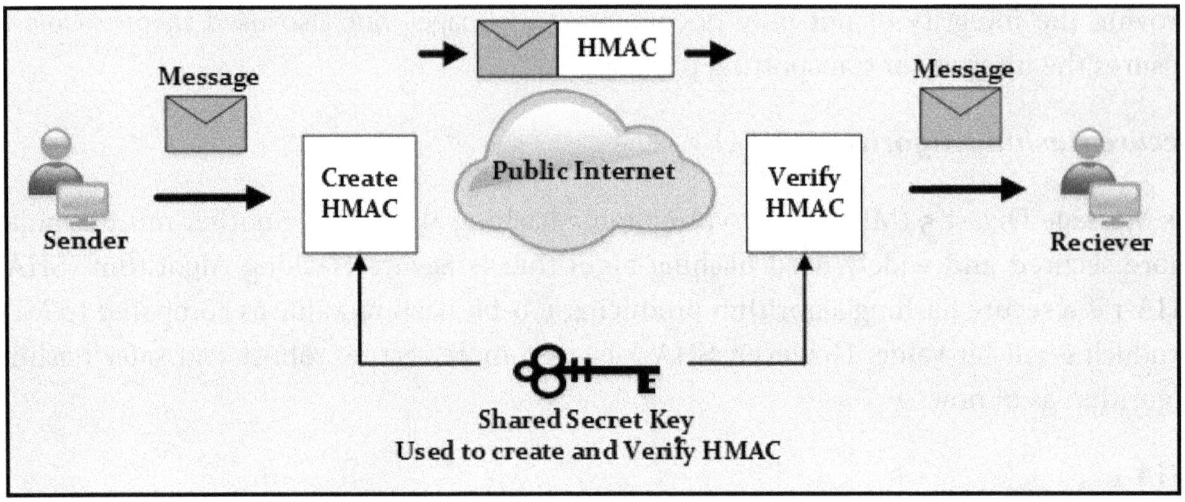

Figure 1-13: HMAC Working Conceptual Diagram

Digital Signatures

In real world, signatures are used to prove someone's identity or its commitment towards some task. In computer networks, digital signatures provide three main benefits: Authentication, Data Integrity, and Non-repudiation.

Digital certificates use methods of hashing and encryption as defined earlier. For example, if Bob and Chris want to make VPN connection, they will use digital certificates to make sure that they are talking to the right device. Let us say that Bob wants to prove his identity to Chris.

In the first step, both Bob and Chris will generate their own public/private key pairs and both will be given digital certificate via common certificate authority. A certificate authority is an entity in charge of handing out digital certificates. Inside a digital certificate is a public key and name of device to which it may belong.

To create a digital signature, Bob will take a packet and create a hash. Then Bob will take this hash and encrypt it using its own private key. When this encrypted hash will be sent to Chris, it will become a *digital signature.*

When Chris receives this packet, he will use Bob's public key (received via Bobs digital certificate) to decrypt this hash. In the second step, Chris will run the same algorithm on the remaining packet to calculate another hash. If both of these hashes are the same, then it means the integrity of data is rock solid.

Identity Certificate: The purpose of identity certificate is similar to root certificate except that it provides the public key and identity of client computer or device. For example, a client router or webserver who wishes to make SSL connections with other peers.

Signed Certificate vs. Self-Signed Certificate

Self-Singed Certificates and Signed Certificates from a Certificate Authority (CA) provide security in the same way. Communications using these types of certificates are protected and encrypted by high-level security. Presence of Certificate Authority implies that a trusted source certifies the communication. The signed security certificate is to be purchased whereas Self-signed certificates can be configured to optimize cost. A Third-party Certificate Authority (CA) requires verification of domain ownership, and other verifications to issue a certificate.

Public Key Infrastructure:

PKI is the combination of policies, procedures, hardware, software, and people that are required to create, manage and revoke digital certificates.

Here are some basic terminologies related to PKI:

IPsec: IPsec is used to protect IP packets and it is used both for remote access VPNs and Site-to-Site VPNs. Another option is to use SSL with remote access VPN. In general, IP security (IPsec) is a combination of algorithms to protect IP packets at Layer 3 of TCP/IP model. For encryption, we can use AES, DES, and 3DES. For hashing, we can use MD5 and SHA. For authentication algorithms, which are used to check peer's identity, we use pre-shared keys and RSA digital certificates. Below are two primary methods of implementing IPsec:

ESP and AH: Encapsulating Security Payload (ESP) and Authentication Header (AH) are used to implement features of IPsec. The only difference between the two is that AH does not support encryption. That is why in most of the cases, we use ESP.

SSL: In a corporate environment, we can implement the security of corporate traffic over the public cloud by using site-to-site or remote VPN. In public, there is no IPsec software running. Normal users also need to do encryption in different cases like online banking, electronic shopping etc. In such situations, SSL comes in to play. The good thing about Secure Socket Layer (SSL) is that almost every single web browser in use today supports SSL. By using SSL, web browsers make an HTTPS based session with server instead of

HTTP. Whenever a browser tries to make HTTPS based session with a server, a certificate request is sent to the server in background. Server in return replies with its digital certificate containing its own public key. Web browser then checks the authenticity of this certificate with certificate authority (CA). Let us assume that the certificate is valid, now the server and the web browser have a secured session between them.

Public and Private Key Pair: Public and Private Key pair work like a team in encryption/decryption process. Public key is exchanged with everyone and private key is kept secret. Every device makes sure that no one has its private key. We encrypt data sent to a particular node by using its public key. Similarly, a private key will be used to decrypt the data. It is also true in the opposite case. If a node encrypts a data with its private key, then a public key will be used for its decryption.

Certificate Authorities: A Certificate Authority (CA) is a computer or entity that creates and issues digital certificates. Number of things like IP address, fully qualified domain name and public key of particular device will be present in a digital certificate. CA also assigns a serial number to the digital certificate and signs the certificate with its own digital signature.

Root Certificate: Root certificate provides public key and other details of CA. An example of one is:

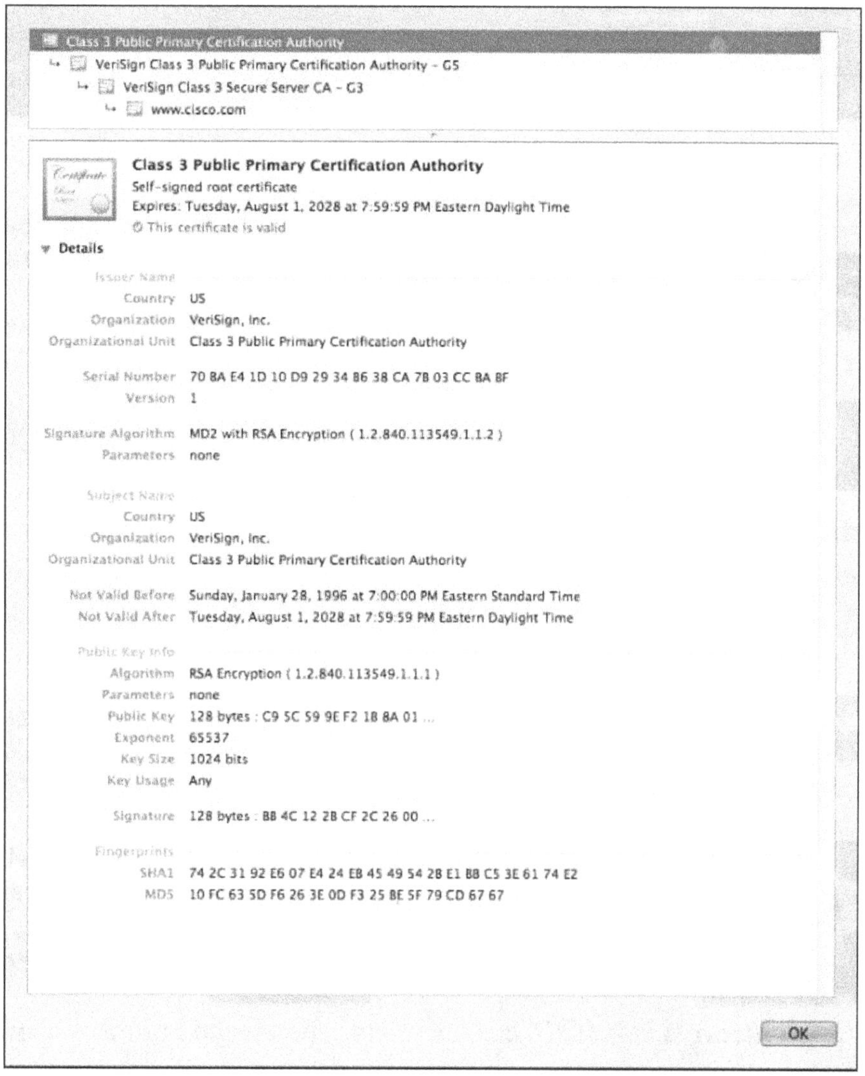

Figure 1-14: Example Root Certificate

There are multiple informative sections in the figure above including serial number, issuer, country and organization names, validity dates, and public key itself. Every OS has its own placement procedure regarding the certificates. Certificate container for specific OS can be searched in the internet to get to the certificates stored in a local computer.

Identity Certificate: The purpose of identity certificate is similar to root certificate except that it provides the public key and identity of client computer or device. For example, a client router or webserver who wishes to make SSL connections with other peers.

Public Key Cryptography Standards: There are many standards available for PKI. These standards control the format and use of certificates. These standards also have Public Key Cryptographic Standards (PKCS) numbers.

Some of the important PKCS standards in use today are:

- **PKCS#1:** Standard for RSA cryptography
- **PKCS#3:** Standard related to Diffie-Hellman key exchange
- **PKCS#10:** States the format of certificate request sent to CA for corresponding in order to apply for digital identity certificate
- **PKCS#7:** This format stats CA response to PKCS#10 with the identity certificate

Simple Certificate Enrolment Protocol: In order to automate the creation and installation of certificates, Cisco, along with other vendors created Simple Certificate Enrolment protocol. This makes installation of root and identity certificate very convenient.

Revoked Certificates: Let us say an identity certificate has been issued to a device and either this certificate is compromised or this device is no longer in use, CA can be contacted to revoke the issued certificate.

The three most popular methods to check whether a certificate has been revoked or not are:

Certificate Revocation List (CRL): CLE lists the serial numbers and names of certificates that had been initially issued by CA but had been revoked due to any specific reason and should not be trusted. CRL may be very long and it can be accessed via HTTP or LDAP to verify the name of any specific certificate on the list.

Online Certificate Status Protocol (OCSP): Clients can send request to OCSP for specific certificate and get response without checking the whole list in case of CRL.

Authentication, Authorization, and Accounting (AAA): AAA service in Cisco also provides means to validate a certificate but it is not used in PKI due to its proprietary nature.

PKI Topologies

There is no universal solution to implement PKI. It depends on network scenario. As number of devices increases, we may have to go from single CA to multiple CAs option as defined below:

- **Single Root CA:** Having a single root CA may work well in small organizations but as the number of devices increases to 40,000 or more, load on single server increases, which may affect the communications going on over the network. Although CA is not involved directly in every communication but it is a good idea to shift things like CRLs to other servers. Overall, it is a good practice to have some fault tolerance in PKI i.e. to have more than one root CA server.
- **Hierarchical CA with Subordinate CAs:** In order to have fault tolerance in our PKI, we need multiple root CAs. To have some chain of authority, we have one root at the top of the command and multiple subordinate CAs. Root CA gives permission to subordinate CAs, which in turn have abilities to issue identity certificates to clients. In this scenario, clients need to have both root certificate and subordinate CA's certificate. Root certificate is used to verify the digital signature of subordinate CA.

In the case of multiple subordinate CAs, clients need to have certificates of all subordinate CAs all the way up to root certificate.

Putting it All Together

In order to summarize the concepts discussed, consider an example of the secured e-mail between Chris and Laurel.

- In order to implement encryption on email, a pair of keys will be used namely Public/Private Key pair.
- Chris will encrypt the message with Laurel's public key and send it to Laurel.
- Let us say a third person, say Mr. Snape, was sniffing the data but he would not be able to decrypt and read the message unless he has Laurel's private key.
- On reception, Laurel will use her private key to read the original message. Private key must not be shared with anyone except the owner.
- Now this public key is shared inside something called digital signature. A digital signature makes sure that only legitimate user can read the original data and end-user can verify that no one has changed the data on its way.
- In order to understand how user makes sure the integrity of data, let us take a simple example of sending a list of numbers to someone over the phone call. Assume that 100 different numbers were written down. In order to verify that all numbers were successfully heard and written down by the person on the other side of phone call, a total number will be reminded to make sure that he knows the total amount of numbers he is assumed to have received.

- In the digital world, users make sure of the integrity of data by using hashes for digital signatures. As an example, let us assume that following sentence is the data Chris sending to Laurel over the public internet

The quick brown fox jumped over the lazy hound

One of the basic hash techniques would be to add all characters and at the end of sentence, so, this number should be included like this:

The quick brown fox jumped over the lazy hound. 46

The sentence above shows that anything between $ signs at the end of message will be the hash of data just received. Now, the end-user after receiving it, can sum the total characters and if it matched 46 then it means that length of data just received is correct. In reality, very complex algorithms, just explained in last topic, are used to perform the hashing of data. Above example only tells about the length of data. Someone may change the message on its way to the receiver and change the hashing part. To prevent such situations, hashed code is send by some secure channel.

Let us say that private key is used to encrypt the hash code, only public key will be used to decrypt the hash, which is available to everyone on public internet. If attacker wants to modify the hash, then a private key would be needed, which is only known to the owner of original message. In this way, a hashing key along with the message is secured by using digital signatures and certificates.

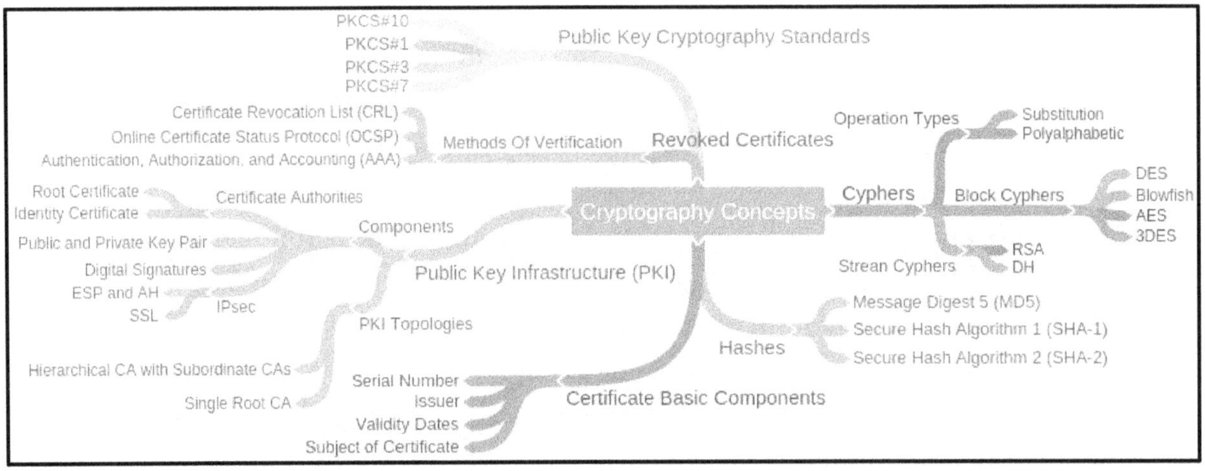

Figure 1-15: Cryptography Concept's Mind Map

Network Topologies

Network topology is designed according to the need of an organisation i.e. how many branches or different offices an organization carries. Each organisation has its own and distinct network topology. Basically, every network has an access, distribution and core layer in its topology, but the topologies are not necessarily the same.

Here are some scenarios of different network topologies.

Campus-Area Network (CAN)

Campus Area Network is a type of network topology where multiple LANs are interconnected but it is not expanded as Wide Area Network (WAN) or Metropolitan Area Network (MAN). CAN provides connectivity and services amongst all the branches and end users of a geographically separated organization like different campuses of a university, multiple offices of an organization, etc. The CAN includes elements listed in the following figure, for each building of corporate office, from internet connectivity to security of end connectivity, and data center devices.

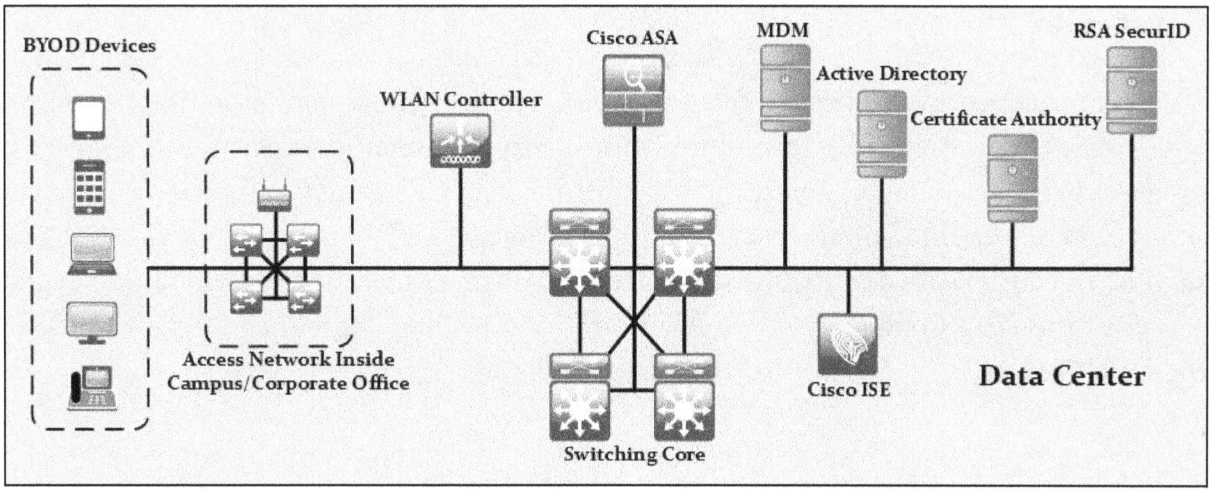

Figure 1-16: Campus Area Network (CAN)

Cloud, Wide-Area Network (WAN)

Cloud and Wide-Area Network helps organizations to expand geographically around the globe. By using WAN and cloud services from service providers usually called "off-sourcing" or "outsourcing", organizations just have to focus on their local connectivity while rest of the network is taken care by the internet service providers. This shows the basic network topology seen under Cloud/Wide-Area Network in use today:

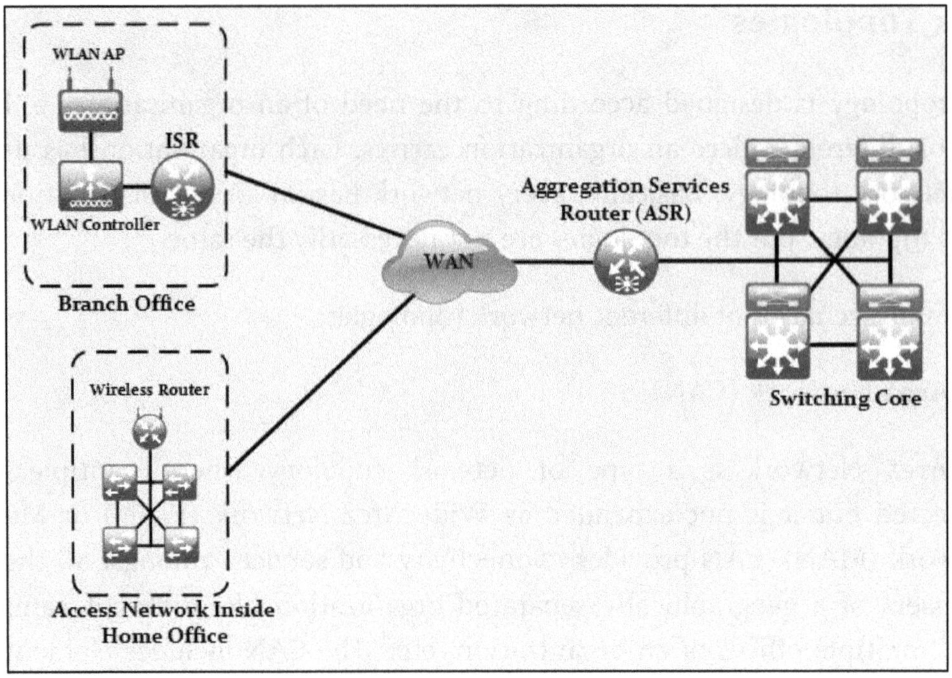

Figure 1-17: Cloud/WAN Network

Data Center

Data center network is usually an offsite facility, where organizations store their sensitive and confidential data. ISPs give interconnectivity between data center and all the different branches of an organization. Most of the Data Center networks use Cisco nexus series switches for interconnectivity. They may also have unified computing system (UCS) servers, voice gateways and CUCM servers for VoIP services. Security is also an important aspect of the Data Centers, set of firewalls are used to filter ingress and egress traffic of the Data Centers.

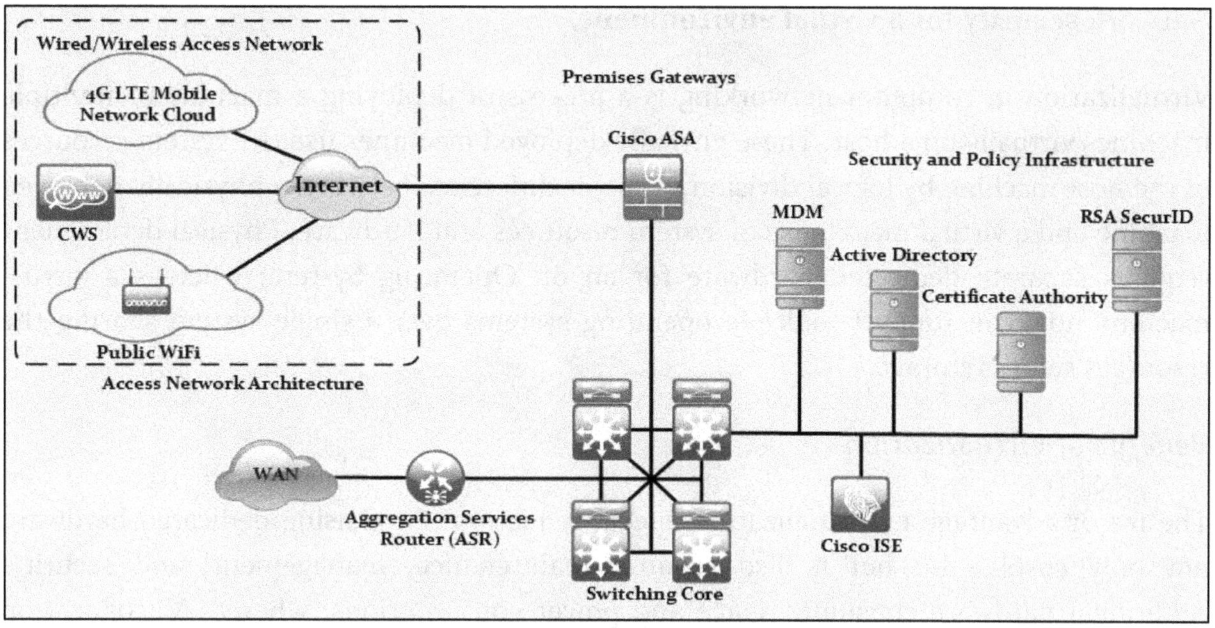

Figure 1-18: Data Center Network Topology

Small Office/Home Office (SOHO)

SOHO is generally a remote office or enterprise environment with small to medium infrastructure. SOHO users are connected to corporate headquarter by using WAN MPLS or some other technology based services provided by service providers. Normally, access switches are used to provide connectivity with SOHO environment.

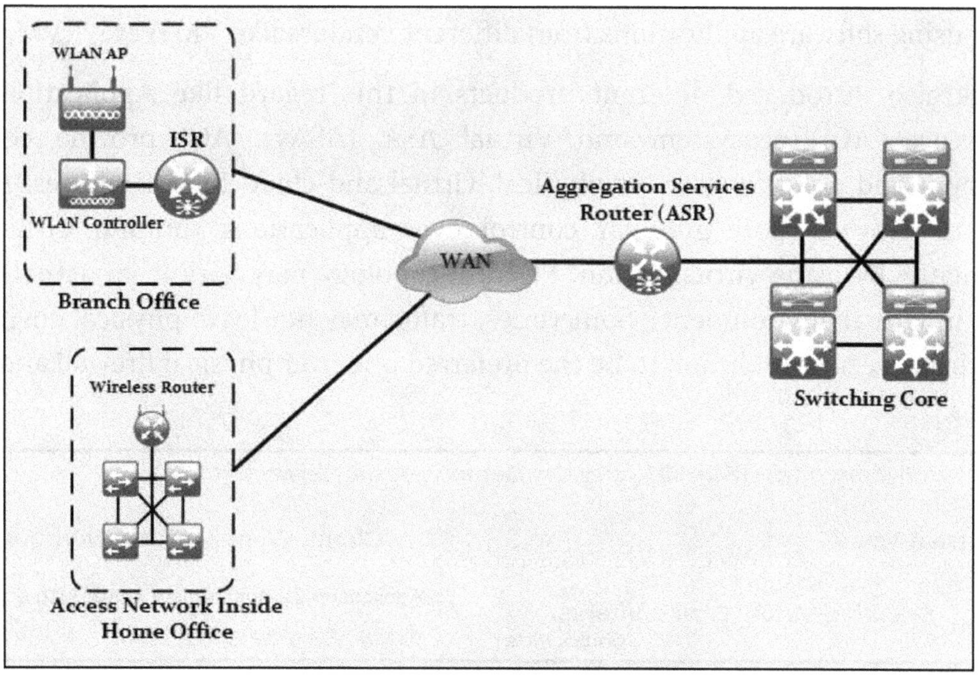

Figure 1-19: SOHO Network Topology

Network security for a virtual environment

Virtualization in computer networking is a process of deploying a machine or multiple machines virtually on a host. These virtually deployed machines use the system resources of the host machine by logical division. A major difference between a physically deployed machine and a virtual machine is of system resources and hardware. Physical deployment requires separate dedicated hardware for an on Operating System, whereas a virtual machine host can support multiple operating systems over a single system sharing the resources such as storage.

Benefits of Virtualization

The major advantage of virtualization is cost reduction. Purchasing dedicated hardware not only costs a lot but it also requires maintenance, management, and security. Additional hardware consumes space and power consumptions, whereas Virtualization supports multiple machines over single hardware. Furthermore, virtualization also reduces administration, management and networking tasks, and ensures efficiency. Virtualization over the cloud is even more effective as there is no need to install even a single hardware. All virtual machines deployed over a host are owned by cloud over the internet. You can easily access them from anywhere any time.

Virtualization concept is taking major portion in current Data Centers in order to reduce the administrative work and increase the flexibility and efficiency. For example, instead of using multiple servers, virtualized Virtual Machines (VMs) can be installed in single high server by using software applications from different vendors like VMWare, KVM, Xen etc.

Cisco has also introduced different products in this regard like Application Centric Infrastructure (ACI) ecosystem and Virtual ASA (ASAv). ACI provide centralized management and policy engine for physical, virtual and cloud infrastructures. ASAv can be used to provide more granular control over applications running within virtual environment. By using virtualization, Physical topology may vary from actual topology (running in virtual environment). Sometimes, traffic may not leave physical environment, making virtual security solution to be the preferred one over physical firewall and security appliances.

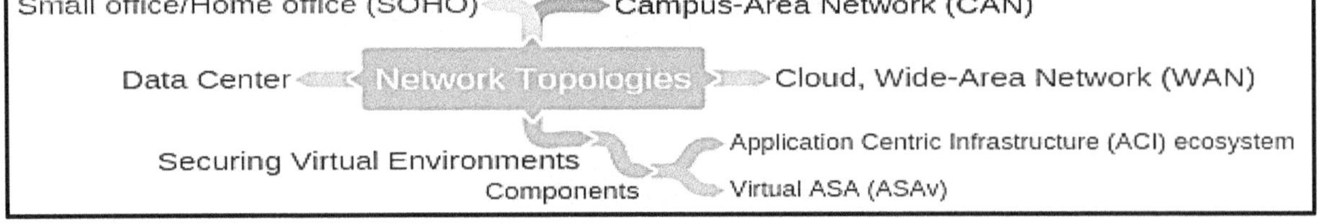

Figure 1-20: Network Topologies Mind Map

Practice Questions

1. What is a ping sweep?
   A. A scanning technique that indicates the range of TCP or UDP port numbers on a host.
   B. A network scanning technique that indicates the number of live hosts in a range of IP addresses.
   C. A solution that provides data security through encryption.
   D. A query and response protocol that identifies information about a domain, including the addresses that are assigned to that domain.

2. Which three are the main components of information security? (Choose any three)
   A. Threat prevention
   B. Authorization
   C. Confidentiality
   D. Countermeasures
   E. Integrity
   F. Availability

3. Which three characteristics describe SIEM technology? (Choose any three)
   A. It provides a comprehensive and centralized view of an IT infrastructure.
   B. It establishes VPN connection.
   C. It provides real-time analysis of logs and security alerts generated by network hardware or application.
   D. It saves data for the long time, so the organizations can have a detailed report of incident.
   E. It prevents man-in-the-middle attack.

4. Databases that categorizes the threats over the internet are known as:
   A. Common Vulnerabilities and Exposures (CVE)
   B. Simple Network Monitoring Protocol (SNMP)
   C. Simple Mail Transfer Protocol (SMTP)
   D. Intrusion Prevention System (IPS)

5. Which of the followings is an availability attack?
   A. Denial of service (DOS) attack
   B. DHCP snooping

C. Botnet
D. Phishing
E. Port security

6. Which of the followings are the attack generating methods? (Choose any three)
   A. Social Engineering
   B. Port security
   C. Reconnaissance
   D. Pharming
   E. DHCP Snooping

7. Which attack denies services reduce the functionality or prevent the access of the resources even to the legitimate users?
   A. Denial-of-Service (DoS) attack
   B. DHCP spoofing
   C. Botnet
   D. Phishing
   E. Pharming

8. Which of the two network security solutions can be used to prevent DoS attacks? (Choose any two)
   A. Virus Scanning
   B. Intrusion Protection Systems (IPS)
   C. Applying User Authentication
   D. Anti-Spoofing Technologies
   E. Data Encryption

9. An attacker with a laptop (rogue access point) is capturing all network traffic from a targeted user. Which type of attack is this?
   A. DHCP spoofing
   B. MAC overflow
   C. Man-in-the-Middle
   D. Whaling

10. What is the characteristic of a Trojan horse?
    A. A Trojan is a self-replicating malware, which infects system, files or programs.
    B. A Trojan horse carries out malicious operations under the guise of a legitimate

program.

C. Malicious software, which is designed to disguise itself misleading users of its true intent.

D. A malicious software application, which delivers ads through pop-up windows on any program's interface.

11. What is the characteristic of a worm malware?

A. A worm must be triggered by an event on the host system.

B. A malicious software application, which delivers ads through pop-up windows on any program's interface.

C. Once installed on a host system, a worm does not replicate itself.

D. A worm is a self-replicating malware, which infects system, files or programs.

12. An attacker is using Wireshark to discover administrative Telnet usernames and passwords. What type of network attack does this describe?

A. Denial of Service

B. Reconnaissance

C. Port Redirection

D. Trust Exploitation

13. Which malicious software is designed to encrypt user's data and then hackers demand ransom payment to decrypt the respective data?

A. Ransomware

B. Scareware

C. Worms

D. Adware

14. Which attack involves a software program attempting to discover a system password by using an electronic dictionary?

A. Denial of Service attack

B. Brute-Force attack

C. IP Spoofing attack

D. Man-in-the-Middle attack

E. Port Redirection attack

15. Which type of network has the topology where multiple LANs are interconnected but it is not expanded as Wide Area Network (WAN) or Metropolitan Area Network

(MAN)?
A. Campus Area Network
B. Cloud and Wide Area Network
C. Data Center
D. Small Office/Home Office (SOHO)

16. The technique of encrypting the clear text data into a scrambled code is called:
A. AAA authentication
B. Cryptography
C. Cisco Discovery protocol (CDP)
D. Cypher text

17. Which type of cryptography uses the same pair of keys on both sides?
A. Asymmetric Key Cryptography
B. Public Key Cryptography
C. Symmetric Key Cryptography
D. Hybrid Key Cryptography

18. The combination of policies, procedures, hardware, software, and people that are required to create, manage and revoke digital certificates is called?
A. Service Level Agreement (SLA)
B. Certificate Authority (CA)
C. Public Key Infrastructure (PKI)
D. None of the above

19. Which kind of potential threat can occur by Instant On in a data center?
A. When the primary firewall in the data center crashes.
B. When an attacker hijacks a VM hypervisor and then launches attacks against other devices in the data center.
C. When the primary IPS appliance is malfunctioning.
D. When a VM that may have outdated security policies is brought online after a long period of inactivity.

20. What role does the Security Intelligence Operations (SIO) play in Network architecture?
A. User authentication
B. Policy enforcement

C. Resource management
D. Identify and stop malicious traffic

21. What is the primary method of network defense for mitigating malware?
    A. Make use of encrypted or hashed authentication protocols.
    B. Install antivirus scanner or software on all hosts.
    C. Deploy intrusion prevention systems on the entire network.
    D. Deploy firewalls.

22. What usually motivates cyber attackers or criminals to attack networks as compared to hacktivists or state-sponsored hackers?
    A. Political reasons
    B. Fame seeking
    C. Network vulnerability testing
    D. Financial gain

23. What purpose does a digital certificate serve?
    A. It makes sure that a website has not been hacked.
    B. It authenticates a website and establishes a secure connection to exchange confidential data.
    C. It provides proof that data has a traditional signature attached.
    D. It ensures that the person who is gaining access to a network device is authorized.

24. Which of the following is a type of encryption algorithm that uses a pair of public and private keys to provide authentication, integrity, and confidentiality?
    A. Symmetric
    B. Shared Secret
    C. Both A and D
    D. Asymmetric

25. Which of the following type of an encryption algorithm uses the same key to encrypt and decrypt data?
    A. RSA
    B. Shared-Secret
    C. Public-Key
    D. Asymmetric

Chapter 02: Secure Access

Technology Brief

Network security is a term that refers to the measures to secure their corporate network and precautions taken to prevent unauthorized access in a network. Unauthorized access results in data loss, data tampering or disclosure of confidential data.

We can reduce the risk of security threats by implementing secure access controls. In today's world, the most common technology to connect employees and customers of an organization from anywhere is Bring Your Own Device (BYOD). BYOD leads end users to connect anytime, anywhere, using any device, which results in an ease of access for all. Being an easy and user-friendly solution to connect endpoints, it is also vulnerable for the organization to keep their access secure and risk for organization's assets.

Before moving towards the different methods of managing the secure access of network devices, first we need to categorize our network infrastructure and the need of security polices in the respective category to build the best possible security solution.

Basic Elements of Network infrastructure

A network infrastructure can be divided into three basic elements or functions, namely:

Management Plane

Management Plane is a logical plane dealing with management traffic and performs management related functions for a network and is capable to coordinate all other plane (Management, Control and Data plane). The management plan is also used to manage a device through the network.

Following are the protocols processed in management plane, these management protocols are used for monitoring and for CLI access:

1. Simple Network Management Protocol (SNMP)
2. Telnet
3. Hyper-Text Transfer Protocol (HTTP)
4. Secure HTTP (HTTPS)
5. Secure Shell (SSH)

Control Plane

Control Plane is often referred to as the brain of network device that deals with signaling, control packets and their operation. This plane deals with routing and control protocols in order to maintain sessions and exchanges protocol information with other devices. Control plane manages routing of a device including ACL and other security controls and policies. This plane is used for managing and controlling any forwarding table that the data plane uses. For example, routing protocols such as OSPF, EIGRP, RIP, and BGP as well as IPv4 ARP, IPv6 NDP, switch MAC address learning, and STP are all managed by the control plane.

Data Plane

Data plane is also known as user plane or forwarding plane. This plane is responsible for the switching of data packets. It is responsible for forwarding frames of packets from its ingress to egress interfaces using protocols managed in the control plane. Here, data is received, the destination interface is looked up, and the forwarding of frames and packets happens, so the data plane relies completely on the control plane to provide solid information.

This table summarizes the above concept and mitigating against risks and vulnerabilities involved in each plane.

Name	Purpose	Examples	Mitigating Against Common Attacks
Management Plane	Allows Network Administrators to access networking devices.	SSH/Telnet Sessions with router/switch, Syslog messages, SNMP traps and get messages etc.	Use of encrypted protocols like SSH/SFTP instead of TELNET/TFTP. Role based access control, Secure NTP, Login restrictions, AAA.
Control Plane	Any kind of traffic, which requires device-processing power.	Routing Protocols path calculation and their updates. Traffic directed to the IP address of Device itself.	Use of authentication feature in routing protocols. Using different control plane features present in specific models of device.
Data Plane	Physical movement of data between networking devices.	Any kind of traffic movement between hosts.	Use of ACLS, STP safeguards, Port Security, Firewalls, IDS / IPS for security.

Table 2-01: Categorization of Traffic Generated in a Network

Secure Management

In this section, we deal with the security measures for the management plane. Below are the recommendations for securing the management plane of a network:

Management Plane Protection (MPP)

Management Plane Protection (MPP) is a network management feature for Cisco IOS devices, which provide the capability to the network administrator to restrict the interfaces either to permit or deny the management packets. Additionally, MPP allows the administrator to configure a secure management interface designated for management packets, which permit the device management traffic.

Strong Password Recommendations

It is a good security practice to implement strong passwords wherever required. Passwords should not include some word or sentence that can be easily guessed through victim's personality or background. The minimum length as suggested by different standards must be followed and must include variable character types like "P@ssw@rd:10".

In this string, different variants make it difficult to break through it. Attackers always try to break password by two common password attacks namely *dictionary* and *brute force attacks*. In dictionary attacks, logging in process is automated using a list of guessable and daily life words. Words keep changing unless correct password is detected. In brute force attacks, instead of using list of words, a combination of characters is used as input to password field. This string keeps incrementing in length to get to the correct password. By using long and complex passwords, we can increase the time to insanely indefinite length before brute force attack can guess our password.

Lockout after Login Failure

We can also set the maximum logging in attempts within specific time period. After those attempts, we can lock the logging in process for specific time. This method can slow down different attacks like brute force as explained above.

User Authentication

Whenever a network administrator is required to access an asset of an organization, username/password combination must be used instead of just password. By using prompt for asking user name and integrating the results of username with AAA server (explained later on), will help us know which user is concerned with the alteration of respective data. Furthermore, we can also use multi-factor authentication and impose custom authentication and authorization policies to ensure and strengthen the authentication process.

Role Based Access Control (RBAC)

It involves the assignment of privilege level according to the specified role of an end user. Let us say in an organization, an IT department is comprised of ten employees. Only two of them, say Chris and John, are supposed to maintain and change the configuration of networking devices like routers, switches, and firewalls while the rest are assigned with some other tasks like *help-desk, network support, IT support* etc. If privilege level 15 is assigned to every person in that department and accidentally someone erased something like the IP addresses from interfaces or even erase flash as well as start-up configuration file, then it would be very difficult to trace the culprit.

Therefore, by implementing RBAC, we can set custom privilege levels and assign them to different users and groups depending on the role of their job. We can set custom privilege levels in between 1 and 15. The user with level 1 will not be able to make changes in configuration and the user with level 15 can do anything from configuration to deleting some data.

Role based CLI Access

Cisco offers Role-based CLI access feature for network administrators to restrict users accessing Cisco IOS command line interface. Role-based CLI access features offer the administrator to define "views". These views are the set of operational commands and configurations. Configuring a view allows selective or partial access to EXEC and Configuration mode commands. CLI views can be of following types:

Root View

A system in a root view has the same privileges as a user with privilege level 15. For creating any other view like CLI view or Super view, the administrator must be in root view.

CLI View

In a CLI view, there is no higher or lower views in specific, it consists of a bundle of specific commands.

Super view

A super view comprises of one or more CLI views, which allow users to define what commands are accepted from certain level and what configuration information is available for users. Users who are in a super view can access all the commands that are configured for any of the CLI views that are part of the super view.

Lawful Intercept View

A system in a lawful intercept view has access to specified commands and configuration information. Specifically, a lawful intercept view allows a user to secure access to lawful intercept commands; these commands are not available for any other view or privilege level.

Parser Views

Another great feature of Cisco IOS is parser views. Parser views do the same thing as custom privilege levels but they have fewer commands and they give a clear configuration view. From implementation point of view, first we define a view and then assign a user or group commands to it. Parser view feature provides granular access control by restricting the authorized users to a certain privilege level where specific set commands are allowed only.

In Band vs Out of Band Management

Generally, management within a network can be imposed using either In-band management or Out-of-band management. The difference between these two options is the communication channel used for these management packets. Following are the two method of implementing management on Cisco devices:

In band management: In this case, network path to access the device for management is same as normal data traffic. It provides ease of management by allowing administer the devices from any node within the network however, sharing the data channel will consume bandwidth.

Out of band management: In out-of-band management, we dedicate a specific channel or interface just for management traffic. Out-of-band management is reliable and avoids interference. Being out of band from data channels, it is harder to attack.

Most of the best management practices related to network states to have both in-band and out-band management. In-band management implies that common protocols like

TELNET and *SSH* should be used for accessing networking devices. Application requiring high quality of service (QoS) like voice or steaming will cause delay in the traffic.

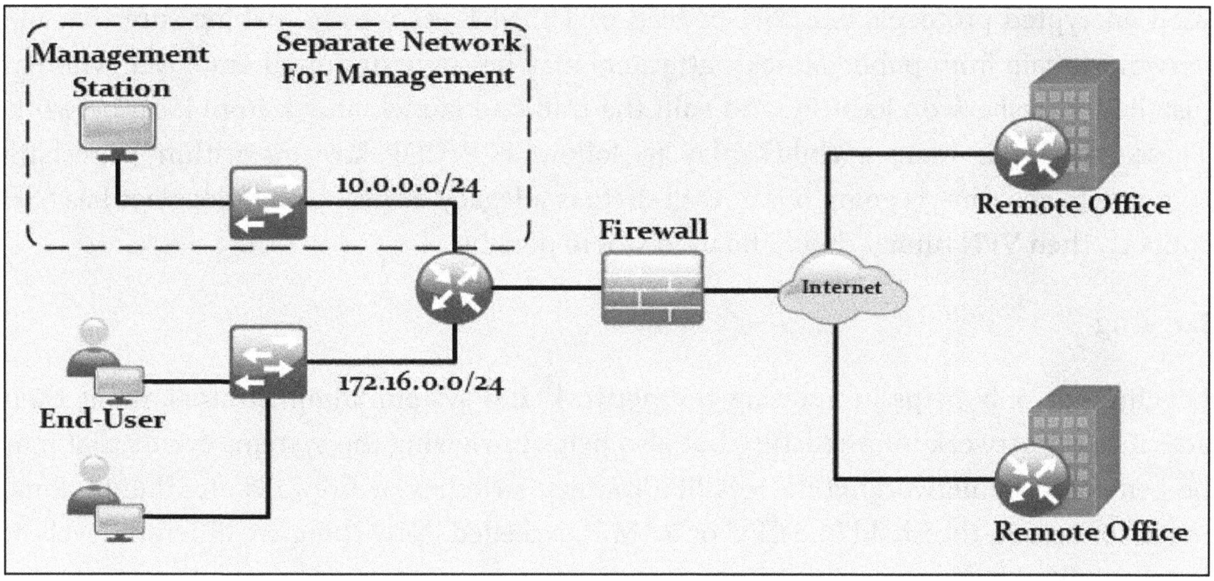

Figure 2-01: Example Scenario for In-Band vs. Out-of-Band Management

In-band and out-band management is a term used globally. It is not vendor specific to Cisco equipment. Normally in out-of-band management, an access server is used to be connected to management port of every single networking device. This access server is then configured with a public IP address with access limited to some specific known hosts. Another case would be to use a specific segment within organization for management purposes (a different VLAN other than end-users' etc.) like shown in the diagram above. If we just focus on the left side of firewall, we can see there are two segments connected to a router. If we use 10.0.0.0/24 network just for management then we can access the router through it in case the 172.16.0.0/24 segment is down due to any reason (for example a switch is choked etc.).

Most people argue and consider *out-of-band* as a useless measure. However, there are scenarios where we may lose the connectivity and we have to visit a site physically to fix some problem. In the scenario above, let us say that we used both segments for access of networking devices as well as data traffic. In case both switches are heavily degraded due to performance issues, link between router and switches is optical fiber based, router is connected to some other city and, there is problem in some remote site, then we have no other option but to visit the site to fix the problem.

Encrypted Protocols for Remote Access

Both in using either *in-band* or *out-of-band* management, the first priority should be to used encrypted protocols like SSH instead of TELNET. As we are making sure that our network is safe from public attacks, attackers may be some disguised employee who has installed *Wireshark* on local PC and sniff the traffic to launch attack from local network. These days, it is mere a child's play to follow TCP/UDP streams within Wireshark software to see what is going on. In case there is a legacy device, which does not has SSH support, then VPN tunnel should be used where possible.

Logging

Logging not only helps in auditing the network and system administrators about their activities on network infrastructure but also helps in viewing the systems events that may be generated by networking devices like routers, switches or firewalls etc. due to some failure or certain threshold like CPU or RAM is exceeded. Now there are different levels of logs generated by these devices.

As far as Cisco devices and Cisco IOS are concerned, it can send log output to the following destinations:

Console: A Router/Switch/Firewall can send log messages to the connected terminal. For example, an attached computer with terminal emulation program running like HyperTerminal.

VTY Lines: Whenever an administrator tries to connect remotely to Cisco devices, a *VTY line* is activated for that *exec session*. Depending on the device model, this number may vary. Terminal Monitor command also needs to be issued at privilege level 15 to see the logs on terminal.

Buffer: In order to save log messages for later analysis, device's internal memory (RAM) can be used. Depending on the size of RAM dedicated for storing log messages, which is named as buffer, these messages are stored on first-in/first-out basis. As RAM is emptied on reboot, so is the buffer.

SNMP Server: Log messages can be sent to the SNMP server in the form of SNMP TRAPs if configured on devices. Normally, SNMPv3 is preferred due to its support for Hashing and Encryption.

Syslog Server: A Syslog server is a dedicated device, whose purpose is to store any kind of log messages directed to it. Depending on the nature of event, which generated the log message, an immediate action may be required by a responsible person otherwise situation may get worse. To categorize the events, Syslog uses eight severity levels from zero to seven with zero being more critical one when system becomes severely degraded.

Name	Level	Description
Emergencies	0	System is unusable
Alerts	1	Immediate Action needed
Critical	2	Critical Condition
Errors	3	Error Condition
Warnings	4	Warning Condition
Notifications	5	Normal but require attention
Informational	6	Informational messages
Debugging	7	Debugging messages with maximum details depending on number of processes for which debugging is enabled

Table 2-02: Syslog Severity Levels and their Descriptions

A Syslog, being the most suitable and usable option, is based on client server architecture. It means there will be a Syslog server and multiple Syslog Clients (different networking devices). Keep it in mind that more detailed log messages will be required than hard drive space for storage. Normally, a RAID technology is also considered where the log belongs to important infrastructure.

As Log messages contain important information, if it is leaked, it may result in very serious attacks on the network. The payload of Syslog messages, which may contain information like IP addresses, username/password of logged in users etc., should be in encrypted form when in transit over the network.

NTP Service: Another important feature of Logging is the time stamp of an event. An attacker may want to change the time settings so that user may be unaware of an event. In order to synchronize the time over the network, *Network Time Protocol (NTP)* is used. Now a day, NTP v3 is widely used due to its support for encryption.

NTP uses *UDP port number 123*. Although Cisco routers can be set to be the NTP Clients of publically available NTP servers, we can set a single device in network infrastructure to be NTP server and all the devices will synchronize their time according to the NTP server. One of the advantages we have by using NTP is to correlate different events. If time is tampered, it would be impossible to find the root cause of main problem.

Lab 2.1: Configure Secure Network Management

Cisco routers and switches come with no password set on login interfaces. Some Cisco devices come with username set to *Cisco* and password set to *Cisco.* Whenever a user tries to login either via console port, Telnet/SSH session, it gets *level 1* access where basic command set is available. One of the commonly used commands at level 1 is *show* command used to show various important information like IP addresses assigned to each interface. When a user enters ***enable*** command at level 1, it gets the level 15 access where complete access of router is available. Now a user can enter into global configuration of Cisco IOS by typing ***configure terminal*** and can change anything. Two important access usernames/passwords identified in above discussion are:

Level 1 username/password prompt: Level 1 access must be allowed after successful attempt of correct username and password, because an attacker can get various information, which can result in reconnaissance attacks.

Enable/level 15 password: If an attacker accesses level 15 of device, implementation of whole security posture is of no good use. Previous versions of Cisco IOS support the *enable password* command. This command is replaced with the *enable secret* command, which increases the security of password phrase by storing it in hashed form in configuration. *Enable password* command stores password in plain text. Additional command of *service password-encryption* is used to store passwords in hashed form but it can be cracked with simple methods.

Mode	Access Method	Prompt	Exit Method
User EXEC mode	Log in.	Router>	Type "logout" command.
Privileged EXEC mode	Type "**enable**" in EXEC mode, to enter privilege mode.	Router#	To return to user EXEC mode, type "disable" command.
Global configuration mode	Type "configure terminal" or "config t" to enter global mode from privileged EXEC mode.	Router(config)#	To return to privileged EXEC mode from global configuration mode, use the exit or end command, or press Ctrl-Z.
Interface configuration mode	Type "interface" command to specify an interface.	Router(config-if)#	To return to global configuration mode, use the exit command. To return to privileged EXEC mode, use the end command, or press Ctrl-Z.

Table 2-03: Command Modes

Another important aspect of accessing the device remotely is using SSH instead of Telnet. Wireshark is a common sniffing tool used to follow the TCP/UDP streams. Telnet does not use encryption, which can result in *Man-in-the-middle* attacks. To enable SSH on Cisco devices, *hostname* and *domain name* are mandatory to be configured before generating RSA keys for SSH. Hostname and domain name can be set in global configuration mode.

Management access should also be limited to specific IP addresses of management station. By entering ***line VTY*** command in global configuration mode, a user can get into special configuration mode related to remote access of Cisco device. Number of Telnet/SSH sessions a device can made depends on specific model number and its series. By entering special configuration mode, ***access-class*** command is used to call Access List in inward direction to allow only management station to access devices.

Let us implement these concepts on the router shown in the diagram below. The number of routers and switches may increase, but the basic concept of security remains the same.

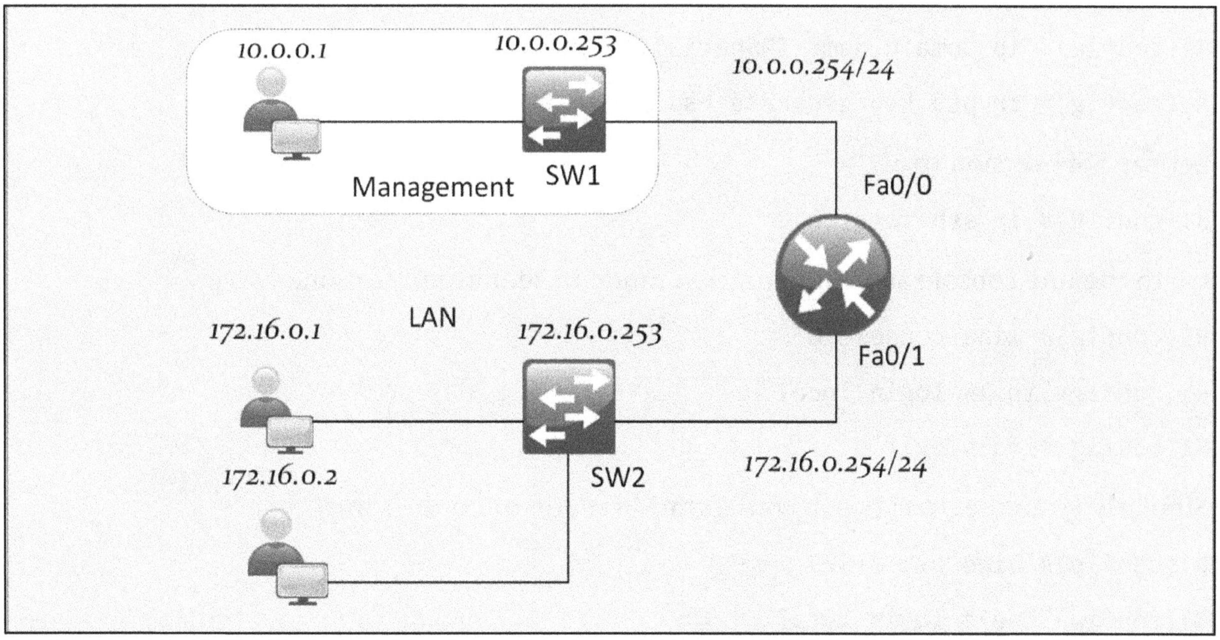

Figure 2-02: Topology diagram

Let us assume that management station has an IP address of *10.0.0.1.* As Cisco devices come with no configurations, we need to access the device via console port for the first time to implement the concepts defined above.

R1:

Enter the level 15 by entering enable on user privilege mode.

```
R1> enable
```

Enter configure terminal to enter the global configuration mode.

```
R1# configure terminal
```

Use enable secret command to set the level 15 password.

Use long string of password with multiple character types.

```
R1(config)# enable secret P@$$word:10
```

Define a username and password with associated privilege level.

```
R1(config)# username IPSpecialist privilege 1 secret P@$$word:10
```

Set the hostname of your choice.

```
R1(config)# hostname R1
```

Set the domain name and RSA for SSH.

```
R1(config)# ip domain name IPSpecialist.net
R1(config)# crypto key generate rsa general-keys modulus 1024
```

Set the SSH version to 2.

```
R1(config)# ip ssh version 2
```

Go to the line console sub configuration mode to set authentication.

```
R1(config)# line console 0
R1(config-line)# login local
R1(config-line)# exit
```

Similarly go to the line vty sub configuration mode to do the same.

```
R1(config)# line vty 0 903
R1(config-line)# login local
```

Enable only SSH. Disable Telnet for being less secured.

```
R1(config-line)# transport input ssh
```

Also, call access list to limit access to only to management-station.

```
R1(config-line)# access-class MGMT-STATION in
R1(config-line)# exit
```

Now define MGMT-STATION named based ACL.

```
R1(config)# ip access-list standard MGMT-STATION
R1(config-std-nacl)# permit host 10.0.0.1
R1(config-std-nacl)# exit
```

Go to line aux sub configuration mode.

```
R1(config-line)# line aux 0
R1(config-line)# login local
```

Verification:

Open PuTTY on management PC. Enter router's IP address. Management PC should be able to access the router through SSH.

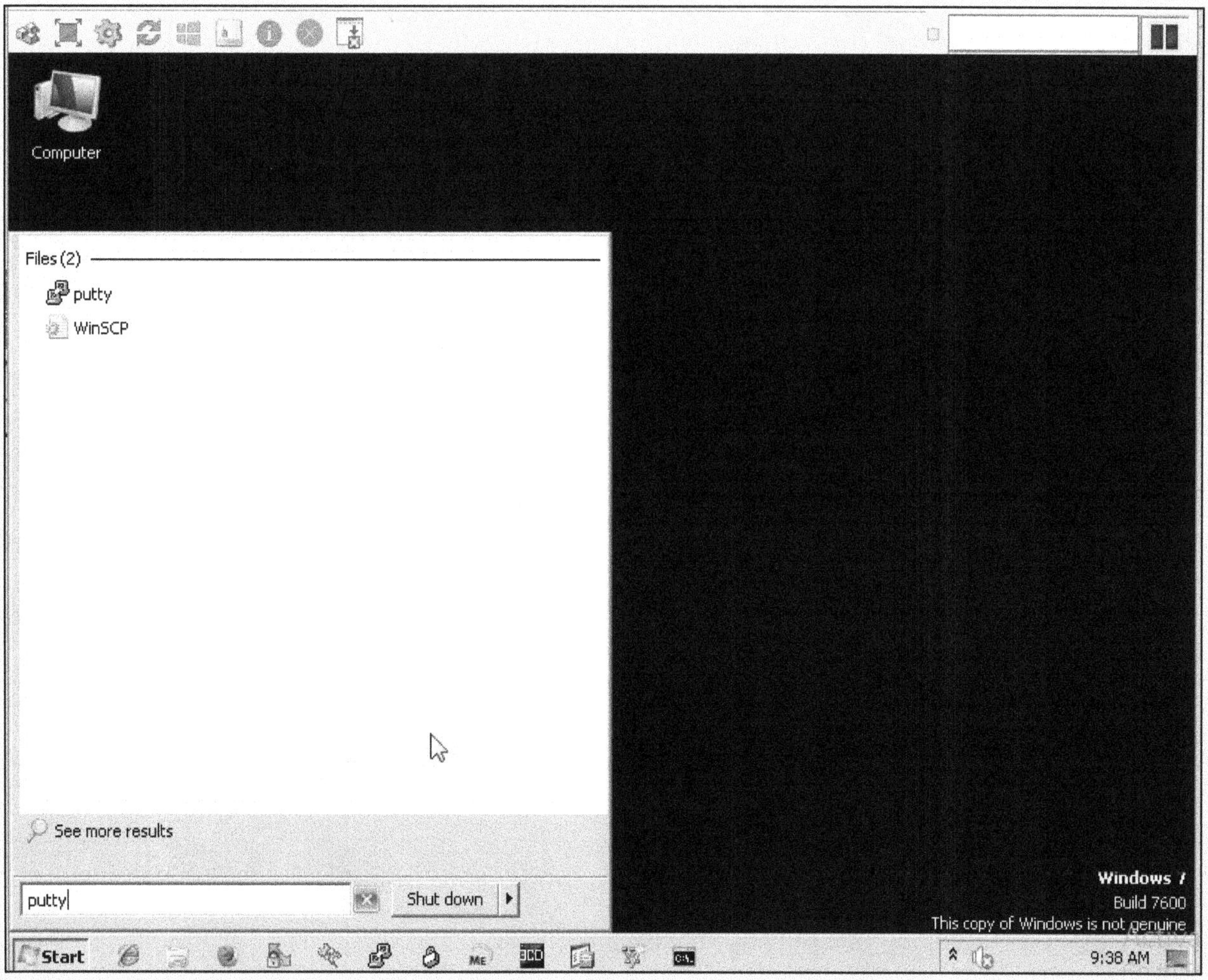

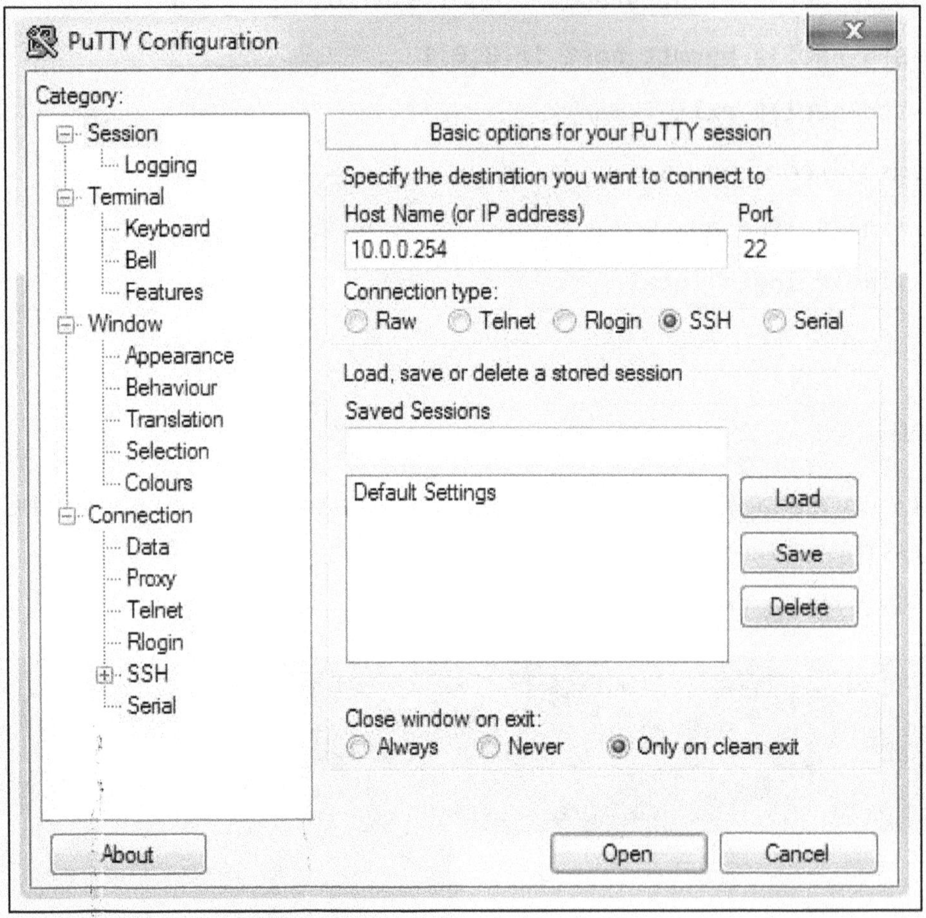

Click "Open" and you will be prompted with login username prompt. Enter "IPSpecialist" as username and "P@$$word:10" as password. You will also be prompted with Putty security alert. Click "Yes" to continue.

After entering the username and password, you should get Level 1 access. Enter Level 15 by entering "enable command" and providing the above-defined password.

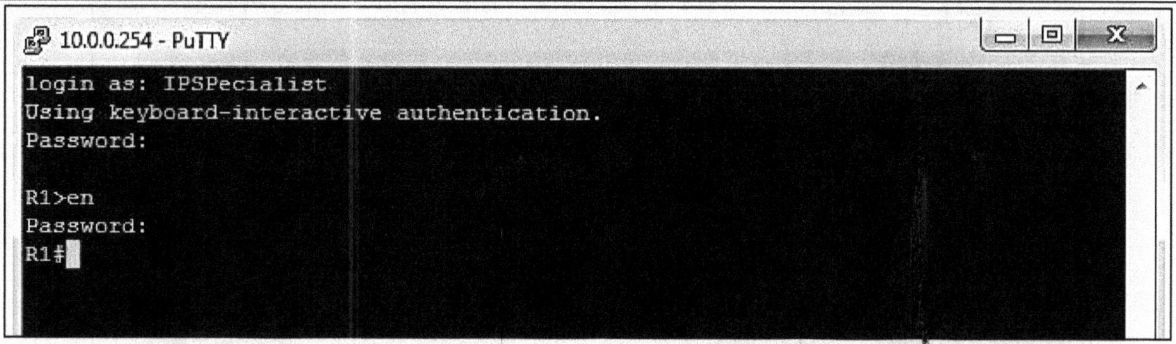

Now close this connection and use telnet instead of SHH. You will not be able to connect through Telnet as SSH is the only allowed option in the configuration.

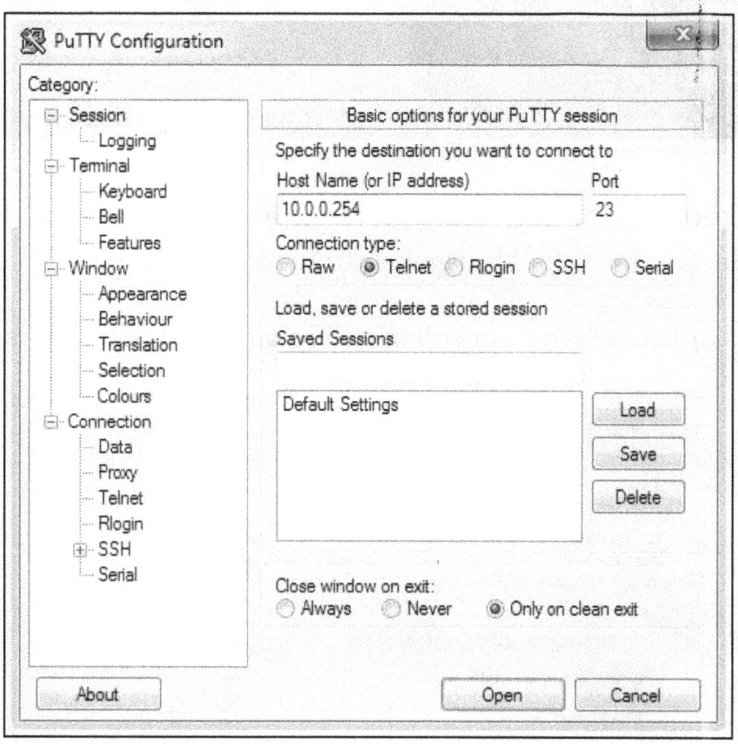

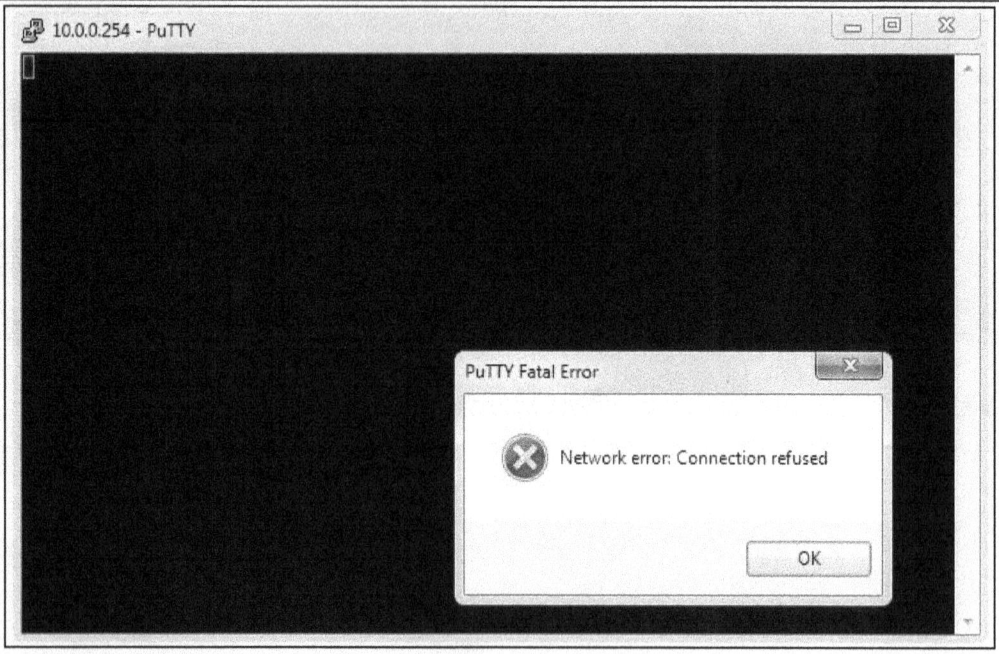

As Management Station is the only user allowed to access router with 10.0.0.1 as source IP address, change the IP address of Management Station to verify it.

Change IP address of *Local Area Connection 2* to 10.0.0.2 and SSH will not work this time.

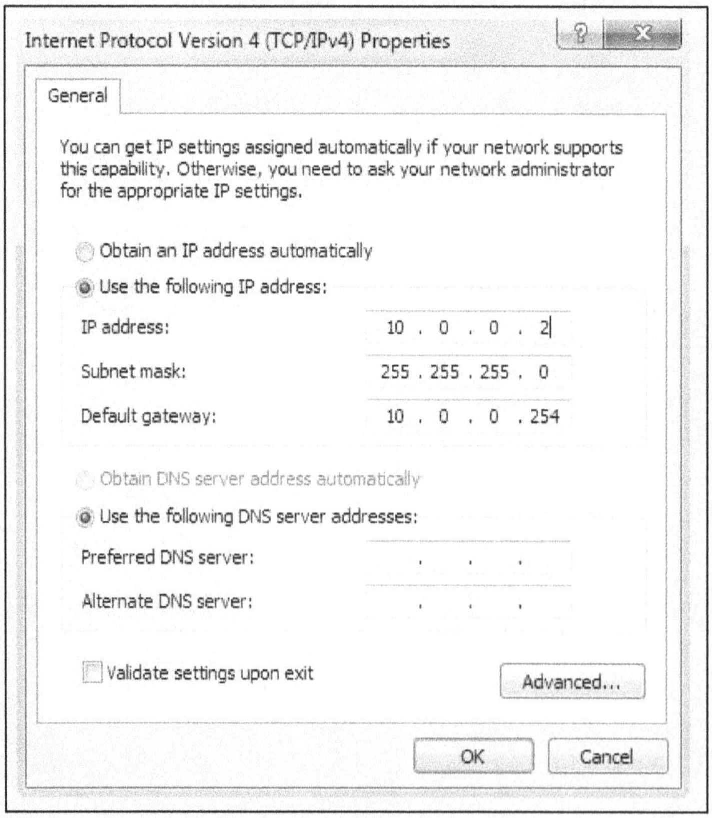

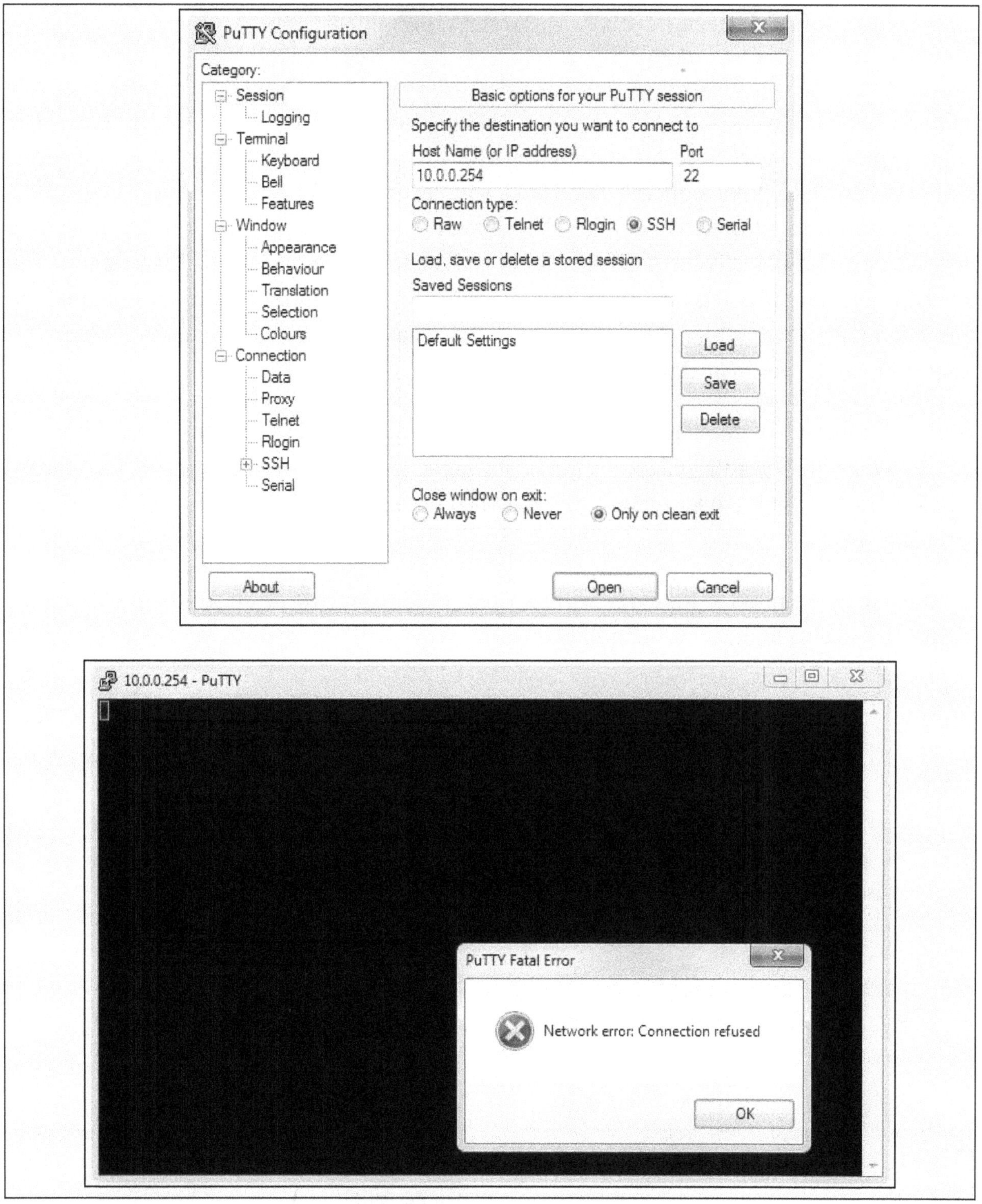

So, by basic Passwords Setting And Filtering Remote Access, we can control network access by authorized or unauthorized users.

Lab 2.2: Custom Privilege Levels And Parser Views

In the previous lab, only Level 1 and Level 15 access had been tested. While Cisco IOS allows users to make different privilege levels from Level 1 to Level 15, it eases the management of network staff itself. By default, privilege level 15 is set on Cisco devices, but level 15 is of great concern regarding the security of device, having access of all configurations to all users is not a good approach of securing the network. Any user with level 15 has all rights to access Cisco routers and switches. To overcome this problem, the concept of least privilege must be implemented, which states that a user should be provided with as limited access as possible while making sure that the tasks assigned to that user can be performed with that limited access.

Another method of implementing the concept above is using *parser views*. Although parser views give clearer look and understanding as compared to custom privilege levels, but it is rarely used. Parser views limit the view or number of commands irrespective of privilege level.

In this lab, the same lab topology will be used. Following two users will be created with respective access limitations defined below:

Username1: IPSpecialist

Password: P@$$word:10

Privilege level: 15

Username2: NetworkSupport

Password: Network$upport:10

Privilege level 4

Allowed Access: User can only change IP address and shutdown interfaces

R1:
Enter the level 15 by entering enable on user privilege mode.
`R1> enable`
Enter configure terminal to enter the global configuration mode.
`R1# configure terminal`

Use enable secret command to set the level 15 password.

Use long string of password with multiple character types.

```
R1(config)# enable secret  P@$$word:10
```

Define a usernames and passwords with associated privilege level.

```
R1(config)# username IPSpecialist privilege 15 secret P@$$word:10
R1(config)# username NetworkSupport privilege 4 secret 0 Network$upport:10
```

Now define the commands associated with custom privilege levels.

```
R1(config)# privilege interface level 4 shutdown
R1(config)# privilege interface level 4 ip address
R1(config)# privilege interface level 4 no shutdown
R1(config)# privilege interface level 4 no ip address
R1(config)# privilege configure level 4 interface
R1(config)# privilege exec level 4 configure terminal
R1(config)# privilege exec level 4 configure
```

Set the hostname of your choice.

```
R1(config)# hostname R1
```

Set the domain name for SSH to work.

```
R1(config)# ip domain name IPSpecialist.net
R1(config)# crypto key generate rsa general-keys modulus 1024
```

Set the SSH version to 2.

```
R1(config)# ip ssh version 2
```

Go to the line console sub configuration mode to set authentication.

```
R1(config)# line console 0
R1(config-line)# login local
R1(config-line)# exit
```

Similarly go to the line vty sub configuration mode to do the same.

```
R1(config)# line vty 0 903
R1(config-line)# login local
```

Enable only SSH. Disable Telnet for being less secured.

```
R1(config-line)# transport input ssh
```

Also, call access list to limit access to only to management-station.

```
R1(config-line)# access-class MGMT-STATION in
R1(config-line)# exit
```

Now define MGMT-STATION named based ACL.

```
R1(config)# ip access-list standard MGMT-STATION
R1(config-std-nacl)# permit host 10.0.0.1
R1(config-std-nacl)# exit
```

Go to line aux sub-configuration mode.

```
R1(config-line)# line aux 0
R1(config-line)# login local
R1(config-std-nacl)# exit
```

Verification

In a real network, we use multiple stations for network staff. However, in virtual environment, same management station with an IP address of 10.0.0.1 will be used to verify the above concept.

Log in to R1 router using putty and SSH as your choice of protocol. When asked for username and password prompt, use NetworkSupport as username and Network$upport:10 as password to log in.

When a user enters *show run* command, which shows running configuration of router, error will be prompted, as it is not allowed at privilege level 4. Show privilege command can be used to see current privilege level.

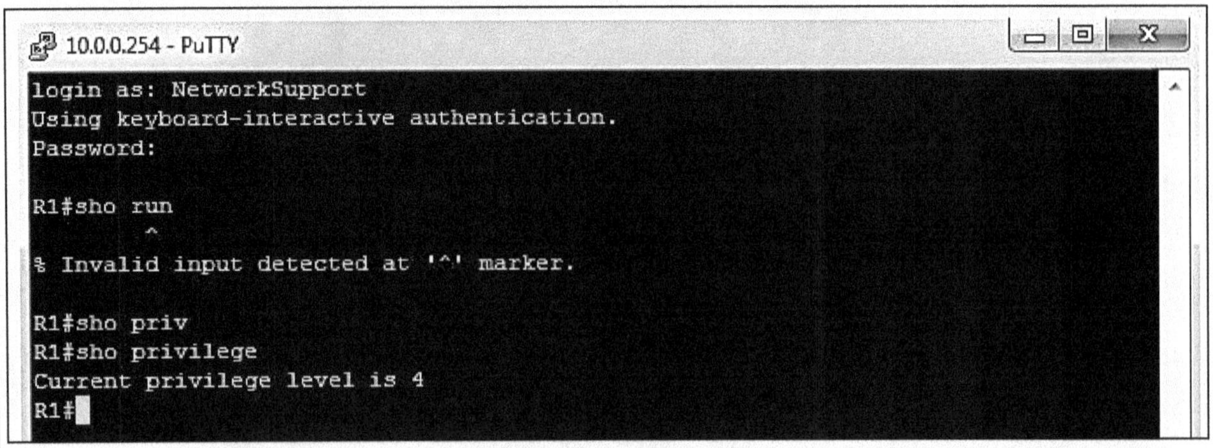

10.0.0.254 - PuTTY
login as: NetworkSupport
Using keyboard-interactive authentication.
Password:
R1#sho run
^
% Invalid input detected at '^' marker.
R1#sho priv
R1#sho privilege
Current privilege level is 4
R1#

As IP addressing and interface shutdown commands are allowed at privilege level 4, very few options are available at sub-configuration mode of specific interfaces.

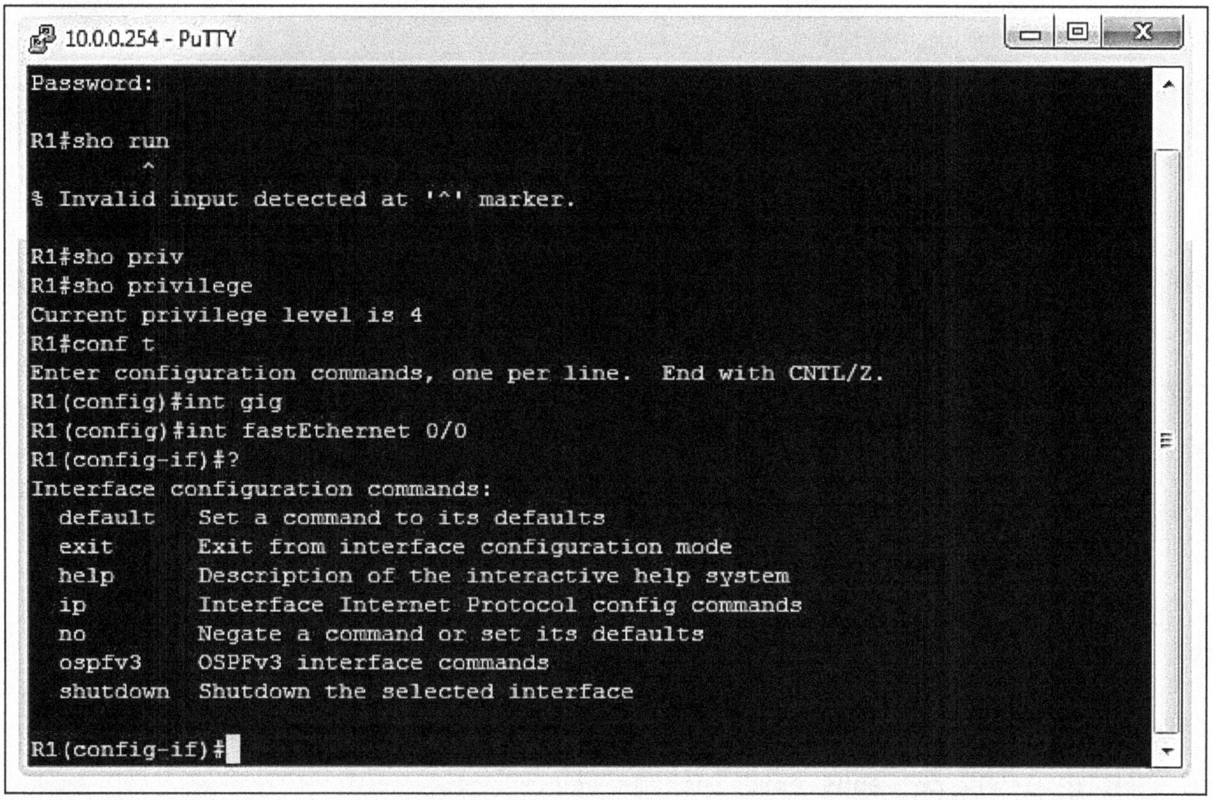
10.0.0.254 - PuTTY
Password:
R1#sho run
^
% Invalid input detected at '^' marker.
R1#sho priv
R1#sho privilege
Current privilege level is 4
R1#conf t
Enter configuration commands, one per line. End with CNTL/Z.
R1(config)#int gig
R1(config)#int fastEthernet 0/0
R1(config-if)#?
Interface configuration commands:
default Set a command to its defaults
exit Exit from interface configuration mode
help Description of the interactive help system
ip Interface Internet Protocol config commands
no Negate a command or set its defaults
ospfv3 OSPFv3 interface commands
shutdown Shutdown the selected interface
R1(config-if)#

In the second part of this lab, same task will be performed by using parser view. The following user will be created in the above lab scenario with respective access limitations defined below:

Username: Chris

Password: P@$$word:10

Privilege level: 15

Associated Parser view: help-desk

Associated set of commands with parser view: Can view *show version, show ip* and *show* commands.

R1:
Parser view required AAA to be enabled first. Enter aaa new-model command.
`R1(config)# aaa new-model`
Use "enable secret" to enter in to root view.
`R1# enable view`
`Password: ***********`
Use show parser view command to check current parser view.
`R1# show parser view`
`Current view is 'root'`
Create new parser view with name help-desk and enter associated commands.
`R1# config t`
`R1(config)# parser view help-desk`
`R1(config-view)# secret P@$$word:10`
`R1(config-view)# commands exec include all show ip`
`R1(config-view)# commands exec include all show version`
`R1(config-view)# commands exec include show`
`R1(config-view)# exit`
Now create a username and associate parser view with it.
`R1(config)# username Chris view help-desk privilege 15 secret P@$$word:10`
Configure the router to use local database for authentication and authorization.
`R1(config)# aaa authorization exec default local`
`R1(config)# aaa authentication login default local`
Two method lists are called in the above command. Method list with name "default" gets active on any kind of access. If we define a custom method list, then it must be called on line console and line vty sub configuration mode.

Verification:

Log in to router R1 with username "Chris" and associated password. Although user has privilege level 15 access, but limited commands will be displayed as defined in help-desk parser view.

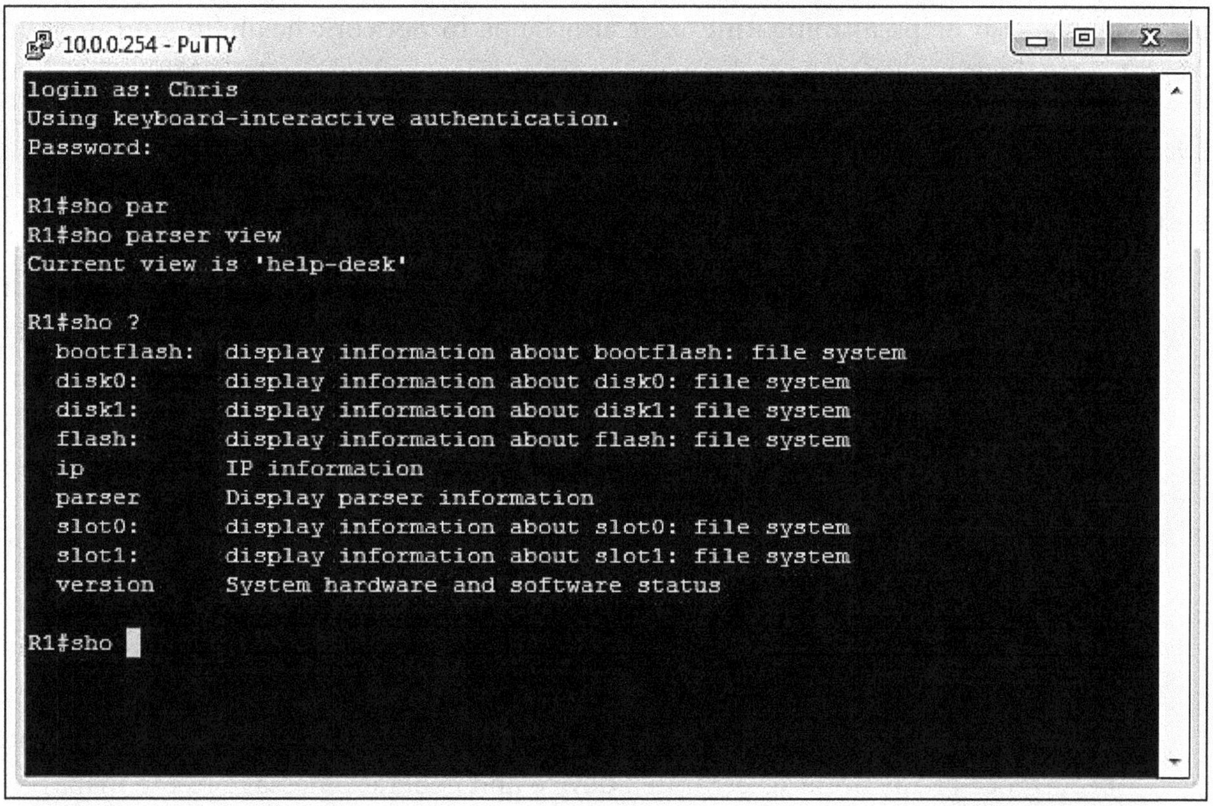

Lab 2.3: Use Of Snmpv3 NTP SCP And Syslog For Secure Access And Management

Simple network management protocol (SNMP) is a protocol that provides the format of messages for communication between managers and agents. SNMP is an application layer protocol, which enables network administer to monitor network health, its performance and helps to troubleshoot the issues. SNMP not only helps in finding the network's problem but also helps in mitigating it, it also helps in network flexibility and growth. Almost every single vendor supports Simple Network Management Protocol (SNMP).

Technically three components are involved in deploying SNMP in a network:

- **SNMP Manager:**

  SNMP manager is a Software application that is running on the management system to control and monitors the network hosts using SNMP. One of the most common network manager is Network Management System (NMS). NMS can either be a dedicated device or an application installed in a system. Commonly used SNMP software are PRTG, Solarwinds, OPManager etc. Free edition of OPManager will be used in this lab scenario.

- **SNMP Agent**:

  All the devices with in a network needs to be managed and come under the category of (SNMP) agent, it is basically a software component within a managed device that maintains the health and performance of that device such as an occurrence of any event or error in a device and generate message to the manager. The agent resides on the routing device (router, access server, or switch). Examples include CPU/RAM usage, interface status etc. UDP port number 161 is used for communication between SNMP agent and SNMP manager.

- **Management Information Base:**

  MIB stands for Management Information Base and is a collection of information organized hierarchically in a virtual database. This is accessed using a protocol such as SNMP.

There are two types of MIBs: -

MIB Types	Description
Scaler	It defines a single object instance.
Tabular	It defines multiple related objects instances.

Table 2-04: Types of Management Information Base (MIB)

Scalar objects define a single object instance whereas tabular objects define multiple related object instances grouped in MIB tables. MIBs are collections of definitions, which define the properties of the managed object within the device to be managed.

This collection of information such as a description of network objects that are organized & managed hierarchically in MIB using SNMP is addressed through Object Identifiers (OIDs). These Object identifiers (OIDs) include MIB objects like String, Address, Counter, Access level and other information.

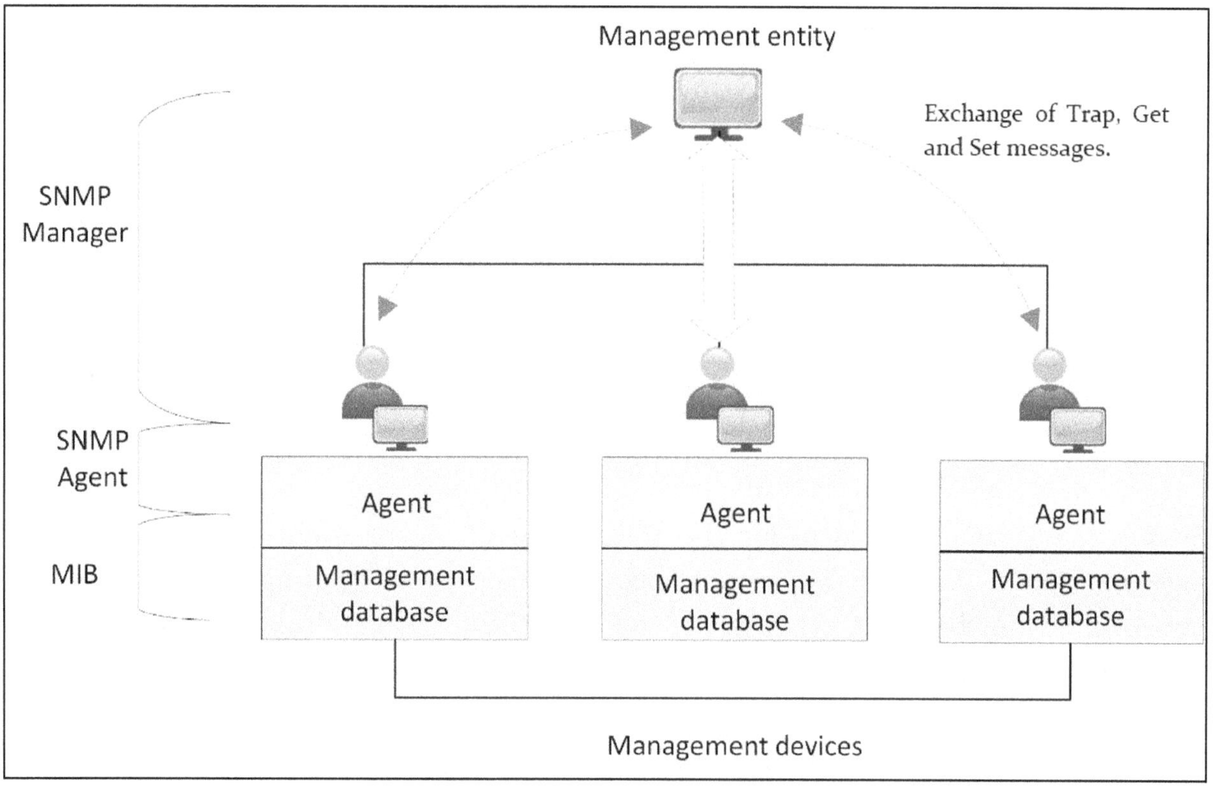

Figure 2-03: Versions of SNMP and Their Features

The features of available SNMP variants are:

SNMP version	Features
V1	No support for encryption and hashing. Plain text community string is used for authentication.
V2c	No support for encryption and hashing either. Some great functions like ability to get data in bulk from agents are implemented in version 2c.
V3	Support for both encryption (DES) and hashing (MD5 or SHA). Implementation of version 3 has three models. NoAuthNoPriv means no encryption and hashing will be used. AuthNoPriv means only MD5 or SHA based hashing will be used. AuthPriv means both encryption and hashing will be used for SNMP traffic.

Table 2-05: Versions of SNMP and Their Features

NTP

Another important aspect of collecting information is the **time** at which that specific event occurs. Attackers may try to change the time stamps setting of router or may introduce rough NTP server in the network to mislead the forensic teams. Network time protocol (NTP) is a protocol that allows networking devices like routers, switches etc. to synchronize their time with respect to the NTP server, so the devices may have more authenticated time settings and generated syslog messages can be observed more easily. This helps in analyzing problems and attacks during troubleshooting. Now, network time protocol (NTP) v3 is used to synchronize computer clock in the network because it supports authentication with NTP server.

Syslog Server

Syslog is a standard protocol for the transaction of log or event messages within a network. Although SNMP traps are enough for daily-based routing maintenance of a network, but for having a granular control over the event monitoring, Syslog server is used. Simply, you need to configure network devices (routers, switches, servers etc.) to generate Syslog or event messages and forward them to the syslog server. It is easily available, as either an open source or a proprietary. Any event like Hits on ACL, login attempts on networking devices along with other features like interface's status are collected by Syslog server.

The only disadvantage of Syslog server is that it generates clear text traffic i.e. the data is not encrypted, so it will be easily available for the unauthorized person. If a user enters a login username and password to perform some action, its password will be sent in clear text to Syslog server. Therefore, encryption needs to be implemented on any kind of syslog traffic, which includes sensitive information like usernames and passwords.

In this lab scenario, management station acts to be a syslog server and SNMP management station at the same time. Router R2 will act as a simulated public internet. This router will also act as a secure NTP server. Router R1 will be configured to get time from this NTP server, which will be used further in Syslog messages timestamps.

The following topology will be used in this lab scenario:

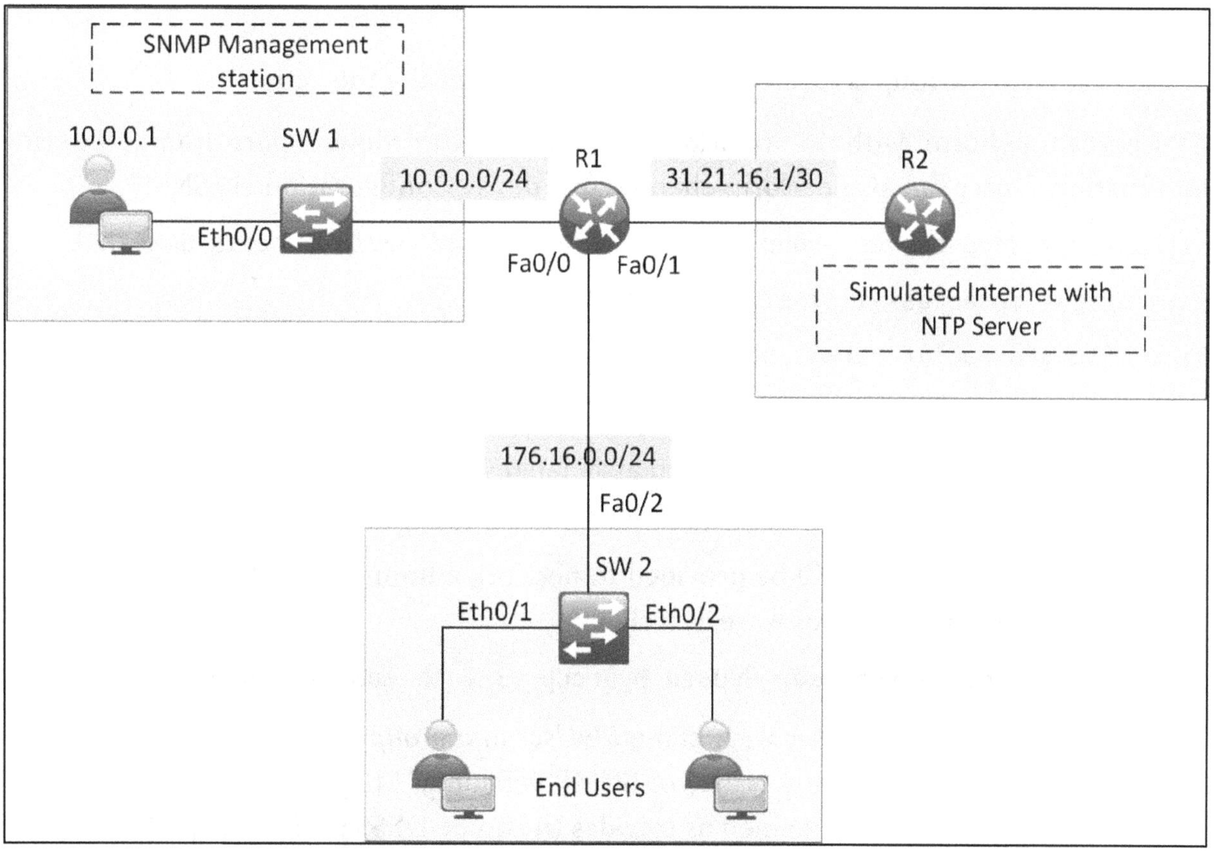

Figure 2-04: Lab 2.3 Topology

It is also assumed that previous labs are properly implemented and tested. Custom privilege levels, parser views and other concepts implemented in previous labs are implemented in this lab as well so that by the end of this section, a complete picture of securing management access will be shown.

R1:

First part of this lab explains the configuration of SNMP v3.

In first step, a view is created. SNMP with default configuration will send every single piece of information defined in its MIB. If specific information needs to be monitored, then only that information should be included in view.

More information regarding MIB hierarchy can be found on Cisco website.

R1(config)# **snmp-server view MyView iso included**

ISO sits on the top of MIB hierarchy. We can view everything related to the device by just including ISO view.

In the next step "a Group is created" to call a view and specify the action.

A user can perform with information provided in the view. Apart from collecting information, a user can also perform changes in a device configuration via SNMP.

R1(config)# **snmp-server group MyGroup v3 auth read MyView access SNMP-ACL**

R1(config)# **ip access-list standard SNMP-ACL**

R1(config-std-nacl)# **permit host 10.0.0.1**

R1(config-std-nacl)# **exit**

In the above command, MyView has been associated with SNMP-ACL. Only hosts defined in SNMP-ACL will receive the SNMP Information.

Further, "a user is created" will be provided to network administrator to be defined in the SNMP management station software as well.

R1(config)# **snmp-server user MyUser MyGroup v3 auth md5 P@$$word:10**

Above command defines a user with name *MyUser in a group MyGroup* with auth model md5 (it can be md5, sha or any other) of SNMP version 3. MD5 is used as algorithm for hashing. Here privacy is also defined as priv des (it can be DES, 33DES AES {128|192|256}).

Configure remote IP address of SNMP management station with SNMP Engine ID of Device.

Use *show snmp engineID* command to get current EngineID.

R1# **show snmp engineID**

```
*Mar  1 00:51:32.659: %SYS-5-CONFIG_I: Configured from console by console
Router#show snmp engineID
Local SNMP engineID: 800000090300C2036F3F0000
Remote Engine ID          IP-addr    Port
```

An SNMP agent is also referred to as SNMP engine. This engine or agent responds to incoming messages (Get, GetNext, GetBulk, Set), and sends trap messages to the SNMP manager. By default, the SNMP Engine ID is made up of enterprise number and the default MAC address. Every SNMP Engine ID or MAC address is unique, so that no other device in a network has the same Engine ID.

Now, associate the engine ID with the IP address of SNMP management station.

```
R1# config t
R1(config)# snmp-server engineID remote 10.0.0.1 800000090300C2036F3F0000
```

Here, 10.0.0.1 is an IP address of SNMP manager, which will get all the SNMP messages.

Configure the desired SNMP management station software.

In this lab, OP Manager free edition is used.

SNMP verification:

Open the Firefox web browser pinned at the start bar of management station and type "localhost". You will get the following screen. Click "First Time User" and then "Login".

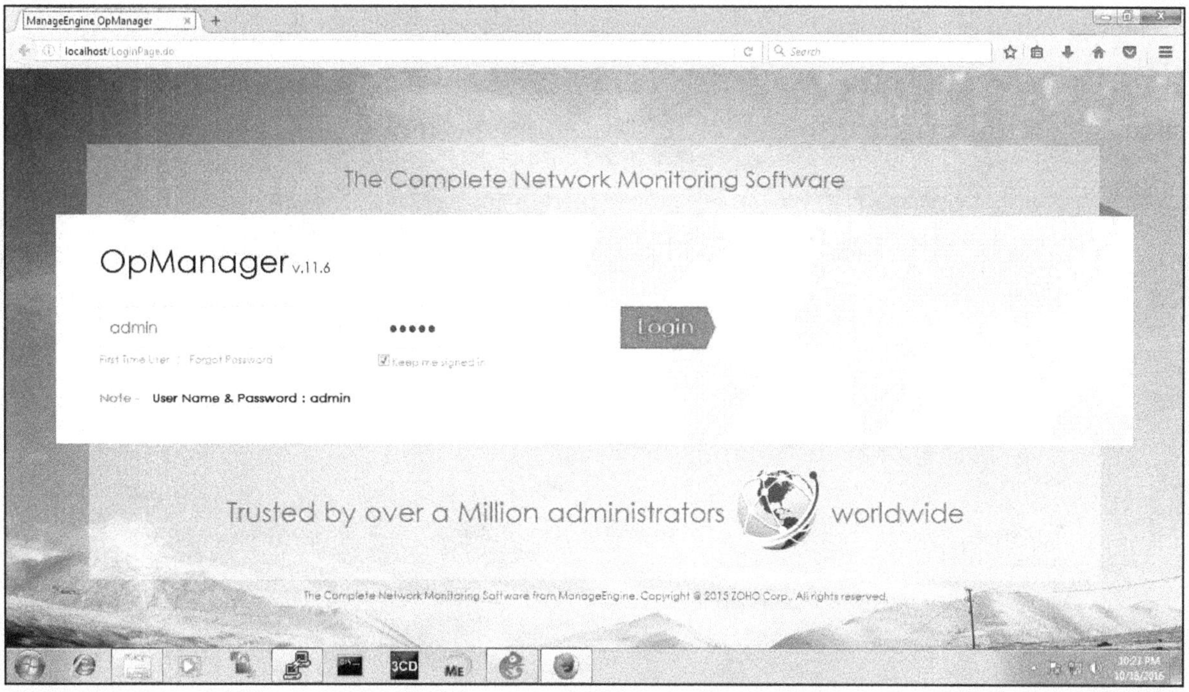

Discovery gives user the ability to find devices on IP address range defined by the user. Enter the out-of-band management address range as shown below:

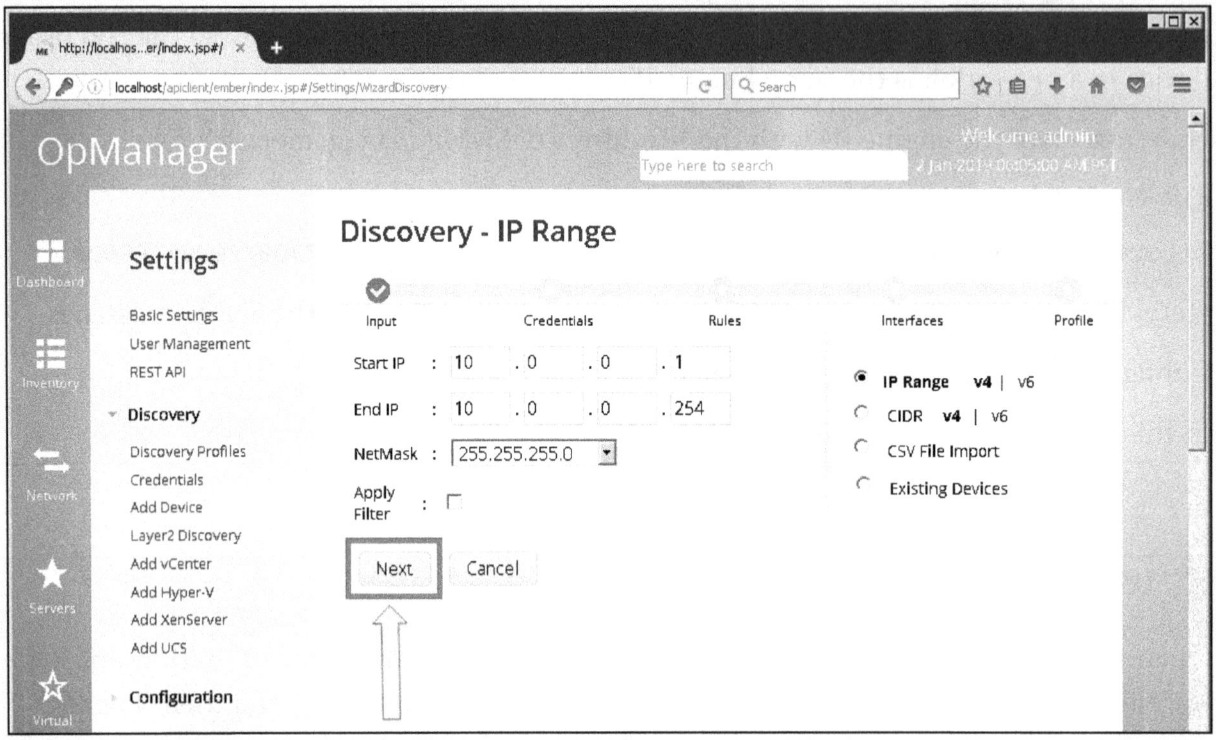

By clicking on "Next", a web page will be prompted for user credentials we defined on R1 and R2 router. Enter the credentials of SNMPv3 AuthNoPriv model. Select MD5 as hashing algorithm as it has to match with R1's configuration.

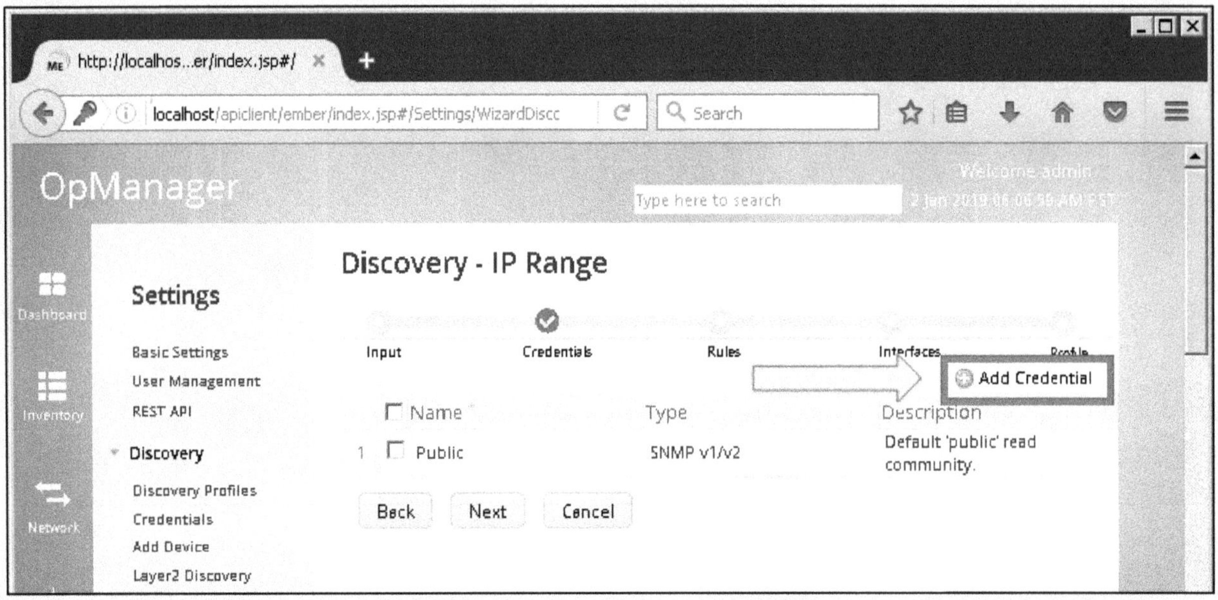

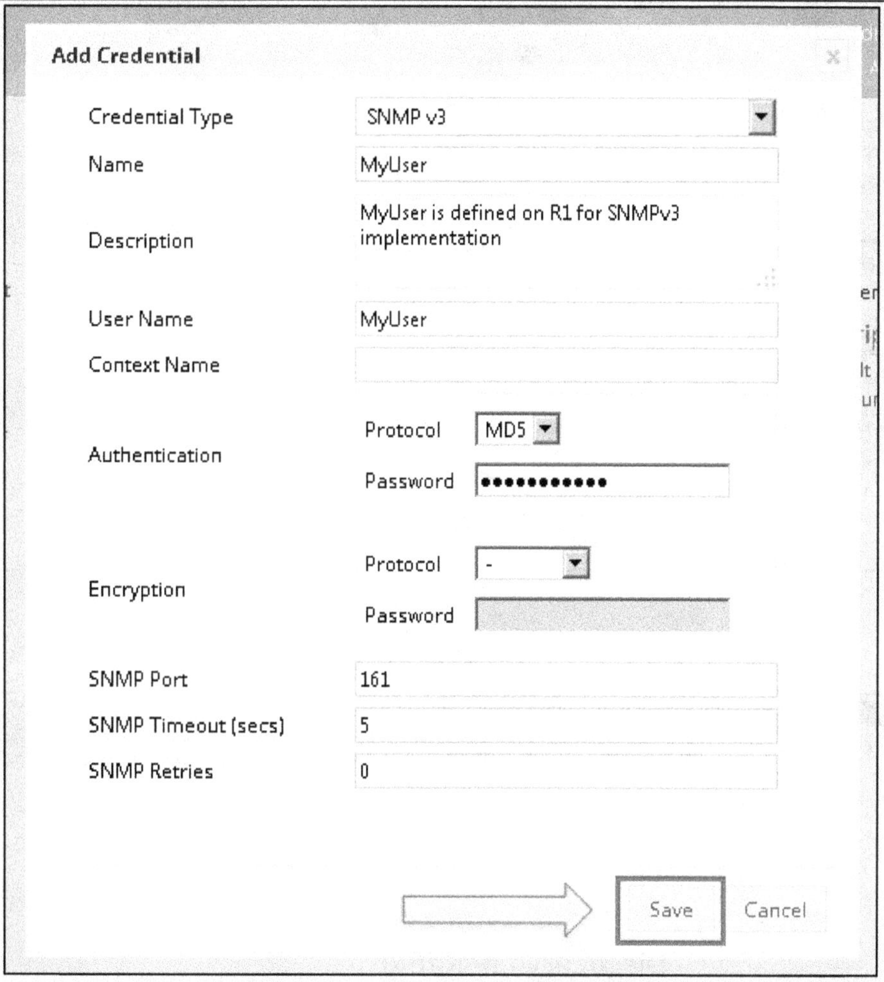
Add Credential
Credential Type
SNMP v3
Name
MyUser
Description
MyUser is defined on R1 for SNMPv3 implementation
User Name
MyUser
Context Name
Authentication
Protocol
MD5
Password
Encryption
Protocol
Password
SNMP Port
161
SNMP Timeout (secs)
5
SNMP Retries
0
Save
Cancel

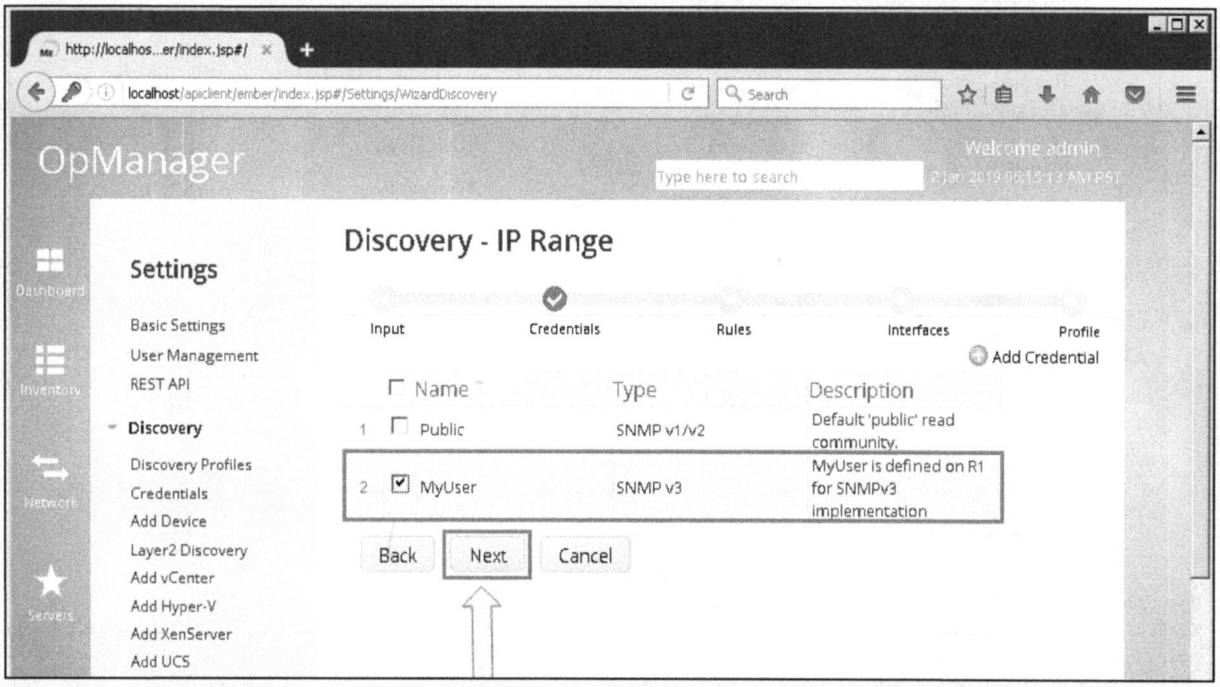
http://localhos...er/index.jsp#/
localhost/apiclient/ember/index.jsp#/Settings/WizardDiscovery
Search
OpManager
Type here to search
Welcome admin
Dashboard
Inventory
Network
Servers
Settings
Basic Settings
User Management
REST API
Discovery
Discovery Profiles
Credentials
Add Device
Layer2 Discovery
Add vCenter
Add Hyper-V
Add XenServer
Add UCS
Discovery - IP Range
Input
Credentials
Rules
Interfaces
Profile
Add Credential
Name
Type
Description
1
Public
SNMP v1/v2
Default 'public' read community.
2
MyUser
SNMP v3
MyUser is defined on R1 for SNMPv3 implementation
Back
Next
Cancel

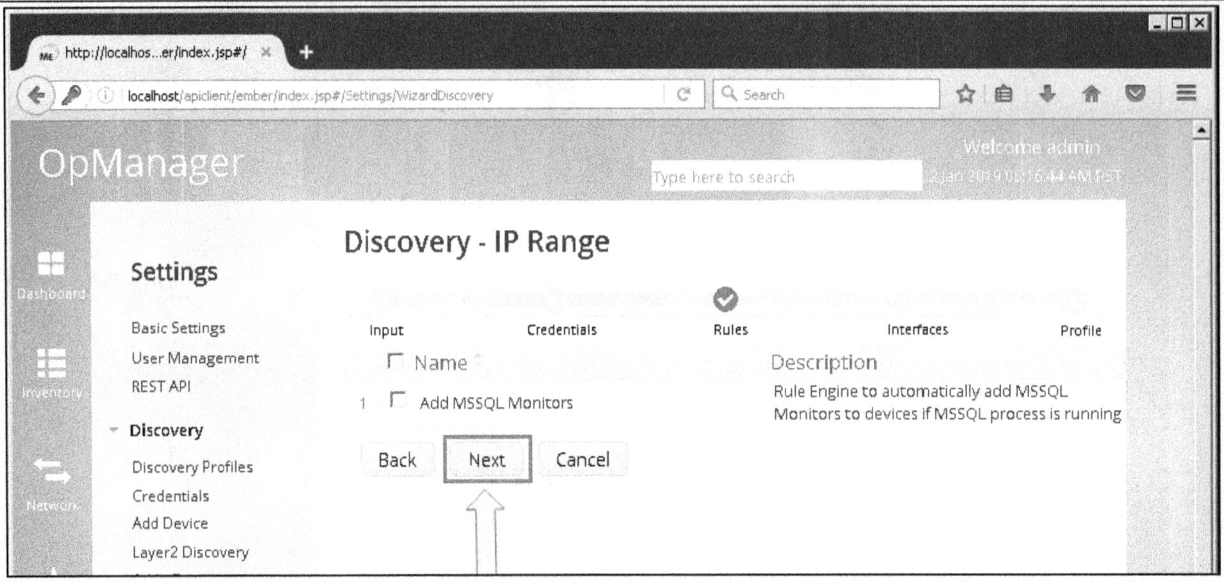

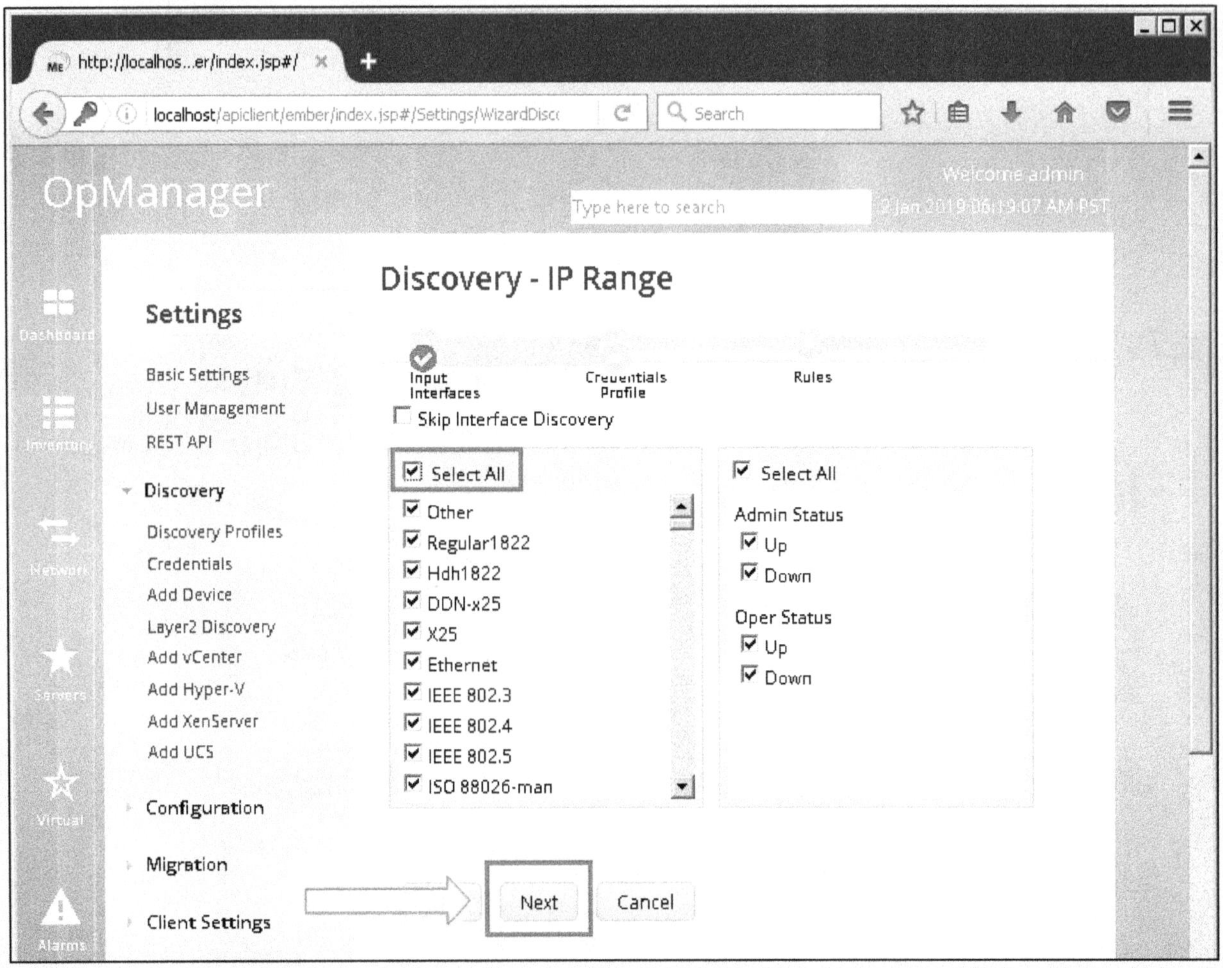

After clicking on "Finish", OPManager will respond to the incoming SNMP traffic.

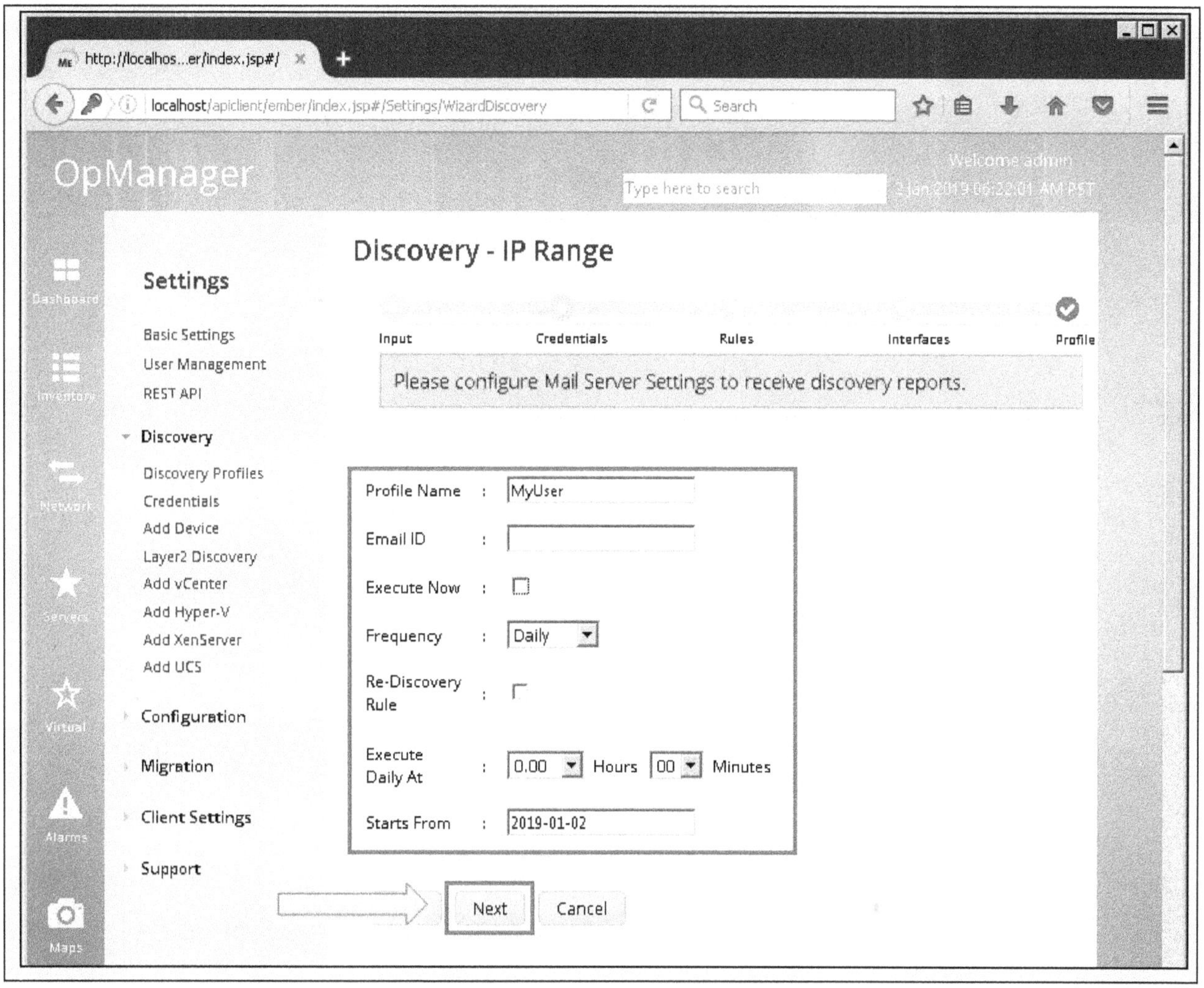
http://localhos...er/index.jsp#/
localhost/apiclient/ember/index.jsp#/Settings/WizardDiscovery
Search
OpManager
Type here to search
Welcome admin
Dashboard
Inventory
Network
Servers
Virtual
Alarms
Maps
Settings
Basic Settings
User Management
REST API
Discovery
Discovery Profiles
Credentials
Add Device
Layer2 Discovery
Add vCenter
Add Hyper-V
Add XenServer
Add UCS
Configuration
Migration
Client Settings
Support
Discovery - IP Range
Input
Credentials
Rules
Interfaces
Profile
Please configure Mail Server Settings to receive discovery reports.
Profile Name :
MyUser
Email ID :
Execute Now :
Frequency :
Daily
Re-Discovery Rule :
Execute Daily At :
0.00
Hours
00
Minutes
Starts From :
2019-01-02
Next
Cancel

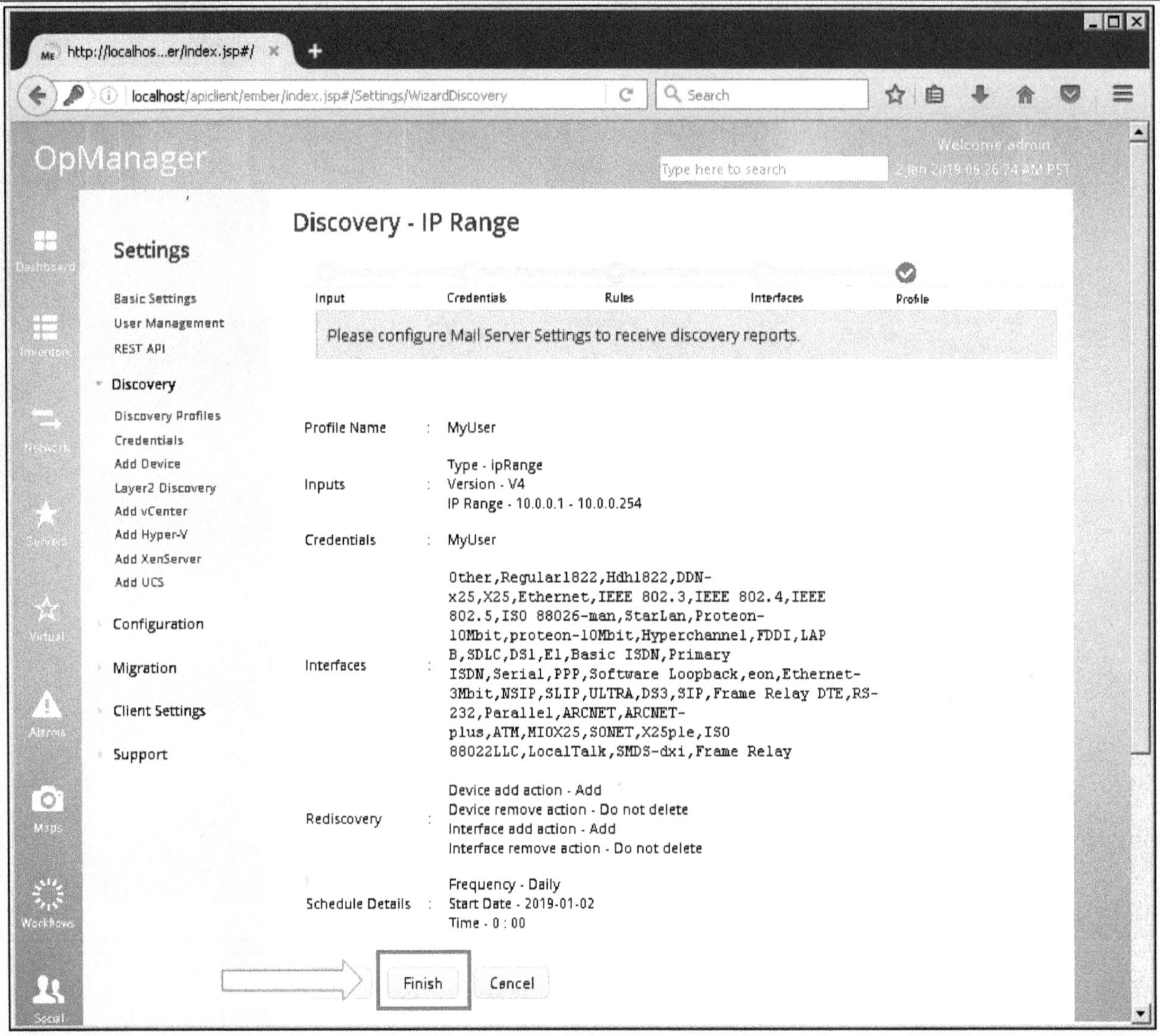

OPManager must identify router R1 after completing discovery process as shown below:

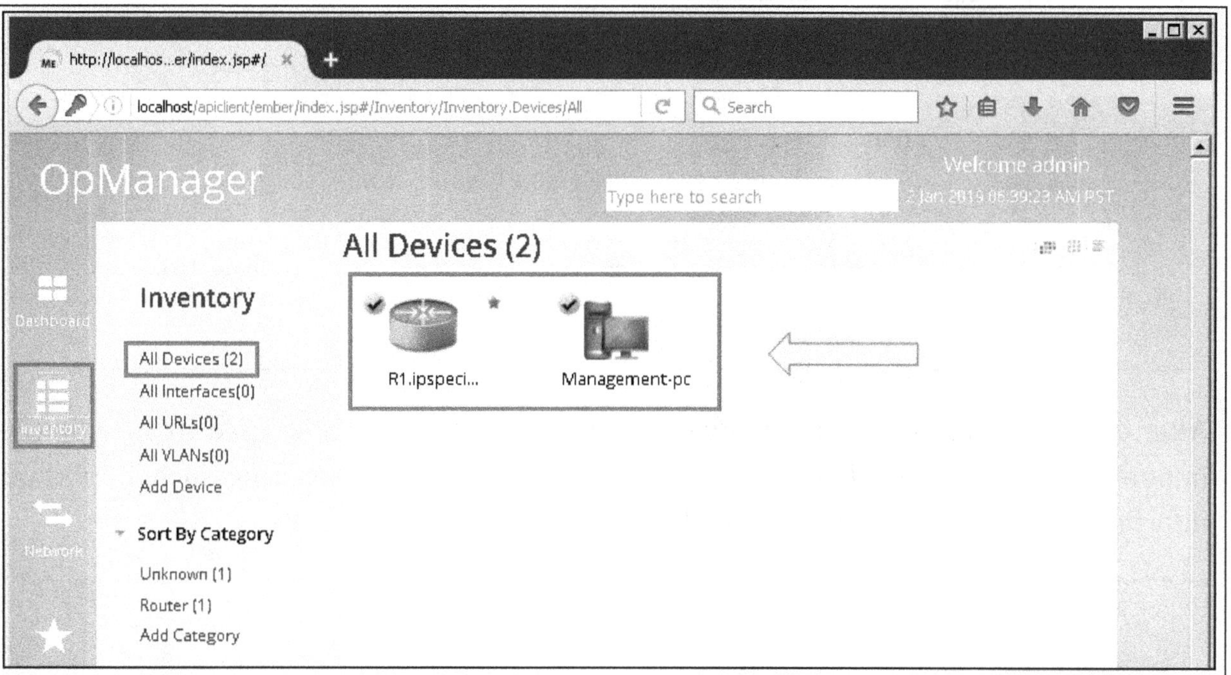

By double clicking on R1.IPSpecialist.net, it is clear that OP Manager has identified router category and its model number along with interfaces and other features.

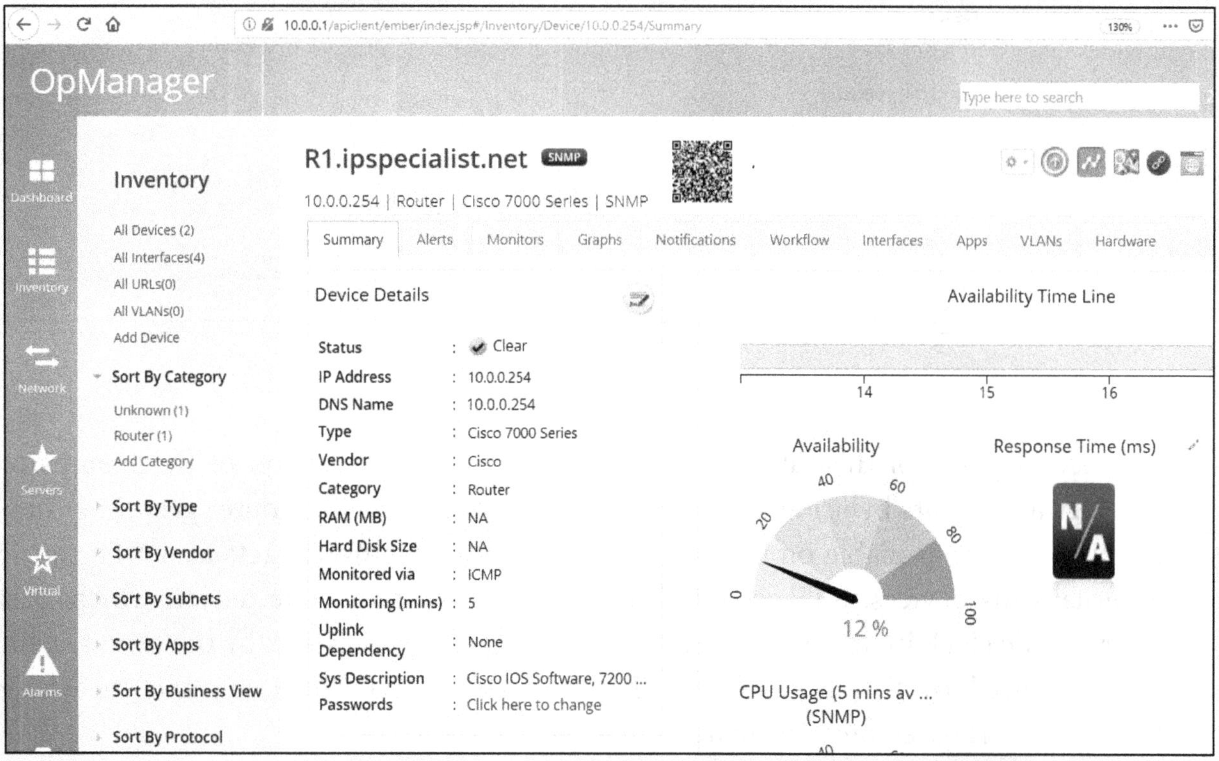

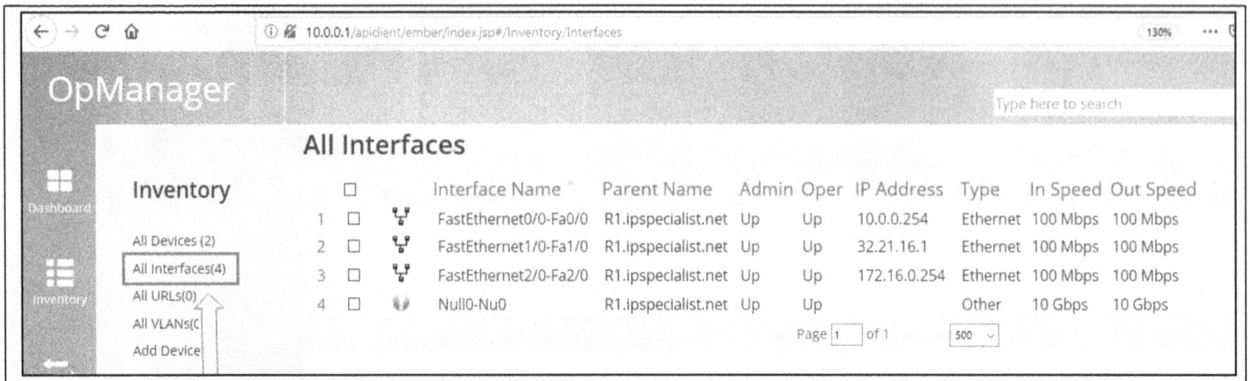

After adding devices from the discovery process, Dashboard can be used to view all the important information related to the devices. Importance of securing such important information displayed by SNMP should be clear at this stage.

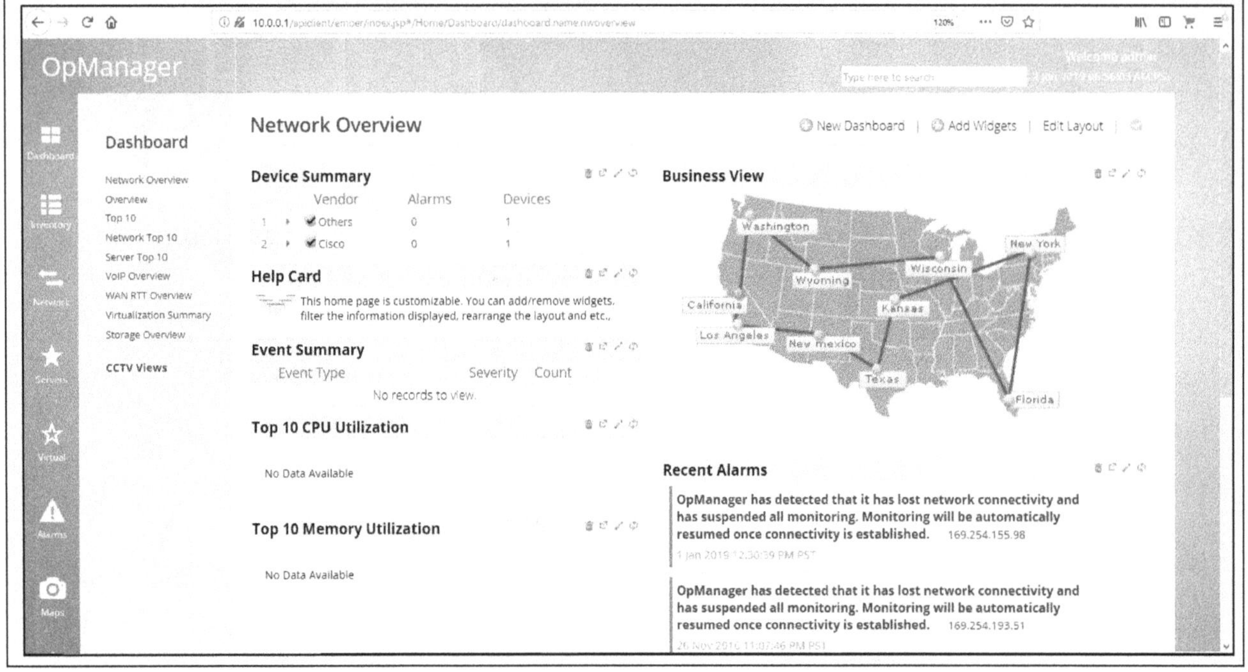

In the second phase of this lab, our main focus is on the correction of timestamps of system logs and events by using NTP. Normally the perimeter edge router gets time from public NTP servers available on the internet. Now, this edge router acts as a NTP server for internal LAN devices. NTP server is also available as standalone device, which uses radio or atomic clock in its operation. NTP helps in correlating events by the time system logs are received by Syslog servers. NTP uses UDP port number 123 and its whole communication is based on coordinated universal time (UTC).

NTP uses a term known as *stratum* to describe the distance between NTP server and device. It is just like TTL number that decreases every hop a packet passes by. Starting from one, stratum number increases by every hop. For example, if we see stratum number 10 on local router, it means that NTP server is nine hops away. Securing NTP is also an important aspect as attacker may change time at first place to mislead the forensic teams who investigate and correlate the events to find the root cause of the attack.

In this part, router R2 will act as NTP server. Route R1 will act as NTP client to R2 and. NTP version3 supports authentication, which will be used in this lab.

R2:

First, set the local clock of router depending on your geographical region

Use *show clock* command to see current time.

R2# **show clock**

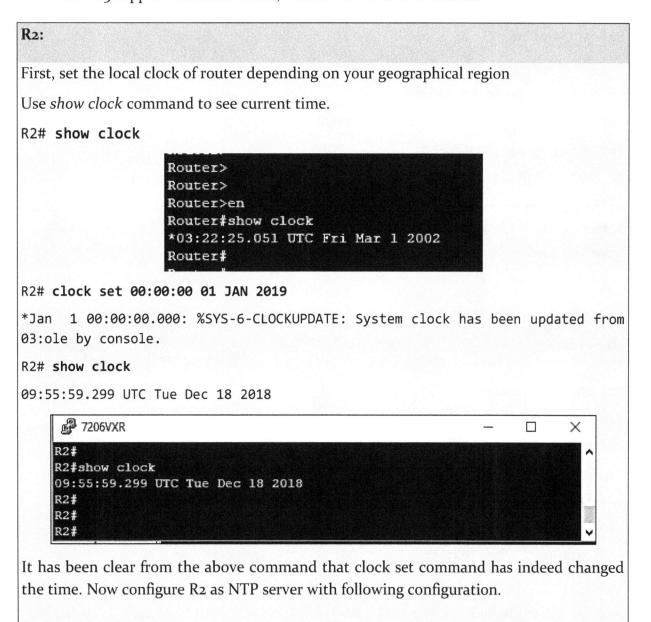

R2# **clock set 00:00:00 01 JAN 2019**

```
*Jan  1 00:00:00.000: %SYS-6-CLOCKUPDATE: System clock has been updated from 03:ole by console.
```

R2# **show clock**

```
09:55:59.299 UTC Tue Dec 18 2018
```

It has been clear from the above command that clock set command has indeed changed the time. Now configure R2 as NTP server with following configuration.

```
R2(config)# ntp master 10
R2(config)# ntp authentication-key 1 md5 P@$$word:10
```

NTP master command configures router R2 as NTP server with 10 as stratum number. In second command MD5 based authentication key is defined.

R1:

Now, access router R1 to configure as NTP client.

First, check the current date of R1 using *show clock* command.

```
R1# show clock
*23:05:39.383 UTC Tue Oct 18 2016
R1(config)# ntp authenticate
R1(config)# ntp authentication-key 1 md5 P@$$word:10
R1(config)# ntp trusted-key 1
R1(config)# ntp server 32.21.16.2 key 1
```

In the above commands, NTP server is assigned with an IP address along with md5 based authentication. Here, key is defined for providing further authentication. NTP trusted-key command specifies which key should be used for authenticating time source.

Verification:

show ntp status command can be used to verify connection with NTP R1(config)#! Server

```
R1# show ntp status
Clock is synchronized, stratum 11, reference is 32.21.16.2
nominal freq is 250.0000 Hz, actual freq is 250.0000 Hz, precision is 2**18
ntp uptime is 98700 (1/100 of seconds), resolution is 4000
reference time is DFC34429.459BB079 (10:02:17.271 UTC Tue Dec 18 2018)
clock offset is -24.0338 msec, root delay is 39.81 msec
root dispersion is 7961.99 msec, peer dispersion is 187.61 msec
loopfilter state is 'CTRL' (Normal Controlled Loop), drift is 0.000000000 s/s
system poll interval is 64, last update was 12 sec ago.
```

```
7206VXR
R1#
R1#
R1#show ntp status
Clock is synchronized, stratum 11, reference is 32.21.16.2
nominal freq is 250.0000 Hz, actual freq is 250.0000 Hz, precision is 2**18
ntp uptime is 98700 (1/100 of seconds), resolution is 4000
reference time is DFC34429.459BB079 (10:02:17.271 UTC Tue Dec 18 2018)
clock offset is -24.0338 msec, root delay is 39.81 msec
root dispersion is 7961.99 msec, peer dispersion is 187.61 msec
loopfilter state is 'CTRL' (Normal Controlled Loop), drift is 0.000000000 s/s
system poll interval is 64, last update was 12 sec ago.
R1#
R1#
```

NTP client consumes some more time than other protocols to synchronize with NTP server (around 5 minutes or more).

Show ntp association command can be used to check the IP address and other information related to NTP server.

```
R1#show ntp associations
```

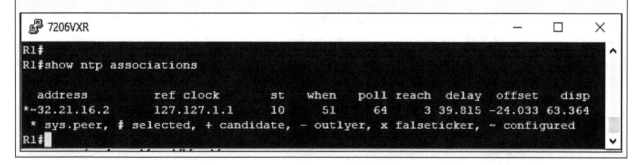

```
7206VXR
R1#
R1#show ntp associations

  address         ref clock       st   when   poll reach  delay  offset   disp
*~32.21.16.2      127.127.1.1     10     51     64     3 39.815 -24.033 63.364
 * sys.peer, # selected, + candidate, - outlyer, x falseticker, ~ configured
R1#
```

In this section of the lab, Syslog logging will be enabled on routers R1 and R2 to send every generated message to the server.

R1:

Specify the IP of syslog server on R1 and make it generate messages to the server.

```
R1(config)# logging 10.0.0.1
R1(config)# logging trap debugging
R1(config)# service timestamps debug datetime msec
R1(config)# service timestamps log datetime msec
```

Logging command is used to specify the IP address of Syslog server. Logging trap command tells router to send every log/event up to debugging level of syslog. Service timestamps command is used to include timestamp in log messages.

To specify the IP of syslog server on R2 and make it generate messages to the server,

the same configuration is replicated on router R2.

R2:

Logging command is used to specify the IP address of Syslog server.

```
R2(config)# logging 10.0.0.1
R2(config)# logging trap debugging
R2(config)# service timestamps debug datetime msec
R2(config)# service timestamps log datetime msec
```

Verification:

Open source 3CDaemon server used in this lab, contains Syslog server along with FTP and other servers. Click on 3CD icon on start menu to start it and view its operations. As OP Manager is also installed on same management station, we may need to stop manage engine service before starting syslog server.

To stop manage engine service, type *services.msc* in start menu and stop the *Manage Engine OPManager* service.

The next figure shows few logs received by Syslog server.

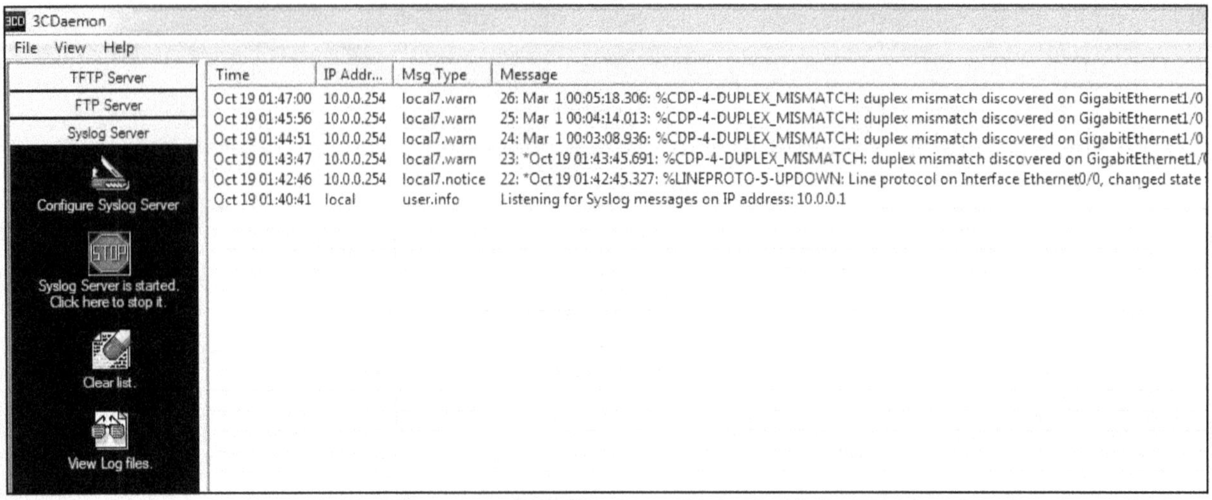

In order to use SCP for file transfer anywhere inside IOS of Cisco devices, we need to enable SCP server option on Cisco devices. Following command is used to make device an SCP server. SSH needs to be enabled first for SCP to work as SCP based sessions use SSH encrypted flow of data.

```
R2(config)# ip scp server enable
```

Any scp supported software can be used from workstation to access any location within Cisco IOS.

Using SCP for file transfer

SCP is a secured copy protocol used for transferring files between client and server machines. SCP uses SSH for data transfer and authentication hence, adds both authenticity and confidentiality during whole transaction. SCP allows users with appropriate authorization level to securely copy any file from that exists in the Cisco IOS File System. A third-party software is also used on workstation to copy files. Similarly, to copy file from one device to another, we can use *copy* command.

In order to configure Cisco device with SCP server's functionality, we first need to configure SSH properly and a username with proper authorization level for SCP to work properly.

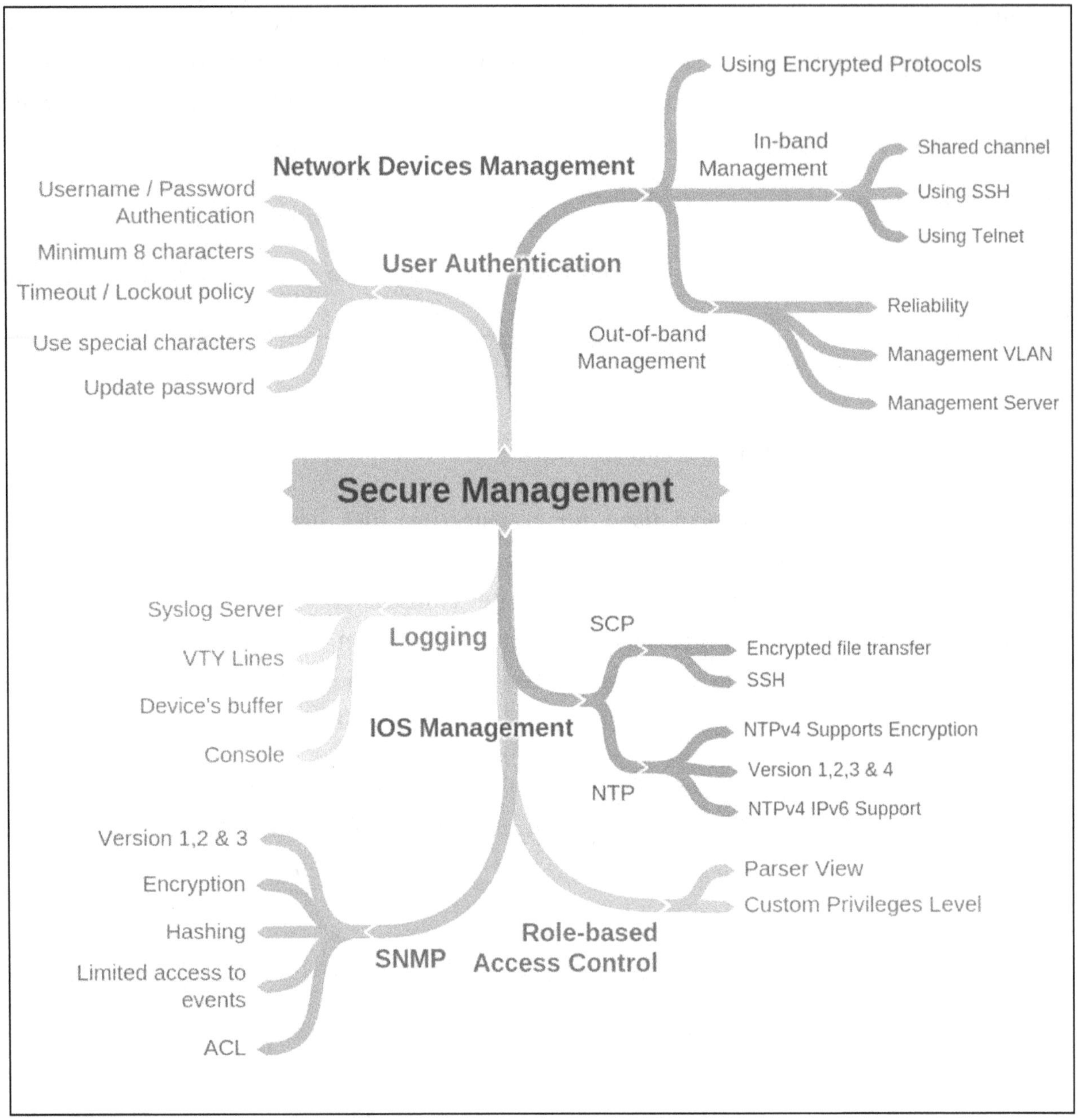

Figure 2-05: Secure Management Mind Map

AAA Concepts

In the previous section, we have discussed different techniques to prevent an attacker from getting unauthorized access to network infrastructure. Those users who are required to access networking devices for maintenance or for configuration also need to have authorization as well as a proper audit trail so that authorized and unauthorized users can be differentiated.

Authentication, Authorization and Accounting (AAA) framework, as its name suggests is used to identify, validate and authenticate a legitimate user on the management plane of a network device. AAA supports both local databases for usernames and passwords as well as configuring an Active Directory (AD). If the network administrator wants multiple users to access the devices in a network, a centralized AD is created, which lists authorized users to authenticate the users.

AAA Components

AAA is a modular framework and it tries to cater all kinds of traffic over the network, whether it is some network administrator trying to access a networking device or some end user trying to send data traffic out of local LAN.

The three main components of AAA are:

Authentication:

Authentication is the process of proving an identity to the system by login identification and a password. It also does the purpose of determining whether the user is the same person he claims to be or not.

It is used in every system, not just in computer networking. In banking system, we need to prove the identity by entering the password before making the transaction. Similarly, if a network administrator needs to access a router or a switch and wants to make some changes, some kind of authentication must be defined on the device. The first but least usable practical solution would be to define the usernames passwords database inside the device. The second option would be the use of some centralized server like Cisco ACS or ISE. In Cisco devices, we can use the combination of both options by defining a *method list,* which states the list of preferred methods for authentication. If one option is not available, then second option will be used and so on. Examples of these methods are explained in Lab Section of AAA.

Authorization:

Authorization determines the access of resources and the operations performed by users according to their role of job.

After authentication of user succeeds, the next step is to deal with is the level of clearance that a user needs to perform his legal actions. A banking example would be perfect in this regard. After entering correct password, we get the authorization to withdraw the maximum cash depending on balance available in bank account. Similarly, there are similar scenarios in computer networking where we need to restrict the access to the user. For example, an end user may need network resources for eight hours a day. Similarly, a network administrator may need commands associated with privilege level 4. Custom as well as default method lists are used to define the authorization in Cisco devices.

Accounting:

Third element of AAA is accounting or auditing, which keeps the track of how the network resources of an organization are being used. Whenever user is authenticated and authorized to specific set of commands of Cisco devices, the set of commands he used while accessing the specific device at the specific time must be recorded. Like authentication and authorization, we also use methods like *default* or *custom method list* to define what should be accounted for and where to send this information.

TACACS+ vs RADIUS Technology:

There are two common security protocols of AAA used to control access in a network, which are RADIUS and TACACS+. These protocols are generally used as a language of communication between a networking device and AAA server.

RADIUS:

Remote Authentication Dial-In User Service (RADIUS) is an access server that uses AAA protocol, it secures remote access of network and network services from unauthorized users. Data transaction between RADIUS and client are authenticated by the use of shared secret key and all the passwords are sent encrypted, so it reduces the possibility of password determination by an unauthorized user even in an unsecured network. RADIUS does authentication and authorization together. RADIUS is an open standard meaning that all vendors can use it in their AAA implementation.

TACACS+:

TACACS+ stands for Terminal Access Control Access Control Server and it is Cisco proprietary. As RADIUS, TACACS+ is also used as a communication between networking device and AAA server. Unlike RADIUS, TACACS+ encrypts the entire packet body, and attaches TACACS+ header to the message body. TACACAS+ ensures reliable delivery between clients and servers as it uses TCP connection, since it is a Cisco proprietary, it has a granular control over Cisco's router and switches. TACACS+ does authentication, authorization and accounting separately, so different methods of controlling AAA functions can be achieved separately.

One of the main differences between RADIUS and TACACS+ is that RADIUS only encrypts password and transacts other RADIUS packets as clear text over the network.

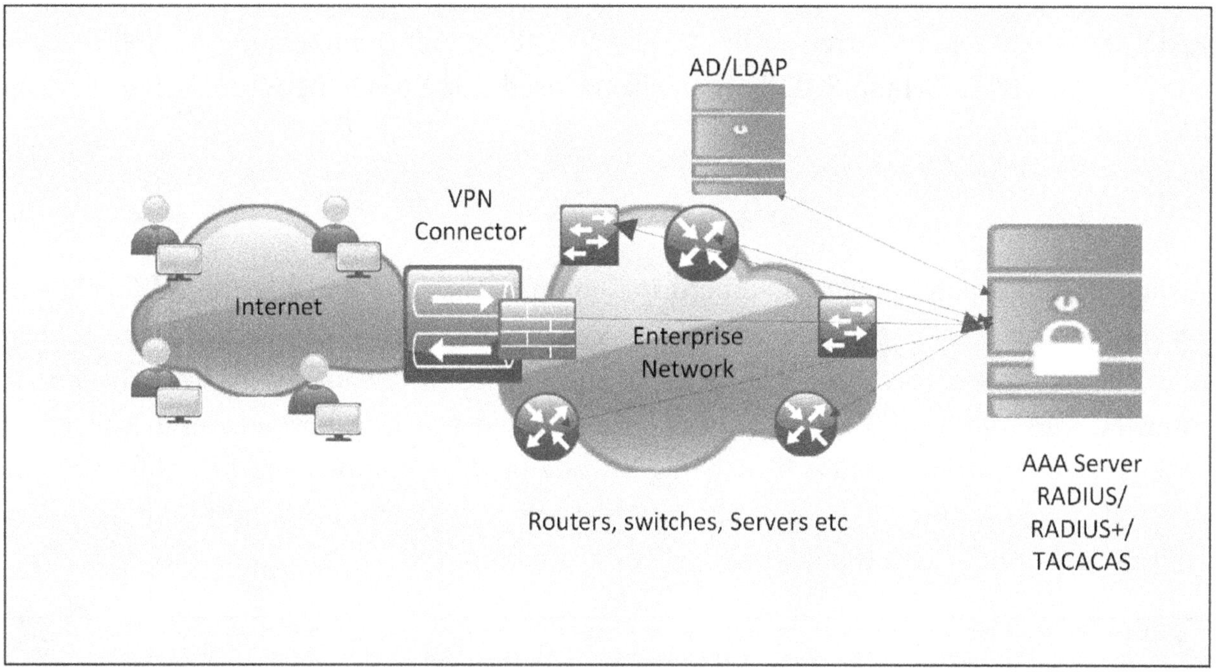

Figure 2-06: Comparison between RADIUS and TACACS+

This table summarizes and compares the unique features of RADIUS and TACACS+.

	TACACS+	**RADIUS**
L4 Protocol	TCP port 49.	UDP ports. 1812/1645 for authentication 1813/1646 for accounting.
Encryption	Encrypts full payload of each packet.	Encrypts only passwords.
Observations	Proprietary to Cisco, very granular control over authorization, separate implementation of AAA.	Open Standard, robust, great accounting features, less granular authorization control. Another protocol named DIAMETER may replace RADIUS in near future with enhanced capabilities.
Primary use	Device administration.	Network access.

Table 2-06: Comparison between RADIUS and TACACS+

In general, when you need to give granular control over commands to network administrator, for example CLI access of some router, access for alteration in authorization of specific group or commands, then TACACS+ is preferred over RADIUS due to its granular control in authorizing which commands should be allowed.

When configuring for end-users to enable them to send their traffic over the network, RADIUS is always preferred over TACACS+. It is not compulsory to follow this convention. TACACS+ and RADIUS can also be used side by side between ACS server and its client devices.

Case Study

A multinational, automobile manufacturing company has a main office in California and several branch offices spanning across the America and rest of the world. Every branch office is connected to the main office via *Site to Site* or *Remote VPN* over the public internet. One of the project managers (who studied the cyber-attacks and leakage of sensitive information because of it being on one of their competitors in California) has ordered you to review the current security posture of the main office and take necessary actions as required. This topology shows one segment of the overall main office network.

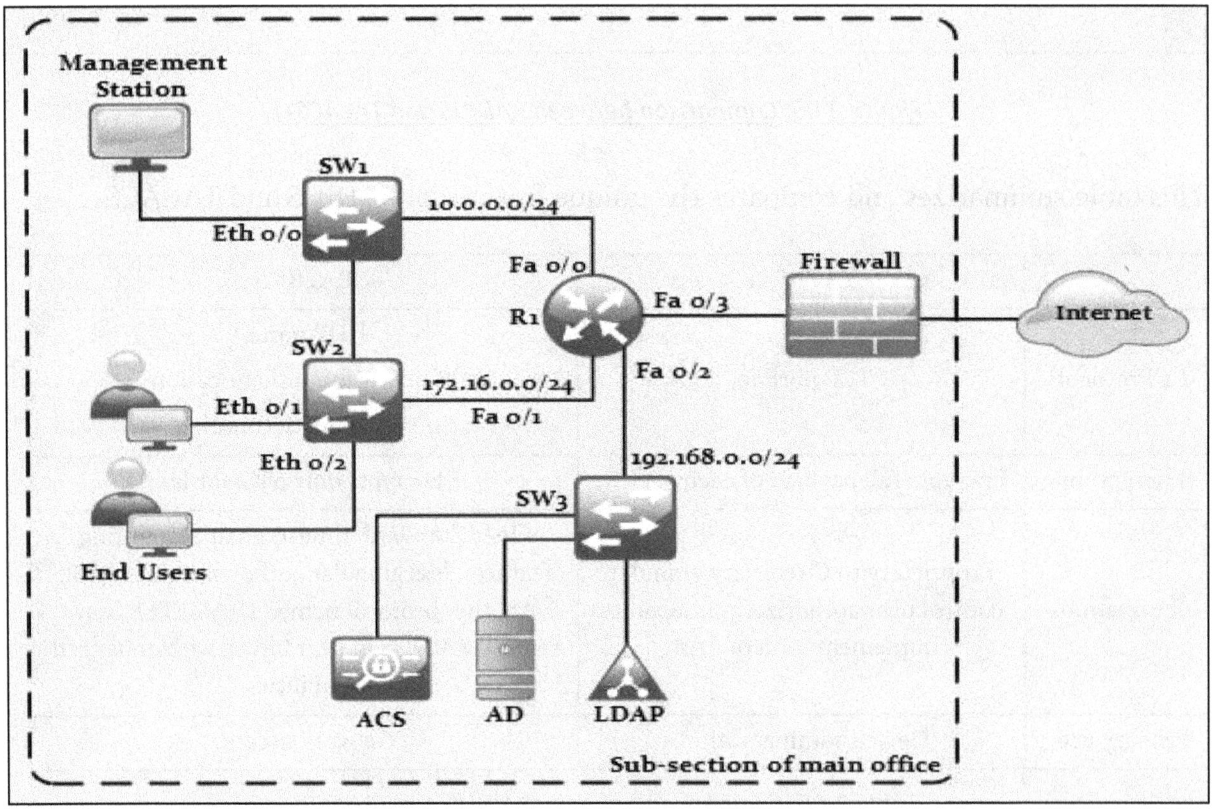

Figure 2-07: Secure Management Case Study

The main focus in the coming labs will be on securing management access of IOS of routers. Switches as firewall will not be discussed yet.

Lab 2.4: Configuring Administrative Access On A Cisco Router Using TACACS+ And ACS Server

In Small Office Home Office (SOHO) environments where a single or few network administrators have complete access of IT infrastructure, the local router database works well for implementing AAA. However, in large enterprises or service provider environments where a large number of network administrator team configure and provide support to overall network design, it becomes tedious to define a local database for Authentication, Authorization and Accounting purposes on every single device. In such scenarios, Cisco proprietary servers like ACS/ISE will be used. By using centralized server for AAA, and every device being configured to verify any request by contacting ACS/ISE, the administration process becomes quite easy.

The following topology will be used in this lab.

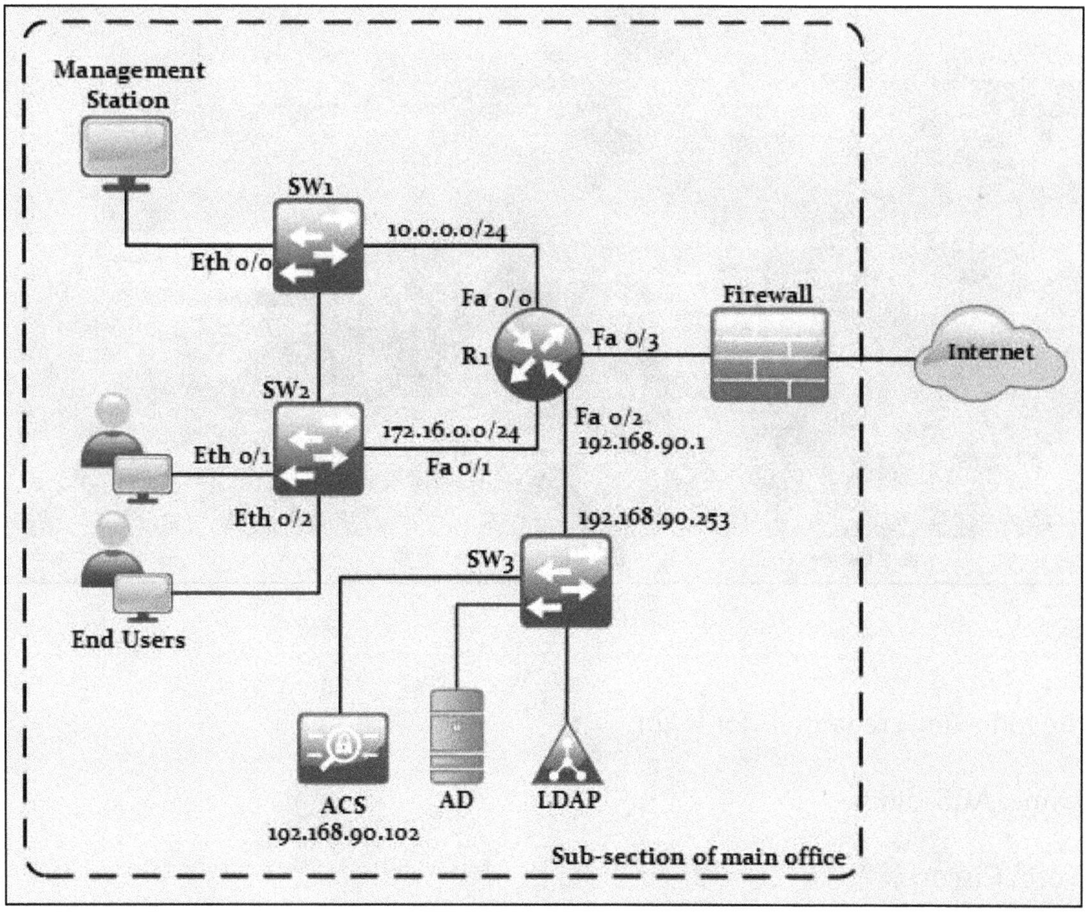

Figure 2-08: Lab 2.4 Topology

In the first part, different user accounts with different privilege levels will be defined on ACS server followed by their configuration and verification on R1, which can be further extended to Switches SW1, SW2 and SW3.

ACS:

Type https:\\192.168.90.102 on web browser of management station to access ACS server.

By accessing the management IP address of ACS, which is 192.168.90.102, a certificate trust alert may appear which can be ignored. After bypassing security exception, the following screen will appear.

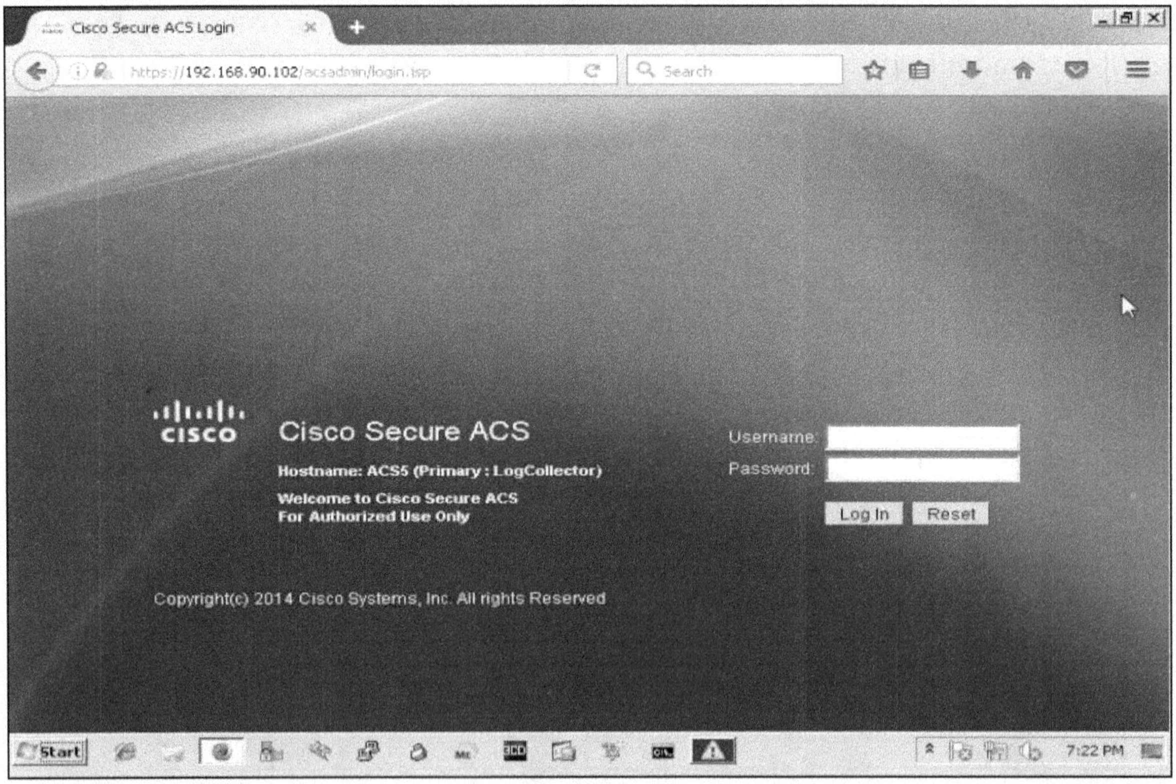

Use the following credentials for login:

Username: ACSadmin

Password: Cisco123

After successful login, the following dashboard will appear.

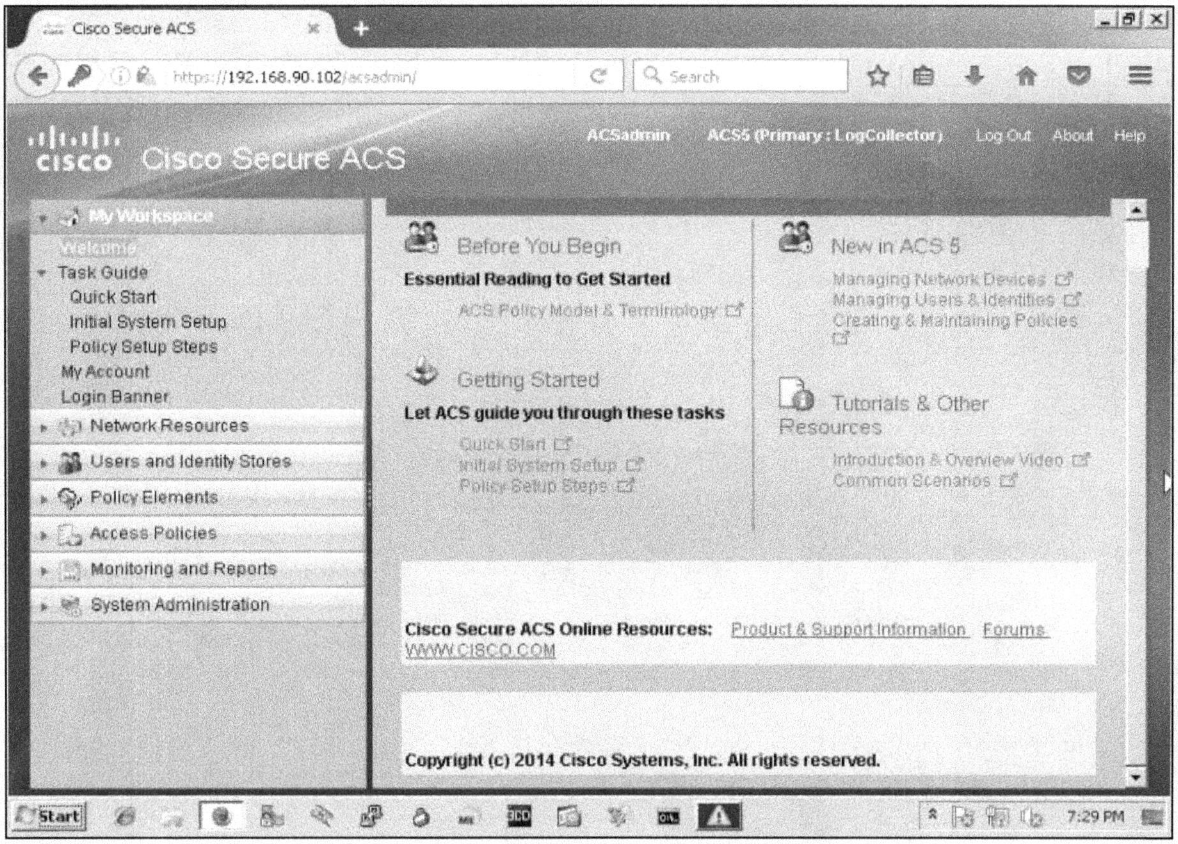

In the previous labs of parser view and custom privilege levels, the following two users were created. Same users will be created in this lab by using ACS.

Username1: IPSpecialist

Password: P@$$word:10

Privilege level: 15

Username2: NetworkSupport

Password: Network$upport:10

Privilege level 4

Allowed Access: User can only change IP address and shutdown interfaces

Click on Policy elements-> Shell profiles -> Create

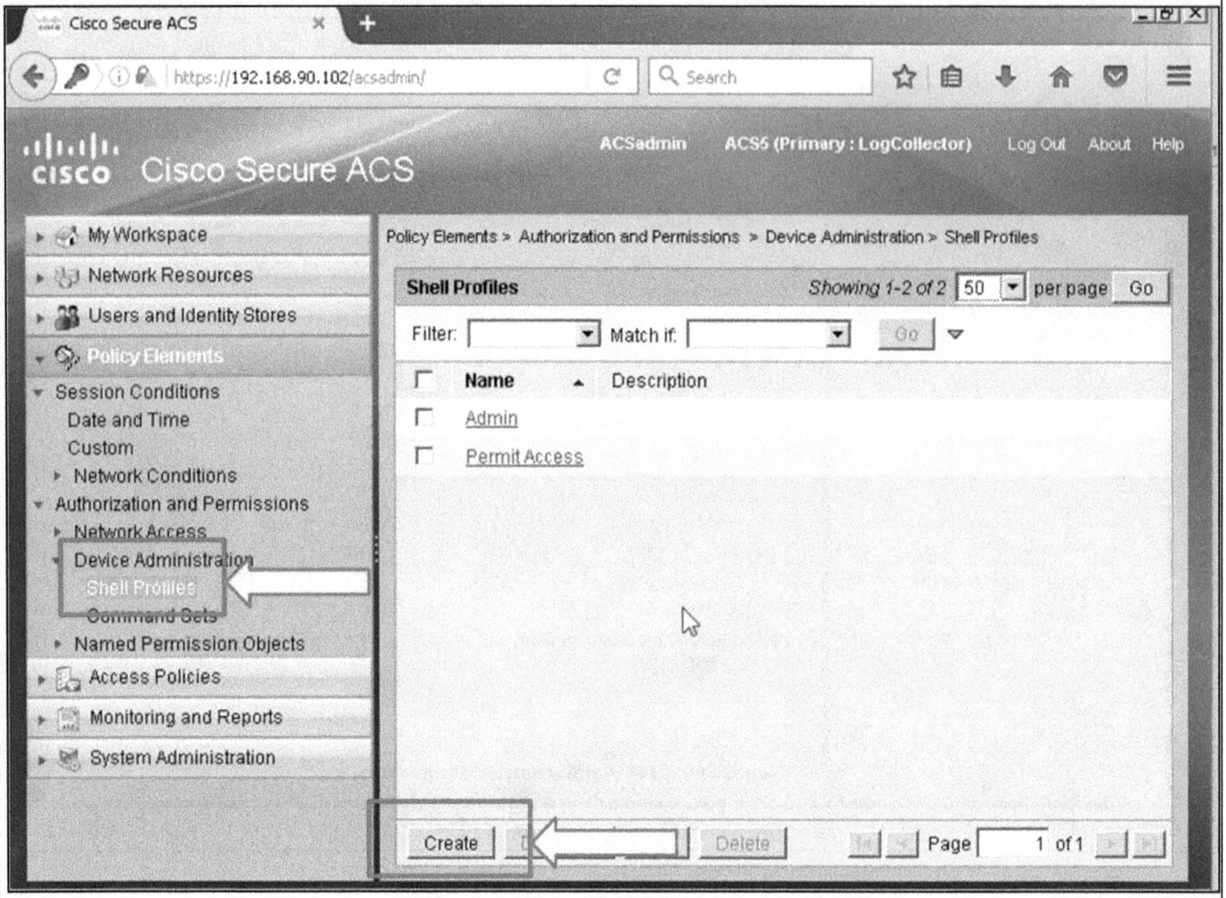

Click on "Common task" to define the privilege level associated with username.

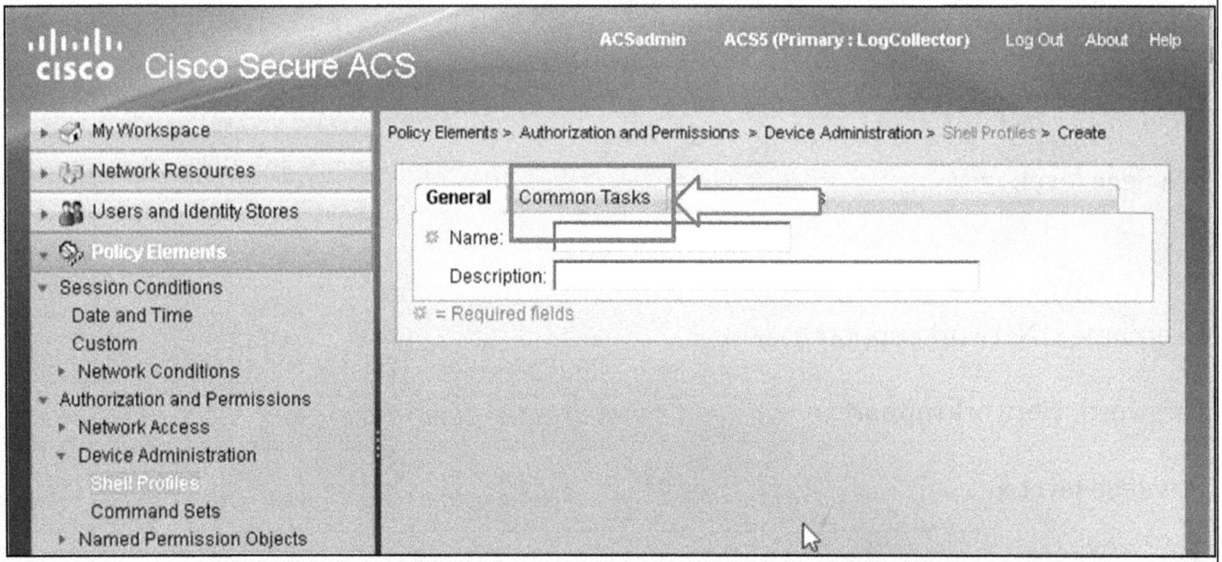

Click on "Submit" to save the intended entry. Similar procedure will be followed for the second username.

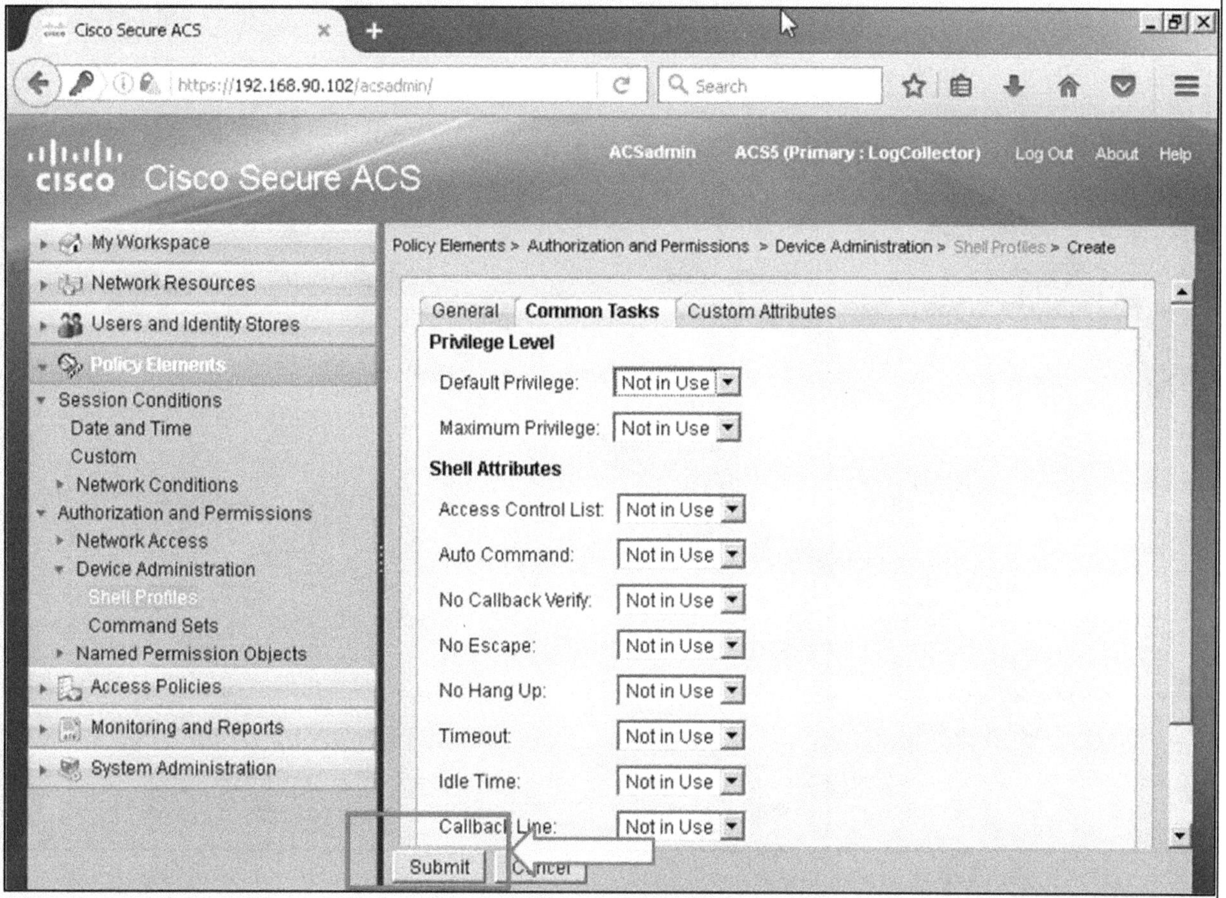

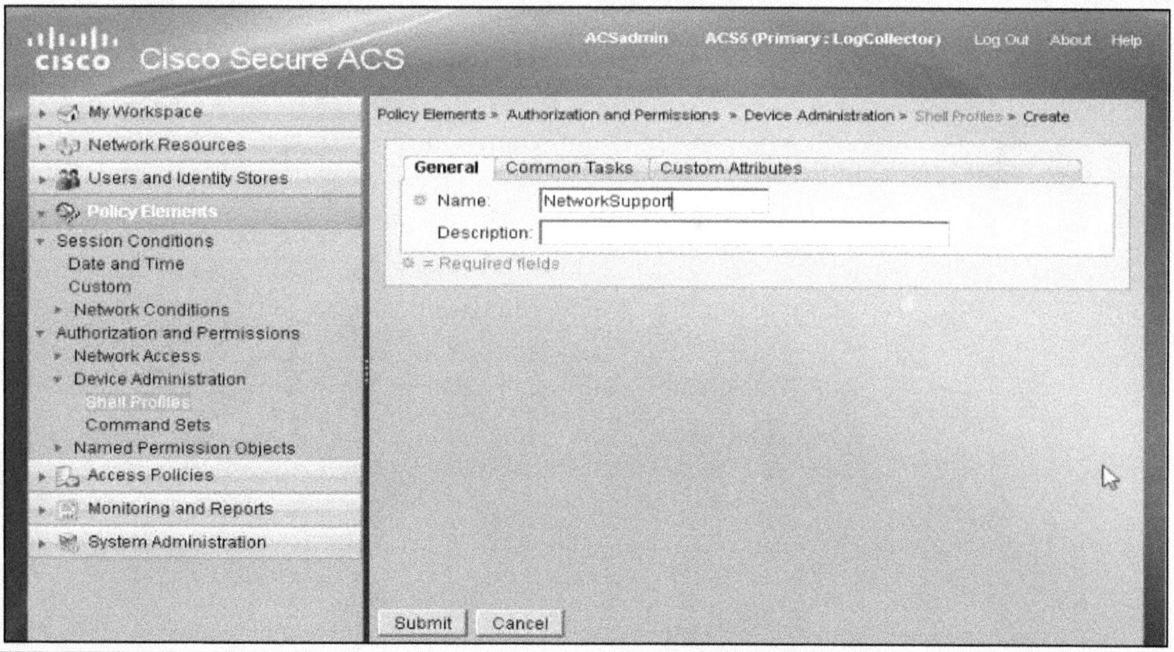

In order to create a profile with specific set of commands, click Policy elements -> Command set -> Create to Create profiles with custom command sets.

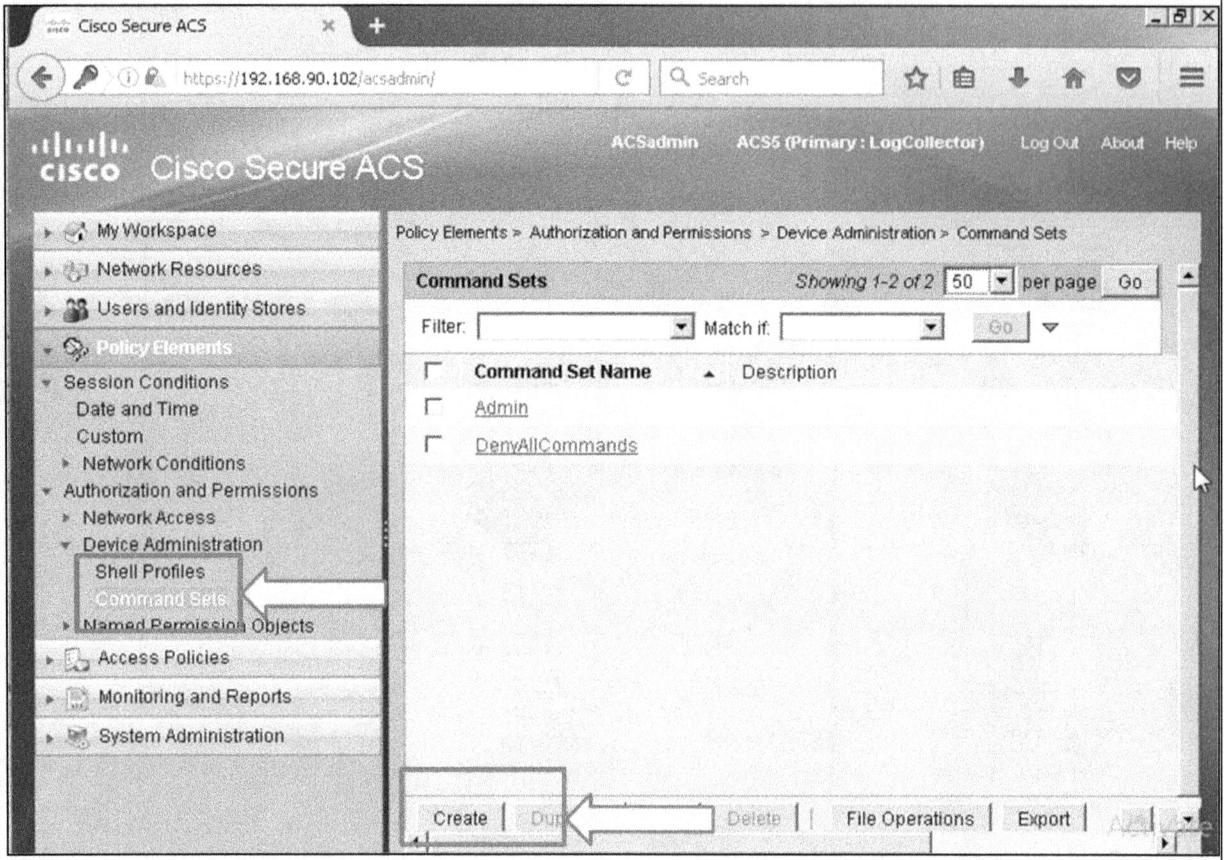

By entering the commands, the following window will open.

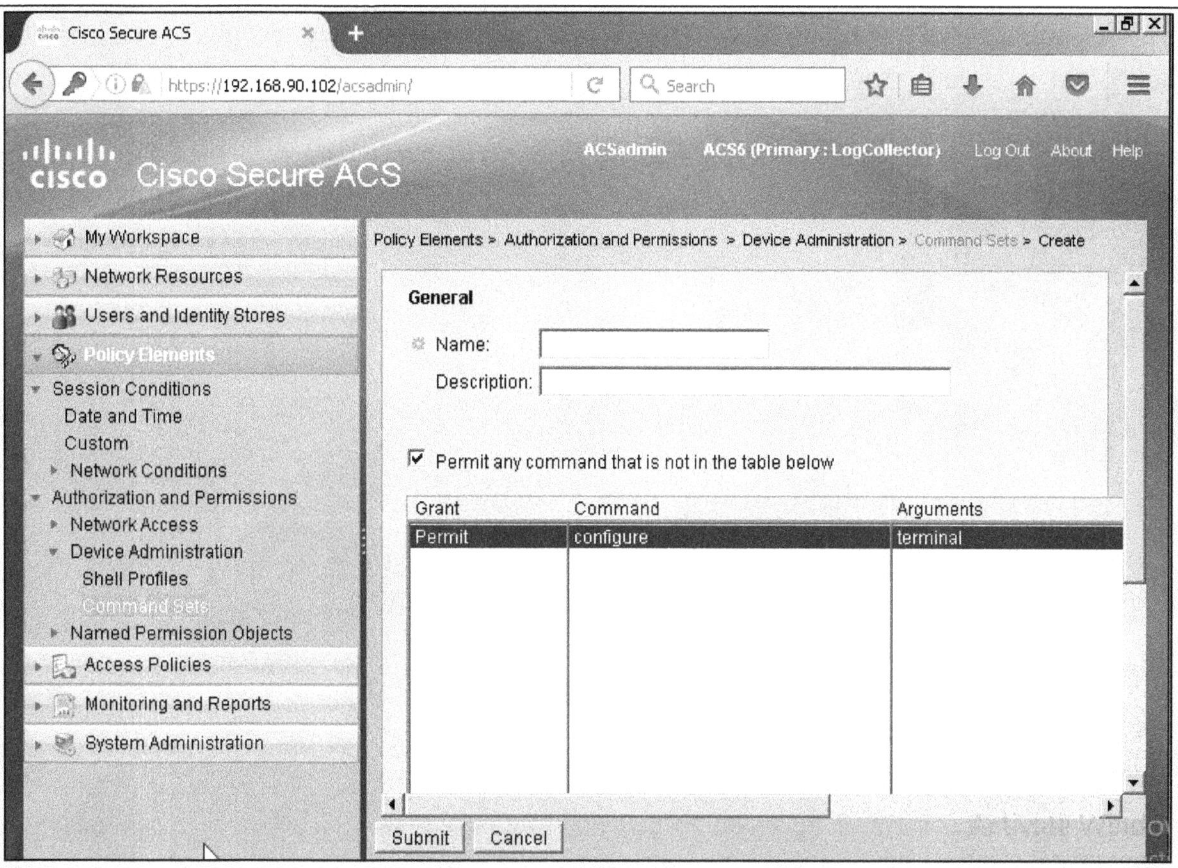

Now, add the user name “NetworkSupport” in name and set administrative access in the column below:

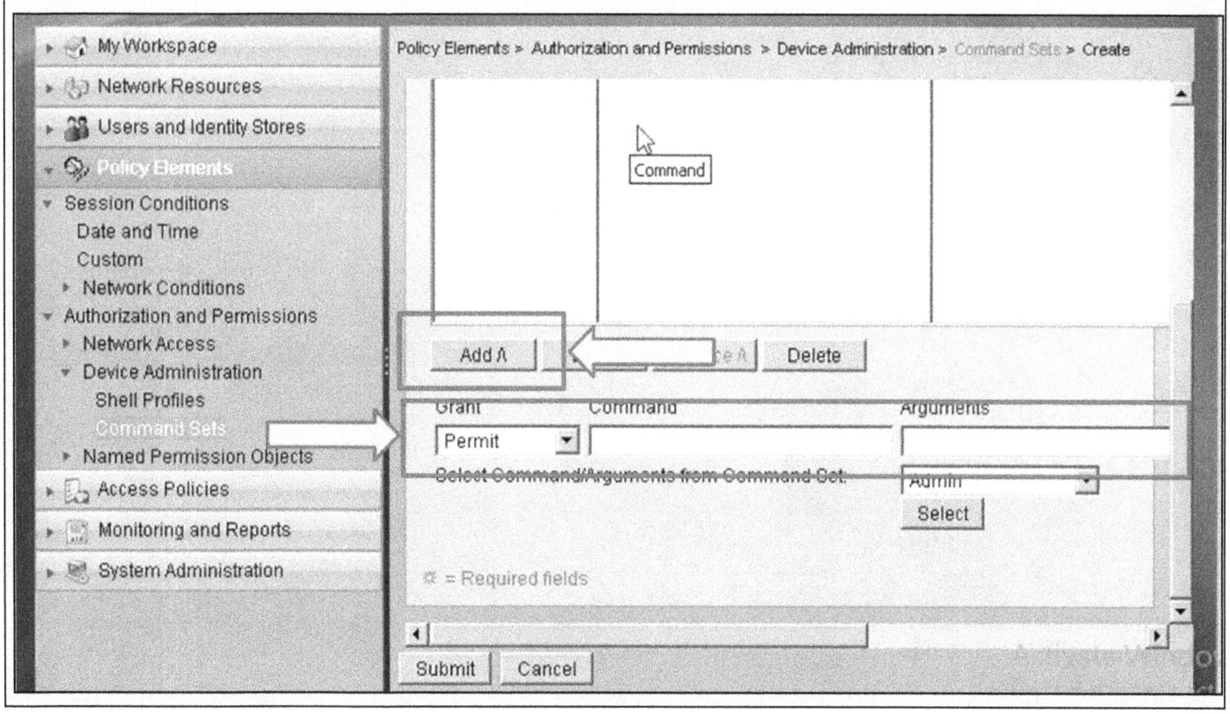

Type "command" in Command's space and "argument" in the Argument's space and then click "Add A" tab to add commands in the column of administrative access, as shown below:

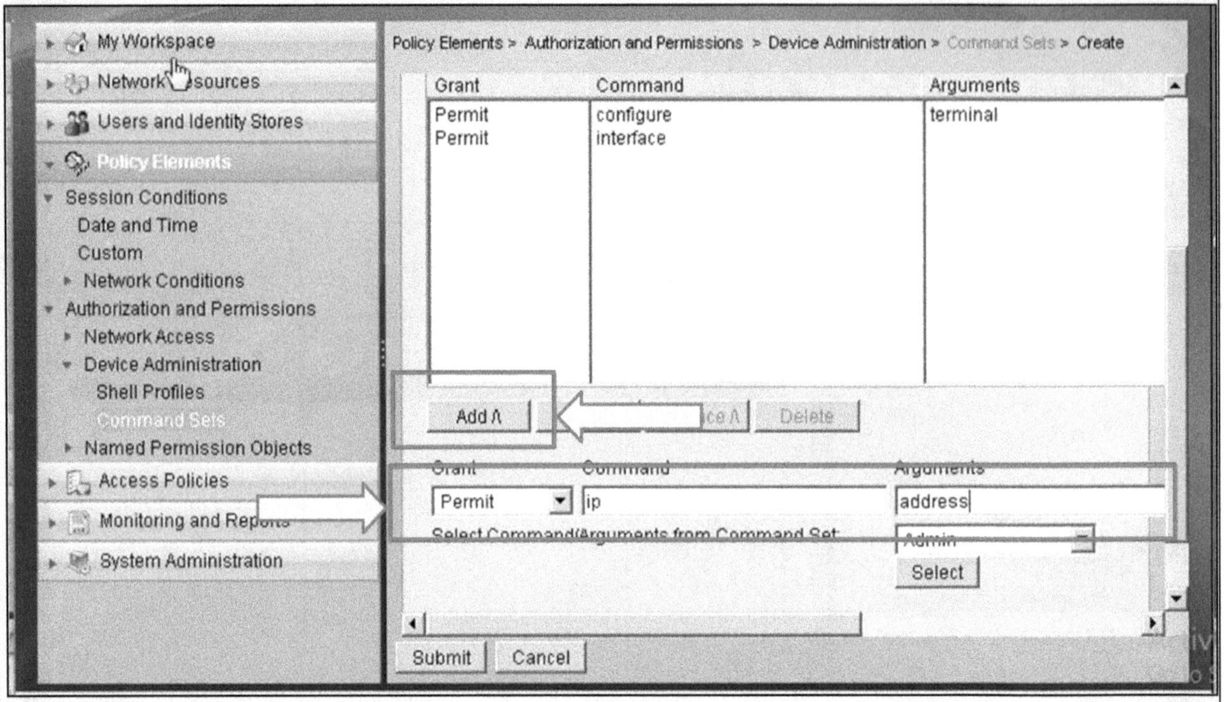

Now, the profile with the name "NetworkSupport" is created as shown below. Click "Submit" to save the profile.

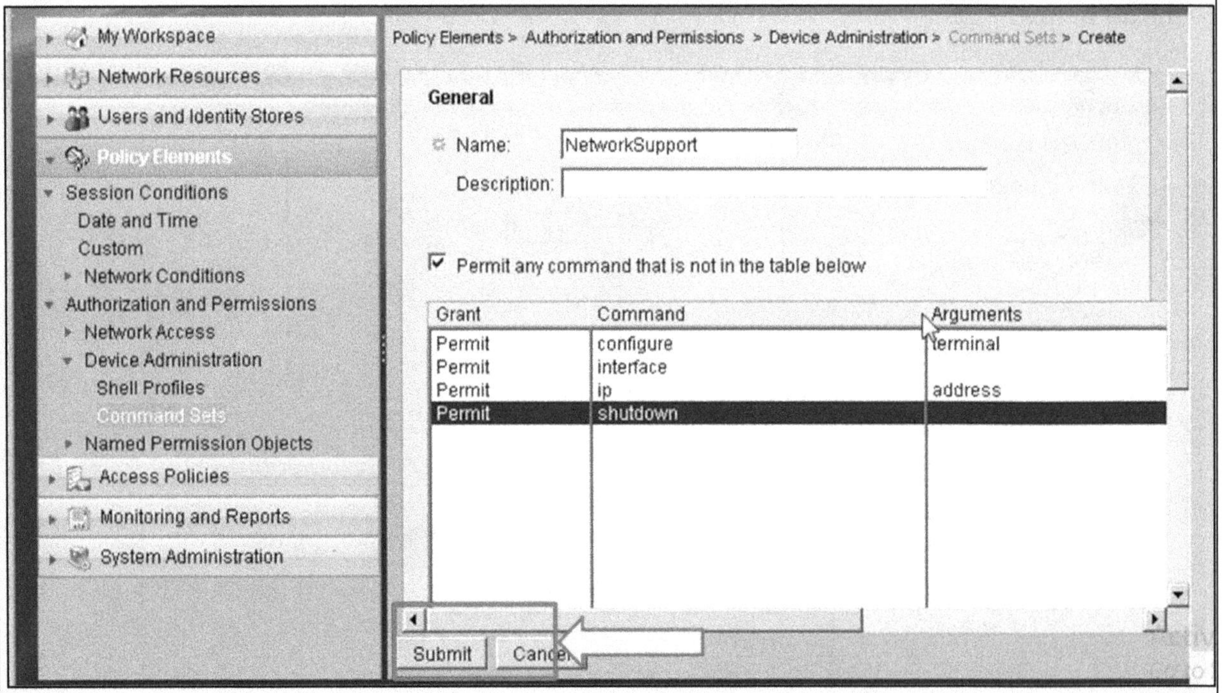

Now, the same steps will be followed for creating a profile of "IPSpecialist".

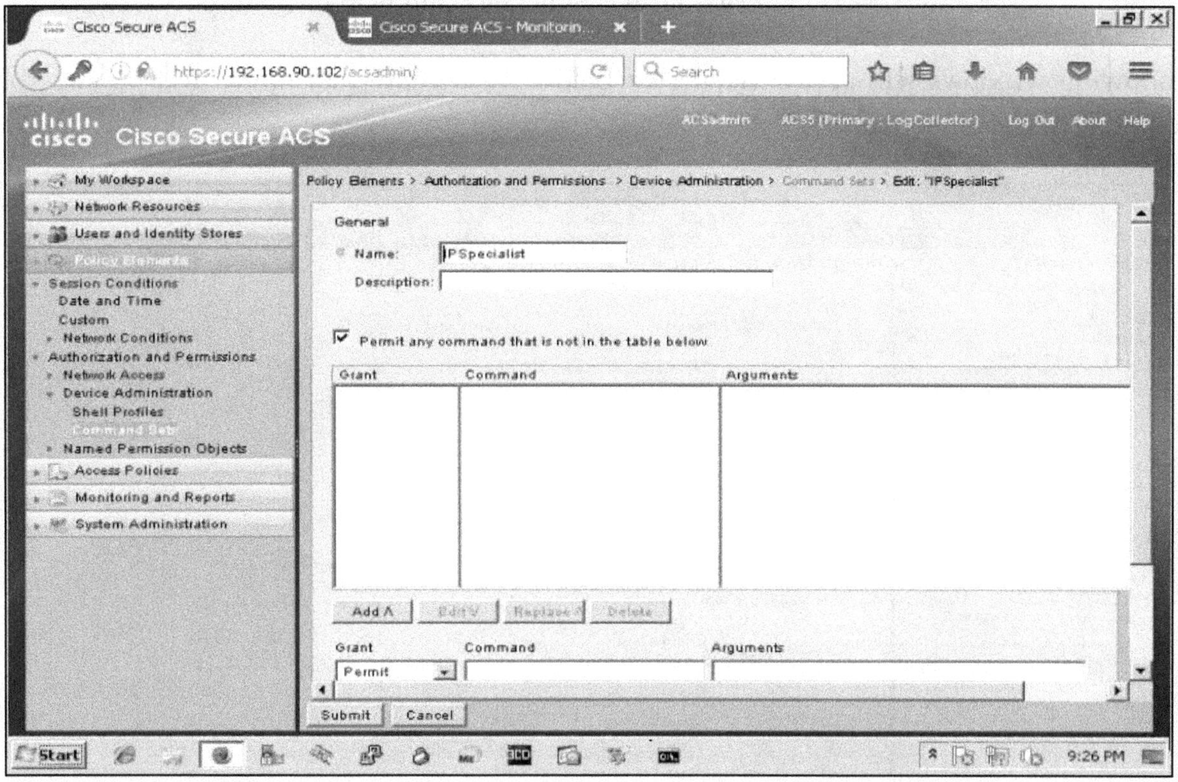

In the next step, usernames will be created and shell profiles along with commands set profiles will be assigned to the respective users.

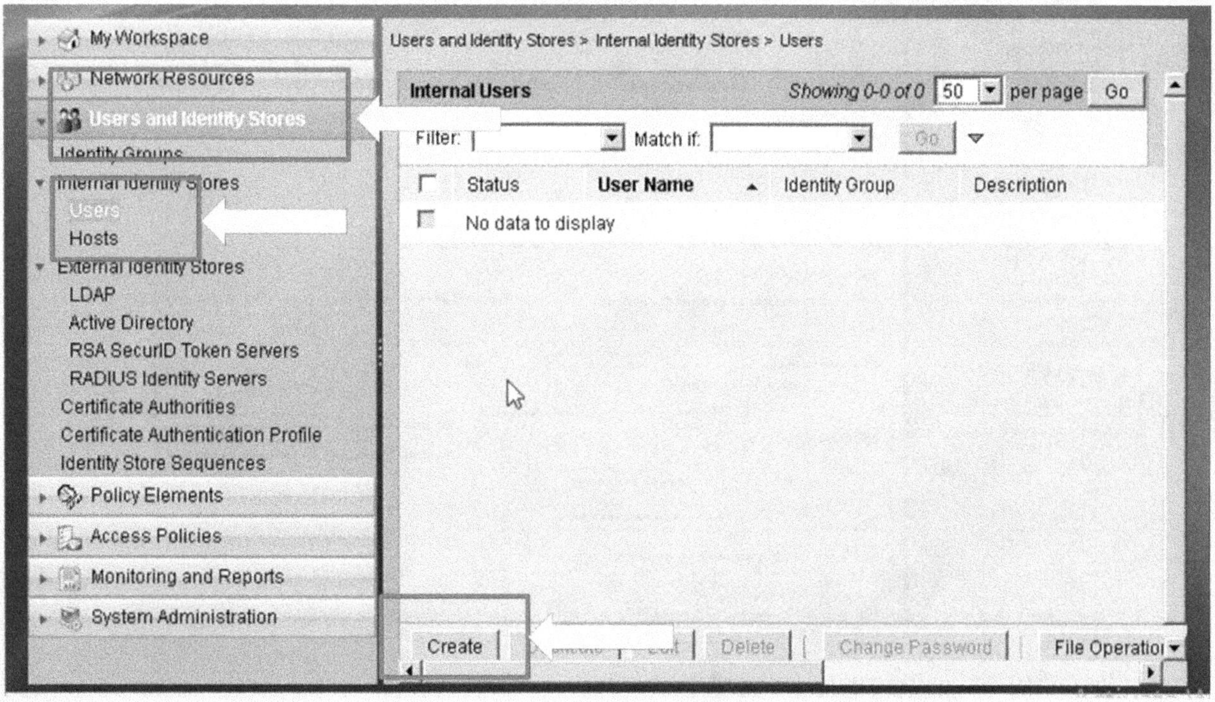

In order to create a new user, click: “Users and Identity Stores” -> “Internal Identity Stores” -> “Users” -> “Create” to create the IPSpecialist and Network Support Usernames.

Following windows will appear as shown below. Now, enter/set name and password as required in the objective.

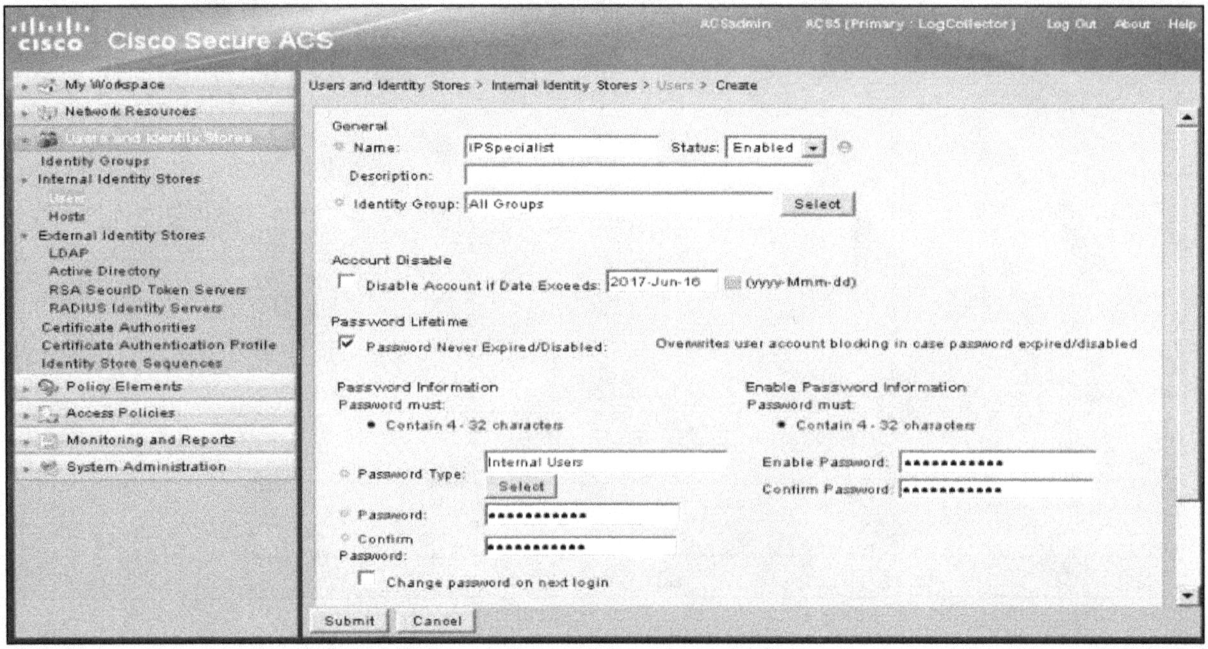

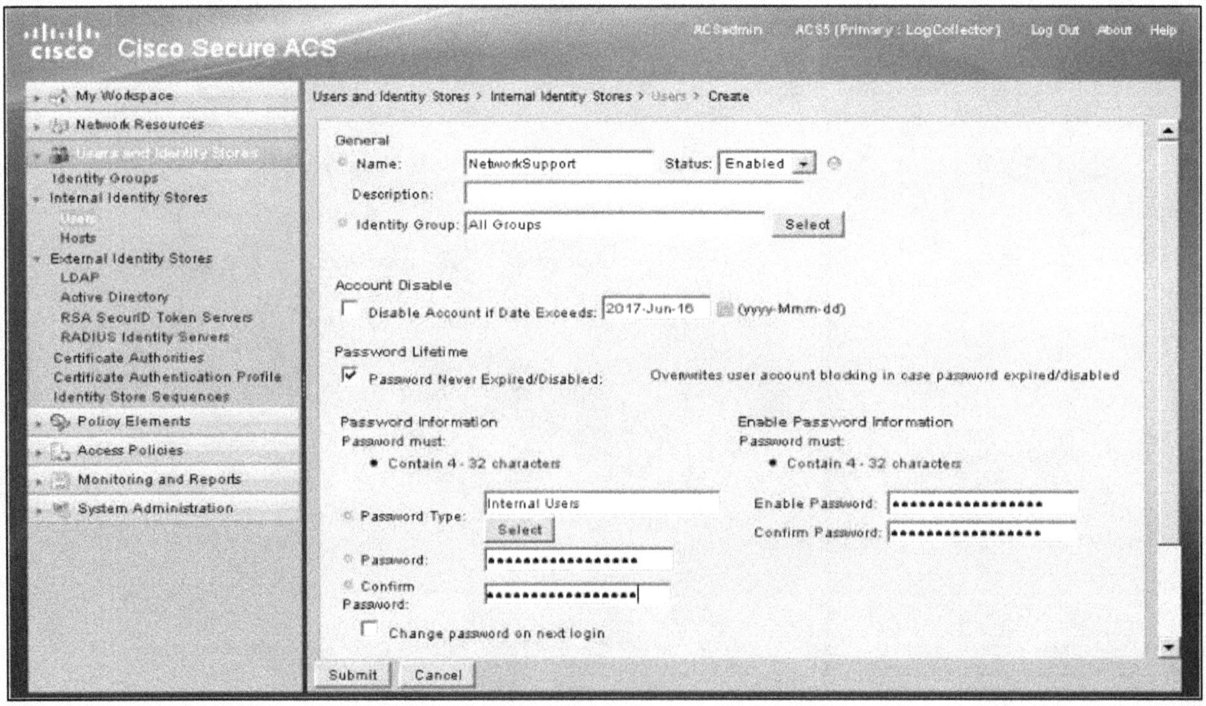

Then click “Submit”, to create respective users.

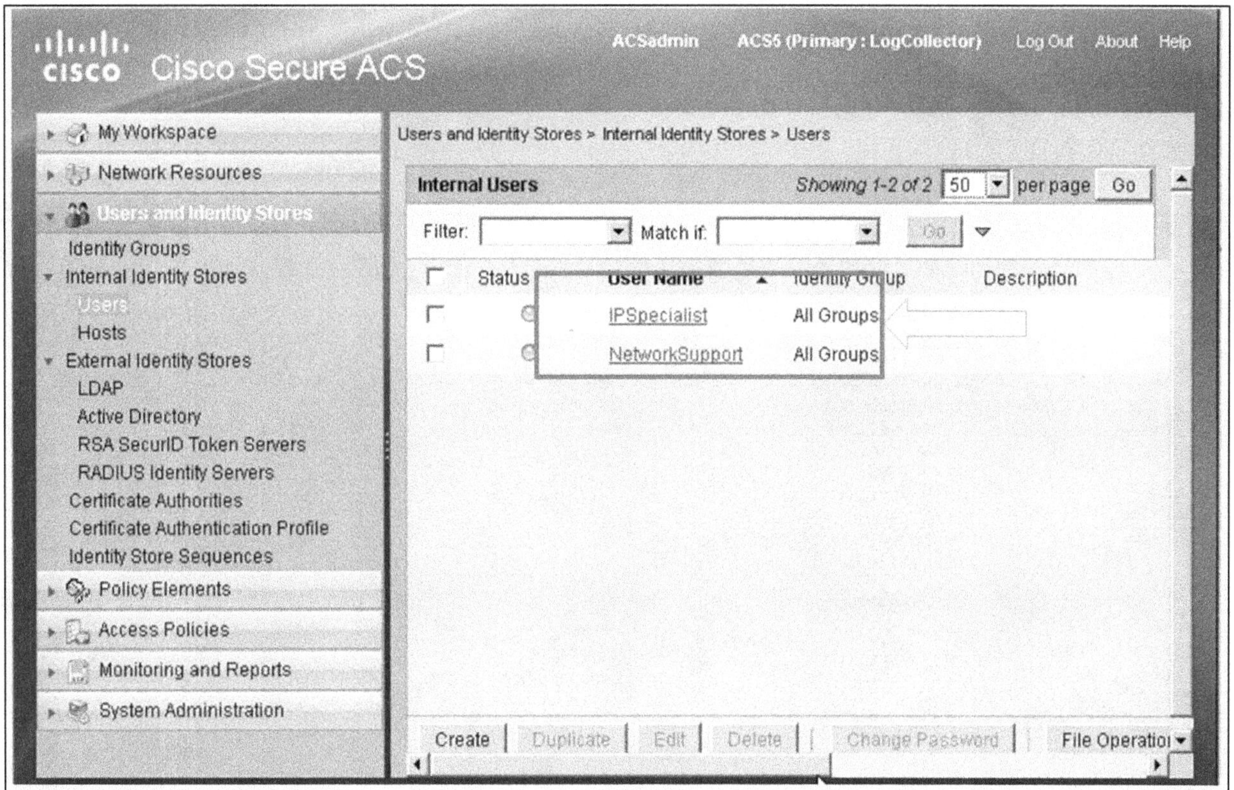

Now, click "Access Policies"-> "Default Device Admin"-> "Authorization" to associate custom command levels and shell profiles with usernames.

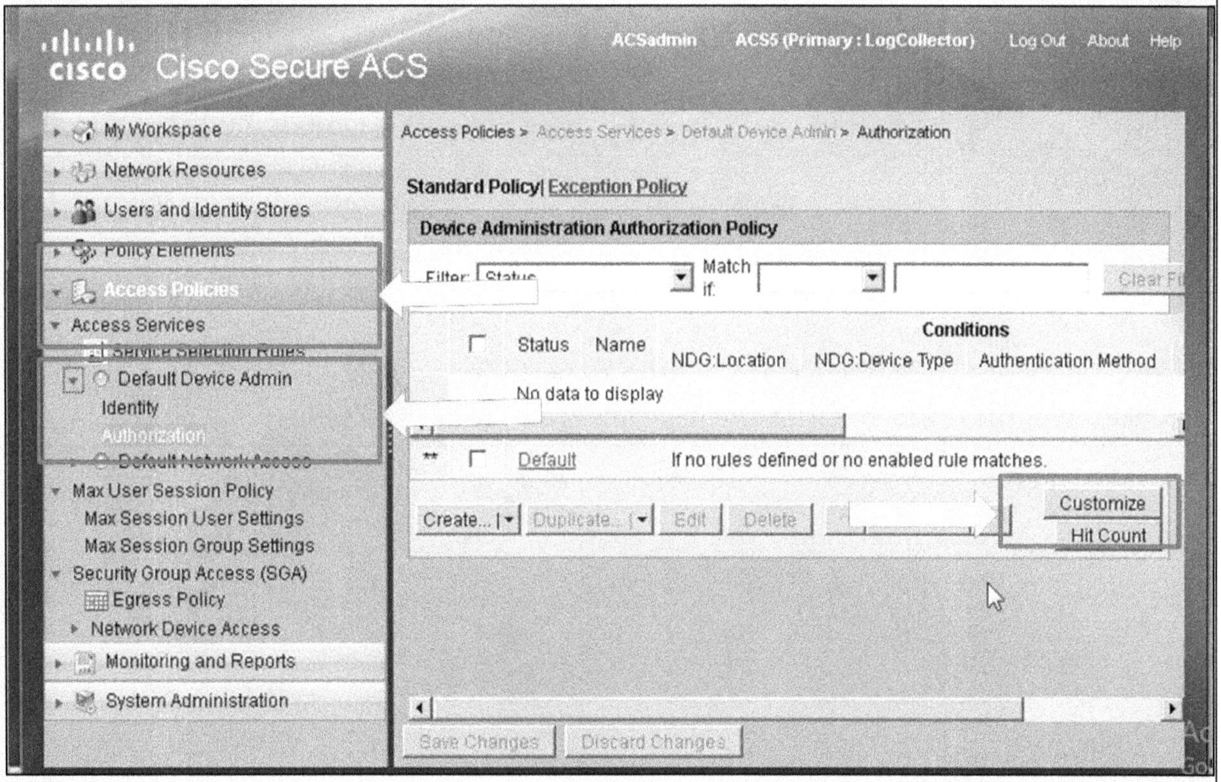

Click "Customize" to select the System Username, Shell profile and Custom Command Sets as assigning factors.

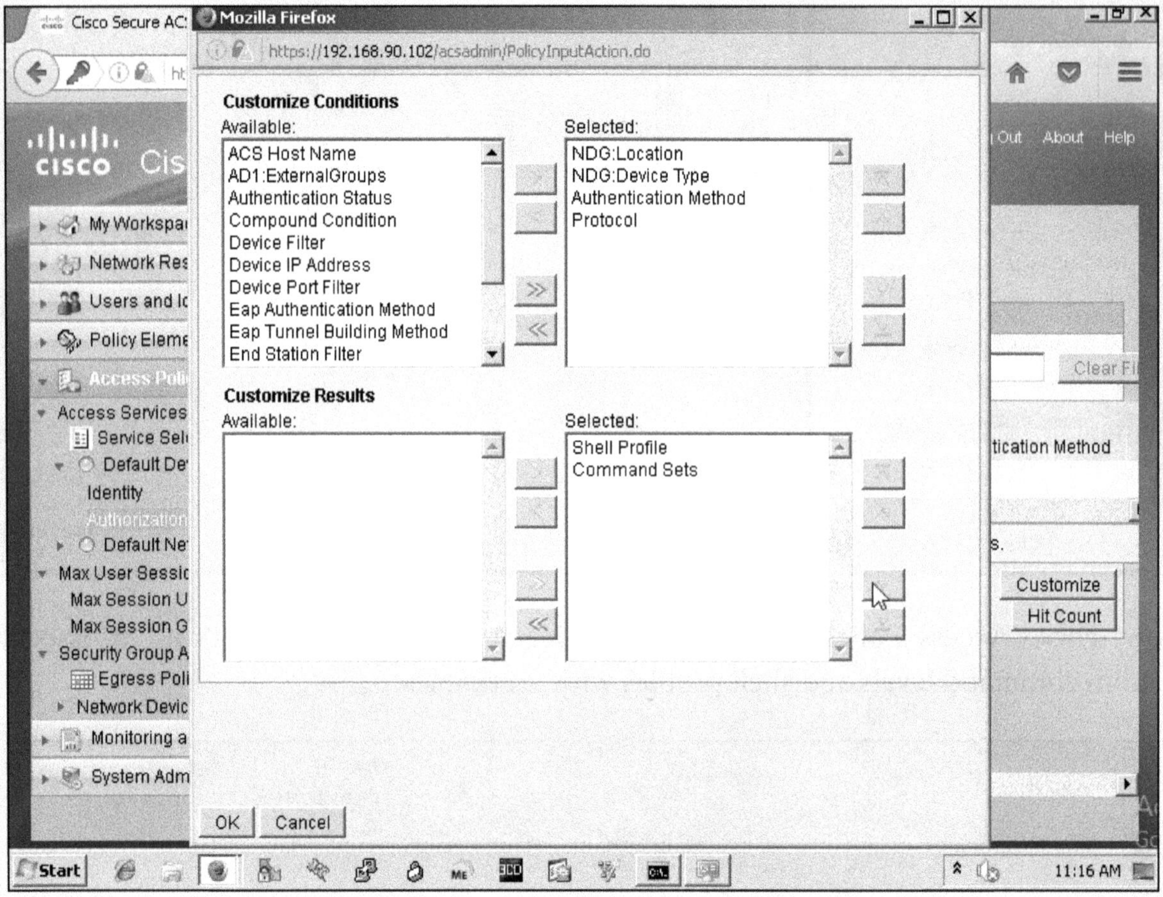

Click "OK".

After clicking ok, press the "Create" button to perform the final task in ACS, which is an association of the username with privilege levels and command sets.

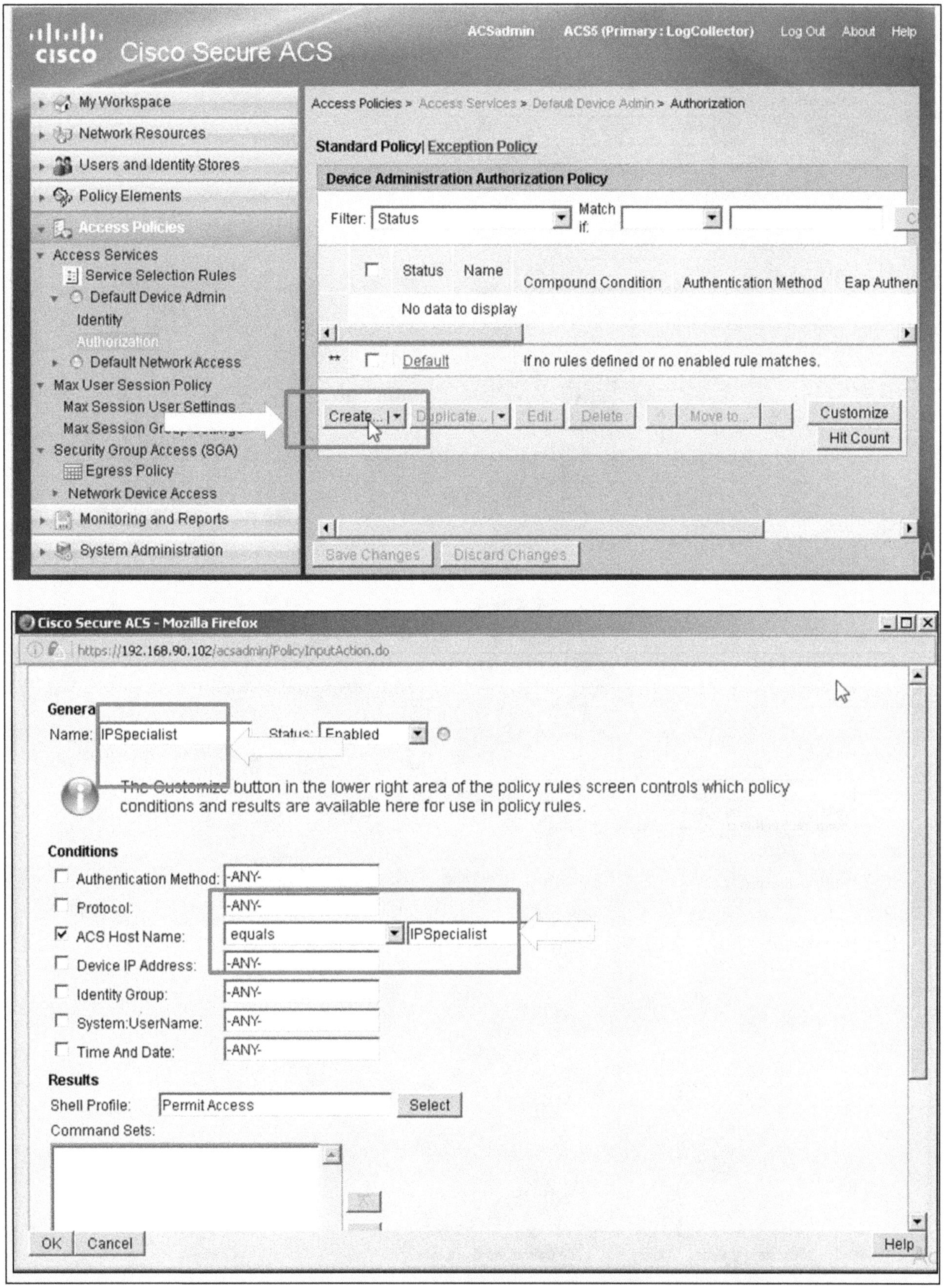
Cisco Secure ACS
ACSadmin
ACS5 (Primary : LogCollector)
Log Out
About
Help
My Workspace
Network Resources
Users and Identity Stores
Policy Elements
Access Policies
Access Services
Service Selection Rules
Default Device Admin
Identity
Authorization
Default Network Access
Max User Session Policy
Max Session User Settings
Security Group Access (SGA)
Egress Policy
Network Device Access
Monitoring and Reports
System Administration
Access Policies > Access Services > Default Device Admin > Authorization
Standard Policy| Exception Policy
Device Administration Authorization Policy
Filter: Status
Match if:
Status
Name
Compound Condition
Authentication Method
No data to display
Default
If no rules defined or no enabled rule matches.
Create...
Duplicate...
Edit
Delete
Move to...
Customize
Hit Count
Save Changes
Discard Changes
Cisco Secure ACS - Mozilla Firefox
https://192.168.90.102/acsadmin/PolicyInputAction.do
Name: IPSpecialist
Status: Enabled
The Customize button in the lower right area of the policy rules screen controls which policy conditions and results are available here for use in policy rules.
Conditions
Authentication Method: -ANY-
Protocol: -ANY-
ACS Host Name: equals IPSpecialist
Device IP Address: -ANY-
Identity Group: -ANY-
System:UserName: -ANY-
Time And Date: -ANY-
Results
Shell Profile: Permit Access
Select
Command Sets:
OK
Cancel
Help

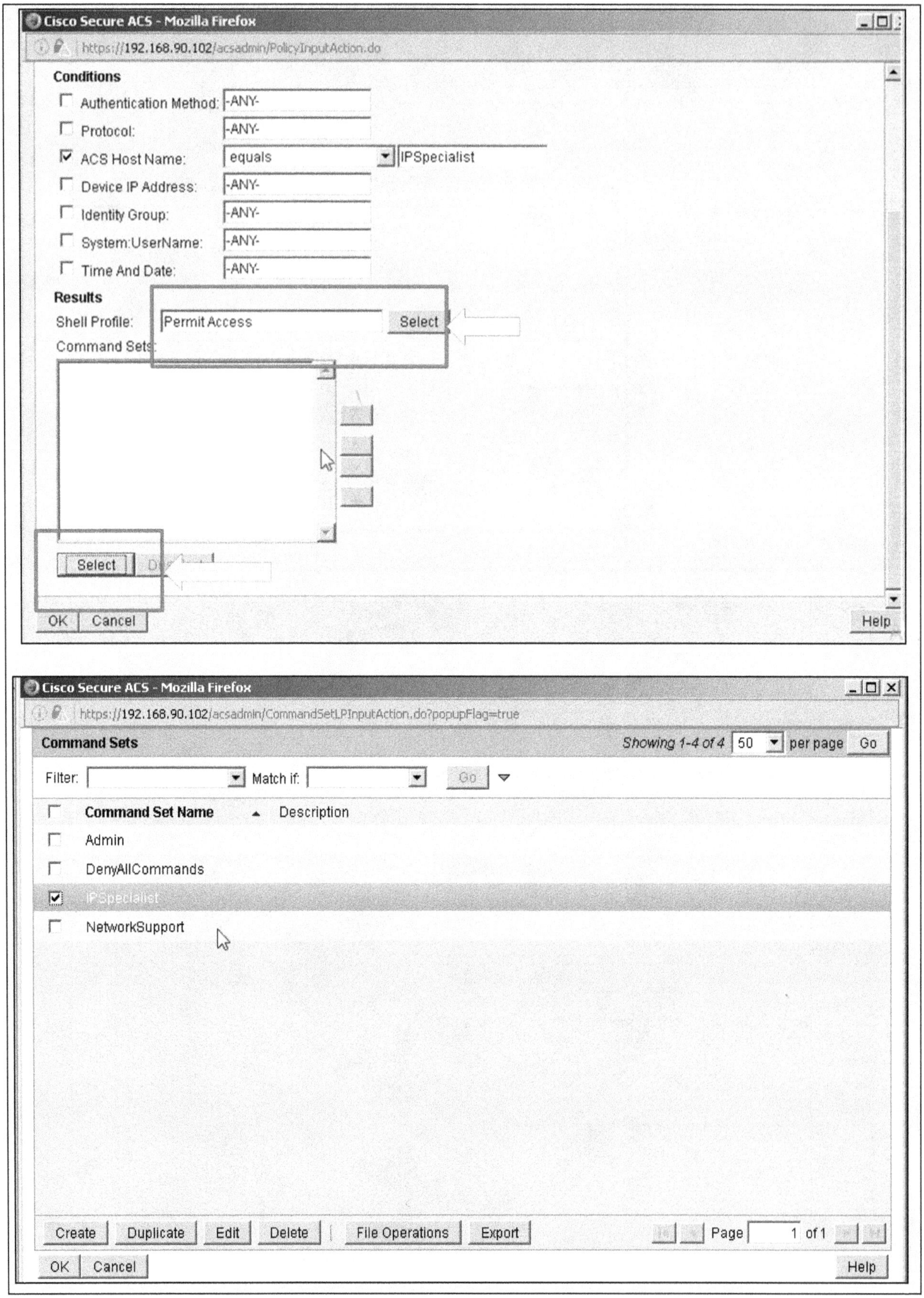
Cisco Secure ACS - Mozilla Firefox
https://192.168.90.102/acsadmin/PolicyInputAction.do
Conditions
Authentication Method: -ANY-
Protocol: -ANY-
ACS Host Name: equals IPSpecialist
Device IP Address: -ANY-
Identity Group: -ANY-
System:UserName: -ANY-
Time And Date: -ANY-
Results
Shell Profile: Permit Access Select
Command Sets:
Select
OK Cancel Help
Cisco Secure ACS - Mozilla Firefox
https://192.168.90.102/acsadmin/CommandSetLPInputAction.do?popupFlag=true
Command Sets
Showing 1-4 of 4 50 per page Go
Filter: Match if: Go
Command Set Name Description
Admin
DenyAllCommands
IPSpecialist
NetworkSupport
Create Duplicate Edit Delete File Operations Export
Page 1 of 1
OK Cancel Help

Click “Ok” to associate the username with the granted access.

Similar procedure will be followed for the next user.

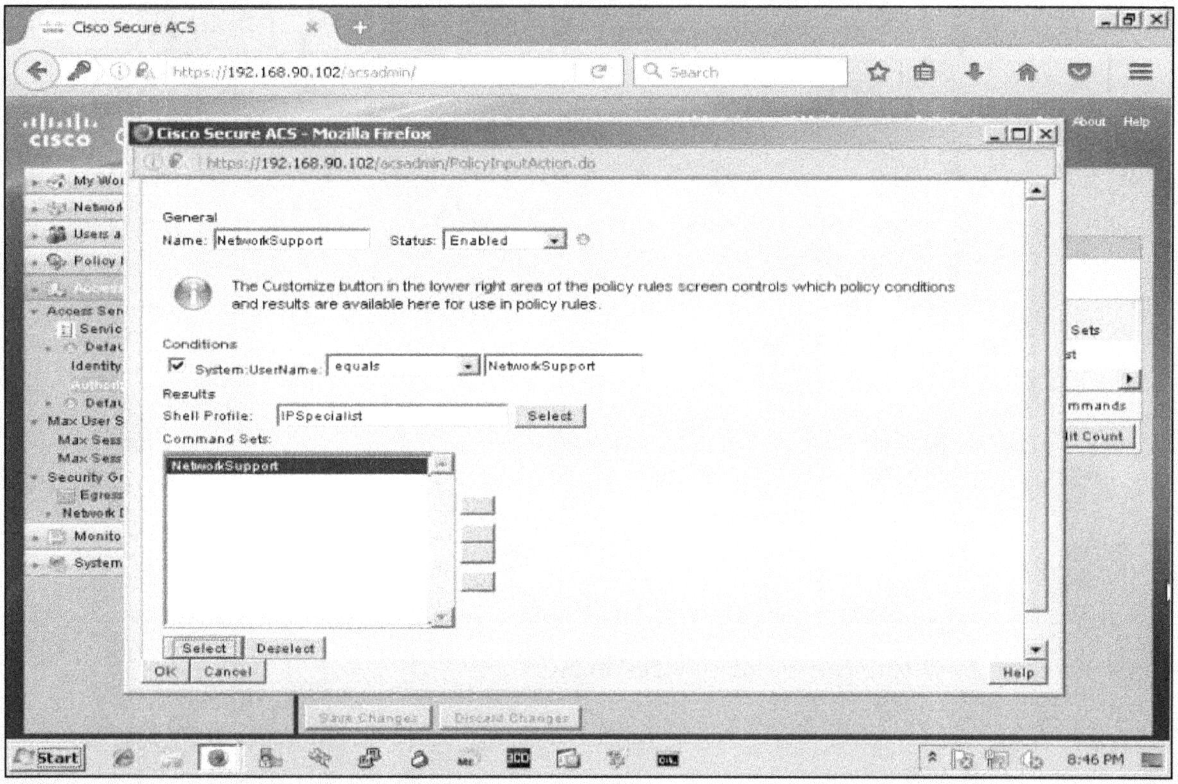

As the choice of protocol between ACS server and network devices is TACACS+ and it uses a shared secret key for allowing devices to communicate with it, let us define the network devices (R1, SW1, SW2 and SW3) IP addresses along with shared secret of P@$$word:10 by clicking “Network Resources” -> “Network Devices and AAA Clients”

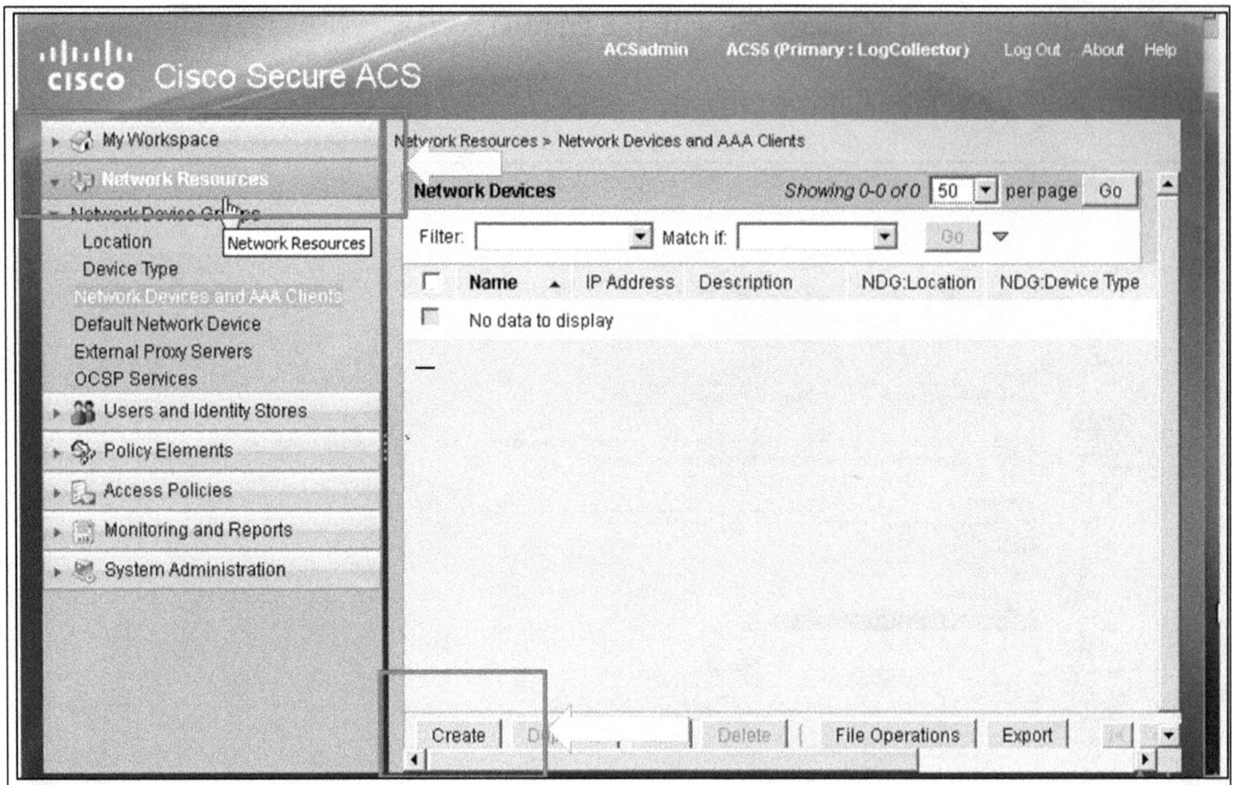

Click “Create” to define the client devices in ACS.

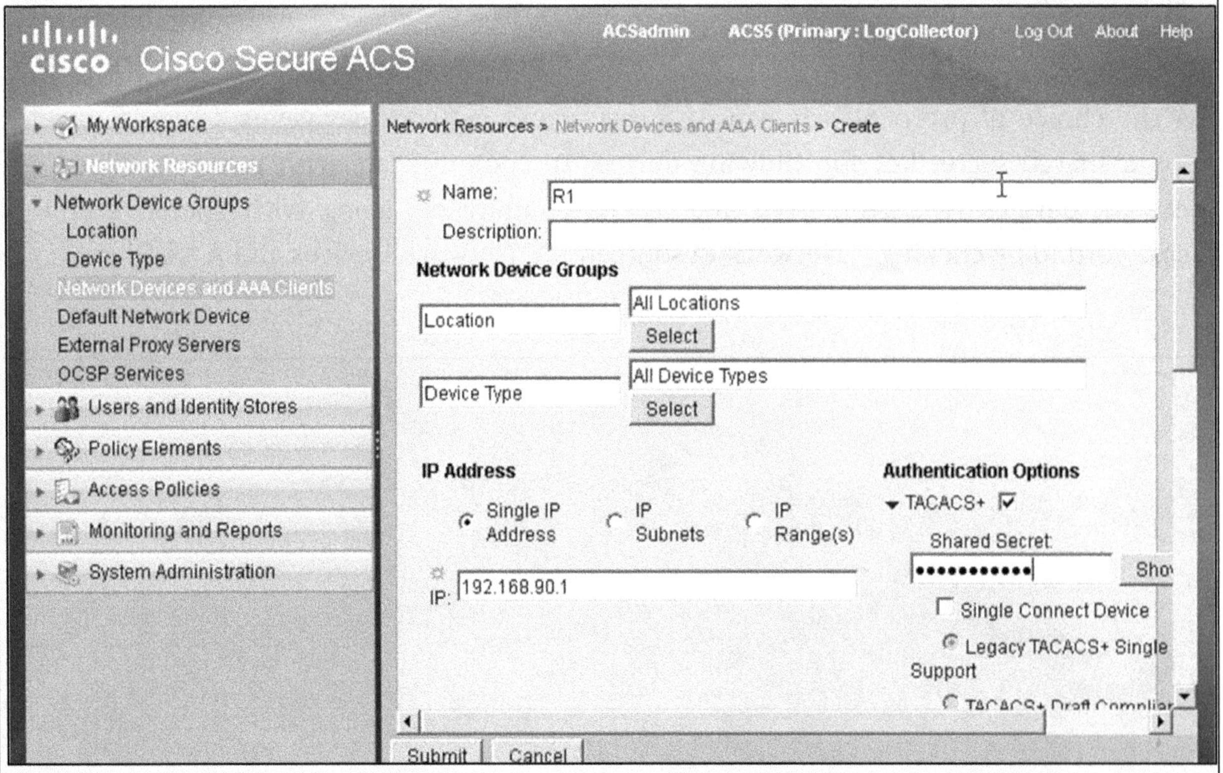

Click “Submit” to save the device.

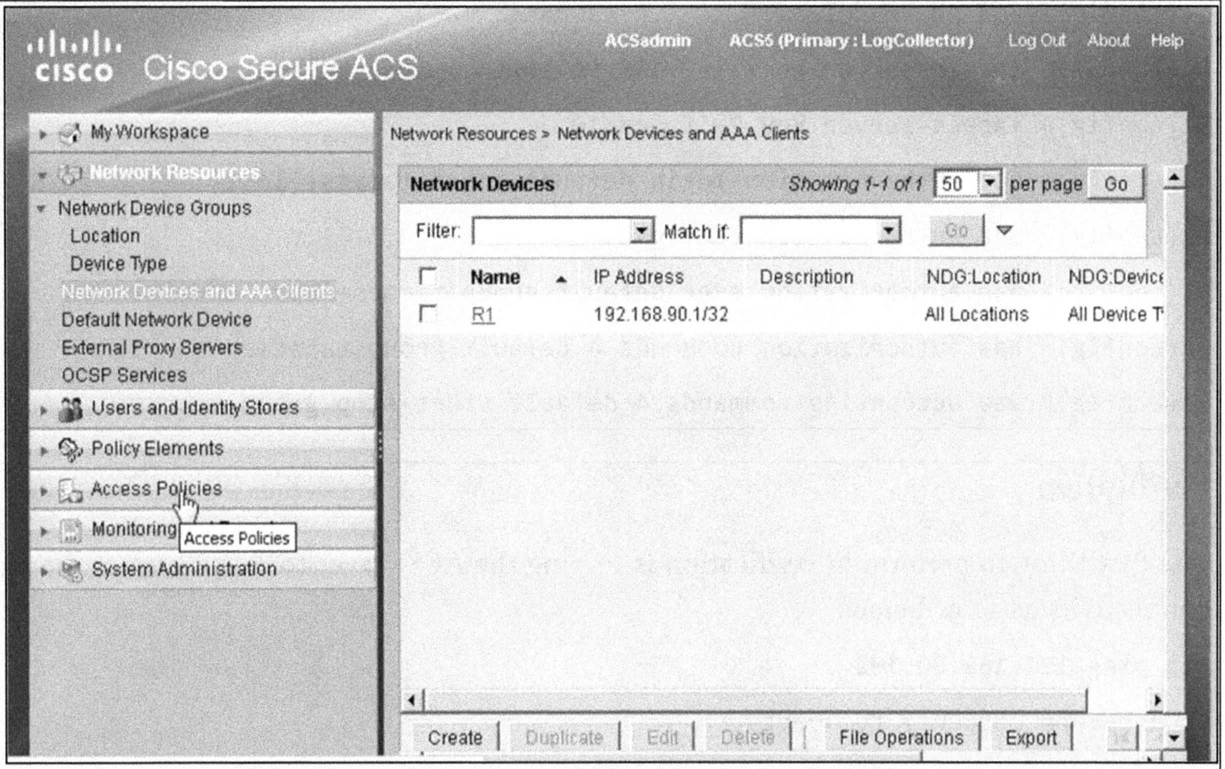

Similarly, Switches SW1, SW2 and SW3 management IP address will be defined here.

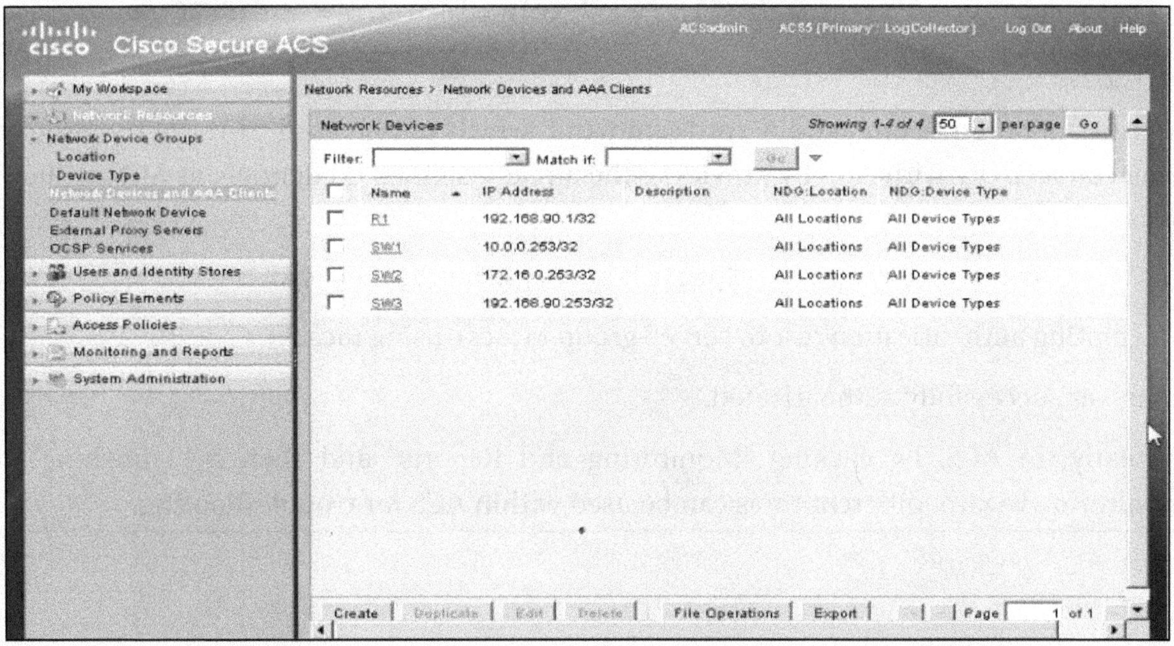

In the next phase of this lab, networking devices will be configured for AAA using TACACS+ protocol, followed by the verification section.

R1

```
R1(config)# aaa new-model
R1(config)# tacacs-server host 192.168.90.102
R1(config)# tacacs-server key P@$$word:10
R1(config)# aaa authentication login default group tacacs+ local
R1(config)# aaa authorization config-commands
R1(config)# aaa authorization exec default group tacacs+
R1(config)# aaa authorization commands 4 default group tacacs+
R1(config)# aaa accounting commands 4 default start-stop group tacacs+
```

Verification

The first thing to perform in verification is to ping the ACS server to make sure of the L3 connectivity as show below:

```
R1# ping 192.168.90.102
Type escape sequence to abort.
Sending 5, 100-byte ICMP Echos to 192.168.90.102, timeout is 2 seconds:
!!!!!
Success rate is 80 percent (4/5), round-trip min/avg/max = 4/9/16 ms
```

Another important command is **test** command, which can be used to verify the protocol level connectivity with ACS by providing the already defined credentials in ACS as shown below.

```
R1# test aaa group tacacs+ IPSpecialist P@$$word:10 legacy
```

Attempting authentication test to server-group tacacs+ using tacacs+,

User was successfully authenticated.

Similarly, in ACS, by clicking "Monitoring and Reports" and then by launching the monitoring wizard, different tools can be used within ACS for troubleshooting.

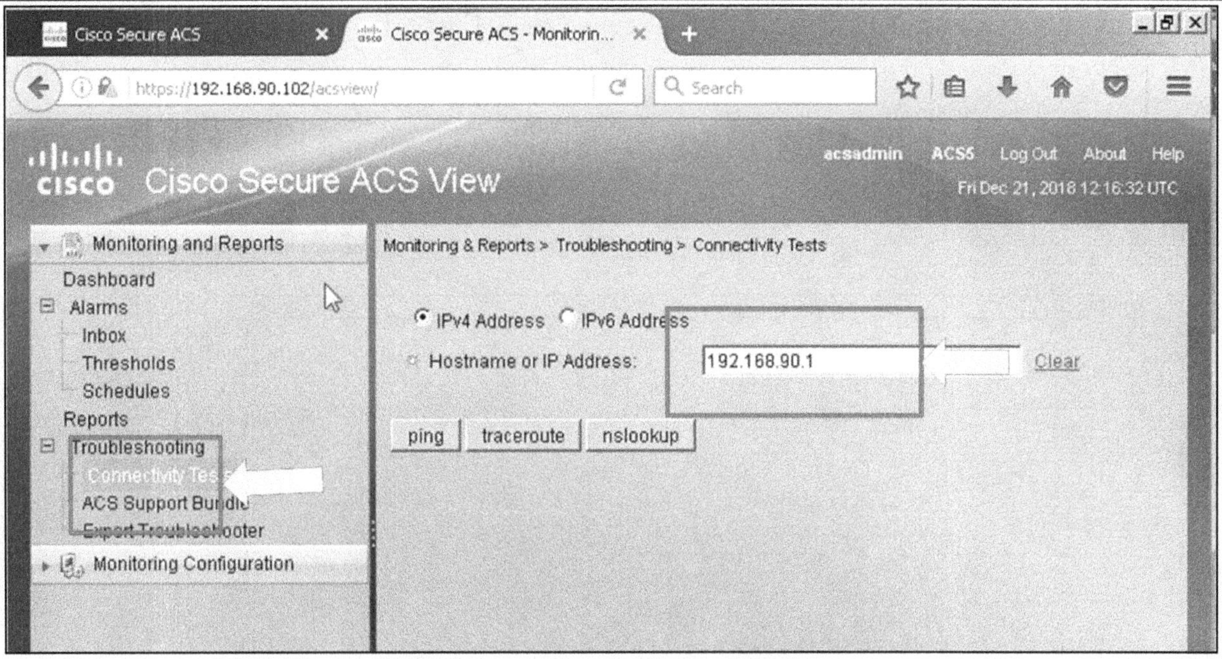
Cisco Secure ACS
Cisco Secure ACS - Monitorin...
https://192.168.90.102/acsview/
Search
Cisco Secure ACS View
acsadmin ACS5 Log Out About Help
Fri Dec 21, 2018 12:16:32 UTC
Monitoring and Reports
Dashboard
Alarms
Inbox
Thresholds
Schedules
Reports
Troubleshooting
ACS Support Bundle
Expert Troubleshooter
Monitoring Configuration
Monitoring & Reports > Troubleshooting > Connectivity Tests
IPv4 Address
IPv6 Address
Hostname or IP Address:
192.168.90.1
Clear
ping
traceroute
nslookup

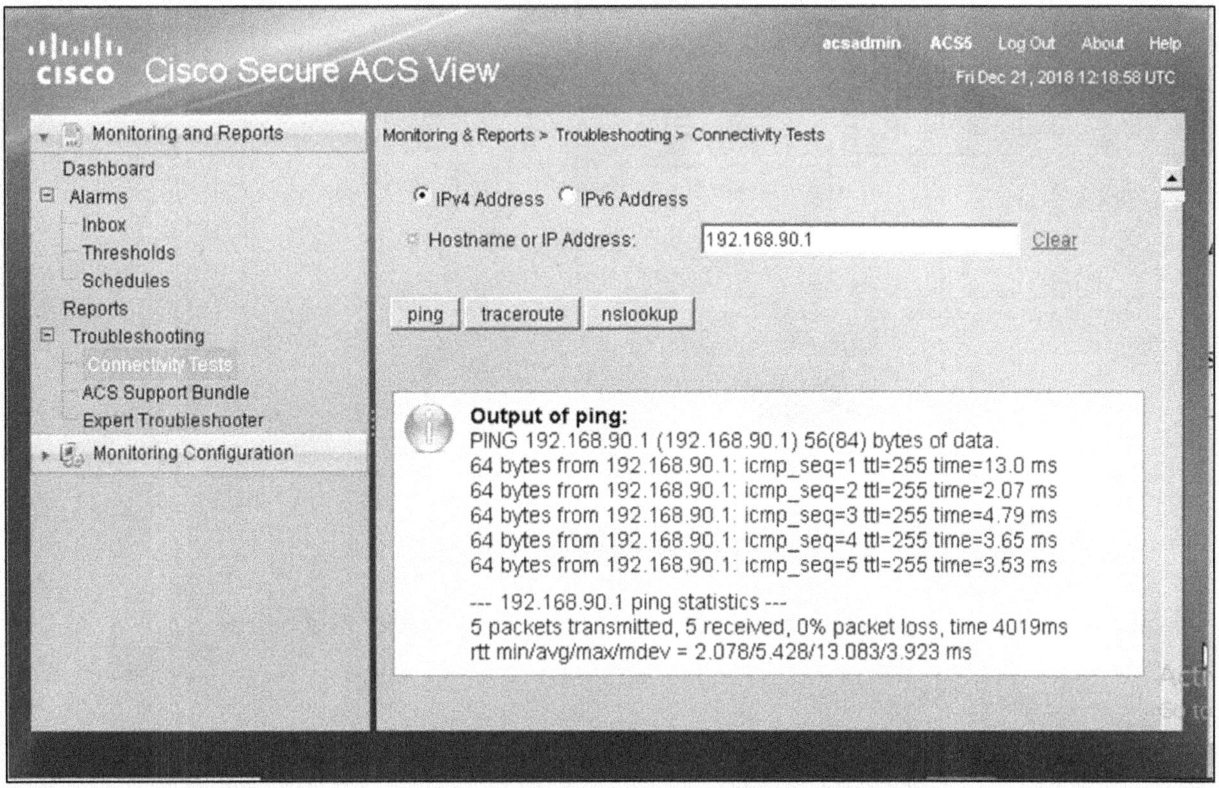
Cisco Secure ACS View
acsadmin ACS5 Log Out About Help
Fri Dec 21, 2018 12:18:58 UTC
Monitoring and Reports
Dashboard
Alarms
Inbox
Thresholds
Schedules
Reports
Troubleshooting
Connectivity Tests
ACS Support Bundle
Expert Troubleshooter
Monitoring Configuration
Monitoring & Reports > Troubleshooting > Connectivity Tests
IPv4 Address
IPv6 Address
Hostname or IP Address:
192.168.90.1
Clear
ping
traceroute
nslookup
Output of ping:
PING 192.168.90.1 (192.168.90.1) 56(84) bytes of data.
64 bytes from 192.168.90.1: icmp_seq=1 ttl=255 time=13.0 ms
64 bytes from 192.168.90.1: icmp_seq=2 ttl=255 time=2.07 ms
64 bytes from 192.168.90.1: icmp_seq=3 ttl=255 time=4.79 ms
64 bytes from 192.168.90.1: icmp_seq=4 ttl=255 time=3.65 ms
64 bytes from 192.168.90.1: icmp_seq=5 ttl=255 time=3.53 ms
--- 192.168.90.1 ping statistics ---
5 packets transmitted, 5 received, 0% packet loss, time 4019ms
rtt min/avg/max/mdev = 2.078/5.428/13.083/3.923 ms

Lab 2.5: Configuring Administrative Access On A Cisco Router Using RADIUS And ISE Server

The main objective of this lab is the same as the previous one but ISE will be used in this lab instead of Cisco's ACS server. The choice of protocol between client devices and ISE will be RADIUS.

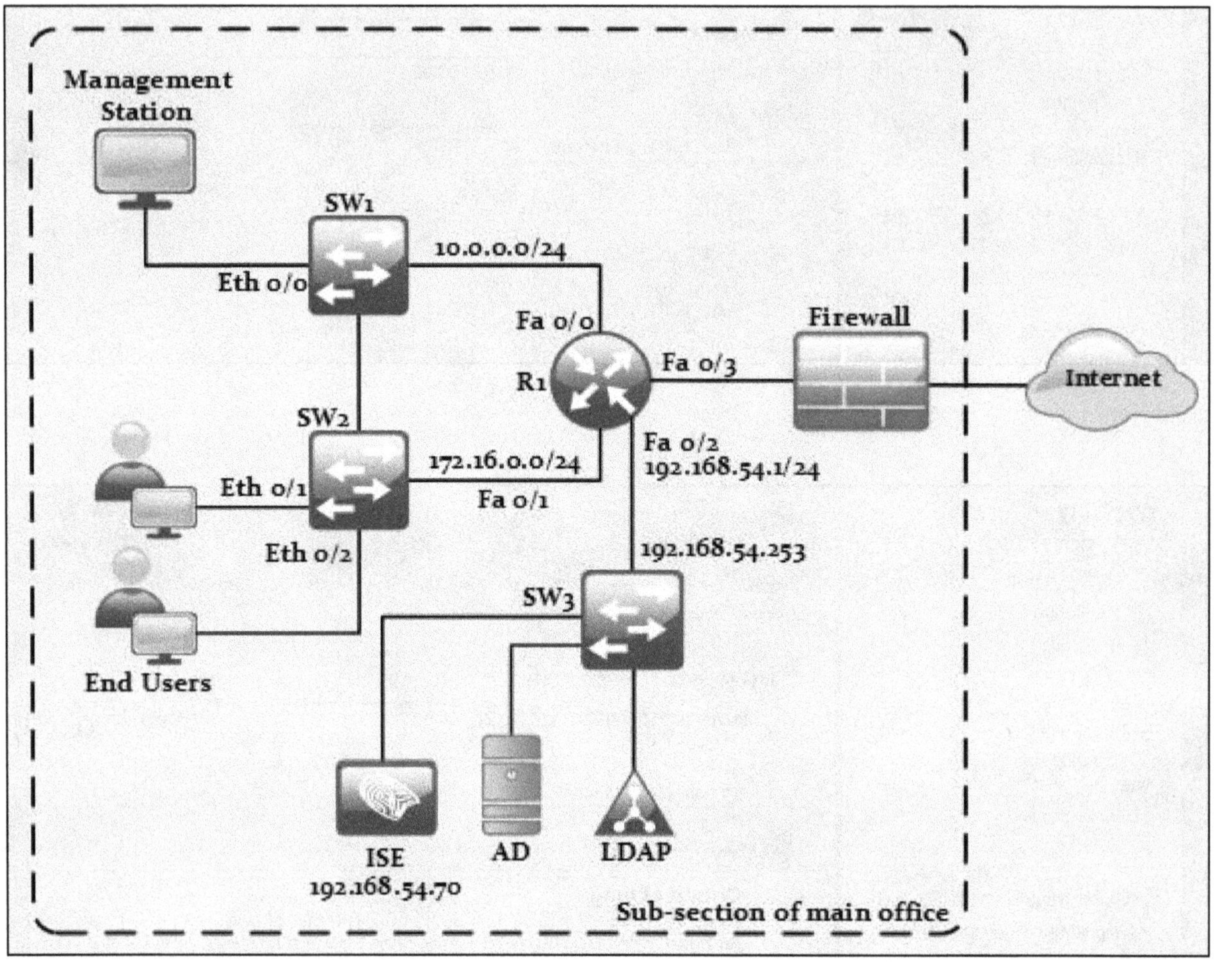

Figure 2-09: Lab 2.5 Topology

Two users will be created with respective access limitations defined below:

Username1: IPSpecialist

Password: P@$$word:10

Privilege level: 15

Username2: ITHelpdesk

Password: P@$$word:20

Privilege level 4

The following topology will be used in this lab.

ISE

By accessing the management IP address of ISE, which is 192.168.54.70, a certificate trust alert may appear which can be ignored, the following screen will appear.

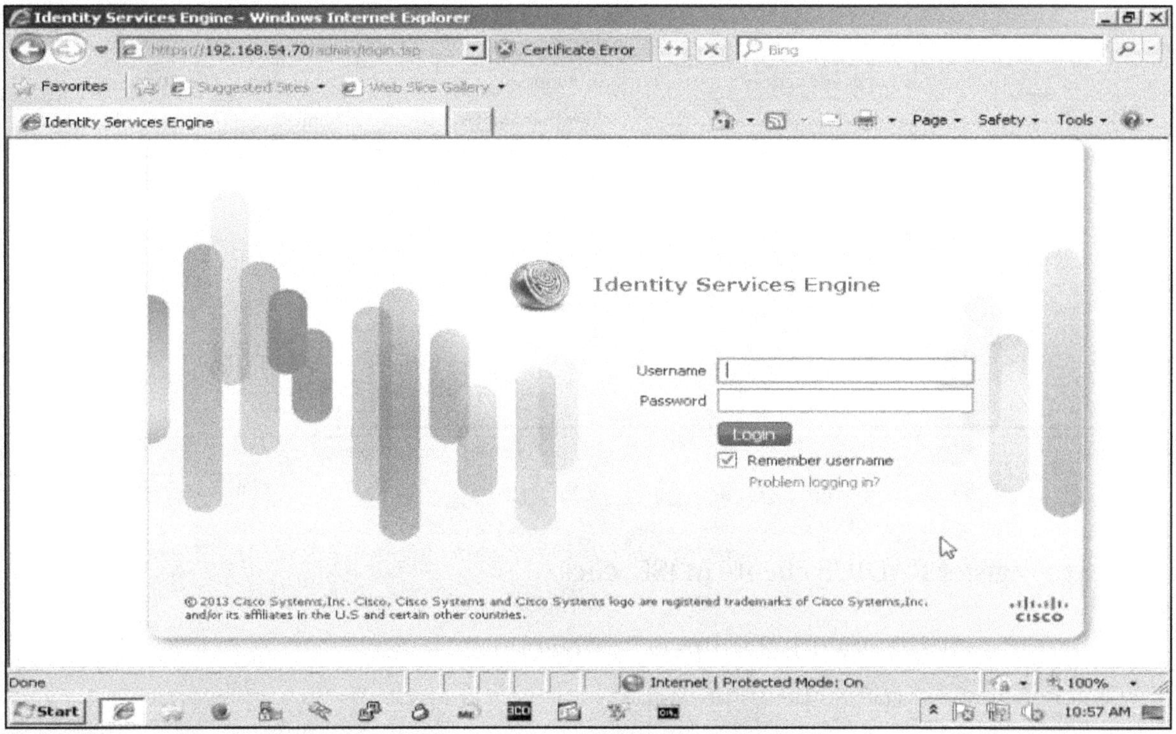

Use the following credentials for login:

Username: admin

Password: Cisco123

After a successful login, the following dashboard will appear.

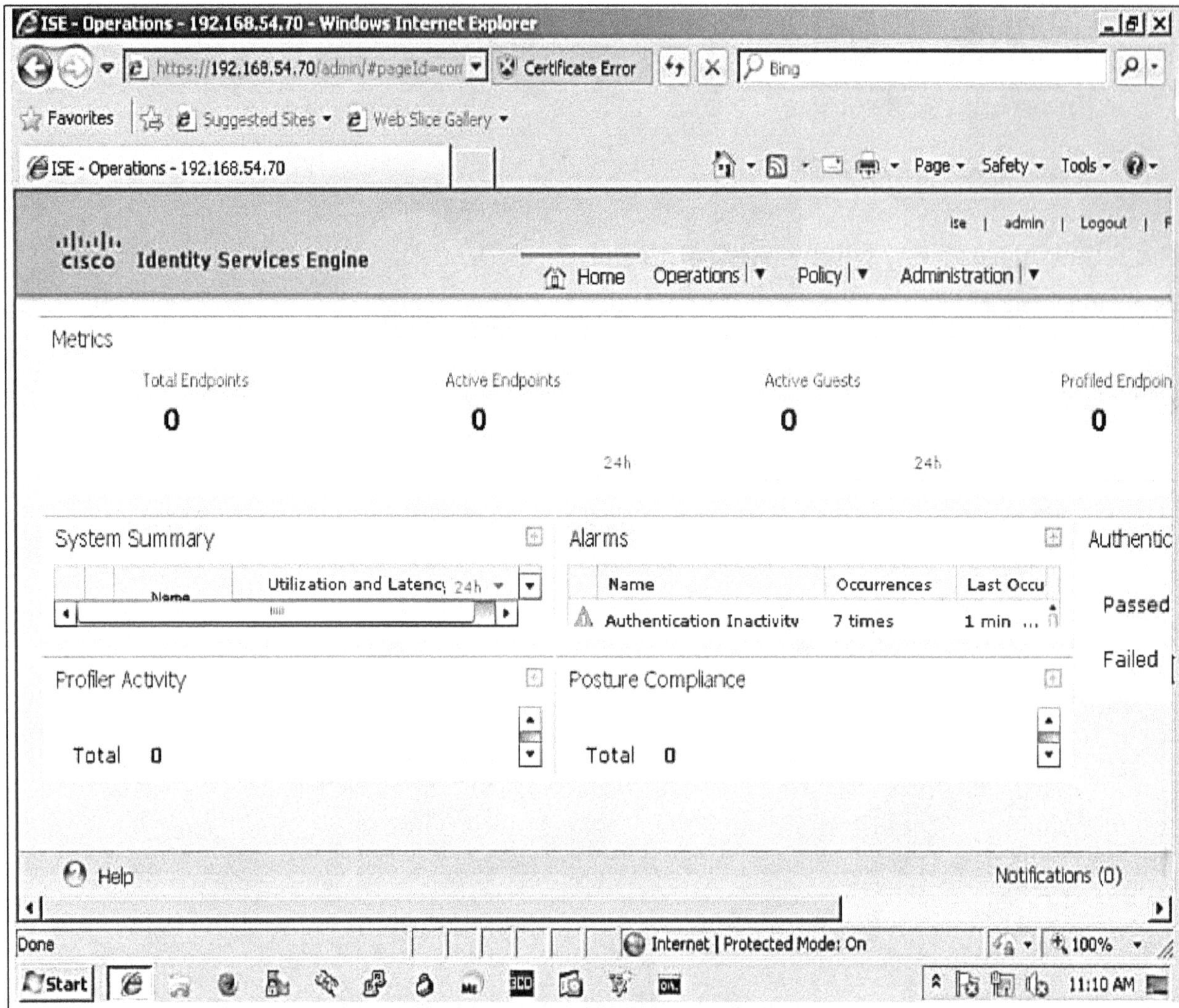

In order to register RADIUS clients in ISE, click

"Administration" -> "Network Resources"-> "Network Devices"

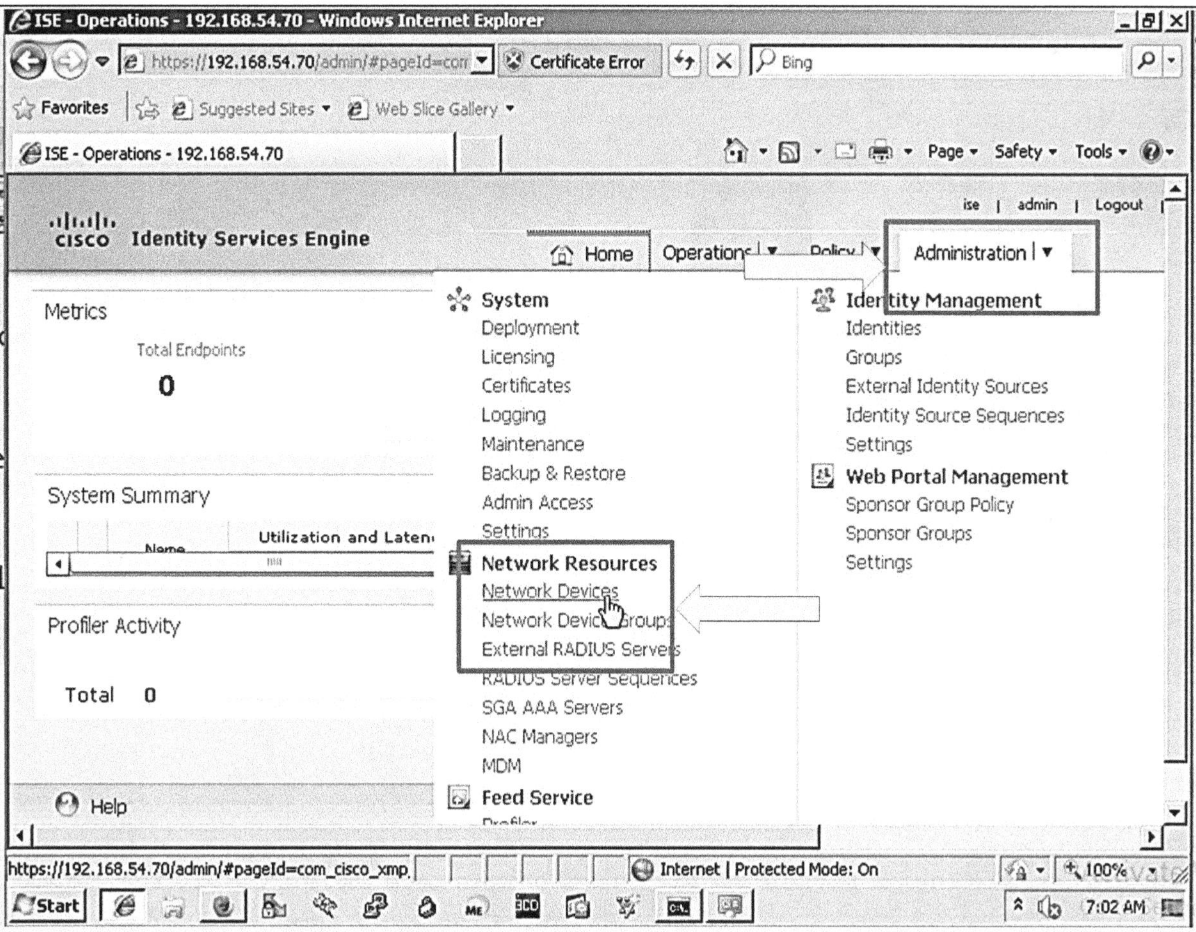

Click "Add" button to actually add new clients.

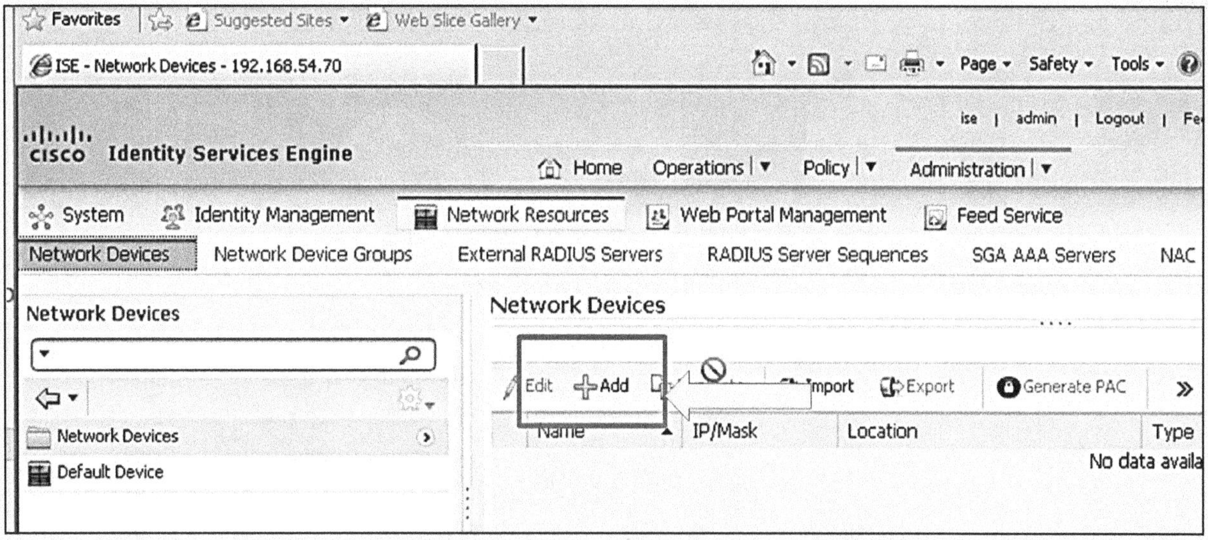

The following screen will appear.

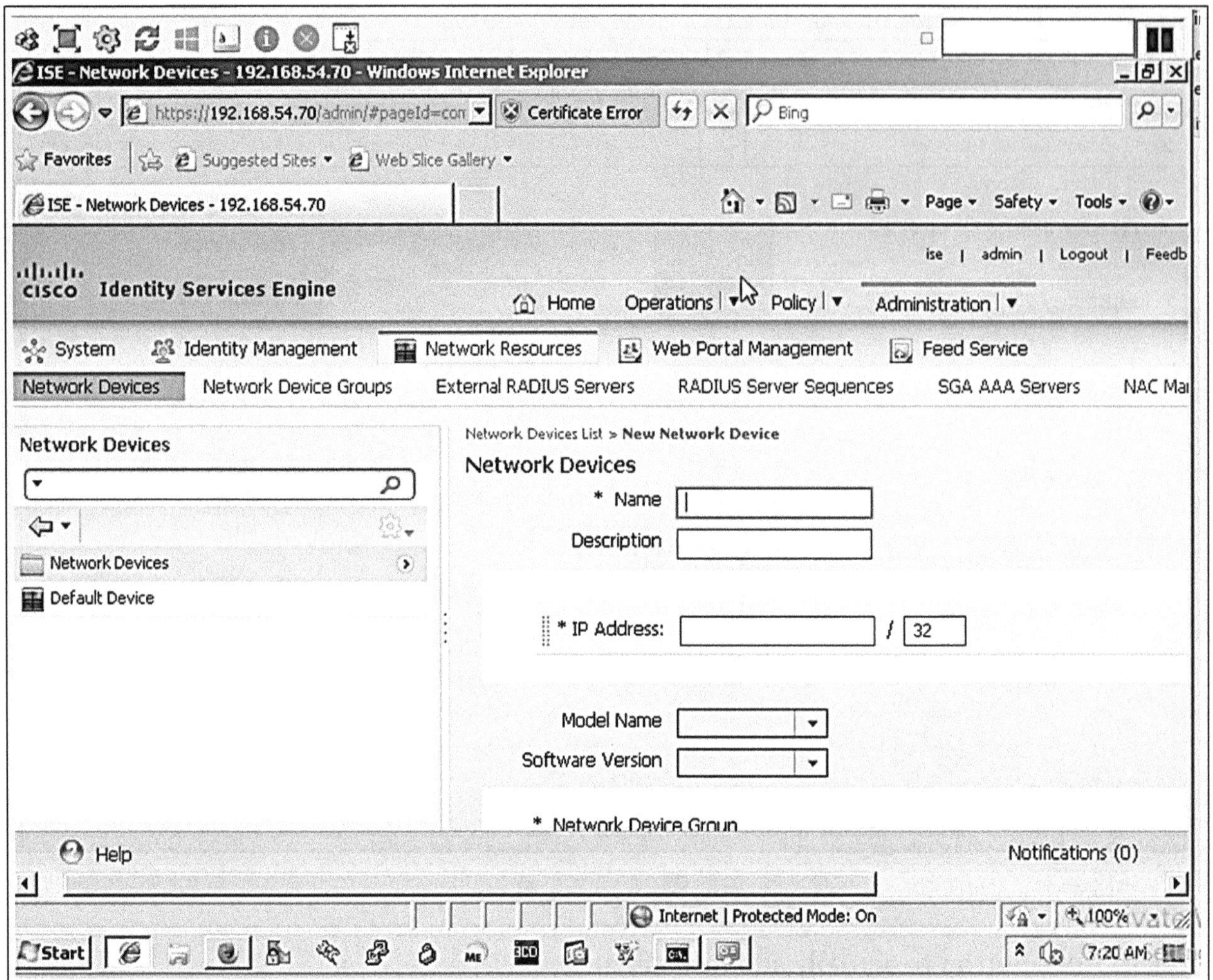

Define the IP address of R1 and P@$$word:10 as radius shared secret.

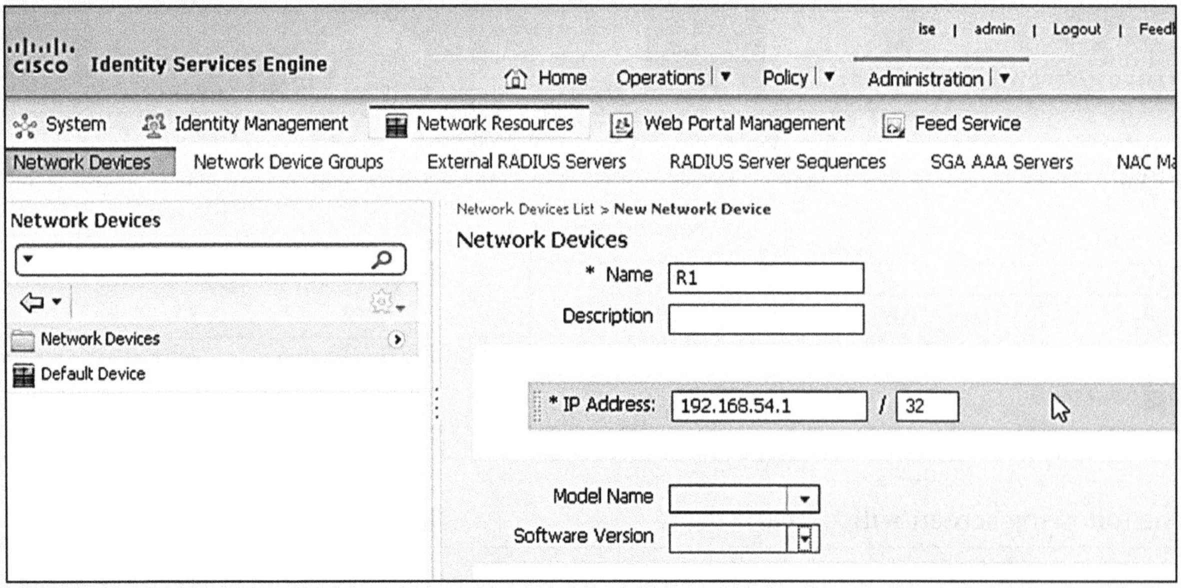

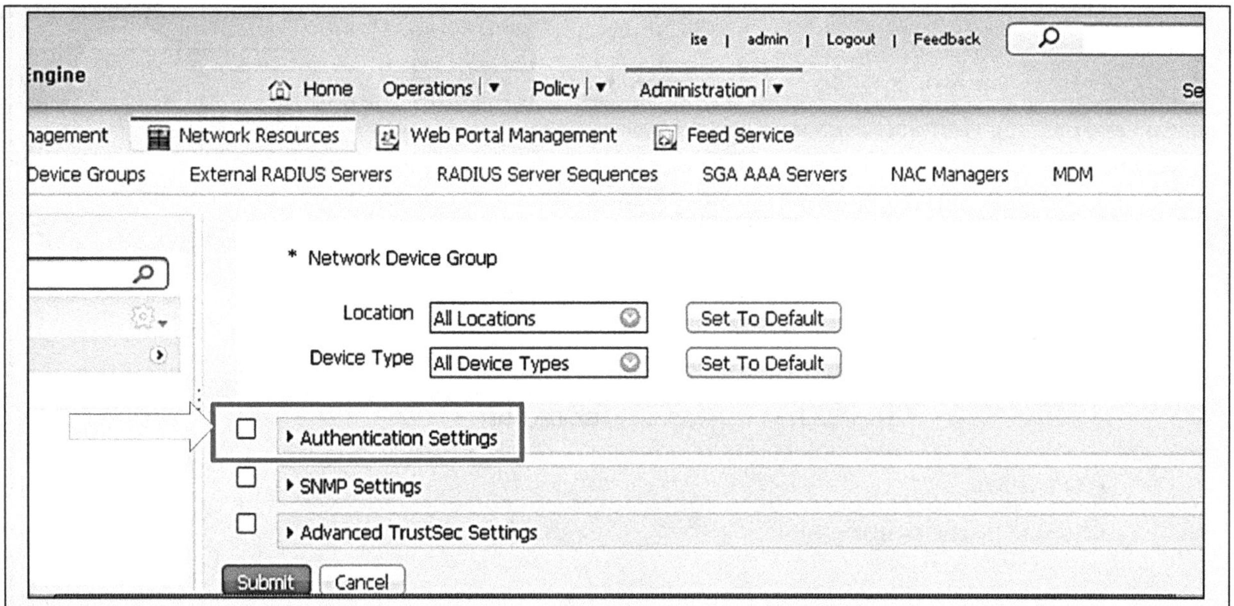
ise | admin | Logout | Feedback
Home
Operations
Policy
Administration
Network Resources
Web Portal Management
Feed Service
External RADIUS Servers
RADIUS Server Sequences
SGA AAA Servers
NAC Managers
MDM
* Network Device Group
Location
All Locations
Set To Default
Device Type
All Device Types
Set To Default
Authentication Settings
SNMP Settings
Advanced TrustSec Settings
Submit
Cancel

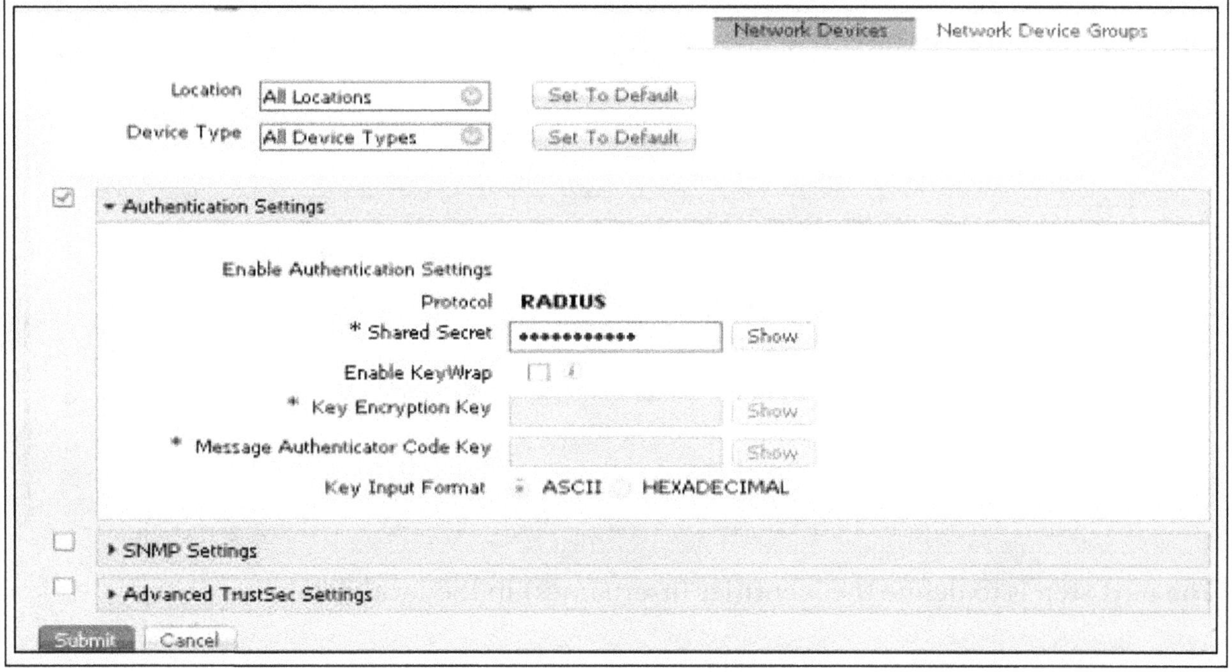
Network Devices
Network Device Groups
Location
All Locations
Set To Default
Device Type
All Device Types
Set To Default
Authentication Settings
Enable Authentication Settings
Protocol
RADIUS
* Shared Secret
Show
Enable KeyWrap
* Key Encryption Key
Show
* Message Authenticator Code Key
Show
Key Input Format
ASCII
HEXADECIMAL
SNMP Settings
Advanced TrustSec Settings
Submit
Cancel

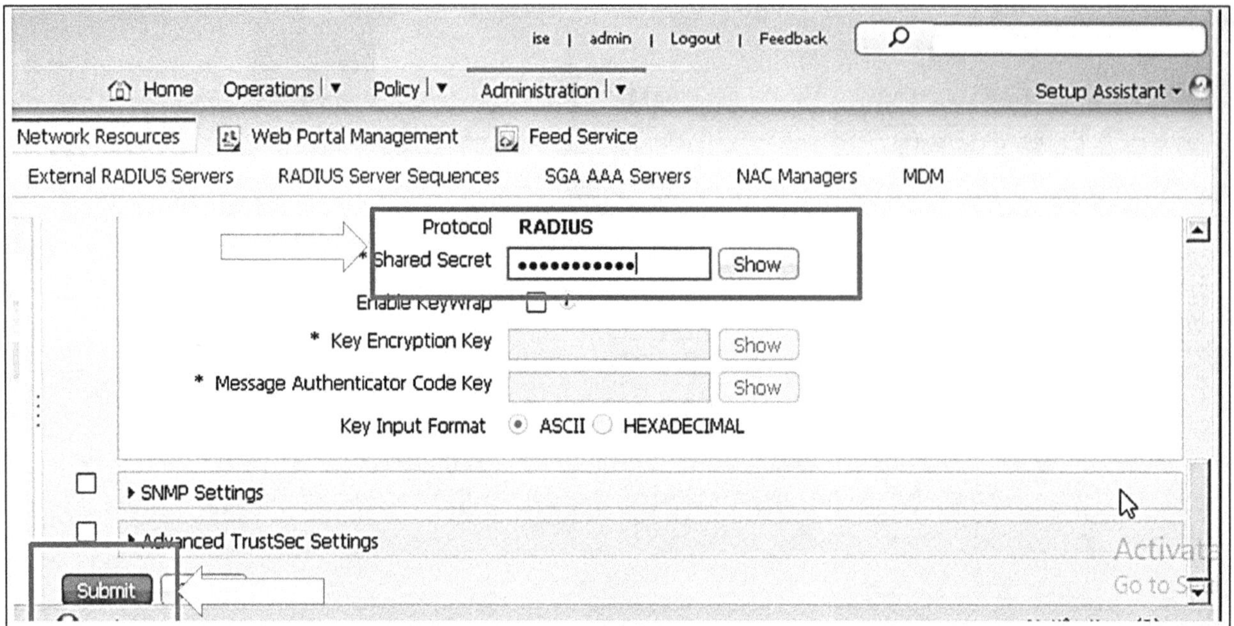

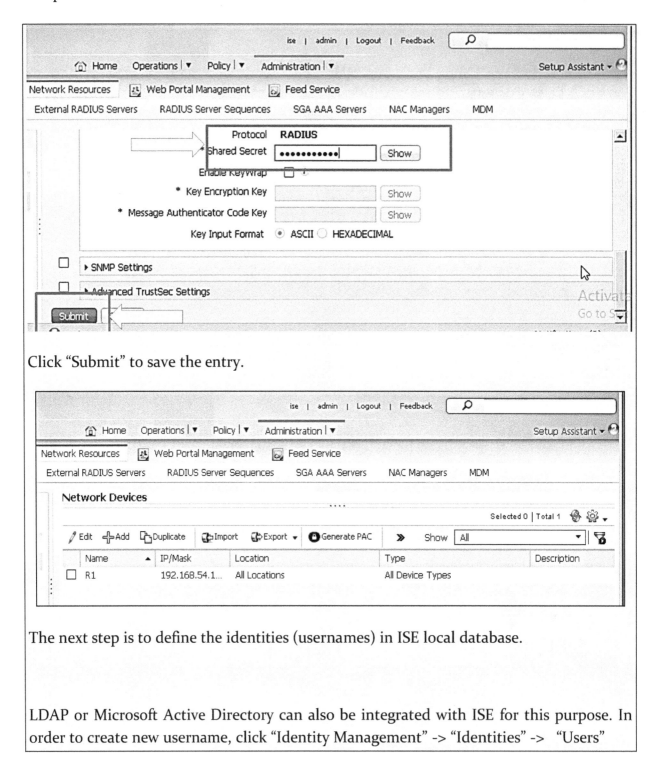

Click “Submit” to save the entry.

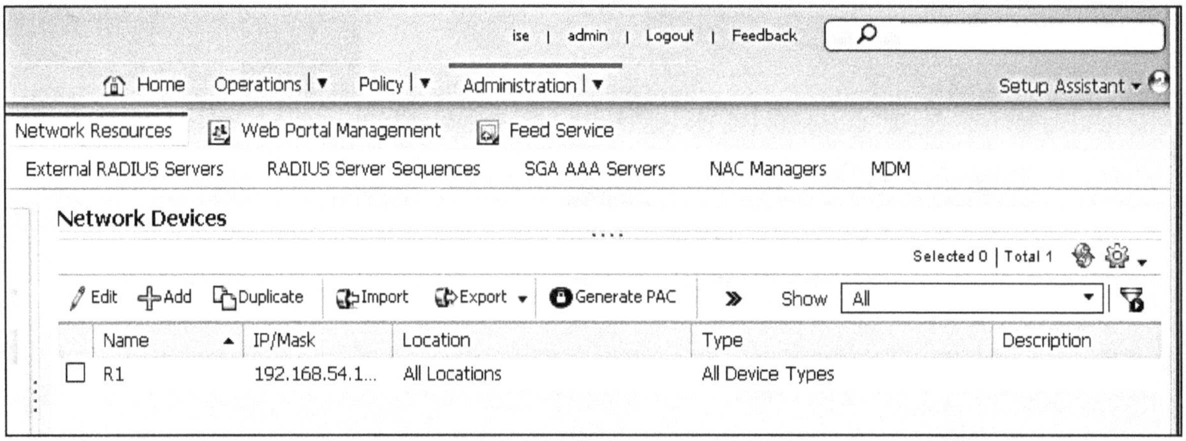

The next step is to define the identities (usernames) in ISE local database.

LDAP or Microsoft Active Directory can also be integrated with ISE for this purpose. In order to create new username, click “Identity Management” -> “Identities” -> “Users”

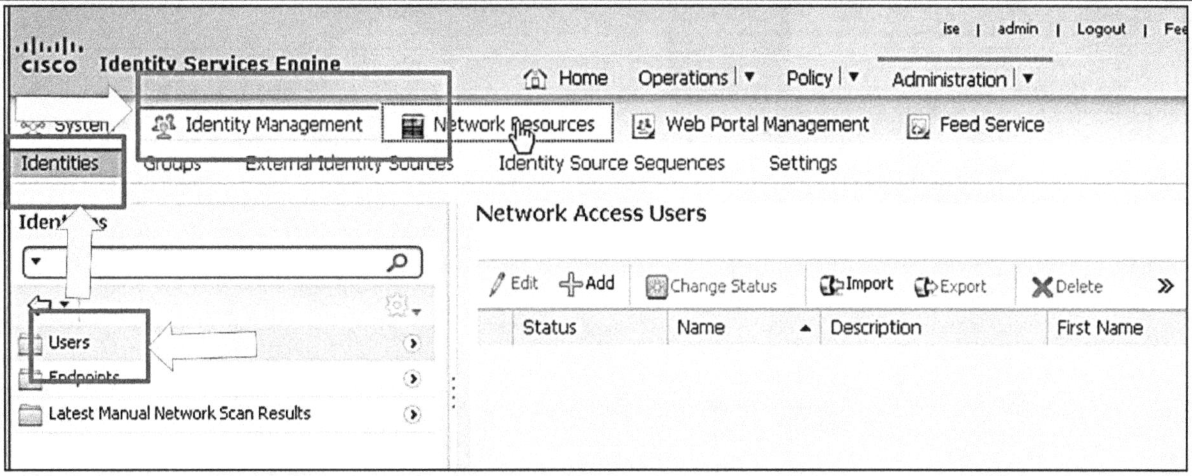

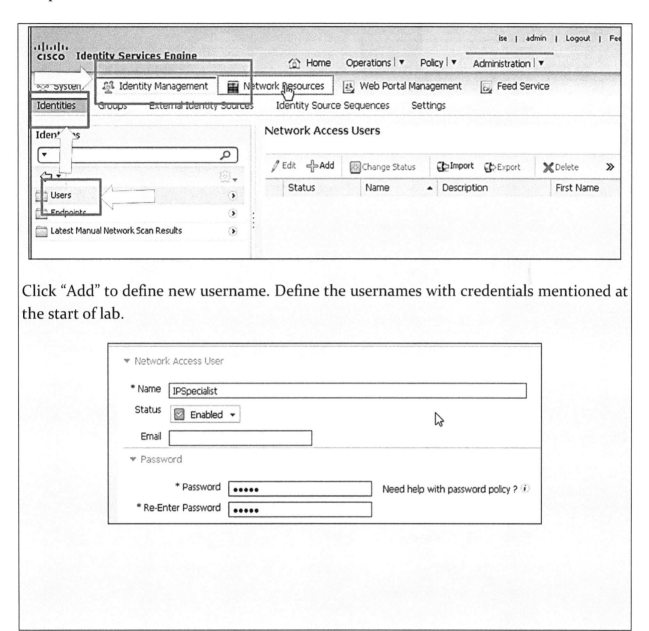

Click "Add" to define new username. Define the usernames with credentials mentioned at the start of lab.

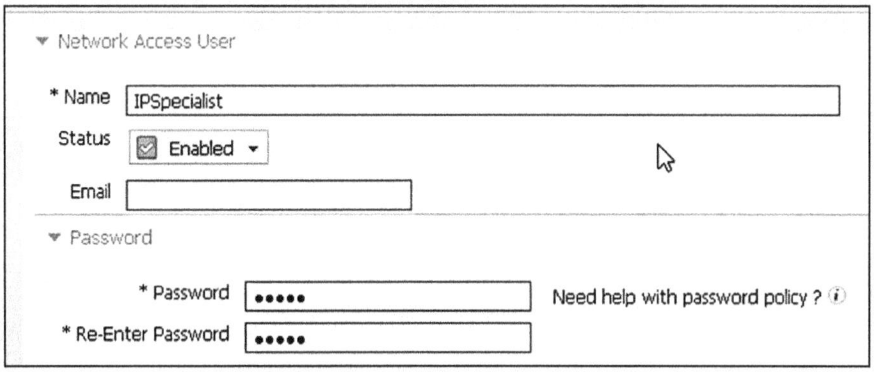

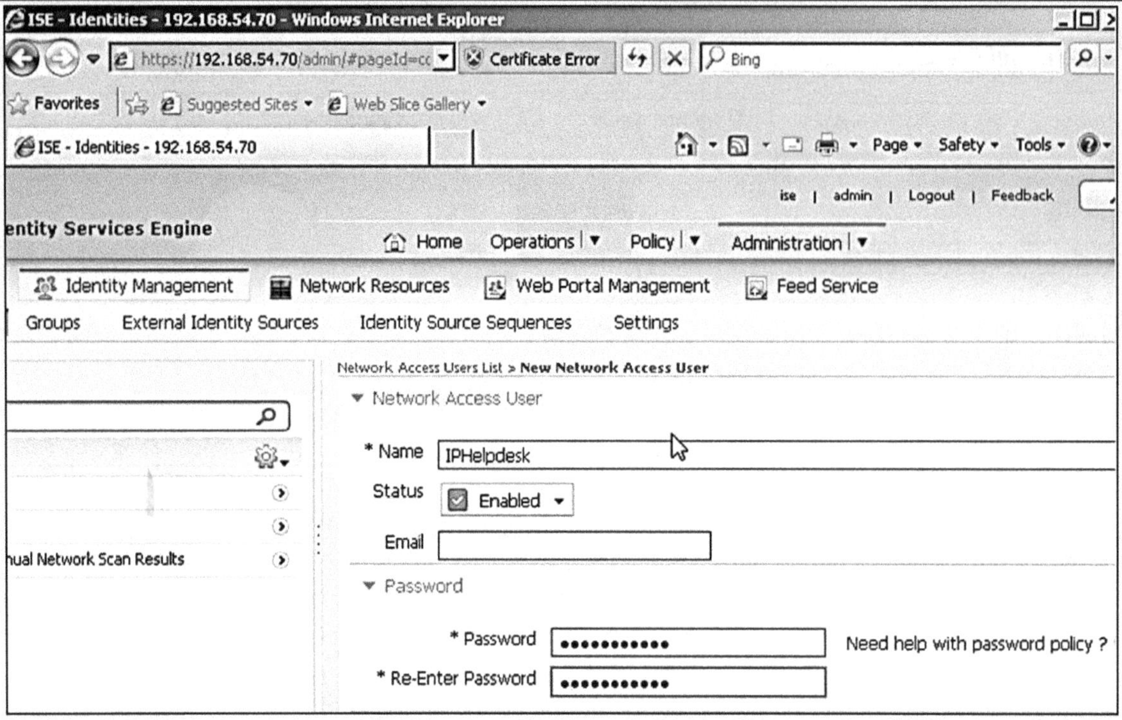

Scroll down a bit and press “Submit” button to save the username entry. Here is the display of users created, shown below:

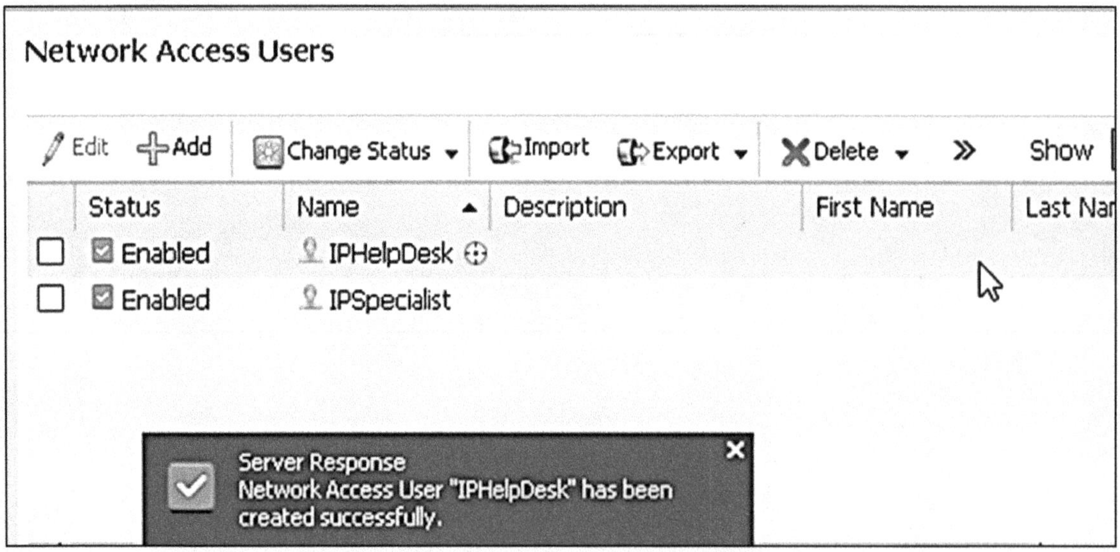

The only remaining task of this lab is to define the authorization policies for the users with different privilege levels. Username “IPSpecialist” should be given privilege level 15 access while ITHelpdesk should be given privilege level 4 according to the objective of lab:

To create two authorization policies for privilege level 15 and privilege level 4.

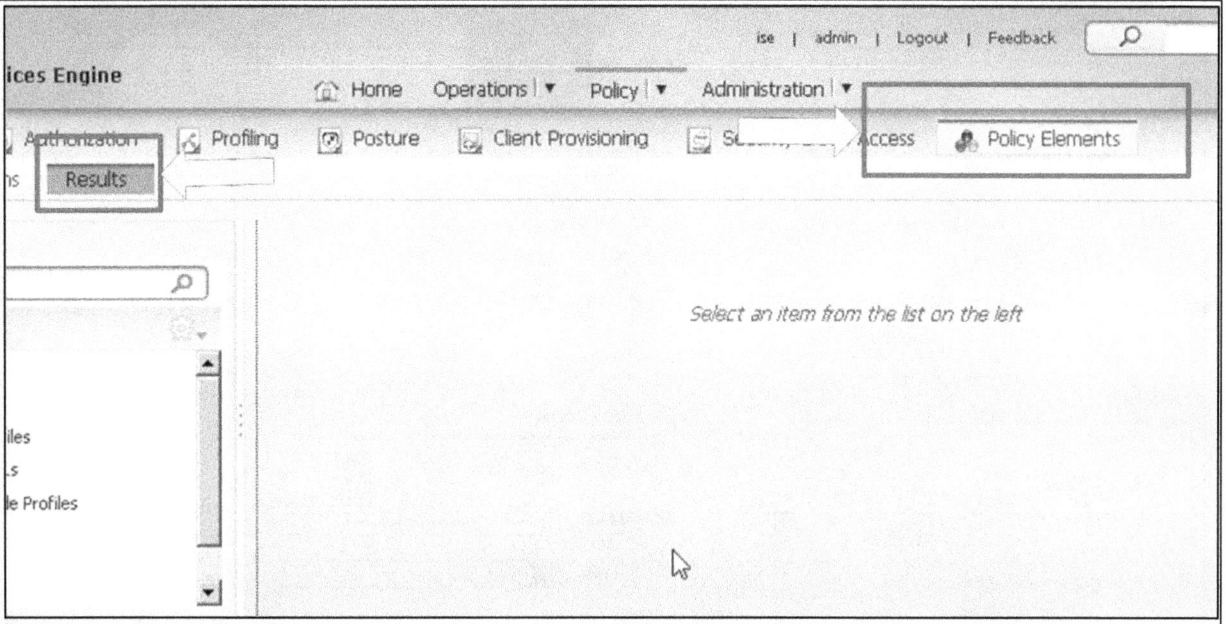

Now, click “Policy” -> “Results” -> “Authorization” -> “Authorization Profiles”

To create new policies, click “Add” to create “Shell_priv_15” policy as shown below:

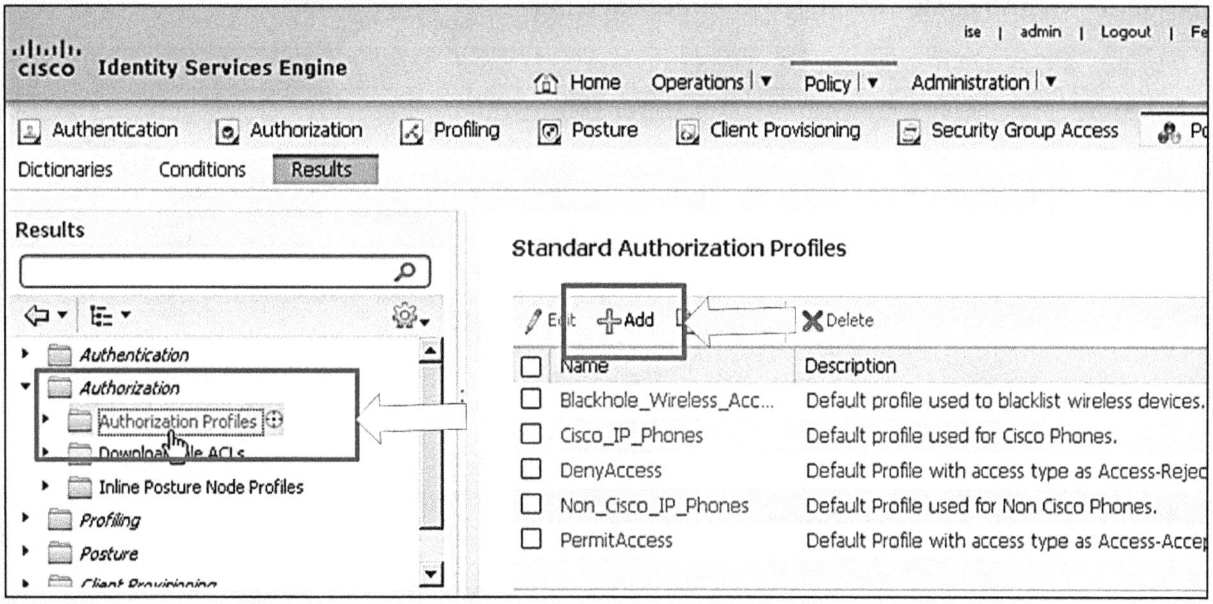

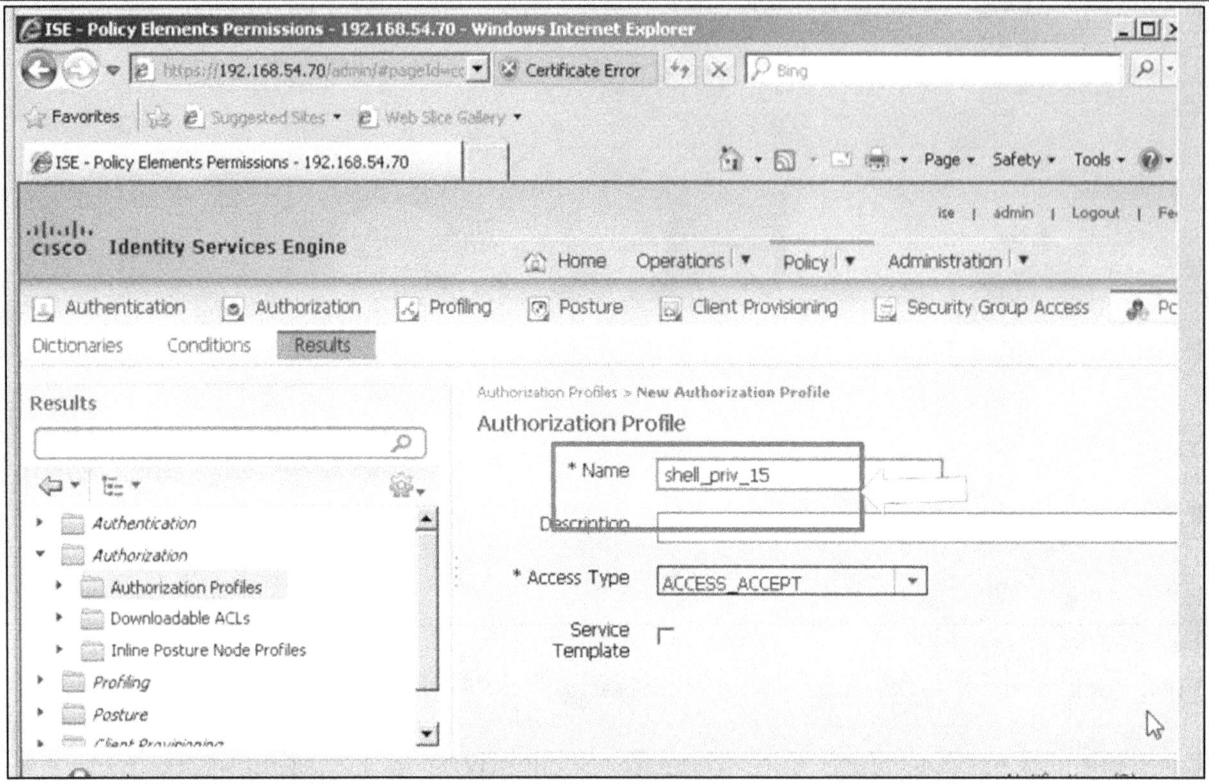

Scroll down and click "Advance Attributes Settings".

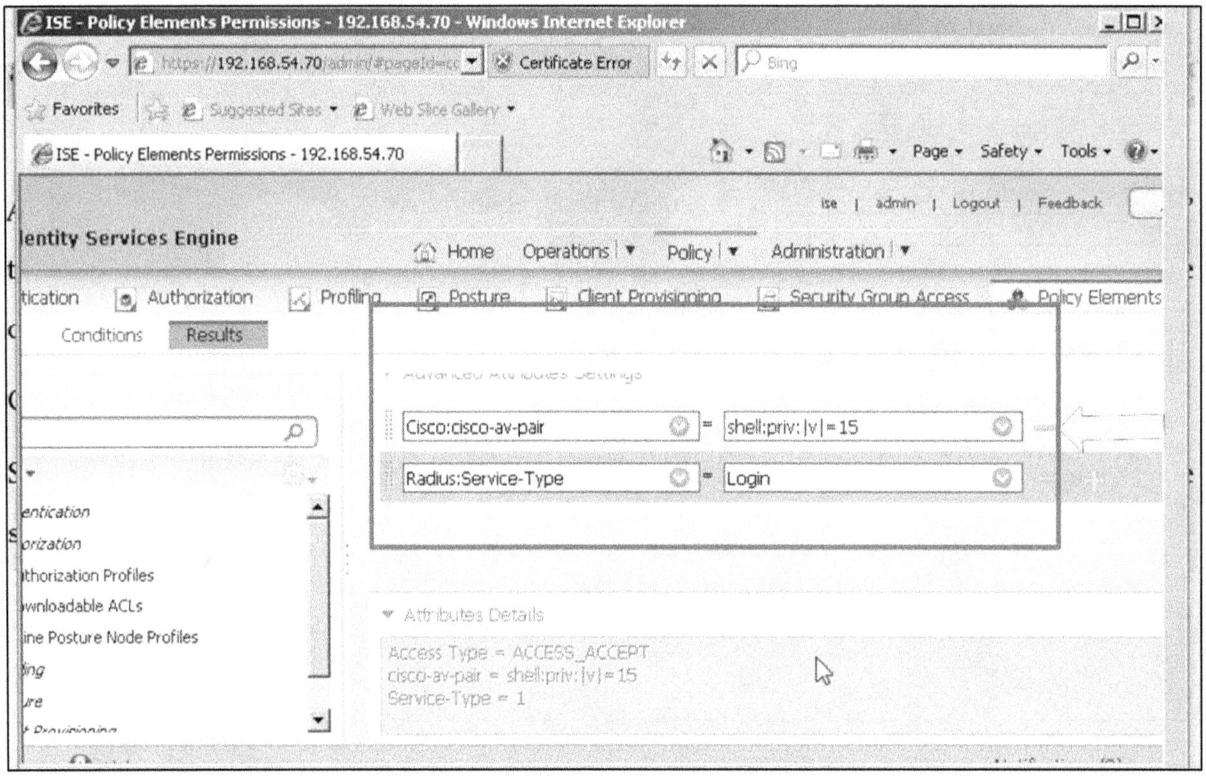

As shown in the figures above, under the tab of "Advanced Attributes Settings", two attributes are defined. First one defines the privilege level while the second one defines the Radius service type.

Click "Submit" to save the attribute profile.

Similar steps will be followed for the username "ITHelpdesk". The only change will be in the shell privilege level attribute "shell:priv:lvl=4".

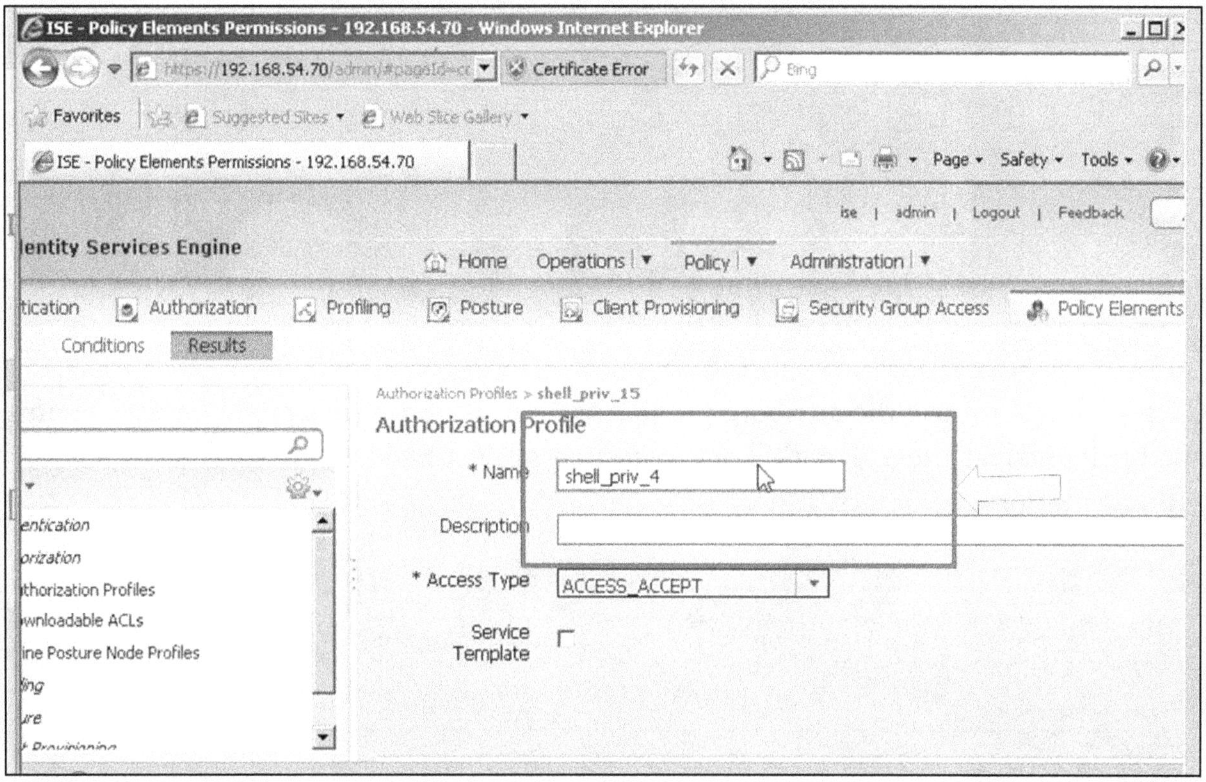

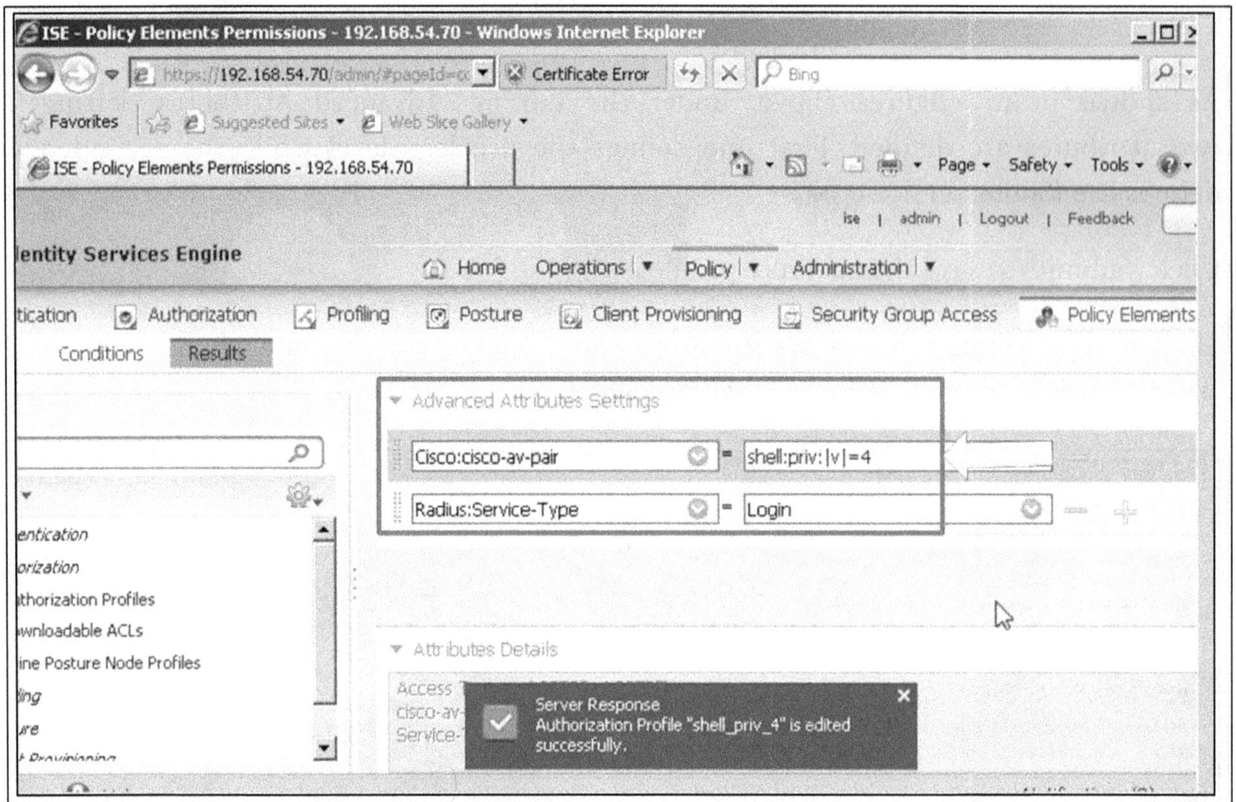

Click "Submit" to save the attribute profile. Authorization policies apply on user groups, not on individual users. For this purpose, two groups need to be created by clicking "Administration" -> "Groups".

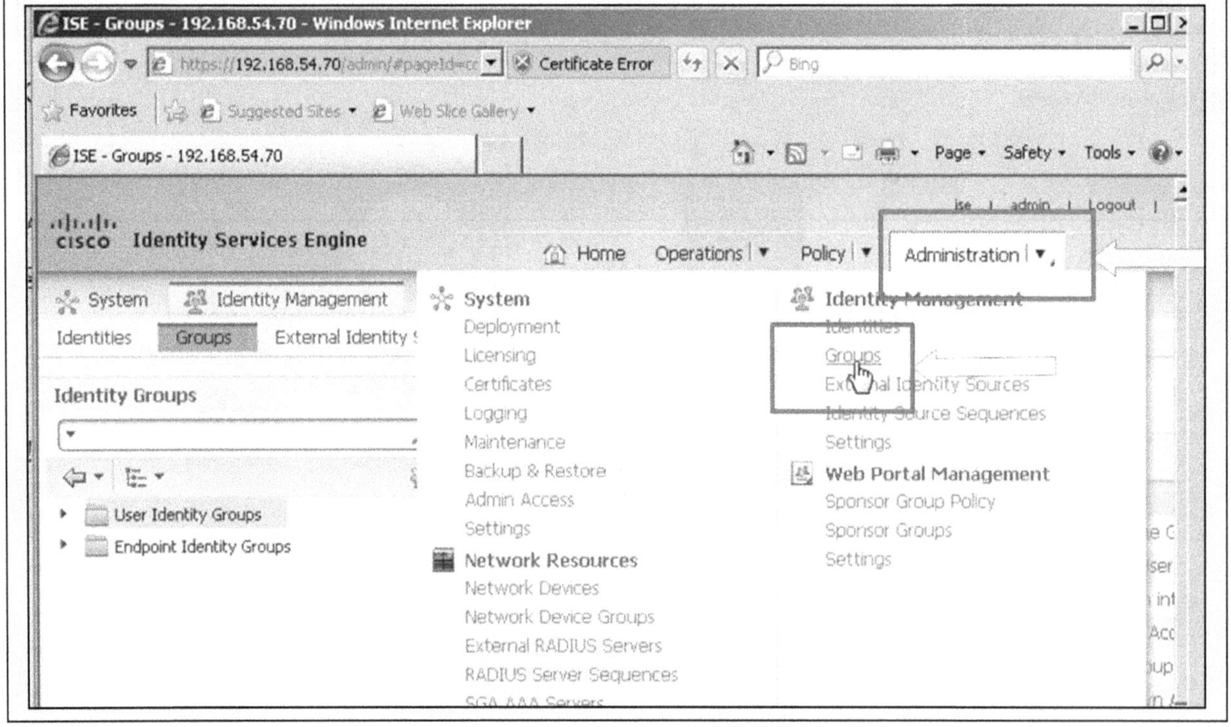

Click "Add" to define new group and add respective users in it.

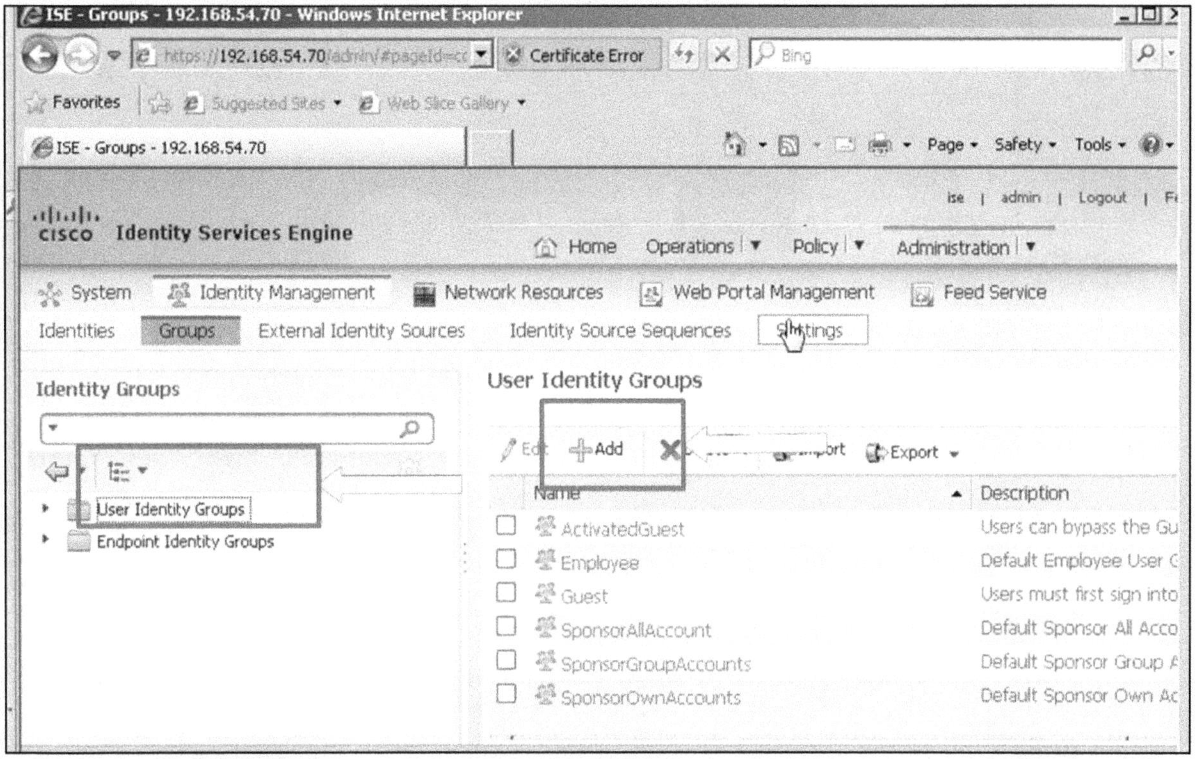

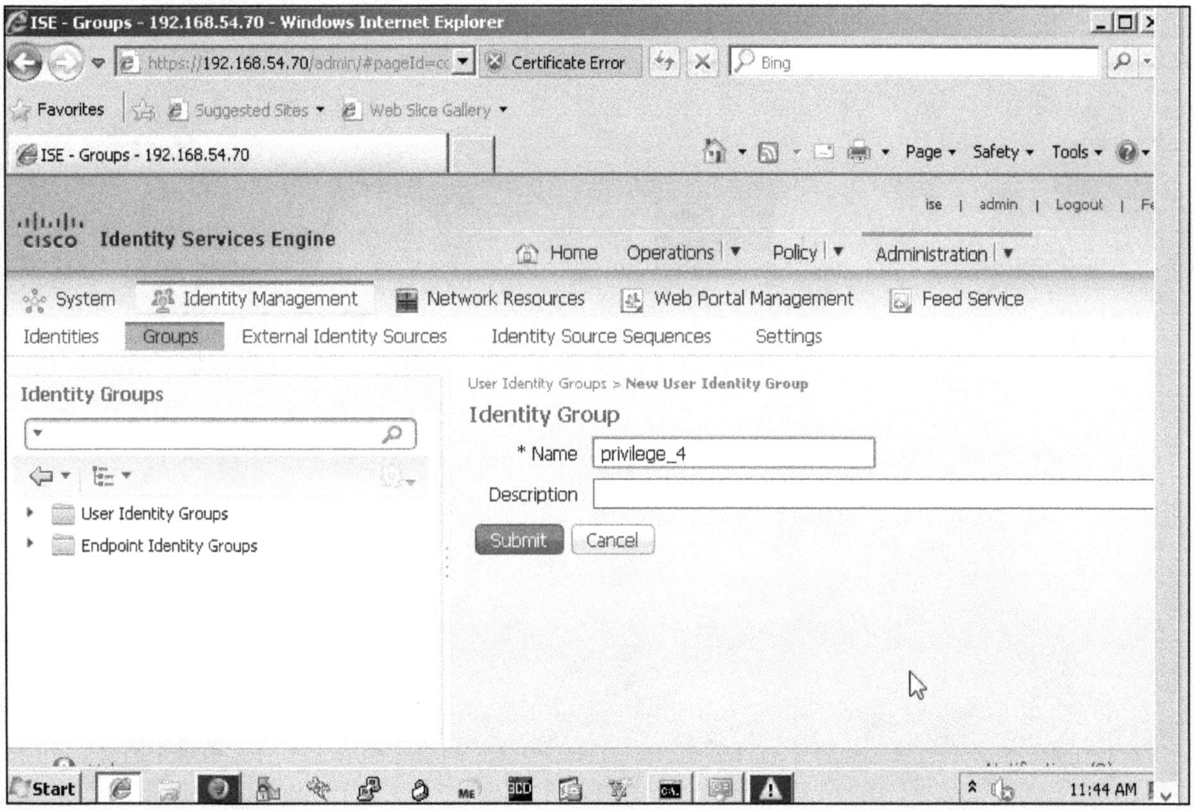

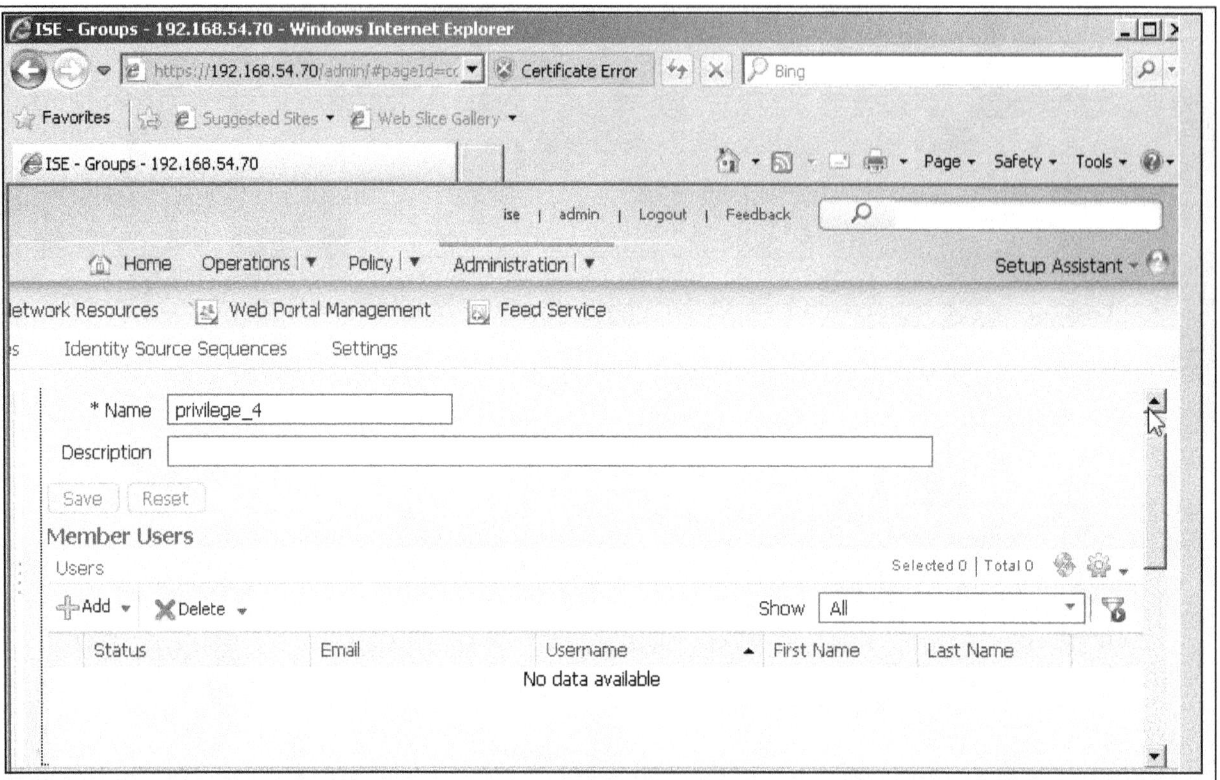
ISE - Groups - 192.168.54.70 - Windows Internet Explorer
Certificate Error
Favorites
Suggested Sites
Web Slice Gallery
ISE - Groups - 192.168.54.70
Page
Safety
Tools
ise | admin | Logout | Feedback
Home
Operations
Policy
Administration
Setup Assistant
Network Resources
Web Portal Management
Feed Service
Identity Source Sequences
Settings
* Name
privilege_4
Description
Save
Reset
Member Users
Users
Selected 0 | Total 0
Add
Delete
Show
All
Status
Email
Username
First Name
Last Name
No data available

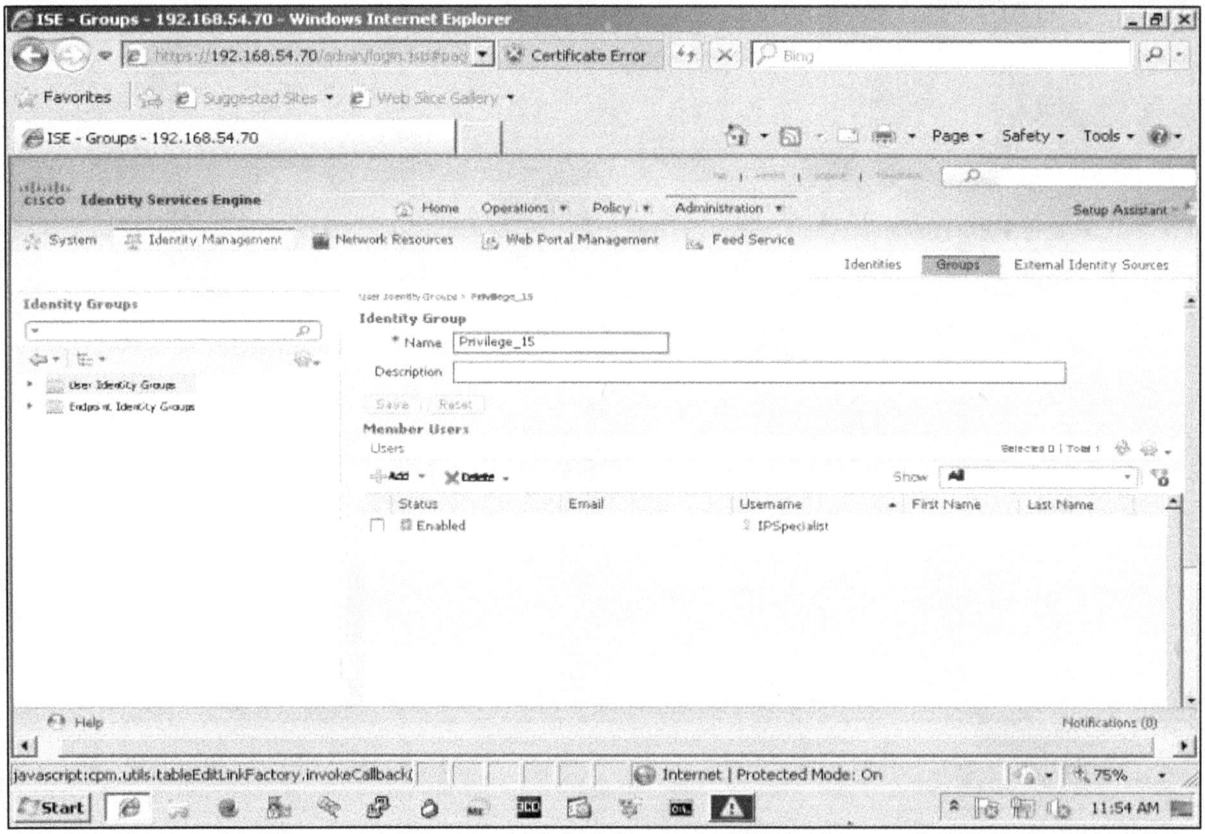
ISE - Groups - 192.168.54.70 - Windows Internet Explorer
Certificate Error
Favorites
ISE - Groups - 192.168.54.70
Page
Safety
Tools
Identity Services Engine
Home
Operations
Policy
Administration
Setup Assistant
System
Identity Management
Network Resources
Web Portal Management
Feed Service
Identities
Groups
External Identity Sources
Identity Groups
Identity Group
* Name
Privilege_15
Description
Member Users
Users
Status
Email
Username
First Name
Last Name
Enabled
IPSpecialist
Help
javascript:cpm.utils.tableEditLinkFactory.invokeCallback(
Internet | Protected Mode: On
75%
Start
11:54 AM

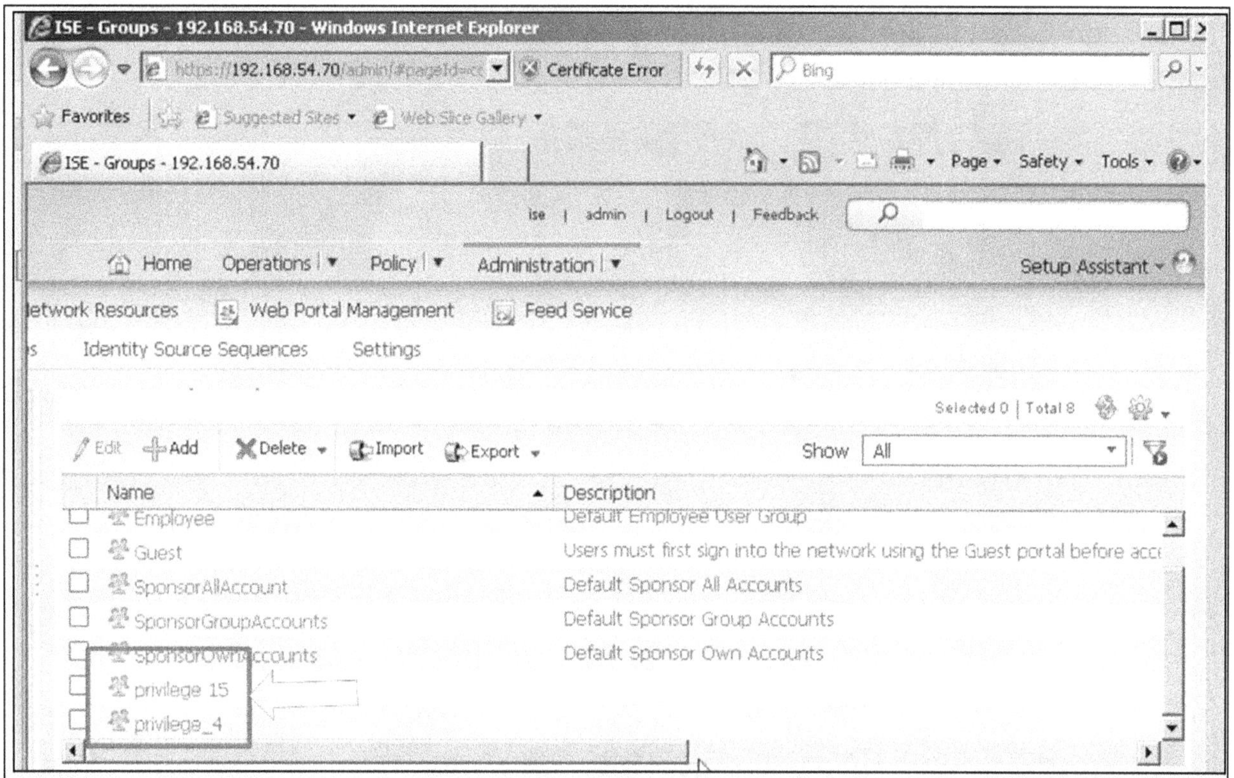

In order to tie Authorization Profiles and User groups together, click “Policy” and then “Authorization” tab.

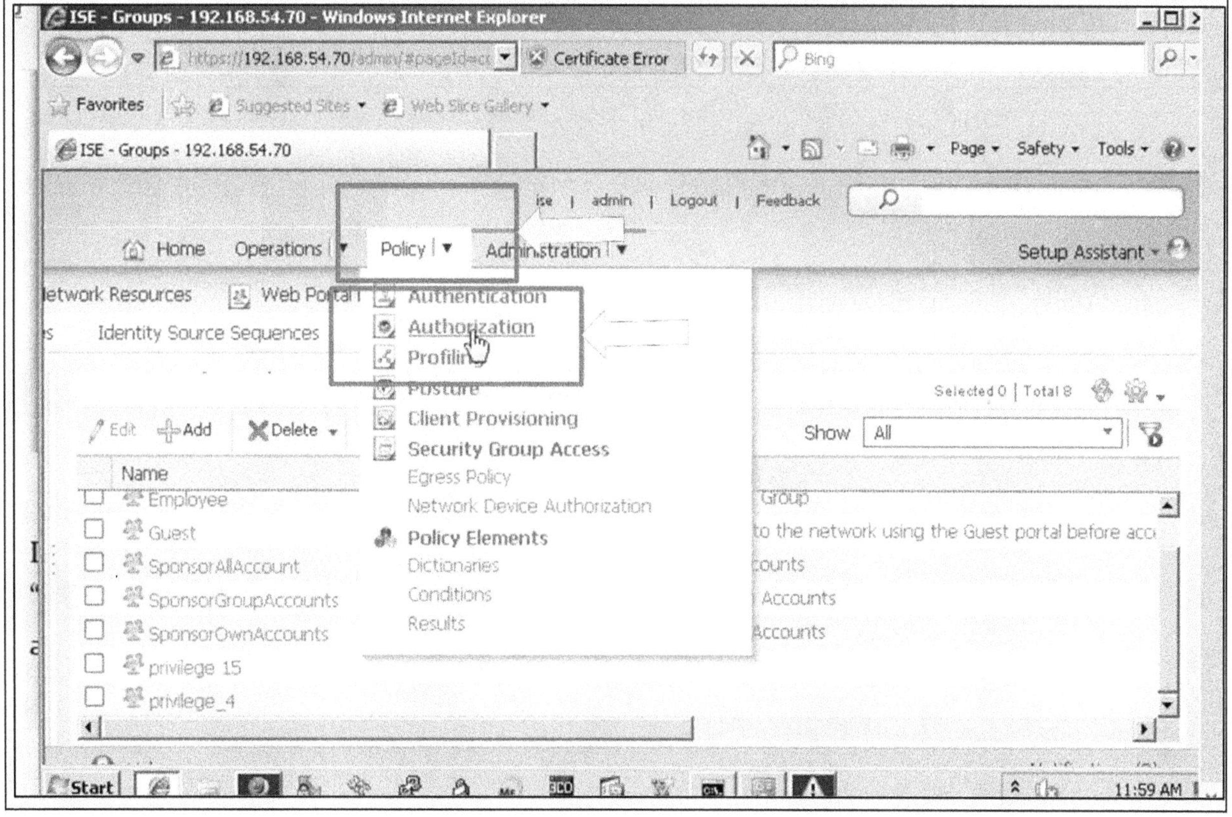

By default, these four authorization rules or policies are defined with default actions that permit access as shown below:

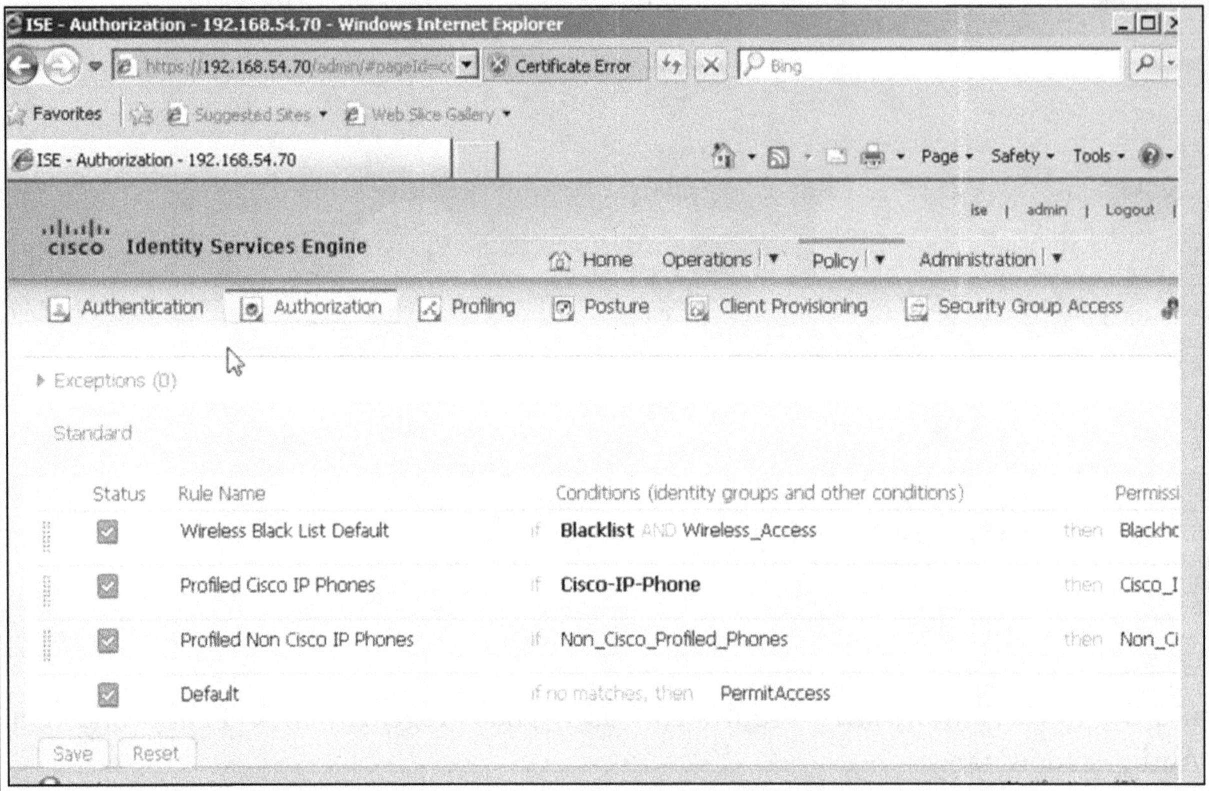

Scroll right and click "Edit" -> "Insert New Rue Above" -> to add two new rules to tie the authorization profiles to two different user privilege groups as shown below:

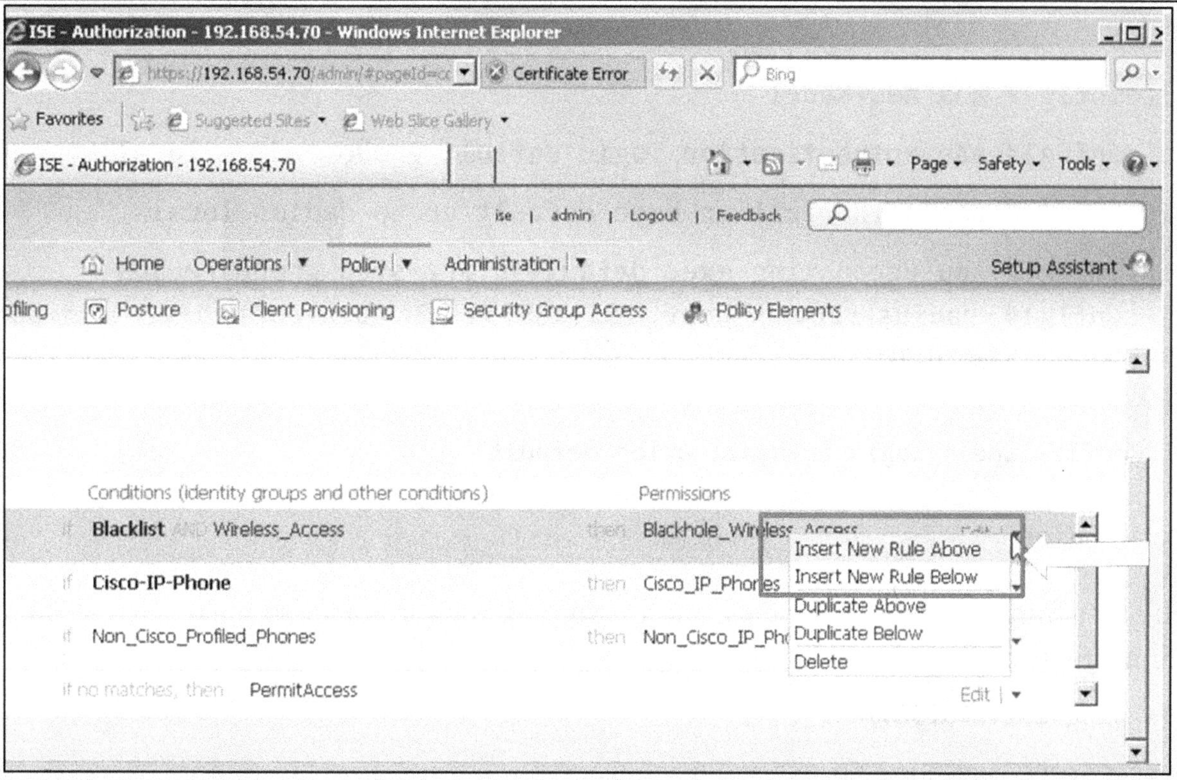
ISE - Authorization - 192.168.54.70 - Windows Internet Explorer
Certificate Error
Favorites
Suggested Sites
Web Slice Gallery
ISE - Authorization - 192.168.54.70
Page
Safety
Tools
ise | admin | Logout | Feedback
Home
Operations
Policy
Administration
Setup Assistant
Posture
Client Provisioning
Security Group Access
Policy Elements
Conditions (identity groups and other conditions)
Permissions
Blacklist AND Wireless_Access
then Blackhole_Wireless_Access
Insert New Rule Above
Insert New Rule Below
Duplicate Above
Duplicate Below
Delete
Cisco-IP-Phone
then Cisco_IP_Phones
Non_Cisco_Profiled_Phones
then Non_Cisco_IP_Ph
if no matches, then PermitAccess
Edit

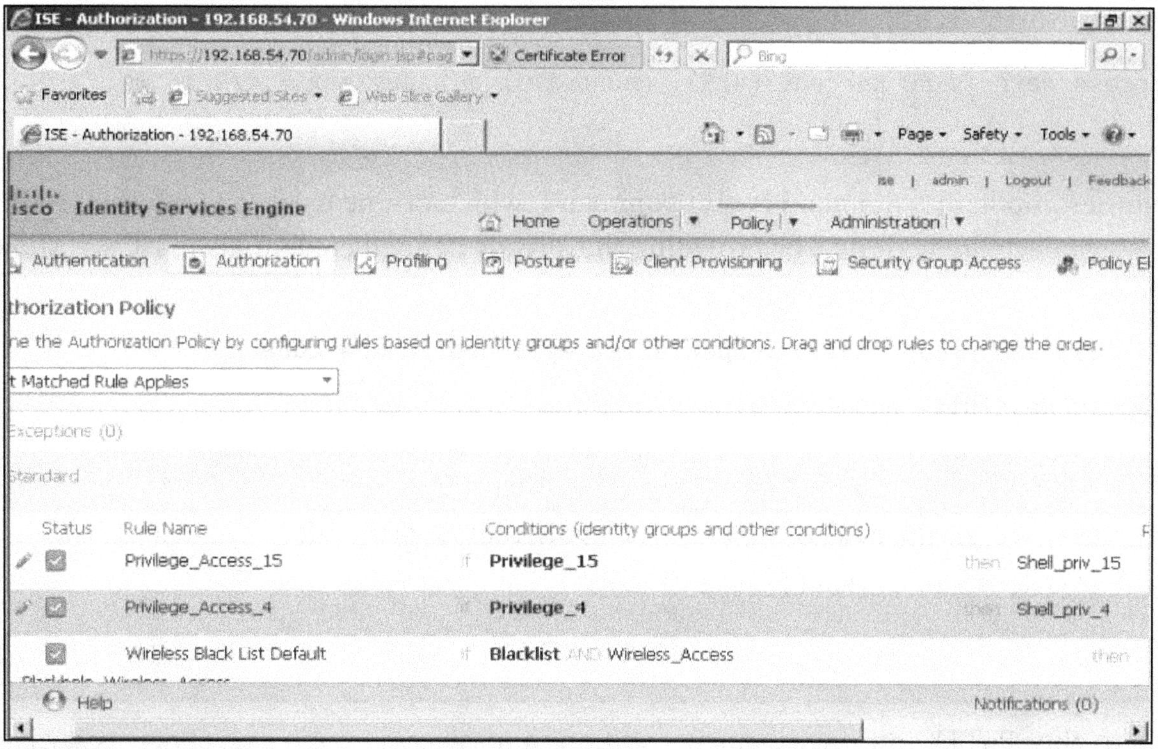
ISE - Authorization - 192.168.54.70 - Windows Internet Explorer
Certificate Error
Favorites
Suggested Sites
Web Slice Gallery
ISE - Authorization - 192.168.54.70
Page
Safety
Tools
ise | admin | Logout | Feedback
Identity Services Engine
Home
Operations
Policy
Administration
Authentication
Authorization
Profiling
Posture
Client Provisioning
Security Group Access
Matched Rule Applies
Exceptions (0)
Standard
Status
Rule Name
Conditions (identity groups and other conditions)
Privilege_Access_15
Privilege_15
then Shell_priv_15
Privilege_Access_4
Privilege_4
Shell_priv_4
Wireless Black List Default
Blacklist AND Wireless_Access
then
Help
Notifications (0)

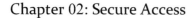

R1

```
R1(config)# aaa new-model
R1(config)# aaa authentication login default group radius local
R1(config)# aaa authorization exec default group radius local
R1(config)# aaa accounting exec default start-stop group radius
R1(config)# radius-server host 192.168.54.70 auth-port 1812 acct-port 1813 key P@$$word:10
R1(config)# line vty 0 903
R1(config-line)# login authentication default
```

Verification

The first thing to perform in verification is to ping the ISE server to make sure of the L3 connectivity as show below:

```
R1# ping 192.168.50.74
Type escape sequence to abort.
Sending 5, 100-byte ICMP Echos to 192.168.50.74, timeout is 2 seconds:
!!!!!
Success rate is 80 percent (4/5), round-trip min/avg/max = 4/9/16 ms
```

Another important command is **test** command, which can be used to verify the protocol level connectivity with ACS by providing the already defined credentials in ACS as shown below

```
R1# test aaa group radius IPSpecialist P@$$word:10 new-code
User successfully authenticated.


R1# test aaa group radius ITHelpdesk P@$$word:20 new-code
User successfully authenticated.
```

Open the PuTTY on management station and access 10.0.0.254. Enter username "ITHelpdesk" and password "P@$$word:20"

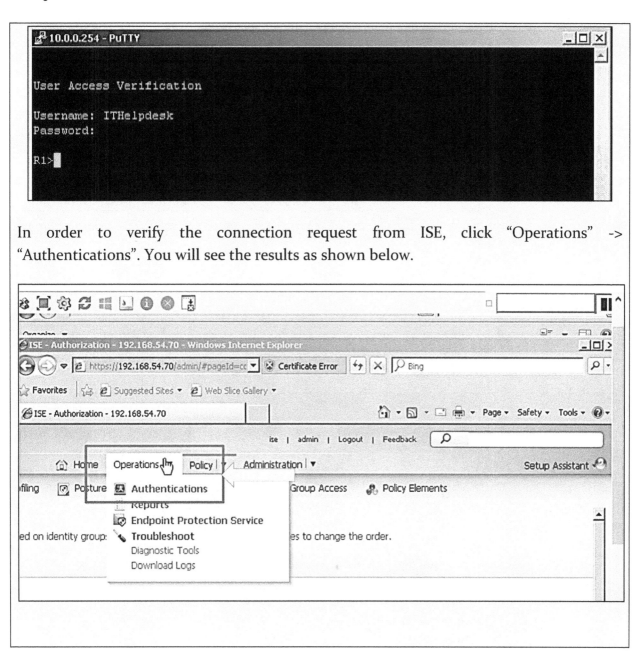

In order to verify the connection request from ISE, click "Operations" -> "Authentications". You will see the results as shown below.

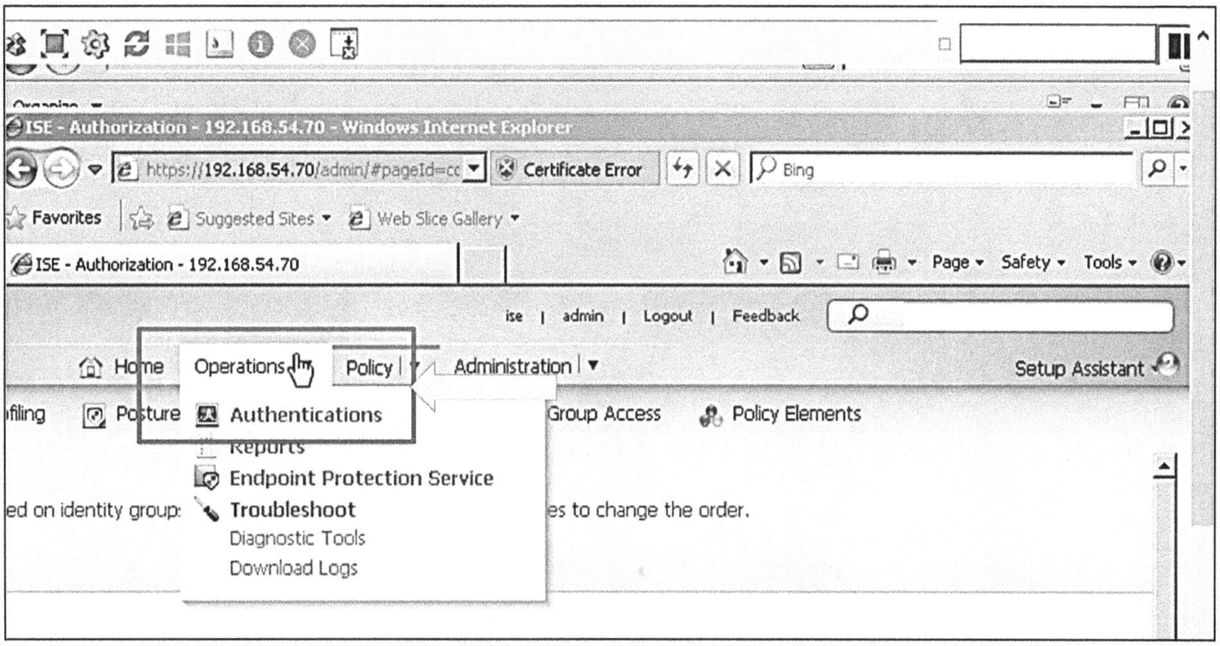

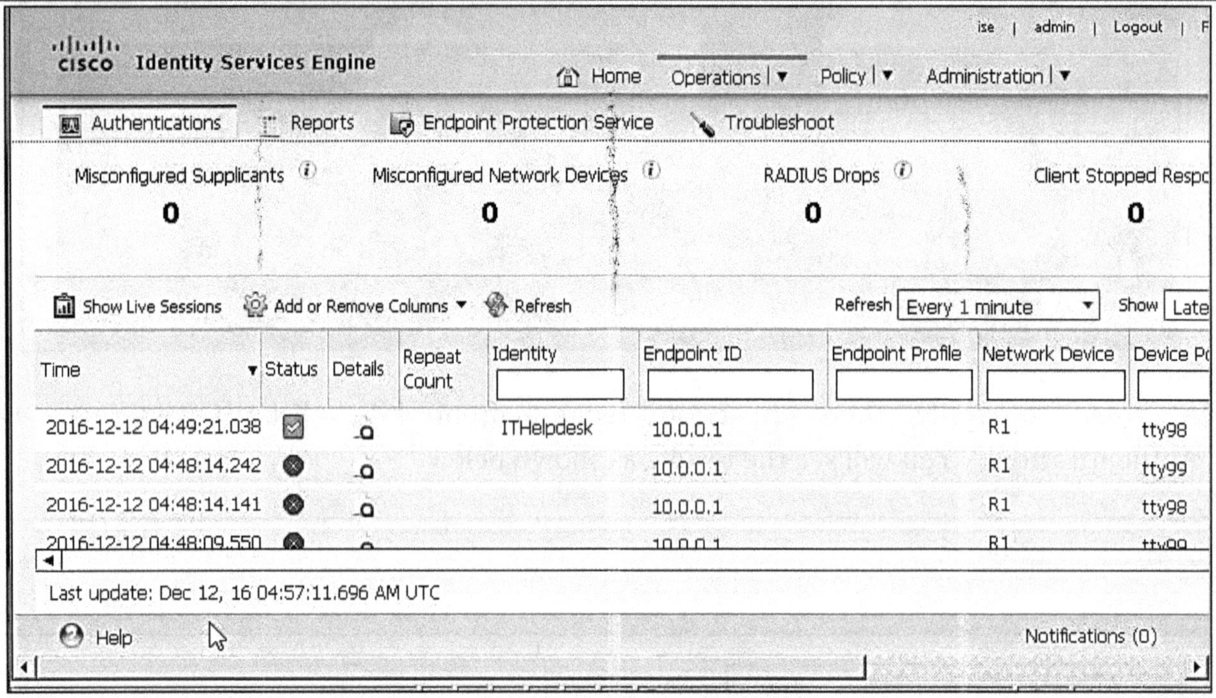

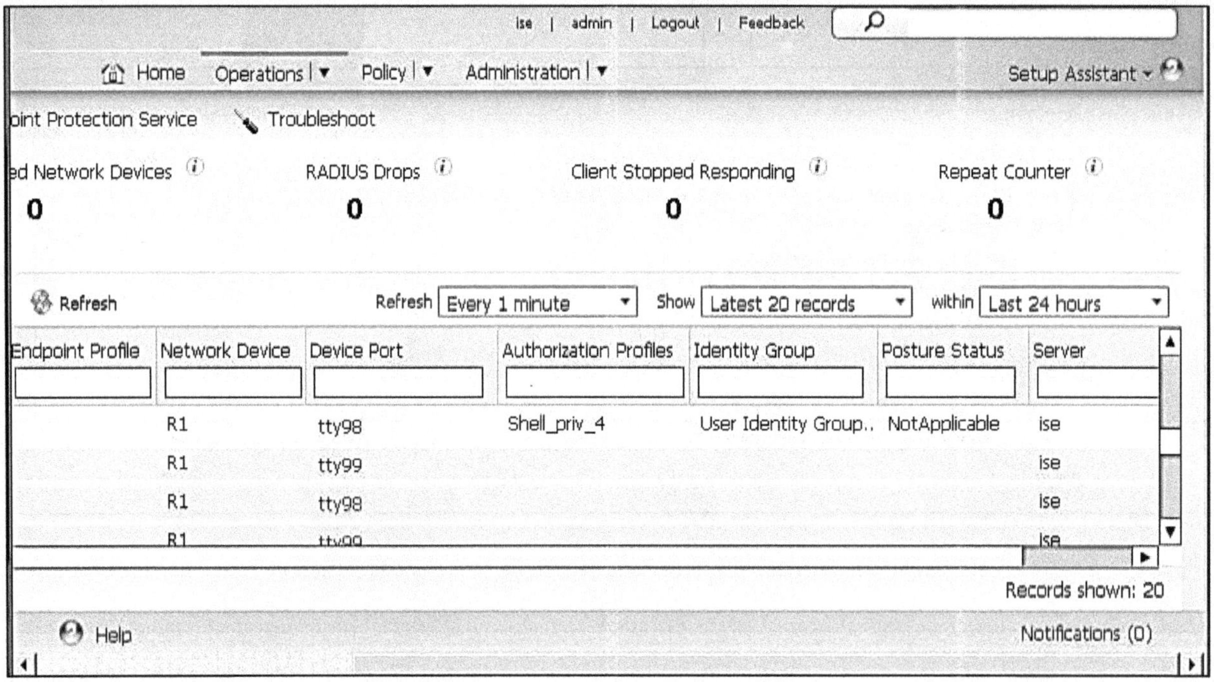

As discussed in chapter 2.0- Secure Access, ACS 5.xx is preferred over ISE 1.xx for device administration due to its support for TACACS+, which has good authorization features. The newer versions of ISE 2.xx has support for TACACS+, which can be used for such purposes.

Techniques for implementing AAA

Cisco provides a number of ways to implement AAA. Over the years, many names have been used for appliances, which implement centralized list of usernames and passwords for access. Two examples are ACS server and Radius Server. Today, two kinds of such proprietary servers exist, namely ACS server and ISE. Few open source implementations like *Free Radius* implemented in Linux is also very popular in an ISP environment.

The following are different options of centralized servers:

1. Cisco Secure ACS solution Engine
2. Identity Service Unit (ISE)

Cisco Secure ACS Solution Engine

In the past years, Cisco sold this solution as hardware appliance with Cisco Access Solution (CAS) server pre-installed. However, it can also be installed on virtualized environment like VMWare in production environment. Any network device that wants to implement AAA, has to become a client of this server, which contains usernames passwords and associated level of authorization with each username. Two protocols are commonly used in communication between client and ACS server namely *TACACS+* and *RADIUS*. Generally, TACACS+ is used for communication between client device and server for giving access to network administrator. Similarly, RADIUS is normally preferred as protocol between device and ACS server for allowing access to end-users of network. However, it is not a hard and fast rule; we can use one of the two at the same time.

It may be time-consuming to enter every single username/password and associated level of authorization in ACS, as majority of organizations who can afford ACS have a very large number of employees. ACS has a nice feature of integration with already running databases containing every single username and passwords. An example of this would be integrating AAA with Microsoft Active Directory.

ACS comes in different forms. It can be installed in older versions of ACS already running Windows based Server. Another option is to purchase hardware appliance from Cisco with pre-installed ACS. Third and the most convenient option is to install ACS in VMWare on ESXi server. The basic functionality and purpose of ACS remains the same regardless of which method of deployment is used.

ACS in Nutshell: In order to explain the full process of ACS giving access to a user over the network, consider the scenario below.

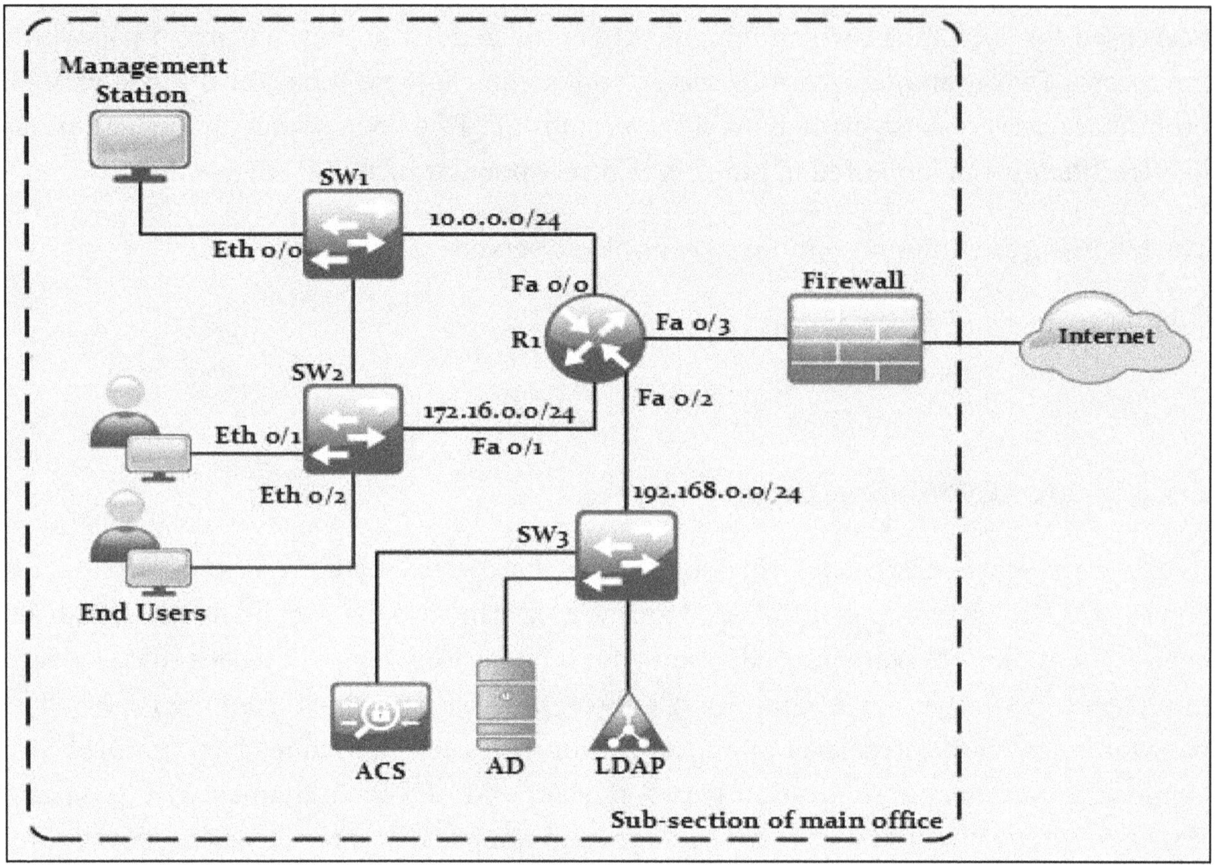

Figure 2-10: ACS in Working Environment

Consider an end user enters an office and tries to login the workstation, or a network administrator who tries to login to a switch or a router or even a firewall. Assume router is configured with using ACS as primary tool for AAA and it is also integrated with Microsoft Active Directory (AD) and LDAP servers. Therefore, the request will first come to a router, which in turn will prompt a username and password request in front of the user. On submission, router will send the requested query to the ACS server, which in turn will contact the LDAP or AD for authenticity of provided username and password. Upon green signal from LDAP or AD, ACS will verify the authorization level of that user and give the green signal to originating network device to allow the specific user for authorized access.

Identity Service Unit ISE

ISE is used for secure access management like ACS. It is a single policy control point for entire enterprise including wired and wireless technologies. Before giving access to endpoints or even networking devices itself, ISE checks their identity, location, time, type of device and even health of endpoints to make sure that they comply with company's policy like antivirus, latest service pack and OS updates etc. Most of the time, people prefer ACS over ISE, although ISE can implement AAA but it is not a complete replacement of ACS.

Integrating AAA with AD

Identity Stores:

An Identity Store is a store or database that is used to authenticate users or endpoints. This Identity Store may reside in AAA Server (Internal Identity Store) or additional external database (External Identity Store) can also connect. These Identity Stores can also be used for attributes required for authorizing policies.

- **Internal Identity Store**

Internal Identity Store or local database that can be used for internal username and password accounts like Cisco ISE that has an internal user database. User accounts stored in the internal user database are referred to as internal users in this Internal Identity store. The internal user database can be used as an internal identity store for local authentication and authorization policies.

- **External Identity Store**

External Identity Stores are the external databases, which are used for authentication for internal and external users. Some external identity stores are LDAP, Active Directory, RSA SecureID Token Server and RADIUS Identity Server. Attributes, Configuration parameters can be defined over External Identity Store user records.

Active Directory (AD)

In a network, keeping track of everything is a very difficult, and time consuming task. If the network is wide enough, it becomes impossible to manage and find resources on a network. Microsoft Windows 2000 server launches Active Directory (AD) to replace Domain functionality. Active Directory is like a phonebook. As phonebooks store information like Name, Contact No, Business, similarly, Active Directory stores the information about organization, sites, system, user, share and much more. It is much more flexible as well. Active Directory is a more efficient way to perform these tasks. Another advantage of Active Directory is that it can be replicated between multiple domain controllers.

Components of Active Directory:

- **Name space or Console tree:**

Active Directory as defined, stores information about multiple users and allows the clients to find objects within namespace or console tree. Namespace or console tree is like DNS, resolving hostname to IP address, similarly, namespace resolve Network object to object themselves.

- **Object:**

Object may be a User, Resource, or System that can be tracked within Active Directory. These Objects can share common attributes.

- **Attributes:**

In an Active Directory, Attributes describe objects like username, full name, description, hostname, IP address and location, etc. It may depend upon the type of the object.

- **Schema:**

The Schema is the set of attributes for any particular object type. It differentiates object classes from each other.

- **Name:**

Each object has a name. These are LDAP distinguished names. LDAP distinguished names allow any object within a directory to be identified uniquely regardless of its type.

- **Site:**

Sites correspond to logical IP subnets, and as such, they can be used by applications to locate the closest server on a network. Using site information from Active Directory can profoundly reduce the traffic on Wide Area Networks.

Lightweight Directory Access Protocol (LDAP)

The Lightweight Directory Access Protocol LDAP is an open standard, application protocol. LDAP is for accessing and maintaining distributed directory information services. A directory service plays an important role by allowing the sharing of information like user, system, network, service, etc. throughout the network. LDAP provides a central place to store usernames and passwords. Applications and Services connect to the LDAP server to validate users.

Authentication and Authorization

RADIUS combines authentication and authorization processes. The access-accept packets sent by the RADIUS server to the client contain authorization information. This makes it difficult to decouple authentication and authorization.

TACACS+ uses the AAA architecture, which separates AAA. This allows separate authentication solutions that can still use TACACS+ for authorization and accounting. For example, with TACACS+, it is possible to use Kerberos authentication and TACACS+ authorization and accounting. After a NAS authenticates on a Kerberos server, it requests authorization information from a TACACS+ server without having to re-authenticate. The NAS informs the TACACS+ server that it has successfully authenticated on a Kerberos server, and the server then provides authorization information.

During a session, if additional authorization checking is needed, the access server checks with a TACACS+ server to determine if the user is granted permission to use a particular command. This provides greater control over the commands that can be executed on the access server while decoupling from the authentication mechanism.

Multiprotocol Support

RADIUS does not support these protocols:

- AppleTalk Remote Access (ARA) protocol
- NetBIOS Frame Protocol Control protocol
- Novell Asynchronous Services Interface (NASI)
- X.25 PAD connection

TACACS+ offers multiprotocol support.

Implement Accounting:

In an AAA model, accounting features are also very much important in security. Accounting command enables tracking the commands, services and resources used by user while accessing the network. Accounting is the measure of resources consumed by a user during access. In accounting, it includes amount of time, amount of data the user has send or received during a session. This accounting is carried in the form of logs of session statistics and usage information. This accounting data is used for authorization control, analysis of resources utilization, billing and planning as well. This accounting is also very much helpful to troubleshoot if network devices are not functioning properly. An example of this is when someone tries to access the network device and is issued a wrong command, which stops the device forwarding the packets. Accounting logs will verify the user who is responsible to issue that command. AAA Accounting is disabled by default.

AAA Accounting Types

- **Network**

To enable Accounting for all network-related service requests (including SLIP, PPP, PPP NCPs, and ARAP protocols) use the network keyword.

- **Exec**

To create a method list that provides accounting records about user EXEC terminal sessions on the network access server, including username, date, start and stop times use the exec keyword.

- **Commands**

To create a method list that provides accounting information about specific, individual EXEC commands associated with a specific privilege level use the commands keyword.

- **Connection**

To create a method list that provides accounting information about all outbound connections made from the network access server use the connection keyword.

- **Resource**

To create a method, provide accounting records for calls that have passed user authentication or calls that have failed to be authenticated.

Accounting Commands

Generating records when client is authenticated and after client disconnection.

```
Router(config)# aaa accounting network default start-stop group radius local
```

Generates records when client is disconnected.

```
Router(config)# aaa accounting network default stop group radius local
```

Generates records for authentication and negotiation failure.

```
Router(config)# aaa accounting send stop-record authentication failure
```

It enables full resources accounting.

```
Router(config)# aaa accounting resource start-stop
```

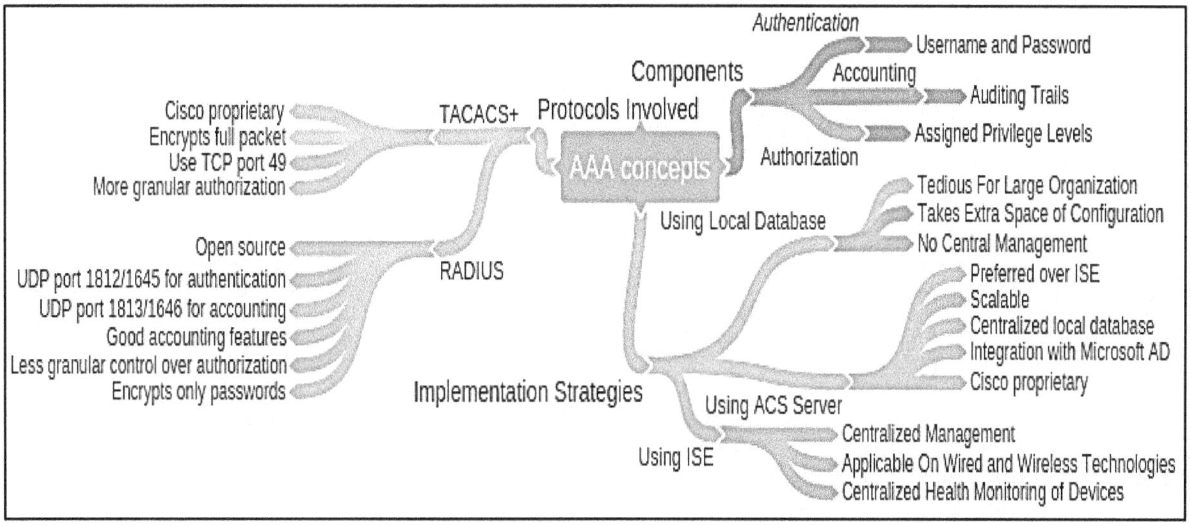

Figure 2-11: AAA Concepts Mind Map

802.1x Authentication

The IEEE 802.1X authentication is an IEEE specification that is used to provide Port-based Network Access Control (PNAC) to the users. This specification is used to restrict unauthorized hosts from connecting to a LAN or WLAN. Each and every host that are intended to connect to the LAN must be authenticated to gain network access.

It is part of the IEEE 802.1 group of networking protocols. IEEE 802.1X commonly uses the Extensible Authentication Protocol over the LAN (EAPOL) protocol to make sure that the initial communication between a wired end user and a switch is secure. In 802.1Xa, initially a host may only use DHCP, ARP and EAPOL until it is authenticated. Once the user is done with authentication, normal network traffic from the host will be permitted to the port.

Wireless LANs offers reachability and economy. End user scalability is achieved without adding new resources to the network. Access point is required to be configured properly and networking is good to go. However, security aspect of WLAN can result in more problems if not configured properly. Kali Linux and Back track have many tools, which can be used to spoof not only MAC address configure on access port but also the passwords of access points.

Implementing IEEE 802.1x provides identity based access control at access layer of network. Almost in every organization, consultants, guests require access to network resources over the same network as regular employees. There is also a possibility that guests may bring along unmanaged devices, which may result in access of unauthorized digital assets of organization. Similarly, as the size of organization increases, the rate of such events increases exponentially.

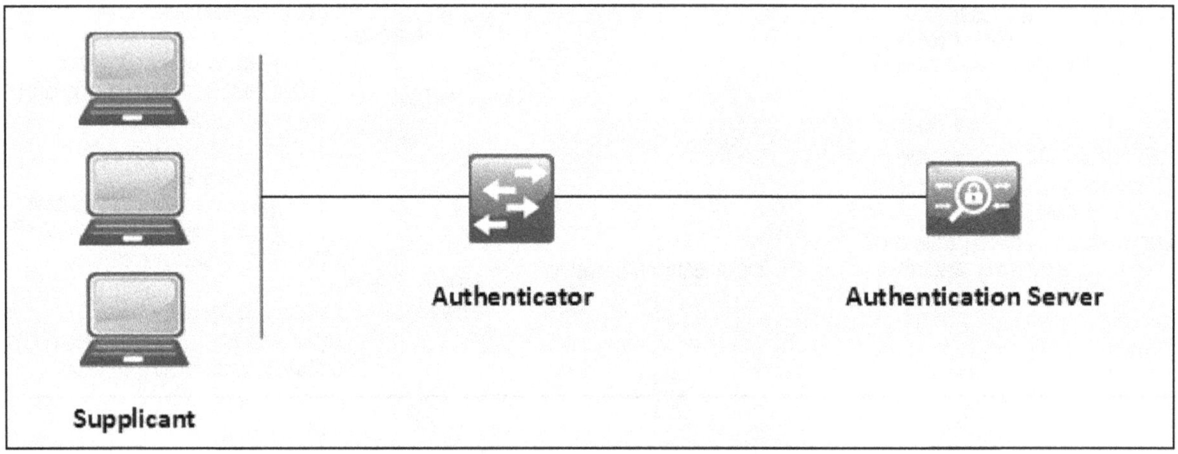

Figure 2-12: 802.1x Authentication

IEEE 802.1x standard states such problems by implementing a three component-based solution namely:

- **Supplicant:** is the end point device that wishes to connect to LAN or WLAN based network.
- **Authenticator:** is a network device (Cisco catalyst switch or Cisco Router or wireless access point). It facilitates the whole process by relying the credentials from end-point to the server and then taking the corresponding action by either shutting down the port or opening it.
- **Authentication Server:** plays a key role in implementing IEEE 802.1x based port security solution. It is typically a server running software, which supports both RADIUS and EAP protocols. Common Implementation of these protocols are NAP

(Network Access Protection) role in Microsoft Server 2008 and 2012, Cisco ACS server also support it and open source implementations like FreeRadius in Linux.

Although implementing 802.1x is a great step towards enhancing the security posture of an organization, it also has some downsides. Following table compares its advantages and disadvantages.

Advantages	Disadvantages
Can be used to authenticate users and devices.	Legacy equipment may be unable to use network services because 802.1x does not provide network access to users who are unable to authenticate.
It can be made transparent to end users.	802.1x may introduce a slight delay till authentication process completes. Some applications may require modification to cater this delay.
Helps in linking IP, MAC and switch ports to users, which enhances the overall visibility over the network.	

Table 2-07: IEEE 802.1x Advantages and Disadvantages

This diagram shows the message sequences followed in whole process of authentication between supplicant, switch and RADIUS server:

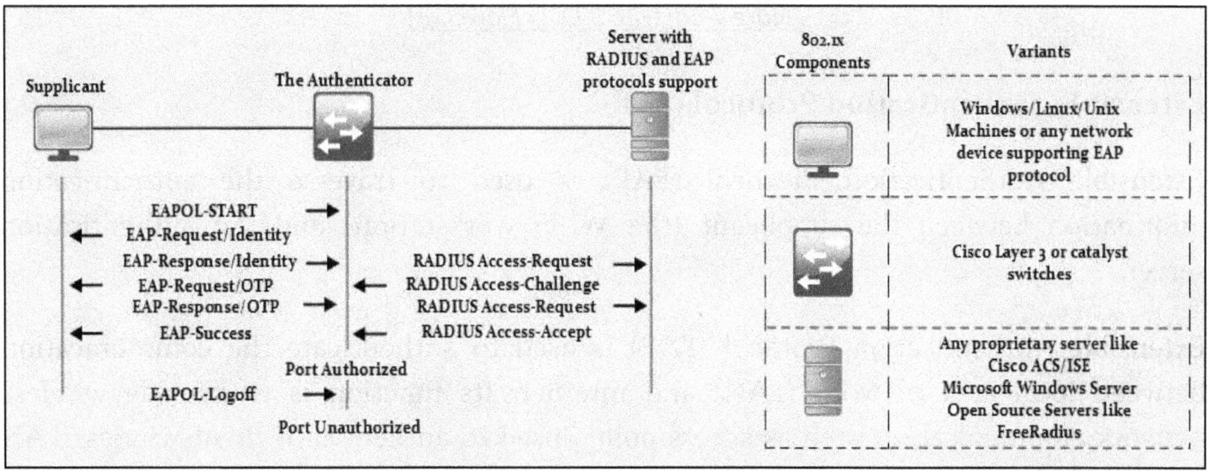

Figure 2-13: IEEE 802.1x Process Diagram

This flow chat further explains the process defined in the previous page:

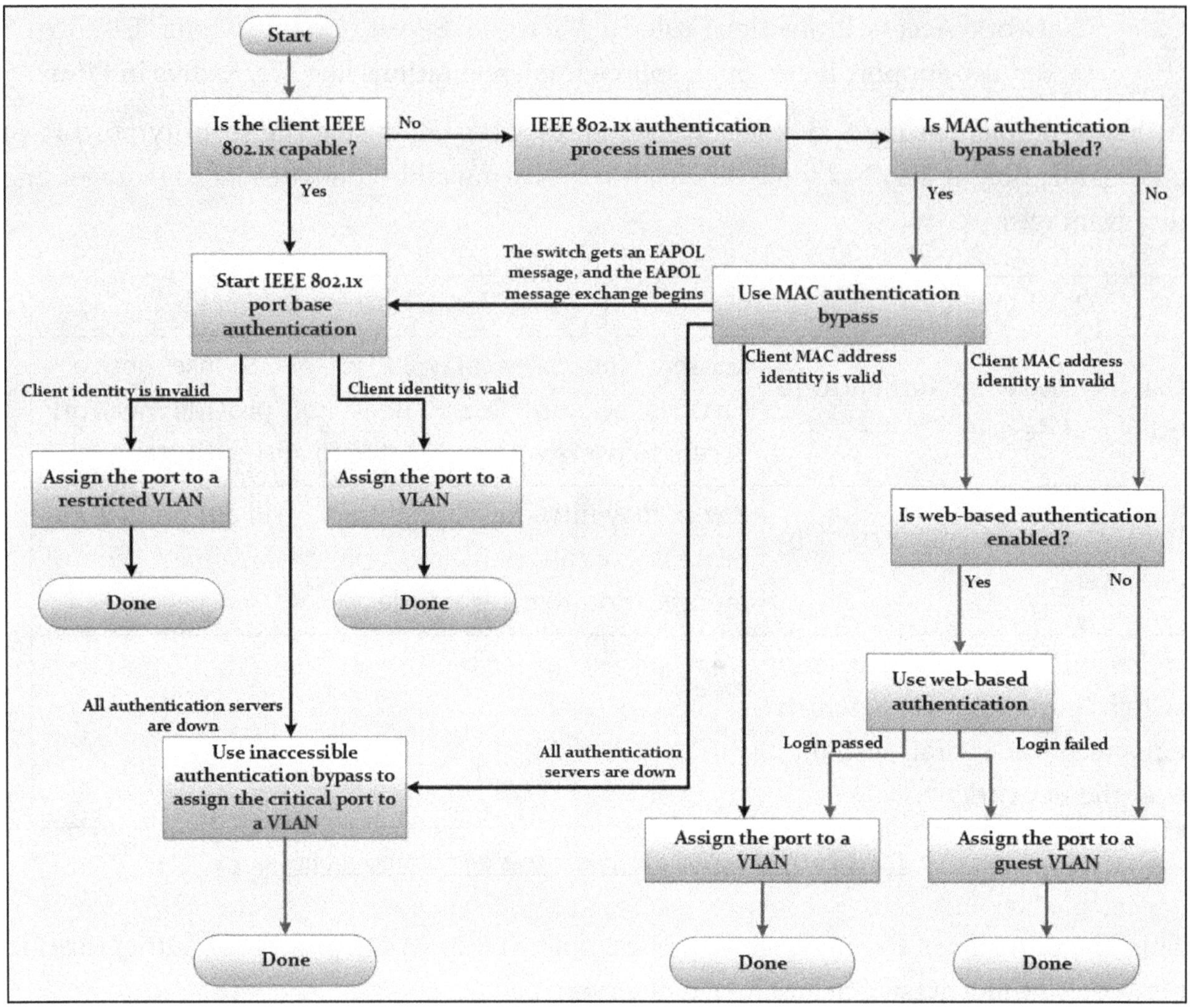

Figure 2-14: IEEE 802.1x Flowchart

Extensible Authentication Protocol (EAP)

Extensible Authentication Protocol (EAP) is used to traverse the authentication information between the supplicant (the Wi-Fi workstation) and the authentication server.

Extensible Authentication Protocol (EAP) is used to authenticate the communication between local area network (LAN) and internet. Its function is to provide wireless network communication such as access points used to authenticate client-wireless/LAN network systems.

EAP is a point-to-point framework that uses a simple request and grant mechanism. Here, for the establishment of connection, a client requests a wireless network connection through the transceiver. The transceiver then gets client's information and forwards it to the authentication server for further processing. In the next step, the authentication server requests client's information from the transceiver. After the whole process of verification, the client can connect to the internet and communicate with the server.

Some of the most commonly used EAP authentication types include:

- **EAP-MD-5**: it provides the basic level of EAP support, by supporting just one-way authentication. There is no mutual authentication between a client and Wi-Fi network. So, it is not recommended for Wi-Fi LAN implementation.
- **EAP-TLS**: it provides certificate based mutual authentication between client and the network. Certificates should be managed on both the sides, so this method is not recommended for large WLAN installations.
- **EAP-PEAP**: it is a protected extensible authentication protocol. It provides a method to traverse authentication data (like password based protocols, via 802.11 networks) securely.
- **EAP-Fast**: it provides flexible authentication via secured tunneling. Here, we use PAC (PROTECTED ACCESS CREDENTIALS) instead of certificates for mutual authentication.

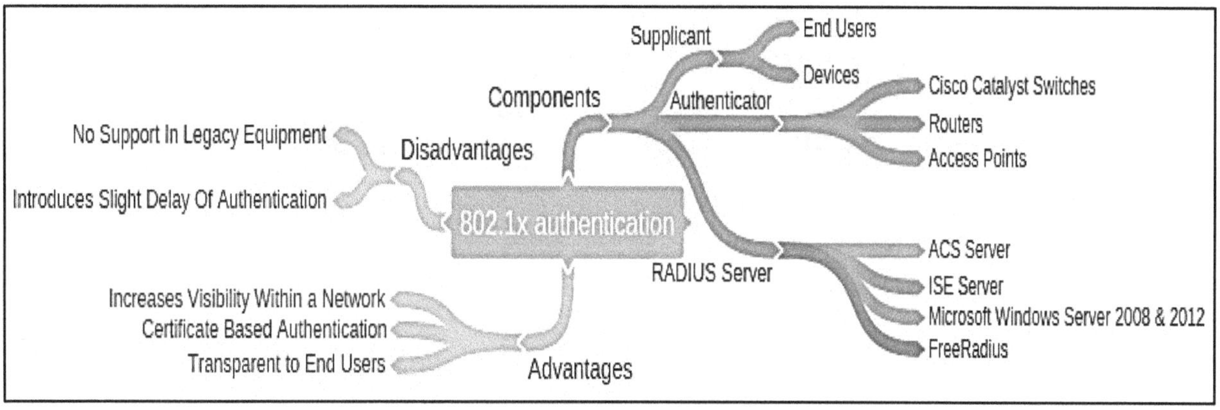

Figure 2-15: IEEE 802.1x Mind Map

Bring Your Own Devices (BYOD)

Bring your own device (BYOD) or bring you own technology (BYOT) refers to the network users who bring their own devices - such as smartphones, laptops and tablet PCs – for their work, they use them instead of company's given devices.

In this section, we will discuss the importance of *Bring Your Own Device (BYOD)* and its high-level architecture. Along from BYOD, one of its management approach known as *Mobile Device Management (MDM)* will also be discussed.

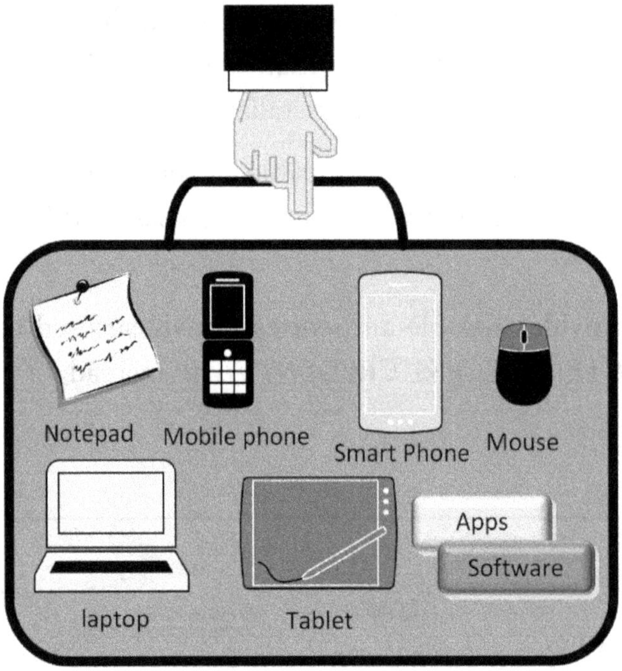

Bring Your Own Device (BYOD)

Although, the concept of BYOD facilitates the end users in many ways, it also increases the risk of threat for the network. The most challenging factor for today's network is to provide seamless connectivity between network and end users while maintaining a good security policy for an organization. Organization's security policies must be constantly reviewed to make sure that bringing any outside device over the corporate network will not result in any security breach or comprise on organization's digital assets.

Some of the reasons that demand BYOD solutions to be implemented in an organization are:

- **Wide variety of consumer devices:** Few years back, the only trend in the organization was to assign a desktop computer to the user and wired connection was the only preferred way of communication. In the 21st century, engineers not only succeeded in attaining higher data rates per second but also resulting in various end user devices. If we look around, we see mobile devices like smartphones, tablets and even laptops, which are constantly communicating with each other over some wired or wireless network. Employees may connect their smartphones over corporate networks during working hours and to the internet when they move to home or some café.
- **No fix time for work:** Few years back, employees were bound to follow a strict 8-hour working environment, but now we can work from home, during traveling, during lunch and even our working rosters are updated on weekly bases. Sometimes, we even work during night to meet the deadlines. Hence, BYOD increases the flexibility of working hours
- **Connecting to corporate from anywhere:** Employees also demand to be connected to the corporate network anytime whether they are in home or in some café. Emergence of wireless networks and mobile networks like 3G/4G also enables them to connect even from the most remote locations on earth.

BYOD Architecture Framework

There are rules in implementing BYOD in an organization. It depends on the company's policy about how flexible they are in accepting and enabling their employees to bring different types of devices along with them. Introducing BYOD in an organization may also result in implementing or deploying new software and hardware features to cater the security aspects of BYOD.

The Cisco BYOD framework is based on *Cisco Borderless Network Architecture* and it tries to implement *Best Common Practices (BCP)* in designing branch office, home office and campus area networks.

This figure shows the Cisco BYOD architecture with a short explanation of each component in the coming section.

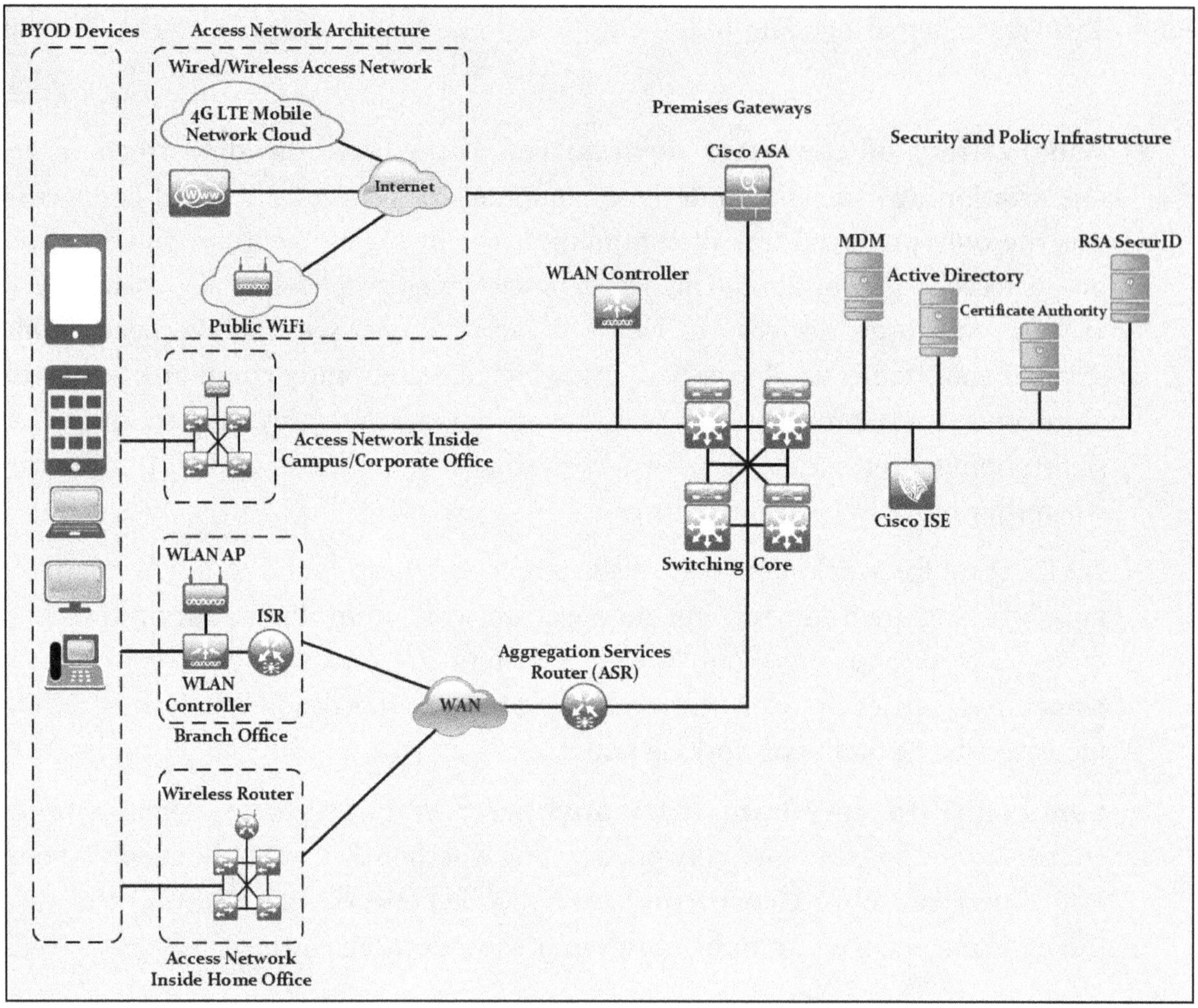

Figure 2-16: BYOD High-Level Architecture

BYOD Devices: These endpoint devices are required to access the corporate network for daily business need. BYOD devices may include both corporate and personally owned devices, regardless of their physical location. During the day, they may be at corporate office and during the night, they may be at some café or food restaurant. Common BYOD devices include smartphones, laptops etc.

Wireless Access Points (AP): Cisco Wireless Access Points (APs) provide wireless connectivity to the corporate network for above defined BYOD devices. Access points are installed physically at campus, branch office, or even at home office to facilitate the employees.

Wireless LAN Controllers: WLAN controllers provide centralized management and monitoring of Cisco WLAN solution. WLAN are integrated with *Cisco Identity Service Engine* to enforce the authorization and authentication on BYOD end-point devices.

Identity Service Engine (ISE): ISE is one of the most critical elements in Cisco BYOD architecture as it implements Authentication, Authorization, and Accounting on BYOD end-point devices.

Cisco AnyConnect Secure Mobility Client: Cisco AnyConnect Client software provides connectivity to corporate network for end users. Its uses 802.1x features to provide access with in campus, office or home office network. When end users need to connect over public internet, AnyConnect uses VPN connection to make sure the confidentiality of corporate data.

Integrated Services Router (ISR): Cisco ISR routers are preferred in BYOD architecture for proving WAN and internet access for branch and home office networks. They are used to provide VPN connectivity for mobile BYOD devices within the organization.

Aggregation Services Router (ASR): Cisco ASR routers provide WAN and internet access for corporate and campus networks. They also act as aggregation points for connections coming from branch and home office to the corporate networks of Cisco BYOD solution.

Cloud Web Security (CWS): Cisco Cloud Web Security provides enhanced security for all BYOD devices, which access internet using public hotspots and 3G/4G networks.

Adaptive Security Appliance (ASA): Cisco ASA provides the standard security solutions at the internet edge of campus, branch and home office networks within BYOD architecture. Apart from integrating IPS/IDS module within itself, ASA also act as termination point of VPN connections made by *Cisco AnyConnect Client* software over the public internet to facilitate the BYOD devices.

RSA securID: RSA securID generates one-time password (OTP) for BYOD devices that need to access the network applications that require OTP.

Active Directory: Active Directory provides centralized command and control of domain users, computers, and network printers. It restricts the access to network resources only to the defined users and computers.

Certificate Authority: Certificate authority can be used to allow access of corporate network to only those BYOD devices, which have valid corporate certificate installed on them. All those devices without certificate may be given no access of corporate network but limited internet connectivity as per defined in corporate policy.

Mobile Device Management

Mobile Device Management (MDM) is a solution that provides a unified management of the entire network (mobile devices, smart phones, tablets, notebooks, Laptops etc.) from a centralized dashboard. The role of Mobile device managers is to manage, monitor and secure mobile devices of end users whether they are organization owned devices or employee-owned devices (BYOD). It makes you deploy software and apps that you used on your PC during office timings.

Now, they can be moved outside the corporate office to home or some other place and still keep you connected, hence making the network more flexible. It not only gives flexibility to the network but makes it secure as well. Following are some of the functions provided by MDM:

- Enforcing a device to be locked after certain login failure attempts.
- Enforcement of strong password polices for all BYOD devices.
- MDM can detect any attempt of hacking BYOD devices and then limits the network access of these affected devices.
- Enforcing confidentiality by using encryption as per organization's policy.
- Administration and implementation of *Data Loss Prevention (DLP)* for BYOD devices. It helps to prevent any kind of data loss due an end user's carelessness.

MDM Deployment Methods

Generally, there are two types of MDM deployment methods, namely:

On-site MDM deployment: On-site/premises MDM deployment involves installation of MDM application on local servers inside corporate data centers or offices and its management is done by local staff available on the site.

The main advantage of implementing the on-site MDM is granular control over the management of the BYOD devices, which increases the level of security to some extent.

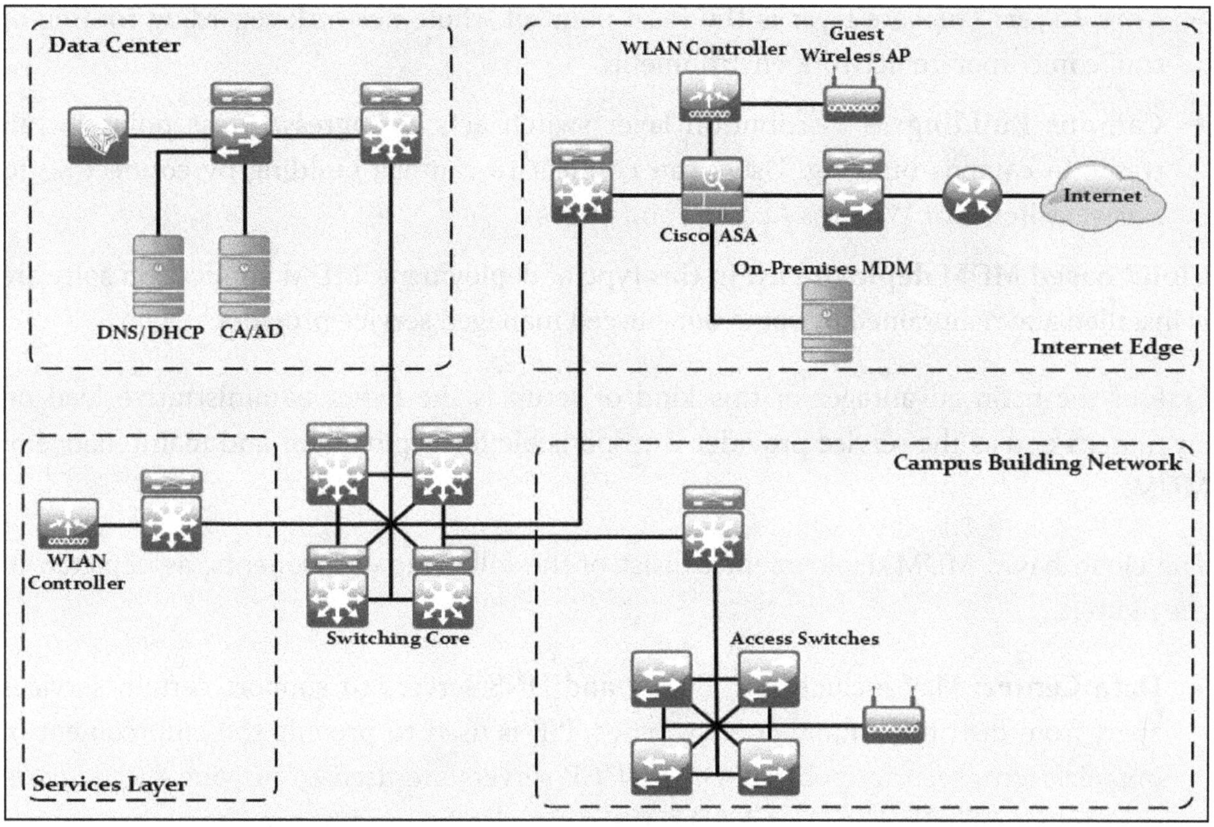

Figure 2-17: On-Premises MDM High Level Deployment Architecture

The on-site/premises MDM solution is consisting of the following architectures:

- **Data Center:** It includes ISE, DHCP, and DNS servers to support certain services apart from distribution and core switches. ISE is used to provide the enforcement of organization's security policies. DNS/DHCP servers are used to provide the network connectivity. Similarly, CA and AD servers can also be used to provide access only to users with valid authentication credentials.
- **Internet Edge:** The basic purpose of this architecture is to provide connectivity to public internet. This layer includes Cisco ASA firewall to filter and monitor all the traffic ingress and egress towards public internet. Wireless LAN Controller (WLC) along with Access Points (APs) are also a part of internet edge to support guest users. One of the key components at internet edge is On-premises MDM solution, which maintains policies and configuration settings of all BYOD devices, connected to the corporate network.
- **Services Layer:** This layer contains Wireless LAN Controller (WLC) for all the APs used by users within corporate environment. Any other service required by corporate users like NTP and its supporting servers can be found in this section.

➢ **Core Layer:** The core layer is the focal point of whole network regarding routing of traffic in corporate network environment.

➢ **Campus Building:** A distribution layer switch acts as ingress/egress point for all traffic in campus building. Users can connect to campus building by connecting to access switches or Wireless Access Points (APs).

Cloud based MDM deployment: In this type of deployment, MDM application software is installed and maintained by some outsourced managed service provider.

One of the main advantages of this kind of setup is the lesser administrative load on customer's end as the service provider is responsible for deployment and maintenance of MDM.

The cloud based MDM deployment consist of the following components, as depicted in the figure:

➢ **Data Center:** May include ISE, DHCP and DNS servers to support certain services apart from distribution and core switches. ISE is used to provide the enforcement of organization's security policies. DNS/DHCP servers are used to provide the network connectivity. Similarly, CA and AD servers can also be used to provide access only to users with valid authentication credentials.

➢ **Internet edge:** Basic purpose of this section is to provide connectivity to public internet. This layer includes Cisco ASA firewall to filter and monitor all the traffic ingress and egress towards public internet. Wireless LAN Controller (WLC) along with Access Points (APs) are also present in internet edge to support guest users.

➢ **WAN:** The WAN module in cloud based MDM deployment provides MPLS VPN connectivity from branch office to corporate office, internet access from branch offices and connectivity to cloud based MDM application software. Cloud based MDM solution maintains policies and configuration settings of all BYOD devices connected to the corporate network.

➢ **WAN edge:** This component acts as focal point of all ingress/egress MPLS WAN traffic entering from and going to branch offices.

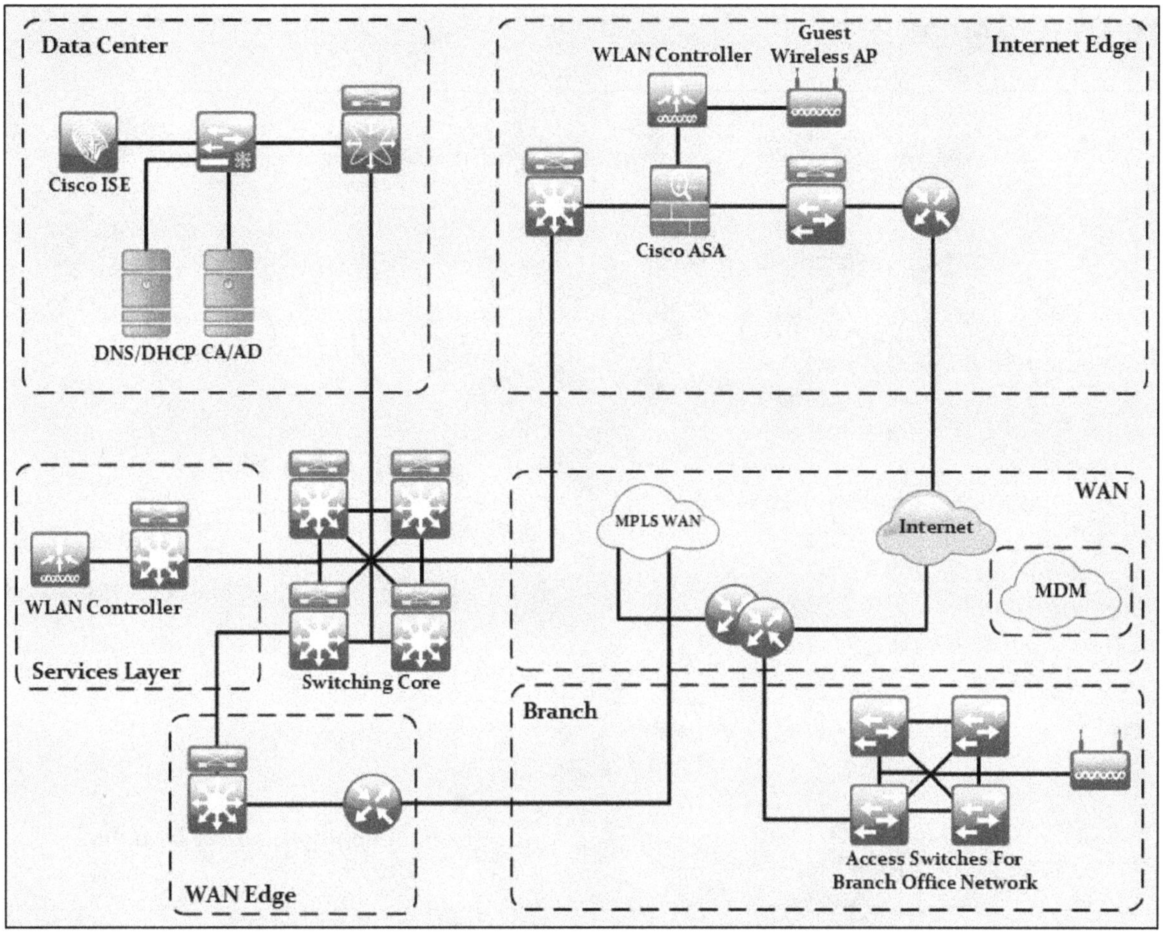

Figure 2-18: Cloud Based MDM Deployment High Level Architecture

- **Services:** This layer contains WLC for all the APs used by users within corporate environment. Any other service required by corporate users like NTP and its supporting servers can also be found in this section.
- **Core Layer:** The core layer is the focal point of whole network regarding routing of traffic in corporate network environment.
- **Branch Offices:** This component comprises of few routers acting as focal point of ingress and egress traffic out of branch offices. Users can connect to branch office network by connecting to access switches or Wireless Access Points (APs).

BYOD Mind Map

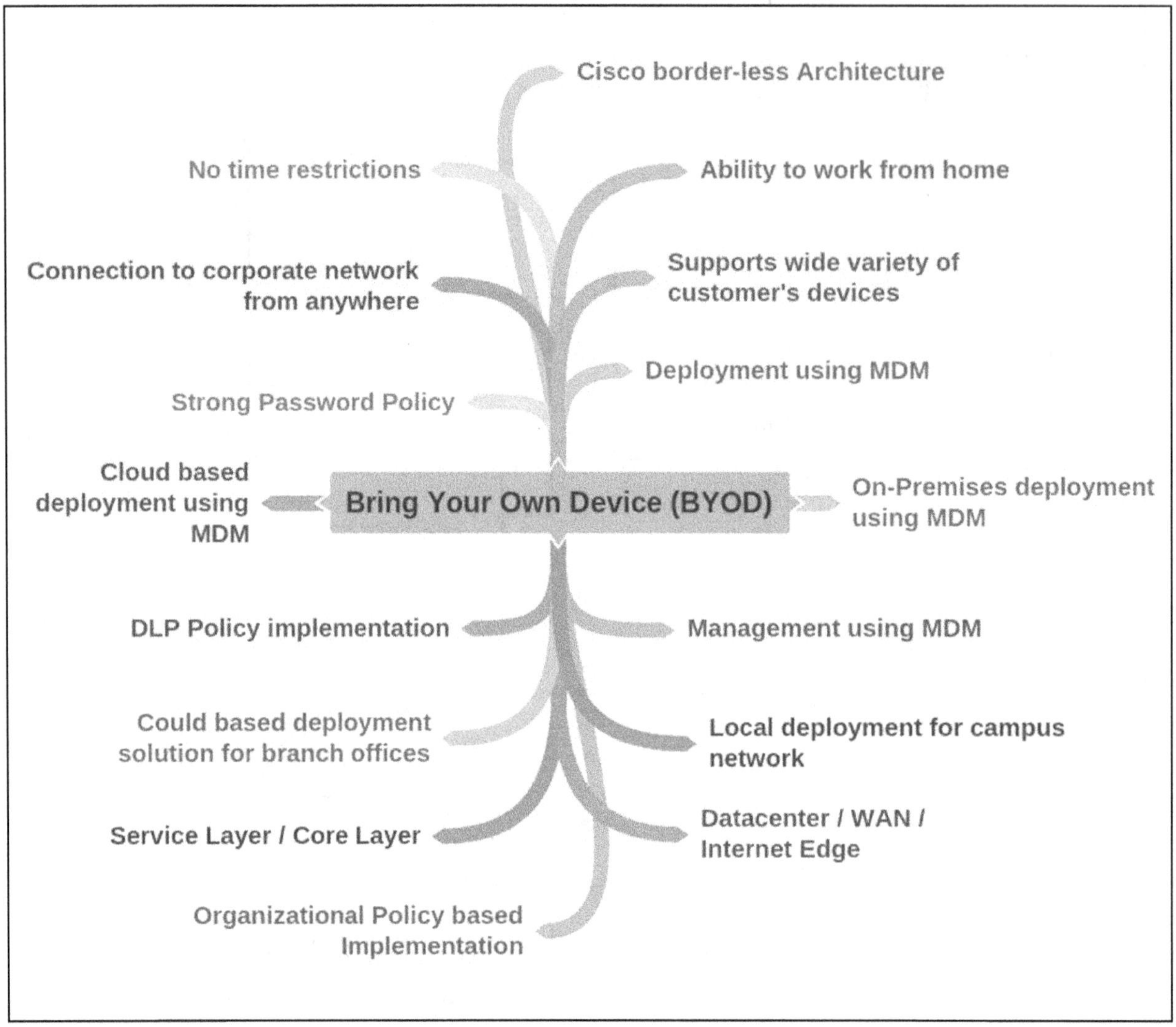

Figure 2-19: BYOD Mind Map

Practice Questions

1. What is the main feature of Control Plane Policing (CoPP)?
   A. Reduce overall traffic by disabling control plane services.
   B. Configuration, management and monitoring of networking devices.
   C. Manage services provided by the control plane.
   D. Restrict unnecessary traffic from overloading the route processor.

2. What are the types of role-based CLI control access feature?
   A. Super view, admin view, config view, CLI view
   B. admin view, Root view, CLI view, Super view
   C. root view, CLI view, Super view, admin view
   D. CLI view, Root view, Super view, Law intercept view

3. By default, what is the privilege level of user account created on Cisco routers?
   A. 0
   B. 1
   C. 15
   D. 16

4. Syslog server uses eight severity levels from zero, which of the following level indicates the critical condition?
   A. 0
   B. 1
   C. 2
   D. 3
   E. 4
   F. None

5. An application-level network monitoring protocol with fewer manager stations and controls a set of agents, known as:
   A. HTML
   B. TCP
   C. SNMP
   D. SMTP

6. Which one is the characteristic of the MIB?
   A. OIDs are organized in a hierarchical structure.
   B. Information in the MIB is rigid.
   C. A separate MIB tree exists for any given device in the network.
   D. Information is organized in a flat manner so that SNMP can access it quickly.

7. _________________ is the process of proving an identity of a user by login identification and a password.
   A. Authorization
   B. Authentication
   C. Accounting
   D. MIB

8. Which AAA security protocol provides encryption of full payload?
   A. RADIUS
   B. TACACS
   C. ISE
   D. ACS

9. What is the requirement to enable the Secure Copy Protocol feature in a network?
   A. A user with privilege level 1 has to be configured for local authentication.
   B. SSH protocol has to be configured and a command must be issued to enable the SCP server side functionality.
   C. Transfer can only occur from SCP clients that are routers.
   D. Telnet protocol has to be configured first on the SCP server side.

10. Which specification or protocol provides port based network access control (PNAC)?
   A. 802.1Q
   B. 802.1
   C. 802.1x
   D. None of the above

11. Which technology provides seamless connectivity between network and end users

while maintaining good security policies for an organization?
A. IOT
B. BYOD
C. SNMP
D. FTP

12. Which solution provides the unified management of the entire network (mobile devices, smart phones, tablets, notebooks, Laptops etc.) from a centralized dashboard?
A. BYOD
B. IOT
C. MDM
D. Big Data

13. Which option can be configured by Cisco AutoSecure?
A. Enable secret password
B. Interface IP address
C. SNMP
D. Syslog

14. After enabling AAA, which three CLI steps are required to configure a router with a parser view? (Choose any three)
A. Create a root view using the parser view view-name command.
B. Associate the view with the law intercept view.
C. Assign groups who can use the view.
D. Create a view using the parser view view-name command.
E. Assign a secret password to the view.
F. Assign commands to the view.

15. In SSH, which three steps are required to configure Router to accept only encrypted SSH connections? (Choose any three)
A. Enable inbound vty SSH sessions.
B. Assign IP addresses.
C. Configure DNS on the router.
D. Configure IP domain name on the router.
E. Enable Telnet sessions.

F. Generate SSH keys.

16. What are the three primary functions of syslog logging service? (Choose any three)
    A. Specifies the size of the logging buffer.
    B. Specifies the database where captured information is stored.
    C. Gathers logging information.
    D. Compares the information to be captured and the information to be ignored.
    E. Authenticates and encrypts data sent revolving inside LAN.
    F. Assigns time stamp to the packets.

17. On which plane or layer do we apply policies to control user traffic?
    A. Data plane
    B. Control plane
    C. Management plane
    D. None of the above

18. Which plane involves the configuration, management and monitoring of networking devices?
    A. Data plane
    B. Control plane
    C. Management plane
    D. None of the above

19. Which of the following version of SNMP supports encryption and hashing?
    A. Version 1
    B. Version 2c
    C. Version 3
    D. All

20. Which protocol allows networking devices to synchronize their time with respect to the NTP server, so the devices may have more authenticated time settings and generated syslog messages?
    A. Syslog
    B. NTP
    C. SNMP

D. SMTP

21. What functional plane is responsible for device-generated packets required for network operation, such as ARP message exchanges and routing advertisements?
   A. Data plane
   B. Control plane
   C. Management plane
   D. Forwarding plane

22. If a user complains about not being able to gain access to a network device configured with AAA. How would the network administrator determine if login access for the user account is disabled or not?
   A. Use the show aaa user command.
   B. Use the show aaa local user lockout command.
   C. Use the show running-configuration command.
   D. Use the show aaa sessions command.

23. Which AAA solution supports both RADIUS and TACACS+ servers?
   A. RADIUS and TACACS+ servers cannot be supported by a single solution.
   B. Implement a local database.
   C. Implement Cisco Secure Access Control System (ACS) only.
   D. Access Control System (ACS).

24. Syslog server uses eight severity levels from zero, which of the following level indicates the WARNING condition?
   A. 0
   B. 1
   C. 2
   D. 3
   E. 4
   F. None

25. Which of the following logging mechanism provides time stamp of an event?
   A. SCP
   B. NTP

C. Syslog logging
D. SNMP

Chapter 03: Virtual Private Network (VPN)

Technology Brief

In the previous chapter, we had discussed about how to prevent unauthorized network access, but network security is not just about securing the end-user, it also includes providing confidentiality, integrity, and availability of data in motion. For example, an end-user accessing organization's resources from home or some cafe over the public internet and if this communication is not secure, then this data can be sniffed or stolen easily. Attackers can also modify the data and can misuse it.

In some cases, a small business organization has multiple offices, they cannot afford leased lines connecting to remote offices and cannot take risk of sending their confidential data over the public internet without any kind of encryption. Therefore, the concept of ***Virtual Private Network (VPN)*** arises where an organization wants to implement confidentiality, integrity and authorization of data in motion over the public internet or some other autonomous system with minimum expenses.

"Virtual Private Network (VPN) is an encrypted communication channel or tunnel between two remote sites over the internet".

VPN is a logical network that allows connectivity between two devices. That devices can either belongs to the same network or connected over a Wide Area Network. As we go deep down into the word VPN. The term "Virtual" here refers to the logical link between the two devices, as the VPN link does not exist separately, it uses internet as a transport mechanism. The term "Private" here refers to the security VPN provides to the connection between the two devices, as the medium of transport is internet, which is not secure and VPN adds confidentiality and data integrity. It encrypts the data and prevents alteration or manipulation of data from unauthorized person along the path.

Following are the key features of VPN technology:

Confidentiality: Only the intended destination's user can understand the data, as data is sent in an encrypted form, data for any other person would be meaningless.

Data integrity: VPN makes sure that the sent data is accurate, secured and remains unaltered end to end.

Authentication: VPN authenticates the peer on both side of the tunnel through pre-shared public or private keys or by using user authentication method.

Anti-replay Protection: VPN technology makes sure that if any VPN packet has been sent for transaction and accounted for, then the exact same packet is not valid for the second time of VPN session; no one can befool VPN peer into believing that the peer trying to connect is the real one.

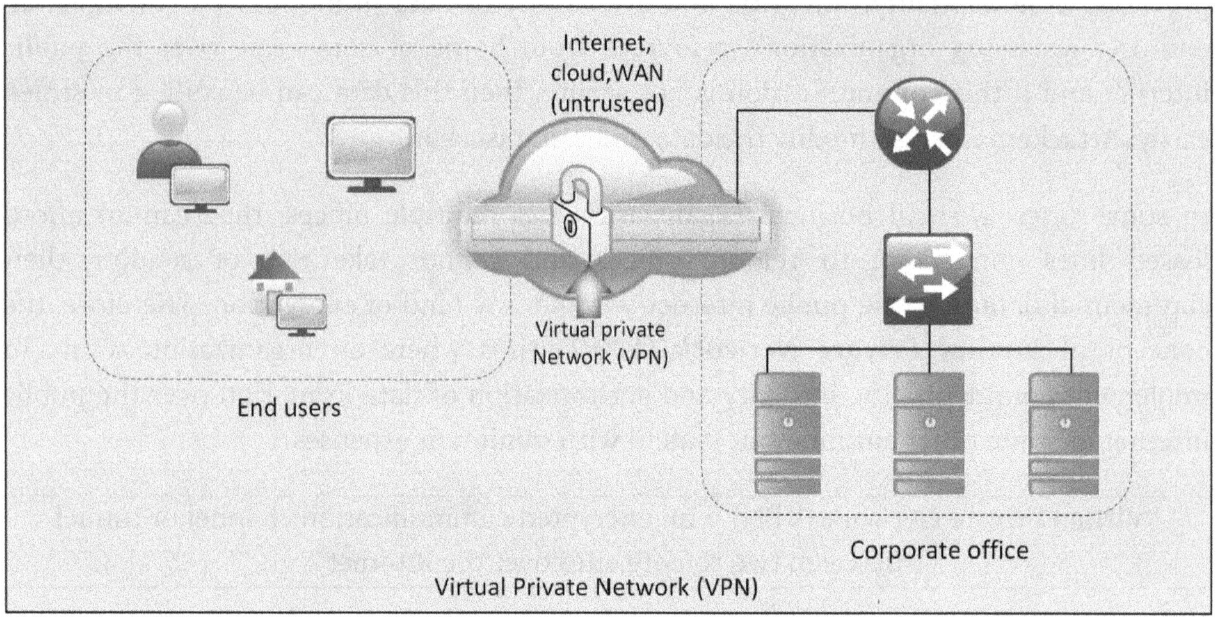

Figure 3-01: Example of Using VPN for Secure Connection

Benefits of using VPN

Using VPN in enterprise or home environment provides many benefits. Some of them are:

- **Security:** VPN uses one of the most advanced encryption and hashing algorithms to provide confidentiality and integrity. Although, latest web browsers have native support for SSL, Cisco's AnyConnect SSL client software also provides SSL based VPN solution. Second most common option is IPsec. It is used for Site-to-Site VPN implementation.
- **Cost:** Connecting the remote offices to most feasible internet service provider and then using VPN for secure connection is so far the most cost effective solution as compared to point-to-point leased lines.
- **Scalability:** Setting up VPN connectivity of newly established remote office with corporate office is quicker in terms of setup than using leased lines.

Types of VPN

1. Remote Access VPN
2. Site-to-Site VPN

Remote Access VPN

A remote access VPN feature allows an end-point to connect to the secure LAN network of an organization. These end-point devices include smartphones, tablets, laptops etc.

For example, consider an employee of an organization who works from different remote locations to provide real-time data to the organization. The organization wants to provide a secure communication channel, which connects the remote employee to the organization's internal network securely. Remote-access VPN provides the solution by allowing the remote employee's device to connect to the corporate headquarters or any other branch of that organization. This is referred as a remote-access VPN connection. Remote-access VPNs uses IPsec or Secure Sockets Layer (SSL) technologies for securing the communication tunnel. Many organizations use Cisco's AnyConnect client for remote access SSL VPNs.

Site-to-Site VPN

A site-to-site VPN securely connects two or more sites that want to connect together over the internet. For example, a corporate office wants to connect to its head office or there are multiple branches that want to connect with each other. This is referred to as site-to-site VPN. Site-to-site VPN usually uses IPsec as a VPN technology.

This figure below shows the conceptual view of two main types of VPN connections:

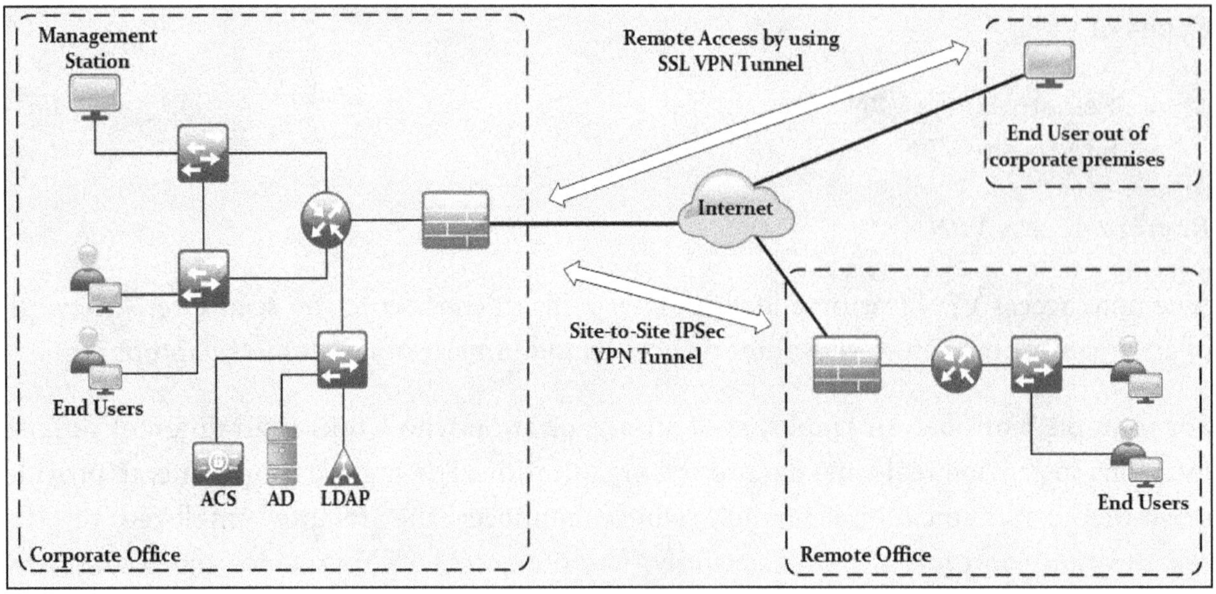

Figure 3-02: Types of VPN

Types of Encryption Protocols in VPN Technology

The following three types of encryption protocols are used in VPN technologies:

- **IPsec:** Used for connecting whole site with another site, IPsec provides security of IP packets at *Network Layer* of TCP/IP stack.
- **SSL:** Supported by latest web browsers and custom-made software for clients, SSL encrypts TCP traffic by using encrypted SSL tunnels.
- **MPLS:** *Multi-Protocol Label Switching (MPLS)* and *L3 MPLS VPN* are normally used by service providers to provide logical connectivity between two sites of an organization. IPsec is then used on top of L3 VPN connectivity to provide encryption.

Before moving towards the further details, let us review the basics of cryptography discussed in chapter 1, as they are the key to understand the VPN technology.

IPsec

IPsec stands for IP security. As the name suggests, it is used for the security of general IP traffic. Internet Protocol Security (IPsec) VPN is the process of establishing and managing VPN connections or services securely over the internet using an IPsec protocol suite. It adds IPsec's security features to VPN network packets.

The power of IPsec lies in its ability to support multiple protocols and algorithms. It also incorporates new advancements in encryption and hashing protocols. The main objective of IPsec is to provide CIA (Confidentiality, Integrity and Authentication) for virtual networks used in current networking environments. IPsec makes sure the above objectives are in action by the time packet enters a VPN tunnel until it reaches the other end of tunnel.

IPsec offers protection of the following aspect of an IP datagram:

- Data origin authentication
- Connectionless data integrity authentication
- Data content confidentiality
- Anti-replay protection
- Limited traffic flow confidentiality

The key components IPsec uses to provide the *CIA* are:

- **Confidentiality:** IPsec uses encryption protocols namely AES, DES and 3DES for providing confidentiality.
- **Integrity:** IPsec uses hashing protocols (MD5 and SHA) for providing integrity. Hashed Message Authentication (HMAC) can also be used for checking the integrity of data.
- **Authentication algorithms:** RSA digital signatures and pre-shared keys (PSK) are two methods used for authentication purposes.

Working of IPsec

The following scenario will be used to explain the concepts involved in IPsec implementation:

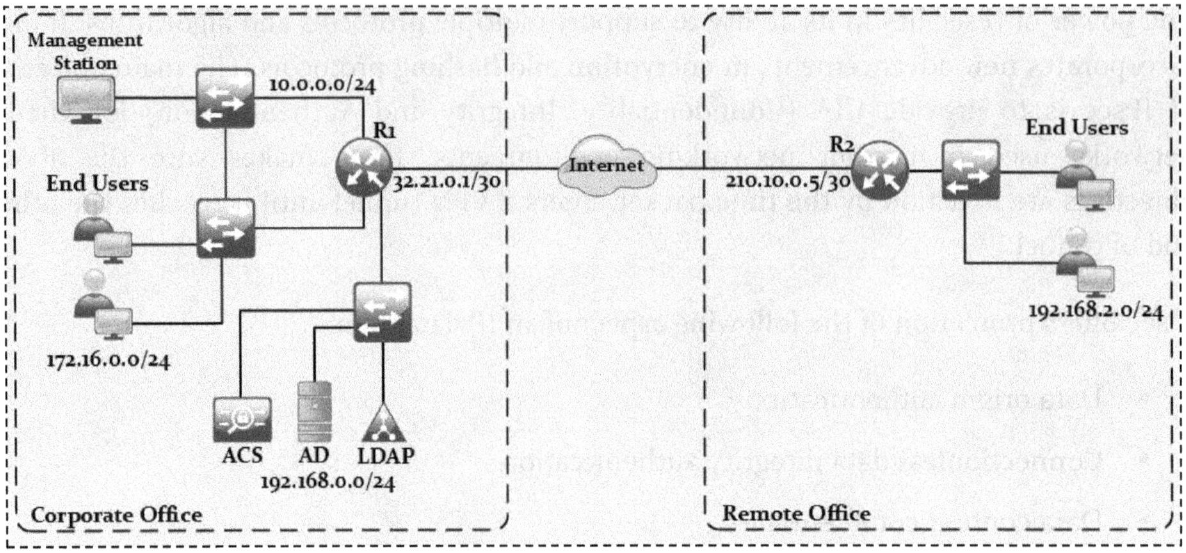

Figure 3-03: Two Sites Connected via Public Internet

Let us assume that router R1 wants to send some encrypted traffic from 172.16.0/0/24 network and then send it from a logical tunnel to R2 over the internet. Encrypted packets after travelling over untrusted network will be decrypted by R2 and send it to the desired client of 192.168.2.0/24 network.

Let us assume that both routers are configured with the correct VPN settings and can ping each other's public IP addresses, which make sure their connectivity at layer 3. "***Security Associations (SAs)***" are established between the two IPsec peers R1 and R2. This pair of routers is known as "***IPsec peers***". These SAs are unidirectional, defining the set of protocols, algorithms and keying information to be used in between IPsec peers.

Both routers will wait for the exchange of traffic from 172.16.0.0/24 and 192.168.2.0/24 to show up on respective interfaces. Normally, both routers will not make VPN connection without the generation of any data traffic. As soon as traffic hits the router, say end-users from R1 tries to connect to end-user of R2, R1 will be the initiator of VPN in this case and will initiate negotiation process with R2.

IKE (Internet Key Exchange) is a key management protocol to authenticate, negotiate and distribute IPsec encryption keys among IPsec peers. IKE also automatically establishes the SAs. The process of IKE negotiations depends on two phases:

1. IKE Phase 1 Negotiation Tunnel
2. IKE Phase 2 Tunnel

Phase 1: IKE Phase 1 Negotiation Tunnel

The phase 1 of IKE offers the negotiations of Security Association (SA) between peers. This association helps the peers to communicate in phase 2. The first step of initiation of VPN between two peers is known as Internet Key Exchange (IKE) phase 1 tunnel. This phase is not used for sending encrypted user traffic. Instead, it is used for securing the management traffic related to VPN connection between two peers. For example, keep alive packets to verify the status of VPN connection, PSK key for authentication between peers and encryption and hashing algorithms used to protect this key etc. are defined in IKE phase 1 tunnel. Two modes are used to define this tunnel namely:

1. Main Mode
2. Aggressive Mode

Main Mode

Main mode negotiations can be further classified as:

1. Main Mode Address
2. Main Mode Fully Qualified Domain Name (FQDN)

Main mode address negotiation is the most secure mode having three two-way exchanges among the initiator of the tunnel and receiver. It is also the default mode for negotiation. Similarly, **Main mode FQDN** requires DNS resolution support to identify the peers. Six different messages are exchanged between the negotiating peers in main mode. The process begins with the source sending proposal to the destination, this proposal carries details about what encryption and authentication protocols will be used, for how long the key will remain activated, etc. The first communication between nodes establishes the basic security policy between the source and destination.

The main mode uses more packets exchange and as a result, it consumes more processing power than aggressive mode.

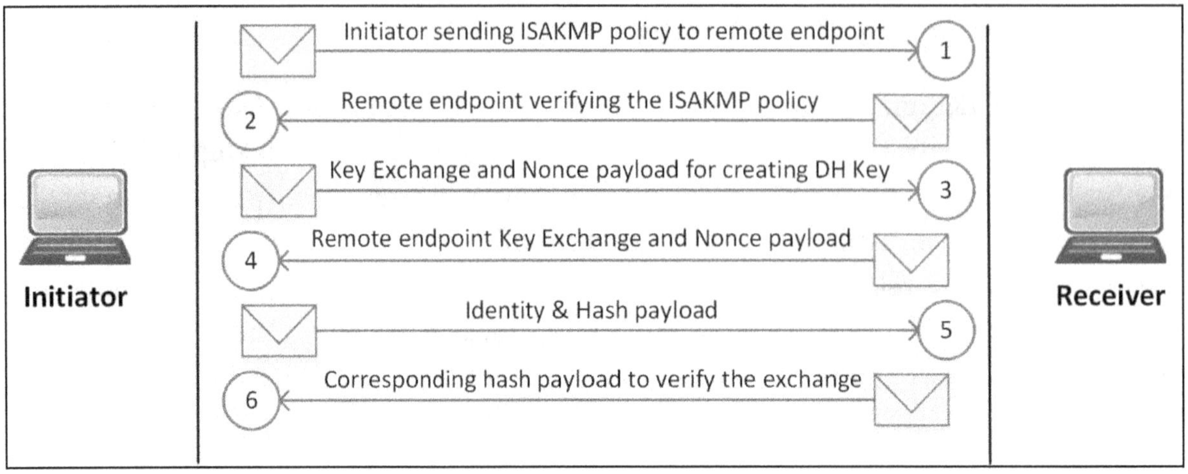

Figure 3-04: Main mode

Aggressive mode

The main goal of aggressive mode is same as main mode. Instead of exchanging six messages, this type for IKE phase 1 tunnel negotiation uses three messages.

1. Initiator of the tunnel sends first packet having information required for generating the DH secret key for the remote end-point. This single packet contains enough information, equivalent to the initial four packets of main mode.
2. Second packet contains the DH secret key from the remote end-point back to initiator.
3. Third packet is again from the initiator, which contains identity and hash payload. Receiver recalculates the hash payload. If it matches, phase 1 is established.

According to the previous discussion, R1 is VPN initiator, thus following these five things must be matched on both routers for *IKE phase 1 tunnel* to succeed:

- **Hashing Algorithm:** Message Digest (MD5) and Secure Hashing Algorithm (SHA) are commonly used in the latest implementations.
- **Encryption Algorithm:** Advanced Encryption Standard (AES), Digital Encryption Standard (DES) or 3DES is used for securing the key and management information used in phase 1. Longer key is preferred, as the longer the key is, the more difficult it is to break.
- **Diffie-Hellman (DH) Group:** It is used to generate symmetrical keys, which may be used by VPN peers for using symmetrical algorithms like *AES*. DH group number refers to the size of key (in bits) used to generate the above-mentioned

key pair. Group 1 uses 768 bits; Group 2 uses 1024 bits while Group 5 uses 1536 bits. DH key exchange itself is asymmetrical in nature but key it generates is symmetrical.

- **Authentication Method:** It is used to verify the authenticity of VPN peers. Two options available are *Pre-Shared Keys (PSK)* and *RSA Signatures* (Certificate based authentication).
- **Lifetime:** As the name suggests, it defines the time after which IKE phase1 tunnel will be torn down if remains idle. Default lifetime is 3600 seconds (equal to one day). Normally a smaller life is desired because a new DH key pair will be generated for each session, which gives an attacker a minor time space to calculate the key pair used for current session before it times out.

The following diagram summarizes the IKE phase 1 tunnel and proposal set (above components) acceptance process.

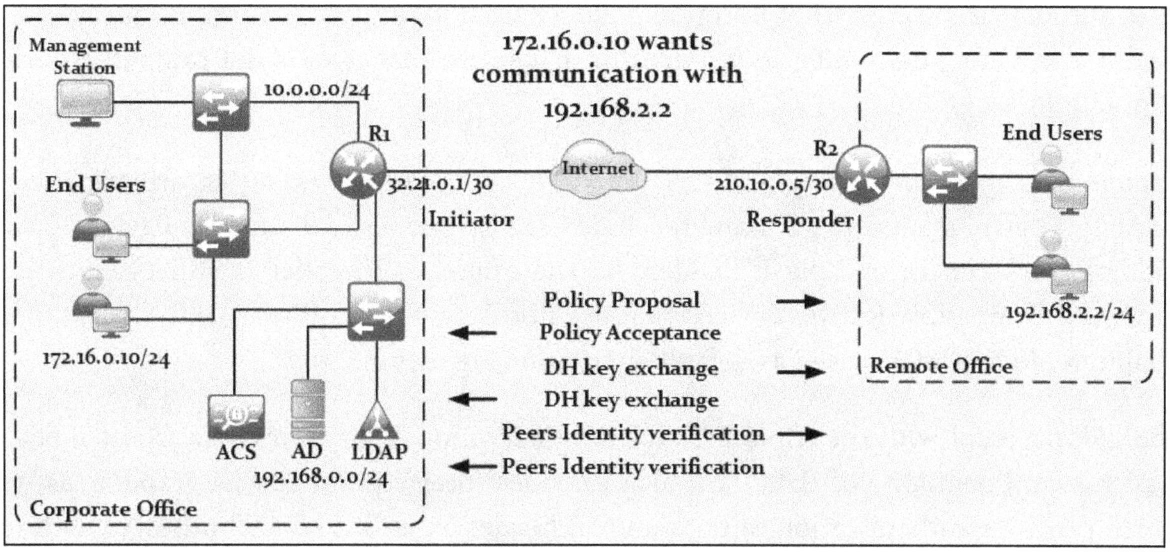

Figure 3-05: IKE Phase 1 Tunnel Establishment

Phase 2: IKE Phase 2 Tunnel

The above-defined phase is used only to secure the management communication between VPN peers. After successful establishment of IKE phase1 tunnel, a second tunnel known as IKE phase 2 tunnel is established, again with mutual agreement, to secure the end user IP traffic. In Phase 2, the channel is prepared for the transfer of data between the networks. IKE Phase 2 uses the keys that were established in Phase 1 and the IPsec Crypto profile, which defines the IPsec protocols and keys used in IKE Phase 2.

From configuration point of view, network administrators are required to create second policy for IKE phase 2-tunnel establishment, although already defined policy for IKE phase 1, tunnel can be used for phase 2.

Securing IP layer with IPsec:

Following are the two standards used in IPsec to secure the communication:

1. Authentication Header (AH)
2. Encapsulating Security Payload (ESP)

Authentication Header (AH) is responsible for authentication services in IPsec framework. AH can also be configured alone, along with ESP and nested in tunnel mode. Authentication provided by AH differs from ESP authentication, it provides external IP header with entire ESP packet. AH is responsible for protecting all fields that does not change in transit like data by using one-way hash. The AH protocol with the HMAC or MD5 authentication algorithm in tunnel mode is used for authentication. Basically, AH is used for providing data integrity services to make sure that data is not tampered during transaction.

Encapsulating Security Payload (ESP) contains six parts including an arbitrary 32-bit number known as Security Parameter Index (SPI), Sequence Number, Payload Data, Padding, Pad Length and Next Header. As the original IP header is still present, it is backward compatible for the devices that are not designed for IPsec. DEC-Cipher Block Chaining Mode (CBC) is used as default encryption algorithm.

The ESP protocol with the triple DES (3DES) encryption algorithm in transport mode is used for confidentiality of data. ESP also provides integrity but not as granular as AH, which provides authentication of data and IP header as well. The ESP protocol with the 56-bit DES encryption algorithm and the HMAC with SHA-1 authentication algorithm in tunnel mode is used for authentication and confidentiality.

Transform Sets

A transform set is a combination of individual security protocols, algorithms and settings to design an IPsec specific security policy for the data traffic. An IPsec transform set specifies a single IPsec security protocol (either AH or ESP) with its corresponding security algorithms and mode. During the Internet security association and key management protocol (ISAKMP), IPsec negotiation that occurs in IKE phase-2, the peers agree to use a specific transform set for protecting the respective data flow. Transform sets combine the following IPsec factors:

- Mechanism for payload authentication—AH transform
- Mechanism for payload encryption—ESP transform
- IPsec mode (transport versus tunnel)

Transform sets equal a combination of an AH transform, plus an ESP transform, plus the IPsec mode (either tunnel or transport mode).

IPsec Working Modes

There are two working modes of IPsec; namely tunnel and transport mode. Each has its own features and implementation procedure.

IPsec Tunnel Mode:

Being the default mode set in Cisco devices, tunnel mode protects the entire IP packet from originating device. It means that for every original packet, another packet is generated with new IP header and sent over the untrusted network to the VPN peer located on other end of logical connection. Tunnel mode is commonly used in case of Site-to-Site VPN where two secured IPsec gateways are connected over public internet using IPsec VPN connection. Consider following diagram:

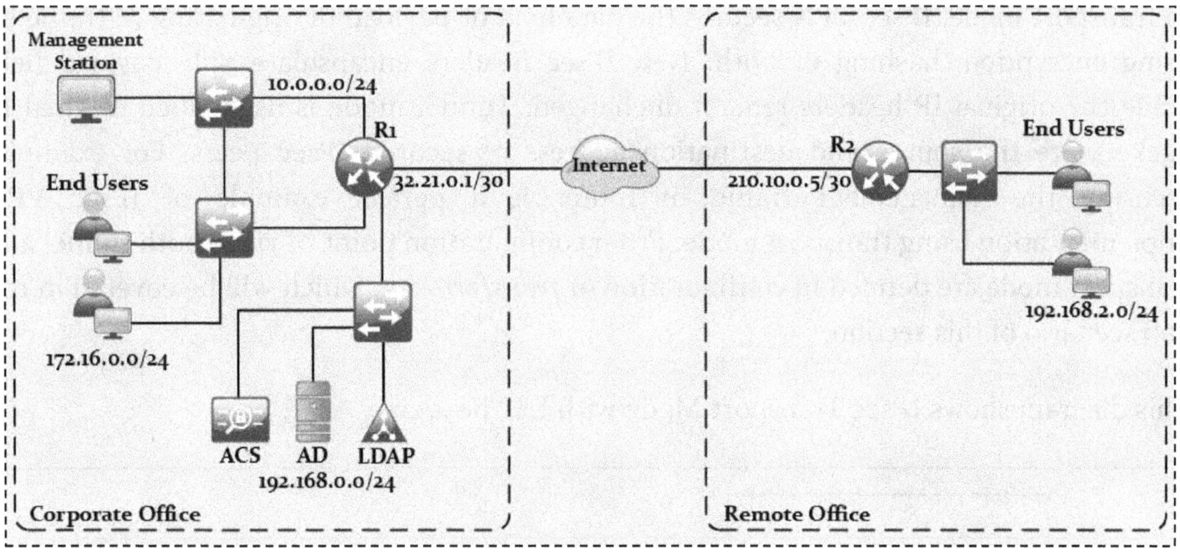

Figure 3-06: IPsec Tunnel Mode

If a client from corporate office tries to communicate with client from remote office and tunnel mode is used for IPsec implementation, then original IP address from both sides will be encapsulated by new IP header and trailer generated by R1 and R2.

The following diagram shows IPsec Tunnel Mode with ESP header:

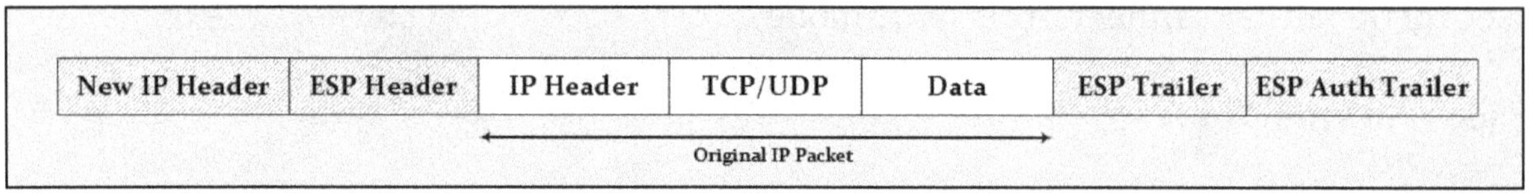

Figure 3-07: IPsec Tunnel Mode with ESP Header

Similarly, when AH is used, the new IP Packet format will be:

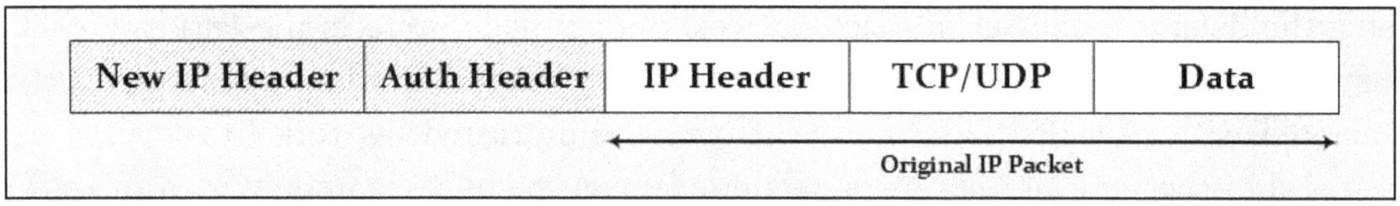

Figure 3-08: IPsec Tunnel Mode with AH Header

IPsec Transport Mode:

In transport mode, IPsec VPN secures the data field or payload of originating IP traffic by using encryption, hashing or both. New IPsec headers encapsulate only payload field while the original IP headers remain unchanged. Tunnel mode is used when original IP packets are the source and destination address of secured IPsec peers. For example, securing the management traffic of router is a perfect example of IPsec VPN implementation using transport mode. From configuration point of view, both tunnel and transport mode are defined in configuration of *transform set*, which will be covered in the Lab scenario of this section.

This diagram shows IPsec Transport Mode with ESP header:

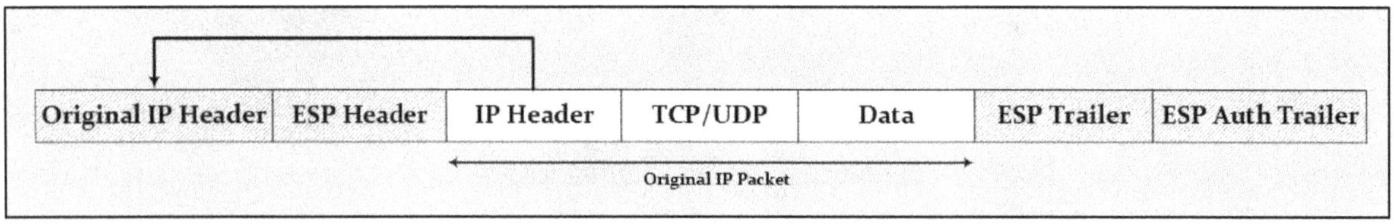

Figure 3-09: IPsec Transport Mode with ESP Header

Similarly, in the case of AH:

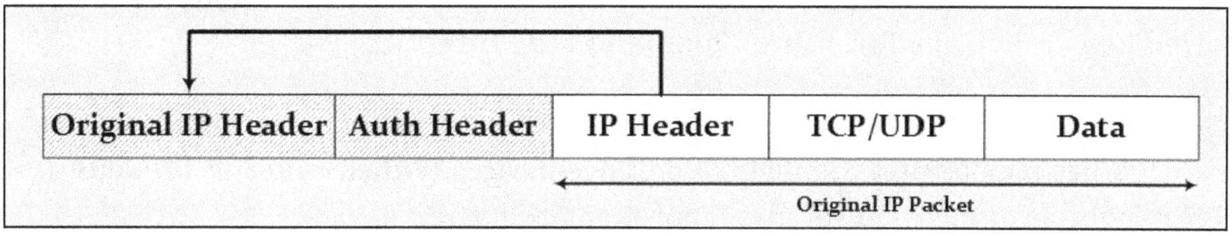

Figure 3-10: IPsec Transport Mode with AH Header

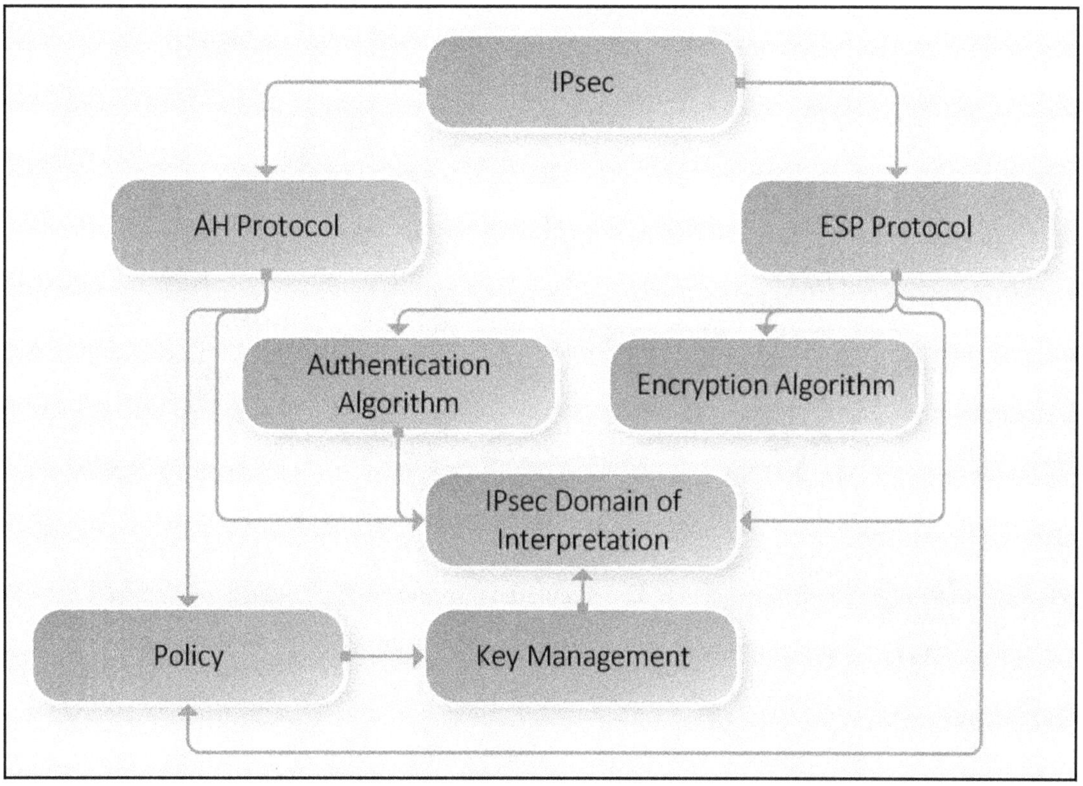

Figure 3-11: IPsec Architecture

Case Study

Consider a scenario, where University "X" has a main campus in New York and branch campuses in California and San Jose. In the current network architecture, all sites are connected to Internet via respective internet service providers. However, the recent project of "Secure and Smart Universities" intends to secure and centralize the sensitive database system of university. During the financial meeting of board, it has been decided to deploy ASA firewall on the edge of main campus while using VPN connections with branch campuses for secure data transaction.

Lab 3.1: Implementation of IPsec site-to-site VPN between Cisco routers with pre-shared key authentication using Command Line Interface

IPsec site-to-site VPN is normally used to connect remote branches with corporate office or with other remote sites. Configured on edge devices (either router or firewall), IPsec VPN is invisible to the end-user from implementation point of view.

This topology will be used in the lab to implement this concept:

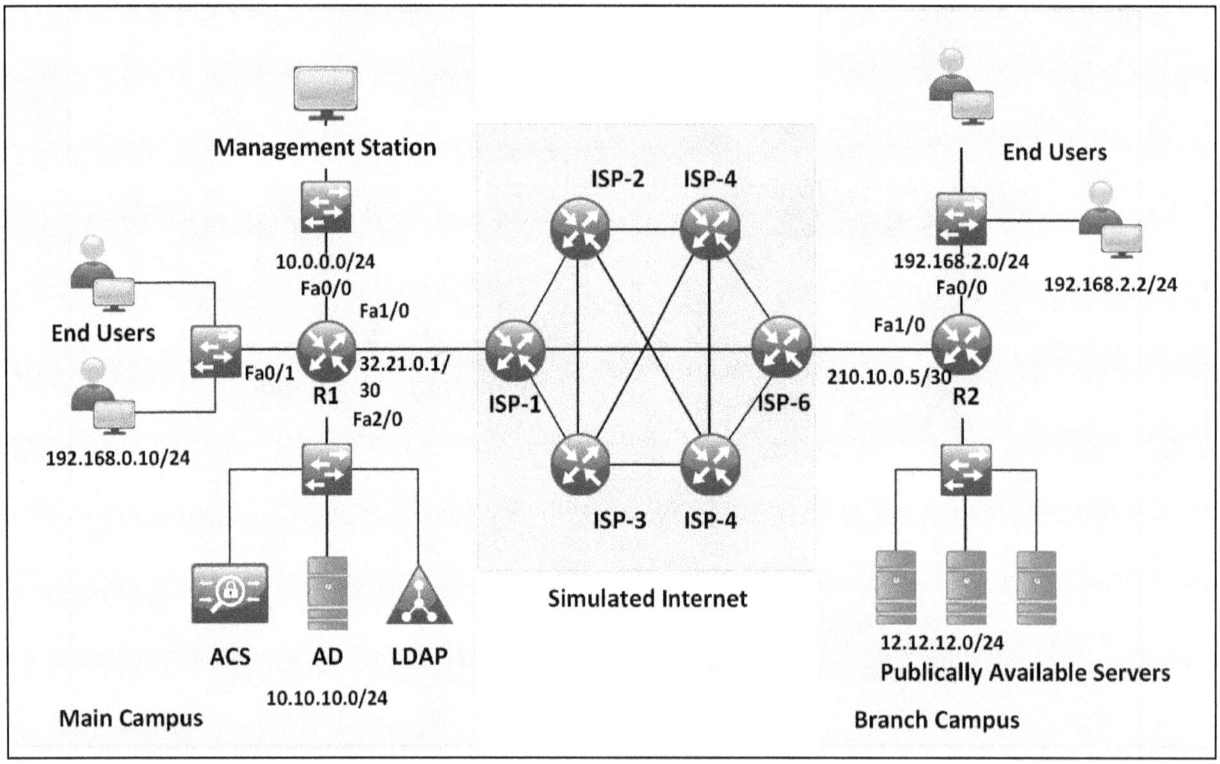

Figure 3-12: Lab 3.1 Topology for IPsec VPN Site to Site Implementation

In the diagram shown above, IPsec VPN will be established between end-users of corporate and remote offices. Every other traffic will flow without any encryption and hashing. IP scheme within Simulated Public Internet is also described in above figure. For example, first two octets are configured as <ISP-A><ISP-B> where A is smallest number of two ISPs followed by second ISP's number. As an example, the link between ISP3 and ISP2 will have an IP address from 23.23.0.0/30. Cisco's proprietary protocol *EIGRP* will be used within internet cloud for dynamic routing. All the concepts learned in previous sections and labs (Password policies etc.) will also be applied in this lab.

In the first part after initial configuration, IPsec VPN will be implemented between remote users followed by the verification section.

Basic IP configuration along with dynamic routing protocol (EIGRP) will be configured on the given topology. Password scheme along with access rights (as discussed in the previous chapter) will be used. Just to recall, that only 10.0.0.1 is allowed to remotely login networking devices. Similarly, a username of ***IPSpecialist*** with secret password of ***P@$$word:10*** has been defined on all routers.

Enable secret password is also ***P@$$word:10***.

If we try to traceroute publically available servers from management station, we should see that packet is going through several hops before hitting the destination.

Traceroute result from a management station is shown below:

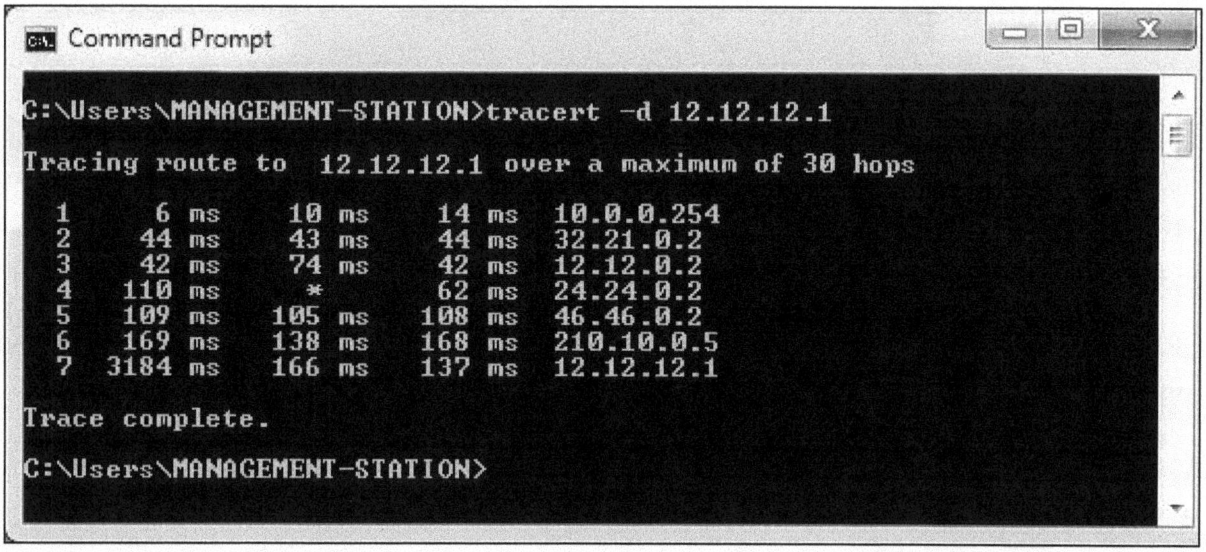

Command Prompt
C:\Users\MANAGEMENT-STATION>tracert -d 12.12.12.1
Tracing route to 12.12.12.1 over a maximum of 30 hops
1 6 ms 10 ms 14 ms 10.0.0.254
2 44 ms 43 ms 44 ms 32.21.0.2
3 42 ms 74 ms 42 ms 12.12.0.2
4 110 ms * 62 ms 24.24.0.2
5 109 ms 105 ms 108 ms 46.46.0.2
6 169 ms 138 ms 168 ms 210.10.0.5
7 3184 ms 166 ms 137 ms 12.12.12.1
Trace complete.
C:\Users\MANAGEMENT-STATION>

Similarly, when we try to ping remote LAN either from management station or from corporate LAN, packets will be dropped by first hop as both LAN networks are not introduced in EIGRP. This is the point, which whole lab surrounds. By using IPsec VPN tunnel, we should be able to reach both LANs by encrypting the IPheader as well as data of both LANs by using publically reachable addresses over the internet.

```
Command Prompt
Microsoft Windows [Version 6.1.7600]
Copyright (c) 2009 Microsoft Corporation.  All rights reserved.

C:\Users\MANAGEMENT-STATION>tracert -d 192.168.2.1

Tracing route to 192.168.2.1 over a maximum of 30 hops

  1    14 ms     4 ms    21 ms  10.0.0.254
  2     *        *        *     Request timed out.
  3     *        *        *     Request timed out.
  4     *        *
```

According to the lab's objective, data from management or end-user LAN to publically available servers should be visible to everyone while traffic to remote LAN should be encrypted and hashed by using IPsec site to site VPN configuration on R1 and R2 routers.

Let us access the R1 router from management station.

R1

Let us create GRE tunnel first to establish point-to-point connection between remote sites.

GRE is a tunnelling protocol and helps to encapsulate many protocols inside IP based tunnels.

A separate subnet will be used for GRE tunnel between R1 and R2. Let us assume 13.13.13.0/30 to be the subnet with the first IP assigned on R1.

```
R1(config)# interface tunnel 12
R1(config-if)# ip address 13.13.13.1 255.255.255.252
R1(config-if)# tunnel mode gre ip
R1(config-if)# tunnel source FastEthernet1/0
R1(config-if)# tunnel destination 210.10.0.5
R1(config-if)# no shutdown
```

Introduce the tunnel 12 network in eigrp.

```
R1(config)# router eigrp 1
R1(config-router)# network 13.13.13.1 0.0.0.3
```

Configuration of IPsec VPN starts from now.

First IKE phase 1 configuration will be performed by using *crypto isakmp* command.

ISAKMP stands for Internet Security Association Key Management Protocol. As the name suggest, it is used for the security and authenticity of pre-shared key defined on both IPsec secure peers.

"Crypto isakmp policy" command defines the different security algorithms used for securing pre-shared key while *"crypto isakmp key"* is used to define the pre-shared key as shown below:

```
R1(config)# crypto isakmp policy 1
R1(config-isakmp)# hash md5
R1(config-isakmp)# encryption des
R1(config-isakmp)# group 2
R1(config-isakmp)# lifetime 3600
R1(config-isakmp)# authentication pre-share
```

The commands above show crypto isakmp policy with locally assigned number of 1, which is defined to use *DES* as encryption algorithm, *MD5* as hashing algorithm, a lifetime period of 3,600 seconds and DH-group of 2. DH-group needs to be same on both sides as it is internally used by IPsec process for transfer and authenticity of pre-shared key.

In the next step, pre-shared key is defined by the following command:

```
R1(config)# crypto isakmp key IPSpecialist:10 address 210.10.0.5
```

Above command shows ***IPSpecialist:10*** as pre-shared key or password between R1 and R2. This password also needs to be same on both IPsec secured peers for IPsec VPN to work. If basic connectivity is good and we can ping 210.10.0.5 from R1 and passwords and above commands are also configured correctly on both R1 and R2 (explained later on) then IKE phase 1 would succeed, followed by generation of second tunnel from securing end user data.

"***crypto IPsec transform-set***" command is used to define the transform set (explained in theoretical portion), which defines the security algorithms used for encryption and hashing of end-user data.

```
R1(config)# crypto IPsec transform-set IPSEC-TRANSFORMSET esp-des esp-md5-hmac
```

The command above shows the definition of *IPSEC-TRANSFORMSET* named transform-set with *DES* and *MD5* as encryption and hashing algorithms respectively. It is a significant name and can be defined suitable to one's understanding. By default, Tunnel mode is selected for IPsec VPN connection type. Tunnel mode means that the whole IP packet (including IP header) will be encapsulated with new IP header by IPsec.

Transform-set is defined now.

Now a specific traffic needs to be defined by using access-list that must be secured by a VPN connection. The following extended access list is defined for VPN connection:

```
R1(config)# ip access-list extended VPN-ACL
R1(config-ext-nacl)# permit ip 192.168.0.0 0.0.0.255 192.168.2.0 0.0.0.255
R1(config-ext-nacl)# permit ip 10.0.0.0 0.0.0.255 192.168.2.0 0.0.0.255
R1(config-ext-nacl)# exit
```

A Crypto map is the last step of configuring IPsec site-to-site VPN.

In crypto-map configuration, IPsec secures VPN peer's address along with desired traffic matched by ACL is defined.

After defining crypto-map, VPN will start working whenever traffic goes out of interface on which this crypto map will be applied.

```
R1(config)# crypto map IPSEC-CRYPTOMAP 1 IPsec-isakmp
% NOTE: This new crypto map will remain disabled until a peer and a valid access list have been configured.
R1(config-crypto-map)# set peer 210.10.0.5
R1(config-crypto-map)#  set transform-set IPSEC-TRANSFORMSET
R1(config-crypto-map)#  match address VPN-ACL
R1(config-crypto-map)#  exit
```

Now this crypto map must be applied on interface tunnel 12 by following command.

```
R1(config)# interface tunnel 12
R1(config-if)# crypto map IPSEC-CRYPTOMAP
R1(config-if)# exit
```

Add static route for 192.168.2.0/24 with tunnel 12 as exit interface.

```
R1(config)# ip route 192.168.2.0 255.255.255.0 13.13.13.2
```

R2

Now, the same set of commands will be configured on R2 router.

```
R2(config)# interface tunnel 12
R2(config-if)# ip address 13.13.13.2 255.255.255.252
R2(config-if)# tunnel  mode gre ip
R2(config-if)# tunnel source FastEthernet1/0
R2(config-if)# tunnel destination 32.21.0.1
R2(config-if)# no shutdown
R2(config-if)# exit

R2(config)# router eigrp 1
R2(config-router)# network 13.13.13.2 0.0.0.3
R2(config-router)# exit

R2(config)# crypto isakmp policy 1
R2(config-isakmp)# encryption des
R2(config-isakmp)# hash md5
R2(config-isakmp)# lifetime 3600
R2(config-isakmp)# group 2
R2(config-isakmp)# authentication pre-share
R2(config-isakmp)# exit

R2(config)# crypto isakmp key IPSpecialist:10 address 32.21.0.1
```

```
R2(config)# crypto IPsec transform-set IPSEC-TRANSFORMSET esp-des esp-md5-
hmac
R2(config)# ip access-list extended VPN-ACL
R2(config-ext-nacl)# permit ip 192.168.2.0 0.0.0.255 10.0.0.0 0.0.0.255
R2(config-ext-nacl)# permit ip 192.168.2.0 0.0.0.255 192.168.0.0 0.0.0.255
R2(config-ext-nacl)# exit
R2(config)# crypto map  IPSEC-CRYPTOMAP 1 IPsec-isakmp
R2(config-crypto-map)# set peer 32.21.0.1
R2(config-crypto-map)# set transform-set IPSEC-TRANSFORMSET
R2(config-crypto-map)# match address VPN-ACL
R2(config-crypto-map)# exit
R2(config)# interface tunnel 12
R2(config-if)# crypto map IPSEC-CRYPTOMAP
R2(config-if)# exit
R2(config)# ip route 192.168.0.0 255.255.255.0 13.13.13.1
R2(config)# ip route 10.0.0.0 255.255.255.0 13.13.13.1
```

Verification

By using "***show ip route***" command on any ISPx router, it is clear that only IPsec secured peer routers know about 192.168.x.x networks. ISP routers only know about the GRE tunnel network. Traffic going to and from 192168.x.x network is encrypted and hashed so it is invisible to ISPx routers.

"***show crypto isakmp sa***" command can be used to check the status of security association, in other words the status of IKE Phase 1. It should show the ACTIVE in column named status.

```
10.0.0.254 - PuTTY
login as: IPSpecialist
Using keyboard-interactive authentication.
Password:

R1>en
Password:
R1#sho cy
R1#sho cry
R1#sho crypto is
R1#sho crypto isakmp sa
IPv4 Crypto ISAKMP SA
dst             src             state          conn-id status
13.13.13.2      13.13.13.1      QM_IDLE           1003 ACTIVE

IPv6 Crypto ISAKMP SA

R1#
```

*"**show crypto isakmp policy**"* command can be used to verify the security algorithms configure on both routers for IKE phase1 negotiation.

```
10.0.0.254 - PuTTY
R1#
R1#show crypto isakmp policy

Global IKE policy
Protection suite of priority 1
        encryption algorithm:   DES - Data Encryption Standard (56 bit keys).
        hash algorithm:         Message Digest 5
        authentication method:  Pre-Shared Key
        Diffie-Hellman group:   #2 (1024 bit)
        lifetime:               3600 seconds, no volume limit
R1#
```

The figure above shows that DES and MD5 are configured as encryption and hashing algorithm for IKE phase 1. It should match on both peers, otherwise the state of security association (*Show crypto isakmp sa*) will not be ACTIVE.

"show crypto map" is also a very handy command, which can be used to verify the *transform-set* settings along with the interface on which crypto map is applied.

```
10.0.0.254 - PuTTY
R1#sho crypto map
Crypto Map IPv4 "IPSEC-CRYPTOMAP" 1 ipsec-isakmp
        Peer = 13.13.13.2
        Extended IP access list VPN-ACL
          access-list VPN-ACL permit ip 192.168.0.0 0.0.0.255 192.168.2.0 0.0.0.255

          access-list VPN-ACL permit ip 10.0.0.0 0.0.0.255 192.168.2.0 0.0.0.255

        Current peer: 13.13.13.2
        Security association lifetime: 4608000 kilobytes/3600 seconds
        Responder-Only (Y/N): N
        PFS (Y/N): N
        Transform sets={
                IPSEC-TRANSFORMSET:  { esp-des esp-md5-hmac  } ,
        }
        Interfaces using crypto map IPSEC-CRYPTOMAP:
                Tunnel12
```

The output above shows that crypto map is applied on interface tunnel 12 with DES and MD5 as encryption and hashing algorithms. It also shows the VPN is being used to categorize the traffic being qualified for VPN connection. It can be seen from above figure that only desired traffic is sent over the VPN connection. Remaining traffic goes straight in to the simulated internet cloud without any alteration. This concept is also known as Split-Tunnelling.

"Show crypto session" command can be used to check the current active VPN sessions as shown below:

```
10.0.0.254 - PuTTY

R1#sho crypto se
R1#sho crypto session
Crypto session current status

Interface: Tunnel12
Session status: UP-NO-IKE
Peer: 13.13.13.2 port 500
  IPSEC FLOW: permit ip 192.168.0.0/255.255.255.0 192.168.2.0/255.255.255.0
        Active SAs: 0, origin: crypto map
  IPSEC FLOW: permit ip 10.0.0.0/255.255.255.0 192.168.2.0/255.255.255.0
        Active SAs: 2, origin: crypto map

R1#
```

Similarly, *"debug crypto"* command allows packet level debugging of different negotiation.

Lab 3.2: Implementation of IPsec Site-to-Site VPN Between Cisco Router and ASA Firewall with Pre-Shared Key Authentication

In this lab, the main objective remains the same. The only change in this lab is that R1 is replaced by ASA Firewall. Configuration of ASA firewall will be done via Adaptive Security Device Manager (ASDM) and CLI while the configuration of R2 router and other devices remains the same.

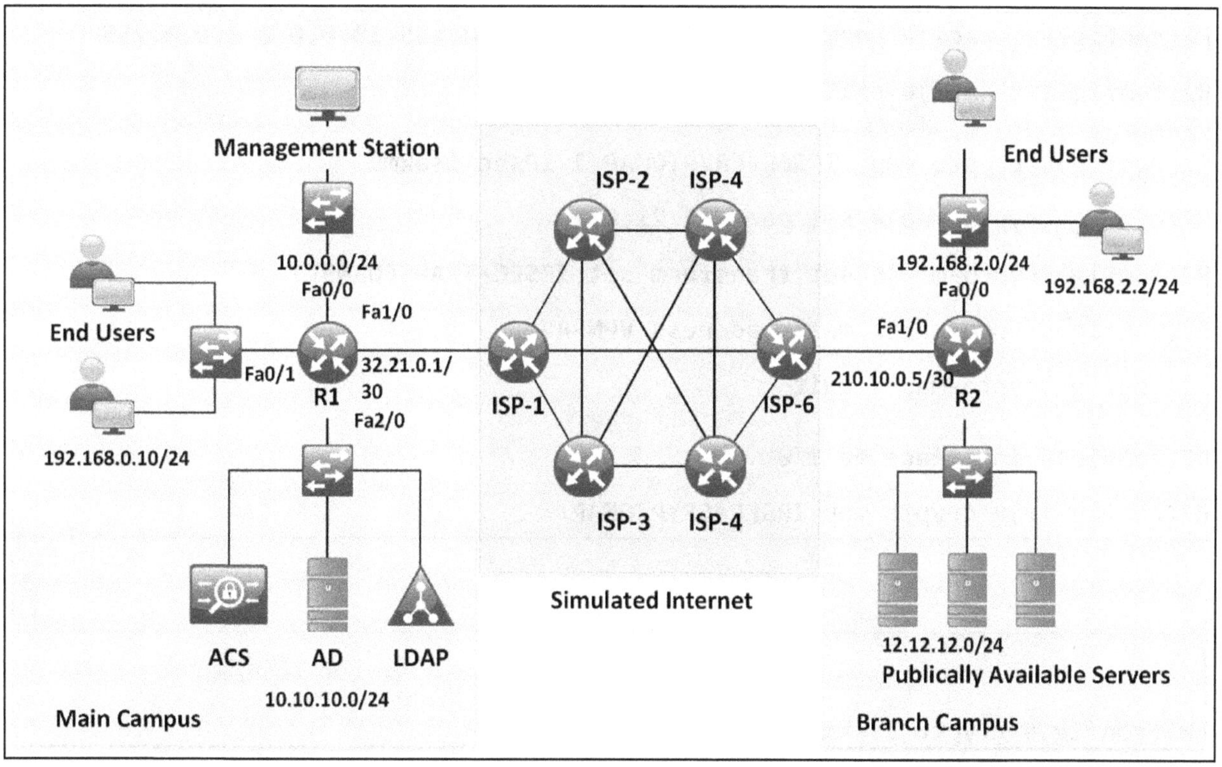

Figure 3-13: Lab 3.2 Topology

R2

In the previous lab, the key concepts were briefly explained as far as IPsec VPN is concerned. In this lab, a quick configuration section of R2 will be done followed by the configuration on FW1 as well.

```
R2(config)# crypto isakmp policy 1
R2(config-isakmp)# encryption des
R2(config-isakmp)# hash md5
R2(config-isakmp)# lifetime 3600
```

```
R2(config-isakmp)# group 2
R2(config-isakmp)# authentication pre-share
R2(config-isakmp)# exit
R2(config)# crypto isakmp key IPSpecialist:10 address 32.21.0.1
R2(config)# crypto IPsec transform-set IPSEC-TRANSFORMSET esp-des esp-md5
R2(config)# ip access-list extended VPN-ACL
R2(config-ext-nacl)# permit ip 192.168.2.0 0.0.0.255 10.0.0.0 0.0.0.255
R2(config-ext-nacl)# exit
R2(config)# crypto map  IPSEC-CRYPTOMAP 1 IPsec-isakmp
R2(config-crypto-map)# set peer 32.21.0.1
R2(config-crypto-map)# set transform-set IPSEC-TRANSFORMSET
R2(config-crypto-map)# match address VPN-ACL
R2(config-crypto-map)# exit
R2(config)# interface fa 1/0
R2(config-if)# crypto map IPSEC-CRYPTOMAP
```

FW1

```
FW1(config)# crypto isakmp policy 1
FW1(config-ikev1-policy)# encryption des
FW1(config-ikev1-policy)# hash md5
FW1(config-ikev1-policy)# lifetime 3600
FW1(config-ikev1-policy)# group 2
FW1(config-ikev1-policy)# authentication pre-share
FW1(config-ikev1-policy)# exit
```

In order to define the crypto pre-shared key associated with certain peer, the following syntax will be used.

```
FW1(config)# tunnel-group 210.10.0.5 type IPsec-l2l
FW1(config)# tunnel-group 210.10.0.5 IPsec-attributes
FW1(config-tunnel-IPsec)# ikev1 pre-shared-key IPSpecialist:10
```

```
FW1(config-tunnel-IPsec)# exit
```

The first command defines the type of tunnel group "210.10.0.5" to be IPSEC site-to-site while the second command along with its sub configuration defines the pre-shared password for IKE Phase 1.

Now, the transform set needs to be defined.

```
FW1(config)# crypto IPsec ikev1 transform-set IPSEC-TRANSFORMSET  esp-des esp-md5-hmac

FW1(config)# access-list VPN-ACL extended permit ip 10.0.0.0 255.255.255.0 192 .168.2.0 255.255.255.0
```

In the last step, crypto map needs to be defined and applied on the outside interface with the following syntax.

```
FW1(config)# crypto map IPSEC-CRYPTOMAP 10 set peer 210.10.0.5

FW1(config)# crypto map IPSEC-CRYPTOMAP 10 set ikev1 transform-set IPSEC-TRANSFORMSET

FW1(config)# crypto map IPSEC-CRYPTOMAP 10 match address VPN-ACL

FW1(config)# crypto map IPSEC-CRYPTOMAP interface outside
```

Unlike Cisco IOS, in ASA the following command needs to be issued in order for IKE process to start working.

```
FW1(config)# crypto ikev1 enable outside
```

Similarly, in ASA, traffic flows from high to low security level, traffic is denied by default. In order to allow access from 192.168.2.0/24 network to 10.0.0.0/24 network, define the following access list and apply it on the outside interface.

```
FW1(config)# access-list 100 permit ip 192.168.2.0 255.255.255.0 10.0.0.0 255.255.255.0

FW1(config)# interface ethernet 2

FW1(config-if)# access-group 100 in interface outside
```

The above command creates an extended ACL and applies on the outside interface with inward direction.

Verification

In order to verify the basic step, you will need to ping an IP address from 192.168.2.0/24 network from the management station. If everything is working correctly, then ping test will be successful. As, shown below:

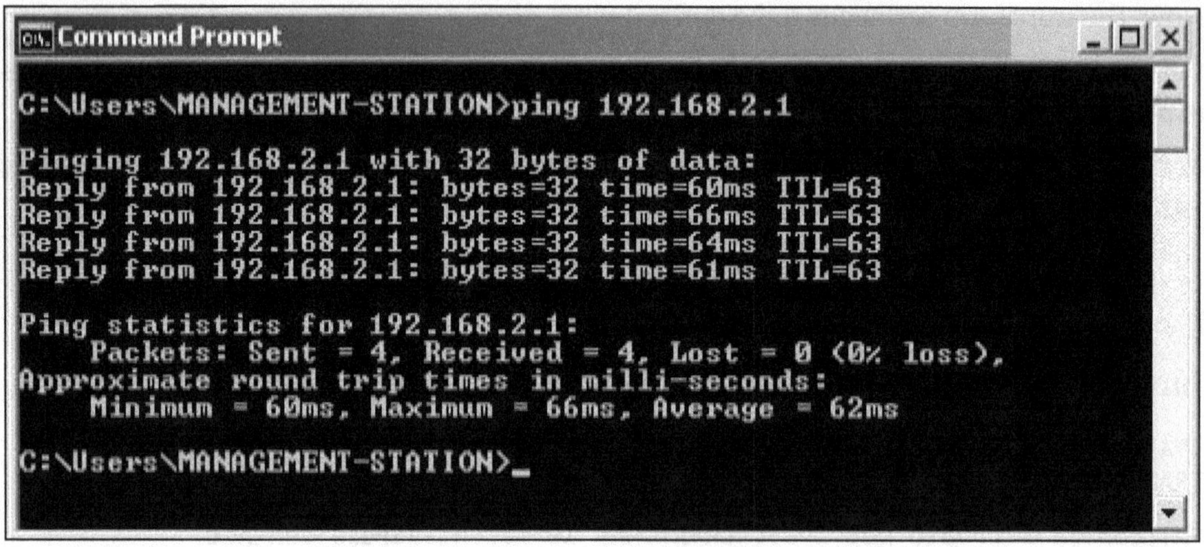

```
Command Prompt
C:\Users\MANAGEMENT-STATION>ping 192.168.2.1

Pinging 192.168.2.1 with 32 bytes of data:
Reply from 192.168.2.1: bytes=32 time=60ms TTL=63
Reply from 192.168.2.1: bytes=32 time=66ms TTL=63
Reply from 192.168.2.1: bytes=32 time=64ms TTL=63
Reply from 192.168.2.1: bytes=32 time=61ms TTL=63

Ping statistics for 192.168.2.1:
    Packets: Sent = 4, Received = 4, Lost = 0 (0% loss),
Approximate round trip times in milli-seconds:
    Minimum = 60ms, Maximum = 66ms, Average = 62ms

C:\Users\MANAGEMENT-STATION>_
```

The "***show crypto isakmp sa***" command can be used to see the current status of Security Association (SA) database. If negotiation between R2 and FW1 is successful, then it should appear as ACTIVE in the command's output as shown below:

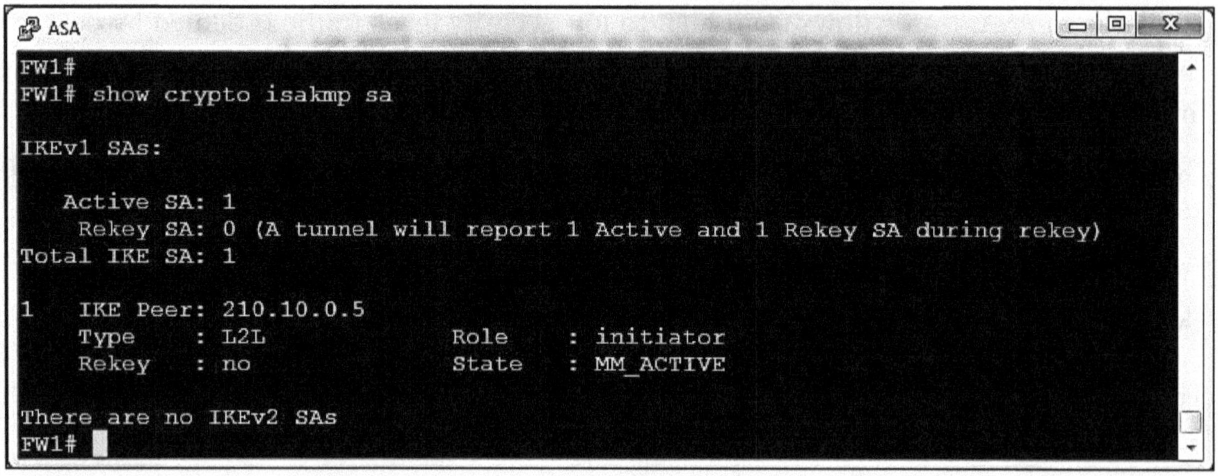

```
ASA
FW1#
FW1# show crypto isakmp sa

IKEv1 SAs:

   Active SA: 1
    Rekey SA: 0 (A tunnel will report 1 Active and 1 Rekey SA during rekey)
Total IKE SA: 1

1   IKE Peer: 210.10.0.5
    Type    : L2L               Role    : initiator
    Rekey   : no                State   : MM_ACTIVE

There are no IKEv2 SAs
FW1#
```

"***Show vpn-sessiondb***" is also another very important command, which can be used to check the total VPN sessions, which are terminated at ASA, as shown below:

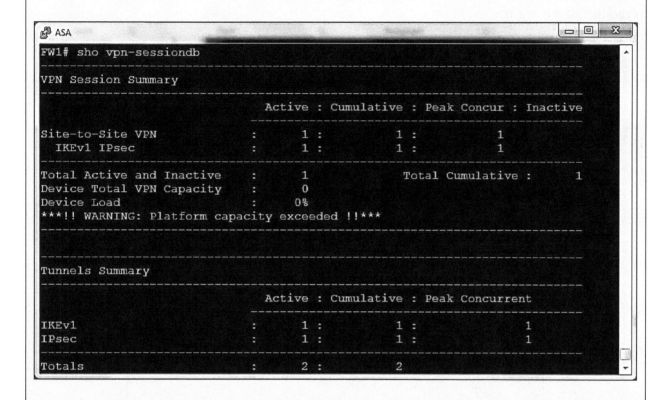

```
FW1# sho vpn-sessiondb
---------------------------------------------------------------------------
VPN Session Summary
---------------------------------------------------------------------------
                              Active : Cumulative : Peak Concur : Inactive
                            -----------------------------------------------
Site-to-Site VPN            :      1 :          1 :           1
  IKEv1 IPsec               :      1 :          1 :           1
---------------------------------------------------------------------------
Total Active and Inactive   :      1             Total Cumulative :      1
Device Total VPN Capacity   :      0
Device Load                 :     0%
***!! WARNING: Platform capacity exceeded !!***
---------------------------------------------------------------------------


---------------------------------------------------------------------------
Tunnels Summary
---------------------------------------------------------------------------
                              Active : Cumulative : Peak Concurrent
                            -----------------------------------------------
IKEv1                       :      1 :          1 :               1
IPsec                       :      1 :          1 :               1
---------------------------------------------------------------------------
Totals                      :      2 :          2
```

Similarly, "***show crypto IPsec sa*** *<detail>*" is another command, which comes very handy during the troubleshooting of the VPN connection.

Similarly, "show access-list <access list Name/Number>" can also be used to check whether intended traffic for VPN session is hitting the ACL or not.

```
FW1# show access-list VPN-ACL

access-list VPN-ACL; 1 elements; name hash: 0xb17dd697

access-list VPN-ACL line 1 extended permit ip 10.0.0.0 255.255.255.0 192.168.2.0 255.255.255.0 (hitcnt=33) 0xf1f41dff
```

IPsec-Site-to-Site Implementation via ASDM

In order to perform the above tasks via ASDM, which is GUI based access of Cisco ASA firewall, click pinned to the task bar of management station, use the following credentials for login:

Username: IPSpecialist

Password: P@$$word:10

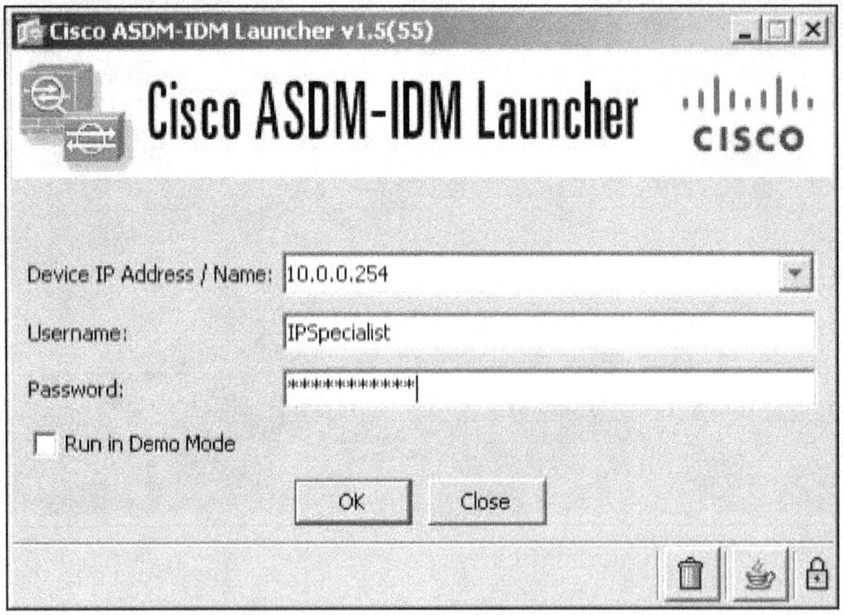

After successful login, the following dashboard should appear:

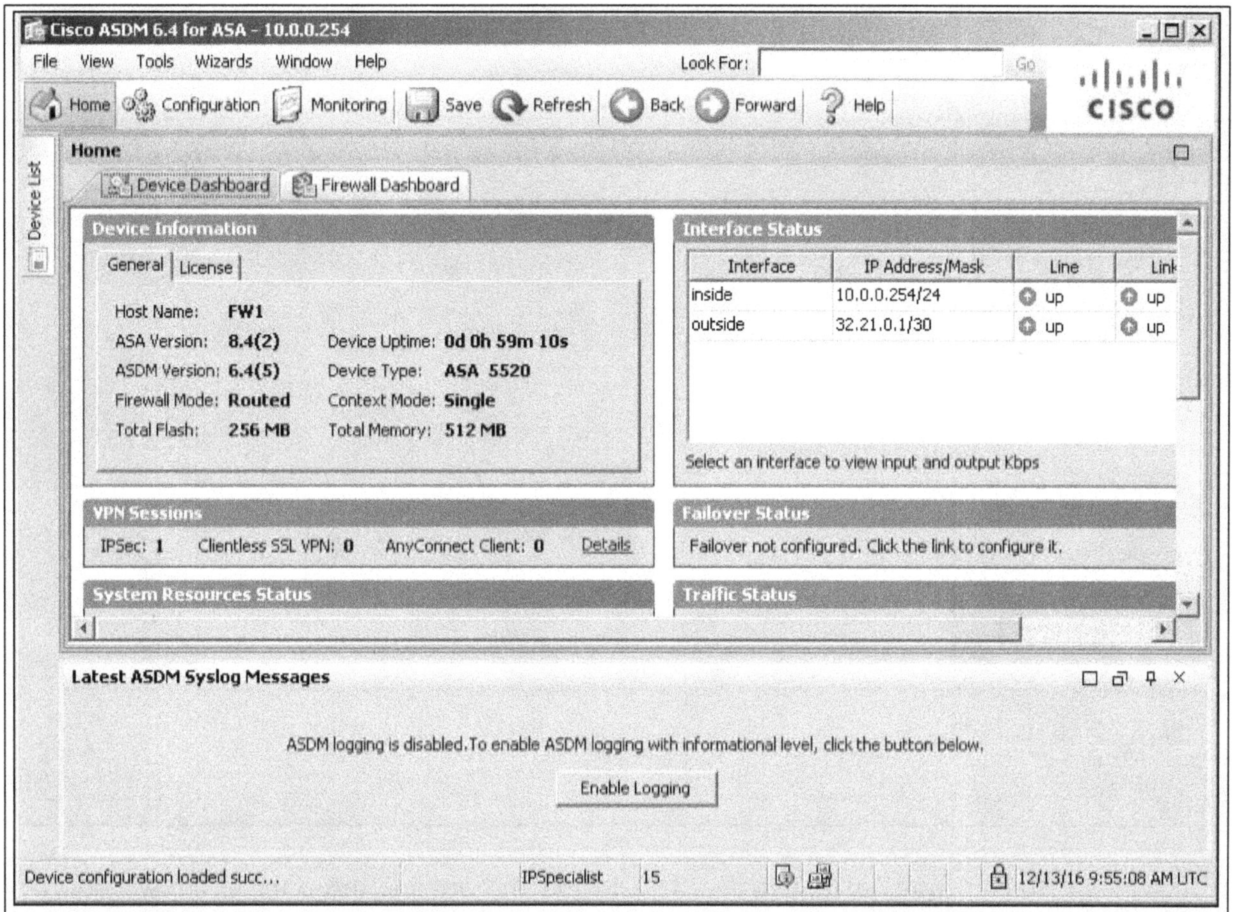

Click "Wizards" -> "VPN Wizards" -> "Site-to-site VPN Wizard" to start an interactive wizard of implementing the above established VPN connection, if CLI is not used for it.

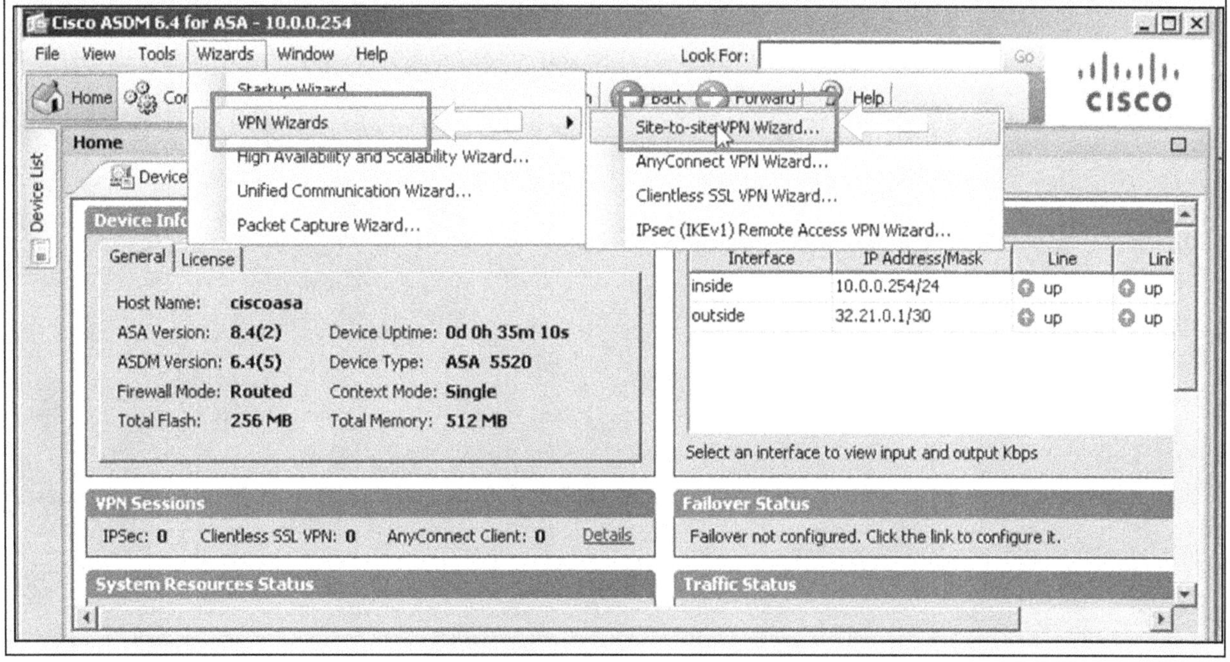

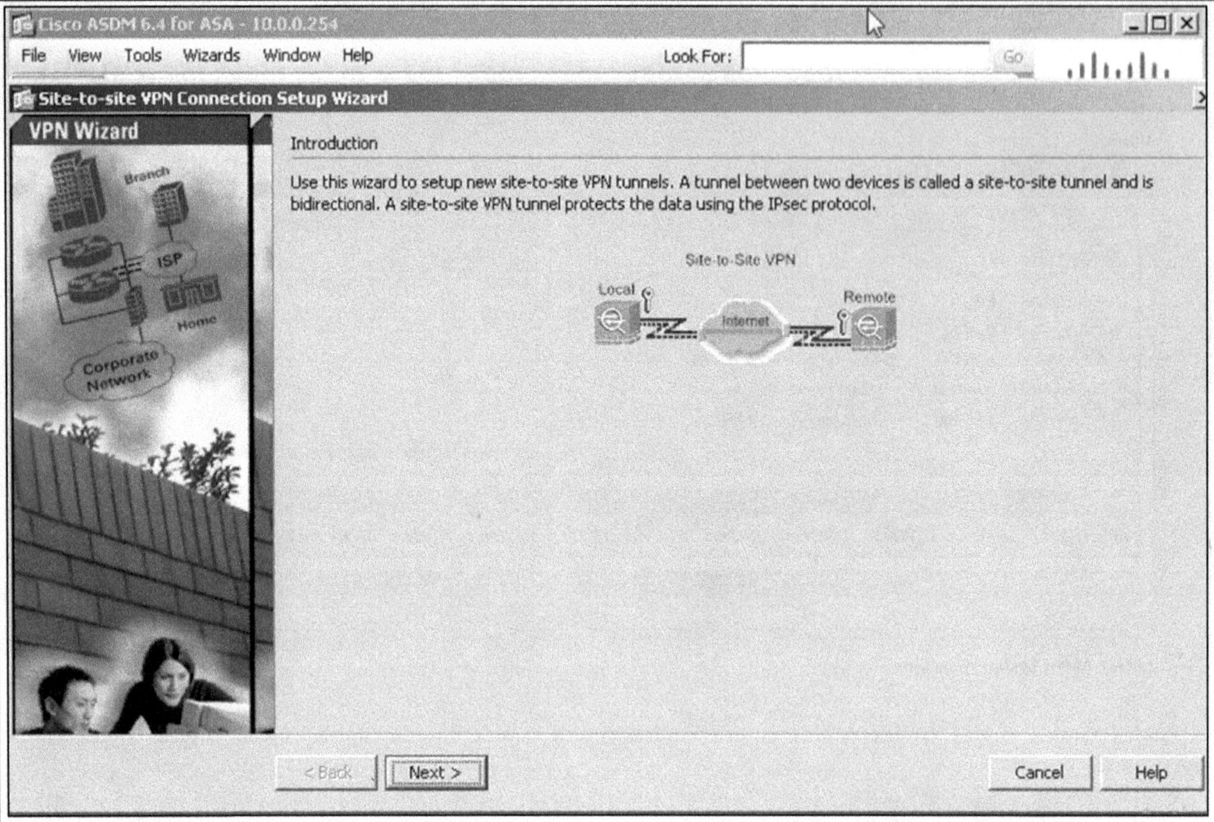

Click "Next" to continue. Enter the peer IP address and outside interface as shown below:

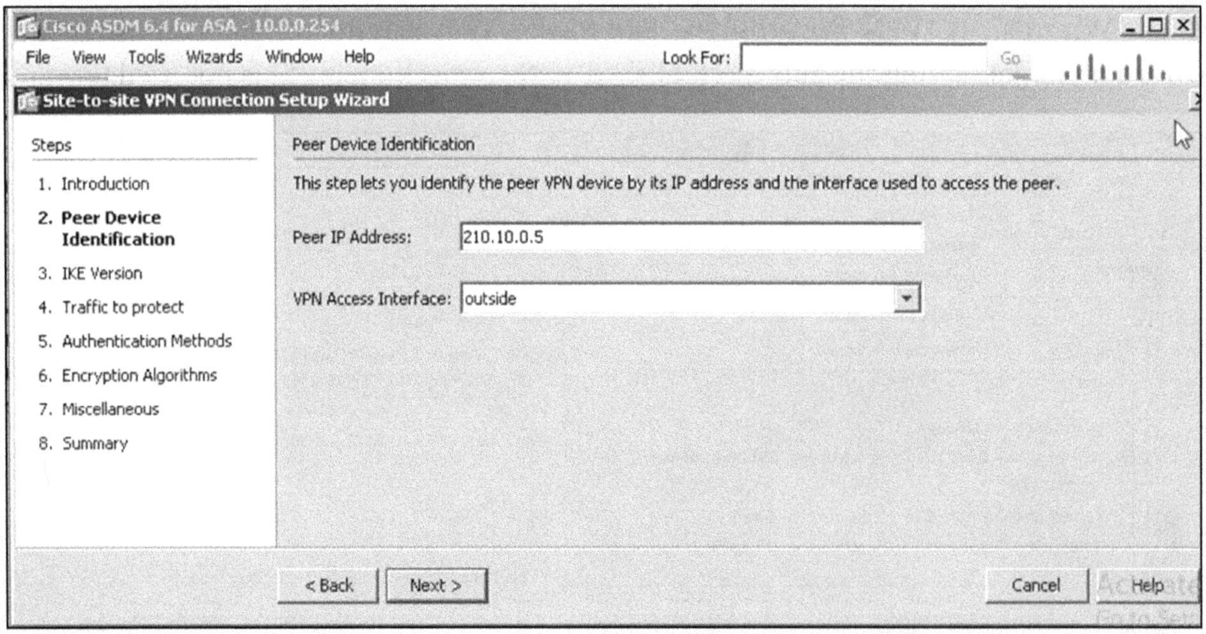

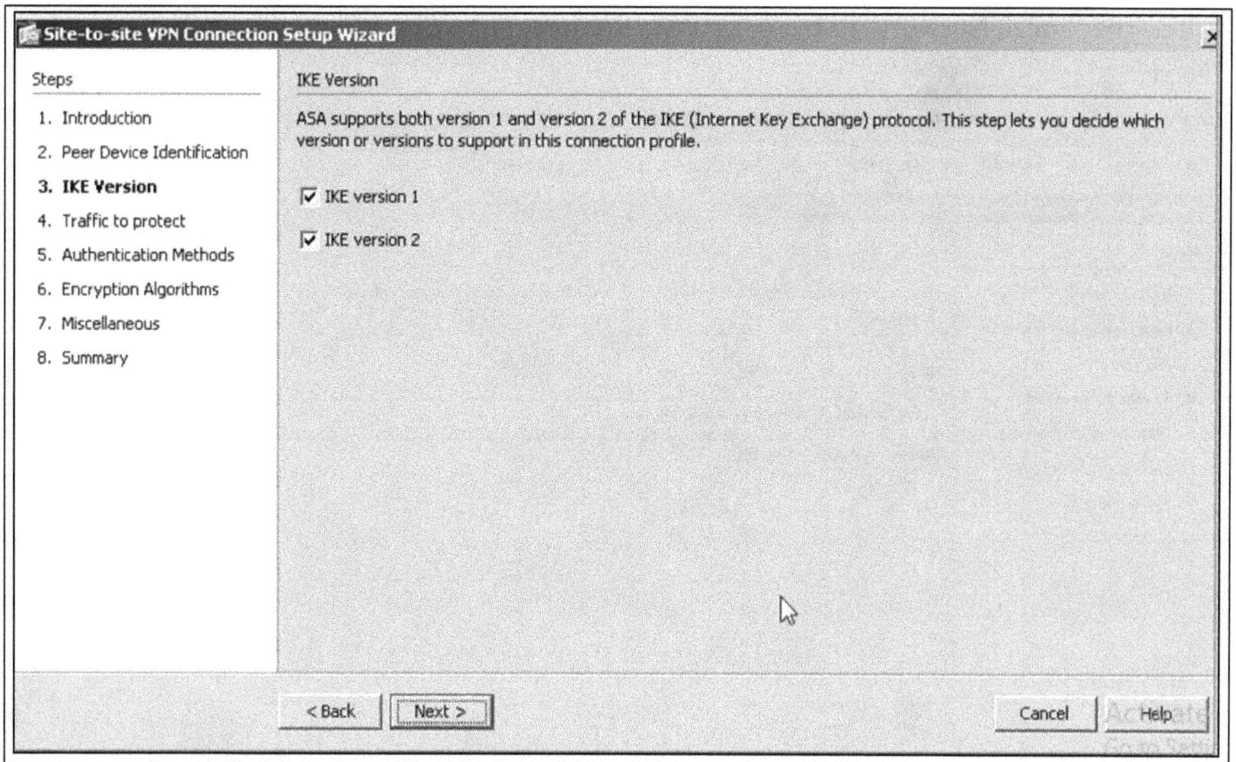

Select "IKE version 1" as it is already used in the CLI configuration of this lab. IKE version 2 has some extra features, which can be reviewed from Cisco website.

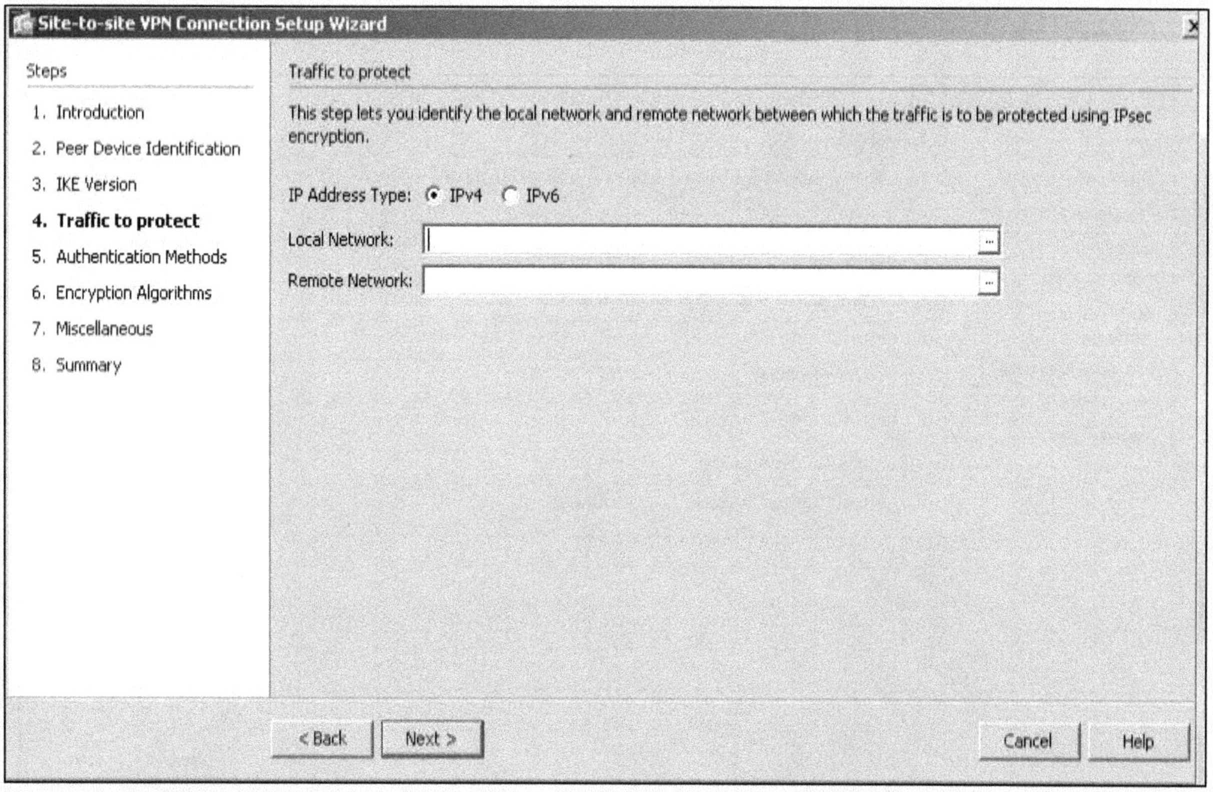

Enter the Local Network 10.0.0.0/24 and Remote Network of 192.168.2.0/24 and click "Next".

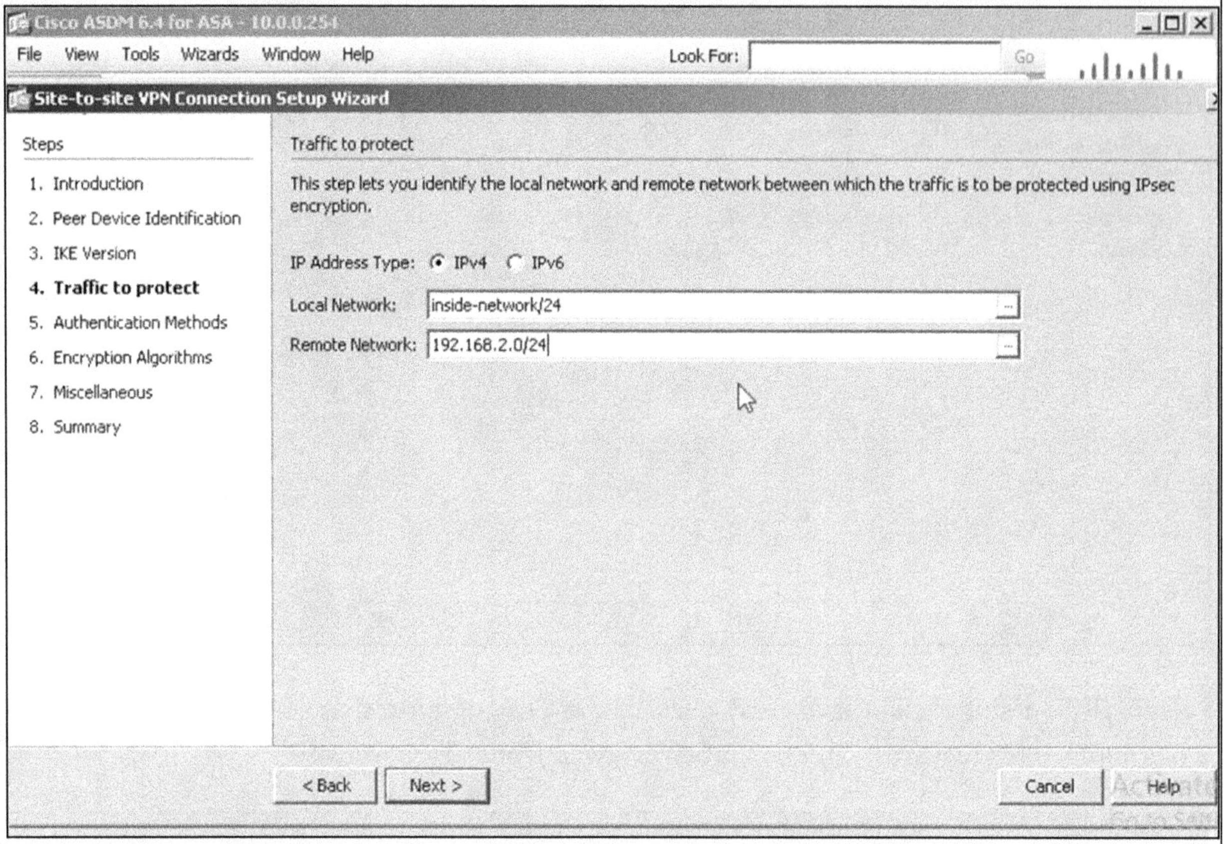

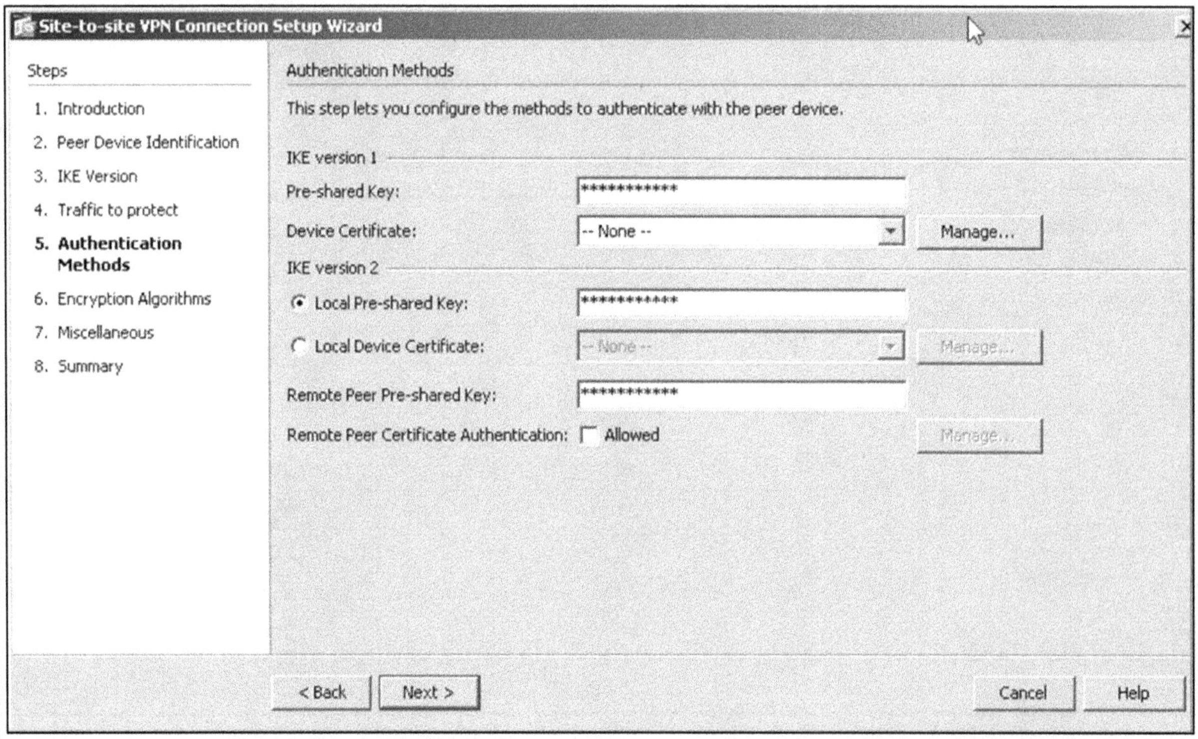

Adjust the IPsec proposal according to the requirements.

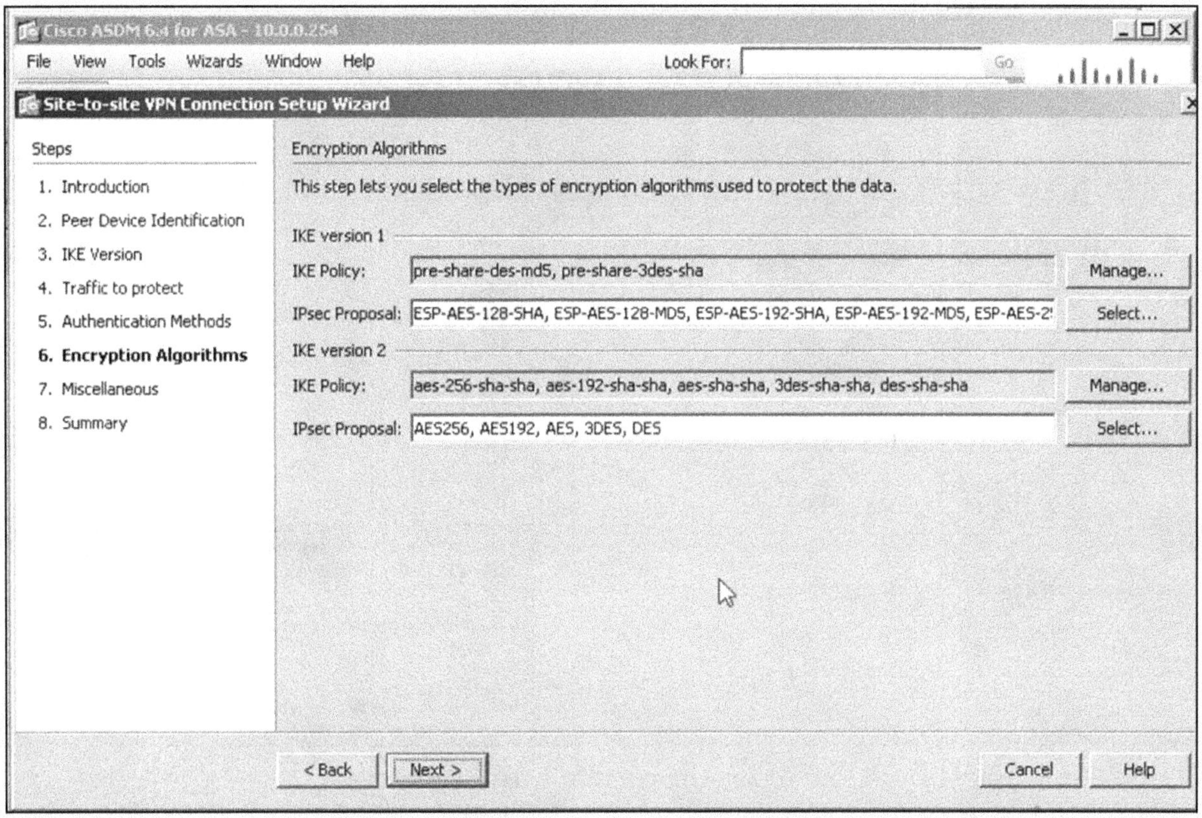

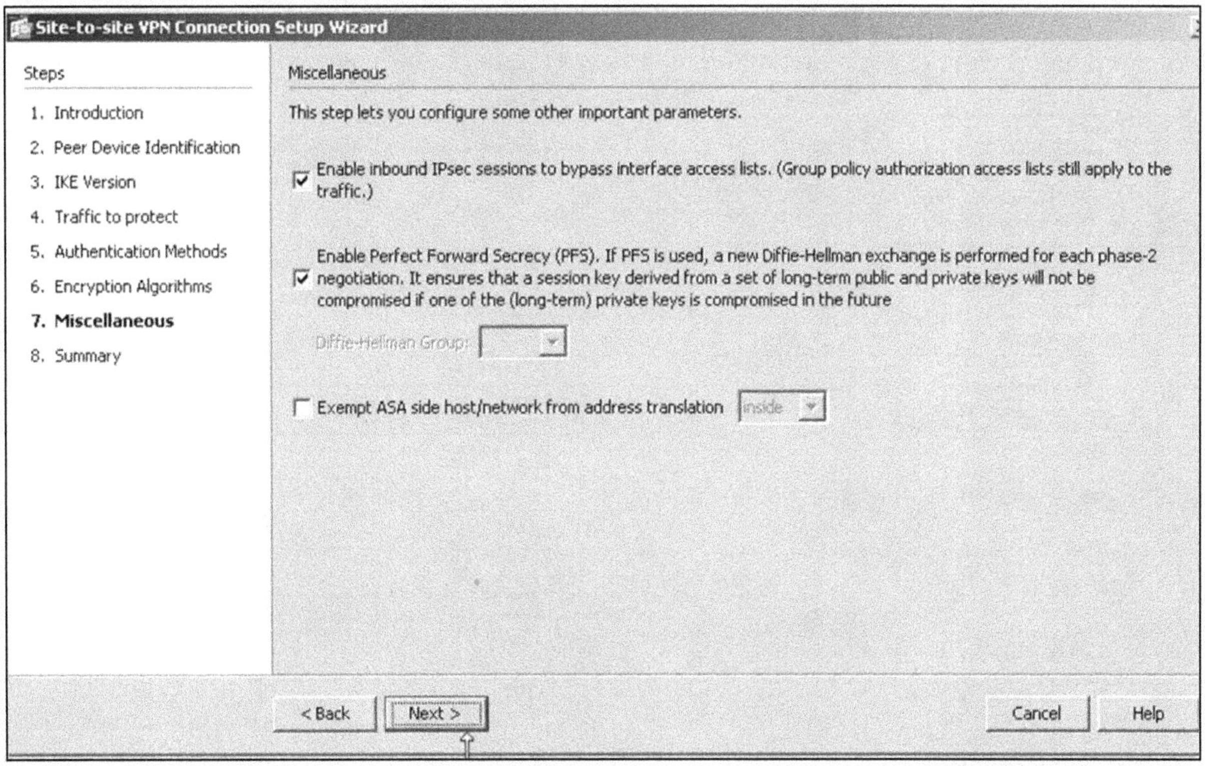

The diagram above shows the miscellaneous settings like exempting NAT etc. Click "Next" to see the summary before finalizing the connection.

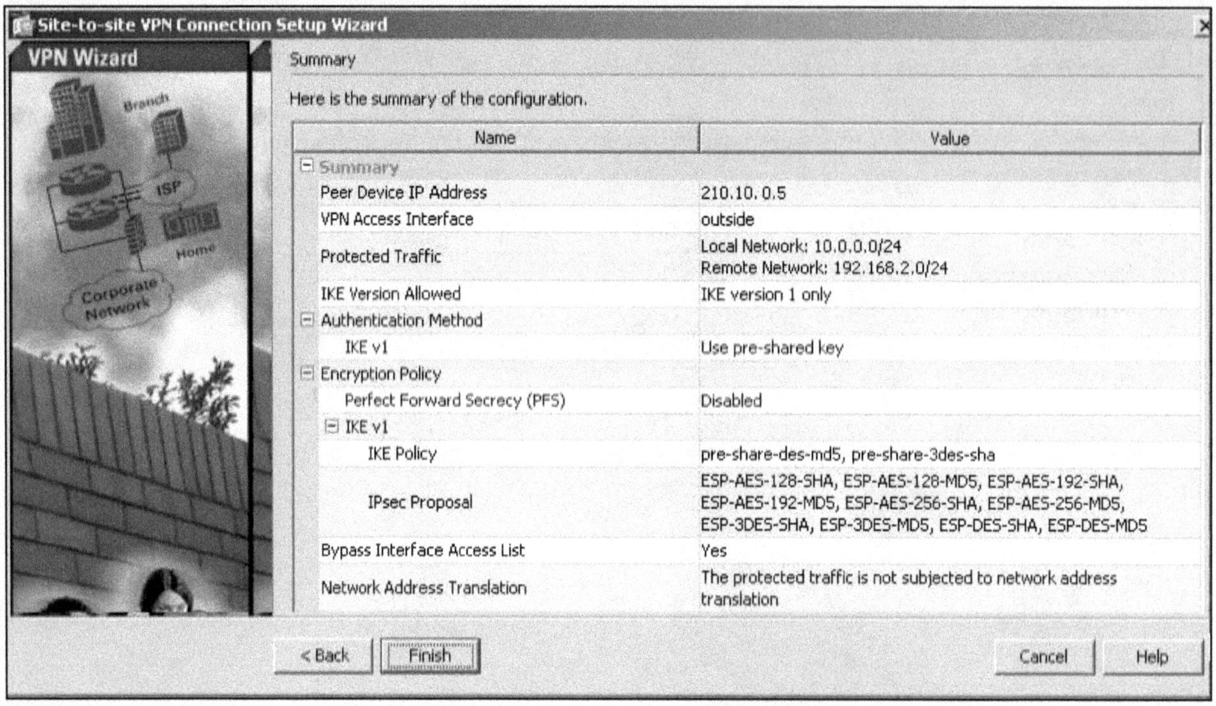

Click "Monitoring" -> "VPN" to see the current active sessions.

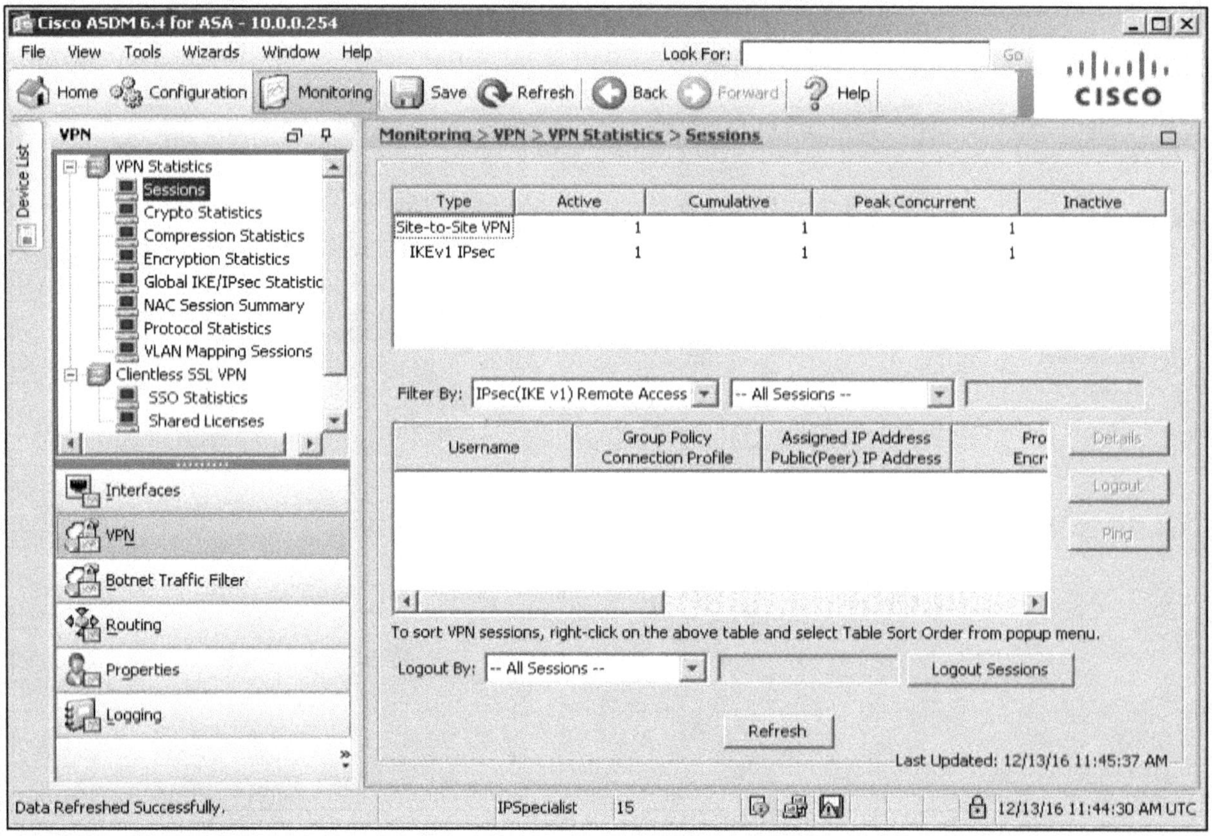

Lab 3.3: Implementation of Remote Access VPN Using CLI and ASDM for Accessing Main Campus from Branch Campus

In this lab, the main objective is to access the main campus network securely from branch office via Remote Access VPN.

The following topology will be used in this lab:

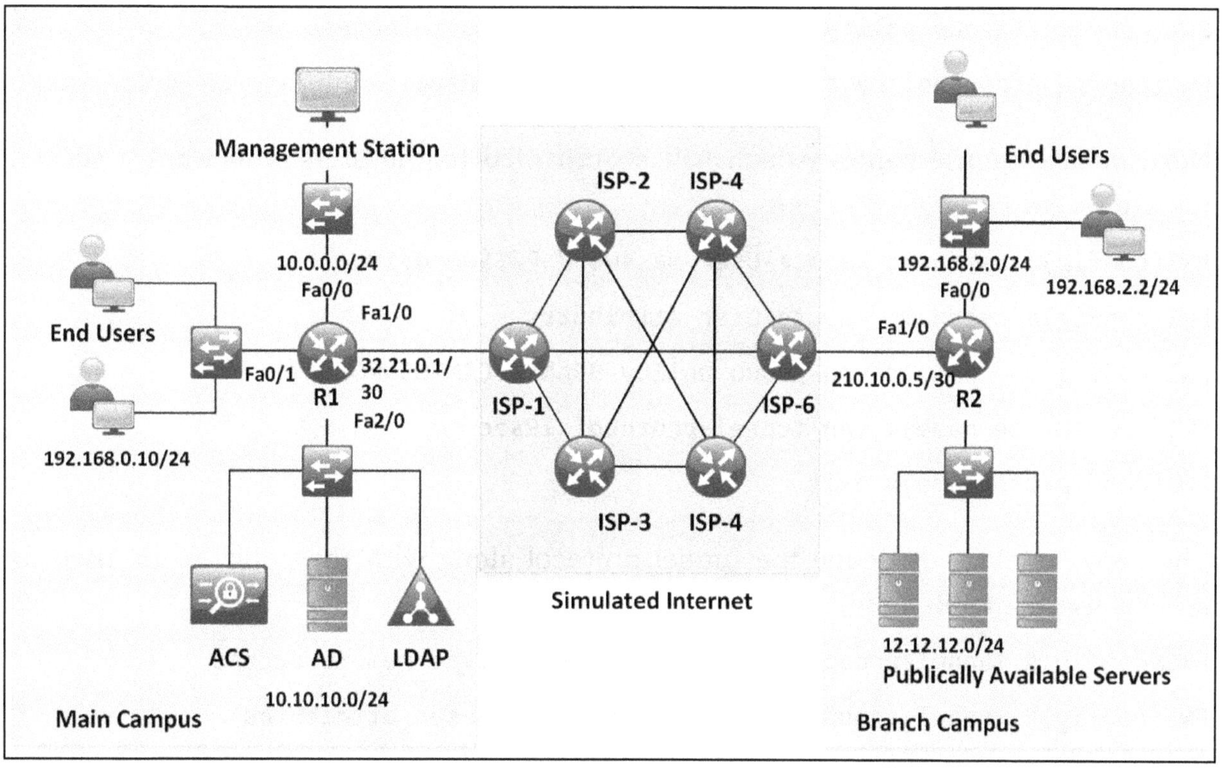

Figure 3-14: Lab 3.3 Topology

In this lab, 10.0.0.0/24 network will be accessed from 192.168.2.0/24 via Remote Access VPN connection.

FW1

```
FW1(config)# crypto isakmp policy 1
FW1(config-ikev1-policy)# encryption des
FW1(config-ikev1-policy)# hash md5
FW1(config-ikev1-policy)# lifetime 3600
FW1(config-ikev1-policy)# group 2
FW1(config-ikev1-policy)# authentication pre-share
```

```
FW1(config-ikev1-policy)# exit
```

Next, define the local pool of IP address for Individual machines who want to connect via remote access VPN.

```
FW1(config)# ip local pool BRANCH-CAMPUS 172.16.0.128-172.16.0.254 mask 255.255.255.0
FW1(config)# group-policy BRANCH-CAMPUS-POLICY internal
FW1(config)# group-policy BRANCH-CAMPUS-POLICY attributes
FW1(config-group-policy)# vpn-tunnel-protocol IPsec
```

Next, create the usernames, which will be provided to the users who want a secured remote access.

```
FW1(config)# username Remote-User password P@$$word:10
FW1(config)# username Remote-User attributes
FW1(config-username)# vpn-group-policy BRANCH-CAMPUS-POLICY
FW1(config-username)# vpn-tunnel-protocol IPsec
FW1(config-username)# exit
```

The above commands define the tunnel protocol along with the policy to be used for specific username "Remote-User".

```
FW1(config)# tunnel-group BRANCH-CAMPUS-GROUP type remote-access
FW1(config)# tunnel-group BRANCH-CAMPUS-GROUP IPsec-attributes
FW1(config-tunnel-IPsec)# pre-shared-key IPSpecialist:10
FW1(config-tunnel-IPsec)# exit

FW1(config)# tunnel-group BRANCH-CAMPUS-GROUP general-attributes
FW1(config-tunnel-general)# address-pool BRANCH-CAMPUS
FW1(config-tunnel-general)# default-group-policy BRANCH-CAMPUS-POLICY
FW1(config)# crypto IPsec ikev1 transform-set BRANCH-CAMPUS esp-des esp-md5-hmac
FW1(config)# crypto dynamic-map BRANCH-CAMPUS 10 set ikev1 transform-set BRANCH-CAMPUS
FW1(config)# crypto map BRANCH-CAMPUS 10 IPsec-isakmp dynamic BRANCH-CAMPUS
FW1(config)# crypto map BRANCH-CAMPUS interface outside
```

The commands above show a tunnel group is created with pre-share key along with specific and general attributes like choice of authentication and encryption protocols. This group along with previously defined username will be used in Cisco any-connect client software for remote access.

In order to enable IKE to start working, issue the following command.

```
FW1(config)# crypto ikev1 enable outside
```

Verification

Open  Cisco VPN Client software on 192.168.2.1, which is the management station of branch campus. The following screen should appear:

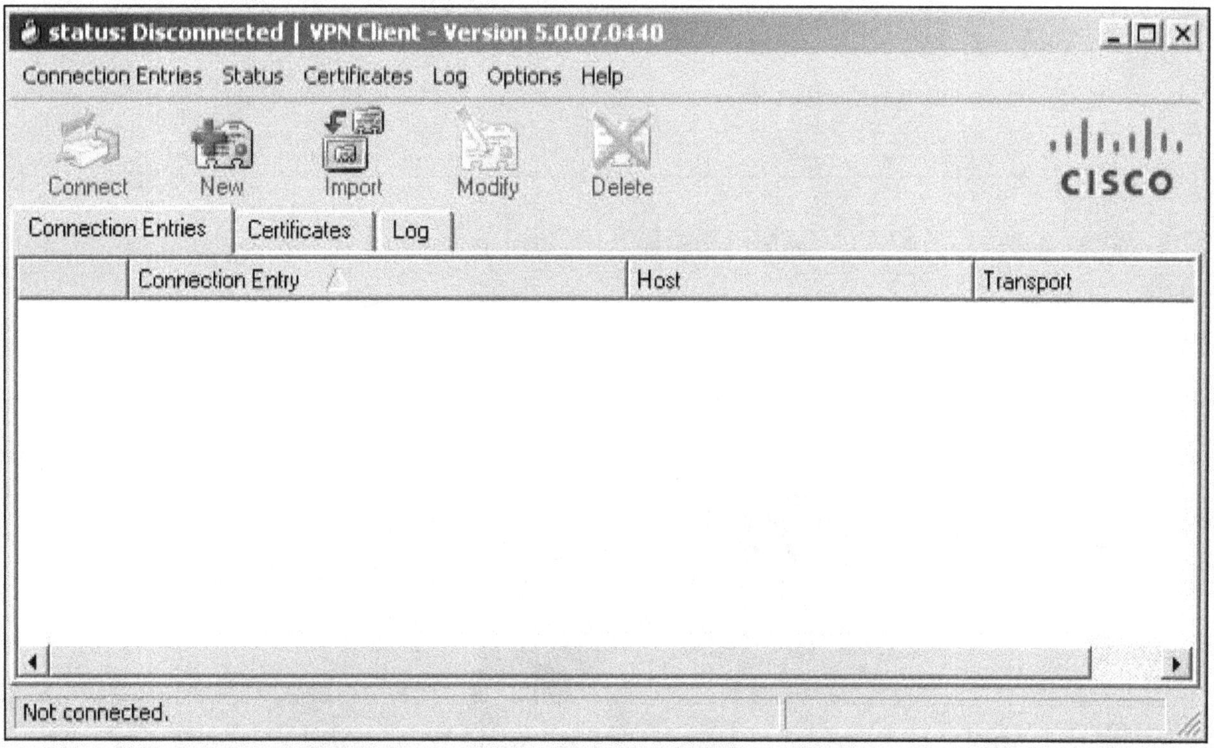

Click  to add new connection.

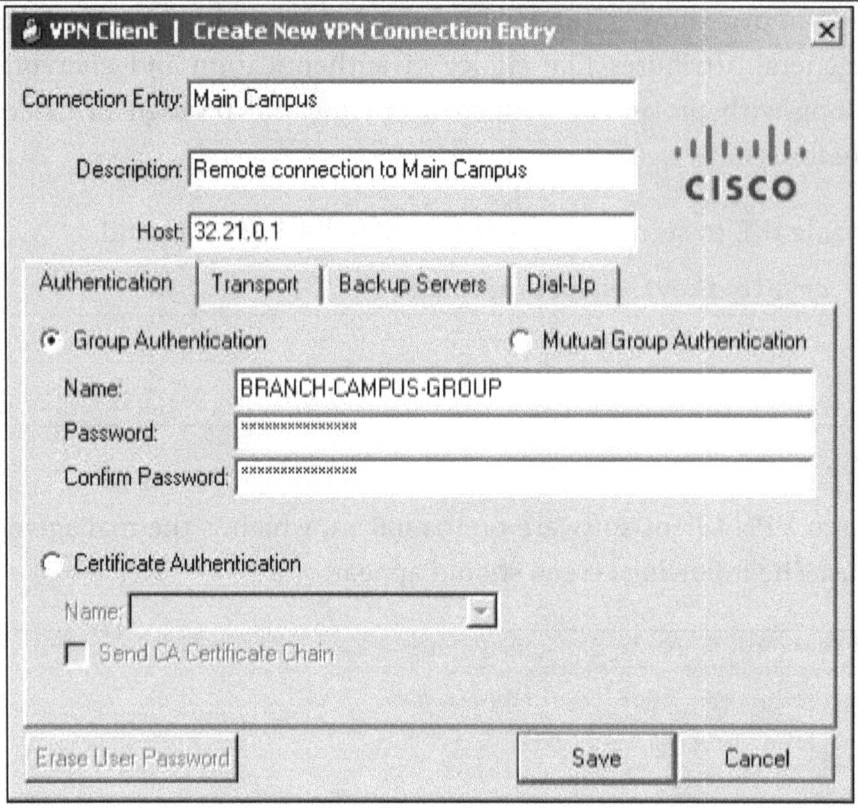

The group name "BRANCH-CAMPUS-GROUP" and password of "IPSpecialist:10" will be used.

Click "Save" to save the remote host. Here, the host IP address is the reachable IP address of the outside interface of ASA firewall. To check the reachability, use the ping test to verify it.

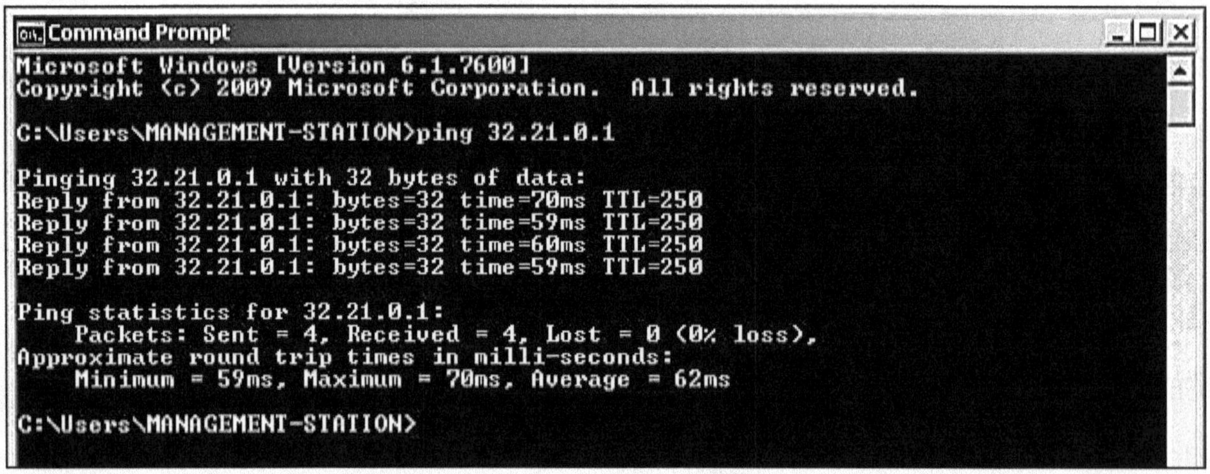
Command Prompt
Microsoft Windows [Version 6.1.7600]
Copyright (c) 2009 Microsoft Corporation. All rights reserved.
C:\Users\MANAGEMENT-STATION>ping 32.21.0.1
Pinging 32.21.0.1 with 32 bytes of data:
Reply from 32.21.0.1: bytes=32 time=70ms TTL=250
Reply from 32.21.0.1: bytes=32 time=59ms TTL=250
Reply from 32.21.0.1: bytes=32 time=60ms TTL=250
Reply from 32.21.0.1: bytes=32 time=59ms TTL=250
Ping statistics for 32.21.0.1:
Packets: Sent = 4, Received = 4, Lost = 0 (0% loss),
Approximate round trip times in milli-seconds:
Minimum = 59ms, Maximum = 70ms, Average = 62ms
C:\Users\MANAGEMENT-STATION>

Click 

to get the remote access of the Main Campus.

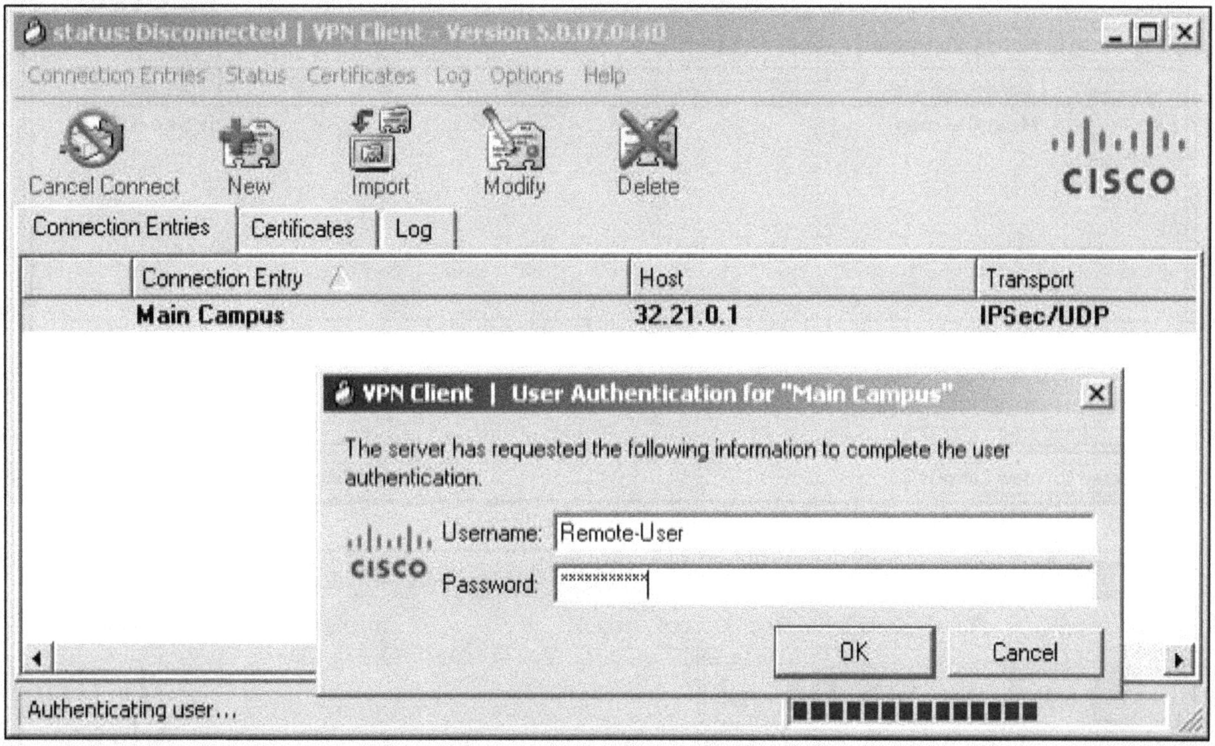

The username of "Remote-User" along with password of "P@$$word:10" already defined in ASA will be used to successfully connect to the Main Campus. Upon successful attempt, the following changes will occur as shown below:

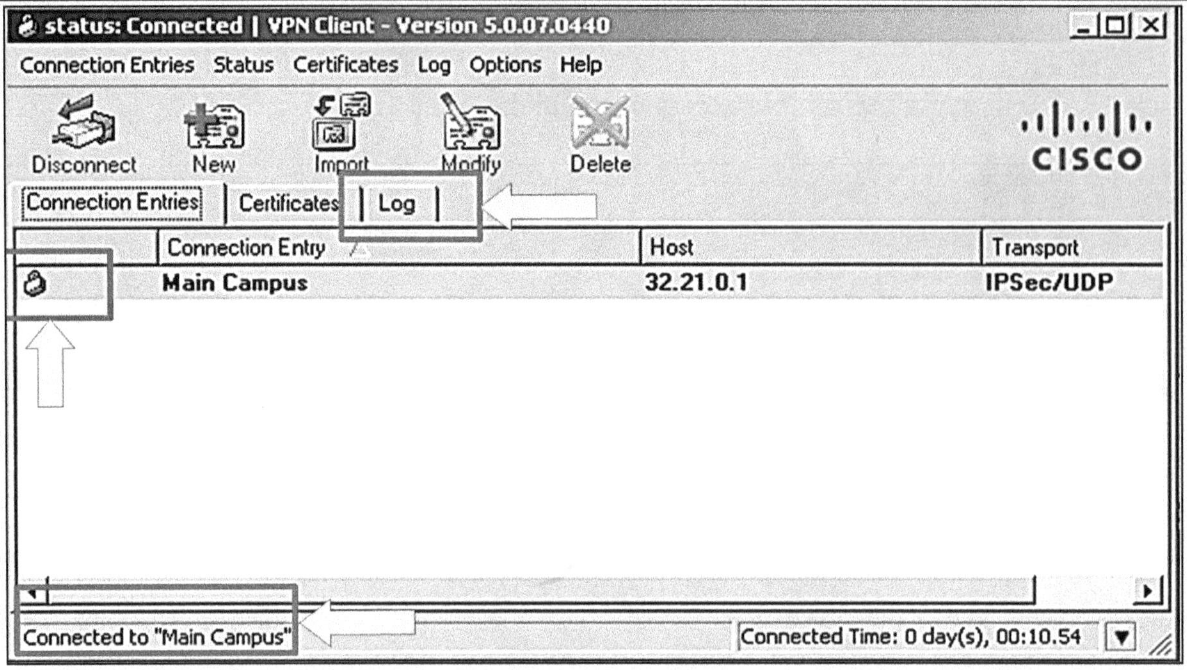

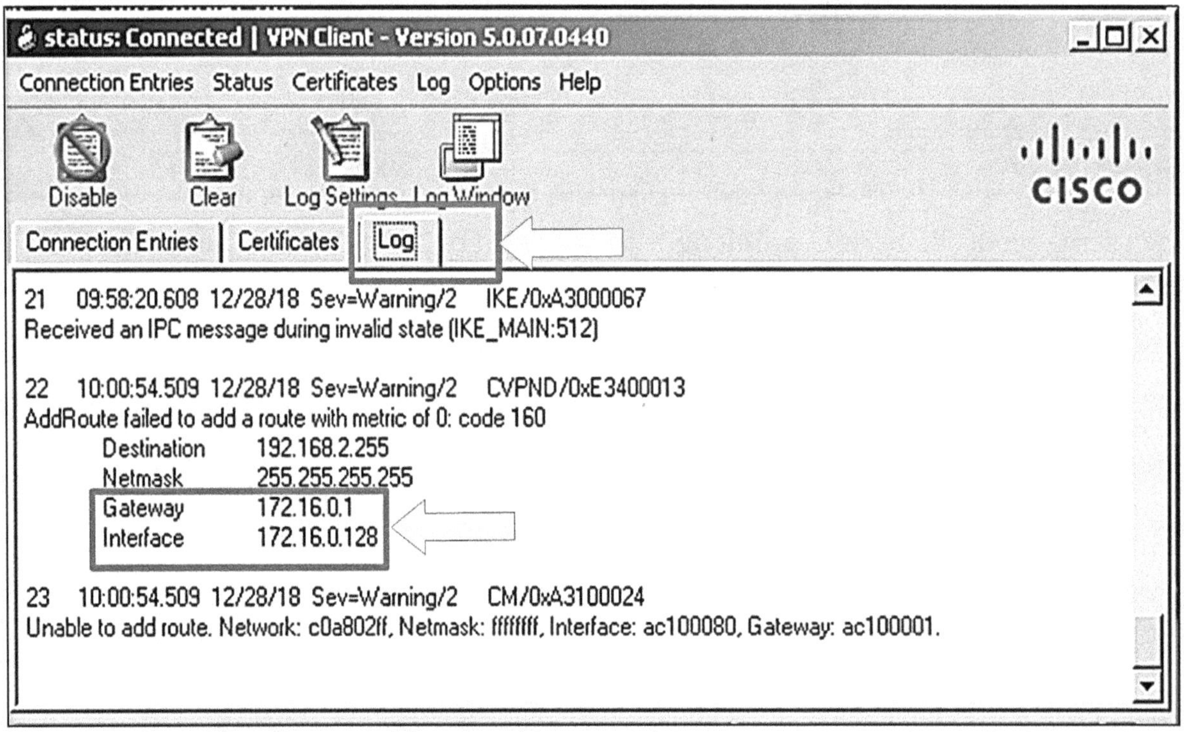

The "show crypto isakmp sa" command can be used to see the current status of security association (SA) database. If negotiation between R2 and FW1 is successful, then it should appear as ACTIVE in above command's output of ASA's CLI as shown below:

```
FW1#
FW1# show crypto  isakmp sa

IKEv1 SAs:

   Active SA: 1
    Rekey SA: 0 (A tunnel will report 1 Active and 1 Rekey SA during rekey)
Total IKE SA: 1

1   IKE Peer: 192.168.2.1
    Type    : user              Role    : responder
    Rekey   : no                State   : AM_ACTIVE

There are no IKEv2 SAs
FW1#
```

"Show vpn-sessiondb" is also another very important command, which can be used to check the total VPN sessions, which are terminated at ASA .

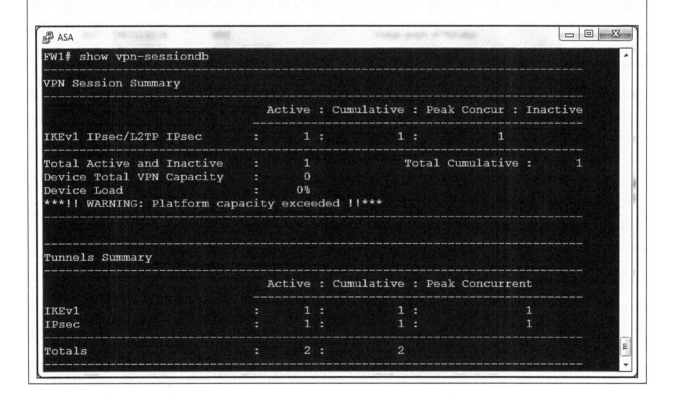

```
FW1# show vpn-sessiondb
---------------------------------------------------------------------------
VPN Session Summary
---------------------------------------------------------------------------
                              Active : Cumulative : Peak Concur : Inactive
                             ----------------------------------------------
IKEv1 IPsec/L2TP IPsec       :      1 :          1 :          1
---------------------------------------------------------------------------
Total Active and Inactive    :      1             Total Cumulative :      1
Device Total VPN Capacity    :      0
Device Load                  :     0%
***!! WARNING: Platform capacity exceeded !!***
---------------------------------------------------------------------------

---------------------------------------------------------------------------
Tunnels Summary
---------------------------------------------------------------------------
                              Active : Cumulative : Peak Concurrent
                             ----------------------------------------------
IKEv1                        :      1 :          1 :               1
IPsec                        :      1 :          1 :               1
---------------------------------------------------------------------------
Totals                       :      2 :          2
---------------------------------------------------------------------------
```

SSL VPN

Cisco features Secure Socket Layer (SSL) VPN or WebVPN in the IOS software, which offers remote user access from anywhere on the internet into the enterprise network through SSL VPN gateway. The SSL VPN gateway established a secure encrypted tunnel from the web browser allowing an easy access solution.

"SSL VPN is a type of virtual private network that uses Secure Socket Layer (SSL) protocol or its successor Transport Layer Security (TLS) protocol to establish a VPN connection between source and destination".

IPsec requires installation of IPsec client software on the client side in order to establish a connection between two sites. Hence, it is called client-server model. Unlike IPsec, in SSL users do not need to install any software on client side to establish SSL VPN connection. Hence, SSL VPN is also known as "Clientless VPN" or "Web VPN". The good thing about Secure Socket Layer (SSL) is that almost every single web browser in use today supports SSL. By using SSL, the web browser makes an HTTPS-based session with the server instead of HTTP. Whenever a browser tries to make HTTPS based session with a server, a certificate request is sent to the server in the background. The server in return replies with its digital certificate containing its public key. The web browser checks the authenticity of this certificate with a certificate authority (CA). Let us assume that certificate is valid, now server and the web browser have a secured session between them.

Note: Cisco also offers Next-Generation SSL VPN Client knwon as Anyconnect VPN client. Cisco Anyconnect VPN is introduced from Cisco IOS Release 12.4(15)T. For older releases, GUI for SSL VPN is accessed, whereas for Cisco IOS Release 12.4(15)T or later releases support GUI for Cisco Anyconnect VPN client.

SSL and TLS for Secure Communication

The terms SSL (Secure Socket Layer) and TLS (Transport Layer Security) are often used interchangeably, and provide encryption and authentication of data in motion. These protocols are intended for a scenario where users want a secured communication over an unsecured network like the public internet. Most common applications of such protocols are web browsing, Voice over IP (VOIP), and electronic mail.

Consider a scenario where a user wants to send an email to someone or wants to purchase something from an online store where credit card credentials may be needed. SSL only spills the data after a process known as 'handshake'. If a hacker bypasses the encryption process, then everything from bank account information to a secret conversation is visible. Malicious users may use this information for personal gain.

SSL was developed by Netscape in 1994 with an intention to protect web transactions. The last version for SSL was version 3.0. In 1999, IETF created Transport Layer Security also known as SSL 3.1, as TLS is, in fact, an adapted version of SSL.

The following are some of the important functionalities SSL/TLS has been designed to do:

- Serve authentication to client and vice versa.
- Select common cryptographic algorithm.
- Generate shared secrets between peers.
- Protection of normal TCP/UDP connection.

Working of SSL & TLS

Working of SSL and TLS is divided into two phases:

Phase 1 (Session Establishment)

In this phase, common cryptographic protocol and peer authentication take place. There are three sub-phases within overall phase 1 of SSL/TLS as explained below:

- **Sub-phase 1**- In this phase, hello messages are exchanged to negotiate common parameters of SSL/TLS such as authentication and encryption algorithms.
- **Sub-phase 2**- This phase includes one-way or two-way authentication between client and server end. A master key is sent by client side by using server's public key to start protecting the session.
- **Sub-phase 3**- The last phase calculates a session key, and cipher suite is finally activated. HMAC provides data integrity features by using either SHA-1 or MD5. Similarly, using DES-40, DES-CBC, 3DEC-EDE, 3DES-CBC, RC4-40, or RC4-128 provides confidentiality features.
  - **Session Keys Creation:** Methods for generating session keys are as follows:
    - *RSA Based.* Using public key of peer encrypts shared secret string.
    - *A fixed DH Key Exchange.* Fixed Diffie-Hellman based key exchanged in a certificate creates a session key.

- *An ephemeral DH Key Exchange.* It is considered to be the best protection option as actual DH value is signed with the private key of the sender, and hence each session has a different set of keys.
- *An anonymous DH Key Exchange without any Certificate or Signature.* Avoiding this option is advised, as it cannot prevent man-in-the-middle attacks.

Phase 2 (Secure Data Transfer)

In this phase, secure data transfer takes place between encapsulating endpoints. Each SSL session has unique session ID, which exchanges during the authentication process. The session ID is used to differentiate between old and new session. The client can request the server to resume the session based on this ID (in case, sever has a session ID in its cache).

TLS 1.0 is considered to be a bit more secure than the last version of SSL (SSL v3.0). Even US Government has also declared not to use SSL v3.0 for highly sensitive communications due to the latest vulnerability named as POODLE. After POODLE vulnerability, most web browsers have disabled SSL v3.0 for most of the communication and services. Current browsers (Google Chrome, Firefox, and others) support TLS 1.0 by default and latest versions of TLS (TLS 1.1 and TLS 1.2) optionally. TLS 1.0 is considered to be equivalent to SSL3.0. However, newer versions of TLS are considered to be far more secure than SSL. Keep in mind that SSL v3.0 and TLS 1.0 is not compatible with each other as TLS uses Diffie-Hellman and Data Security Standard (DSS) while SSL uses RSA.

Apart from a secured web browsing, HTTPS, SSL/TLS can also be used for securing other protocols like FTP, SMTP, and SNTP, and many others.

Options for SSL Based VPN Implementation

The various options, which are used to implement SSL VPN in corporate environment are:

Features	Clientless SSL VPN	Clientless SSL VPN with Port Forwarding Features	Cisco AnyConnect VPN Client Software
Popular names	Web VPN	Thin client	SSL client software
Installation requirement on client side	No installation required	Some configuration required for port forwarding etc.	AnyConnect client software needs to be installed on client machines

User experience	User can experience access through a specific web browser window or URL	User can experience access through a specific web browser window or URL	Full access to corporate network makes user feel like they are physically present at corporate site
Clients Support	SSL Supported machines	SSL and Java supported machines	SSL supported machines
Flow of data traffic	SSL server acts as a proxy for user traffic	SSL server acts as a proxy for user traffic	Client IP addresses remains the same. It is the duty of VPN peers to securely forward the traffic to end-users

Table 3-01: Methods for Implementing SSL VPN

Comparison Between SSL and IPsec

Although IPsec based VPN has better security footprint than SSL based VPNs, one of the major advantages of using SSL VPN is its ease of use and deployment. Cisco *AnyConnect* client software along with some open source softwares can be used to connect to corporate office from anywhere in the world. The next table summarizes the basic comparison of SSL with IPsec.

Features	SSL	IPsec
Supported Applications	Web based applications Email and file sharing applications. Custom applications with support for SSL.	Setting on edge networking devices make end-user settings unchanged.
Ease of use	Easy to deploy.	Requires complex settings on edge devices, which may be challenging for a non-technical staff.
Security	Moderate. Any device can connect initially. After entering correct username and password, it will allow access to corporate resources.	Strong security. Edge devices can filter users by using access list.

Table 3-02: IPsec vs SSL Comparison

Lab 3.4: Implementation of SSL Clientless and AnyConnect VPN Using CLI and ASDM for Accessing Main Campus from Branch Campus

In this lab, the main objective is to access the main campus network securely via Clientless and AnyConnect SSL VPN, which provides web browser based secured access.

The following topology will be used in this lab:

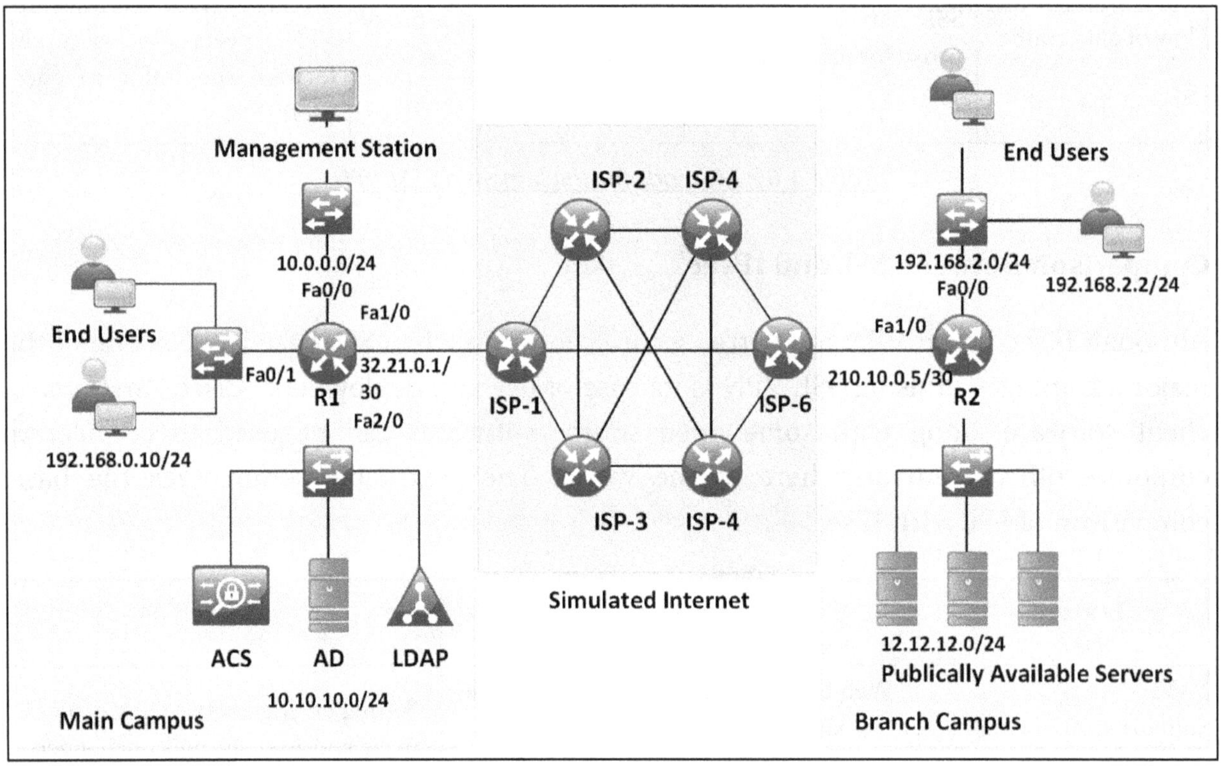

Figure 3-15: Lab 3.4 Topology

SSL AnyConnect VPN Configuration

Access the firewall FW1 via Main Campus' Management station via ASDM. Click  pinned to the task bar of management station, use the following credentials for login: Username: **IPSpecialist** Password: **P@$$word:10**

After a successful login, the following dashboard should appear:

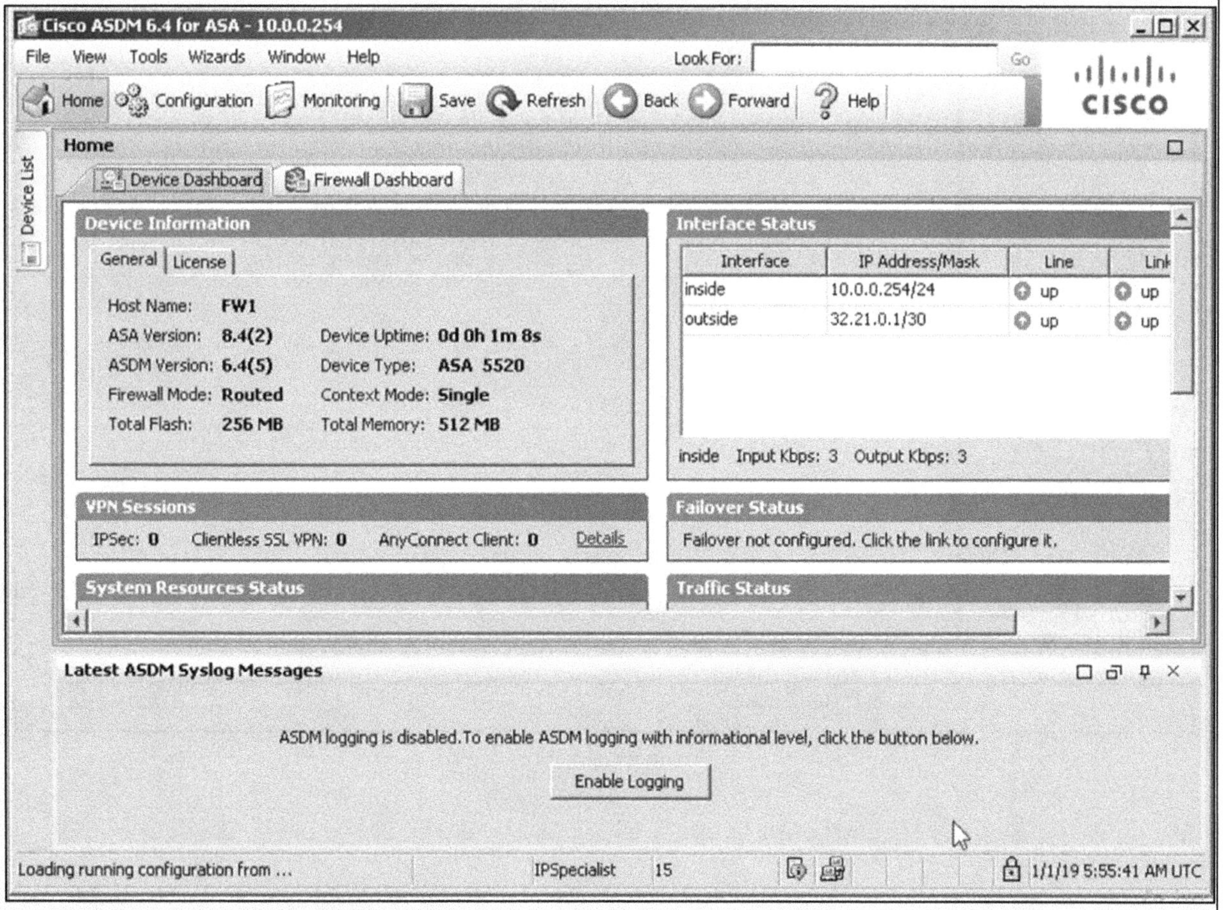

Click: "Wizards"-> "VPN Wizards"-> "AnyConnect VPN Wizards" to start an interactive wizard of implementing the above SSL AnyConnect VPN.

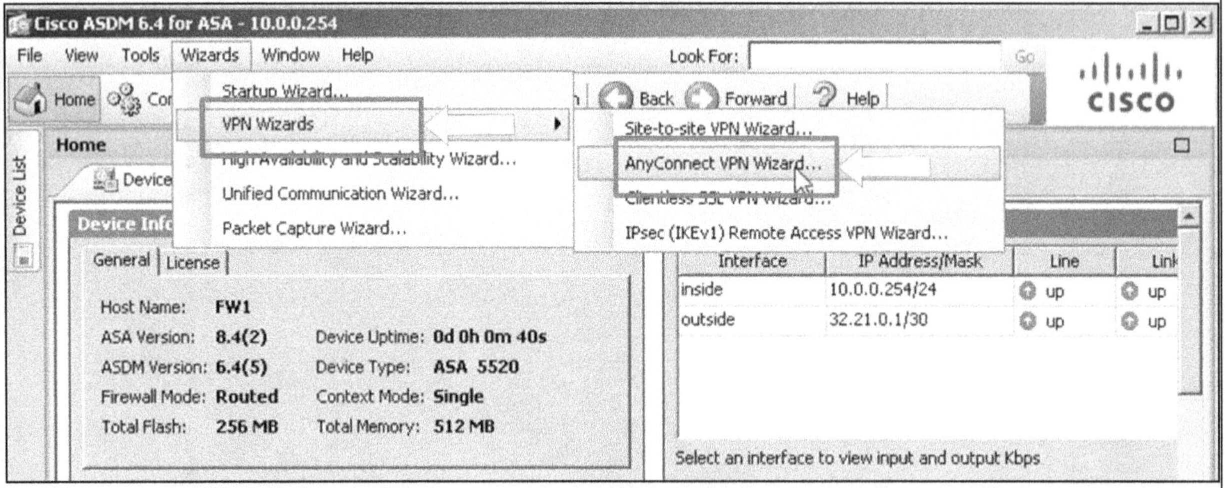

Click "Next" to continue.

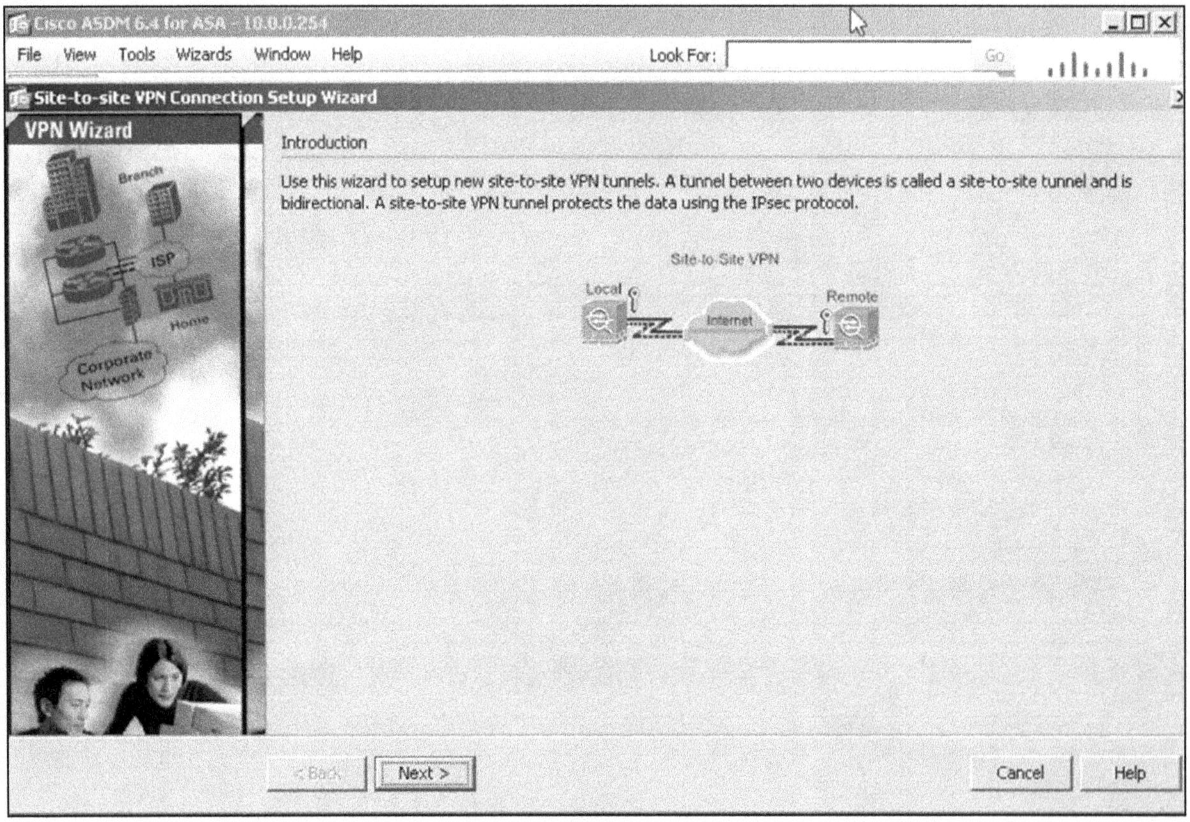

Select a profile name from where user wants to connect to the main office through VPN.

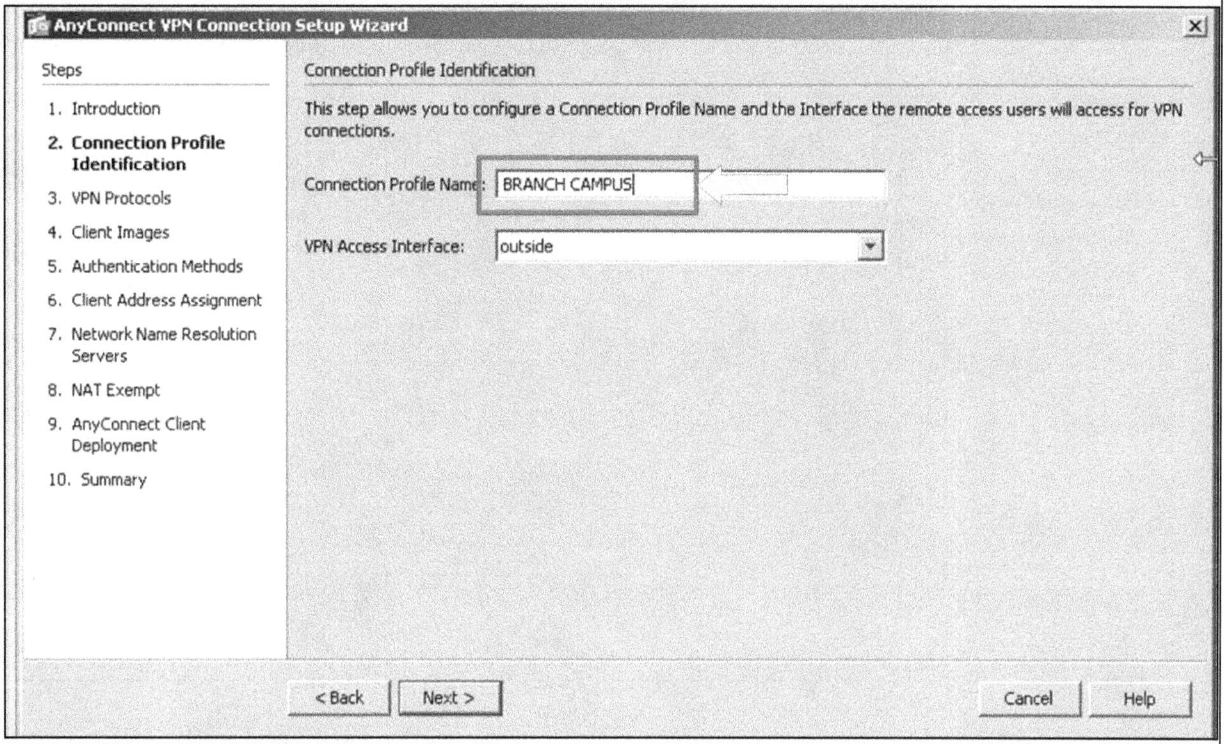

Select only "SSL" option as IPsec Anyconnect VPN was already implemented in last section.

Click "Next".

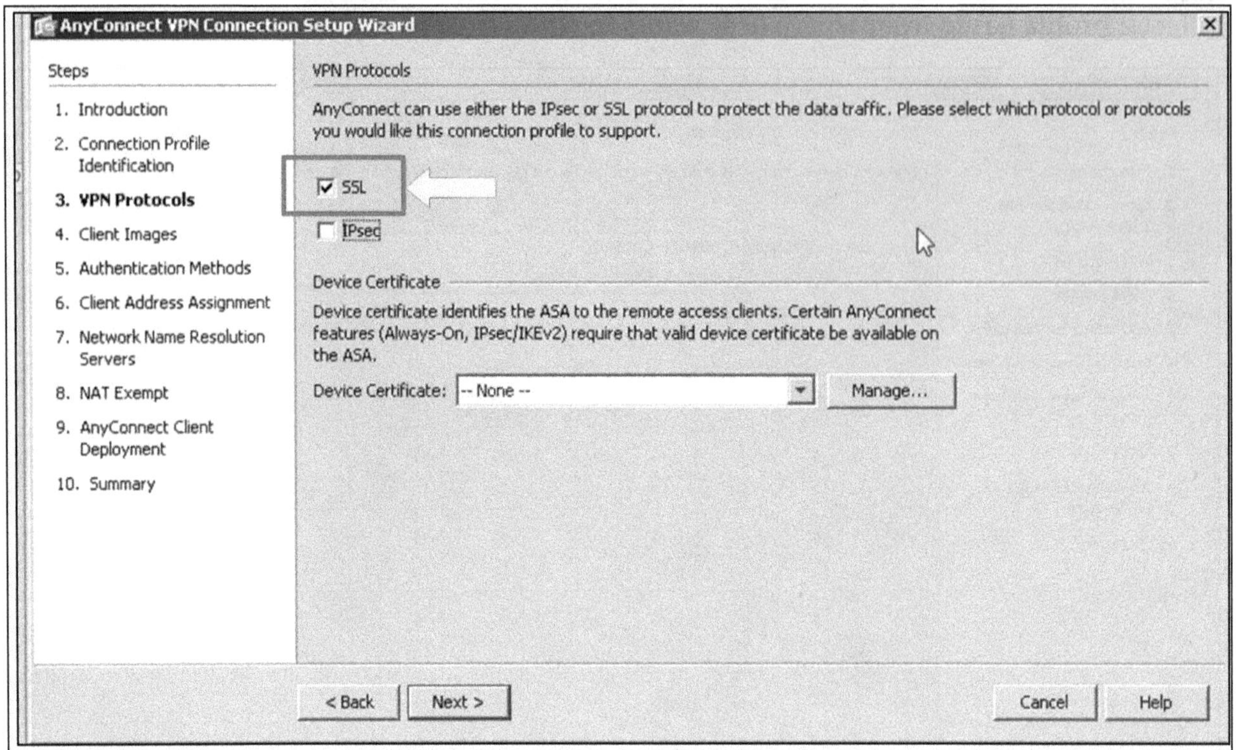

Click "Add" and provide the path for correct any-connect client package path.

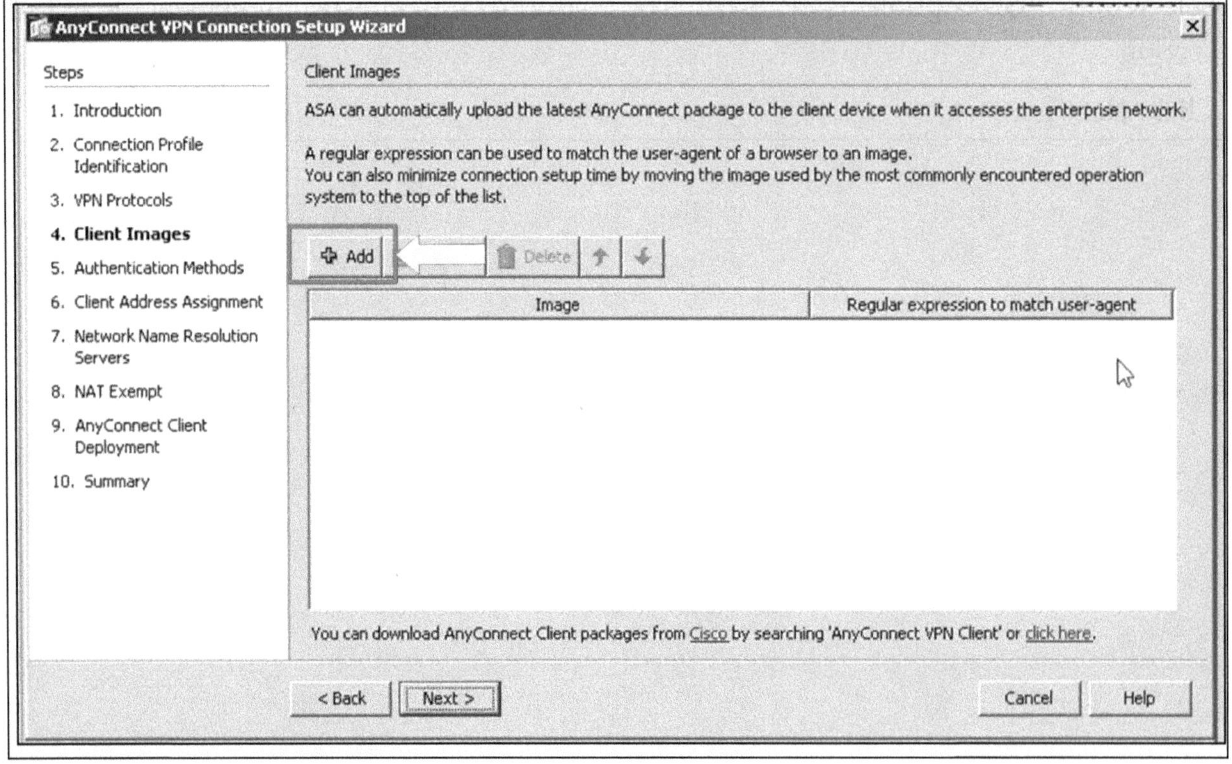

Next, the path for anyconnect client package will be asked; which is available in the "downloads" folder of management station. Select the package for "Windows" as the client used in this lab is Microsoft Windows 7 based.

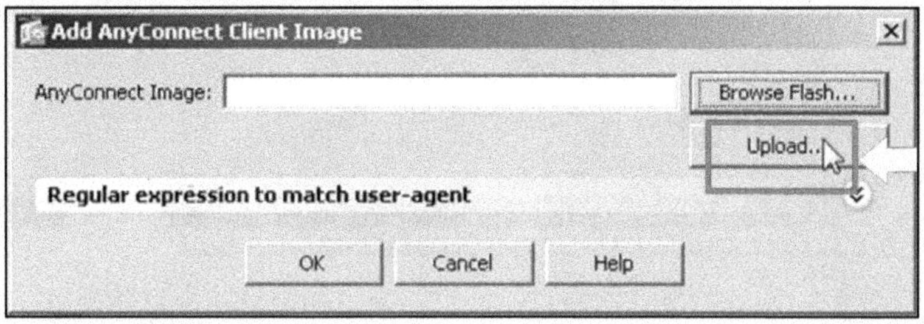

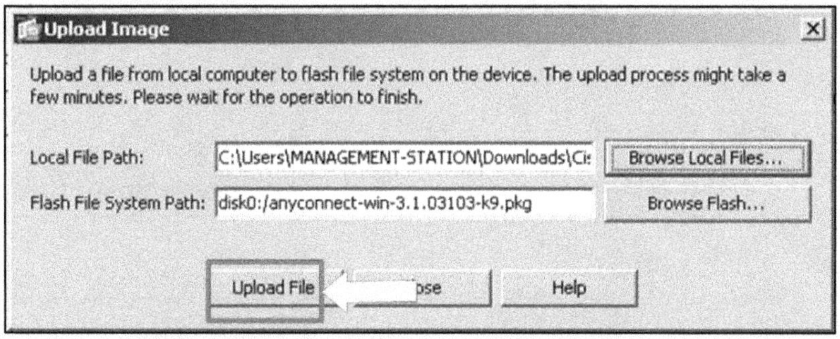

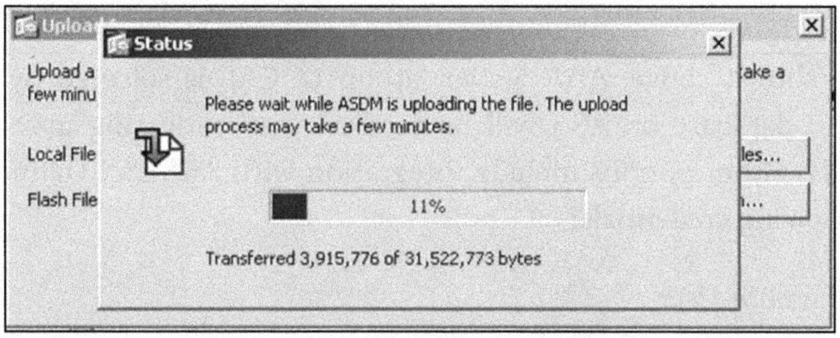

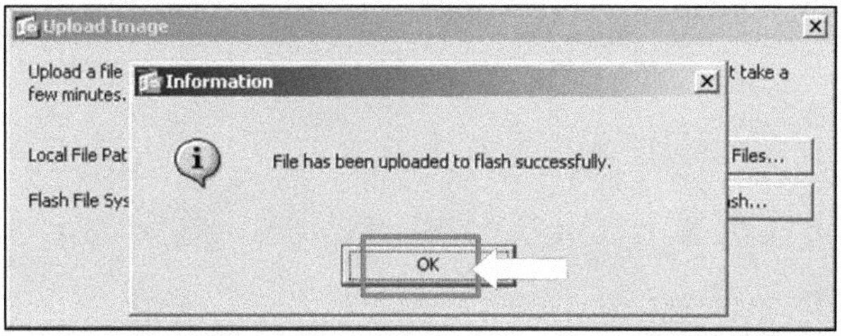

After successfully uploading the file, click "Next". The following dialog will appear:

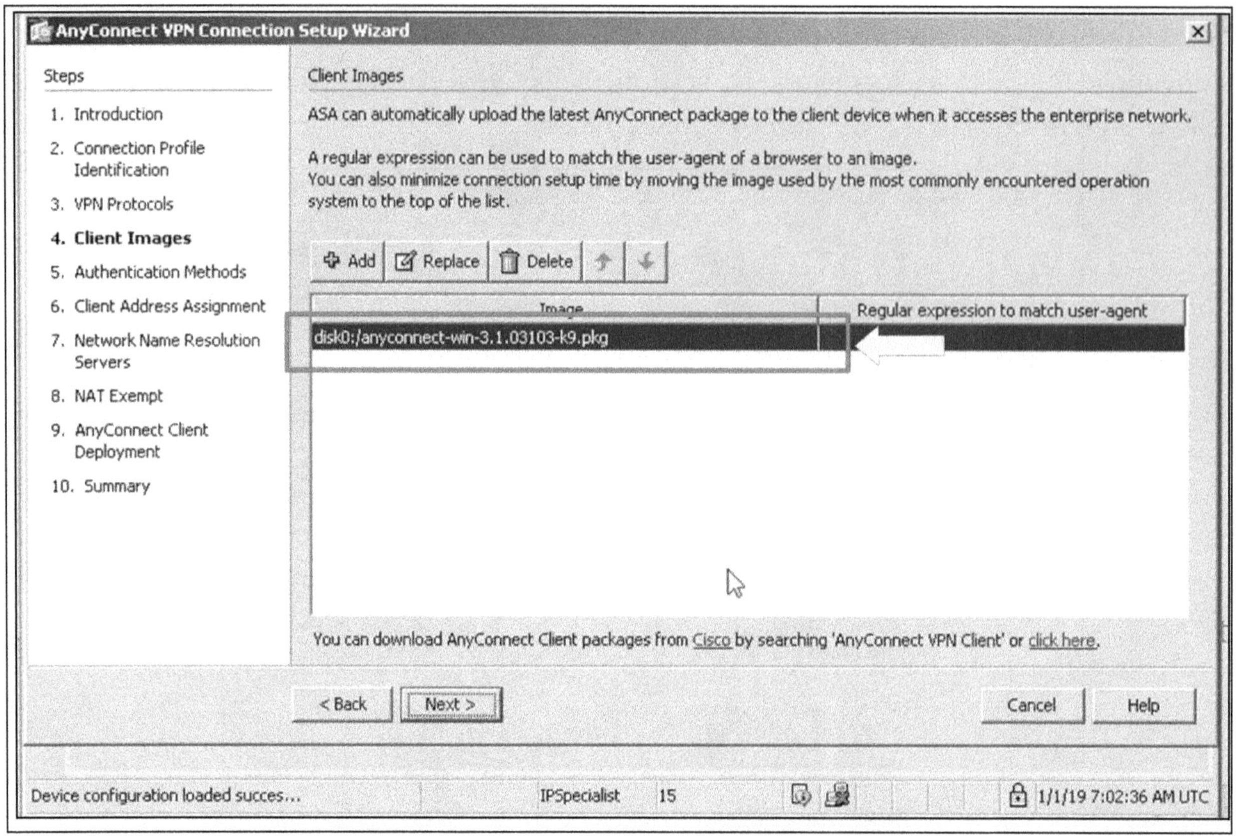

In the diagram shown above, AAA Server Group LOCAL is selected by default, which means that local database on ASA will be used for authenticating users who wants to connect via VPN. Other options include integration with ACS etc. Define the username by using the following credentials:

Username: Remote-User

Password: P@$$word:10

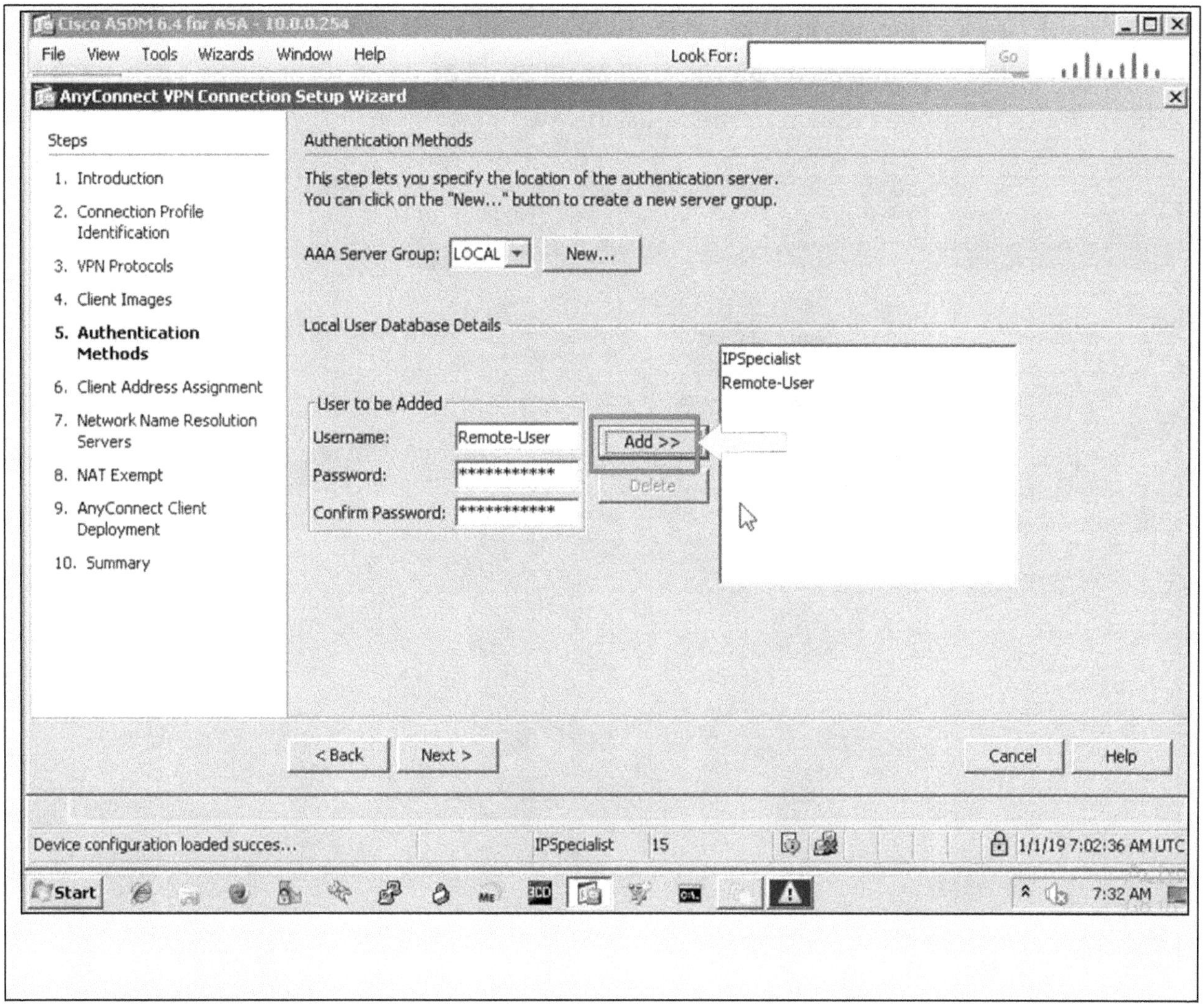
Cisco ASDM 6.4 for ASA - 10.0.0.254
File View Tools Wizards Window Help
Look For:
Go
AnyConnect VPN Connection Setup Wizard
Steps
1. Introduction
2. Connection Profile Identification
3. VPN Protocols
4. Client Images
5. Authentication Methods
6. Client Address Assignment
7. Network Name Resolution Servers
8. NAT Exempt
9. AnyConnect Client Deployment
10. Summary
Authentication Methods
This step lets you specify the location of the authentication server.
You can click on the "New..." button to create a new server group.
AAA Server Group: LOCAL
New...
Local User Database Details
User to be Added
Username: Remote-User
Password:
Confirm Password:
Add >>
Delete
IPSpecialist
Remote-User
< Back
Next >
Cancel
Help
Device configuration loaded succes...
IPSpecialist
15
1/1/19 7:02:36 AM UTC
Start
7:32 AM

In the figure shown above, click "New" to define a pool of IP addresses, which will be used to assign IPs to the connected clients. Define IP range of 172.16.0.127 - 172.16.0.254 /24 in Add IP Pool's prompt as shown in the figure below:

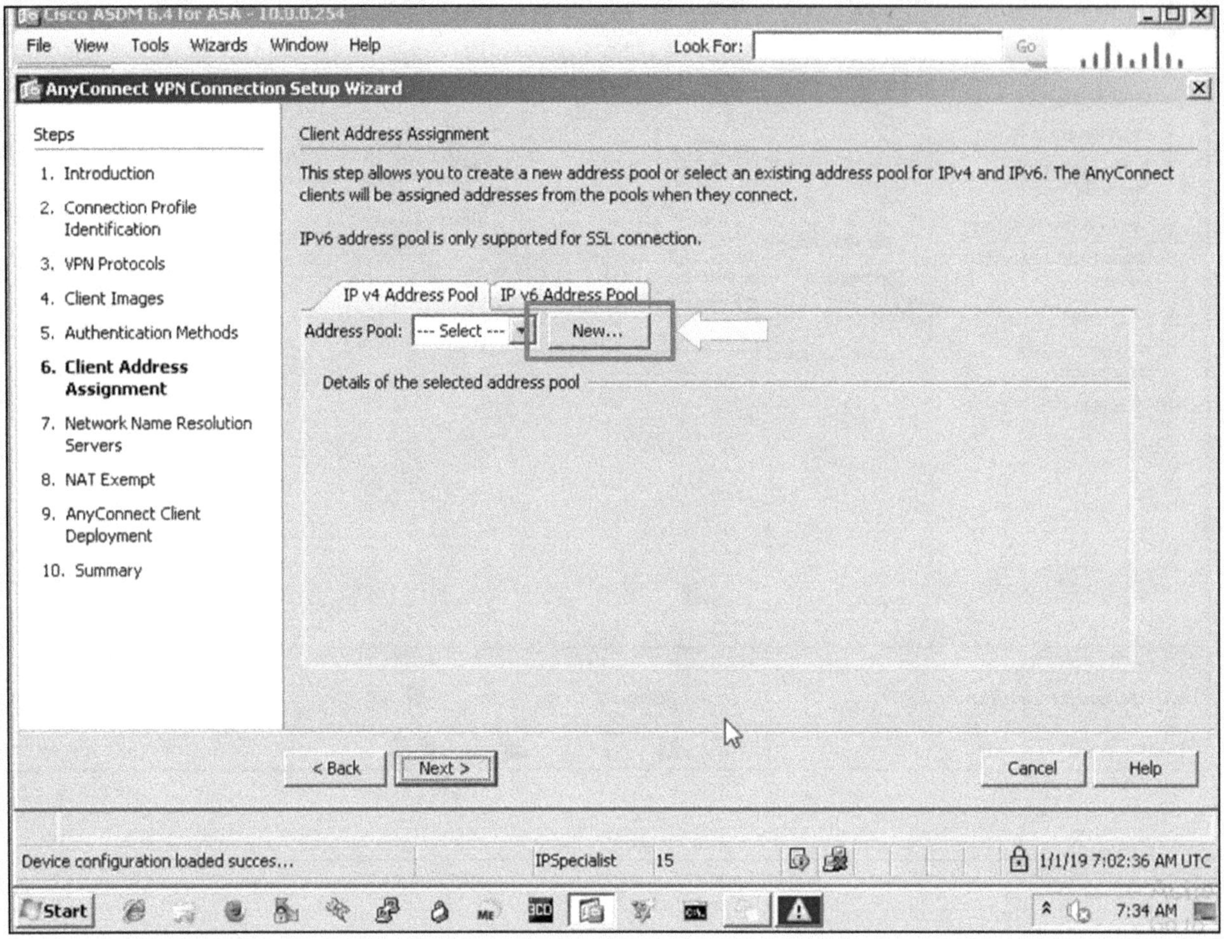

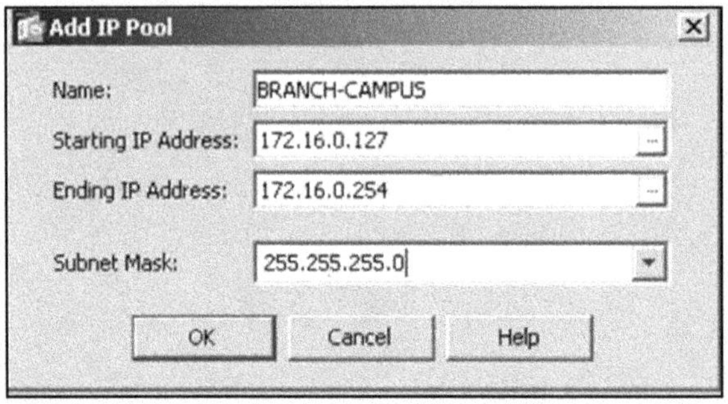

Click "Next" to continue.

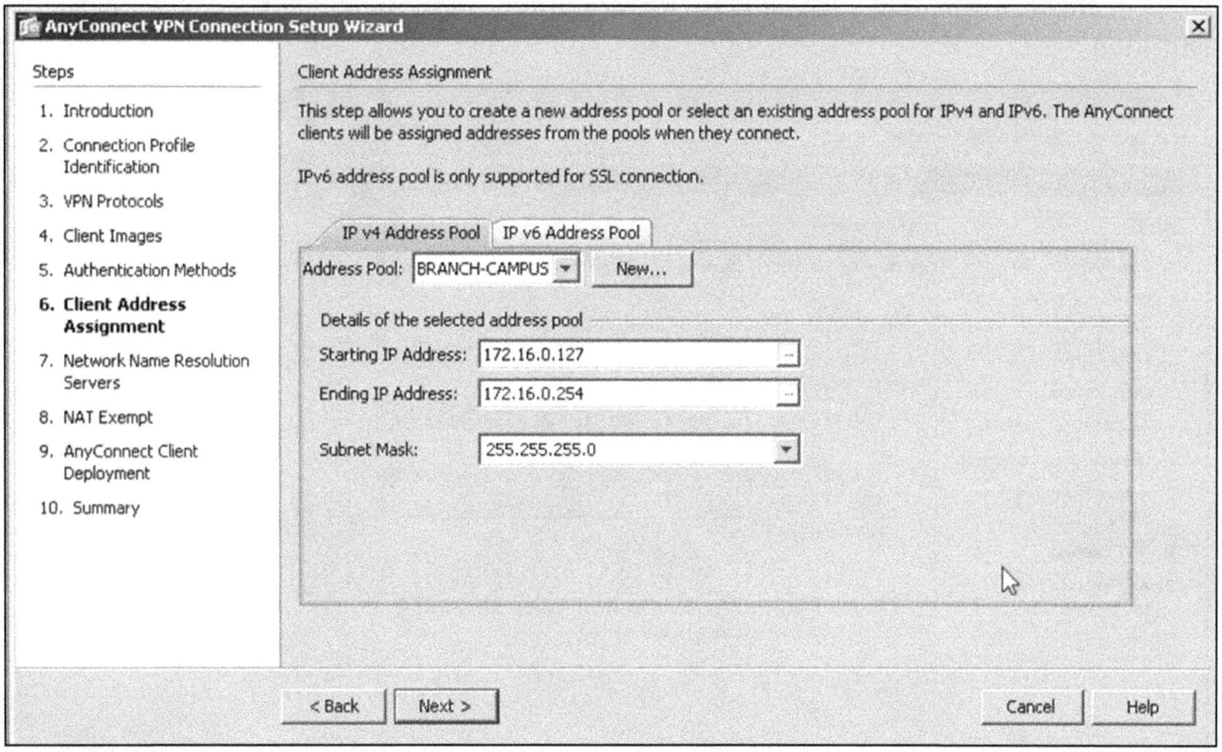

Here, DNS server is not needed in our lab scenario; however, use the outside interface IP address and "ipspecialist.net" as domain name as shown below:

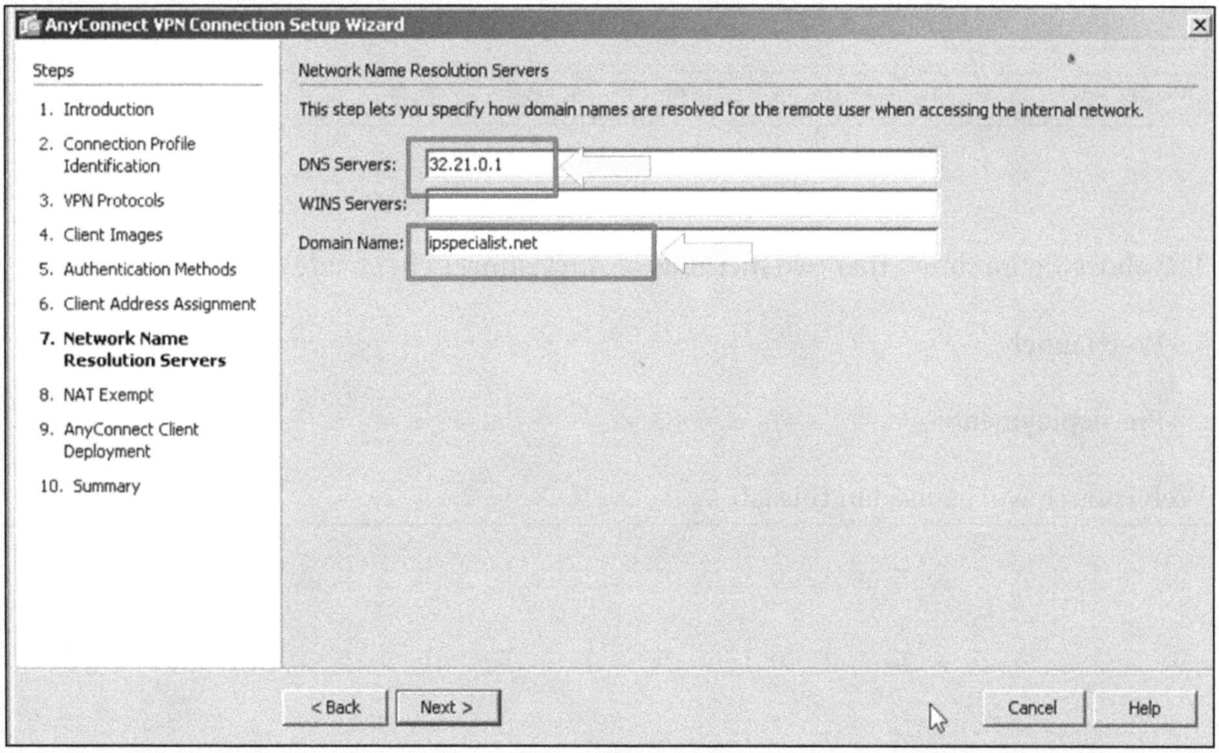

As Real Public Internet Cloud is not involved in our case, it is safe to exempt the traffic coming from the inside interface to be exempted from being NAT. Click "Next" to continue.

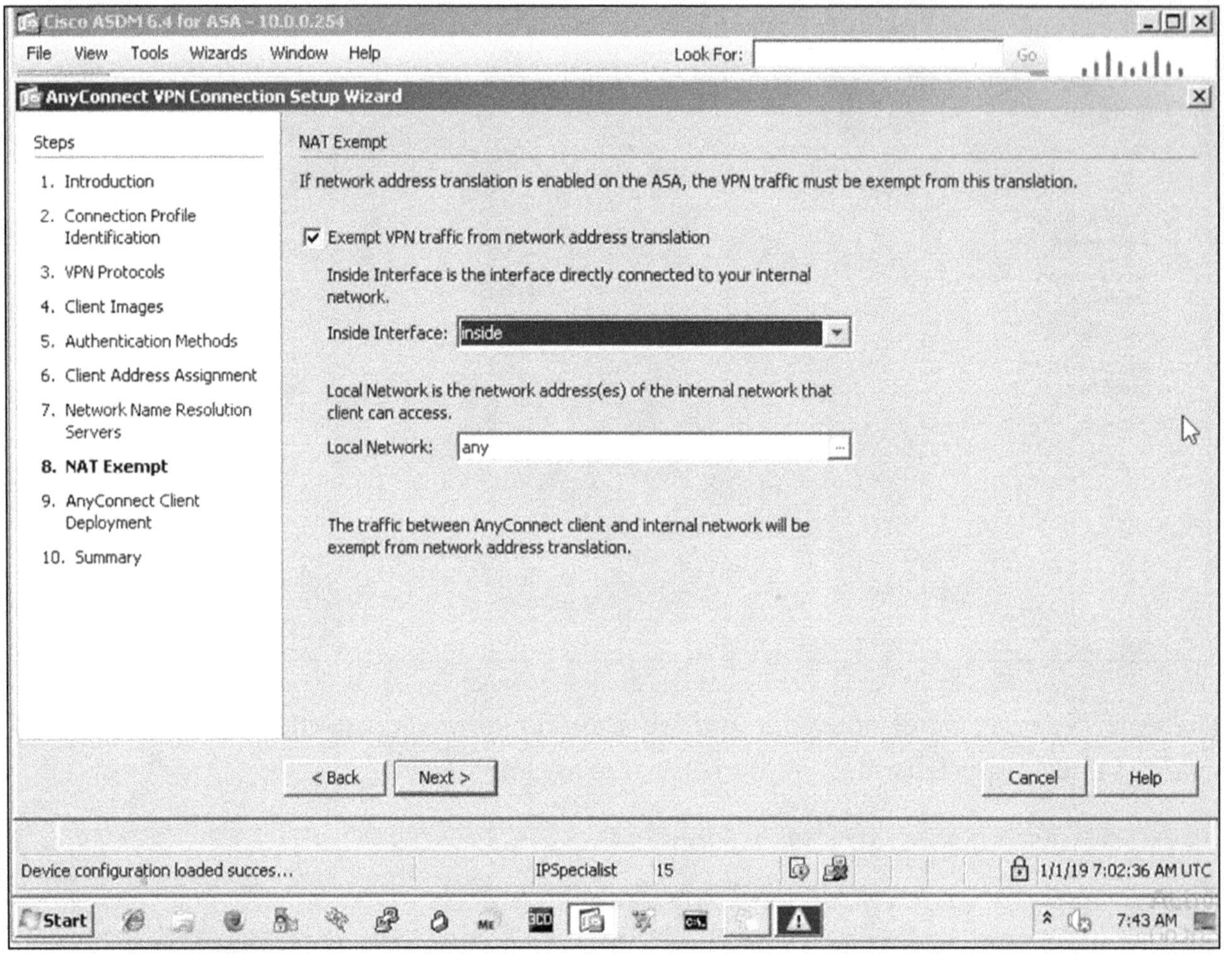

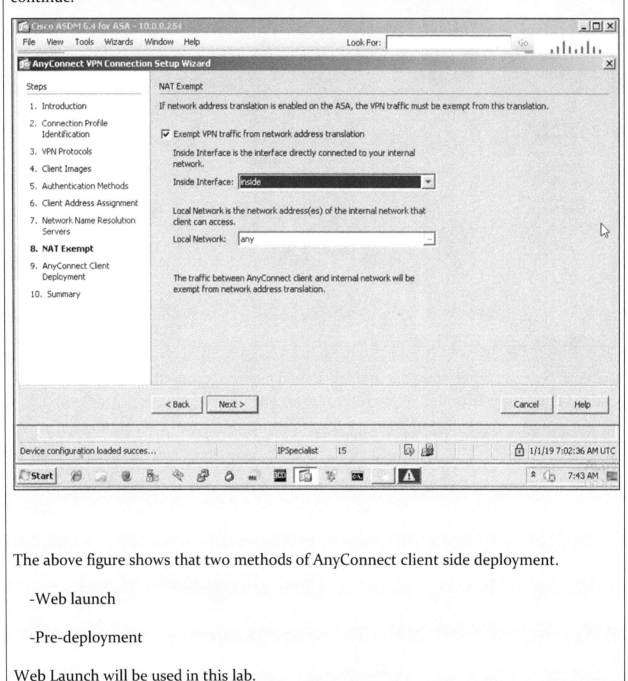

The above figure shows that two methods of AnyConnect client side deployment.

-Web launch

-Pre-deployment

Web Launch will be used in this lab.

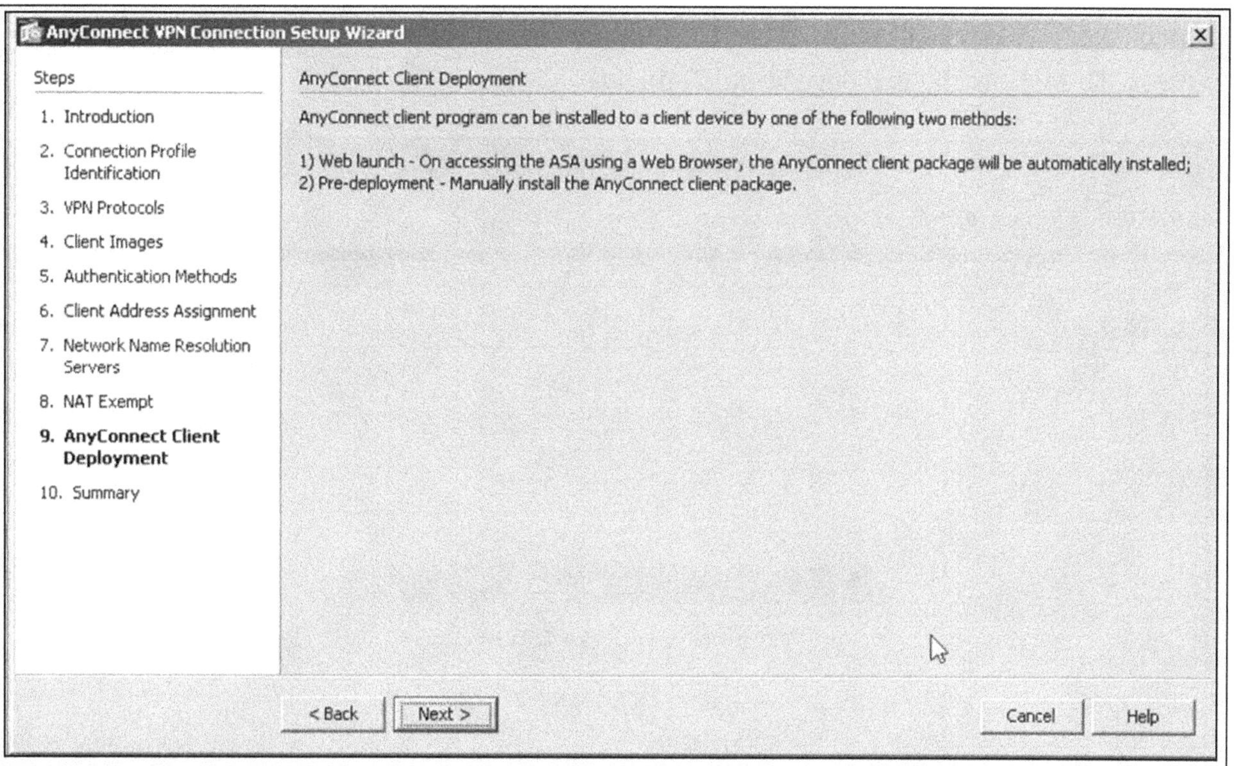

The figure below shows the overall summary of configured SSL AnyConnect VPN. Click "Finish" and jump to Branch office management station for client side configuration.

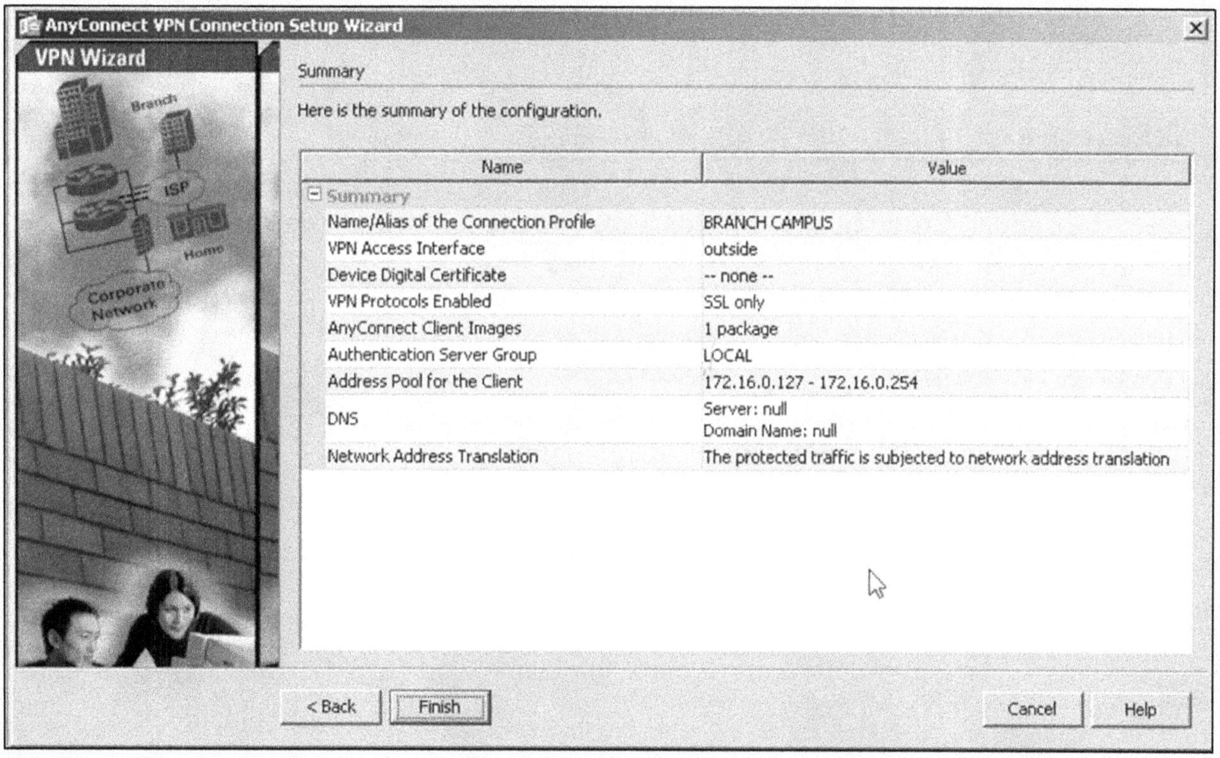

Open the web browser and enter the outside interface IP address of ASA for secure access. The following web page should appear.

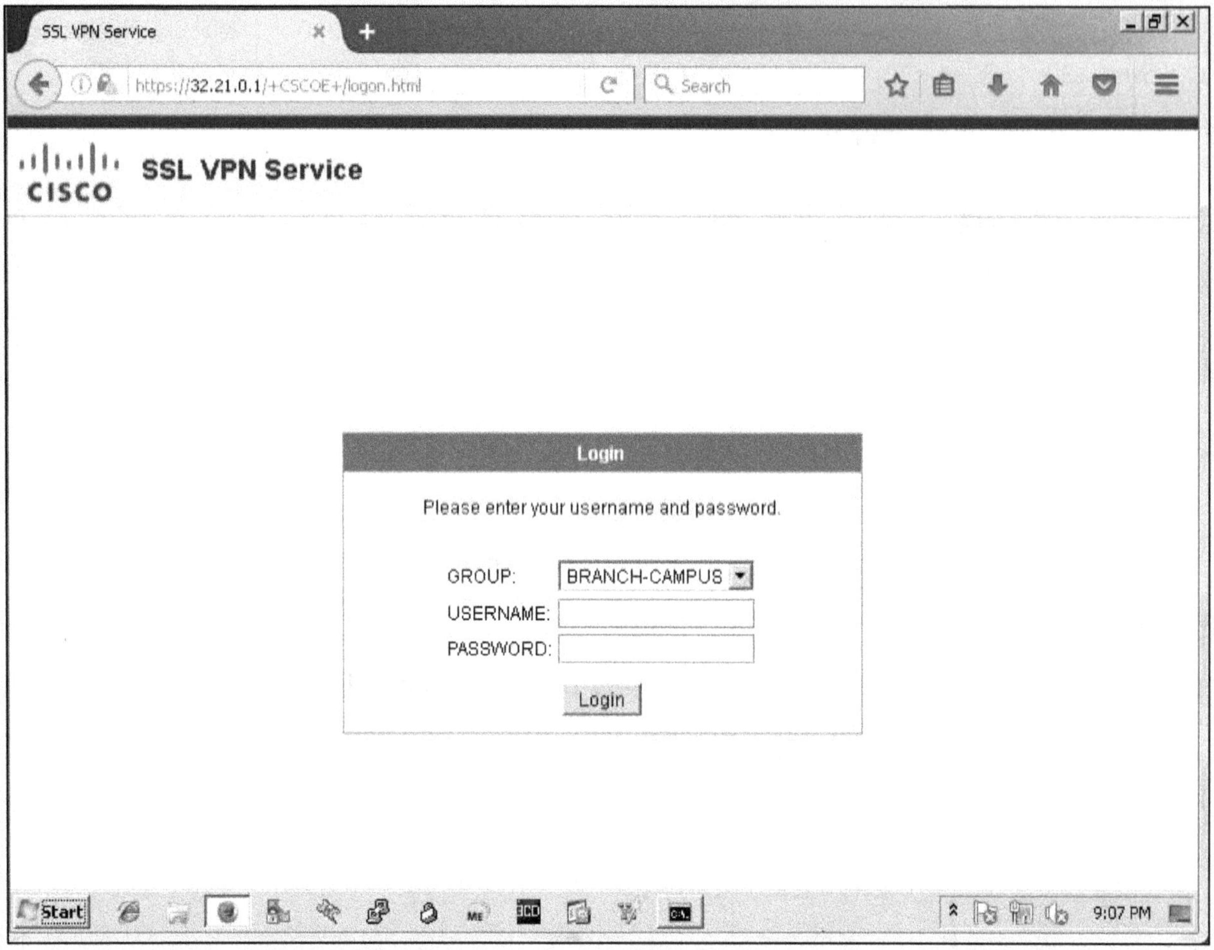

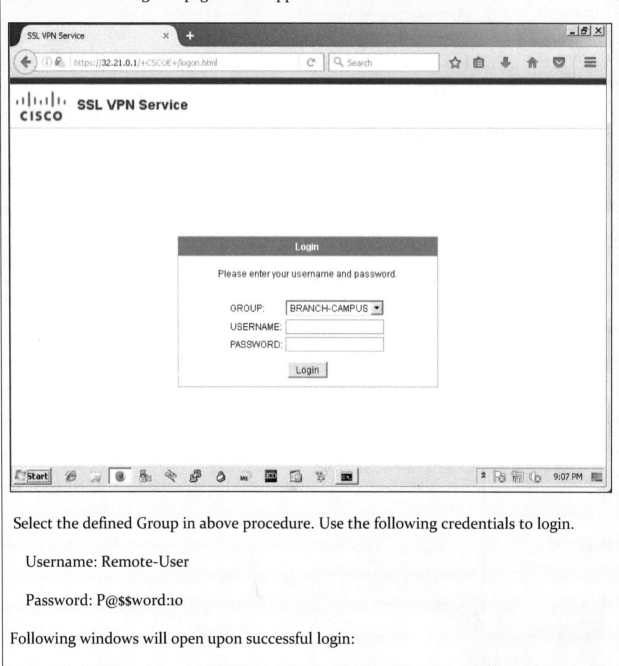

Select the defined Group in above procedure. Use the following credentials to login.

Username: Remote-User

Password: P@$$word:10

Following windows will open upon successful login:

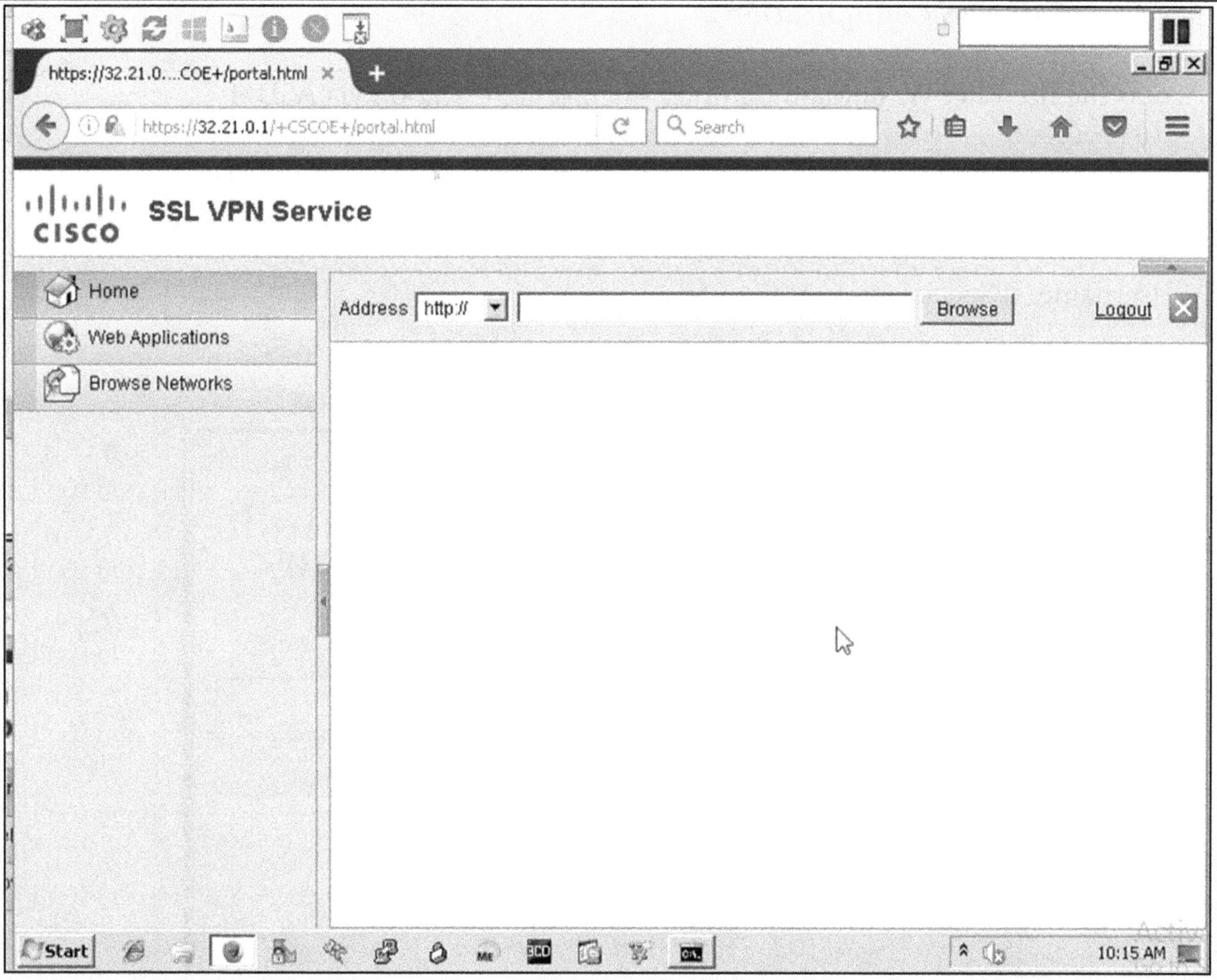
https://32.21.0....COE+/portal.html
https://32.21.0.1/+CSCOE+/portal.html
Search
cisco
SSL VPN Service
Home
Web Applications
Browse Networks
Address
http://
Browse
Logout
Start
10:15 AM

SSL Clientless VPN Configuration

Access the firewall FW1 of Main Campus' Management station via ASDM.

Click  pinned to the task bar of management station and use the following credentials for login:

Username: IPSpecialist

Password: P@$$word:10

After successful login, following dashboard should appear:

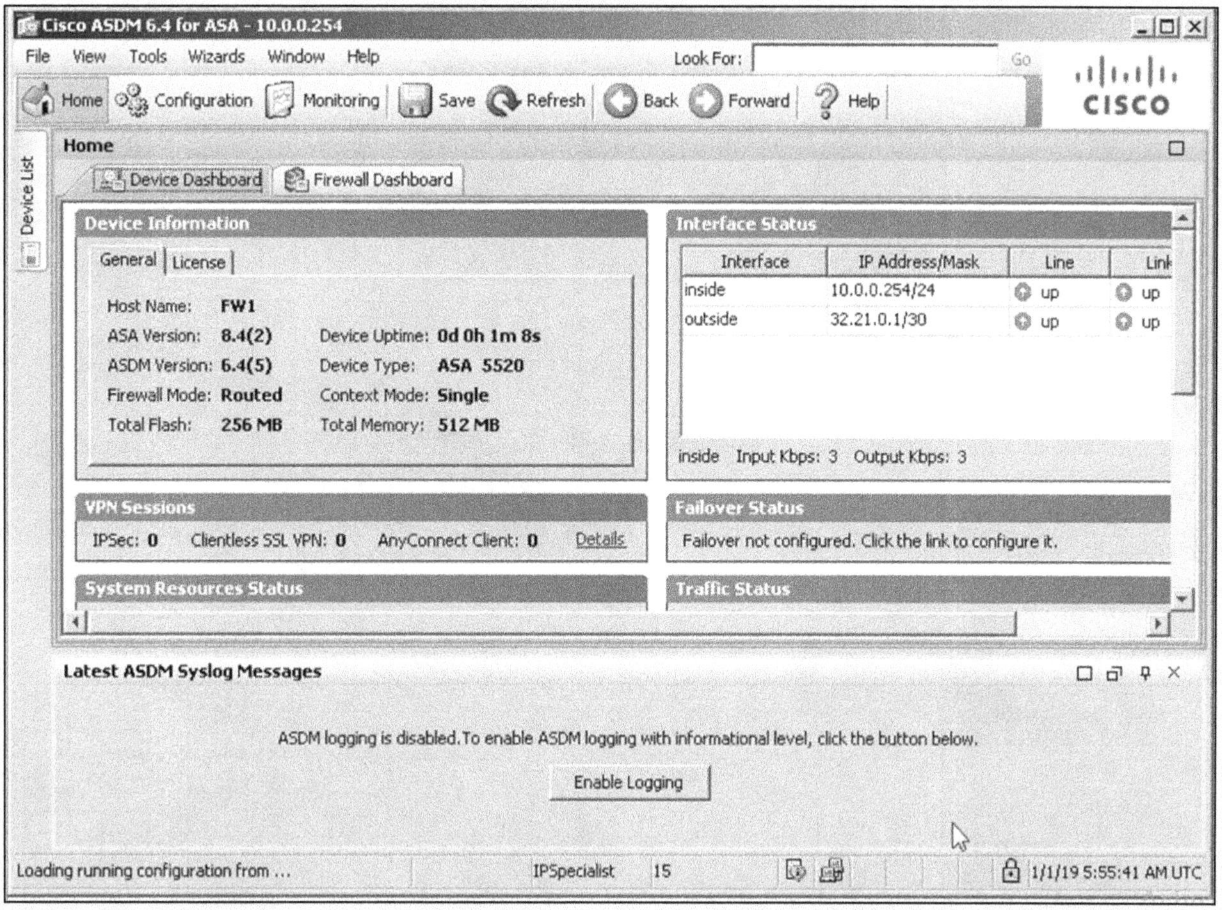

Click "Wizards" -> "VPN Wizards" -> "Clientless SSL VPN Wizards" to start an interactive wizard of implementing the above SSL AnyConnect VPN.

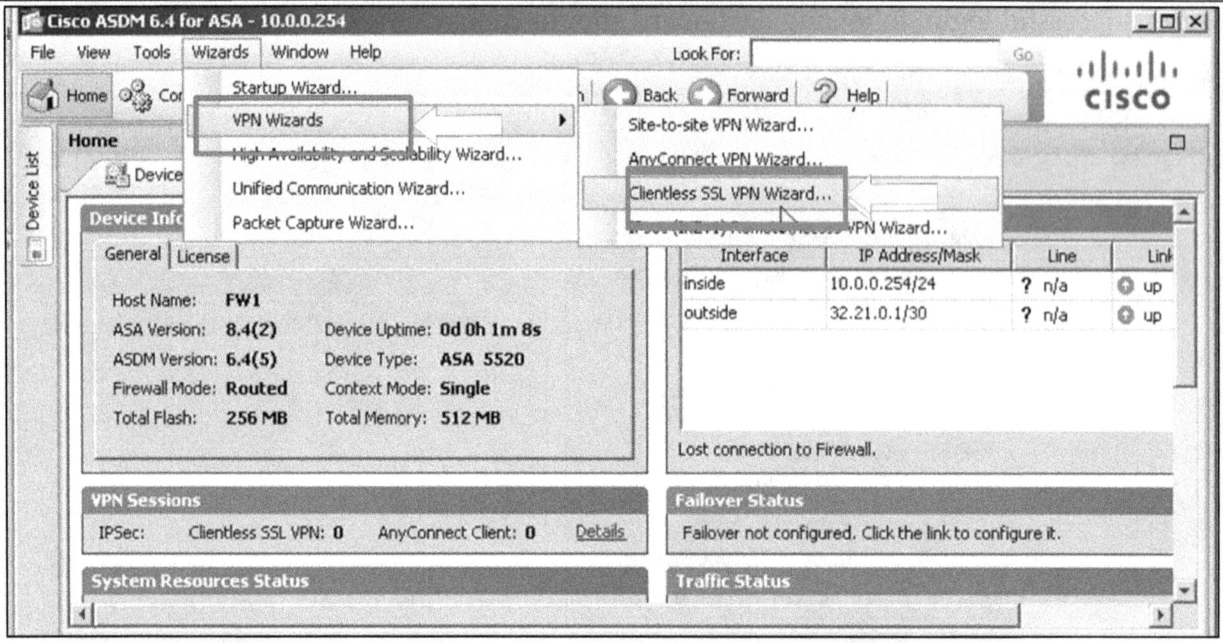

Click "Next" to continue.

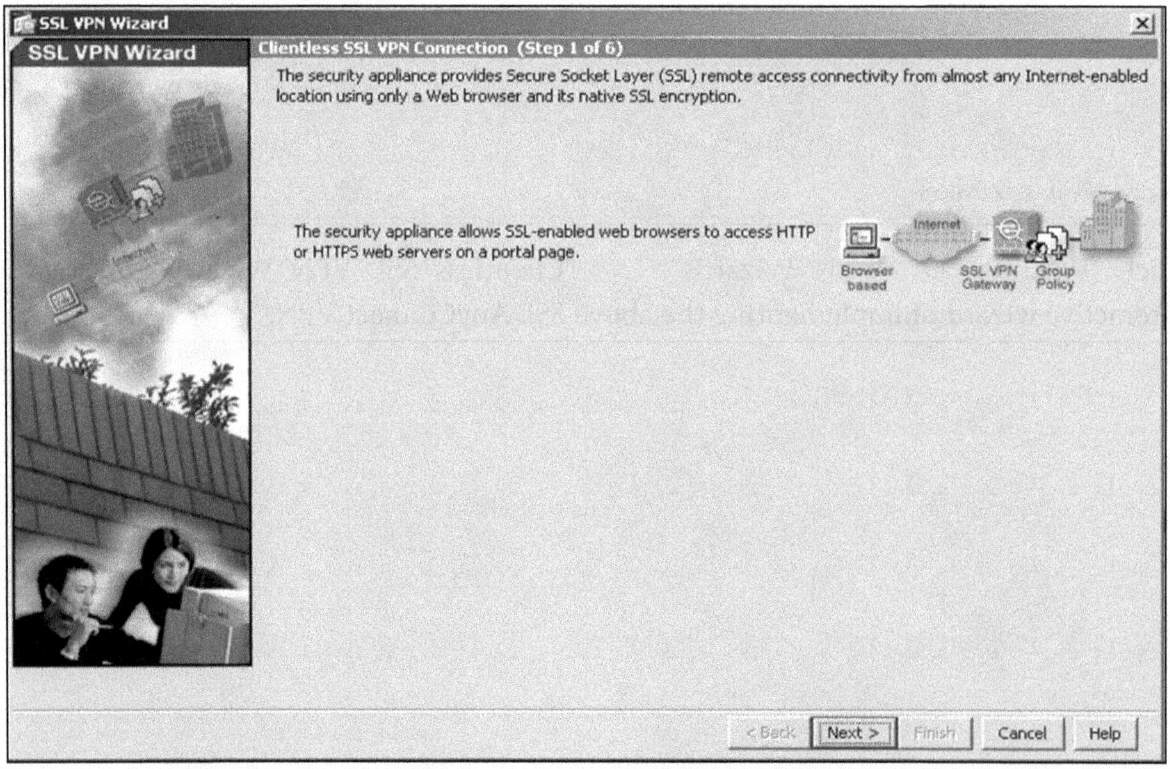

As shown in the figure above, Name the connection "BRANCH-CAMPUS" and click "Next".

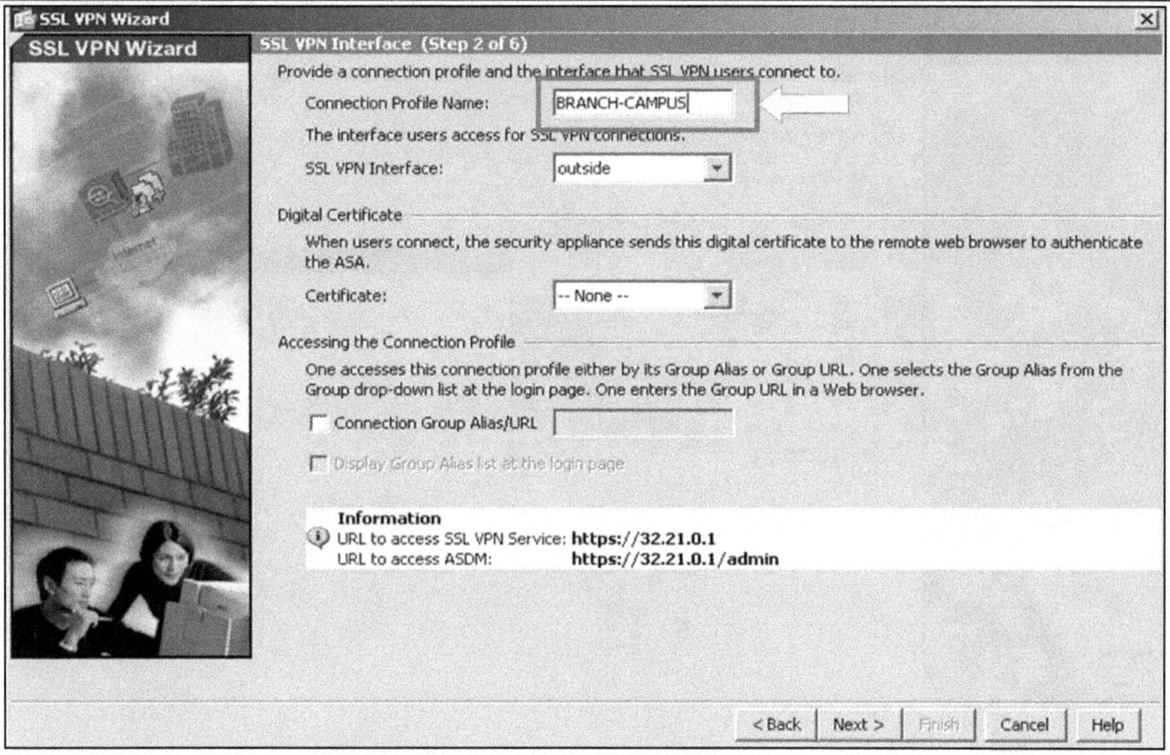

As shown in the figure above, local database on ASA will be used for authenticating users who want to connect to the main branch via VPN. Other options include integration with ACS etc. Define username with following credentials:

Username: Remote-User

Password: P@$$word:10

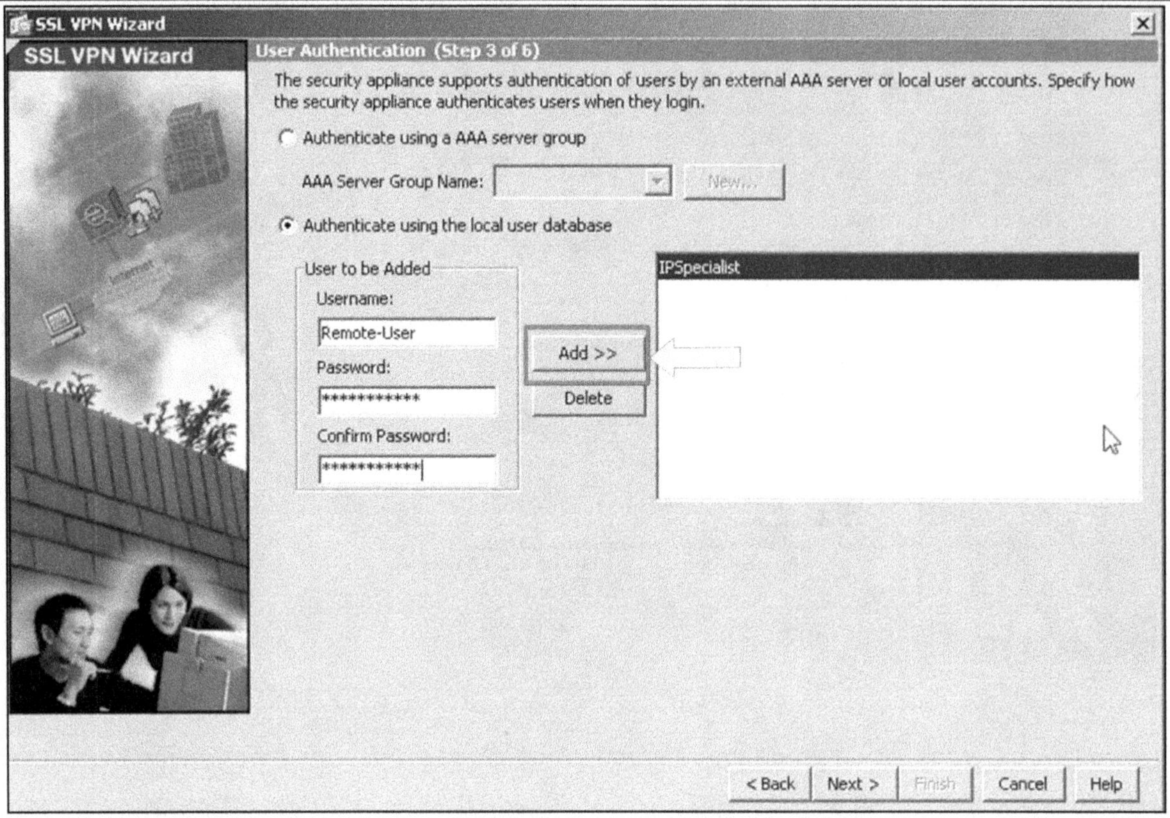
SSL VPN Wizard
SSL VPN Wizard
User Authentication (Step 3 of 6)
The security appliance supports authentication of users by an external AAA server or local user accounts. Specify how the security appliance authenticates users when they login.
Authenticate using a AAA server group
AAA Server Group Name:
New...
Authenticate using the local user database
User to be Added
Username:
Remote-User
Password:
Confirm Password:
Add >>
Delete
IPSpecialist
< Back
Next >
Finish
Cancel
Help

Select "Group Policy" for users.

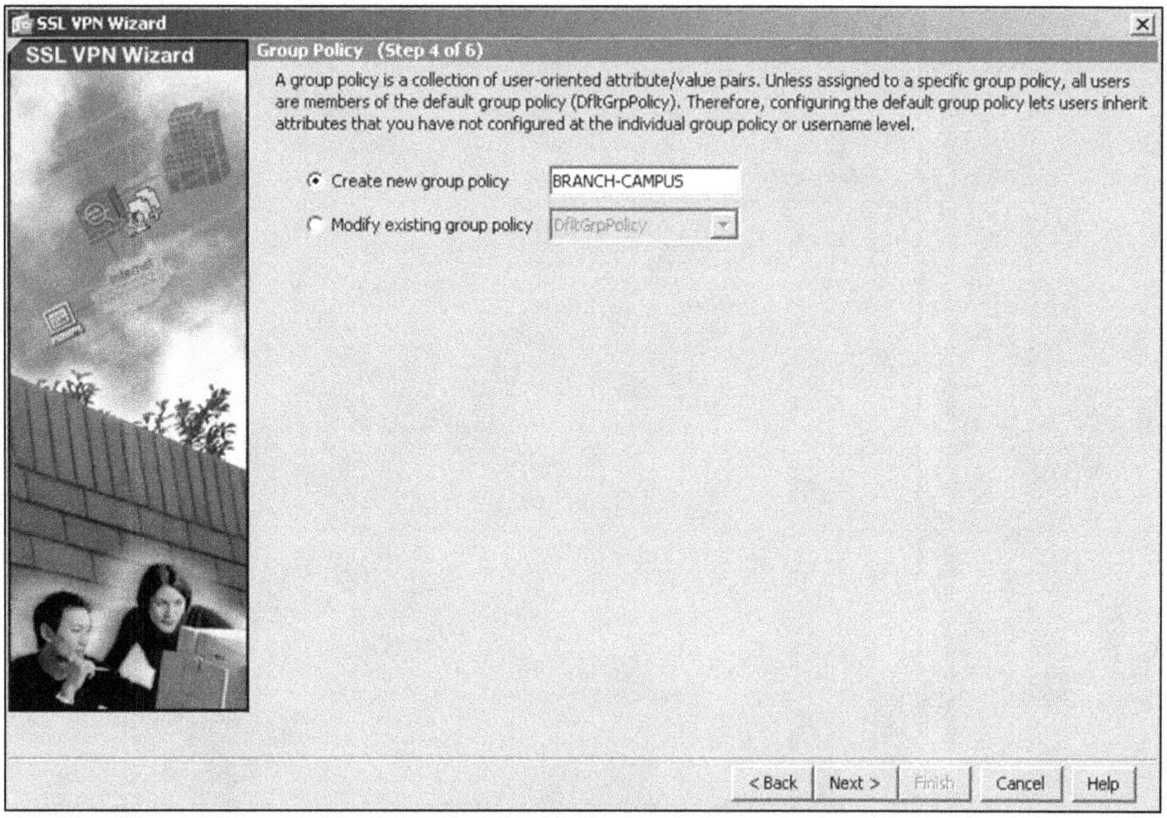

By Clicking on the "Manage" button, custom web URLs can be added, which can be accessed by users after connecting via clientless SSL VPN, but here, we selected "None" in the bookmark list.

The figure shown above, gives you the summary of SSL VPN link.

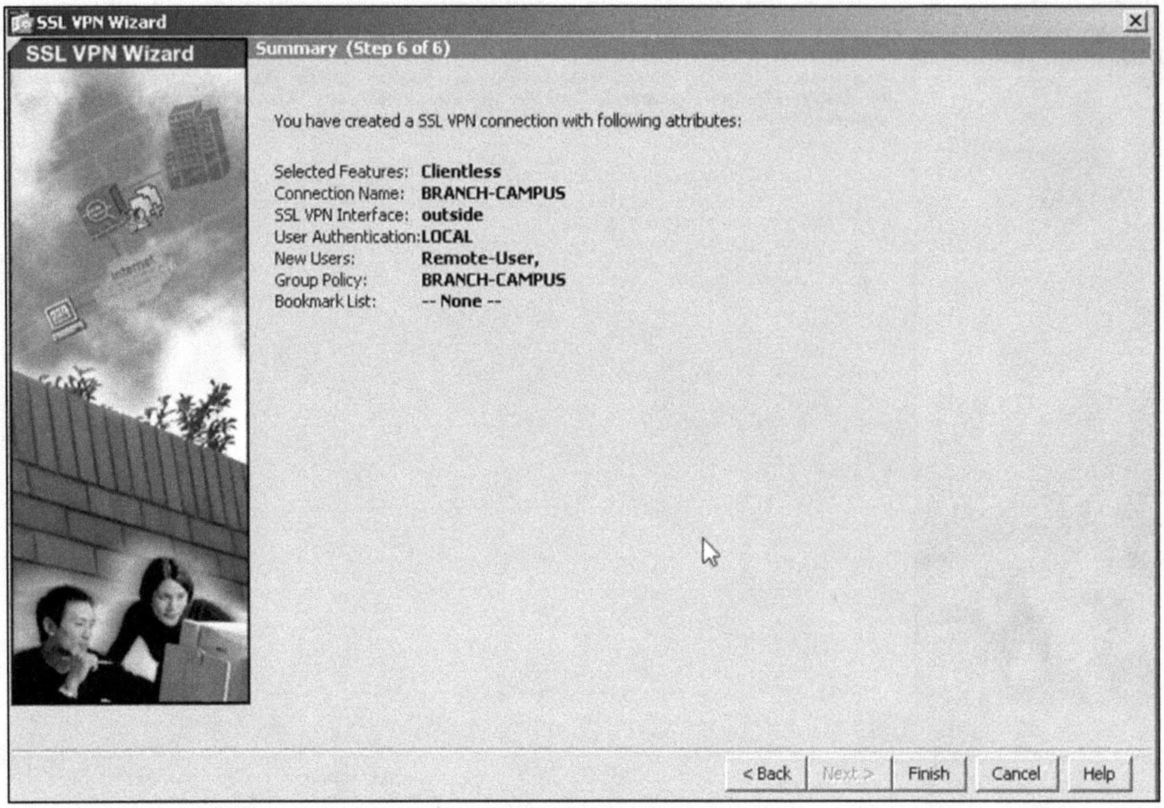

Click "Finish" to store and save the settings. Access the ASA via CLI and issue the following commands:

```
FW1(config)# webvpn
FW1 (config-webvpn)# no anyconnect-essentials
```

By default, the "AnyConnect Essentials license" is used instead of the other licenses, but you can disable the AnyConnect Essentials license in the configuration to restore the use of other licenses, by using "no anyconnect-essentials" command.

Let us move to the branch campus' management station and access the ASA's outside interface IP address. The following dialog should appear:

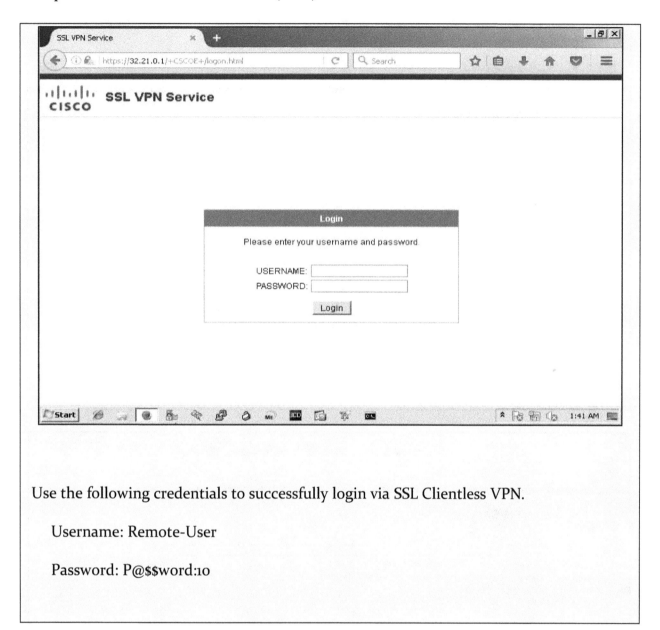

Use the following credentials to successfully login via SSL Clientless VPN.

Username: Remote-User

Password: P@$$word:10

SSL VPN Service
https://32.21.0.1/+CSCOE+/logon.html
Search
CISCO
SSL VPN Service
Login
Please enter your username and password.
USERNAME: Remote-User
PASSWORD:
Login
Start
1:43 AM

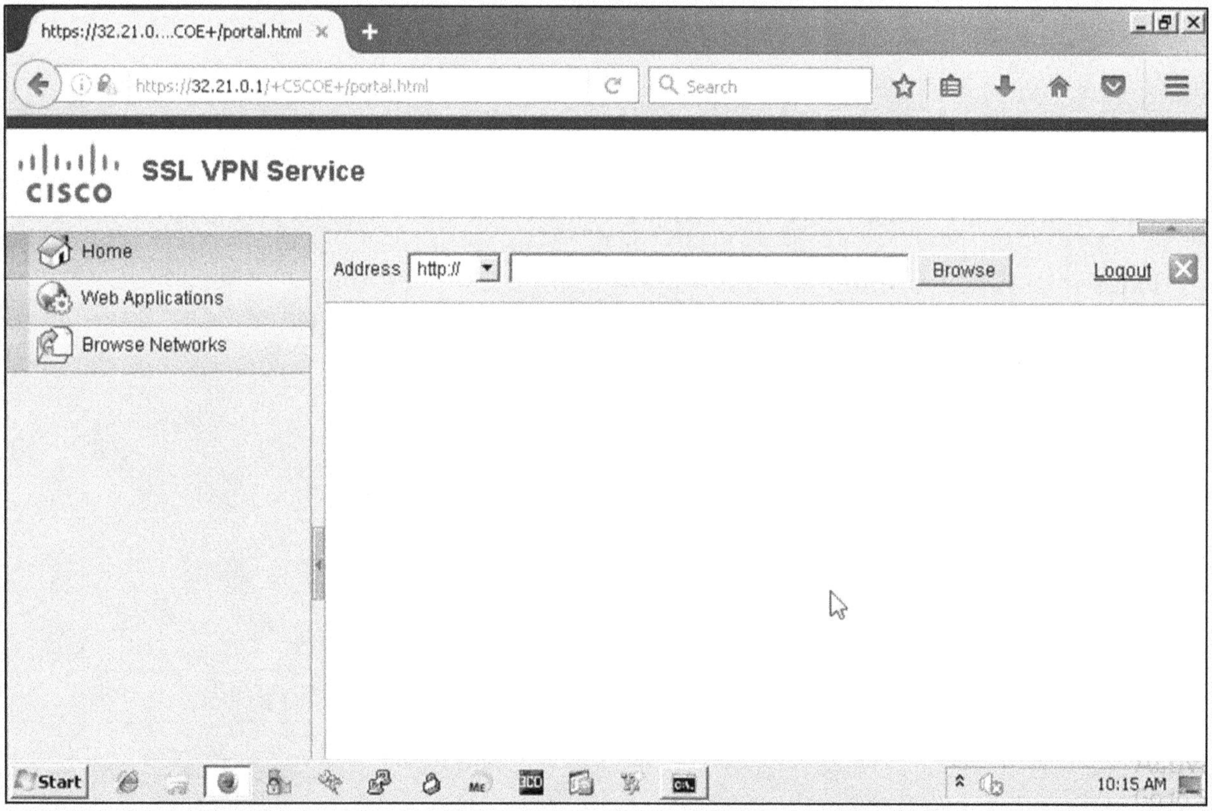
https://32.21.0....COE+/portal.html
https://32.21.0.1/+CSCOE+/portal.html
Search
CISCO
SSL VPN Service
Home
Web Applications
Browse Networks
Address
http://
Browse
Logout
Start
10:15 AM

In order to check the active VPN connections via ASDM, click: “Monitoring” -> “VPN” -> “VPN Statistics” -> “Sessions”.

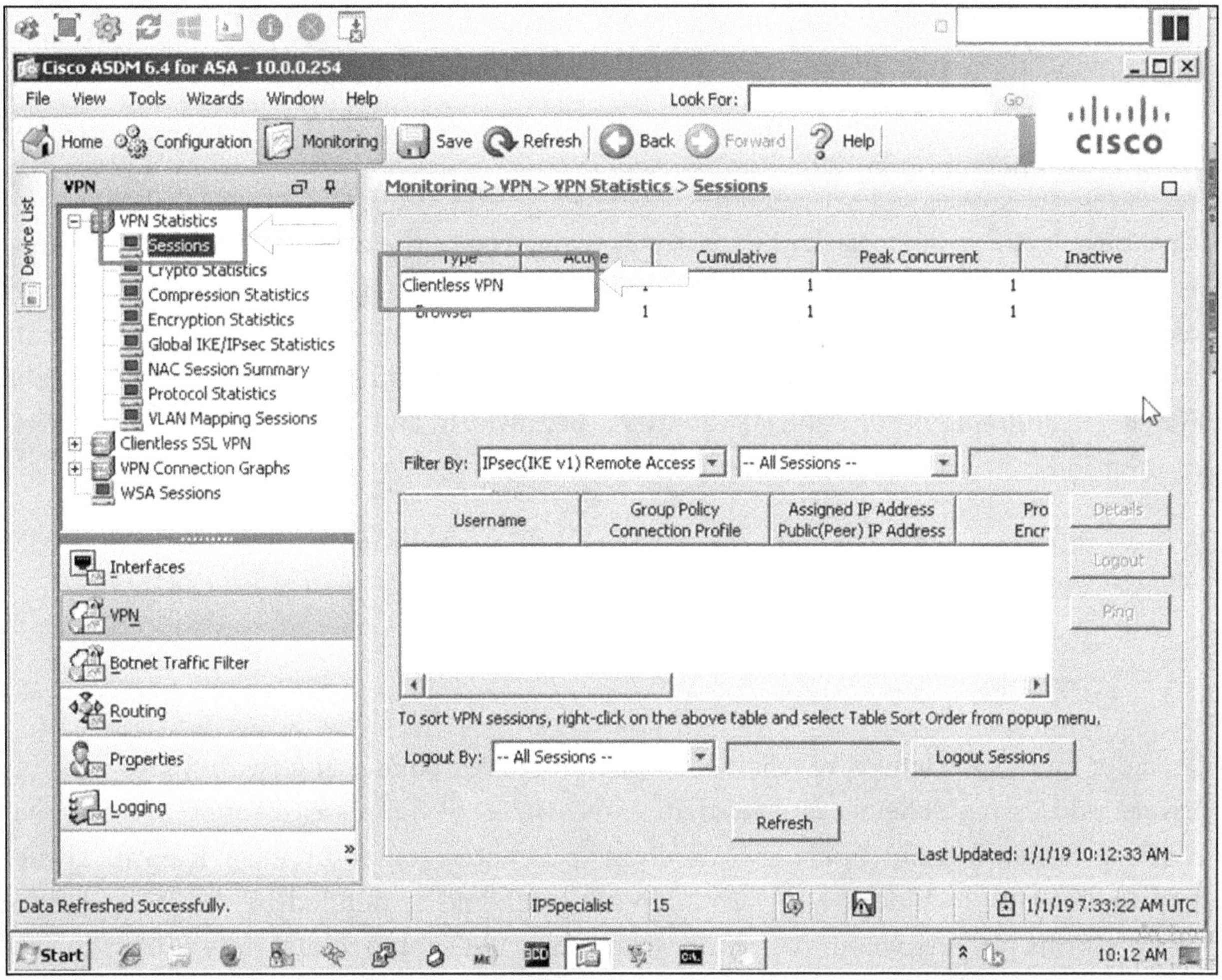

Multi-Protocol Label Switching (MPLS)

Multiprotocol Label Switching (MPLS) and MPLS Layer 3 VPNs are the VPN services provided by the internet service provider to allow an organization with two or more branches to have logical connectivity between the sites using the service provider's network for transport. This is also a type of VPN and called MPLS L3VPN, but it doesn't provide any encryption by default.

It enables data flow to be easier and faster as compared to the other methods of data flow. As it uses short path labels instead of IP addresses for routing network packets. It uses labels for making routing decisions. The label based routing mechanism enables a data packet to move on any protocol. The label contains the routing information, such as the source IP address, destination IP address, bandwidth and other factors like socket information.

In this chapter we will not go into the details of MPLS, as our main focus will be on IPSEC and SSL VPN.

NAT Traversal

Consider a scenario where VPN is not implemented for connecting two remote sites. As private addressing schemes are used in LAN, these IP addresses cannot move across public internet without NATing. Therefore, perimeter router or edge firewall always perform NATing to hide the private addressing scheme as defined in RFC 1918. Device that performs NATing will make a local database or NAT table to make sure that the data transaction is just between its source and destination.

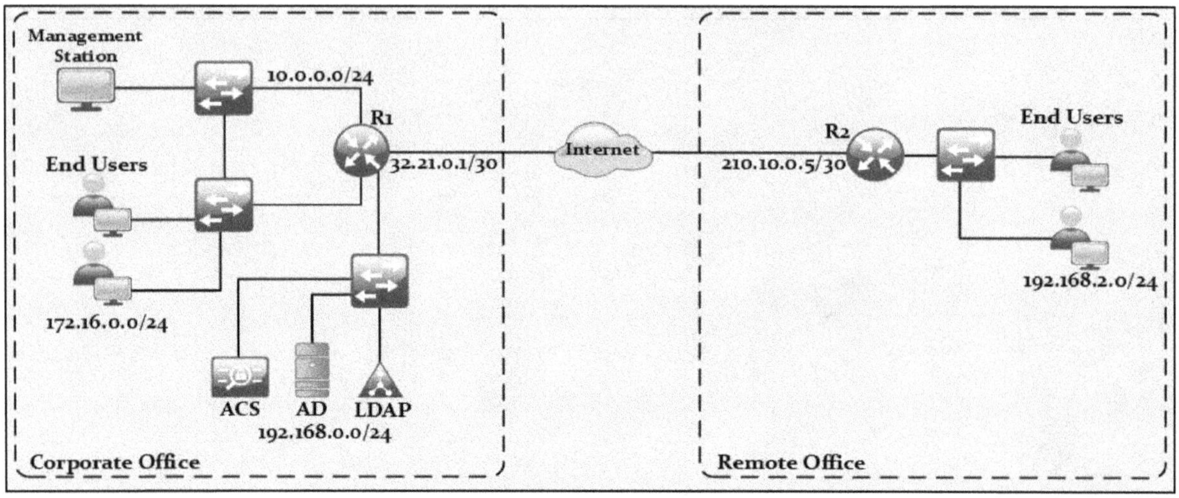

Figure 3-16: NAT Traversal Feature

For example, 172.16.0.10 wants to reach Google's DNS. Then NAT table will look like:

Original Source IP	Translated Source IP	Source Port	Destination IP	Destination Port
172.16.0.10	32.21.0.1	41101	8.8.8.8	80
172.16.0.10	32.21.0.1	41102	8.8.8.8	80
172.16.0.10	32.21.0.1	41103	8.8.8.8	80

Table 3-03: NAT Conversion

Now, consider a scenario where two sites want to establish a VPN connection between them. Here, a problem arises when VPN is established with *Encapsulation Security Payload (ESP).* Although, VPN provides great features like confidentiality and integrity by encapsulating the original payload and IP header in a User Datagram Protocol (UDP) wrapper, which allows the packets to travel across NAT devices. Suppose that a client from corporate office wants to connect to remote office and VPN configured on both routers then new IP packets will look as shown in the figure below:

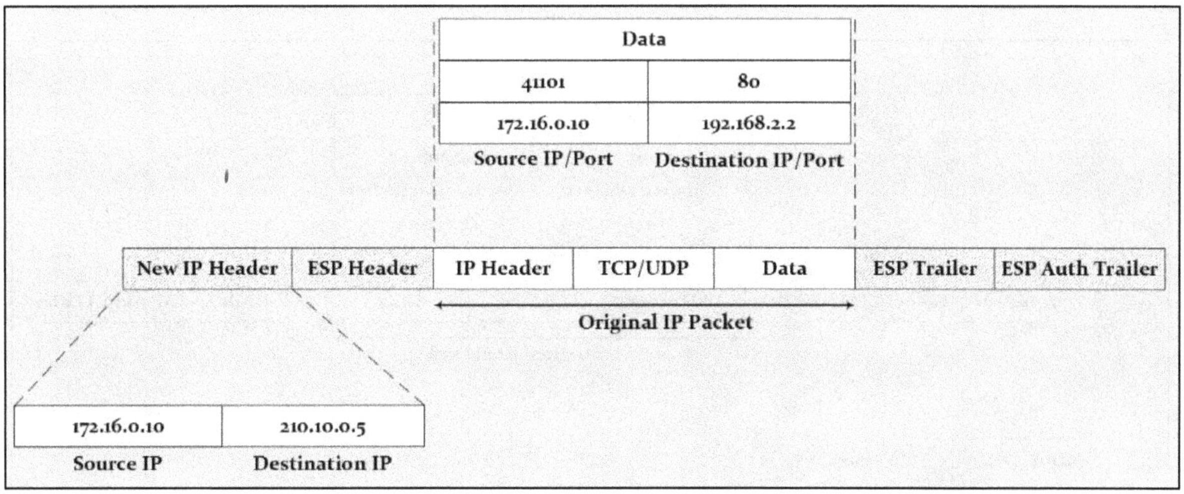

Figure 3-17: IPsec without Nat-Traversal

Usually, there are 4 parameters that provides normal flow of data packets between source and destination during transaction. These are: Source IP, Source port, Destination IP and Destination port.

These parameters let your data packet know how to arrive at the right destination and how to respond back to the source. The **IP address** simply tells you the "TO" and "FROM" of the data packet, just like the address of a house. The **Port number** serves as a sub address of your destination. For example, a mailbox outside your house, but if it is an apartment building, which has many residents or sub houses at a single address, there would be individual mailboxes for all, so that is how port number serves its purpose, it targets the right mailbox or sub address of the main address. The combination of address and port number is called "Socket" and this combination is really important as it leads you to the accurate destination.

Nonetheless, the problem arises where a user wants to establish an ESP connection behind the device, which performs NATing. The process of NATing involves the manipulation of IPheader and TCP/UDP port information to maintain a NAT table, but here, NATing device is unable to do so because the data packet is encapsulated inside the ESP packet. Therefore the device that performs NATing is unable to maintain translation table with packets after ESP encapsulation, which results tearing down of IPsec tunnel.

NAT-Traversal solves the problem above by encapsulating the datagram with a UDP packet. By doing so, source and destination ports will also be included inside a new packet and NATing will work successfully in this case. Now packet arrangement will look like:

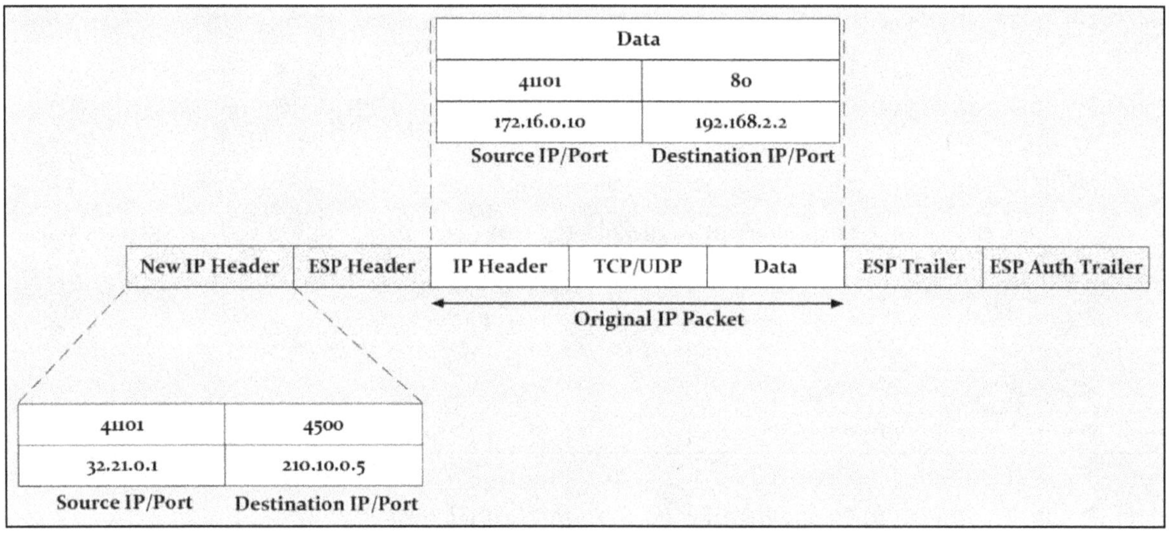

Figure 3-18: IPsec with Nat-Traversal

One important thing about NAT-Traversal is that both secure VPN peers needs to support NAT-Traversal feature, otherwise it will be of no use if any one of them does not support it.

Hair-pinning

Hair-pinning is a method where a packet goes out from an interface, instead of moving towards the internet it makes a hairpin turn, and returns back to the same interface. Usually it seems useless, but it does serves a purpose.

Consider the following scenario where two remote sites have established VPN connection with corporate office by Hub/Spoke fashion and corporate router acting as hub.

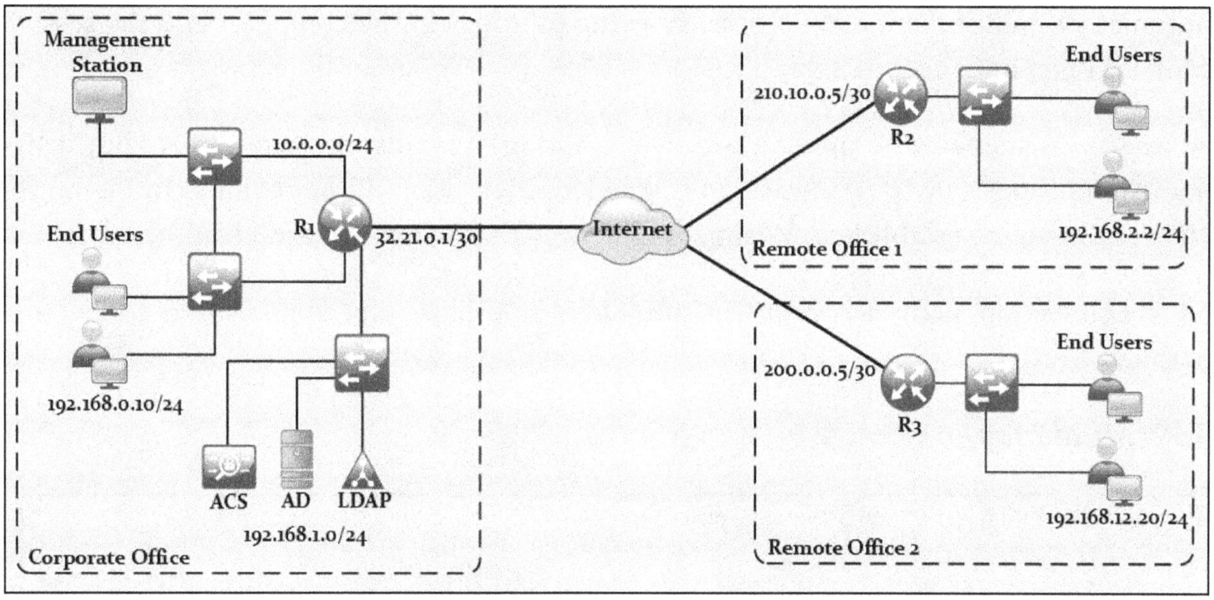

Figure 3-19: IPsec Hair-pinning

If remote office #1 wants secure communication with remote office #2, then data will be sent to the hub in first step. Hub will decrypt the data and encrypt it again to send it over the logical link with the remote site #2. In short, when router/firewall needs to send the data over the same link the data is received, then *hair-pinning* feature needs to be enabled.

Split-Tunnelling

Using IPsec for securing IP traffic either by encryption, hashing or using both, is a very CPU intensive process. In order to optimise the network by using VPN connection for only specific traffic, split tunnelling feature is used. By using *access list,* only required traffic goes encrypted over logical tunnel while remaining traffic like internet surfing or local traffic goes out of gateway without any alteration. Hence, by using split-tunnelling, end-users can use both *Local Area Network (LAN)* for normal usage and *secure SSL connection* for accessing corporate network at the same time.

Always-On

Always-on is one of the features used with *Cisco's AnyConnect* Client software for SSL based VPN. When enabled, end-users will not be able to access public network resources like internet surfing until and unless a VPN session is active. This feature allows an automatic establishment of VPN session as the user logs in the computer and the session remains open until user logs out.

Always-on is supposed to provide security to end user against security threats but it has some limitations as well. If *always-on* is enabled, then user will be required to log-on for VPN session to be established. Without login, no VPN session will establish.

VPN connection with *always-on* feature does not have any support for connecting through a proxy.

VPN Mind Map

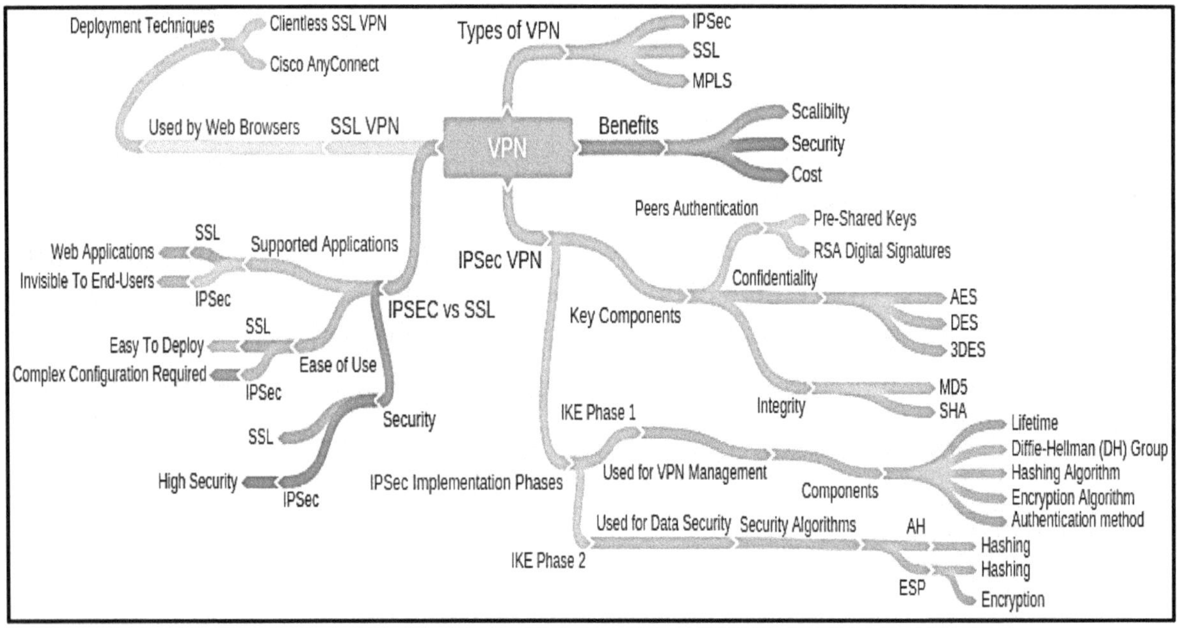

Figure 3-20: VPN Mind Map

Practice Questions

1. Which statement best describes a VPN connection?
   A. VPNs use virtual connections to create a secure tunnel over a public network.
   B. VPNs use dedicated physical connections to transfer data between connected users.
   C. VPNs use logical connections to create public networks over the Internet.
   D. VPNs use open source virtualization software to create the tunnel through the Internet.

2. Which are the key features of VPN technology? (Choose any four)
   A. Confidentiality
   B. Virtualization
   C. Data integrity
   D. Authentication
   E. Anti-replay Protection
   F. Authorization

3. Which of the following VPN offers end-user connectivity?
   A. Site-to-site VPN
   B. Remote access VPN
   C. Hybrid VPN
   D. None

4. Which of the following VPN technologies are used today? (Choose any three)
   A. IPsec
   B. SSL
   C. HTTPS
   D. MPLS
   E. SMTP

5. Which of the protocol provides confidentiality integrity, and authentication services and is a type of VPN?
   A. ESP
   B. IPsec
   C. MD5

D. AES

6. What three protocols must be permitted for the establishment of IPsec site-to-site VPNs? (Choose any three)
   A. SSH
   B. AH
   C. ISAKMP
   D. NTP
   E. ESP
   F. HTTPS

7. During the establishment of an IPsec VPN tunnel, when is the security association (SA) created?
   A. During Phase 1
   B. During Phase 2
   C. During both Phase 1 and 2
   D. None of the above

8. Which action takes place during the IKE Phase 2 exchange of IPsec peer establishment?
   A. Negotiation of IKE policy sets
   B. Exchange of keep alive packets
   C. Negotiation of IPsec policy
   D. Exchange of Hello packets

9. Which of the following statements describe the IPsec protocol framework? (Choose any two)
   A. AH provides integrity and authentication.
   B. ESP provides encryption, authentication, and integrity.
   C. AH uses IP protocol 40.
   D. AH provides encryption and integrity.

10. Which of the two IPsec protocols are used to provide data integrity?
    A. AES
    B. DH

C. MD5
D. RSA
E. SHA

11. Which of the following protocols must be allowed for an IPsec VPN tunnel establishment and operation? (Choose any two)
A. 501
B. 500
C. 51
D. 168
E. 50

12. Which one is the characteristic of remote-access VPNs?
A. The VPN configuration is identical between the remote devices.
B. The VPN connection is initiated by the remote user.
C. Internal hosts have no knowledge of the VPN.
D. Information required to establish the VPN must remain static.

13. Which mode of IPsec encapsulate only payload field while the original IP headers remain unchanged?
A. Tunnel mode
B. Transport mode
C. Both tunnel and transport mode
D. None of the above

14. Which of the VPN is provided by the internet service provider to allow an organization with two or more branches to have logical connectivity between the sites using the service provider's network for transport?
A. SSL
B. IPSec
C. MPLS
D. None of the above

15. What purpose does NAT-Traversal feature serves?
A. Disables NAT for VPN clients

B. Allows NAT to work transparently on one or both ends of the VPN connection
C. Makes NAT to be used for IPv6 addresses
D. Upgrades NAT for IPv4

16. The situation where VPN traffic that is received by an interface is routed back out that same interface is known as ___________.
A. GRE
B. MPLS
C. Hair-pinning
D. Split-tunnelling

17. Refer to the exhibit. Which algorithm is used here for providing confidentiality?

```
R1(config)# crypto isakmp policy 1
R1(config-isakmp)# hash md5
R1(config-isakmp)# encryption des
R1(config-isakmp)#group 2
R1(config-isakmp)#lifetime 3600
R1(config-isakmp)#authentication pre-share
```

A. RSA
B. Diffie-Hellman
C. DES
D. AES

18. Which is the best transform amongst all to provide protection?
A. crypto ipsec transform-set ESP-DES-SHA esp-3des esp-sha-hmac
B. crypto ipsec transform-set ESP-DES-SHA esp-des esp-sha-hmac
C. crypto ipsec transform-set ESP-DES-SHA esp-aes esp-des esp-sha-hmac
D. crypto ipsec transform-set ESP-DES-SHA esp-aes-256 esp-sha-hmac

19. What is the main function of the Diffie-Hellman algorithm inside the IPsec framework?
A. Provides encryption

B. Provides authentication
C. Allows peers to exchange shared keys
D. Guarantees message delivery

20. Refer to the exhibit. Which algorithm is used here for providing data integrity?

```
R1(config)# crypto isakmp policy 1
R1(config-isakmp)# hash md5
R1(config-isakmp)# encryption des
R1(config-isakmp)#group 2
R1(config-isakmp)#lifetime 3600
R1(config-isakmp)#authentication pre-share
```

A. SHA
B. MD5
C. DES
D. AES

Chapter 04: Secure Routing & Switching

Technology Brief

In the previous chapter, we have discussed about securing the data in motion over the internet. One aspect of network security is securing the end-user's data traffic along with access and management of networking devices. Another aspect of network security is to secure the traffic generated by networking device itself. In an organization, a network administrator should be aware of and have a command on different types of traffic that is traversing in their networks. Traffic analysis and monitoring is essential part of network security as it helps network administrator to effectively troubleshoot and resolve the problems when they occur.

Let us take an example of access-list. We can apply it to an interface in any direction to filter the traffic. However, access-list applied to the interface has nothing to do with the traffic generated on that interface by the device itself. Similarly, various routing as well as Layer 2 protocols along with application layer programs generate broadcast/multicast traffic, which creates another dimension of generating an attack on a network.

Security on Cisco Routers

Routing is one of the most essential parts of networking infrastructure that keeps a network running, and it is an absolutely necessary measure to secure it. There are always threats through which routing can be compromised, for example, from the injection of illegitimate updates specially designed to disturb the routing tables. Attackers generally target the routing devices, the routing information or the peering sessions to disturb the routing process.

The router's main function is to learn and traverse routing information, and to forward the data packets through the most appropriate paths from source to destination. Usually, routers are the target of some common sort of attacks designed to compromise end users and servers, such as password stealing, privilege escalation, buffer overflows, and social engineering.

In chapter 2, namely secure access, we have discussed different techniques related to the security of management plane of Cisco IOS. One of the most prominent features already discussed is the assignment of different privilege levels to the employees according to their job description or tasks assigned to them. It is better to have a quick review of different privilege levels, secure management and CLI access using parser views from chapter 2.

In this section, we will discuss most of the concepts discussed in this section are related to securing the routers and switches features and protocols by using limited yet important security features of Cisco IOS.

Cisco ISO Resilient Configuration Feature

Consider a scenario where an employee named Laurel had created one of the worst situations for the networking team by erasing the flash drive of the router. To make situation even worse, she dared to delete the start-up configuration as well. If nobody had noticed what she had done, then on the next reboot, the device would have entered into ***rommon mode*** as flash drive and start-up configuration file would be erased already. The only option left for networking team was to visit the site physically and to use TFTP service to reload the router in the working condition by first restoring the flash followed by placing the start-up configuration in NVRAM.

In order to mitigate such situations, Cisco IOS has a great feature of "***resilient configuration***", which makes a backup copy running IOS image and configuration to mitigate the accidental or malicious attempts of erasing flash and NVRAM of the device.

Limitations: Although it is a great feature, it has some limitations in some cases. Creating a backup file of IOS image along with configuration file needs space to store it. Even though IOS image size is always in MBs, devices have limited storage capabilities. It may be required to have only one IOS in flash in order to have a backup image of it.

This feature disables only by connecting to a device via console port. Remote session does not allow reverting the resilient IOS feature.

Command to see the files created by this feature is "***show secure bootset***". Normally, "***dir***" command lists the files in a directory but *dir* command does not list the secured files created by this feature. Similarly, a *rommon* mode can also be used to see and copy backup files into working condition as *rommon* mode does not have same restrictions as Cisco IOS.

Here are the following configuration steps needed to implement resilient feature on routers and switches.

```
Router> enable

Router# configure terminal
```

Following command is used for IOS image secure backup.

```
Router(config)# secure boot-image
```

Similarly, following command is used for secure configuration backup in persistent storage.

```
Router(config)# secure boot-config
Router(config)# end
```

In order to verify whether the above command is working or not, use the following command:

```
Router# show secure bootset
```

Restoring an Archived Configuration

Consider a situation where flash and NVRAM of the router has been erased due to any reason. Luckily, the IOS reliant feature was enabled. Now it is time to restore the router to its previous state by using the following procedure:

As router is powered on, rommon mode will appear. As flash does not contain any valid IOS image, dir [filesystem] is used for listing files in a directory.

```
rommon 1> dir slot1:
```

boot [partition number]: [filename] command is used to boot from the secured copy of IOS image.

```
rommon 2> boot slot1: c3745-js2-mz
```

Now reload the router. As there is no start-up configuration, router prompts for initial configuration wizard. Use the following commands to use the secure start-up configuration file.

```
Router> enable
Router# configure terminal
```

Use the following command to get the secure configuration in a file.

```
Router (config) # secure boot-config restore slot1:rescue-cfg
```

The above command copies the secure configuration into a file named rescue-cfg. You can use any name for this file. Use the following command to copy the configuration from the above file in to the running configuration.

```
Router# copy slot1:rescue-cfg running-config
```

Secure Routing Protocols

In a networking environment, there are two broad categories of protocols namely *routed protocols* and *routing protocols*. Routed protocols include IPv4 and IPv6 and are used to move the user data traffic across the network. Routing protocols are used by routers to exchange the routing table entries i.e. network segments information with other routers under a common administrative domain. Examples of routing protocols are EIGRP, OSPF and RIP.

For example, in a small-office/home-office situation where a single router may be used for inter-VLAN routing as well as for the communication with public internet like shown below, a single default route pointing towards the service provider's end is perfectly fine.

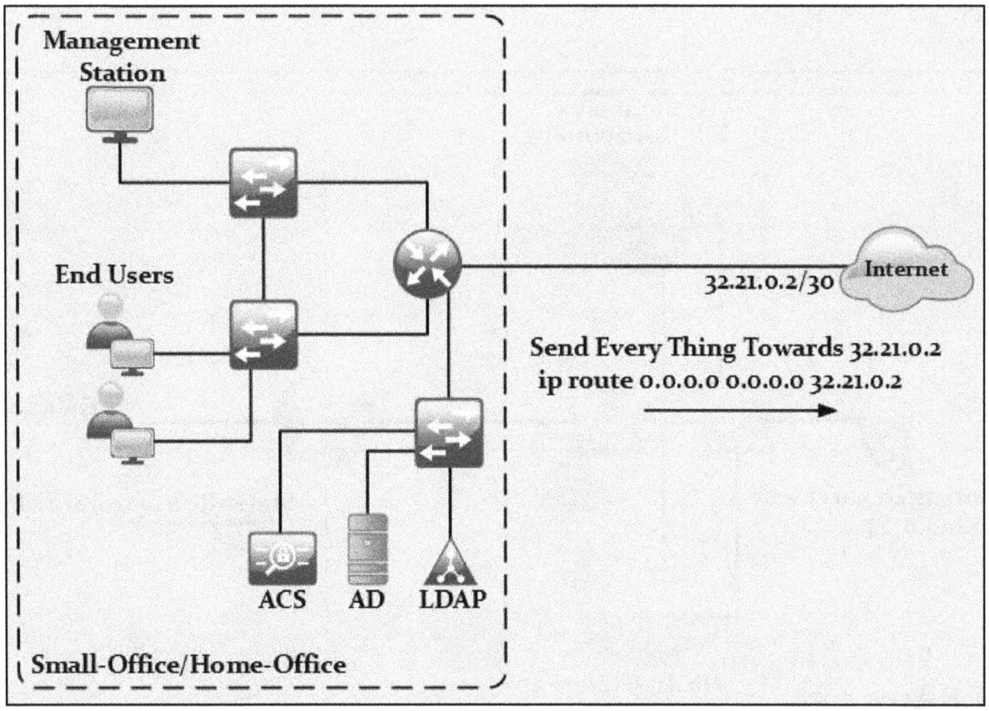

Figure 4-01: Static Route for Small-Office/Home-Office

In such cases, a router is not generating routing protocol information as static route is used. In networking topologies where number of networks running in an organization is relatively small, static routing may provide best security, but when we talk about multinational organizations where offices are spanned over a large geographical region, then static routing will not be suitable. In such situations, dynamic routing protocols are used where routers under a common administrative domain know how to reach a specific subnet depending on unique route preference mechanism of each protocol. For example, *EIGRP*, a Cisco proprietary protocol uses multiple features like bandwidth, delay reliability MTU and load of interfaces along different paths to select the best one for specific network. Similarly, *Open Shortest Path First (OSPF)* is another popular IGP protocol, used extensively due to its open source implementation. It is normally a first choice as dynamic protocol in a multi-vendor network topology.

Security Concerns related to dynamic routing

Although dynamic protocols simplify the job of network administrative team, it also creates some security concerns as well. One of the major problems with dynamic routing protocols is their use of broadcast or multicast traffic. Most IGP routing protocols in use today generates multicast traffic for neighbour discovery and information sharing. Consider a scenario where an organization is using OSPF as dynamic routing protocol, as shown below:

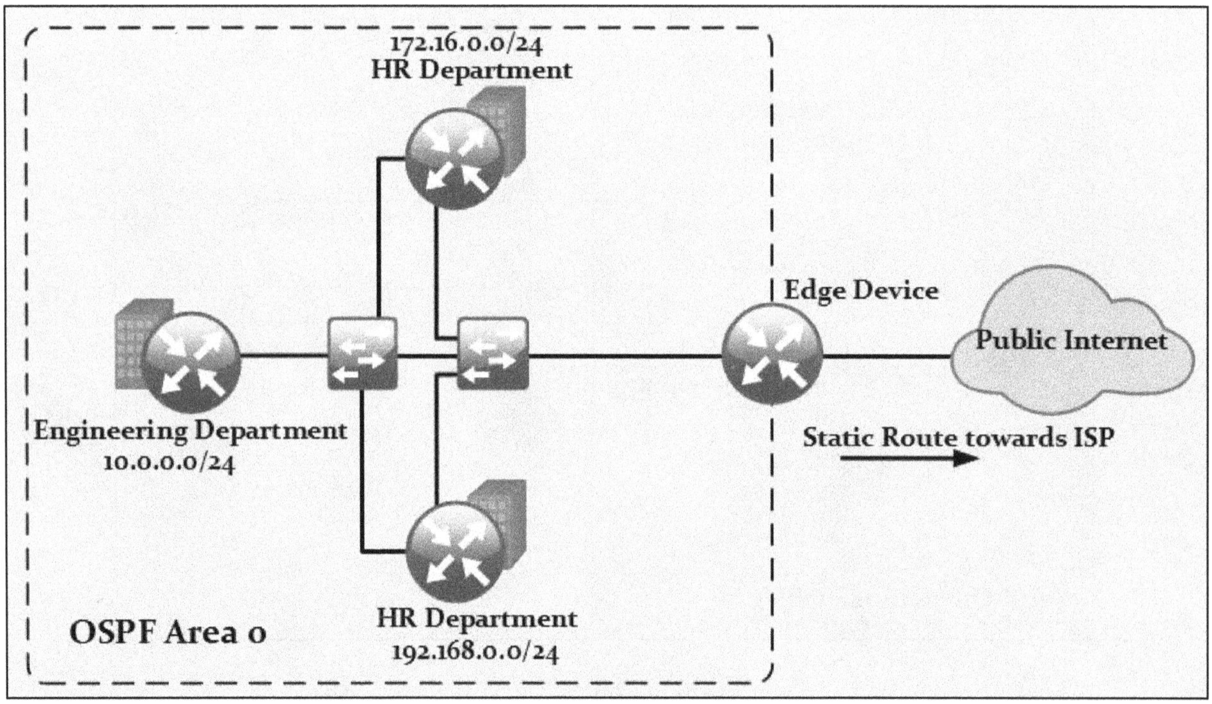

Figure 4-02: OSPF Instance within an Organization

In the diagram above, perimeter edge device, a router in this case will redistribute the default route in to the OSPF domain. Now, consider the scenario shown below where an attacker gets a chance to connect his laptop, running a simulation software like GNS3, to broadcast multi-access network connecting different department's routers.

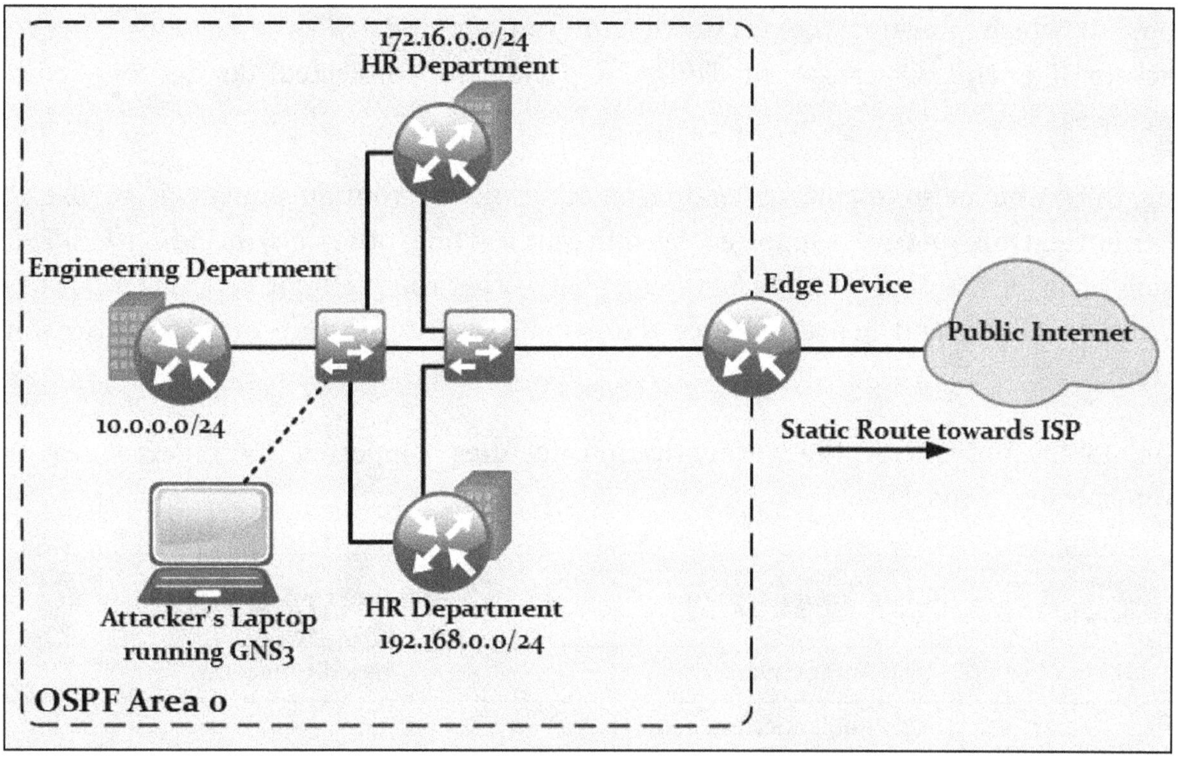

Figure 4-03: Attack on OSPF Routing Instance

The first thing the attacker wants to do is to run the sniffing software like *Wireshark* to receive the multicast packets sent to 224.0.0.5/224.0.0.6 addresses used by OSPF. Attacker can sniff the routing updates to find out the IP addressing scheme running within the OSPF domain along with the important information like OSPF area number, DR/BDR election details and default route as well.

After getting enough information, an attacker can run emulation software like *GNS3* and introduce it into the broadcast multi-access network as DR router. After becoming DR, attacker can introduce a default route with in OSPF domain by redistribution. Now every single router will send the traffic to the attacker as next hop and the attacker will either act as man-in-the-middle attack or alter the packets and send it to the original next hop router, which is Edge device as shown above. In this way, an attacker can sniff every single packet of an organization easily.

In order to mitigate such attacks, security of routing protocols needs to be implemented. If possible, **unicast traffic** must be used instead of multicast or broadcast traffic within routing domain so that no one is able to receive routing information.

Similarly, the concept of **Passive Interface** must be implemented within the routing domain, which prevents the transaction of routing updates or neighbour discovery packets like *HELLO* packet or *UPDATE* packet to connected devices on specific interfaces.

The third and most important feature of securing the routing domain is to use the **authentication feature** supported by different routing protocols including OSPF. By using MD5 for hashing, route updates along with other routing information will not be in clear text format and hence enhance the overall security posture of network to some extent.

This table summarizes the authentication features supported by different routing protocols in use today:

Routing Protocol	Authentication Options	Default Route Update Traffic Nature
RIP v1	No Authentication	Periodic broadcast
RIPv2	No Authentication Clear / Plaintext Authentication MD5	Periodic Multicast. 224.0.0.9
EIGRP	No Authentication MD5	Multicast on change. 224.0.0.10
OSPF	No Authentication Clear / Plaintext Authentication MD5	Multicast 224.0.0.[5,6]

Table 4-01: Authentication Support in Different Routing Protocols

Lab 4.1: Implementation of Links Authentication within the OSPF Domain

Case Study

The national billing and clearance company 'X' has corporate headquarter located at New York with branch offices in different cities. Having more than 500+ employees with confidential data, organization invested a huge amount of money by purchasing next generation firewalls as countermeasure of recent cyber-attacks in the city. However, a recent audit report still shows vulnerabilities in the current security posture of the IT infrastructure.

According to the recent audit report, it has been decided to implement the security of devices involved in the forwarding of data within corporate headquarter including router, switches and servers. The next figure represents one of the most critical segments of the company's IT infrastructure. All configuration implemented in this section will be related to the security of this segment.

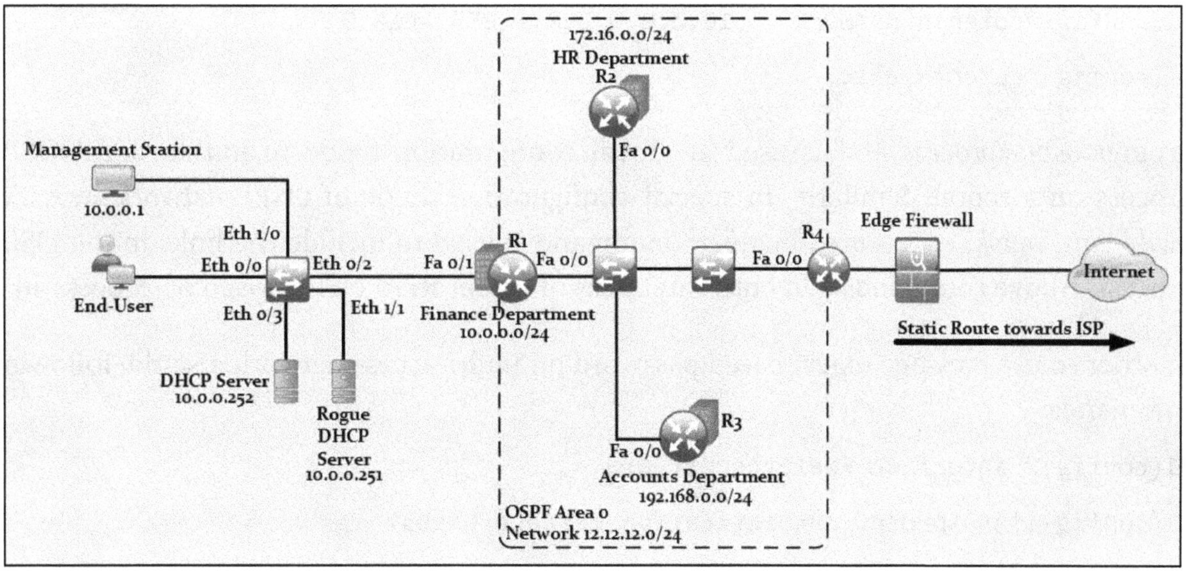

Figure 4-04: Secure Routing and Switching Case Study

Implementing the authentication feature of routing protocols helps in preventing malicious router from becoming the neighbour and thus, manipulating the routing table of corporate devices. As shown above, *OSPF Area 0* needs to be configured between common multi access networks. Configuration will be started from router R1. As long as the correct password is used, OSPF neighbour-ship will succeed followed by the adjacency process. A *Message-Digest* based password of *P@$$word:10* will be used on links in this lab. In this lab, IOU based Layer 2 switch will be used for implementing security concepts related to switching part explained previously in the theoretical section.

Due to the usage of IOU, management station shown in the diagram above will be emulated by a router with an IP address of 10.0.0.1 and it will be used to *SSH* the devices remotely. Assume that, all the concepts learned and implemented in the previous lab sections, for example access from management station and default passwords used in previous labs are already applied in this lab.

R1

Assume that Basic IP addressing, password and access policies ve already been implemented in Base Configuration of this lab. In order to use OSPF as dynamic routing protocol following commands will be used in global configuration mode:

```
R1(config)# router ospf 1
R1(config-router)# network    12.12.12.1 0.0.0.255 area 0
R1(config-router)# network    10.0.0.0 0.0.0.255 area 0
R1(config-router)# exit
```

"router ospf <process-id>" is used at global configuration mode to initiate local OSPF process on a router. Similarly, in special configuration mode of OSPF *network <x.x.x.x> <wild-card-mask> area <area-number>* command is used to include the links in the OSPF process. Above commands add both interfaces of router R1 in OSPF area 0 of process-id 1.

In order to use message digest based password on multi-access network, use the following commands:

```
R1(config)# interface FastEthernet 0/0
R1(config-if)# ip ospf authentication message-digest
R1(config-if)# ip ospf authentication-key P@$$word:10
```

As OSPF has the concept of adding a link in to the OSPF domain rather than a network like EIGRP. So this feature is also applied on the interface-level although it can also be defined under the OSPF process-ID. First, command shown above defines the authentication type to be message digest. In the second command, authentication password is defined. Same set of commands will be applied on other routers to make OSPF neighbour-ship and adjacency process successful.

R2

In order to represent the LAN segment of HR department on R2, loopback interface will be created and introduced in the router OSPF process.

```
R2(config)# interface loopback 1
R1(config-if)# ip address 172.16.0.1 255.255.255.0
R1(config-if)# exit

R2(config)# router ospf 1
R2(config-router)# network 12.12.12.2 0.0.0.255 area 0
R2(config-router)# network 172.16.0.1 0.0.0.255 area 0
```

As no password is currently defined, no neighbour-ship will be established. By using "*debug ip packet*" command, it will be clear that router sends multicast packets but does not get any response form R1 as no authentication is configured yet. Similarly, *show "ip ospf neighbor"* command will show nothing.

```
R2# debug ip packets

*Nov  1 00:45:59.823: IP: s=12.12.12.2 (local), d=224.0.0.5 (FastEthernet 0/0), len 76, sending broad/multicast
*Nov  1 00:45:59.831: IP: s=12.12.12.2 (local), d=224.0.0.5 (FastEthernet 0/0), len 76, sending full packet
```

```
R2(config)# interface FastEthernet 0/0
R2(config-if)# ip ospf authentication message-digest
R2(config-if)# ip ospf authentication-key P@$$word:10
```

As soon as above commands will be entered, neighbour-ship process will succeed as authentication method and password matches on both ends. This can be confirmed by using *show "ip ospf neighbour"* command.

R2# **show ip ospf neighbour**

```
R2
R2#show ip ospf neighbor

Neighbor ID     Pri   State           Dead Time   Address         Interface
12.12.12.1        1   FULL/BDR        00:00:35    12.12.12.1      FastEthernet0/0
R2#
```

By default, configuration loopback interface of R2 will be represented by /32 mask on other routers. To make it look like LAN subnet, following commands will be used:

R2(config)# **interface loopback 1**

R2(config-if)# **ip ospf network point-to-point**

Same set of commands will be applied on routers R3 and R4 to make the multi-access networks being password secured.

R3

R3# **config t**

R3(config)# **interface loopback 1**

R3(config-if)# **ip address 192.168.0.1 255.255.255.0**

R3(config-if)# **ip ospf network point-to-point**

R3(config-if)# **exit**

R3(config)# **router ospf 1**

R3(config-router)# **network 12.12.12.3 0.0.0.255 area 0**

R3(config-router)# **network 192.168.0.1 0.0.0.255 area 0**

R3(config-router)# **exit**

R3(config)# **interface FastEthernet 0/0**

R3(config-if)# **ip ospf authentication message-digest**

R3(config-if)# **ip ospf authentication-key P@$$word:10**

Following messages will be received as soon as correct password is entered on an interface.

***Nov 1 00:58:32.919: %OSPF-5-ADJCHG: Process 1, Nbr 172.16.0.1 on FastEthernet 0/0 from LOADING to FULL, Loading Done**

***Nov 1 00:58:33.155: %OSPF-5-ADJCHG: Process 1, Nbr 12.12.12.1 on FastEthernet 0/0 from LOADING to FULL, Loading Done**

Show ip ospf neighbour command can be used to further verify the neighbour-ship success.

R3# **show ip ospf neighbor**

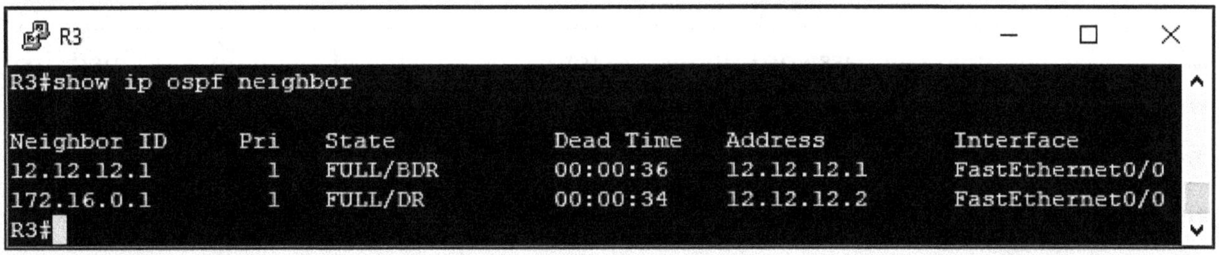

R4

R4# **config t**

R4(config)# **router ospf 1**

R4(config-router)# **network 12.12.12.4 0.0.0.255 area 0**

R4(config-router)# **exit**

R4(config)# **int FastEthernet 0/0**

R4(config-if)# **ip ospf authentication message-digest**

R4(config-if)# **ip ospf authentication-key P@$$word:10**

Show ip ospf neighbour command can be used to further verify the neighbour-ship success.

R4# **show ip ospf neighbor**

```
R4#show ip ospf neighbor

Neighbor ID     Pri   State           Dead Time   Address         Interface
12.12.12.1        1   FULL/BDR        00:00:33    12.12.12.1      FastEthernet0/0
172.16.0.1        1   FULL/DR         00:00:33    12.12.12.2      FastEthernet0/0
192.168.0.1       1   2WAY/DROTHER    00:00:36    12.12.12.3      FastEthernet0/0
R4#
```

Cisco Exam Objectives cover the authentication feature of OSPF but knowing the authentication feature of other IGP protocols like RIP and EIGRP is also important. Consider a scenario where RIP is used instead of OSPF in above routers. If authentication is desired, then following commands will be used. This section is just for further understanding. Do not bother to apply these commands on the lab.

R4

In OSPF, we defined the password under the interface. In RIP, a key chain is defined first, which states the key to be used as authentication password between the peers.

```
R4# configure terminal
R4(config)# key chain IPSPECIALIST
R4(config-keychain)# key 1
R4(config-keychain-key)# key-string P@$$word:10
R4(config-keychain-key)# exit
```

In the next step, this key chain will be called on the interface level.

```
R4(config)# interface FastEthernet 0/0
R4(config-if)# ip rip authentication mode md5
R4(config-if)# ip rip authentication key-chain IPSPECIALIST
R4(config-if)# exit
```

The same kind of syntax is used in case of EIGRP as shown below:

R4

```
R4(config)# key chain IPSPECIALIST
R4(config-keychain)# key 1
R4(config-keychain-key)# key-string P@$$word:10
R4(config-keychain-key)# exit
```

```
R4(config-keychain)# exit
R4(config)# interface FastEthernet 0/0
R4(config-if)# ip authentication mode eigrp 1000 md5
R4(config-if)# ip authentication key-chain eigrp 1000 IPSPECIALIST
```

Above commands shows a key chain named *IPSPECIALIST* is defined first followed by its calling for *EIGRP autonomous system number 1000* on interface FastEthernet 0/0

Securing the Control Plane

As discussed in chapter 2, a network infrastructure can be divided into three basic elements or functions, namely:

1. Management Plane
2. Control Plane
3. Data Plane

Control Function/Plane:

This plane involves the transaction of control packets. Control packets carry signaling traffic and routing operations for a router. Control packets are generated from a router and are destined for a router. This plane involves the calculation of best routes in the network for traffic, filtering of data i.e. which packet to be sent to the next level or which packet to be discarded, device discovery and many more. Examples include CPU usage by routing protocols. Similarly, any kind of traffic directed for networking device itself etc. The feature in Cisco IOS is Control Plane Policing (CoPP)

Control Plane Policing and Protection

Control-function/plane carries many kind of traffic, which consumes processing usage of networking device. As we already know, every networking device has some embedded processing unit, which performs everything from calculating best routes in the network to the data filtering and many more. Examples include CPU usage by routing protocols similarly, any kind of traffic directed for networking device itself etc.

As this section describes management and minimization of processing power of network devices, it is important to discuss the different techniques by which Cisco devices manage and process IP traffic.

Here is a quick review of some basic types of switching, which helps you to understand which switching technique is best for forwarding packets and which is good for device's processing unit.

Process Switching: Process switching is one of the oldest technique of switching, but it is also considered as the slowest forwarding technique as it consumes the processing and computation power more.

In process switching, all packets that enters the router is treated independently and can take a different path to the same destination. In process switching, the workload of CPU increases because it has to process each packet separately, and transaction of packets through different routes might cause the packets to arrive at the destination out of sequence. It also increases the workload of destination host as well, as it requires more time and resources to place the packets back together in the correct sequence, which utilizes more CPU time and somehow degrades performance to some extent.

Fast Switching: By early 90s, Cisco came up with more advanced and redefined form of switching for the forwarding of IP Packets. Fast Switching is cache-based IP forwarding process. Cisco started to use the cache of most recently used destination addresses along with exit interfaces. The packet from the source within the interrupt handler uses a cache of destination through address lookup to find the outgoing interface, the IP next hop and outbound layer-2 header. This improved the efficiency of packet forwarding and device's processing power to some level.

In Fast Switching, when the first packet of a session is getting out of an interface, a route is saved from source to destination and placed in a route cache. This route cache will be used for all the packets belonging to the same destination, so all packets belonging to that session take the same route.

Cisco Express Forwarding: Now a day, *Cisco Express Forwarding (CEF)* is the default option selected for control plane's working mechanism. In CEF, switching cache makes the route for the session in advance even before any packets need to be processed. CEF uses two main components to perform its function: The **Forwarding Information Base (FIB)** and the **Adjacency Table**. The FIB more or less works like a routing table but with faster searching capabilities. The FIB makes the forwarding decision for the destination of the packet. It contains information like next hops, prefixes and the outgoing interfaces. The Adjacency table carries the information about directly connected next hops. CEF's performance has improved to a significant level by using multiple caches of networking information at hardware level and it is change triggered. It means that CEF's view to layer 3 information will be updated only when there is a change in network layer topology.

In general, IP data traffic at control plane has two broad categories:

- **Receive adjacency traffic:** Any kind of traffic for which next hop is device itself will fall in this category. For example, SSH traffic for remotely accessing the device etc. As this kind of traffic will be handled by CEF, *show ip cef* can be used to see the list of total hits against the control plane of device.
- **Special processing for data plane traffic:** Here are some of the reasons why data plane's traffic also hits control plane and ultimately use extra processing power of the device:

Logs generated by Access-Lists: If keyword *Log* is used at the end of access list entries, then log will be generated by the device itself every time the entries have been matched.

Generating ARP requests: Anytime an ARP entry missing on switch, the router will force the device to generate a broadcast for ARP, which will ultimately involve the CPU of the device.

ICMP messages: ICMP is commonly used for troubleshooting purposes. Its messages also require CPU processing power of the device.

Time-to-live expiry: Any packet with TTL less than or equal to 1 will result in generation of ICMP Time Exceed messages.

IP Fragmentation: IP Fragmentation also utilizes the processing power of the device. Some other features like *Unicast Reverse Path Forwarding* also utilizes CPU power.

How to Manage Device's Computational Power?

In order to effectively manage the resources of a device, Control Plane Policing (CoPP) is implemented which identifies specific traffic type and limits its rate that is reaching the control plane of the device.

Let us assume that Distributed Denial of Service (DDOS) attack has been launched against specific networking device by sending *ICMP* traffic towards it. If control plane policing is not implemented to limit the rate of *ICMP* traffic a device can receive, then it will badly effect the overall performance of the system as almost all resources of that device will be effected by this attack.

Control Plane Policing can be implemented by granular use of **Access Control Lists (ACLs)** and **logging features** of the device.

Another great feature to secure the control plane is the use of **Control Plane Protection (CPPr)** feature. *CPPr* gives granular control over the traffic entering the control plane of device. *CCPr* divides the traffic into three broad categories namely traffic for any physical or logical interface of device, data plane traffic that requires some processing before forwarding and Cisco Express Forwarding error or informational messages.

Although it works exactly in the same line as *CoPP*, we can also filter or rate-limit of the above defined traffic in a more granular way than *CoPP*.

Lab 4.2: Limiting the ICMP Traffic Towards First Hop by Control Plane Policing

According to the concepts learned in Control Plane Policing (CoPP) and Control Plane Protection (CPPr), unnecessary traffic towards the router can be filtered to improve the efficiency of networking device. In this lab, control plane policing will be implemented to filter the ICMP traffic towards router R1 from Finance Department LAN. Lab objective will be resumed from the previous lab in order to remain focused on original task as much as possible. Here is the following lab topology:

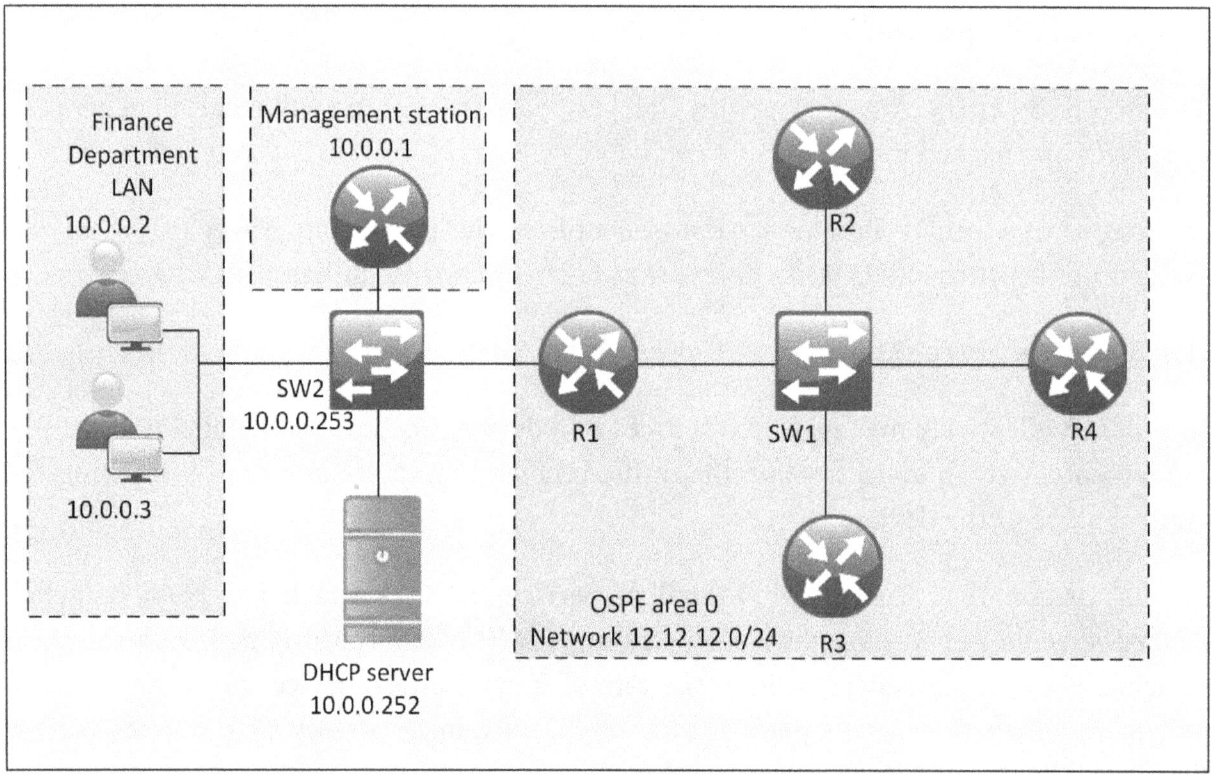

Figure 4-05: Control Plane Policing

R1

Ping command with increased size should be used first in order verify that traffic is allowed before filtering is applied at control plane.

Following commands are executed from management station, which is emulated by a router in this lab.

```
MGMT-STATION# ping 10.0.0.254 repeat 10 size 1000

Type escape sequence to abort.

Sending 10, 1000-byte ICMP Echos to 10.0.0.254, timeout is 2 seconds:

!!!!!!!!!!

Success rate is 100 percent (10/10), round-trip min/avg/max = 8/26/44 ms
```

Above results shows that a total of (10 x 1000) bytes were used in above ping test. In order to limit it, say to 5000, following commands will be used:

```
R1(config)# class-map match-all ICMP-FILTER
R1(config-cmap)# match access-group name ICMP-FILTER-ACL
R1(config-cmap)# exit
R1(config)# policy-map CoPP
R1(config-pmap)# class ICMP-FILTER
R1(config-pmap-c)#  police 160000 conform-action transmit  exceed-action drop
violate-action drop
R1(config-pmap-c)# exit
R1(config)# ip access-list extended ICMP-FILTER-ACL
R1(config-ext-nacl)# permit icmp 10.0.0.0 0.0.0.255 host 10.0.0.254
```

In above commands, a class map is created with name *ICMP-FILTER* to match the ICMP traffic from Finance Department's LAN to 10.0.0.254. Then in a policy-map with the name, *CoPP* is created with *police* command to drop traffic greater than 160,000 bits per second.

Same configuration is also used in QOS implementation via Modular QoS CLI (MQC), but in the lab above policy map will be applied on software based control plane of device rather than the physical or logical interface.

R1(config)# **control-plane**

R1(config-cp)# **service-policy input CoPP**

***Nov 1 10:26:38.391: %CP-5-FEATURE: Control-plane Policing feature enabled on Control plane aggregate path**

VERIFICATION

In the verification part, ping test will be used with same packet size as used before implementing the control plane policing and protection.

MGMT-STATION# **ping 10.0.0.254 repeat 10 size 1000**

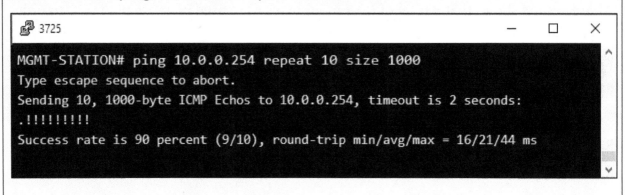

```
3725
MGMT-STATION# ping 10.0.0.254 repeat 10 size 1000
Type escape sequence to abort.
Sending 10, 1000-byte ICMP Echos to 10.0.0.254, timeout is 2 seconds:
.!!!!!!!!!
Success rate is 90 percent (9/10), round-trip min/avg/max = 16/21/44 ms
```

Similarly, "*show policy-map control-plane*" command shows the statistics of actions defined in policy map.

```
R1# show policy-map control-plane
 Control Plane

  Service-policy input: CoPP

    Class-map: ICMP-FILTER (match-all)
      10 packets, 10140 bytes
      5 minute offered rate 0 bps, drop rate 0 bps
      Match: access-group name ICMP-FILTER-ACL
      police:
          cir 160000 bps, bc 5000 bytes, be 1500 bytes
        conformed 9 packets, 9126 bytes; actions:
          transmit
        exceeded 1 packets, 1014 bytes; actions:
          drop
        violated 0 packets, 0 bytes; actions:
          drop
        conformed 0 bps, exceed 0 bps, violate 0 bps

    Class-map: class-default (match-any)
      90 packets, 14400 bytes
      5 minute offered rate 0 bps, drop rate 0 bps
      Match: any
```

Common Layer 2 Attacks

If you want to make your corporate or private network secure, you not only need to implement some security policies but you also need to be aware of the vulnerabilities that attackers can use to exploit your network. These vulnerabilities can give attackers access to the network and help them to control, steal or manipulate information from your network.

Following are the best security practices for overall network infrastructure, including layer 2 technologies:

- It is a good idea to change the native VLAN ID from default value of 1 to some unused VLAN number.
- Port security feature should be used by allowing limited number of MAC addresses on a single port.
- DTP negotiation should be disabled to stop attackers from making a trunk port with a switch.

- Cisco Discovery Protocol (CDP) should be disabled to prevent an attacker getting the overall view of networking topology. CDP works at layer 2 and may help an attacker to redesign the attack according to the physical topology of network. Similarly, if Link Layer Discovery Protocol (LLD) is used which is IEEE implementation of CDP, then it must be disabled as well.
- When deploying new switch, shutdown all unused ports and change the access VLAN assigned to them to some unused VLAN in the whole network.

Here is the description of some of the layer 2 attacks:

STP Attack

Spanning tree protocol (STP) is a protocol that ensures there is only one active link between networking devices. STP is a layer 2 protocol that usually runs on switches and bridges to prevent loop formation in redundant paths within a network.

STP uses 802.1D IEEE algorithm, for detecting loops in a network and then removes the loops by shutting down redundant paths between two networking devices, as it ensures there must be just one active link between the devices.

In this protocol one switch is selected as the root bridge. This is done by manipulating a switch priority, the switch with the lowest bridge priority is the root bridge.

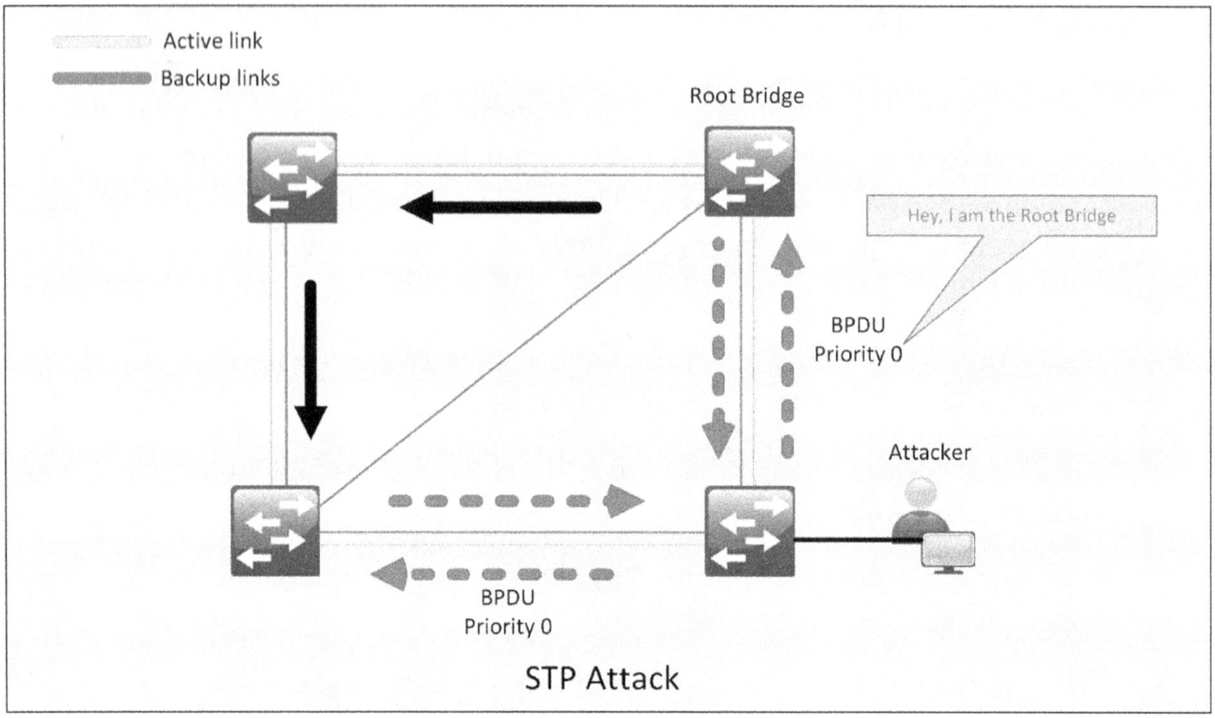

Figure 4-06: STP Attack

In STP attack, an attacker may somehow get the access of switch ports of a network so that he could place a rogue switch in a network and can manipulate the spanning tree protocol. Here, an attacker tries to make his switch a "root switch" and gets the ability to see all traffic that is intended to pass through the root switch.

ARP Spoofing Attack

ARP is a stateless protocol that is used within a broadcast domain to ensure the communication by resolving the IP address to MAC address mapping. It is in charge of L3 to L2 address mappings. ARP protocol ensures the binding of IP addresses and MAC addresses.

In ARP spoofing, an attacker sends forged ARP packets over Local Area Network (LAN). In the case, switch will update the attacker's MAC Address with the IP address of a legitimate user or server. Once attacker's MAC address is learned with the IP address of a legitimate user, the switch will start forwarding the packets to attacker intending that it is the MAC of the user. Using ARP Spoofing attack, an attacker can steal information by extracting from the packet received intended for a user over LAN. Apart from stealing information, ARP spoofing can be used for: -

- Session Hijacking
- Denial-of-Service Attack
- Man-in-the-Middle Attack
- Packet Sniffing
- Data Interception
- Connection Hijacking
- VoIP Tapping
- Connection Resetting
- Stealing Password

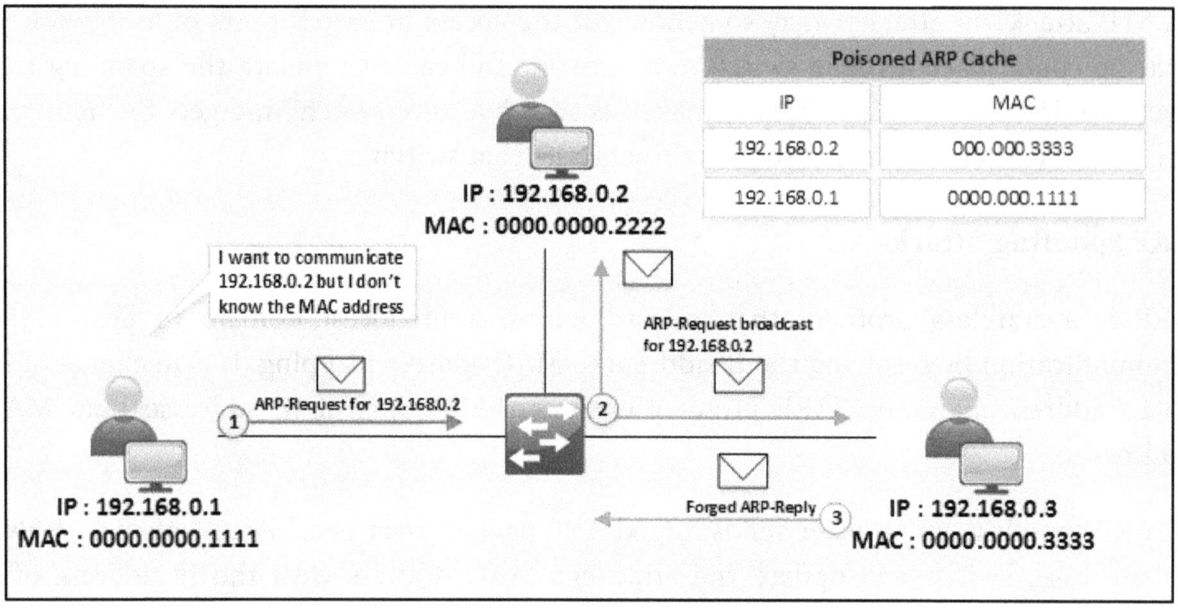

Figure 4-07: ARP Spoofing Attack

(ARP spoofing is a type of attack in which an attacker actively listens for ARP broadcasts and sends its own MAC address for the given IP address. Now if an attacker provides its MAC address against the IP address of default gateway of LAN then man-in-the-middle attack will be easily launched without much effort. Dynamic Arp Inspection (DAI) feature of Cisco IOS helps to mitigate such kind of attacks.)

MAC Spoofing/Duplicating

Media Access Control Address is in short known as MAC address or physical address of a device. MAC address is 48-bits unique identification number that is assigned to a network device for communication at data link layer. MAC address is comprised of Object Unique Identifier (QUI) 24-bits and 24-bits of Network Interface Controller (NIC). In case of multiple NIC, the device will have multiple unique MAC addresses.

MAC Spoofing is a technique of manipulating MAC address to impersonate the legitimate user or launch attack such as Denial-of-Service attack. As we know, MAC address is built-in on Network Interface Controller, which cannot be changed, but some drivers allow changing the MAC address. This masking process of MAC address is known as MAC Spoofing. Attacker sniffs the MAC address of users, which are active on switch ports and duplicate the MAC address. Duplicating the MAC can intercept the traffic and traffic destined to the legitimate user may direct to the attacker.

How to Defend Against MAC Spoofing

In order to defend users against MAC spoofing, DHCP Snooping, Dynamic ARP inspections are effective techniques to mitigate MAC spoofing attacks. Additionally, Source guard feature is configured on client facing switch ports.

IP source guard is a port-based feature, which provides Source IP address filtering at Layer 2. Source guard feature monitors and prevents the host from impersonating another host by assuming the legitimate host's IP address. In this way, the malicious host is restricted to use its assigned IP address. Source guard uses dynamic DHCP snooping or static IP source binding to match IP addresses to host on untrusted Layer 2 access ports.

Initially, all type of inbound IP traffic from the protected port is blocked except for DHCP packets. When a client receives an IP address from the DHCP server, or static IP source binding by the administrator, the traffic with an assigned source IP address is permitted from that port. All bogus packets will be denied. In this way, Source guard protects from the attack by claiming a neighbor host's IP address. Source guard creates an implicit Port Access Control List (PACL).

CAM Table/MAC Address Table Overflows

As routers have routing table stored in RAM for making routing decisions. Likewise, layer 2 devices have content addressable memory or MAC table, which dynamically learn and store the MAC addresses of the attached devices. MAC table helps the switch to track of where to send the traffic for specific learned MAC addresses. Just like routing table, MAC address table is also stored in Random Access Memory (RAM) and CPU allocates specific memory space for it along with other programs, which require CPU as well as RAM. Kali Linux or Back Track have tools, generates random MAC addresses. By using such tools, MAC address table of layer 2 device will overflow within minutes. The next frame being hit on any interface of layer 2 device will result in broadcast to all ports and switches may start behaving as if a hub, which did not have the memory space to store ARP entries.

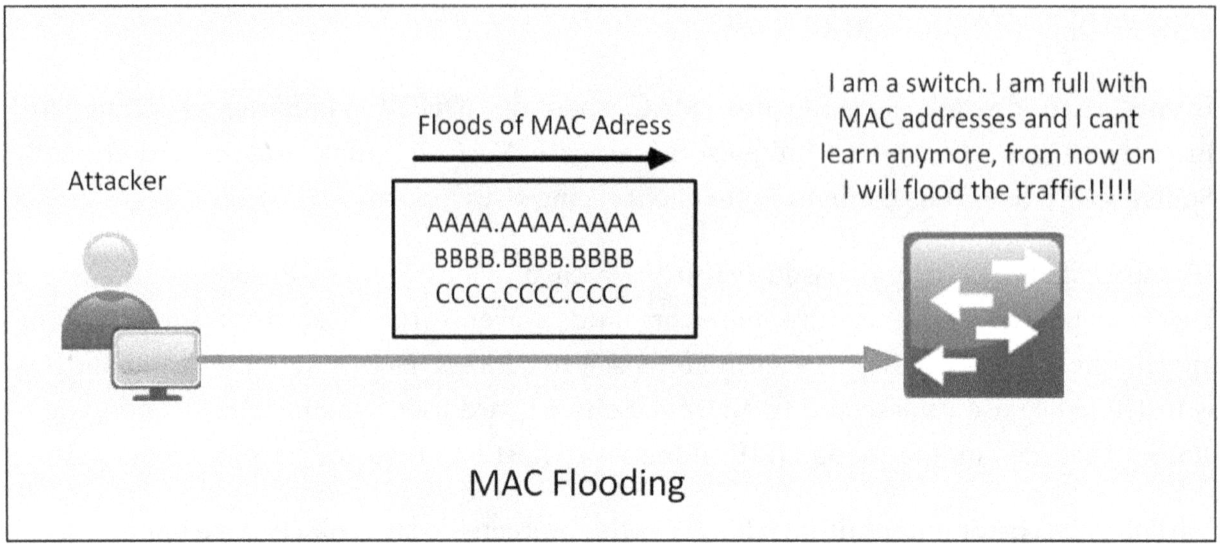

Figure 4-08: MAC Flooding

Apart from the previously discussed security threats and their mitigation procedure, it is a good idea to have multiple VLANs in network and implement inter-VLAN routing for required subnets.

CDP/LLDP Reconnaissance

The Cisco Discovery Protocol (CDP) is a mechanism introduced by Cisco, for the ease of management system to automatically learn about devices connected to the network. Usually, CDP runs on Cisco's routers, switches and other devices but it can also run on some network devices that belong to other vendors. By using CDP, network devices periodically advertise their own information to the other devices connected on the network, this information is worth sharing as it helps to keep the track of networking devices in a large network, making the availability of device's information for each other. However, this information is available to anyone who is "listening", which means that an attacker just has to see the CDP packet in order to obtain information about the connected devices.

By default, exchange of CDP packets are enabled on all interfaces of Cisco devices and they are sent in clear text, which makes an ease for an attacker to see the packet and gain information about the network devices in an organization, which then make an attacker use this information to exploit a known vulnerability against the device. Solution of this problem is to disable CDP on non-management interfaces.

VLAN hopping

The VLAN architecture provides easy network maintenance and improves an overall performance of the network, but it somehow makes the network vulnerable to attack as well.

One of the major threat to VLAN is VLAN hopping attack. In a VLAN hopping attack, an attacker can get the information of all VLANs running in a network. It enables visibility of traffic from one VLAN to another VLAN without using any router. An attacker exploits the feature of automatic trunking port, which is usually by default enabled. Here an attacker configures a host to spoof a rogue switch to use Dynamic trunking protocol (DTP) signalling and 802.1Q signalling to establish trunk with the connecting switch. If an attacker gets successful in establishing a trunk link between switch and the host, then he can access all the VLANS on the switch and can transact traffic on all the VLANs.

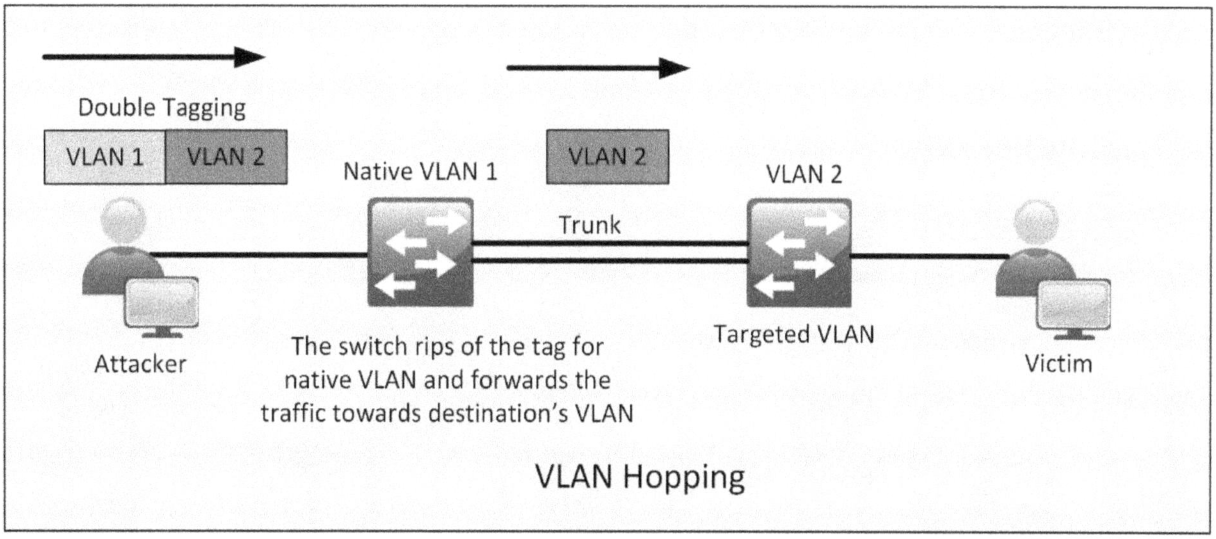

Figure 4-09: VLAN Hopping

A VLAN hopping attack can be performed in one of two ways:

- **801.q Double Tagging:** An attacker can Spoof DTP messages from the attacking host to cause the switch to enter trunking mode. Here, he applies double tagging the first tag comprises of native VLAN to bypass trunking and other tag is of victim's VLAN to reach the victim. So that, the attacker can send traffic tagged with the target VLAN, and the switch simply delivers the packets to the destination.

- **Switch Spoofing:** An attacker may introduce a rogue switch and enable trunking. Then attacker can then get all the VLANs on the rogue switch from the victim's switch.

DHCP Spoofing

Dynamic configuration host protocol (DHCP) is normally used in a network to provide IP address, subnet mask, gateway and DNS to the clients.

In DHCP spoofing attack, the attacker places a rogue DHCP server on the network. As clients get connected to the network and request an IP address from a DHCP pool and if the device gets a response from the rogue server first, the rogue server will assign any address and other information to the client. Thus, making the attacker steal the information almost invisibly.

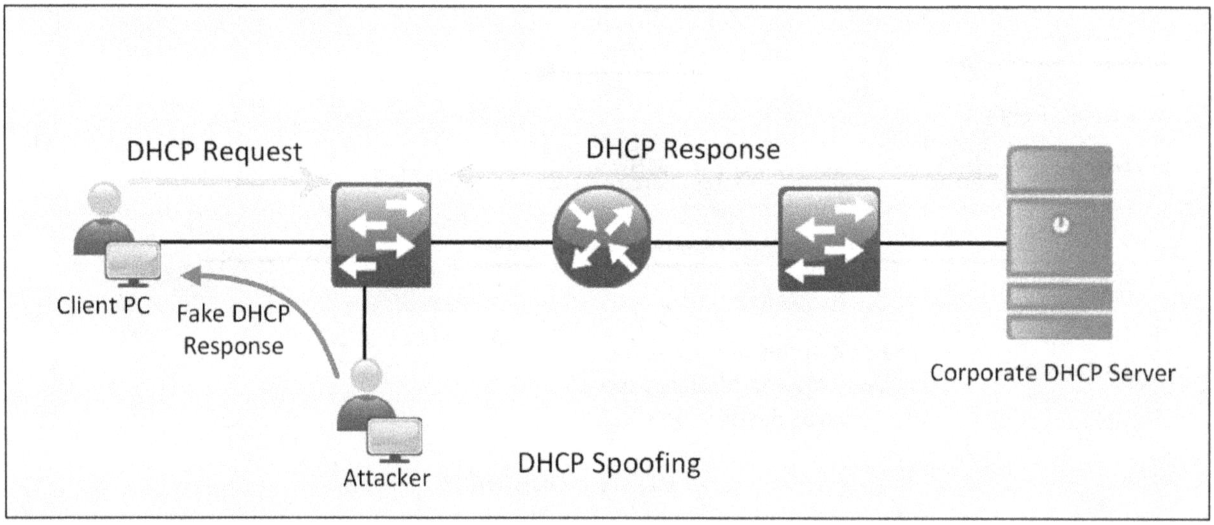

Figure 4-10: DHCP Spoofing

Mitigation procedures

This section deals with some of the mitigation techniques of layer 2 attacks, discussed above.

DHCP Snooping

DHCP Snooping is a security feature designed by Cisco, to mitigate the issues created by rogue DHCP servers.

It is a security feature that behaves like a firewall between trusted DHCP servers and untrusted hosts. DHCP snooping validates the DHCP messages either received from the legitimate source or from an untrusted source and filters out the invalid messages.

It is actually very easy for someone to bring a DHCP server in a corporate environment, accidentally or maliciously. *DHCP Snooping* is all about protecting against it.

Consider a scenario of a corporate network as shown in the figure below:

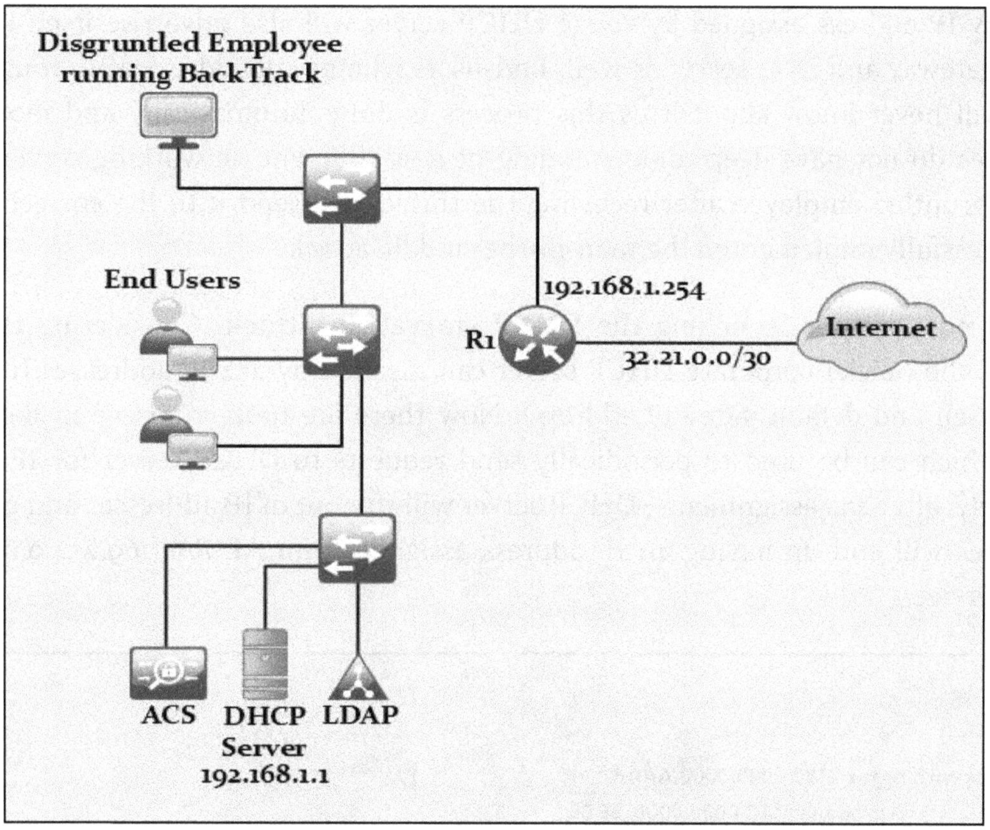

Figure 4-11: Rogue DHCP Server in Corporate Environment

As shown in the diagram above, a DHCP server is running with an IP address of *192.168.1.1*. Let us consider a disgruntled employee say, Bob, has some administrative issues at work and has decided to bring an embedded device next day in the office. On the embedded device, Bob has installed Back Track, which is a Linux distribution commonly used for penetration testing and ethical hacking. On the next day, Bob Plugged the Back Track based embedded device into this workstation's port and started listening to the DHCP requests from different end-devices. A DHCP is a four-step process as show below:

D – Discover ent by end-devices for discovering DHCP server

O – Offer Response from DHCP server for corresponding *Discover* message

R – Request Sent by end-devices as request for IP address to DHCP server

A – Acknowledge Response of DHCP server for *Request* message

Due to the broadcast nature of these steps, request will be listened by both DHCP servers. Now, any IP address assigned by rouge DHCP server will also advertise itself to be the default gateway and DNS server as well. End-users who get IP address from rouge DHCP server will never know about it as this process is done automatically and most of the employees do not have deep understanding of how different networking services work. Now disgruntled employee after receiving the traffic, will send it to the correct gateway and successfully implemented the man-in-the-middle attack.

Another possibility is launching the **DHCP starvation attack**. Considering the above scenario, the official corporate DHCP server can assign only 252 IP addresses (excluding DHCP itself and default gateway address). Now there are tools available in Back Track Linux, which can be used to periodically send requests to DHCP server for IP address. Ultimately, after 252 assignments, DHCP server will run out of IP addresses and corporate employees will end up having an IP address assigned from APIPA (169.254.0.0 address space) service.

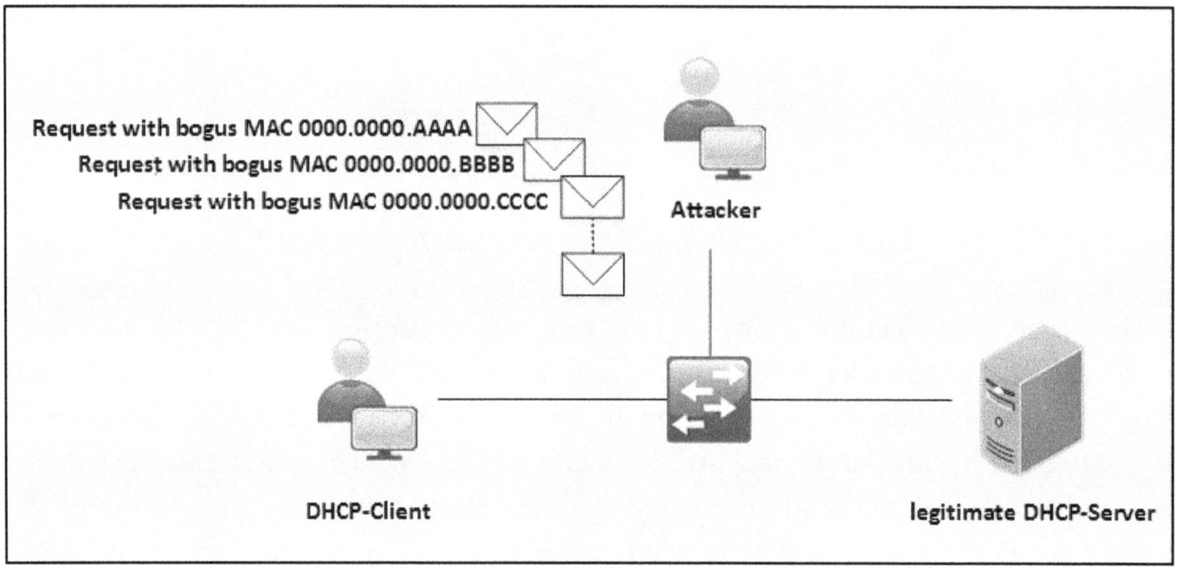

Figure 4-12: DHCP Starvation Attack

In order to mitigate such attacks, DHCP snooping feature is enabled on networking devices to identify the only trusted ports from DHCP traffic either in ingress or egress direction is considered legitimate. Any access port who tries to reply the DHCP requests will be ignored because device will only allow DHCP process from trusted port as defined by the networking team.

Lab 4.3: Protecting the Network Infrastructure from Rogue DHCP Server by Implementing DHCP SNOOPING Feature

In this lab, our main focus is to protect the official DHCP server of the corporate office. IP DHCP Snooping feature helps in protecting clients from getting IP address from rogue DHCP server set up by an attacker or disgruntled employee. In order to implement advanced security features, which are not supported by native switches of GNS3, IOUS based switch will be used in this lab to perform security contents related to switching.

Here is the following lab topology:

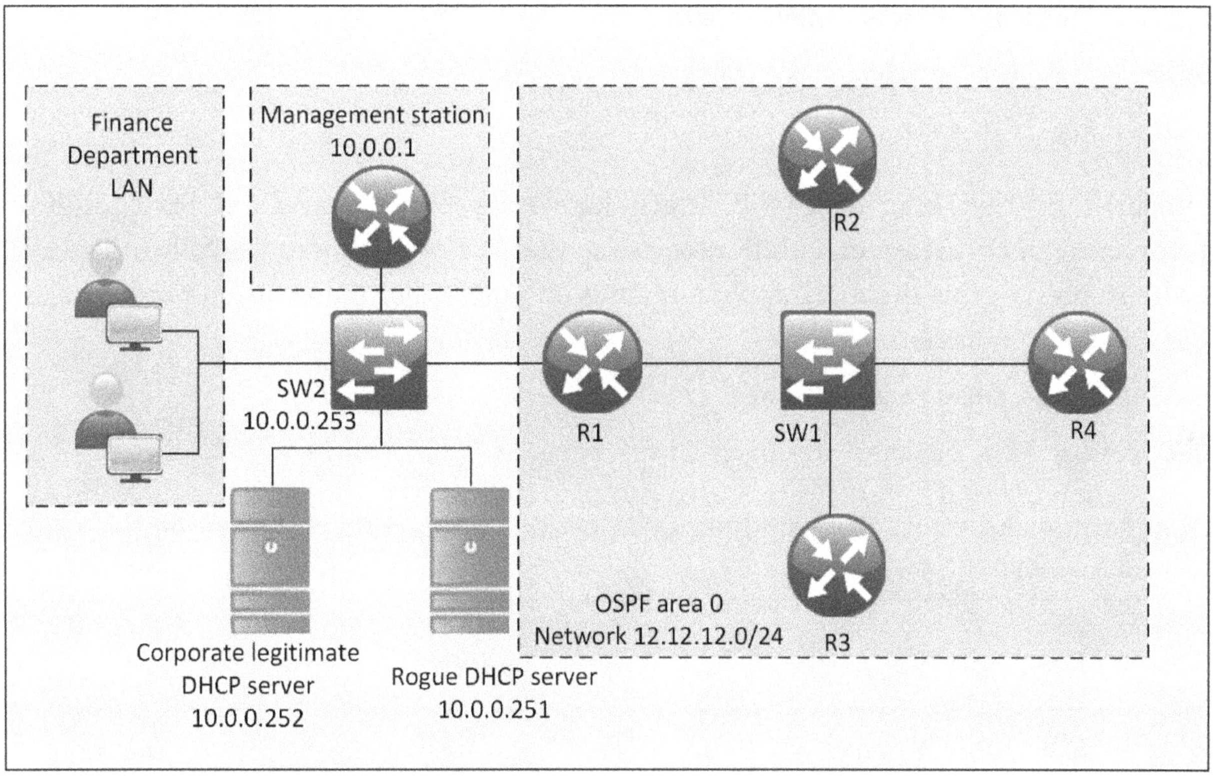

Figure 4-13: Presence of Rogue DHCP Server in Corporate Environment

LAN Switch of Finance Department

In order to implement DHCP Snooping, the following command is executed first.

```
SW2# configure terminal
SW2(config)# ip dhcp snooping
```

As the security of clients in different VLANs is of major concern, following command is used to enable it for different VLANs.

```
SW2(config)# ip dhcp snooping vlan 1
```

As only one VLAN is used in our scenario, so DHCP snooping is enabled for vlan 1.

Secondly, a switch port, which is connected to corporate DHCP server, is declared as trusted port for DHCP communication by using the following command.

```
SW2(config)# interface Ethernet 0/3
SW2(config-if)# ip dhcp snooping trust
SW2(config-if)# exit
```

Similarly, another kind of DHCP attack known as DHCP starvation may result in hammering of DHCP server with IP requests so that DHCP pool becomes fully utilized. In order to prevent this situation, apply rate limit on ports other than trusted ports by using the following command:

```
SW2(config)# interface Ethernet 1/1
SW2(config-if)# ip dhcp snooping limit rate 25
```

Above command shows that rate limit of 25 packets per second is applied on the switch port of rogue DHCP server.

VERIFICATION:

Before starting the verification process, open the console of PCs of finance department and enter the following command so that they get the IP address from legitimate DHCP server.

```
VPCS> ip dhcp
```

DORA IP 10.0.0.4/24 GW 10.0.0.254

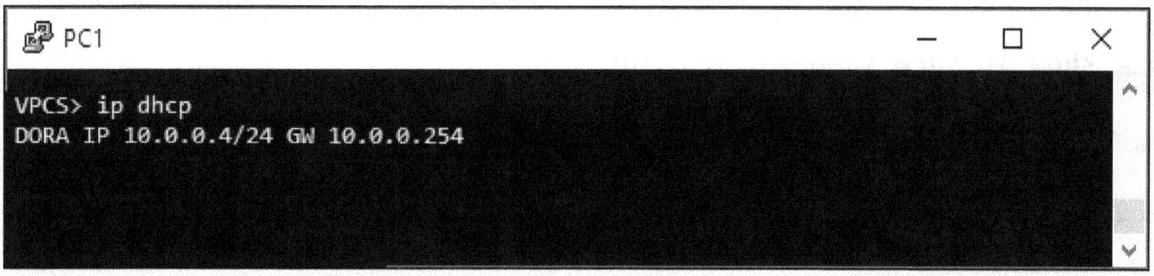

In order to verify that DHCP snooping is actually working, shutdown the port of corporate DHCP server and then restart one of the PC representing the Finance Departments LAN segment. The DORA process will not be completed and client will eventually use APIPA addressing rather than accepting IP from rogue DHCP Server.

Similarly, "*show ip dhcp snooping*" command can be used to see the trusted and untrusted ports.

SW2# **show ip dhcp snooping**

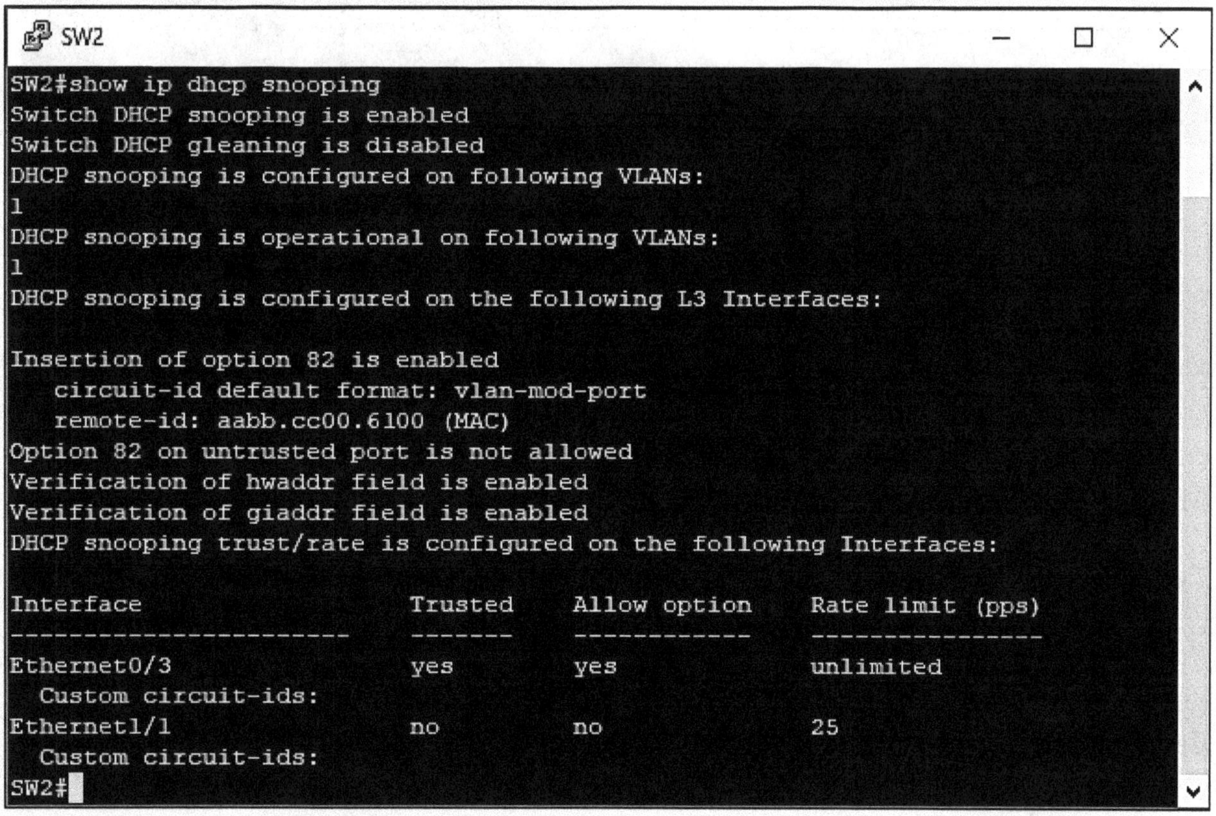

Similarly, *"show ip dhcp snooping binding"* command can be used to display client lists with legitimate IP addresses assigned to them.

```
SW2# show ip dhcp snooping binding
```

MacAddress IpAddress Lease(sec) Type VLAN Interface

------------------ --------------- ---------- ------------- ---- ---------- ----------

00:50:79:66:68:07 10.0.0.4 85960 dhcp-snooping 1 Ethernet0 /0

00:50:79:66:68:08 10.0.0.5 85030 dhcp-snooping 1 Ethernet0 /1

Total number of bindings: 2

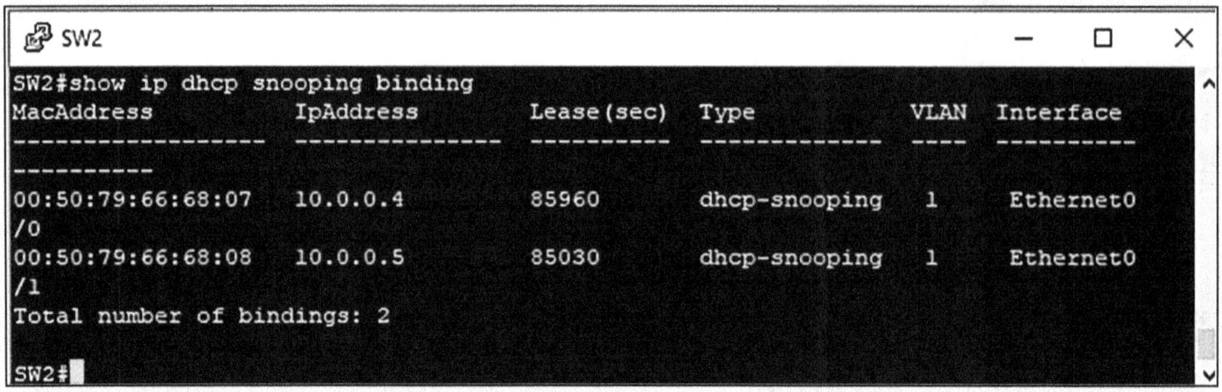
SW2
SW2#show ip dhcp snooping binding
MacAddress IpAddress Lease(sec) Type VLAN Interface
------------------ --------------- ---------- ------------- ---- ----------
----
00:50:79:66:68:07 10.0.0.4 85960 dhcp-snooping 1 Ethernet0
/0
00:50:79:66:68:08 10.0.0.5 85030 dhcp-snooping 1 Ethernet0
/1
Total number of bindings: 2
SW2#

Dynamic ARP Inspection (DAI)

DAI is used with DHCP snooping, IP-to-MAC bindings can be a track from DHCP transactions to protect against ARP poisoning (which is an attacker trying to get your traffic instead of to your destination). DHCP snooping is required in order to build the MAC-to-IP bindings for DAI validation.

Port Security

Port Security is used to bind the MAC address of known devices to the physical ports and violation action is also defined. So if an attacker tries to connect its PC or embedded device to the switch port, then it will shut down or restrict the attacker from even generating an attack. In dynamic port security, you configure the total number of allowed MAC addresses, and the switch will allow only that number simultaneously, without regard to what those MAC addresses are.

If a switch detects an unbinded MAC-address on a port, there are three actions defined in Cisco IOS for the violation against configured MAC address: switch will shut down the port, restrict the port or protect the port.

Cisco Switch offers port security to prevent MAC attacks. You can configure the switch either for statically defined MAC addresses only, or dynamic MAC learning up to the specified range, or you can configure port security with the combination of both as shown below. The following configuration on Cisco Switch will allow a specific MAC address and 4 additional MAC addresses if the switch has learned the static MAC address.

Lab 4.4: Implementing Port Security, Dynamic ARP Inspection (DAI) and Disabling Cisco Discovery Protocol

Dynamic *ARP* inspection helps to mitigate the common attack of *ARP* spoofing in which an attacker tries to reply *ARP* requests and sends its own *MAC* address, and this results in man-in-the-middle attacks.

Cisco Discovery Protocol is used to dynamically find and list the different attributes of attached devices on different interfaces. As in our lab scenario, if we take an example of OSPF area 0 segment, each router is connected to three other routers via Layer 2 switch. Similarly, Router of Finance Department is connected to two switches. Although *CDP* helps a lot in documenting the topology of network, it may also result in severe consequences at the same time. So, it is a good idea to disable it in a production networking environment.

All such kind of attacks happens after connecting the malicious device to the switch or router. Port Security is used to bind the MAC address of known devices to the physical ports and violation actions are also defined. So, if an attacker tries to connect its PC or embedded device to the switch port, then it will shut down or restrict the attacker from even generating an attack.

Here is the following lab topology:

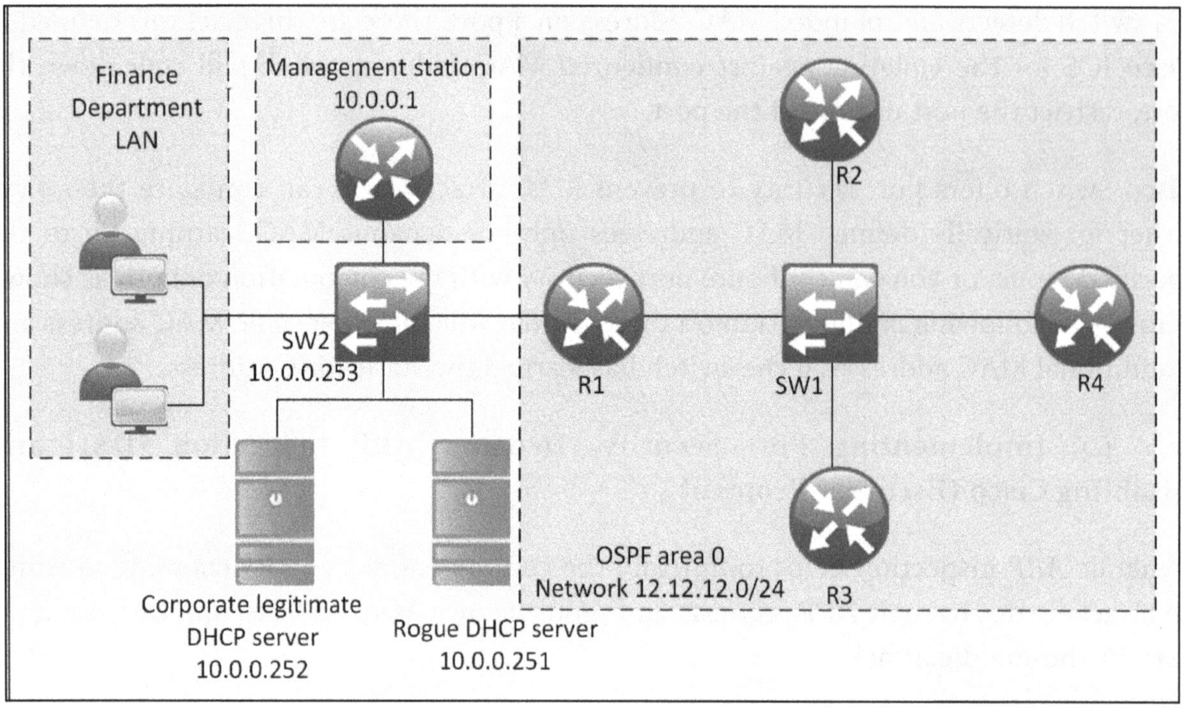

Figure 4-14: Port Security, Dynamic ARP Inspection (DAI) and Disabling Cisco Discovery Protocol

Configuration of this lab will start from IOU based Layer 2 switch up to the router R4 as shown in diagram of case study of this section.

In order to implement the concept of port security. The MAC address of PCs representing the finance department's LAN and router representing the management station is noted with the following command:

SW2# show mac address-table dynamic

SW2

```
SW2#show mac address-table dynamic
          Mac Address Table
-------------------------------------------

Vlan    Mac Address       Type        Ports
----    -----------       --------    -----
   1    0050.7966.6807    DYNAMIC     Et0/0
   1    0050.7966.6808    DYNAMIC     Et0/1
   1    c201.3fbe.0001    DYNAMIC     Et0/2
   1    c209.36f9.0000    DYNAMIC     Et0/3
   1    c20b.3631.0000    DYNAMIC     Et1/1
   1    c20c.3597.0000    DYNAMIC     Et1/0
Total Mac Addresses for this criterion: 6
SW2#
```

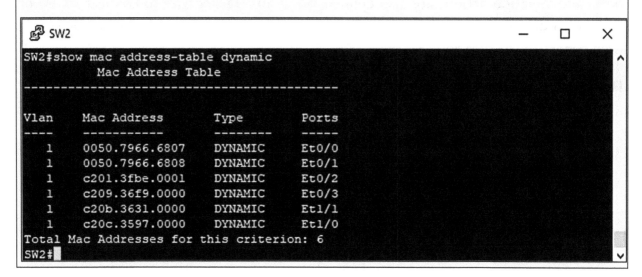

MAC address to be bound on Ethernet 1/0 is a management station simulated by router. This mac address will be changed from CLI to verify the effect of port security and its violation.

In order to implement port security, following commands are used.

```
SW2(config)# interface ethernet 0/0
SW2(config-if)# switchport mode access
SW2(config-if)# switchport port-security mac-address 0050.7966.6807
SW2(config-if)# switchport port-security maximum 1
SW2(config-if)# switchport port-security violation shutdown
SW2(config-if)# switchport port-security
SW2(config-if)# exit
SW2(config)# interface ethernet 0/1
SW2(config-if)# switchport mode access
SW2(config-if)# switchport port-security mac-address 0050.7966.6808
SW2(config-if)# switchport port-security maximum 1
SW2(config-if)# switchport port-security violation shutdown
SW2(config-if)# switchport port-security
SW2(config-if)# exit
SW2(config)# interface ethernet 0/2
SW2(config-if)# switchport mode access
SW2(config-if)# switchport port-security mac-address c201.3fbe.0001
SW2(config-if)# switchport port-security maximum 1
SW2(config-if)# switchport port-security violation shutdown
SW2(config-if)# switchport port-security
SW2(config-if)# exit
SW2(config)# interface ethernet 0/3
SW2(config-if)# switchport mode access
SW2(config-if)# switchport port-security mac-address c209.597e.0000
SW2(config-if)# switchport port-security maximum 1
SW2 (config-if)# switchport port-security violation shutdown
```

```
SW2(config-if)# switchport port-security
SW2(config-if)# exit
SW2(config)# interface ethernet 1/0
SW2(config-if)# switchport mode access
SW2(config-if)# switchport port-security mac-address c20c.5017.0000
SW2(config-if)# switchport port-security maximum 1
SW2(config-if)# switchport port-security violation shutdown
SW2(config-if)# switchport port-security
SW2(config)# interface ethernet 1/1
SW2(config-if)# switchport mode access
SW2(config-if)# switchport port-security mac-address c20b.3631.0000
SW2(config-if)# switchport port-security maximum 1
SW2(config-if)# switchport port-security violation shutdown
SW2(config-if)# switchport port-security
```

Above commands show how to bind a single MAC address on specific port along with violation action if a user with some other MAC address tries to connect to the same port. "*switchport port-security maximum 1*" allows only one MAC address statically defined by "*switchport port-security mac-address <MAC-ADDRESS>*" command. After defining the port-security main parameters, "*switchport port-security*" command needs to be configured on port for port security to start working.

VERIFICATION

Following command is used to verify the port security status of a port along with the violation action

```
SW2# show port-security interface Ethernet 1/0
```

```
SW2

SW2#show port-security interface ethernet 1/0
Port Security              : Enabled
Port Status                : Secure-up
Violation Mode             : Shutdown
Aging Time                 : 0 mins
Aging Type                 : Absolute
SecureStatic Address Aging : Disabled
Maximum MAC Addresses      : 1
Total MAC Addresses        : 1
Configured MAC Addresses   : 1
Sticky MAC Addresses       : 0
Last Source Address:Vlan   : 0000.0000.0000:0
Security Violation Count   : 0

SW2#
```

Now change the MAC address of the router's port connected to Switch interface Ethernet 1/0 by following commands and then check the status of Ethernet 1/0 on SW2.

MGMT-STATION# **config t**

MGMT-STATION(config)# **int fastEthernet 0/0**

MGMT-STATION(config-if)# **shutdown**

MGMT-STATION(config-if)# **mac-address AAAA.BBBB.CCCC**

MGMT-STATION(config-if)# **no shutdown**

SW2

SW2#show port-security interface Ethernet 1/0

```
SW2
SW2>en
SW2#show port-security interface ethernet 1/0
Port Security              : Enabled
Port Status                : Secure-shutdown
Violation Mode             : Shutdown
Aging Time                 : 0 mins
Aging Type                 : Absolute
SecureStatic Address Aging : Disabled
Maximum MAC Addresses      : 1
Total MAC Addresses        : 1
Configured MAC Addresses   : 1
Sticky MAC Addresses       : 0
Last Source Address:Vlan   : AAAA.BBBB.CCCC:1
Security Violation Count   : 1
```

In order to restore the port to secure up, restore the MAC address of the port to default value and enter *shutdown* command followed by *no shutdown* command.

```
MGMT-STATION# config t
MGMT-STATION(config)# int fastEthernet 0/0
MGMT-STATION(config-if)# shutdown
MGMT-STATION(config-if)# mac-address c20c.5017.0000
MGMT-STATION(config-if)# no shutdown
```

SW2

```
SW2(config)# interface ethernet 1/0
SW2(config-if)# shutdown
SW2(config-if)# no shutdown
*Nov 1 17:38:56.371: %LINK-3-UPDOWN: Interface Ethernet0/0, changed state to up
*Nov 1 17:38:57.379: %LINEPROTO-5-UPDOWN: Line protocol on Interface Ethernet1/0, changed state to up
```

SW2# **show port-security interface ethernet 1/0**

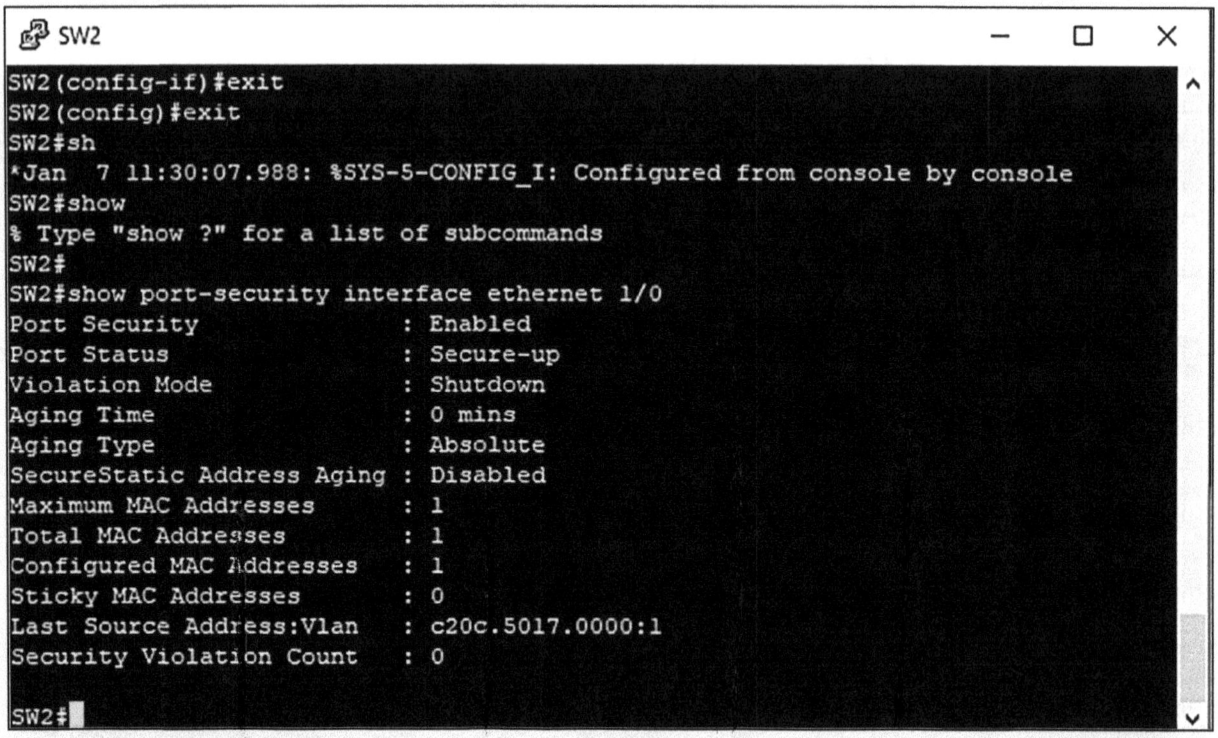

```
SW2
SW2(config-if)#exit
SW2(config)#exit
SW2#sh
*Jan  7 11:30:07.988: %SYS-5-CONFIG_I: Configured from console by console
SW2#show
% Type "show ?" for a list of subcommands
SW2#
SW2#show port-security interface ethernet 1/0
Port Security              : Enabled
Port Status                : Secure-up
Violation Mode             : Shutdown
Aging Time                 : 0 mins
Aging Type                 : Absolute
SecureStatic Address Aging : Disabled
Maximum MAC Addresses      : 1
Total MAC Addresses        : 1
Configured MAC Addresses   : 1
Sticky MAC Addresses       : 0
Last Source Address:Vlan   : c20c.5017.0000:1
Security Violation Count   : 0

SW2#
```

```
SW2# ping 10.0.0.1
```

```
Type escape sequence to abort.
Sending 5, 100-byte ICMP Echos to 10.0.0.1, timeout is 2 seconds:
.!!!!
Success rate is 80 percent (4/5), round-trip min/avg/max = 9/10/11 ms
!
```

In the second phase of this lab, *CDP* will be disabled by running the following commands from global configuration mode.

SW2

```
SW2# show cdp neighbors
```

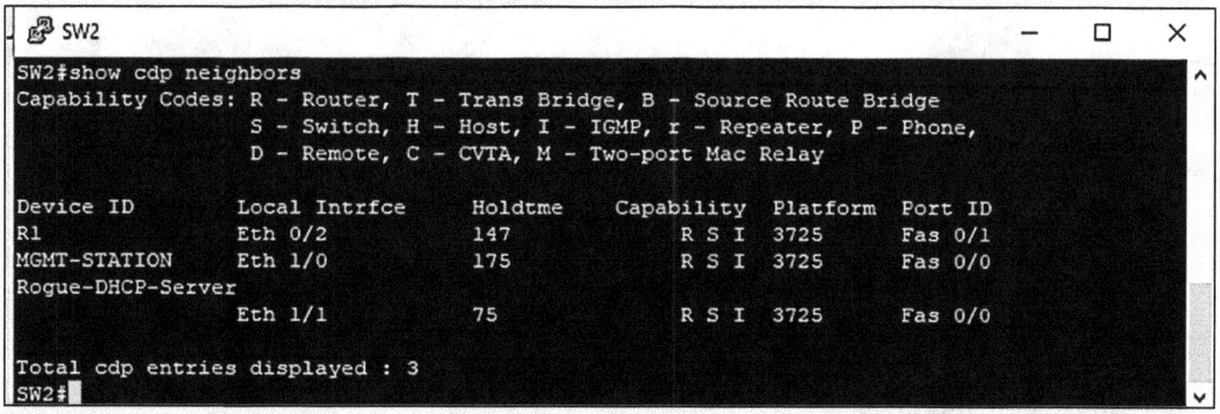

```
SW2#show cdp neighbors
Capability Codes: R - Router, T - Trans Bridge, B - Source Route Bridge
                  S - Switch, H - Host, I - IGMP, r - Repeater, P - Phone,
                  D - Remote, C - CVTA, M - Two-port Mac Relay

Device ID        Local Intrfce     Holdtme    Capability  Platform  Port ID
R1               Eth 0/2           147             R S I  3725      Fas 0/1
MGMT-STATION     Eth 1/0           175             R S I  3725      Fas 0/0
Rogue-DHCP-Server
                 Eth 1/1           75              R S I  3725      Fas 0/0

Total cdp entries displayed : 3
SW2#
```

R1

```
R1# show cdp neighbors
```

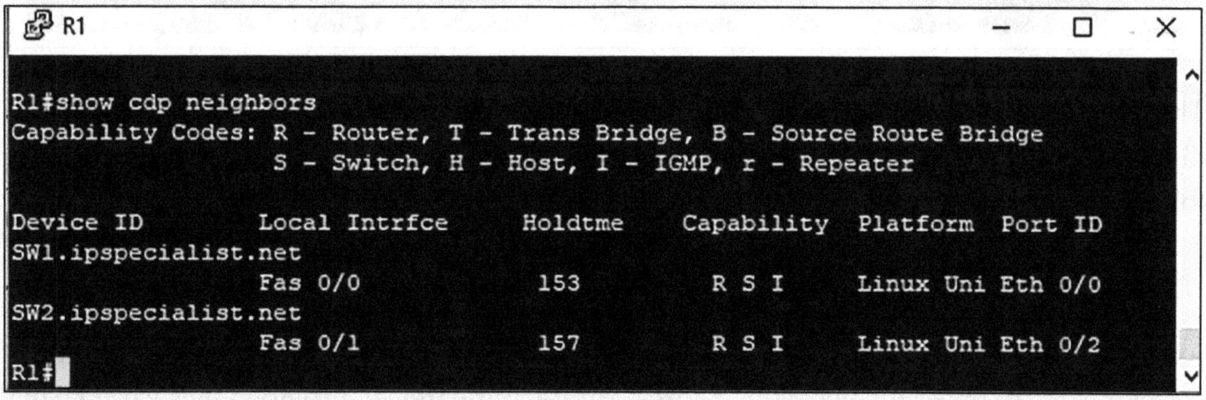

```
R1#show cdp neighbors
Capability Codes: R - Router, T - Trans Bridge, B - Source Route Bridge
                  S - Switch, H - Host, I - IGMP, r - Repeater

Device ID        Local Intrfce     Holdtme    Capability  Platform  Port ID
SW1.ipspecialist.net
                 Fas 0/0            153         R S I     Linux Uni Eth 0/0
SW2.ipspecialist.net
                 Fas 0/1            157         R S I     Linux Uni Eth 0/2
R1#
```

Above command shows different devices connected to the switch and also shows their capabilities. To disable it globally, use the following command:

SW2

SW2(config)# do show cdp neighbors

```
SW2(config)#do show cdp neighbors
Capability Codes: R - Router, T - Trans Bridge, B - Source Route Bridge
                  S - Switch, H - Host, I - IGMP, r - Repeater, P - Phone,
                  D - Remote, C - CVTA, M - Two-port Mac Relay

Device ID        Local Intrfce     Holdtme    Capability  Platform  Port ID
DHCP-SERVER      Eth 0/3           92              R S I  3725      Fas 0/0
R1               Eth 0/2           120             R S I  3725      Fas 0/1
MGMT-STATION     Eth 1/0           92              R S I  3725      Fas 0/0
Rogue-DHCP-Server
                 Eth 1/1           92              R S I  3725      Fas 0/0

Total cdp entries displayed : 4
SW2(config)#
```

SW2(config)# **no cdp run**

Above command will disable the *CDP* on every interface of the device. In order to disable *CDP* on specific interface, use the following command:

SW2(config-if)# **no cdp enable**

SW2# **show cdp neighbors**

```
SW2#show cdp neighbors
% CDP is not enabled
SW2#
```

This single command of *no CDP run* will be applied on every device where we want to disable it. In order to implement the Dynamic ARP Inspection for specific *VLAN,* use the following command at global configuration mode:

SW2(config)# **ip arp inspection vlan 1**

As soon as above command is entered, switch will start inspecting the ARP traffic. If attacker tries to inject its own *MAC* address for default gateway provided by secure DHCP server *(IP DHCP Snooping Feature),* switch will check it against *"show ip dhcp snooping binding"* table and will reject the rogue *ARP* traffic.

BPDU Guard

As discussed earlier, Spanning Tree Protocol (STP) is a layer 2 technology and its main function is to make a loop free network at Layer 2 of TCP/IP stack. STP does this by selecting a *Root Bridge* in a network and making a loop free network with respect to *Root Bridge*. Like every other protocol, selecting root bridge is done by comparing some parameters of every single layer 2 device in a network. This parameter is known as Bridge Protocol Data Unit (BPDU). Inside BPDU is MAC address of the device and 2-byte value known as Bridge Priority.

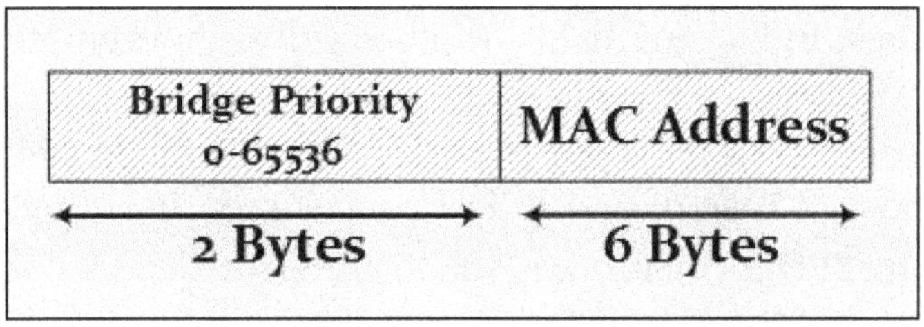

Figure 4-15: BPDU Packet Arrangement

By default, Bridge Priority is 32768, which can be changed later. Every switch shares BPDU with other switches. Switch with the lowest Bridge ID will become the root bridge. As Default Bridge Priority is same on all devices, MAC address becomes the focal point of STP elections in default conditions. A switch with the lowest mac address will become the root bridge. Consider the following switch arrangement, where STP election for the root bridge is going to take place.

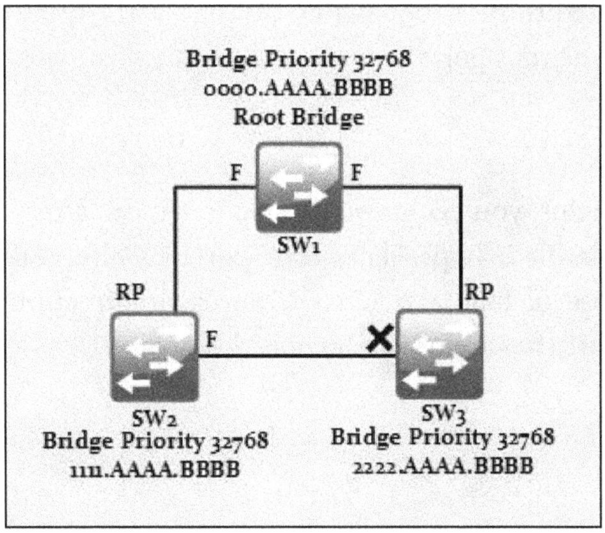

Figure 4-16: STP Root Bridge Election Process

Switch *SW1* is elected as Root Bridge due its lowest MAC address hence, is best bridge ID. Now every traffic forwarding will be done via *SW1*. In the next step, root port will be selected on remaining switches, which is selected according to the best path cost to the root bridge. In the third step, remaining ports are checked and specific ports will be shut down to make the network loop free.

In the above discussion, the importance of BPDU packet is obvious. If an attacker gets a chance to connect his switch to the above switch segment and sends illegal BPDU packets stating itself to have best BPDU guard, all switches will align themselves according to it.

In order to prevent this situation, BPDU guard feature must be enabled on access ports, which disables the port in case of any BPDU packet seen in inbound direction. Once a port is disabled due to BPDU violation, it will show error-disabled state. To bring up the interface back again, *shutdown* command must be issued followed by *no shutdown* command.

Root Guard

Root guard is another feature for STP, which prevents less worthy switch from becoming the root bridge. Apart from BPDU Guard, if there is administrative limitation within an organization and switch from someone's administrative domain is connected to another switch whose configuration and management is someone else's responsibility, then Root Guard is enabled on ports connecting to other switch to prevent the STP topology by ignoring messages related to new root switch on that port. Apply this feature to all ports which should not become root ports.

Loop Guard

Loop Guard feature helps you to prevent loop creation after STP is converged and redundant links are disabled. It prevents root ports or alternate ports from becoming designated ports in case of failure it leads towards unidirectional link. This feature is applicable to all the ports that are or can be non-designated.

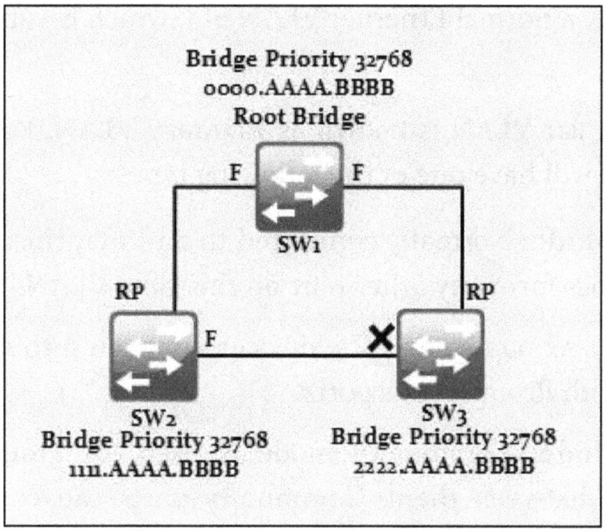

Figure 4-17: Loop Creation After STP Convergence

Considering the diagram above, let us say that port of switch *SW2* gets down due to any reason then error-disabled port of switch SW3 may come up and enter in to forwarding state. If this port of switch SW2 comes up again then a loop is again created in the above switching segment. STP will take some time to converge again. In order to prevent such situations, *Loop Guard* feature must be enabled on port, which disables the port in case no BPDU packet is received on it.

VLAN Security

Private VLANs

Private VLAN (PVLAN) is used to further divide a single VLAN into sub-VLANs. PVLANs also require a layer three device like a router in order to communicate with other VLANs.

Security Implications of a PVLAN

A private VLAN divides a VLAN into subdomains, making you to isolate the ports on the switch from each other. A subdomain consists of a primary VLAN and one or more secondary VLANs. All VLANs in a private VLAN domain share the same primary VLAN, while we can have many secondary VLANs. The secondary VLAN ID differentiates one secondary subdomain from another. Unlike normal VLANs, which use a unique subnet for every broadcast domain, hosts in different PVLANs can belong to same IP subnet while still requiring layer three device for inter-PVLAN communication.

As an example, consider a normal Ethernet VLAN of 1, which is sub-divided in two private VLANs 2 and 3.

VLAN 1, which is a regular VLAN is known as **Primary VLAN**. Ports assigned to normal and sub-divided VLAN will have one of the following types:

- **Promiscuous Mode:** Normally connected to a router, this port is allowed to send and receive frames form any other port on the same VLAN.
- **Isolated Mode:** As name suggests, devices connected to isolated ports will only communicate with Promiscuous ports.
- **Community Mode:** Community mode is used for group of users who want communication between them. Community ports can communicate with other community port members and with Promiscuous ports.

The next diagram further explains this concept.

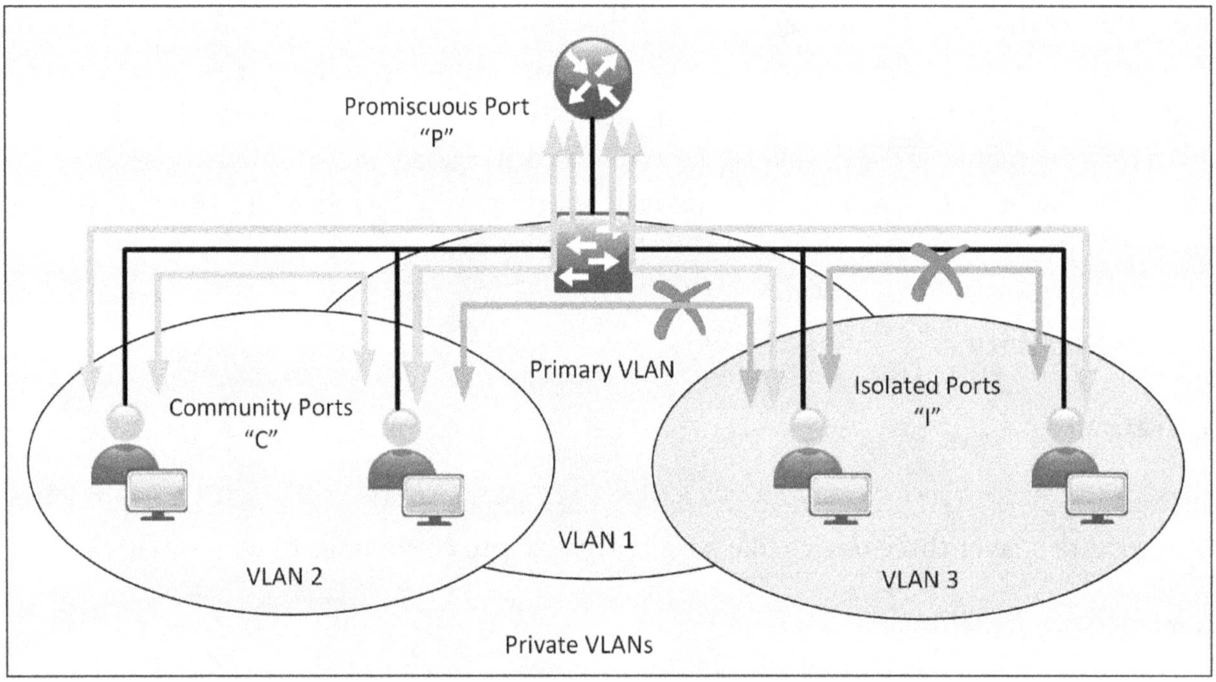

Figure 4-18: Private VLANs within Primary VLAN

In short, on the top of hierarchy is the Primary VLAN, which is the regular VLAN 1 in our scenario. It will be used to forward traffic from Promiscuous mode based ports to Isolated and Community mode based ports.

After Primary VLAN, comes the **secondary VLAN,** which will be either Isolated or Community based on requirements.

Isolated VLAN: It just forwards traffic from isolated ports to Promiscuous ports.

Community VLAN: It forwards traffic within community ports and to the promiscuous ports.

PVLANs are normally used in shared environments like ISP co-location where same subnet may be used for all customers but their traffic is logically isolated from each other due to PVLANs. Using Private VLAN (PVLAN) provides the security and isolation features at the same time.

Native VLAN

By default, VLAN 1 is referred to as native VLAN. Usually, in Cisco's LAN connection, the switch leaves the native VLAN untagged on 802.1Q trunk ports. So, why is it so important to tag native VLAN packets? The practice of sending native VLAN's packet untagged can lead your network towards security vulnerability.

For example, if a user B1 connects to an access port of a switch that is assigned to VLAN 1 on SW1 and then he sends a broadcast frame to SW1, when SW1 receives that frame, it simply forwards that broadcast frame to SW2. This is because the frame belongs to the native VLAN and both the switches agree to use the same native VLAN. Here, they ignore 802.1Q tagging. When the receiving switch SW2 receives a frame on a trunk port, it assumes that the packet belongs to native VLAN as it lacks tagging.

Previously in this chapter, we have discussed how VLAN hopping makes your network vulnerable. Now here, we will cover some of the mitigation techniques.

Security Implications of a Native VLAN

The 802.1q is an IEEE standard, which determines how to handle tagged or untagged frames sent or received on an 802.1q trunk port. If we proactively configure both ends of 802.1q trunk with a native VLAN, then all other traffic will be sent with a VLAN tag, but native VLAN's traffic will be sent untagged and this feature can be exploited by an attacker.

Here are some precautionary measures to overcome the problems discussed above:

- Disable trunking on all access ports.

- Disable auto-trunking and enable manual-trunking.
- Change the native VLAN to a VLAN other than VLAN1.
- Tag the native VLAN traffic in order to prevent against 802.1Q double-tagging attack to exploit network vulnerability.

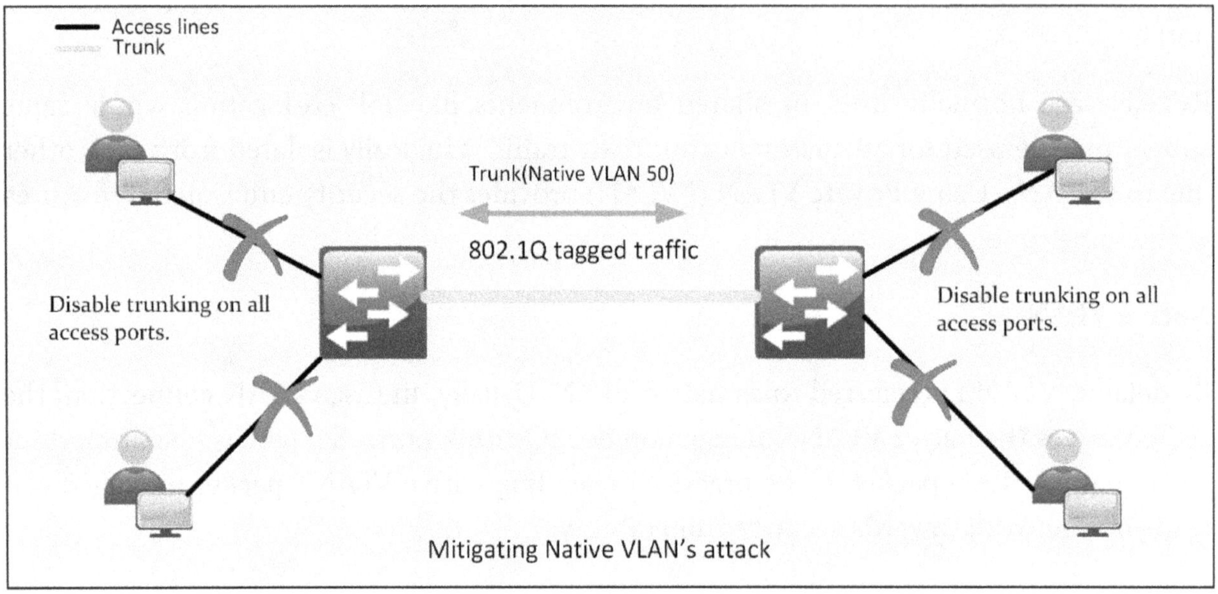

Figure 4-19: Mitigating Native VLAN Attack

Mind Map

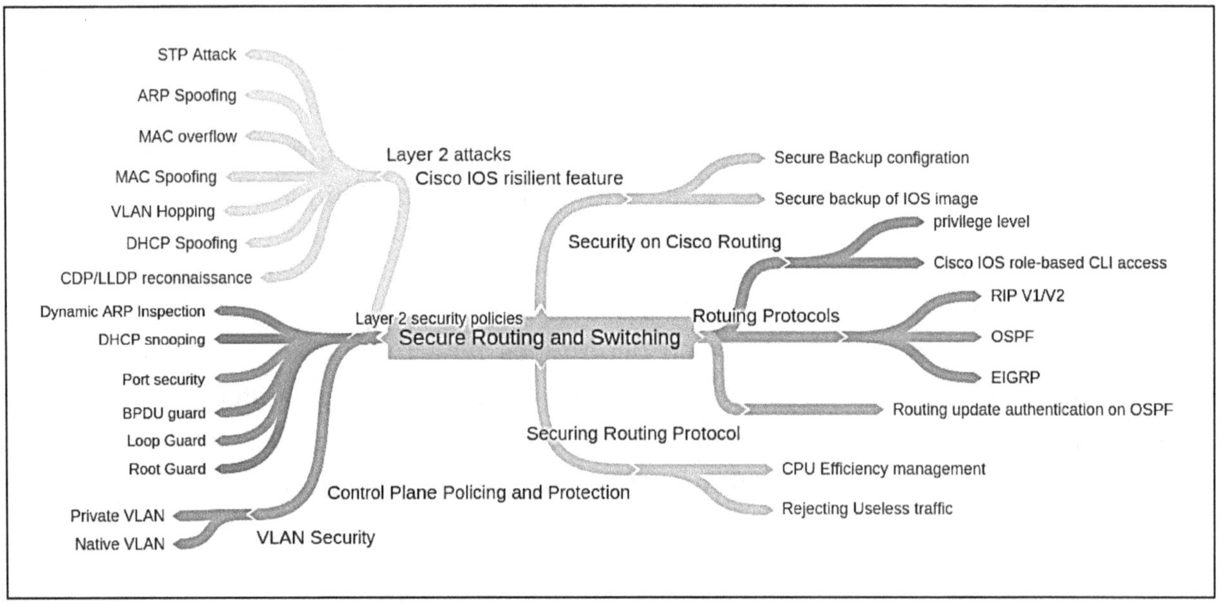

Figure 4-20: Secure Routing and Switching Mind Map

Practice Questions:

1. In order to implement security on all company routers, which two commands must be issued to implement authentication via the password "IPSpecialist" for all OSPF-enabled interfaces in the backbone area of the company network? (Choose any two)
   A. area 1 authentication message-digest
   B. area 0 authentication message-digest
   C. ip ospf message-digest-key 1 md5 IPSpecialist
   D. username OSPF password IPSpecialist
   E. enable password IPSpecialist

2. What purpose does the command "ip ospf message-digest-key key md5 password" serve?
   A. To configure OSPF MD5 authentication globally on the router
   B. To enable OSPF MD5 authentication on a per-interface basis
   C. To facilitate the establishment of neighbor adjacencies
   D. To enable OSPF MD5 authentication on a per-port basis

3. Which of the followings is the characteristic of the Cisco IOS Resilient Configuration feature?
   A. It creates a secure working copy of the bootstrap startup program.
   B. Once issued, the secure boot-config command automatically upgrades the configuration archive to a newer version.
   C. A snapshot of running configuration of the router can be taken and securely archived in a storage device.
   D. The secure boot-image command works properly when the system is configured to run an image from a TFTP server.

4. What purpose does the show "ip ospf neighbour" command serve?
   A. Shows the list of active interfaces
   B. Shows the list OSPF neighbors
   C. Shows the list best routes
   D. All of the above

5. Which type of switching cache makes the route for the session in advance even before any packets need to be processed?
   A. Process switching
   B. Fast switching
   C. Cisco Express Forwarding (CEF)
   D. None of the above

6. What are the two main components of Cisco Express Forwarding (CEF) that are needed to perform its function? (Choose any two)
   A. Forwarding Information Base (FIB)
   B. Routing table
   C. Adjacency table
   D. MAC table

7. What is the main function of Control Plane Policing (CoPP) feature?
   A. Disable all control plane services to reduce overall traffic
   B. Direct all excess traffic to the route processor
   C. Manage services provided by the data plane
   D. Restricts unnecessary traffic from overloading the route processor

8. Which of the following are common layer 2 attacks?
   A. STP attack
   B. MAC Spoofing
   C. MAC table overflow
   D. VLAN hopping
   E. ALL

9. A type of an attack in which an attacker actively listens for ARP broadcasts and sends its own MAC address for given IP address is known as ____________.
   A. STP attack
   B. ARP Spoofing

C. MAC table overflow
D. VLAN hopping

10. A technique of manipulating MAC address to impersonate the legitimate user or launch an attack such as Denial-of-Service attack is known as ____________.
A. STP attack
B. MAC Spoofing
C. MAC table overflow
D. VLAN hopping

11. Which of the following methods serve as the mitigation technique for DHCP spoofing?
A. Port security
B. Dynamic ARP inspection
C. DHCP Snooping
D. Cisco discovery protocol (CDP)

12. Which of the followings is the mitigation technique of layer 2 attacks?
A. Port security
B. Dynamic ARP inspection
C. DHCP Snooping
D. All of the above
E. None

13. Which feature of STP prevents loop creation after STP is converged and redundant links are disabled?
A. BPDU guard
B. Loop guard
C. Root guard
D. None of the above

14. Which of the followings is the characteristic of port security?

A. It binds the MAC address of known devices to the physical port and associates it with violation action
B. It determines the best route for routing
C. It provides authentication and encryption
D. None of the above

15. What purpose does the "show ip dhcp snooping binding" command serve?
A. Shows the list of active interfaces
B. Shows the list OSPF neighbors
C. Shows the list best routes
D. Shows clients list with the legitimate IP addresses assigned to them

16. In which type of an attack does an attacker sends bogus requests for broadcasting to DHCP server with spoofed MAC addresses to lease all IP addresses in DHCP address pool?
A. STP attack
B. MAC Spoofing
C. MAC table overflow
D. DHCP Starvation

17. How can you prevent a VLAN hopping attack? (Choose any three)
A. Disable auto-trunking and enable manual-trunking
B. Enable auto-trunking
C. Change the native VLAN to a VLAN other than VLAN1
D. Always consider VLAN 1 as native VLAN
E. Tag the native VLAN traffic in order to prevent against 802.1Q double-tagging attack to exploit network vulnerability

18. What causes can lead to buffer overflow?
A. Overloading a system by downloading and installing too many software updates on a system at one time
B. If there is an attempt to write more data to a memory location than that location

can hold

C. Overloading too much information to two or more interfaces of the same device, leading to packet dropping

D. All of the above

19. Which type of VLAN-hopping attack may be prevented by configuring any other VLAN as the native VLAN rather than VLAN 1?

A. DTP spoofing

B. DHCP spoofing

C. VLAN double-tagging

D. DHCP starvation

20. In order to mitigate VLAN hopping attacks, which of the following protocol should be disabled?

A. STP

B. DTP

C. ARP

D. CDP

21. On which type of port, can isolated port forward traffic to on a private VLAN?

A. On a community port

B. On a promiscuous port

C. On an isolated port

D. None of the above

22. What security measures prevent CAM table overflow attacks?

A. DHCP snooping

B. Dynamic ARP Inspection

C. IP source guard

D. Port security

23. In spanning Tree Protocol (STP), what security benefit is gained from enabling

BPDU guard on Portfast enabled interfaces?

A. It prevents rogue switches from being part of a network
B. Assigns root bridges
C. It prevents buffer overflow attacks
D. Prevents Layer 2 loops

24. Which of the following VPN solutions allows the establishment of a secure remote-access VPN tunnel between a web browser and the ASA?

A. clientless SSL
B. clientless IPSec
C. client-based SSL
D. client-based IPSec

25. Which of the following protocols supports secure access provided by Cisco AnyConnect?

A. SSL only
B. IPsec only
C. SNMP
D. Both SSL and IPsec
E. None of the above

Chapter 05: Cisco Firewall Technologies

Technology Brief

In the previous chapter, we have discussed about secure routing and switching methods. Nevertheless, in today's world, we also need to be aware of one of the most powerful network security tool and that is firewall. Being aware of the core concepts and deployment techniques of multi-vendor firewalls as well as the related technologies, play a key role in the selection of an employee for network security's job.

Firewall

Firewalls are physical devices or software that defend an internal network or system from unauthorized access by using traffic filtering feature. Firewalls are an essential mechanism to fight against the malicious activities on the internet.

The primary function of using a dedicated device named as firewall at the edge of corporate network is isolation. Firewall prevents the direct connection of internal LAN with internet or outside world. This isolation can be performed in multiple ways:

- **A Layer 3 device**- uses an Access List for restricting specific type of traffic on any of its interfaces.
- **A Layer 2 device**- uses the concept of VLANs or Private VLANs (PVLAN) for separating the traffic of two or more networks.
- **A dedicated host device**- with software installed on it. This host device, also acting as proxy, filters the desired traffic while allowing the remaining traffic.

Although the features above provide isolation in some sense, following are the few reasons a dedicated firewall appliance (whether in hardware or software) is preferred in production environments:

Risks	Protection by firewall
Access by untrusted entities	Firewalls try to categorize the network into different portions. One portion is considered as trusted portion like internal LAN. Public internet and interfaces connected to untrusted network are considered as untrusted portion. Similarly, servers accessed by untrusted entities are placed in a special segment known as demilitarized zone (DMZ). By allowing only specific access of these servers, like port 90 of web server, firewall hides the functionality of network device, which makes it difficult for attackers to understand the physical topology of the network.
Deep Packet Inspection and protocols exploitation	One of the interesting features of dedicated firewall is their ability to inspect the traffic further than just IP and port level. By using digital certificates, Next Generation Firewalls available today can inspect traffic up to layer 7. Firewall can also limit the number of established as well as half open TCP/UDP connections to mitigate DDoS attacks.
Access Control	By implementing local AAA or by using ACS/ISE servers, firewalls can permit traffic based on AAA policy.
Antivirus and protection from infected data	By integrating IPS/IDP modules with firewall, malicious data can be detected and filtered at the edge of the network to protect the end-users.

Table 5-01: Firewall Risk Mitigation Features

Although firewall provides great security features as discussed in the table above, any misconfiguration or bad network design may result in serious consequences. Another important deciding factor of deploying firewall in current network design depends on whether current business objectives can bear the following limitations:

- **Misconfiguration and Its Consequences:** The primary function of firewall is to protect network infrastructure in a more elegant way than a traditional layer 3/2 devices. Depending on different vendors and their implementation techniques, many features need to be configured for a firewall to work properly. Some of these features may include Network Address Translation (NAT), Access-Lists (ACL), AAA base policies and so on. Misconfiguration of any of these features may result in leakage of digital assets, which may have financial impact on the business. In short, complex devices like firewall also require deep insight knowledge of equipment along with general approach of deployment.
- **Applications and Services Support:** Most of the firewalls use different techniques to mitigate the advanced attacks. For example, NATing is one of the most commonly used feature in firewalls and it is used to mitigate the reconnaissance attacks. In situations where network infrastructure is used to

support custom-made applications, it may be required to re-write the whole application in order to properly work under new network changes.

- **Latency:** Just as implementing NATing on a route adds some end-to-end delay, firewall along with heavy processing demanding features add a noticeable delay over the network. Although high-end devices of Cisco Adaptive Security Appliance (ASA) series and other vendor's equipment have a very small throughput delay, some applications like Voice Over IP (VOIP) may require special configurations to deal with it.

Another important factor to be considered while designing the security policies of network infrastructure is using the layered approach instead of relying on single element. For example, consider the following scenario:

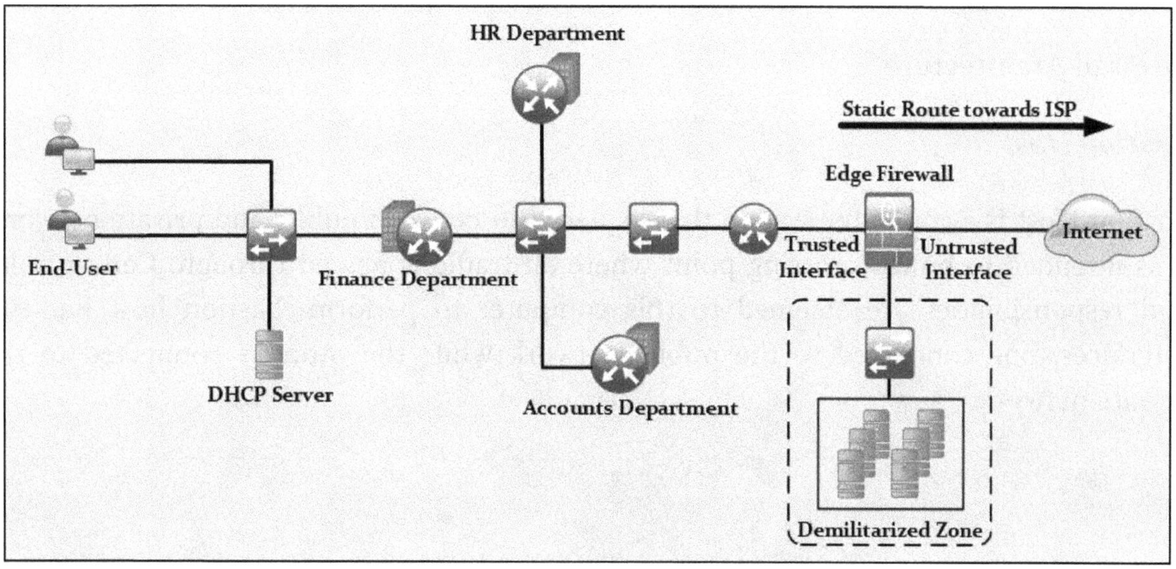

Figure 5-01: Positioning Firewall in Production Environment

The figure 5-01 shows a typical scenario of SOHO and mid-sized corporate environment where whole network infrastructure is supported by couple of routers and switches. If the edge firewall is supposed to be the focal point of security implementation, then any slighter misconfiguration may result in high scale attacks. In general, a layered security approach is followed and packet passes through multiple security checks before hitting the intended destination.

The position of firewall varies in different design variants. In some designs, it is placed after the perimeter router of corporation while in some designs; it is placed at the edge of the network as shown in figure. Irrelevant of position, it is a good practice to implement the layered security in which some of the features like unicast reverse path forwarding, access-lists, etc. are enabled on perimeter router. Features like deep packet inspection, digital signatures are matched on firewall. If everything looks good, then packet is allowed to hit the intended destination address.

Network layer firewalls permit or drop IP traffic based on Layer 3 and 4 information. A router with access-list configured on its interfaces is a common example of network layer firewall. Although very fast in operation, network layer firewalls do not process/ perform deep packet inspection techniques and detect any malicious activity.

Apart from acting as first line of defense, network layer firewalls are also deployed with in internal LAN segments for enhanced layered security and isolation.

Firewall Architecture

Bastion Host

Bastion Host is a computer system that is placed in between public and private network. It is intended to be the crossing point where all traffic is passed through. Certain roles and responsibilities are assigned to this computer to perform. Bastion host has two interfaces, one connected to the public network while the other is connected to the private network.

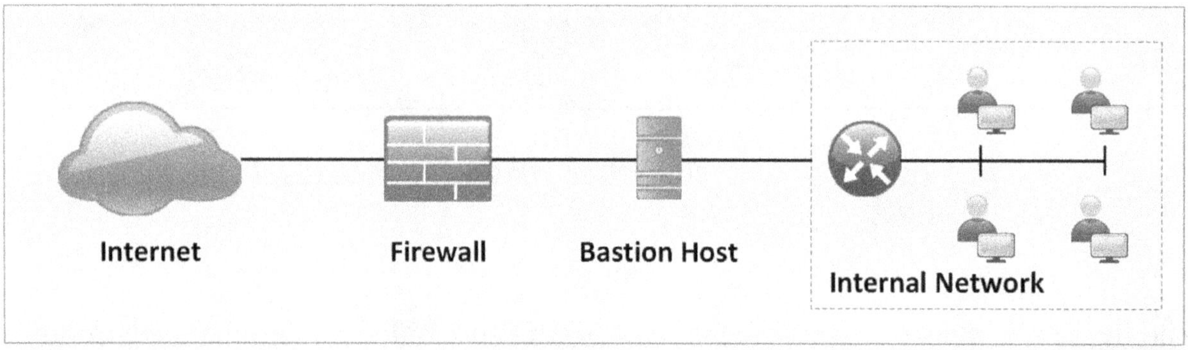

Figure 5-02: Bastion Host

Screened Subnet

Screened Subnet can be set up with a firewall with three interfaces. These three interfaces are connected with Internal Private Network, Public Network, and Demilitarized Zone (DMZ). In this architecture, each zone is separated by another zone hence the compromise of one zone will not affect another zone.

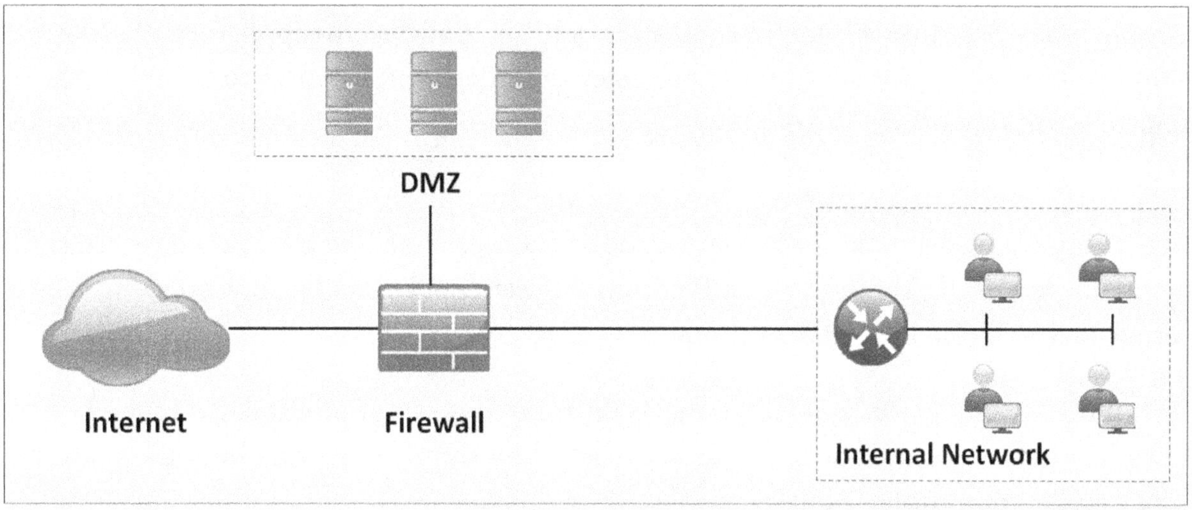

Figure 5-03: Screened Subnet

Multi-Homed Firewall

Multi-Homed firewall refers to two or more networks where each interface is connected to its network. It increases the efficiency and reliability of a network. A firewall with two or more interfaces allows further subdivision.

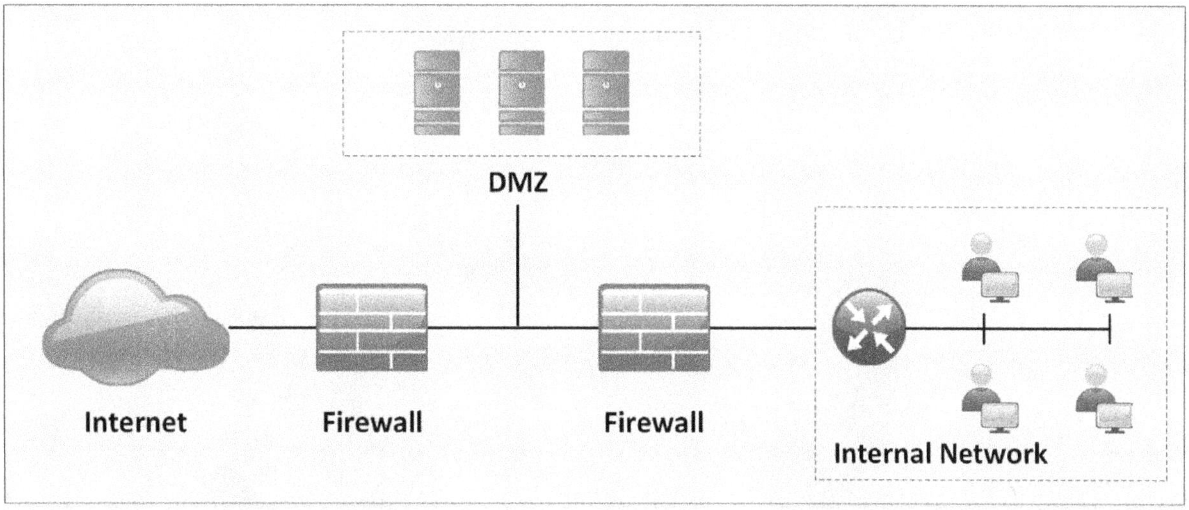

Figure 5-04: Multi-Homed Firewall

Demilitarized Zone (DMZ) Firewalls

IOS zone-based firewalls are specific set of rules, which may help to mitigate mid-level security attacks in environments where security is also meant to be implemented via routers. In zone-based firewalls (ZBF), interfaces of devices are placed in different and unique zones like (inside, outside or DMZ) and then policies are applied on these zones. Naming conventions for zones must be easier to understand in order to be helpful at the hour of troubleshooting.

ZBFs also uses Stateful filtering, which means that if the rule is defined to permit originating traffic from one zone, say inside, to another zone like DMZ, then return traffic would automatically be allowed. Traffic from different zones can be allowed using policies permiting the traffic in each direction.

One of the advantages of applying policies on zones instead of interfaces is that whenever new changes are required at the interface level, then simply removing or adding interface in particular zone applies policies on it automatically.

ZBF may use the following feature sets in its implementation:

- Stateful Inspection
- Packet Filtering
- URL Filtering
- Transparent Firewall
- Virtual Routing Forwarding (VRF)

This figure shows the scenario explained above:

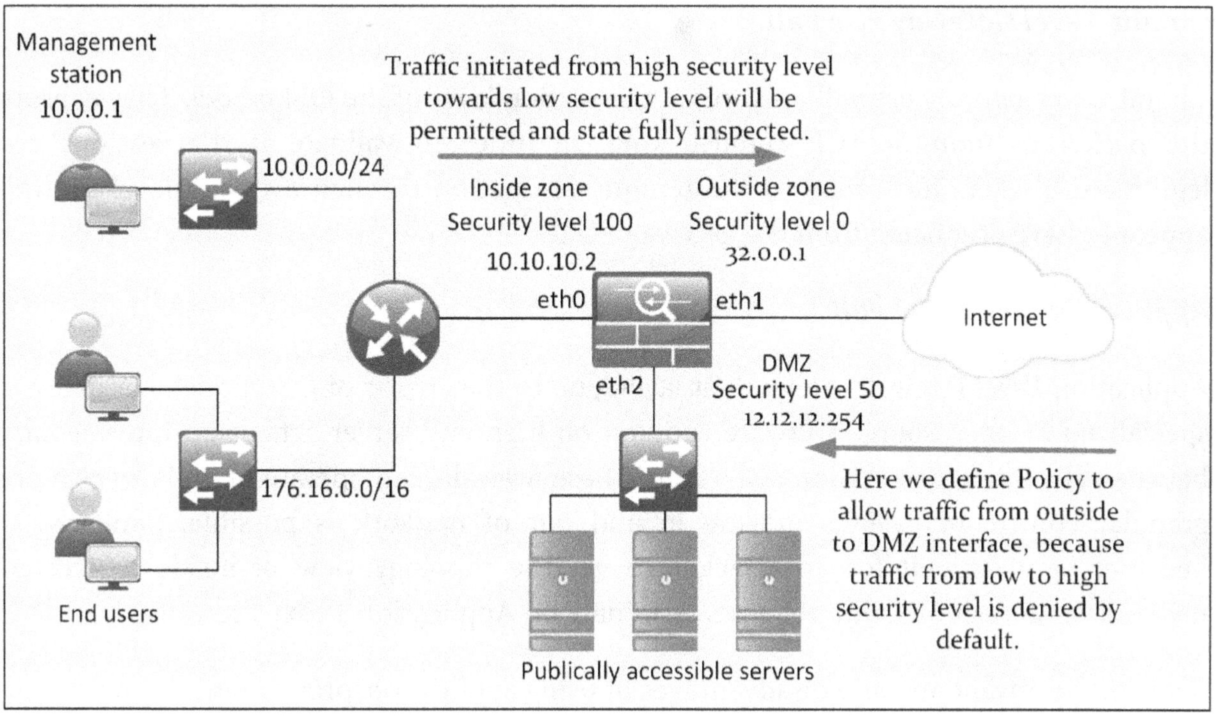

Figure 5-05: Cisco IOS Zone-Based Firewall Scenario

Types of Firewall

Packet Filtering Firewall

Packet Filtering Firewall includes the use of access-lists to permit or deny traffic based on layer 3 and layer 4 information. Whenever a packet hits an ACL configured layer 3 device's interface, it checks for a match in an ACL (starting from the first line of ACL).

This table shows the advantages and disadvantages of using packet-filtering techniques:

Advantages	Disadvantages
Ease of implementation by using permit and deny statements	Cannot mitigate IP spoofing attacks; An attacker can compromise the digital assets by spoofing IP source address to one of the permit statements in the ACL
Less CPU intensive than deep packet inspection techniques	Difficult to maintain when ACLS size grows
Configurable on almost every Cisco IOS	Cannot implement filtering based on session states
Even a mid-range device can perform ACL based filtering	Scenarios in which dynamic ports are used, a range of ports will be required to be opened in ACL, which may also be used by malicious users

Table 5-02: Advantages and Disadvantages of Packet Filtering Techniques

Circuit-Level Gateway Firewall

Circuit Level gateway firewall operates at the session layer of the OSI model. They capture the packet to monitor TCP Handshaking, in order to validate if the sessions are legitimate. Packets forwarded to the remote destination through a circuit-level firewall appear to have originated from the gateway.

Application-Level Firewall

Application Level Firewall can work at layer 3 up to the layer 7 of OSI model. Normally, a specialized or open source software running on high-end server acts as an intermediary between client and destination address. As these firewalls can operate up to layer 7, more granular control of packets moving in and out of network is possible. Similarly, it becomes very difficult for an attacker to get the topology view of inside or trusted network because connection requests terminate on Application/Proxy firewalls.

Some of the advantages and disadvantages of using application/proxy firewalls are:

Advantages	Disadvantages
Granular control over the traffic is possible by using information up to layer 7 of OSI model.	As proxy and application firewalls run in software, a very high-end machine may be required to fulfil the computational requirements.
Indirect connections between end devices make it very difficult to generate attack.	Just like NAT, not every application has support for proxy firewalls and few amendments may be needed in current applications architecture.
Detailed logging is possible as every session involves the firewall as intermediary.	Another software may be required for logging features, which take extra processing power.
Any commercially available hardware can be used to install and run proxy firewalls on it.	Along with computational power, high storage may be required in different scenarios.

Table 5-03: Advantages and Disadvantages of Application/Proxy Firewalls

Stateful Multilayer Inspection Firewall

As the name depicts, this saves the state of current sessions in a table known as a stateful database. Stateful inspection and firewalls using this technique normally deny any traffic between trusted and untrusted interfaces. Whenever an end-device from trusted interface wants to communicate with some destination address attached to the untrusted interface of the firewall, its entry will be made in a stateful database table containing layer

3 and layer 2 information. Following table compares different features of Stateful inspection-based firewalls.

Advantages	Disadvantages
Helps in filtering unexpected traffic	Unable to mitigate application layer attacks
Can be implemented on a broad range of routers and firewalls	Except for TCP, other protocols do not have well-defined state information to be used by the firewall
Can help in mitigating denial of service (DDoS) attacks	Some applications may use more than one port for a successful operation. Application architecture review may be needed in order to work after the deployment of Stateful inspection based firewall.

Table 5-04: Advantages and Disadvantages of Stateful Inspection Based Firewalls

Transparent Firewalls

Most of the firewalls discussed above work on layer 3 and beyond. Transparent firewalls work exactly like above mentioned techniques but the interfaces of firewall itself are layer 2 in nature. IP addresses are not assigned to any interface, you may think of it like a switch with ports assigned to some VLAN. The only IP address assigned to transparent firewall is for management purposes. Similarly, as there is no addition of extra hops between end-devices, user will not be able to be aware of any new additions in network infrastructure and custom-made applications may work without any problem.

Next Generation (NGFW) Firewalls

NGFW is relatively a new term used for latest firewalls with advanced feature set. This kind of firewall provides in-depth security features to mitigate against known threats and malware attacks. An example of next generation firewalls is Cisco ASA series with FirePOWER services. NGFW provides complete visibility in to network traffic users, mobile devices, virtual machine (VM) to VM data communication etc.

Personal Firewalls

Personal firewalls also known as desktop firewalls, which help the end-user's personal computers from general attacks from intruders. Such firewalls appear to be great security line of defense for users who are constantly connect to internet via DSL or cable modem. Running in the background, personal firewalls help by providing inbound and outbound filtering, controlling internet connectivity to and from the computer (both in domain based and workgroup mode), and altering the user for any attempts of intrusions.

Proxy Firewalls

Proxy firewall is an old type of firewall, which serves as the gateway from one network to another network for a specific application. Proxy servers can provide additional features such as security and content caching, which have impacts on the overall throughput capabilities and the applications they can support. Proxy firewalls and application level firewalls are almost the same.

Design and Deployment Considerations for Firewalls

The best industry practices related to deployment of firewalls are:

- Firewall should be the primary element in the overall security posture of network infrastructure.
- Access policy that starts with "deny" statement first followed by specific permit statements is recommended over "permit" first and then explicit deny all statements.
- It is recommended to place firewalls at the edge of network facing the untrusted network with respect to the organization.
- Logging feature of firewall must be properly implemented. Many open sources as well as specialized software are available to display Syslog messages and generate alerts for custom defined levels for forensic investigations.
- Physical security as well as access management of premises where firewall is deployed must be made sure of.

Comparing Stateful & Stateless Firewalls

Stateless firewalls

Initially, the firewalls analyze data packets just to see if they match the particular sets of rules, and then the firewalls decide how to forward or drop the packets accordingly. This type of packet filtering is referred to as stateless filtering because the access control list inspects only the IP addresses. This type of filtering does not care whether a packet is part of an existing data flow, particular state, port or protocol, or not. Each packet is analyzed individually based solely on the values of certain parameters in the packet header, this is somehow similar to ACLs packet filtering.

Stateless firewall monitors network traffic and allow, restrict or block packets based on static values like source and destination addresses. They are not aware of data flows and traffic patterns.

Sometimes, a stateless firewall filter is also known as an access control list (ACL), because it does not state-fully analyze traffic and it is not aware of the communication path. The basic purpose of a stateless firewall filter is to use packet filtering to enhance security. Packet filtering lets you take the decision and actions based upon the policies you applied. Stateless firewalls are faster and can perform better under heavier traffic loads.

Stateful Firewalls

Stateful firewalls analyze the state of connections in data flows during packet filtering. They analyze whether the packet belongs to an existing flow of data or not. Stateful firewalls can see traffic streams from one end to another. They know about the communication paths and they can apply different IP Security (IPsec) functions such as encryption and tunneling. Stateful firewalls lets you know about different TCP connections or port states whether open, open sent, synchronized, synchronization acknowledge or established. Stateful firewalls are better at identifying unauthorized access from anywhere.

Stateful firewall is able to maintain the state of every connection either incoming or outgoing through the firewall and thus replaces long lines of configuration. When the traffic wants to go out through a firewall, the packet will be first matched against a firewall rule list to check whether the packet is allowed or not. If this packet type is allowed to go out through the firewall, then the process of ***Stateful*** filtering will begin.

Usually, ***Stateful*** firewall uses the traffic that is using the Transport control protocol (TCP). TCP is ***Stateful*** to begin with because TCP maintains a track of its connections by using source and destination address, port number and IP flags. Three-way handshake will begin a connection (SYN, SYN-ACK, ACK) and a two-way exchange (FIN, ACK) will sum up the connection. This process makes keeping track of the connection's state easier.

State or Session Table

By default, Stateful packet filtering is enabled on ASA, which means that firewall will keep track of every session initiated from trusted network to untrusted network. When the first packet from source hits the trusted interface of ASA, its entry will be made in Stateful database. As its name depicts, this saves the state of current sessions in a table known as Stateful Database. This database is also called state table or session table. The incoming traffic of connection will only be allowed if source address and port number matches the saved state in the ***Stateful*** table. Stateful firewall records session states and other related details including source and destination IP addresses, sequences, flags, acknowledgement numbers and other details into the state table of all communication sessions passing through the firewall. Whenever a connection is permitted, an entry is recorded. For upcoming requests toward the firewall of same connection, firewall compares the entry in its state table for same validating the information i.e. source and destination address, source and destination ports and protocols to determine the validity of the session.

Function of State Table

The connection begins with the initial request for a connection from an inside host (SYN). This will initiate an entry in the firewall's state table. If the destination host responds and returns a packet (SYN, ACK) to set up the connection, then the state table keeps the entry of this as well. At last, the initial host will send the final packet (ACK) in the connection setup to confirm the establishment. Here the connection will be established. Once a connection is established between the two devices, communication can easily be done between hosts. This state entry will be maintained in the state table as long as the connection remains established or until a timeout occurs for that session. Finally, FIN and ACK messages will be exchanged to end up the session.

Cisco IOS Zone Based Firewalls

IOS zone based firewalls (ZBFW) are specific sets of rules, which may help to mitigate mid-level security attacks in the environment where security is also meant to be implemented via routers. In zone based firewalls (ZBFW), interfaces of devices are placed to different and unique zones like (inside, outside or DMZ) and then policies are applied on these zones. Naming conventions for zones must be easier to understand in order to be helpful at the time of troubleshooting.

ZBFs also uses Stateful filtering, which means that if rule is defined to permit originating traffic from one zone, say inside, to another zone like DMZ, then return traffic would automatically be allowed. In order to allow originating traffic from both zones, two separate permit policies need to be applied.

One of the advantages of applying policies on zones instead of interfaces is that whenever new changes required at interface level, then simply removing or adding interface in particular zone automatically applies policy on it.

ZBF may use the following feature set in its implementation:

- Stateful inspection
- Packet filtering
- URL filtering
- Transparent firewall
- Virtual Routing Forwarding (VRF)

Most of the features defined above are already explained in the previous sections. Virtual Routing Forwardings (VRFs) are logical routing tables, used to divide the global routing table in to multiple ones. Such features are useful in situations where one physical device is used to provide security feature to multiple clients. By creating virtual firewall for each client and VRF because of it, makes troubleshooting as well as design a little bit cleaner as every client's configuration will be independent to each other.

Consider an example of small-office/home-office where a limited number of users only require internet access. In this case, only two zones would be sufficient to implement the IOS zone based firewall. Interface of router connecting to the internal LAN users can be placed in zone named, say inside. Similarly, interfaces connected to public internet can placed in another zone named as outside. In the second process, policies should be applied to permit traffic for required scenarios. For example, from inside to outside zone, HTTP/HTTPS traffic needs to be allowed

Similarly, in the case of corporate environment where multiple servers are meant to be accessed by outside world, for example as ISP, which provides hosting services to different clients, another zone needs to be created named as DMZ. Comparing this scenario with the small office home office, another policy will be needed to permit traffic from outside zone to DMZ zone.

This figure shows the scenario explained above:

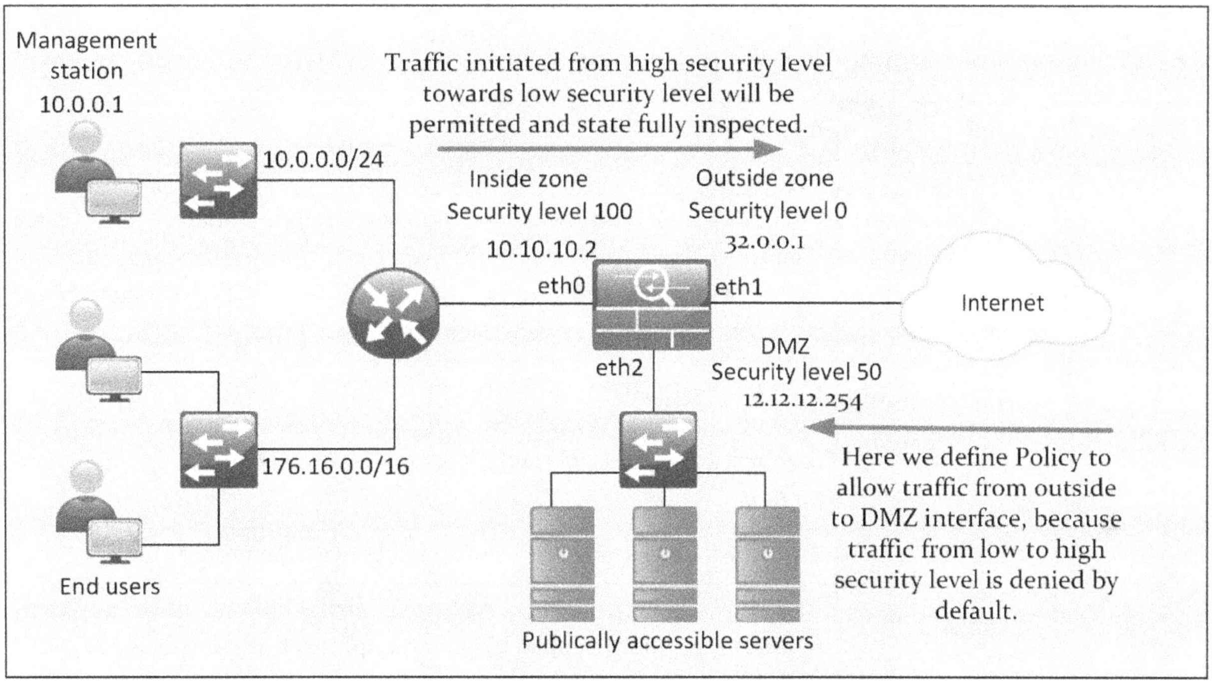

Figure 5-06: Cisco IOS Zone Based Firewall Scenario

Cisco Common Classification Policy Language (C3PL)

Cisco common classification policy language is the framework used to implement the IOS zone based firewalls in Cisco devices. The steps involved are:

Class Maps

Class maps are used to filter out the traffic that needs to be inspected. Traffic can be filtered by using information from Layer 3 up to Layer 7 of OSI model. ACL can also be referred in a class map for the purpose of identifying traffic. Similarly, multiple match statements can also be used within single class map where every single match statement (a match-all condition) or even a single entry can be considered as a match (a match-any condition). By default, a class-map with name *class-default* is created in Cisco IOS, which can be used to match any kind of traffic hitting the device's interfaces.

Policy Maps

Policy maps are used to perform a specific kind of action on traffic matched by class maps. By referring a class-map, policy map can either inspect (Stateful inspection of traffic), permit (permit the traffic but no Stateful inspection), drop the traffic or generate a log of it. A policy map is processed on top to bottom fashioned just like ACL and if multiple class maps are called within a single policy map, traffic would be matched until the match is found. If no class-map satisfies the traffic, then default action of implicit deny will be applied.

The following table summarizes the policy map actions:

Policy Map Action	Explanation	Application
Inspect	Permit the traffic and perform Stateful inspection	This option should be used to allow traffic, initiated from users connected with trusted interface, towards the untrusted destination. Router will make entry for each session in state table or database for such connections while denying everything from everywhere.
Pass/Permit	Permit the traffic without Stateful inspection	In some cases, reply traffic is not expected for initiated session. For example, a UDP Traffic in a Client/Server Architecture may be unidirectional in nature and does not require inspection to be applied on it.
Deny	Deny the traffic	Traffic, which is desired to be dropped between the zones.
Log	Log the traffic	In order to add the logging feature in above options, for example, to monitor the traffic dropped by policy map, this feature will also be used.

Table 5-05: Policy Map Actions and Their Applications

Service Policies:

This command finally implements the policy, defined in policy-map applied on specific zone pair. As from previous discussions, a zone-pair is just a unidirectional flow of traffic from one zone to another zone. For example, in the figure above, two zone pairs need to be defined, one for inside to outside zone and second for traffic from outside to zone named as DMZ.

Without ZBFW configured, whenever a packet hits one of the interfaces of router, it will be matched for more specific entry in the routing table, which will eventually result in either forwarding or drop action. In case of ZBFW in place, Stateful database along with defined policy-map may also be checked before routing the packet to correct interface.

The following table summarizes the action performed as traffic is intended to be moved between interfaces lying in different zones.

Ingress interface zone membership	Egress interface zone membership	Policy definition on zone pair	Action
No	No	Does not matter	Forward the traffic
No	Yes	Does not matter	Drop the traffic
Yes (Zone X)	Yes (Zone X)	Does not matter	Forward the traffic
Yes (Zone X)	Yes (Zone B)	No	Drop the traffic
Yes (Zone X)	Yes (Zone B)	Yes	Policy is applied. Action of permit or deny will be applied as defined in the policy

Table 5-06: Service Policy Actions and Their Applications

In short, implementing the ZBFW on Cisco's IOS involves the steps depicted in the figure next page.

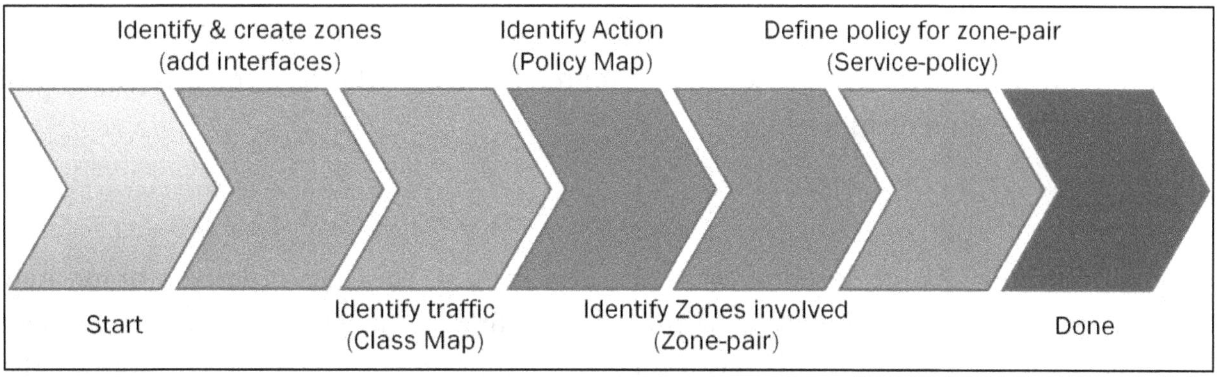

Figure 5-07: Steps Involved in Implementing ZBFW

Self-Zone

Any kind of traffic directed towards the router itself is considered to be part of self-zone. For example, management traffic can be considered as part of self-zone. Similarly, traffic generated by router itself is also the part of self-zone. In Cisco devices, traffic to the self-zone either in ingress direction or in egress direction is permitted by default. However, filtering can be done on traffic directed towards the router by creating a zone pair (involving the self-zone) and applying policy to it. Contrary to named zones created for user traffic, if a zone pair involving self-zones is created but no policy is applied on it, traffic will be permitted. It is summarized in following table:

Originating traffic zone membership	Destination traffic zone membership	Policy definition on zone pair	Action
Self-Zone	Zone X	No	Forward the traffic
Zone X	Self	No	Forward the traffic
Self-Zone	Zone X	Yes	Policy is applied. Action of permit or deny will be applied as defined in the policy
Zone X	Self-Zone	Yes	Policy is applied. Action of permit or deny will be applied as defined in the policy

Table 5-07: Self-Zone Actions and Their Applications

Following are some characteristics of Self-Zone

- The "Self" zone is a default zone.
- All traffic to any router interface is allowed until explicitly denied.
- A zone-based firewall rule that includes the Self zone applies to local traffic.
- The Inspect action is not allowed in rules that apply to the Self zone.
- IOS firewalls support examination of TCP, UDP and H.323 traffic only.
- All IP addresses configured on the router belong to the Self zone, regardless of interface zone membership.

Case Study

A small office of a home-based consultancy firm in New York has ordered a brand new firewall device for the protection of their confidential data. Due to some unforeseen reasons, the shipment of product has been delayed for two months. In the meantime, the boss of the company has ordered to implement the IOS zone based firewall until the company gets their order. Basically, IOS zone based firewall has three zones and the traffic will be divided between these three zones according to the required flow of traffic.

Here is the diagram of company's architecture shown below:

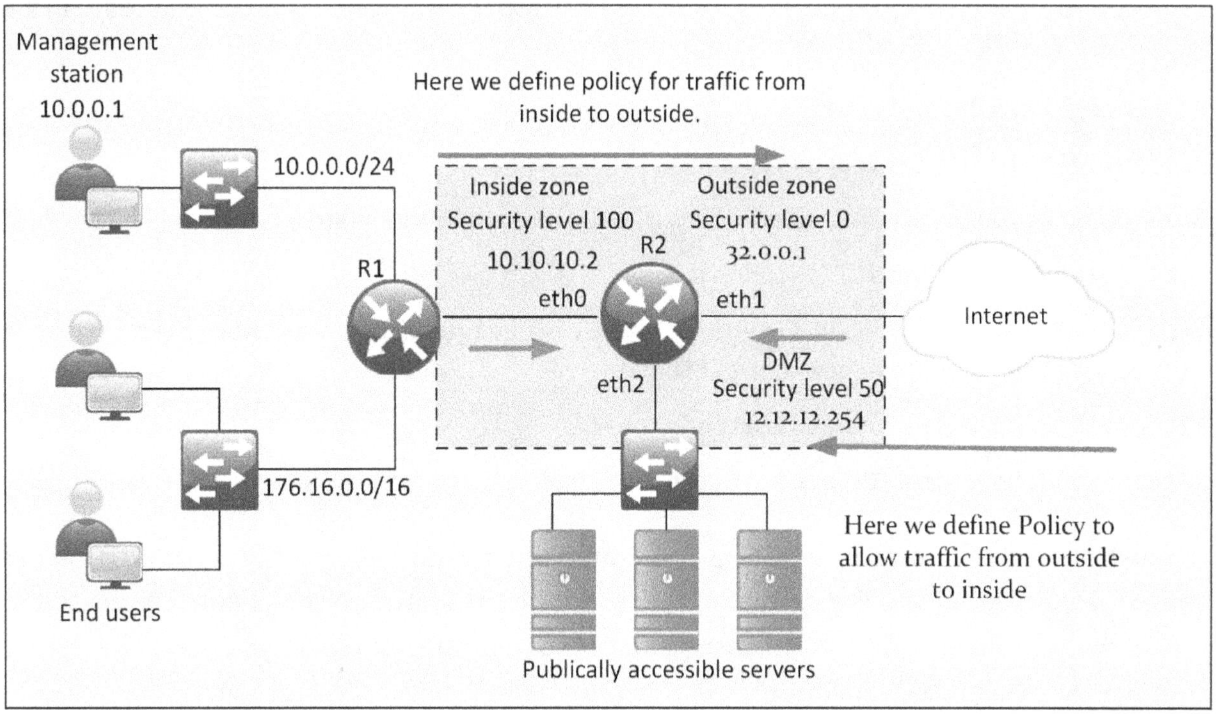

Figure 5-08: Firewall Technologies Case Study Scenario

Lab 5.1: Implementation of Zone-Based Firewalls (Zone to Zone)

In this lab, three zones, namely inside, outside, and DMZ will be created on Router R1. According to company's requirement, traffic from inside zone is only allowed to go towards the outside zone. Similarly, DMZ zone can only be accessible from outside zone. The basic IP addressing scheme is also mentioned in the diagram shown above. The default access username and password scheme is same as used in the previous lab.

R2

Initially, there is no configuration for defining zones on the router, so now there are no zones. Therefore, everyone can get access from the internet. If we ping from simulated internet router R3 to management station, we will get the following response:

```
R3# ping 10.0.0.1
Type escape sequence to abort.
```

```
Sending 5, 100-byte ICMP Echos to 10.0.0.1, timeout is 2 seconds:
!!!!!
```

Similarly, DMZ can access the internal network. It can also be verified from ping test.

In order to enable HTTP and HTTPS access on router R2, following commands will be used:

```
R2(config)# ip http server
R2(config)# ip http secure-server
% Generating 1024 bit RSA keys, keys will be non-exportable...
[OK] (elapsed time was 1 seconds)
*Nov  8 09:10:47.707: %PKI-4-NOAUTOSAVE: Configuration was modified.  Issue
"write memory" to save new certificate
R2(config)# ip http authentication local
R2(config)# username IPSpecialist privilege 15 secret P@$$word:10
```

It must be noted that after entering the command for enabling HTTPS (ip http secure server), a new certificate is generated, which will be presented to the clients connected to it via web browser. This certificate will prove the authenticity of router R2 to its connecting clients. Second important thing to be noted is that, web access required at least one user with privilege level 15 to be defined on device. For this purpose, previous username has been recreated with privilege level 15 access. Now clients connecting via this username will directly get level 15 access.

After opening the Cisco Configuration Professional, following screen will be displayed:

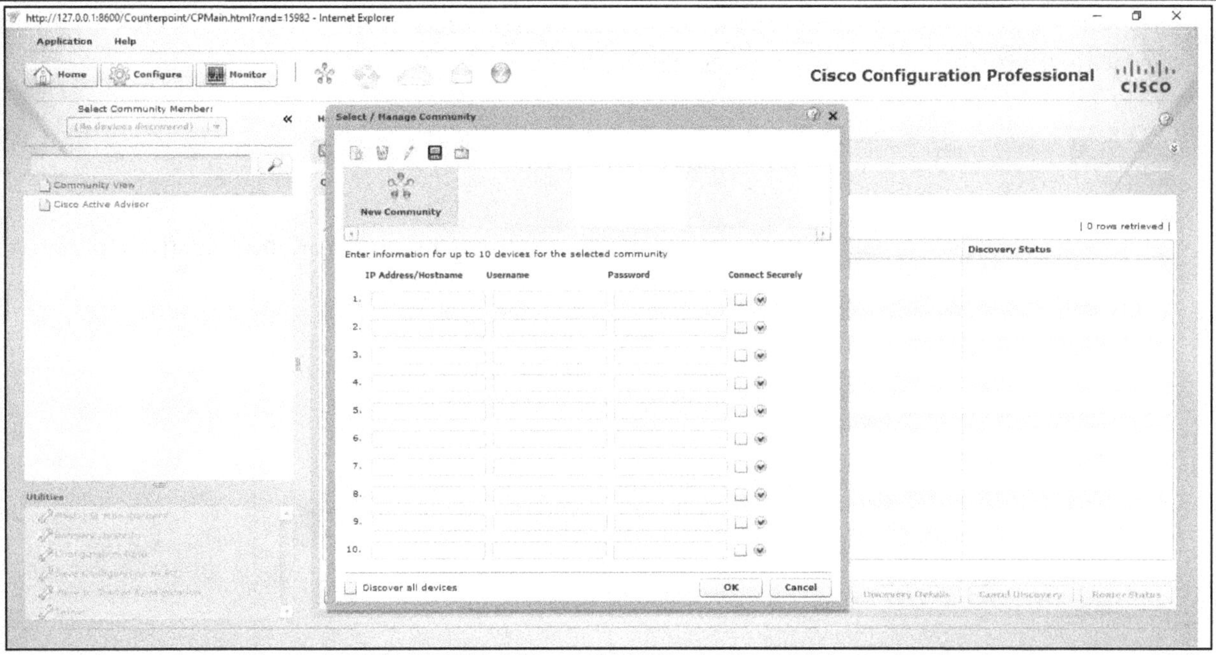

A community is just a grouping of commonly accessed devices in your network. As SSH is only option allowed in our scenario, click connect remotely and provide the SSH port along with the IP address of R2 router (192.168.0.2). Name this community to be IPSpecialist, username be "IPSpecialist" with password "P@$$word:10". Tick the "Connect Securely" checkbox and click "OK".

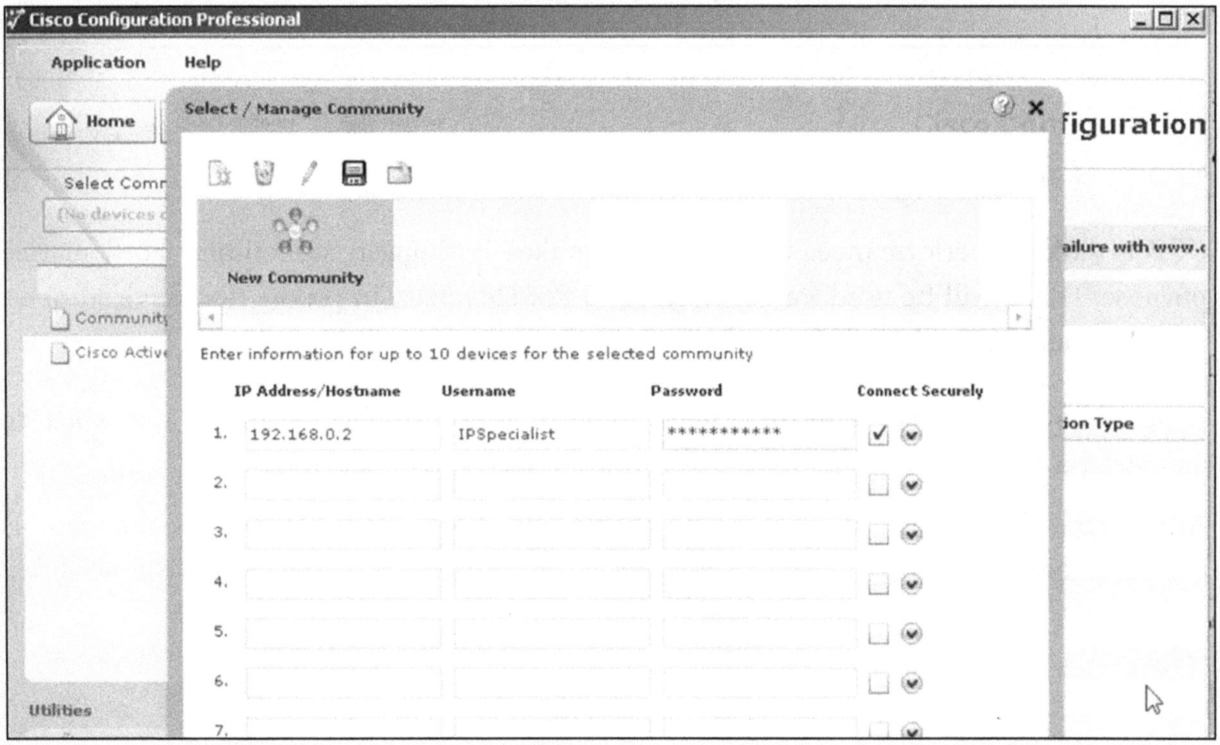

If you enter the correct password in the above fields, following dialog box related to the security alert certificate will prompt on the screen.

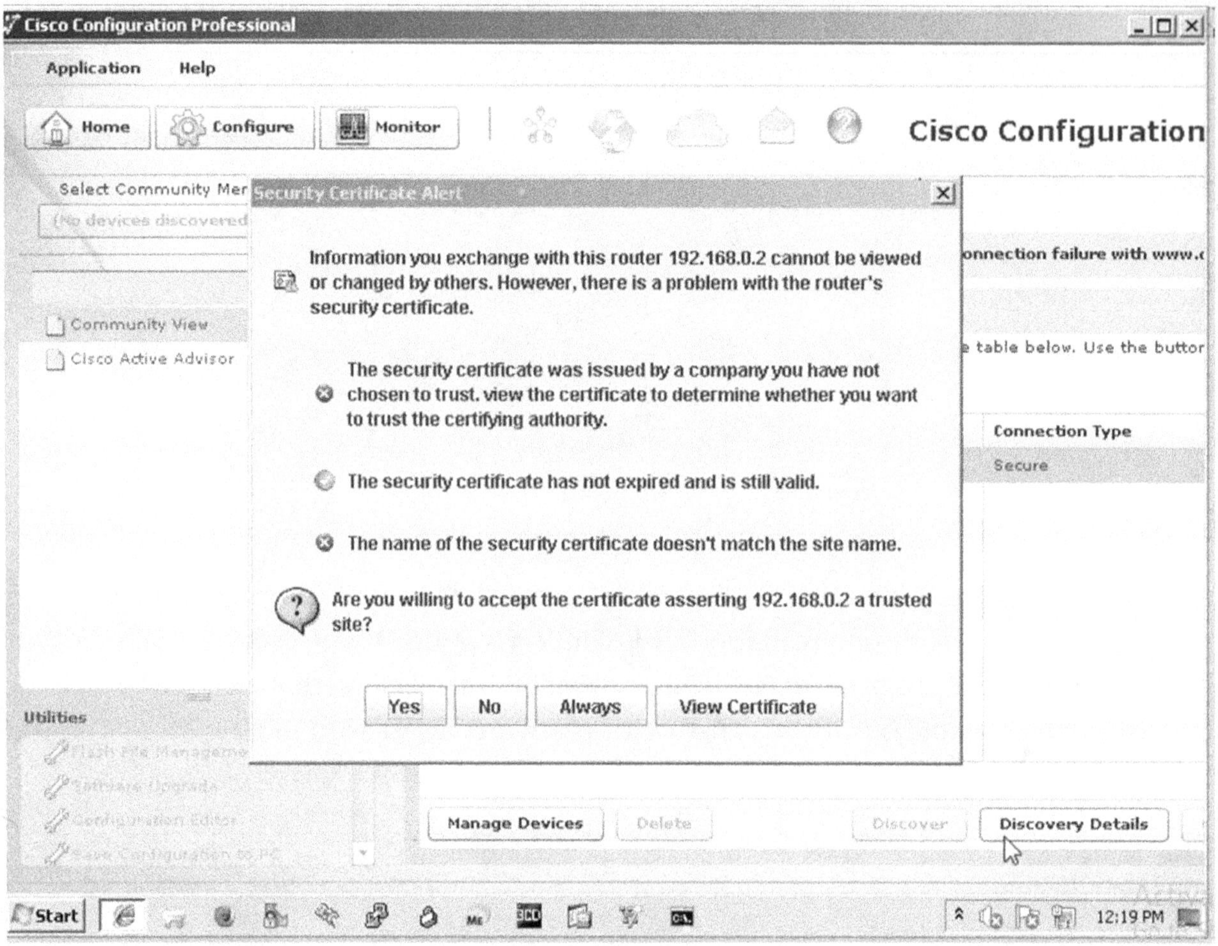

Click "Yes" to start configuring R2 from GUI of CCP.

CCP is slow in performance. Using HTTPS makes it sluggish sometimes. For practice purpose, HTTP will be used for connecting to R2. However, in production environment, HTTPS would be used.

Repeat the above steps but this time, uncheck the "Connect Securely" checkbox to connect via HTTP.

After successful connection, router's hostname and discovery status will be changed, as shown below:

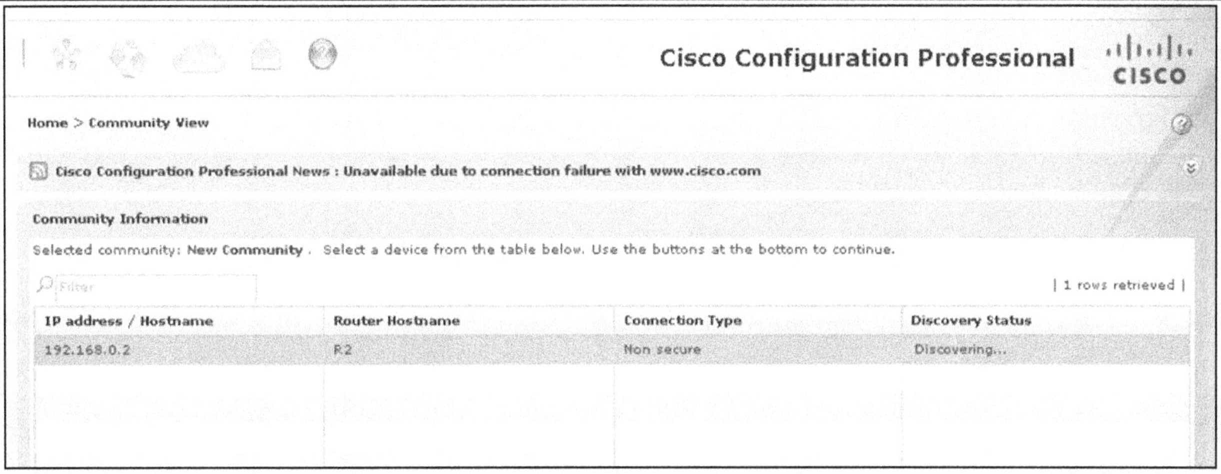

Now the original task of this lab begins by defining the zones, adding interfaces to the zones and applying the policy action defined in the lab objectives.

By clicking on the "Configure" button, go to "Security" > "Firewall" > "Firewall".

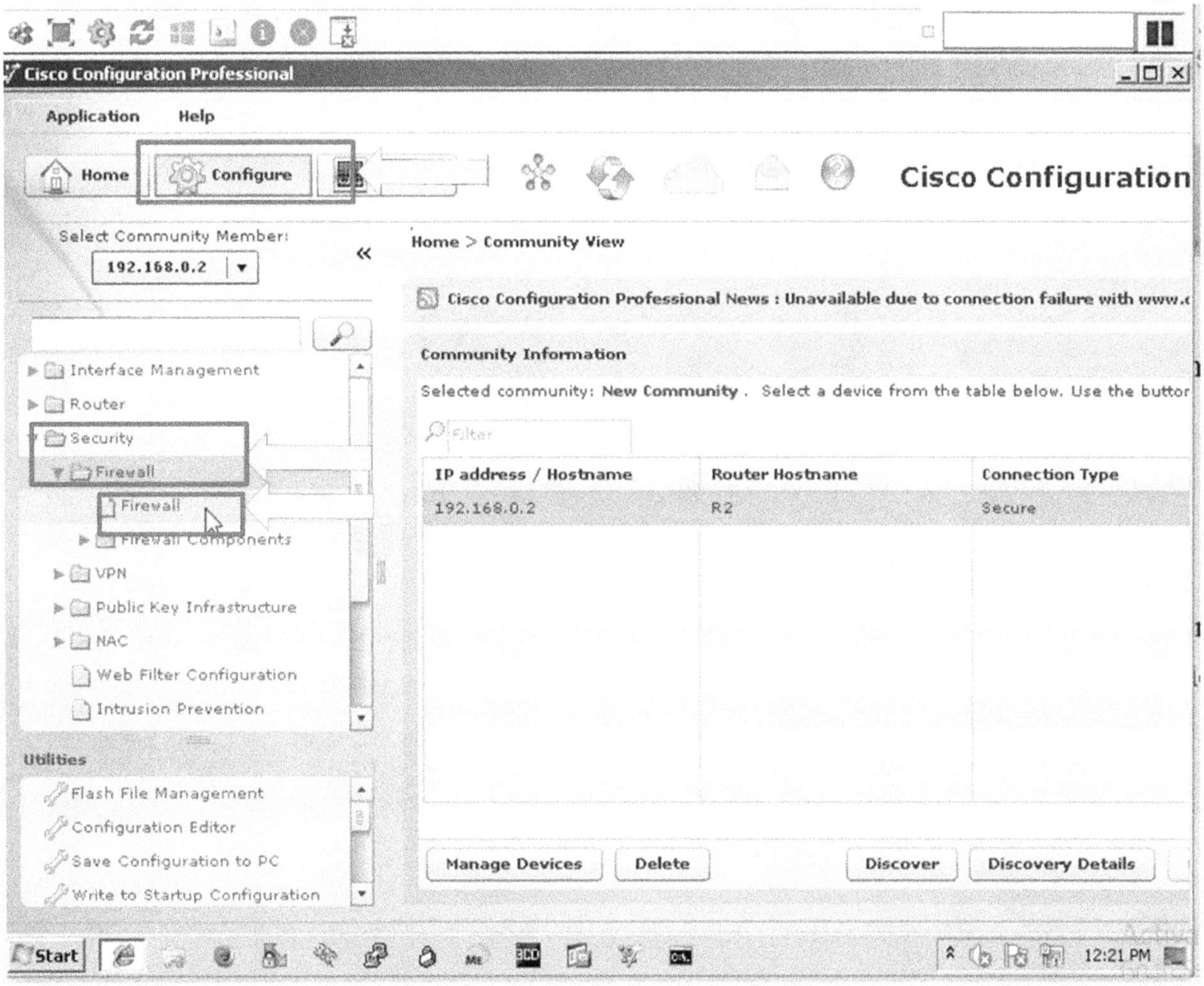

Here, two options will be shown. In basic firewall configuration mode, only inside and outside zone based scenarios are entertained. Second option will be used in this lab, which is for advanced firewall scenarios, containing DMZ zone as well.

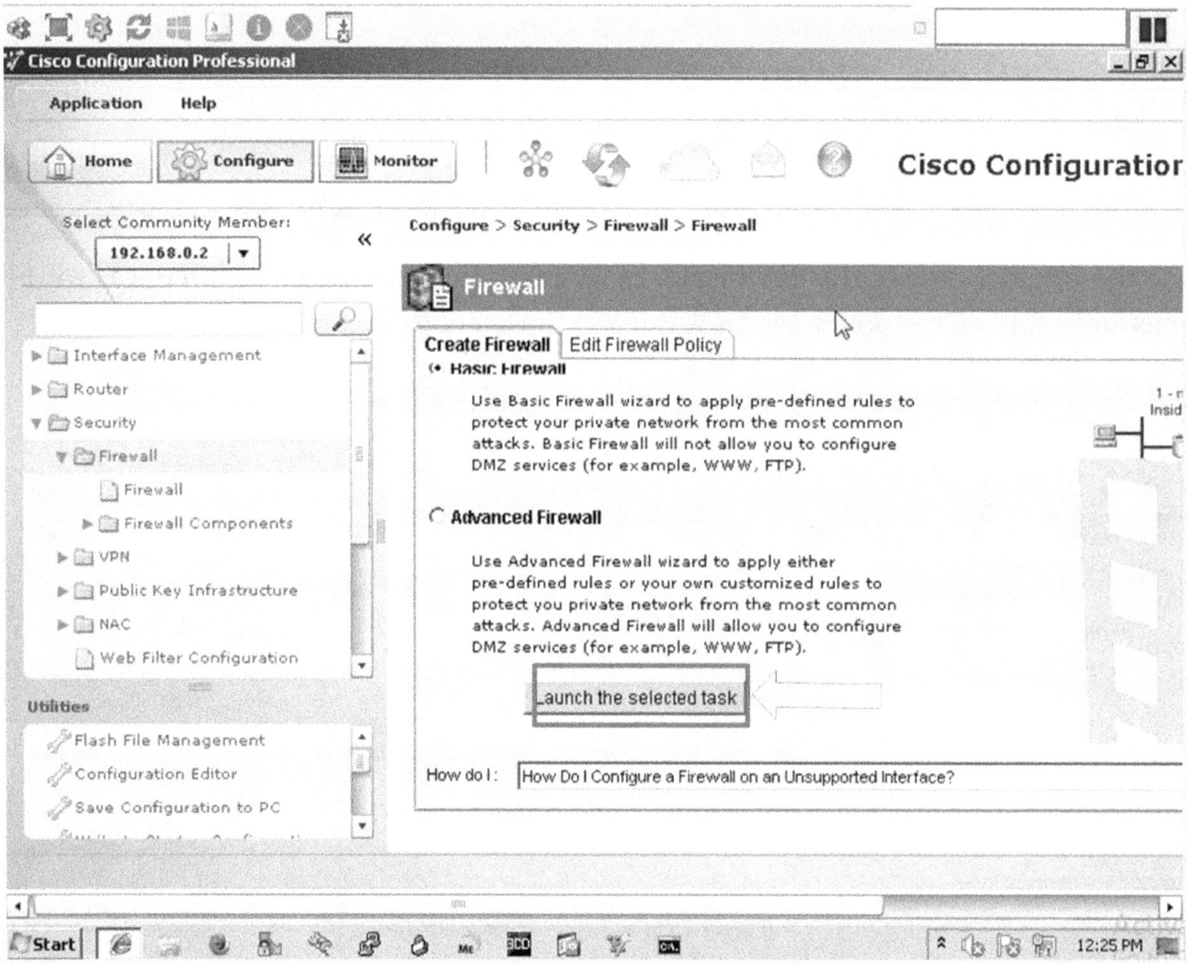

Now, Click on "Launch the selected task" button to start the interactive session in which requirements to implement the zone base firewall will be asked accordingly. Following screens will be shown one by one:

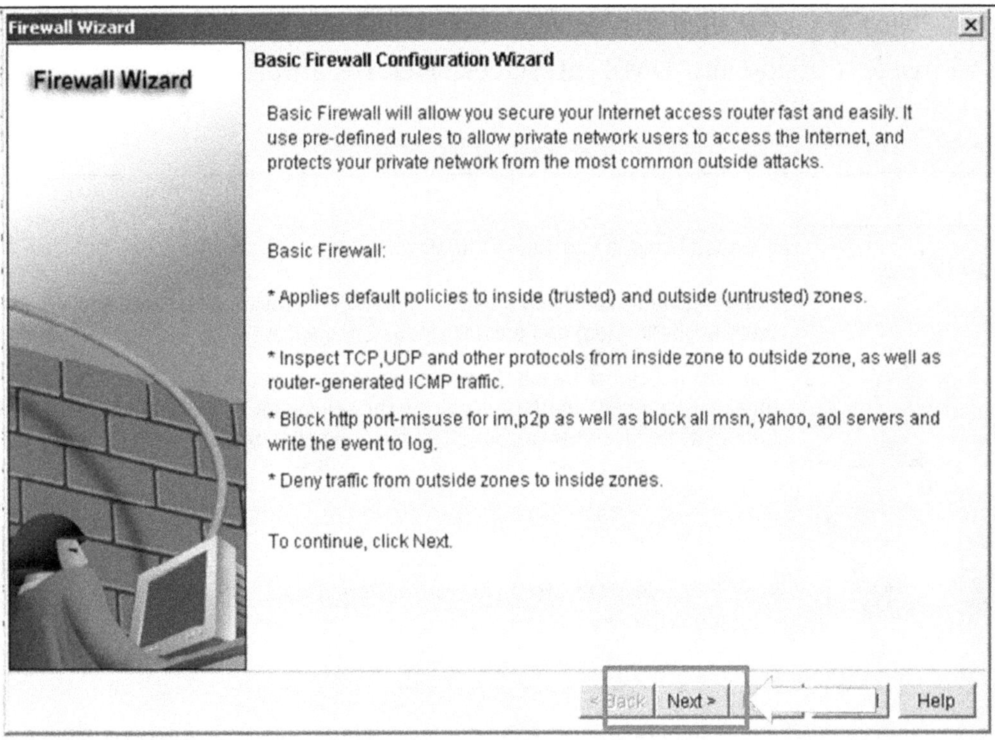

The above wizard starts with explaining some of the features of IOS based firewalls. Click "Next".

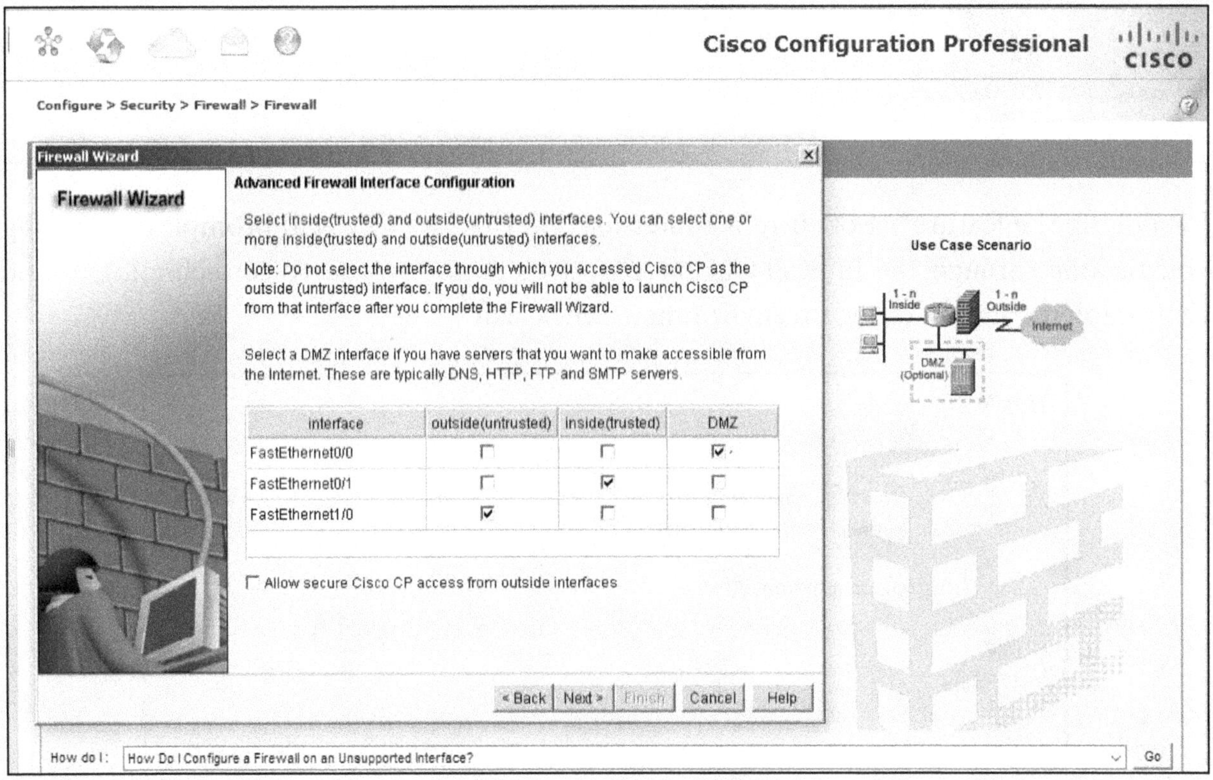

By clicking "Next", a new dialog box will appear, asking for the interfaces, which are working as inside, outside and DMZ interfaces. Tick the interfaces accordingly and click "Next".

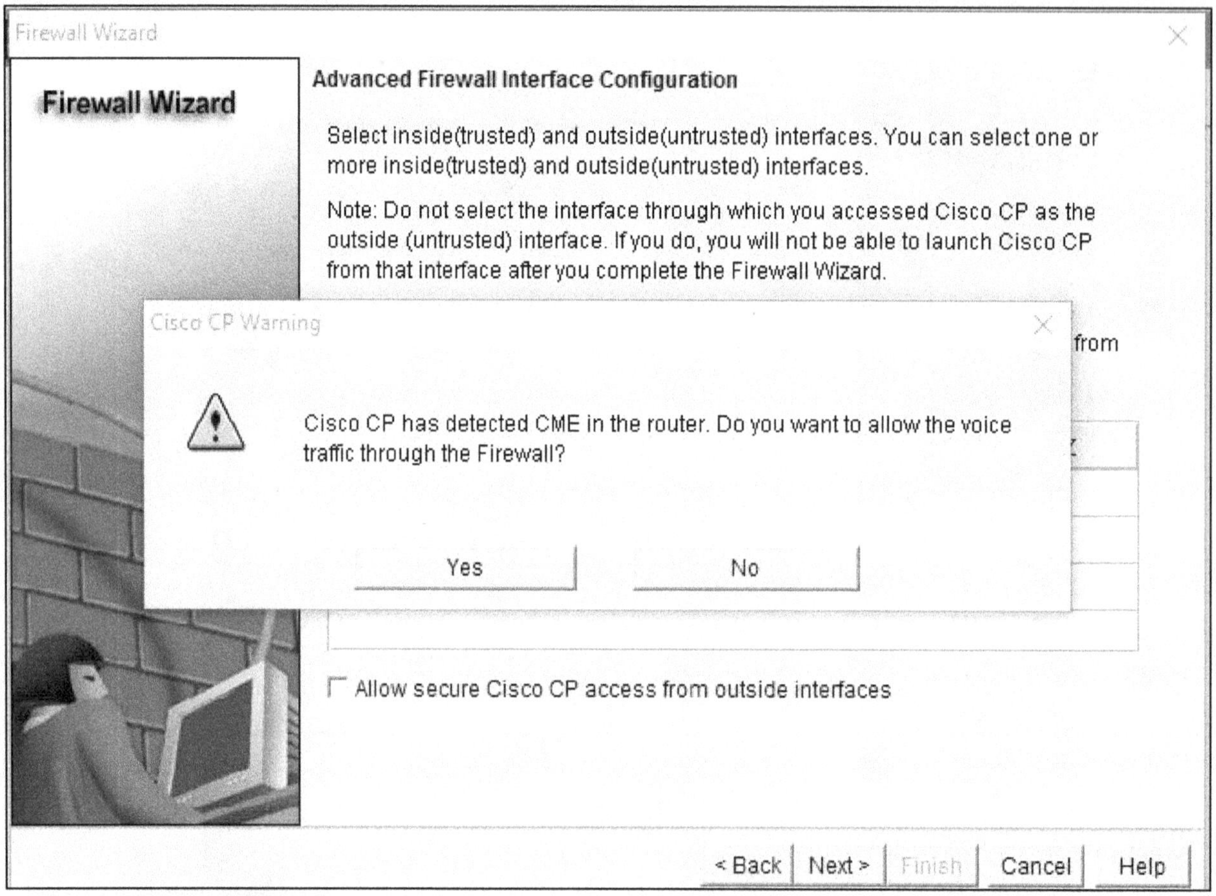

By judging the feature set of current router used in this lab, CCP will prompt for allowing voice traffic through the firewall. As current focus is not on the voice technologies and their implementation in secure environment, click "No".

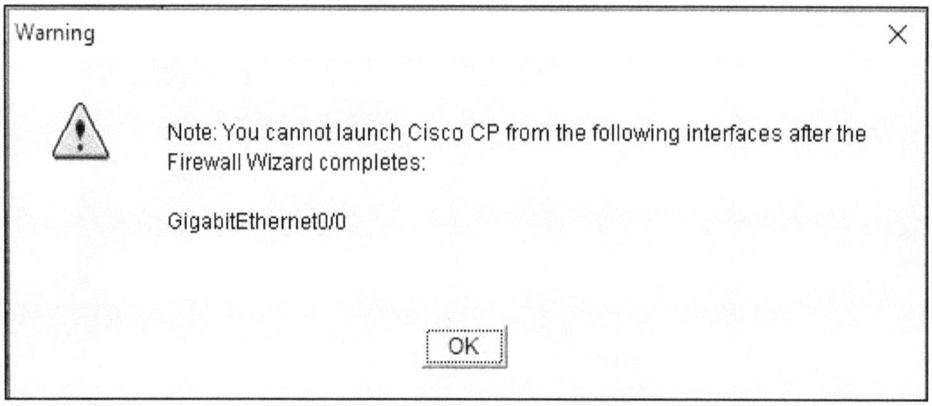

The dialogue box above shows the first security feature by disabling the access to router from interface connected to untrusted network. Click "Ok".

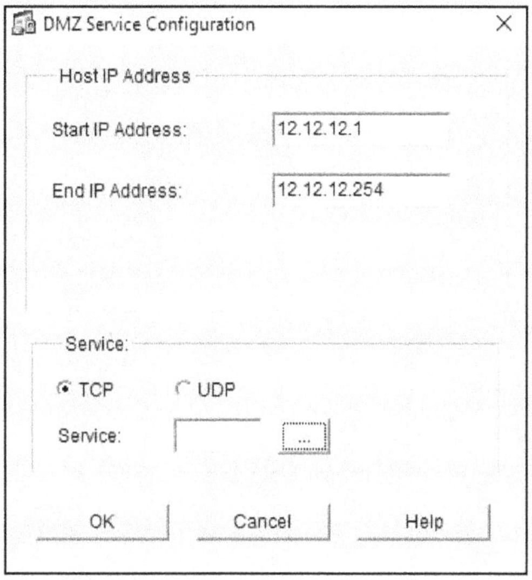

CCP firewall wizard will ask for the traffic allowed from outside interface to DMZ interface. For the purpose of this lab, provide the IP address range of DMZ segment along with the TCP port number 23 for telnet feature.

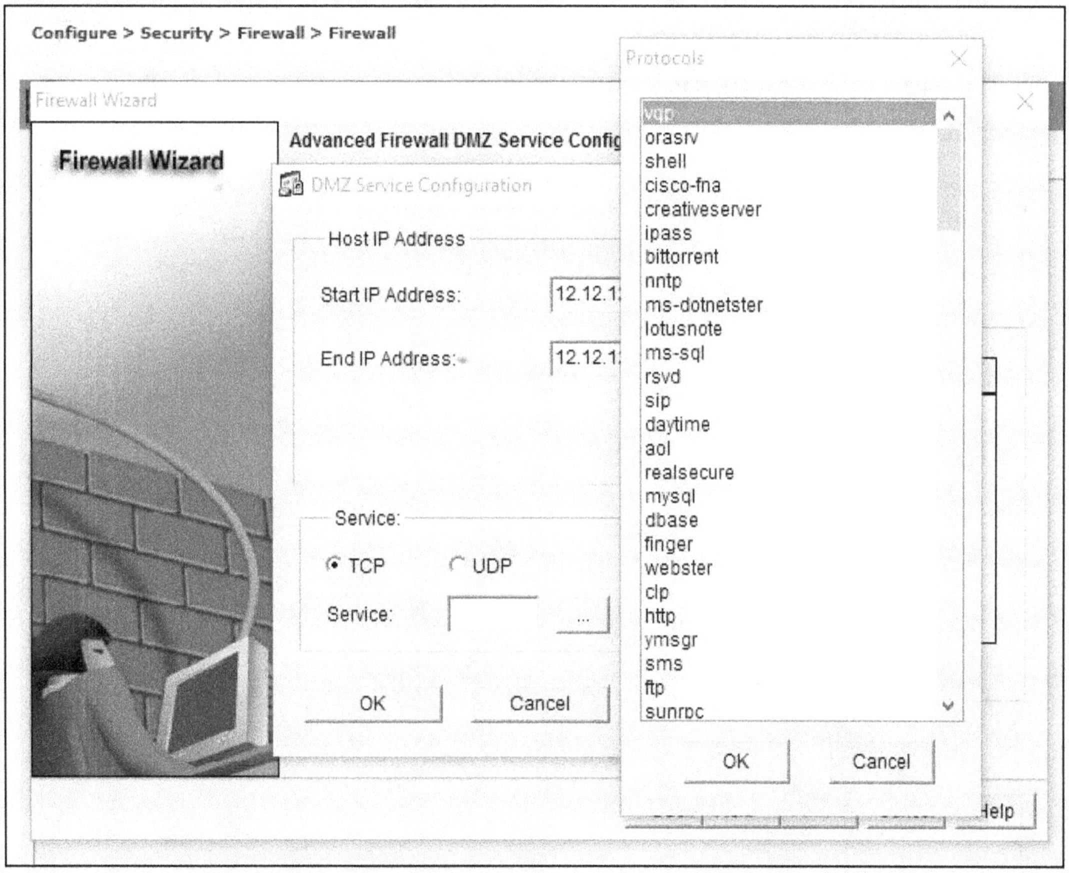

After selecting "TELENT" service, click "Next".

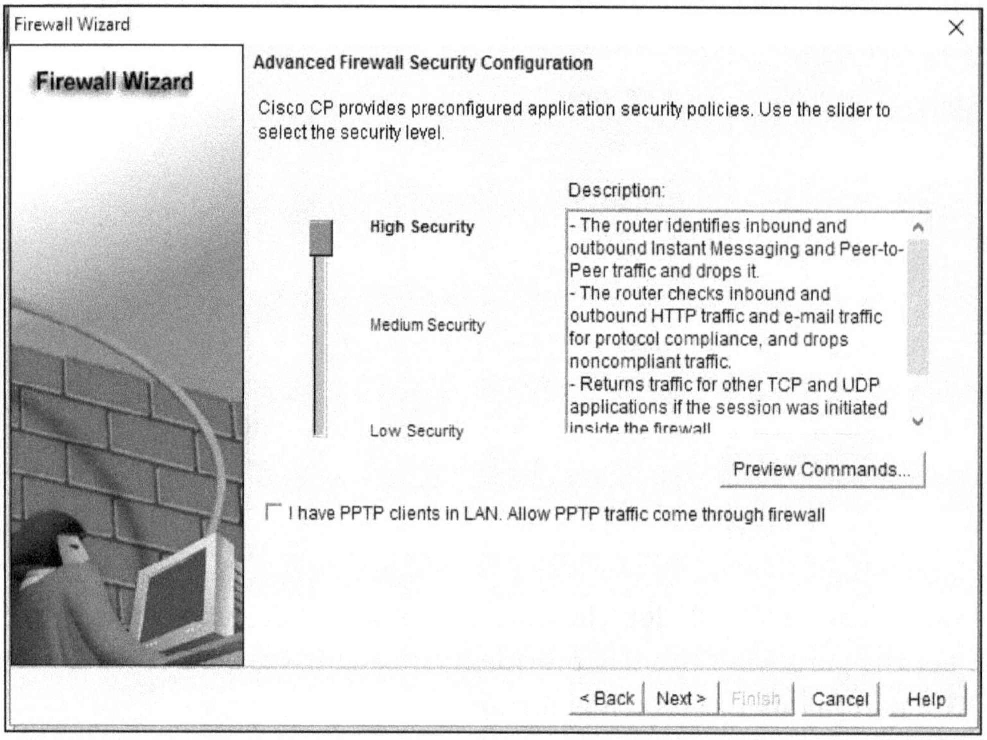

While configuring ZBFW, three security levels are represented along with the description of security features provided by each security level.

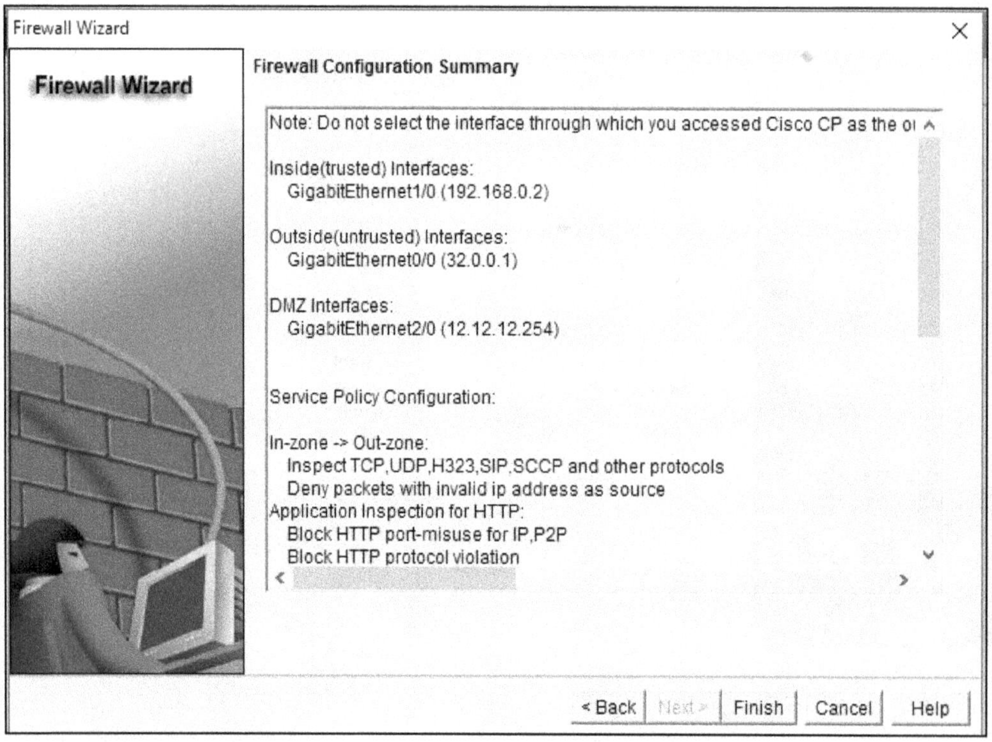

Before applying the configuration, firewall configuration summary can be double checked to make sure that we are going to apply the right policy. Following is the firewall policy applied in this lab:

Note: Do not select the interface through which you accessed Cisco CP as the outside (untrusted) interface. If you do, you will not be able to launch Cisco CP from that interface after you complete the Firewall Wizard.

```
Inside(trusted) Interfaces:
   FastEthernet0/1 (192.168.0.2)

Outside(untrusted) Interfaces:
   FastEthernet1/0 (32.0.0.1)

DMZ Interfaces:
    FastEthernet0/0 (12.12.12.254)

Service Policy Configuration:
 In-zone -> Out-zone:
    Inspect TCP,UDP,H323,SIP,SCCP and other protocols
    Deny packets with invalid ip address as source
Application Inspection for HTTP:
    Block HTTP port-misuse for IP,P2P
    Block HTTP protocol violation
    Block HTTP request methods other than post,head,get
   Block http request response containing non-ascii characters
   Application Inspection for Instant Messaging:
   Block all services of msn,yahoo,aol with log action
Application Inspection for P2P:
    Block file transfer over edonkey,fasttrack,gnutella and kazaa2
    Block text-chat over edonkey
Application Inspection for Email:
   Block invalid command for imap,pop3
    Block SMTP session with data length over 5 MB

 Self -> Out-zone:
    Inspect router generated ICMP traffic
 Out-zone -> Self:
    Deny all other traffic.

 DNS Configuration:
    Primary DNS:10.0.0.254
    Secondary DNS: Not set
```

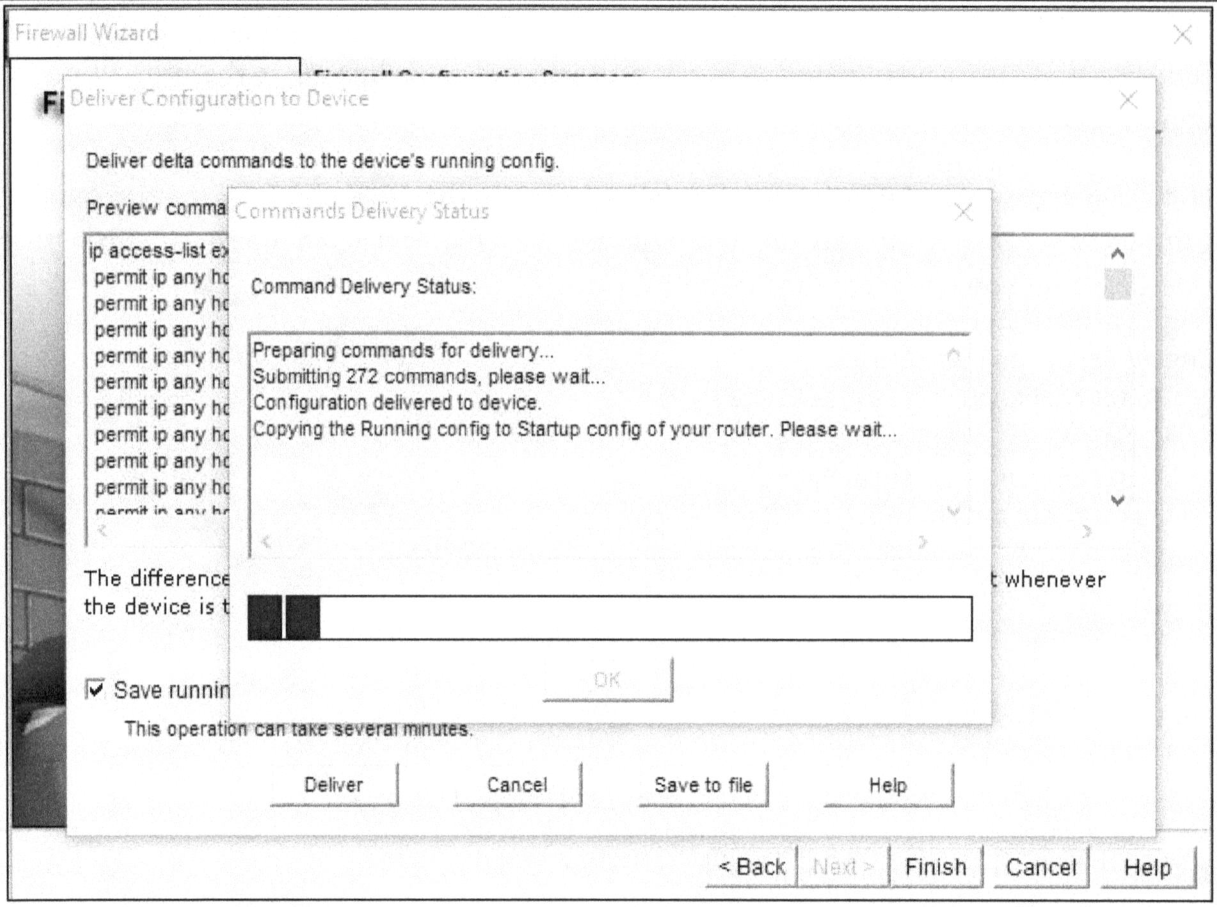

By clicking the "Deliver" button, actually applies the configuration as shown in the figure above.

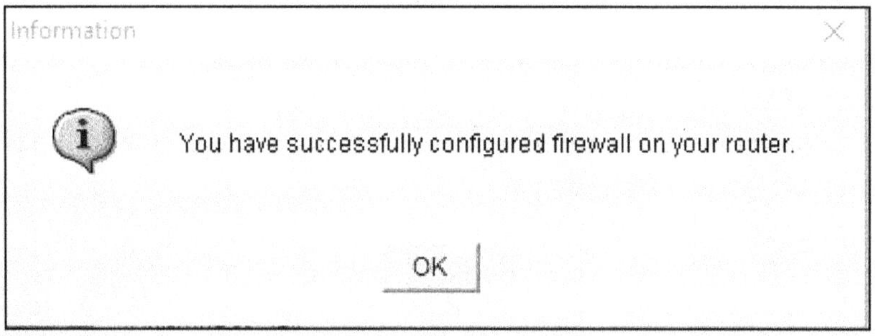

For verification of different features like inspection form inside to outside, click button "Monitor" and then "Security"-> "Firewall Status" to monitor the current active sessions, dropped packets etc. For example, by pinging the 32.0.0.2, which is the IP address of simulated internet, an ICMP based active session from inside to outside zone will appear as shown below:

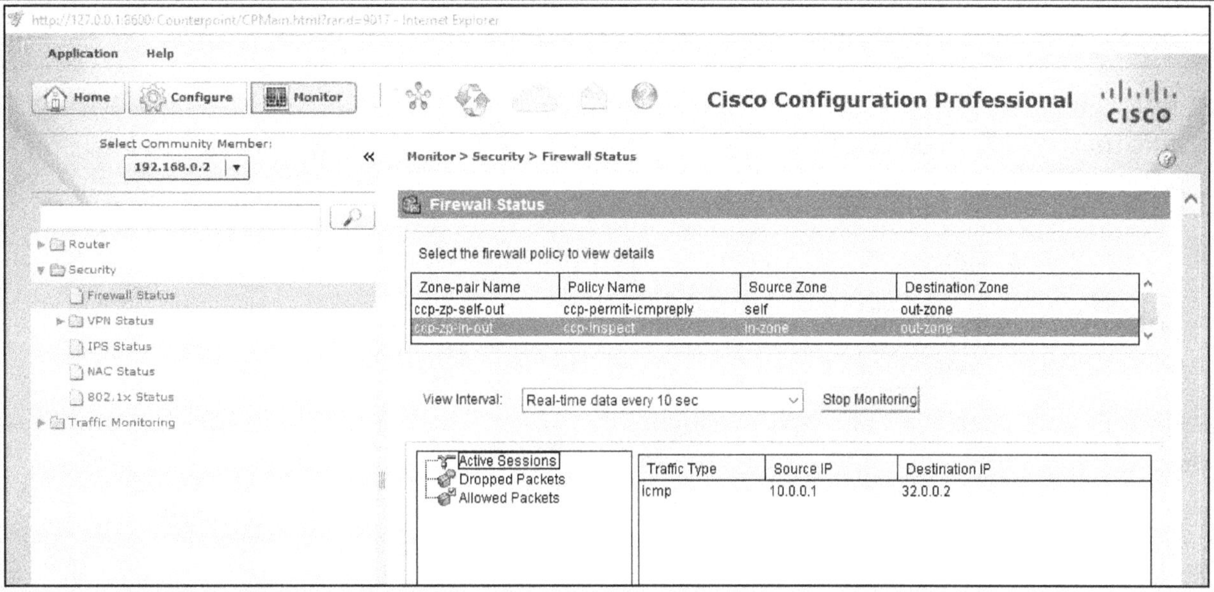

Due to very large configuration settings applied by CCP based firewall implementation, "*show running-config*" command can be used to see the class-maps and policies applied by CCP.

Configuration of Zone based Firewall from CLI

Although CLI commands of ZBFW (*zone-to-zone* as well as *self-zone*) can also be checked from "*show running-config*" command. However, the following section shows general commands of implementing class-maps, policy-maps and then applying policy on an interface.

```
R2 (config) # class-map type inspect match-any IPSPECIALIST-CLASS-MAP
R2(config-cmap)# match protocol telnet
R2(config-cmap)# match protocol icmp
R2(config-cmap)# exit
```

In the above commands, a class map with name *IPSPECIALIST-CLASS-MAP* is defined with matching only telnet and ICMP traffic.

```
R2(config)# policy-map type inspect IPSPECIALIST-POLICY-MAP
R2(config-pmap)# class type inspect IPSPECIALIST-CLASS-MAP
R2(config-pmap-c)# inspect
R2(config-pmap-c)# exit
```

```
R2(config-pmap)# exit
```

A policy map named as *IPSPECIALIST-POLICY-MAP* is configured to define the action on traffic matched by *IPSPECIALIST-CLASS-MAP.*

```
R3(config)# zone security inside
R3(config-sec-zone)# exit
R3(config)# zone security outside
R3(config-sec-zone)# exit
R3(config-sec-zone)# zone-pair security in-to-out source inside destination outside
R3(config-sec-zone-pair)# service-policy type inspect MY-POLICY-MAP
R3(config-sec-zone-pair)# exit
```

As policy map needs to be applied on a zone-pair, first zones named *inside* and *outside* are created. Then zone-pair command is used to create a zone-pair with direction specified by *in-to-out* keyword.

```
R2(config)# interface FastEthernet1/0
R2(config-if)# description Interface belongs to outside zone
R2(config-if)# zone-member security outside
R2(config-if)# exit
R2(config)# interface FastEthernet0/1
R2(config-if)# description Interface belongs to inside zone
R2(config-if)# zone-member security inside
R2(config-if)# exit
R2(config)#
```

Finally, interfaces are added to the specific zones. Whenever *TELNET* and *ICMP* traffic from interfaces places in *inside* zone towards interfaces placed in *outside* zone will hit, Stateful-inspection will be performed.

Note: Below command can be used to configure policy for self-zone

R2(config)# **zone-pair security** *zone-pair-name* **source** {source-zone-name | ***self default***} **destination** {destination-zone-name | ***self default***}

Network Address Translation

Private addresses are used to allow devices to communicate with in an organization locally. However, private IPv4 addresses are not routable over the Internet. In order to access devices and resources outside of the local network, a private address must first be converted into a public address. The mechanism of translating private addresses into public addresses is called Network Address Translation (NAT). This makes a device with IPv4 private address to communicate over the internet.

NAT is one of the most widely used features in Cisco and other vendor's networking devices. Consider the following diagram, which acts as a reference for discussion in this section.

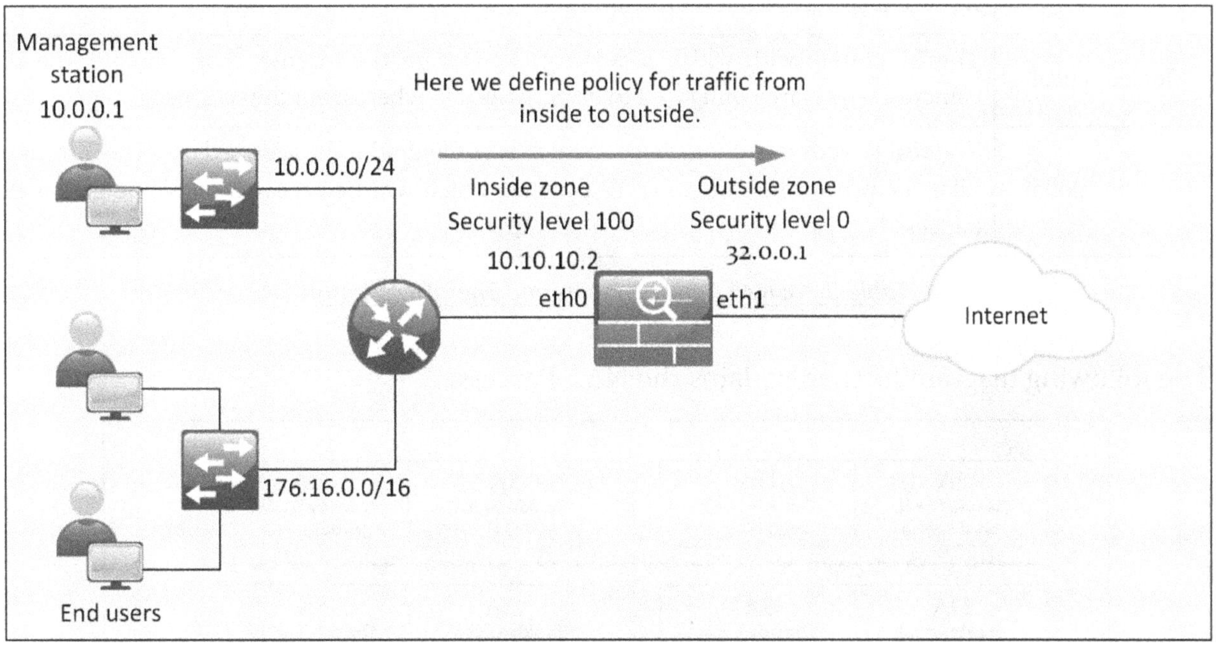

Figure 5-09: Example Scenario for NAT

As shown in the diagram above, end-users along with management network is using private addressing scheme as defined in RFC 1918. If the end user wants to communicate with the other end user over the internet, a public IP address will be needed. Firewall will not be having any connectivity problem because of globally reachable IP address of 32.0.0.1/30 assigned to one of its interfaces. In order to allow the internal or trusted network to communicate with public internet, NAT feature is used by the either firewall or router by swapping the source address field in IP header of originating packets with either its own global address or with pool of global addresses (assigned by service providers).

The implementation of NAT or PAT not only hides thousands of users behind single or group of global IP addresses, it also helps in mitigating some types of attack. Without knowing that which global IP address is assigned to the internal device, connecting with specific internal devices from outside world is even more difficult.

NAT Terminologies: In Cisco's implementation of NAT, whether in routers or firewalls, very specific terminologies are used, for example, inside local, outside global, etc. Following table summarizes the different terminologies of NAT/PAT.

NAT Term	Description
Inside Local	The original IP address of host from trusted network. For example 172.16.0.5 has been assigned to end users in diagram above.
Inside Global	The global address, either of router's interface IP or of one from pool, which will represent the client out on the internet.
Outside Local	The IP address with which a device is known on the internet. For example, the IP cameras, which are configured to be accessed anywhere from the internet.
Outside Global	The real IP address of host device, which is configured to be accessed over the internet. Like the private IP address of IP camera, which will be accessed via some global IP address.

Table 5-08: NAT Terminologies and Their Description

The following diagram further explains the NAT Process:

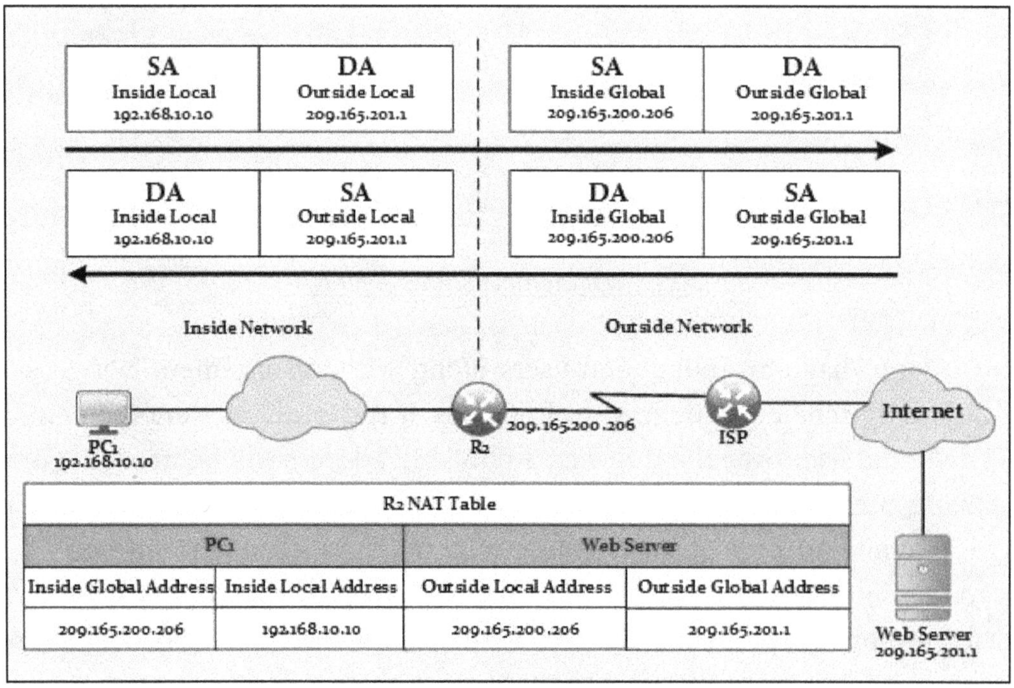

Figure 5-10: NAT Process in Action

Port Address Translation:

The mapping of multiple private IPv4 addresses to a single public IPv4 address or a few addresses is known as Port Address Translation or PATing or NAT overload. Port address translation or PAT is a subset of NAT. Instead of representing each unique private IP address with unique global or real IP address, PAT uses a combination of different port numbers with unique IP addresses. Now, port numbers may vary from 1024 to 65535, which seems enough for one's need. In PAT, each private address is assigned to a unique port number, so multiple private addresses can be mapped to one or to a few public addresses.

However, in case the number of sessions exceeds than the total port numbers, PAT will use the next globally available IP address from the pool, if available. In PAT, the ISP assigns one public address to the router and with that, several members of the company can simultaneously access the Internet. This is the most common form of NAT.

The following table summarizes the different NAT/PAT types and their description.

Options	Description	Application
Static NAT	Static NAT maps one internal IP to one globally reachable IP address (One-to One). For example, if internal LAN consists of 100 users, then 100 global IP addresses will be needed for each of them to be able to communicate over the internet.	As this is not the feasible option for LAN users, this option is normally used for special cases like for servers available in Demilitarized Zone (DMZ), which are accessible publically by general users. By using the static one-to-one mapping of server's original IP address with one of the global IP address from POOL and then entering the global IP address in DNS table, users can access it by name for example www.ipspecialist.net
Dynamic NAT	Dynamic NAT is used where users may need to send traffic for small intervals (Many-to-Many). As a result, router can dynamically assign that address to some other user or end-device that needs global address for sending traffic to public internet. However, traffic may be dropped for extra clients when every global IP address from pool is assigned to internal devices. In order to avoid such situations, dynamic PAT is used.	For example, a pool of six global IP address can serve only six internal LAN users at a time. Client coming at seventh number will have to wait for one the global address to be released and then assign to it.
Dynamic PAT	This option is widely used for internal LAN users who want to access internet	In normal scenarios, single IP address is enough to serve the broad range of users, however

	(Many-to-One). By using the single IP assigned to the router interface along with the range of Port numbers, which vary from 1024 to 65535, thousands of users can hide behind it.	another IP address from global addresses pool, if available, can be used in case of shortage of ports along with one IP address.
Policy NAT/PAT	In this type, NAT/PAT is performed only when specific traffic is generated matched by Access-List.	It is widely used where we require traffic forwarding with any match against the policy rules.

Table 5-09: NAT/PAT Types and Their Description

Lab 5.2: Implementation of Security Levels and NAT/PAT Types

In order to make an interface of firewall operational, the following things are required:

- An IP address (depending on its operational mode)
- Security level (varying between 0 and 100)
- Name assigned to it

In the first part of this lab, different interfaces will be made operational followed by implementation and verification of different types of NAT/PAT, as shown in the diagram below:

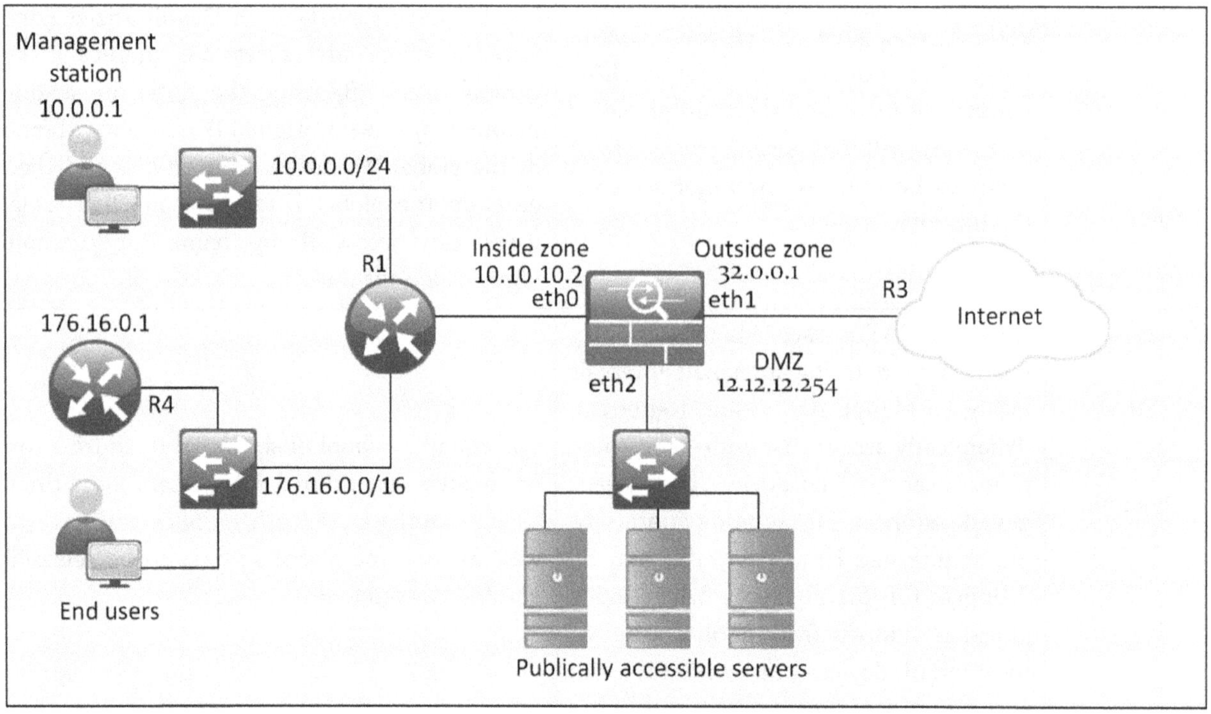

Figure 5-11: Lab 5.2 Network Topology

As explained earlier, in order to make ASA interface operational, assignment of IP address along with security level and name needs to be set first. As shown in the lab topology, three interfaces need to be made operational. The following commands are used for this purpose:

```
Ciscoasa> enable
Password: ***********
Ciscoasa#
```

Same password scheme will be used, as done in previous labs.

```
Ciscoasa# configure terminal
Ciscoasa(config)# interface Ethernet1
Ciscoasa(config-if)# ip address 32.0.0.1 255.255.255.252
Ciscoasa(config-if)# nameif outside
Ciscoasa(config-if)# security-level 0

Ciscoasa(config)# interface Ethernet0
Ciscoasa(config-if)# ip address 10.10.10.2 255.255.255.252
Ciscoasa(config-if)# nameif inside
Ciscoasa(config-if)# security-level 100

Ciscoasa(config)# interface Ethernet2
Ciscoasa(config-if)# ip address 12.12.12.254 255.255.255.0
Ciscoasa(config-if)# nameif dmz
Ciscoasa(config-if)# security-level 50
```

After making interfaces operational, only directly connected interfaces will be reachable from ASA itself. Following static routes will be used for inside traffic on ASA:

```
Ciscoasa(config)# route inside 10.0.0.0 255.255.255.0 10.10.10.1 1
Ciscoasa(config)# route inside 172.16.0.0 255.255.255.0 10.10.10.1 1
```

Before implementing static NAT for management LAN, let us ping test from management station (10.0.0.1) to simulated internet, which is 32.0.0.2.

```
C:\Users\MANAGEMENT-STATION>ping 32.0.0.2

Pinging 32.0.0.2 with 32 bytes of data:
Request timed out.
Request timed out.
Request timed out.
Request timed out.

Ping statistics for 32.0.0.2:
    Packets: Sent = 4, Received = 0, Lost = 4 (100% loss),
```

As internet router does not have routes for inside networks, it will not be able to route packets destined for 10.0.0.0/24 and 172.16.0.0/24 networks. "*debug ip packet*" command will show the following results:

```
R1# debug ip packet

*Nov 11 23:30:15.063: IP: s=10.0.0.1 (FastEthernet0/0), d=32.0.0.2, len 60, input feature, MCI Check(88), rtype 0, forus FALSE, sendself FALSE, mtu 0, fwdchk FALSE

*Nov 11 23:30:15.067: IP: tableid=0, s=10.0.0.1 (FastEthernet0/0), d=32.0.0.2 (FastEthernet0/0), routed via RIB

*Nov 11 23:30:15.071: IP: s=10.0.0.1 (FastEthernet0/0), d=32.0.0.2 (FastEthernet0/0), len 60, rcvd 3

*Nov 11 23:30:15.075: IP: s=10.0.0.1 (FastEthernet0/0), d=32.0.0.2, len 60, stop process pak for forus packet

*Nov 11 23:30:15.079: IP: s=32.0.0.2 (local), d=10.0.0.1, len 60, unroutable
```

Configuring Static NAT:

The output shown above, clearly shows that network (10.0.0.0/24) is un-routable. To work around this problem, static NAT will be implemented for management station.

```
Ciscoasa(config)# object network MANAGEMENT-STATION
Ciscoasa(config-network-object)# host 10.0.0.1
Ciscoasa(config-network-object)# nat (inside,outside) static interface
```

The first command creates a network object with the name MANAGEMENT-STATION.

In the second command, a host is defined with IP address 10.0.0.1, which is the IP address of the management station.

The third command actually implements the static NAT for management station. The inside, outside shows the direction of originating traffic i.e. from inside interface to outside interface. The keyword *"static"* interface tells the ASA to use outside interface IP address as source address for traffic that originates from management station towards network attached to the outside zone or interface.

VERIFICATION

In order to verify the static NAT, let us telnet the 32.0.0.2 from management station (10.0.0.1).

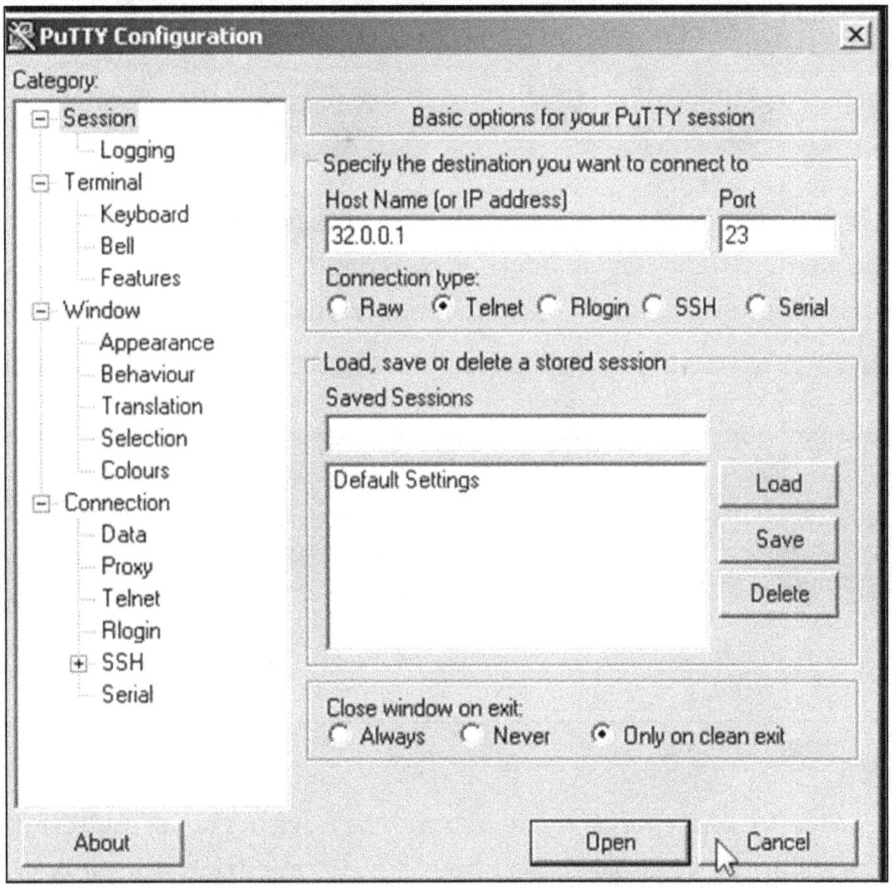

If there is no configuration error, then the above screen prompting for username/password will appear.

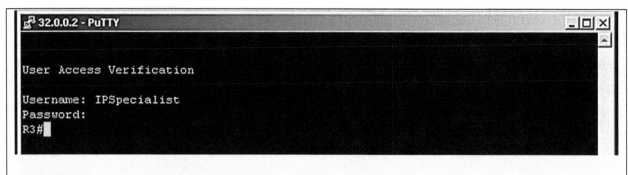

```
32.0.0.2 - PuTTY

User Access Verification

Username: IPSpecialist
Password:
R3#
```

"Show xlate" command can be used on ASA to see current sessions passing through the ASA firewall along with nature of the session.

```
ASA1
ASA1# show xlate
1 in use, 1 most used
Flags: D - DNS, i - dynamic, r - portmap, s - static, I - identity, T - twice
NAT from inside:10.0.0.1 to outside:32.0.0.1
    flags s idle 0:00:08 timeout 0:00:00
ASA1#
```

The figure shown above, clearly shows that NAT session from 10.0.0.1 to 32.0.0.1 is established. Similarly, *"show nat"* is another command, which can be used to further see the number of translated and un-translated connections.

```
ASA1
ASA1# show nat

Auto NAT Policies (Section 2)
1 (inside) to (outside) source static MANAGEMENT-STATION interface
    translate_hits = 2, untranslate_hits = 0
```

Configuring Dynamic NAT:

Similarly, in order to implement the dynamic NAT with global address pool for End User's LAN the following commands will be used. A static route for global pool will also be configured on router representing the simulate internet.

```
Ciscoasa(config)# object network END-USER-LAN

Ciscoasa(config-network-object)# subnet 172.16.0.0 255.255.255.0

Ciscoasa(config-network-object)# nat (inside,outside) static 202.0.0.1
```

VERIFICATION

In order to verify the static NAT, let us telnet the 32.0.0.2 from Router R4 (172.16.0.1).

R4

```
Username: IPSpecialist
Password:
R4#telnet 32.0.0.2
Trying 32.0.0.2 ... Open


User Access Verification

Username: IPSpecialist
Password:
R3#
```

Here R3 is the ISP's router with the IP address of 32.0.0.2.

Configuring Static PAT:

In the last CLI based configuration part of this lab, static PAT entries for DMZ servers will be configured in order to allow their access from outside interface. Now, the second address from global address pool 202.0.0.2/30 will be used for DMZ access from outside world.

```
Ciscoasa(config)# object network DMZ-SERVER-1
Ciscoasa(config-network-object)# host 12.12.12.1
Ciscoasa(config-network-object)# nat (dmz,outside) static 202.0.0.2 service tcp telnet 8080
```

The above commands configure static PAT for DMZ Server 12.12.12.1 tcp port number 23 with 202.0.0.2 with tcp port number 8080. As explained earlier, traffic from low security level to high security level is dropped by default behaviour of ASA. So access-list permitting the tcp port of 12.12.12.1 from outside interface network needs to be configured and applied on outside interface with following commands:

```
Ciscoasa(config)# access-list ALLOW-DMZ-SERVER extended permit tcp any host 12.12.12.1 eq telnet
Ciscoasa(config)# interface Ethernet 1
Ciscoasa(config-if)# access-group ALLOW-DMZ-SERVER in interface outside
```

VERIFICATION

In order to verify the static PAT, let us telnet the 12.12.12.1 from router simulating the internet *R3* but using IP address and port of 202.0.0.2:8080 as shown below:

```
R3
R3#
R3#telnet 202.0.0.2 8080
Trying 202.0.0.2, 8080 ... Open


User Access Verification

Username: IPSpecialist
Password:
R2#
R2#
```

Similarly, on ASA "*show nat*" and "*show xlate*" commands can be used to verify successful translation hits and current sessions established via firewall. It should be noted that one entry for either NAT or PAT would work for connection originated from either direction (depending on access-list applied on interface).

```
ASA1
ASA1# show nat

Auto NAT Policies (Section 2)
1 (inside) to (outside) source static MANAGEMENT-STATION interface
    translate_hits = 2, untranslate_hits = 0
2 (dmz) to (outside) source static DMZ-SERVER-1 202.0.0.2   service tcp telnet 8
080
    translate_hits = 0, untranslate_hits = 1
3 (inside) to (outside) source static END-USER-LAN 202.0.0.1
    translate_hits = 1, untranslate_hits = 0
ASA1# show xlate
3 in use, 3 most used
Flags: D - DNS, i - dynamic, r - portmap, s - static, I - identity, T - twice
NAT from inside:10.0.0.1 to outside:32.0.0.1
    flags s idle 0:22:28 timeout 0:00:00
TCP PAT from dmz:12.12.12.1 23-23 to outside:202.0.0.2 8080-8080
    flags sr idle 0:00:26 timeout 0:00:00
NAT from inside:172.16.0.0/24 to outside:202.0.0.1/24
    flags s idle 0:14:53 timeout 0:00:00
ASA1#
```

Another way to implement this lab is to use ASDM, which is graphical method of managing the ASA firewall. ASDM comes pre-loaded with ASA in flash drive. In order to enable HTTP web access for specific host or subnet, following commands will be used:

```
Ciscoasa(config)# http server enable

Ciscoasa(config)# http 10.0.0.1 255.255.255.255 inside

Ciscoasa(config)# ssl encryption 3des-sha1 des-sha1 aes128-sha1 aes256-sha1
rc4-md5 rc4-sha1
```

These first two commands allow http based web access only to management-station from inside interface. The third command configures the supported SSL types to be used between ASDM and management-station web access software like Google Chrome etc.

To access the ASA firewall via webpage, access https://10.10.10.2, which is the inside interface IP of ASA.

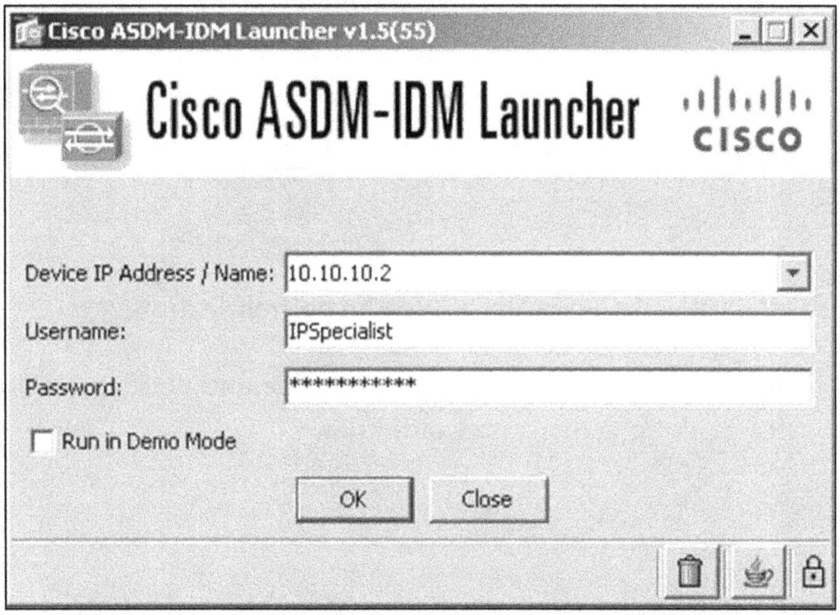

The IP address of ASA along with the login credentials will be required. Enter the IP address of 10.10.10.2, "IPSpecialist" as username and "P@$$word:10" in the password field and then click "OK".

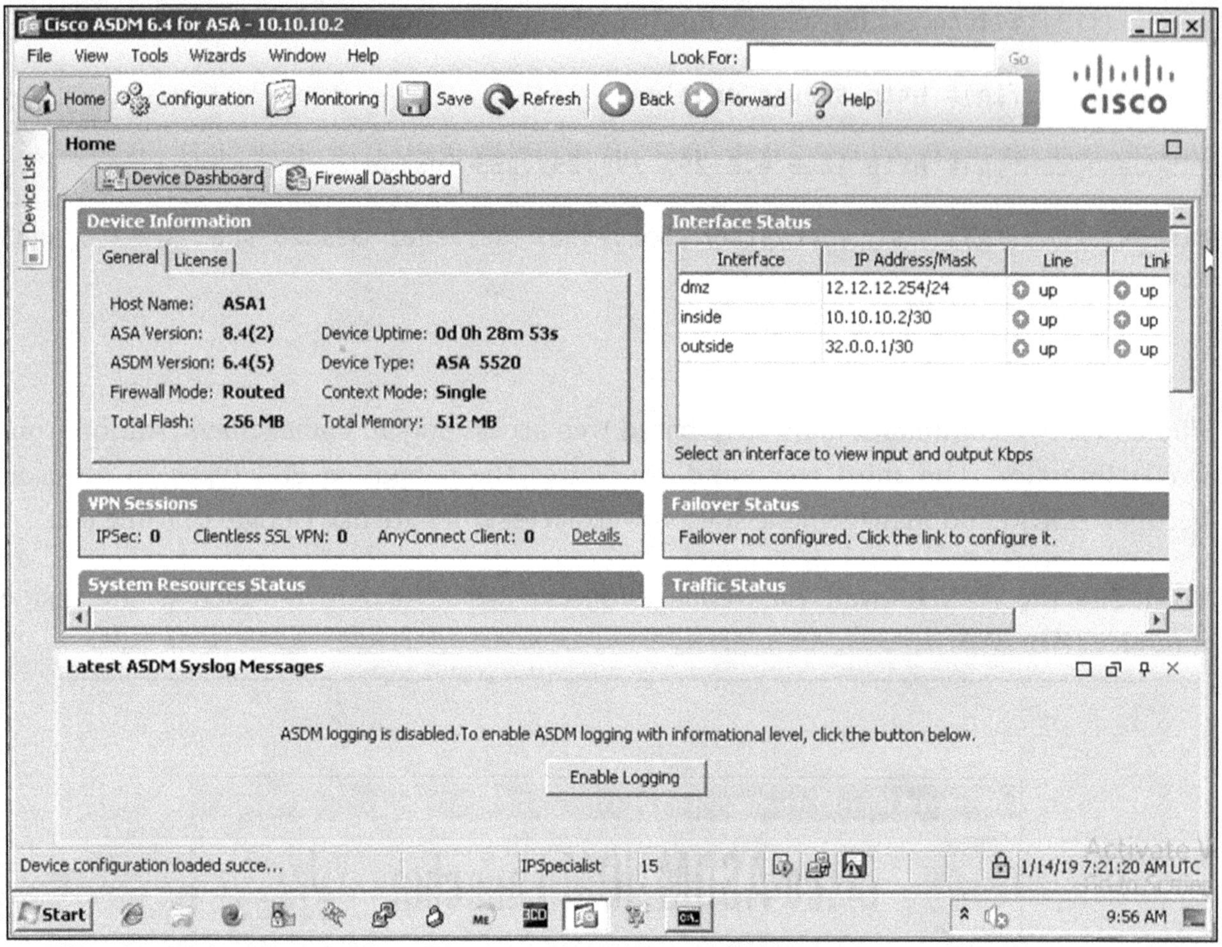

The following dashboard will open upon successful authentication.

Click the "Configuration" button present on top left side and click "Interfaces" settings to see the current settings along with any new addition.

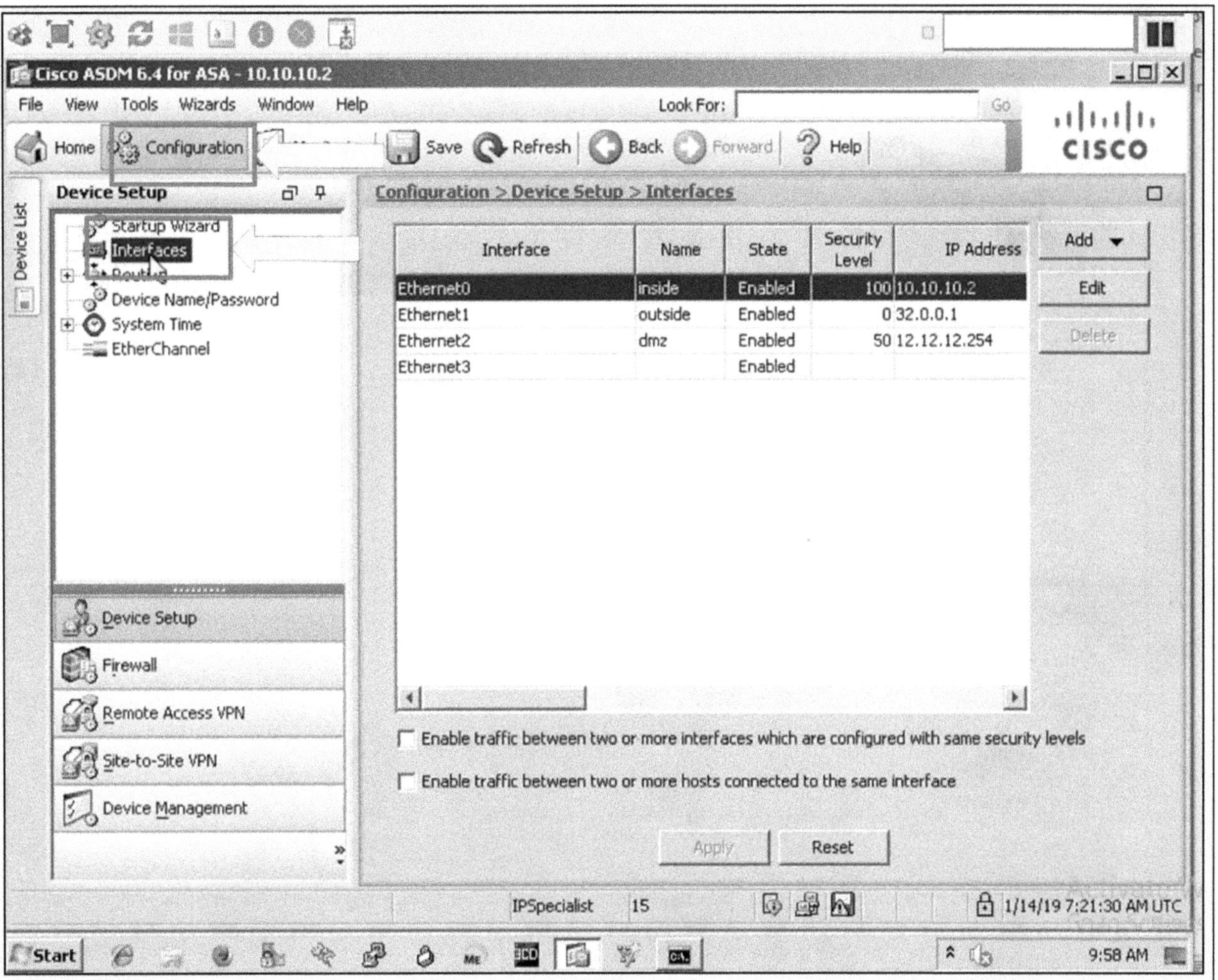

Now, click the “Edit” button to edit the interfaces.

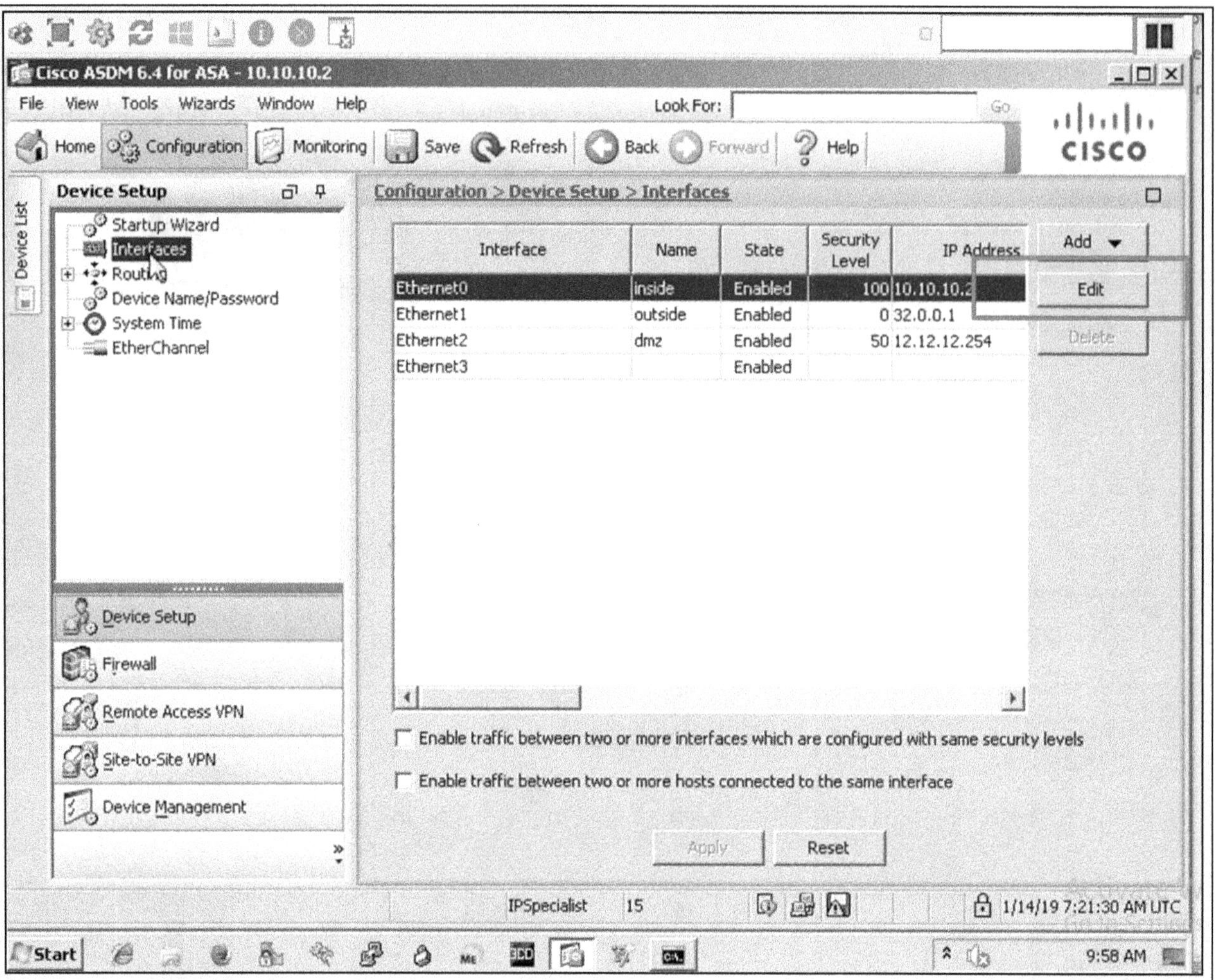

On clicking the "Edit" button, the following windows will prompt:

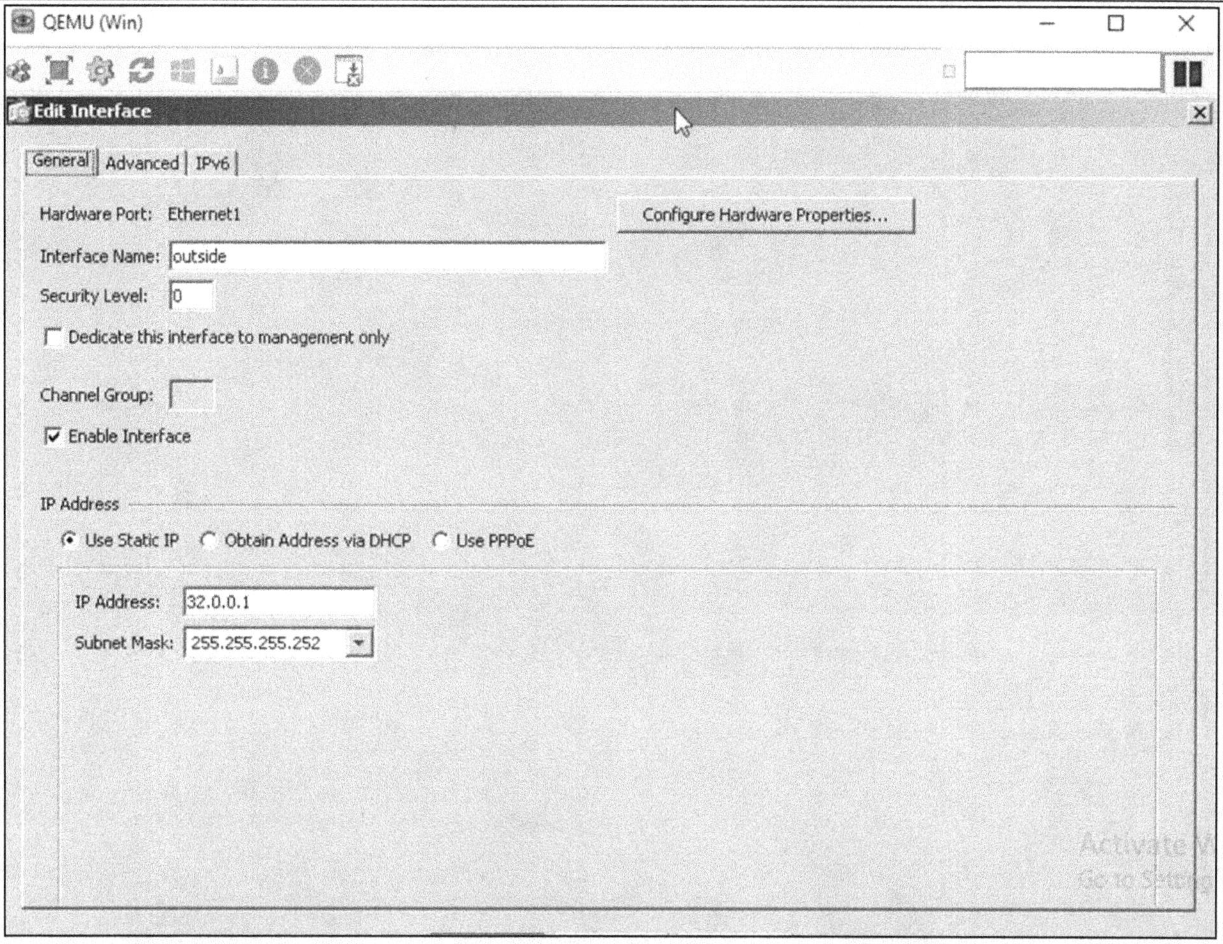

By clicking on the “Edit” button, the current setting can be changed. As shown in the figure shown above, interface with name *outside* has been assigned security level of 0 along with IP address of 32.0.0.1.

Similarly, by clicking on the “Routing” tab, Static as well as dynamic routing can be configured on ASA as shown in the figure below:

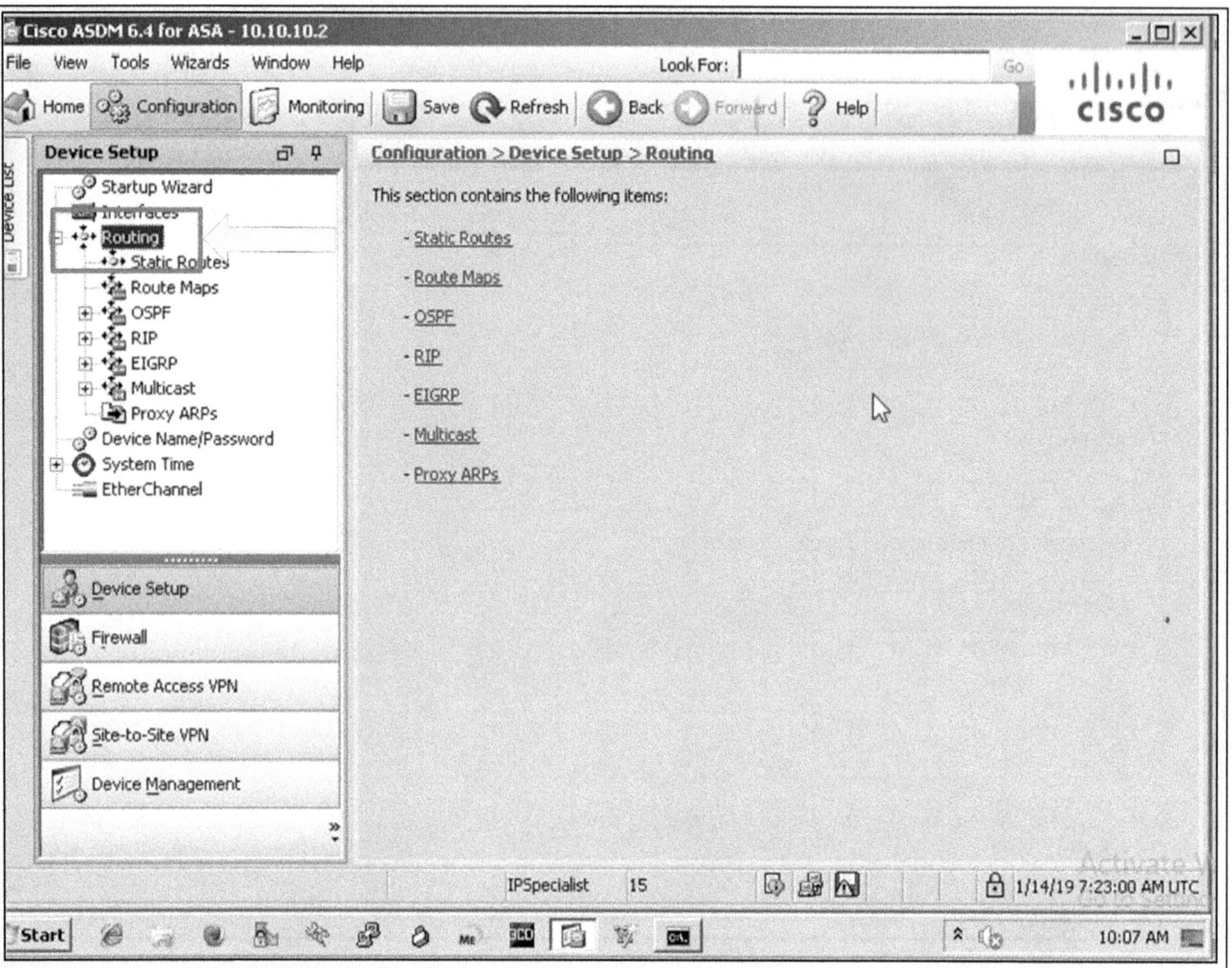

On clicking the "Edit" button, following windowns will prompt up:

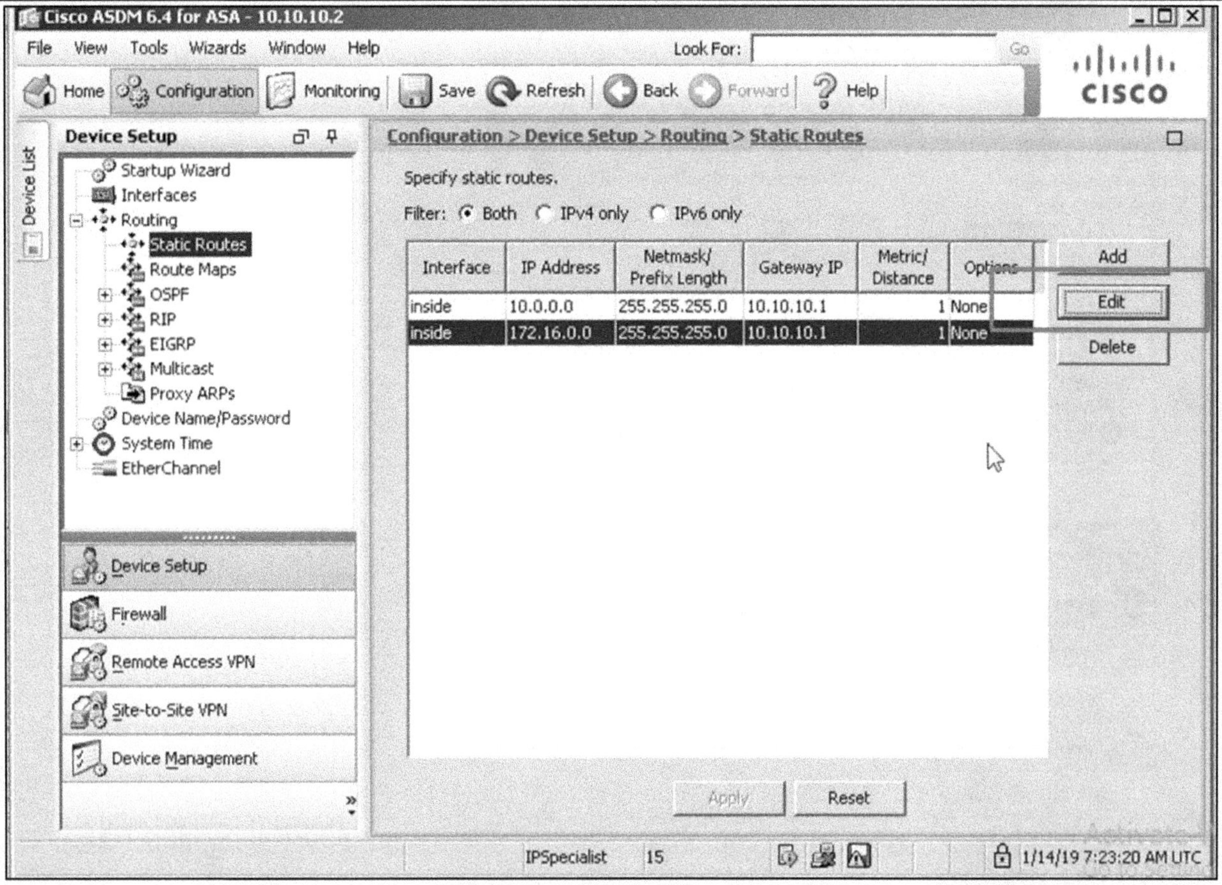

Now, click on the "Edit" button, to edit static routes.

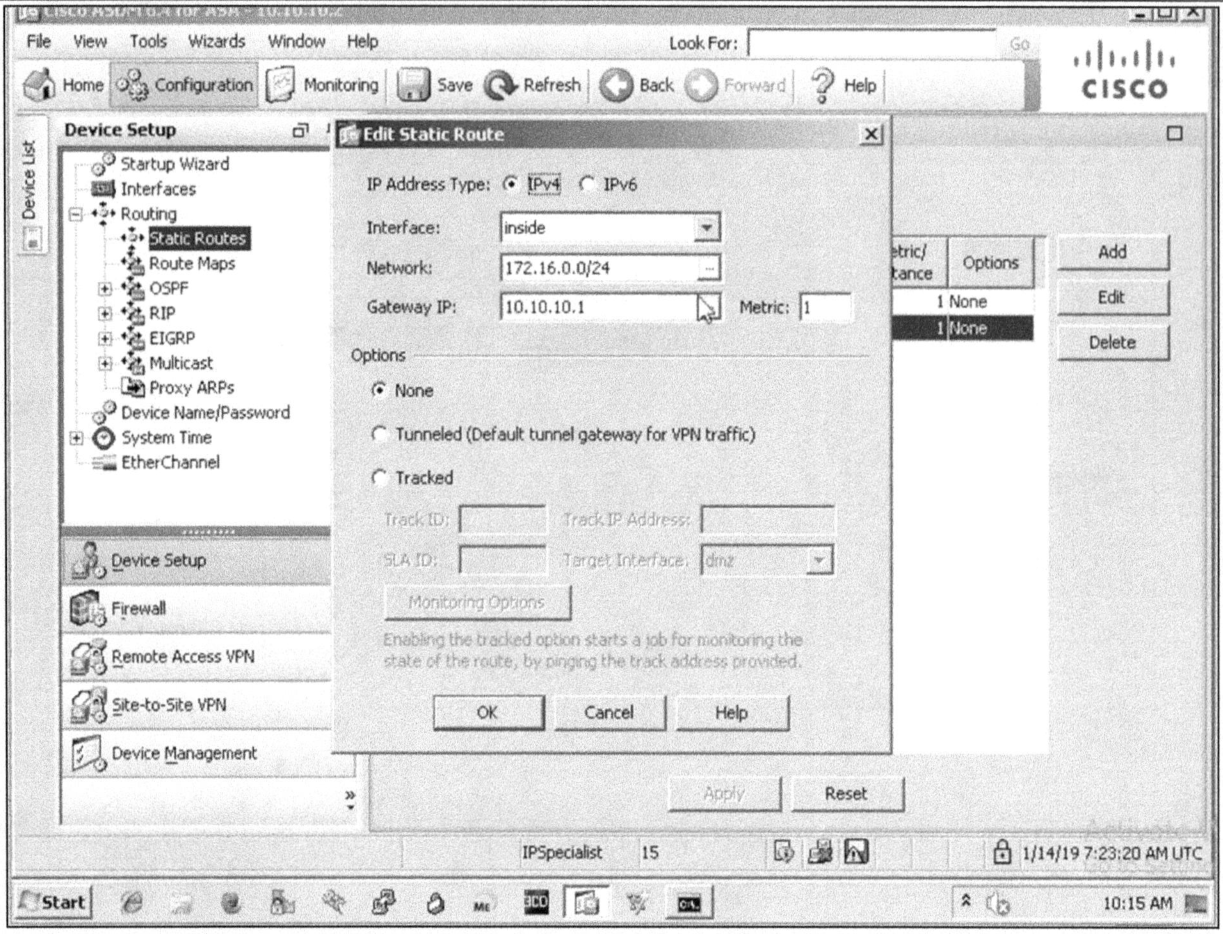

Click on NAT Rules to see currently applied as well as configuring new NAT rules. As this lab is configured via CLI commands in first Phase, which is why different NAT rules are shown in the figure below:

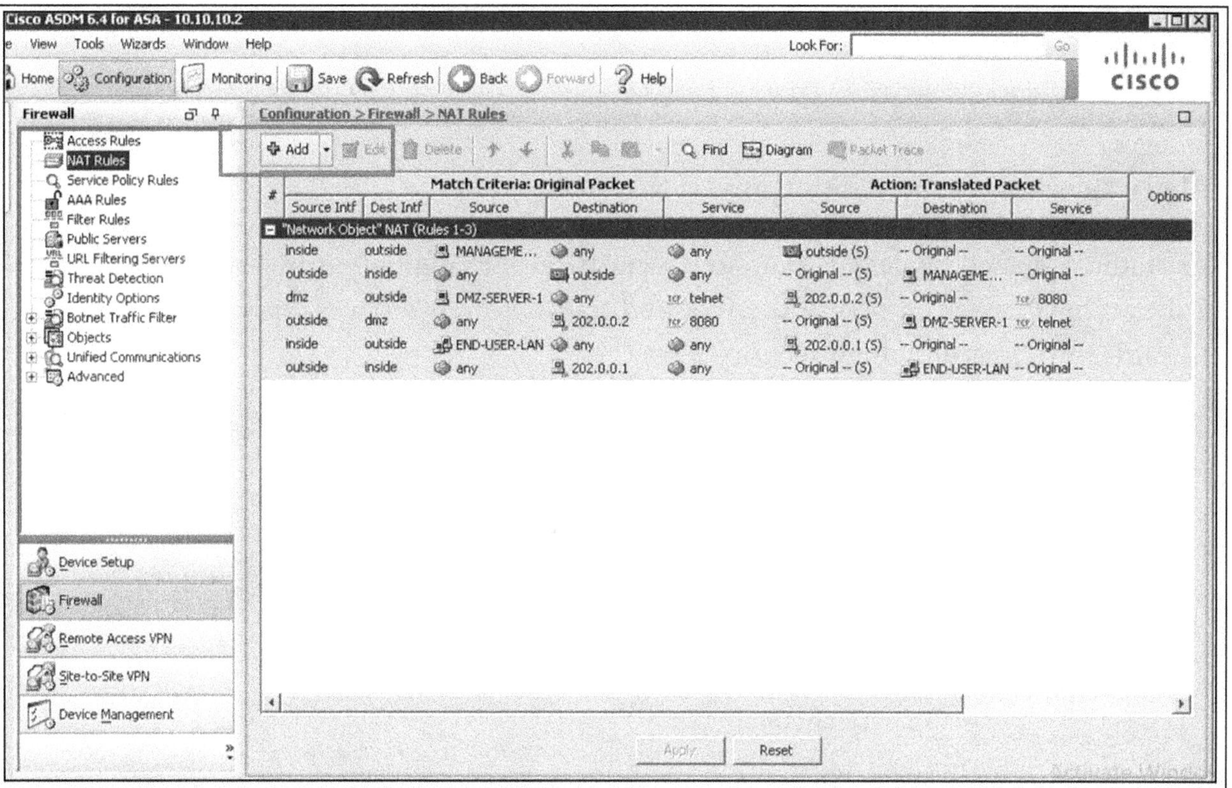
Cisco ASDM 6.4 for ASA - 10.10.10.2
View Tools Wizards Window Help
Look For:
Home Configuration Monitoring Save Refresh Back Forward Help
Firewall
Configuration > Firewall > NAT Rules
Access Rules
NAT Rules
Service Policy Rules
AAA Rules
Filter Rules
Public Servers
URL Filtering Servers
Threat Detection
Identity Options
Botnet Traffic Filter
Objects
Unified Communications
Advanced
Add Edit Delete Find Diagram Packet Trace
Match Criteria: Original Packet
Action: Translated Packet
Source Intf Dest Intf Source Destination Service Source Destination Service Options
"Network Object" NAT (Rules 1-3)
inside outside MANAGEME... any any outside (S) -- Original -- -- Original --
outside inside any outside any -- Original -- (S) MANAGEME... -- Original --
dmz outside DMZ-SERVER-1 any telnet 202.0.0.2 (S) -- Original -- 8080
outside dmz any 202.0.0.2 8080 -- Original -- (S) DMZ-SERVER-1 telnet
inside outside END-USER-LAN any any 202.0.0.1 (S) -- Original -- -- Original --
outside inside any 202.0.0.1 any -- Original -- (S) END-USER-LAN -- Original --
Device Setup
Firewall
Remote Access VPN
Site-to-Site VPN
Device Management
Apply Reset

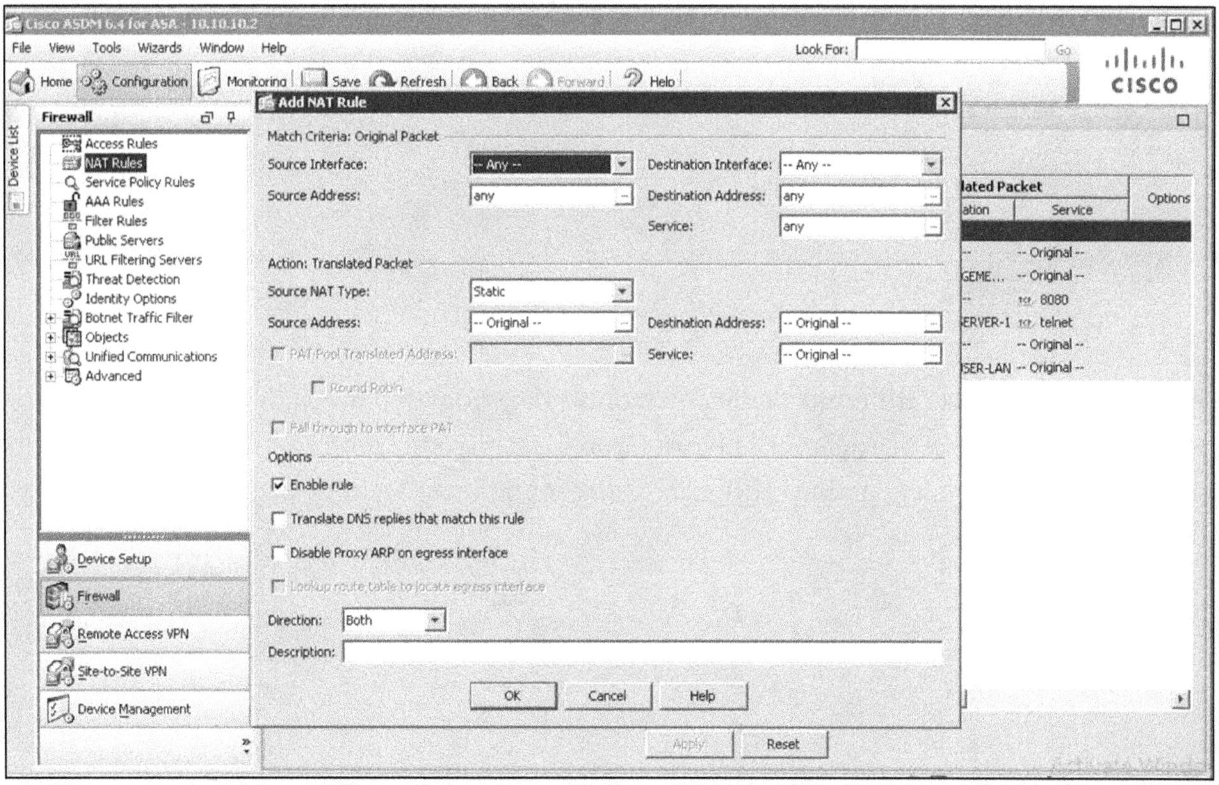
Cisco ASDM 6.4 for ASA - 10.10.10.2
File View Tools Wizards Window Help
Add NAT Rule
Match Criteria: Original Packet
Source Interface: -- Any --
Destination Interface: -- Any --
Source Address: any
Destination Address: any
Service: any
Action: Translated Packet
Source NAT Type: Static
Source Address: -- Original --
Destination Address: -- Original --
PAT Pool Translated Address:
Service: -- Original --
Round Robin
Fall through to interface PAT
Options
Enable rule
Translate DNS replies that match this rule
Disable Proxy ARP on egress interface
Lookup route table to locate egress interface
Direction: Both
Description:
OK Cancel Help
Apply Reset

Above figure shows the addition of new NAT rule.

As traffic is denied by default from low security level to high security level, “Access Rules” Tab can be accessed to permit the required traffic from interfaces with low security level towards interfaces with high security level.

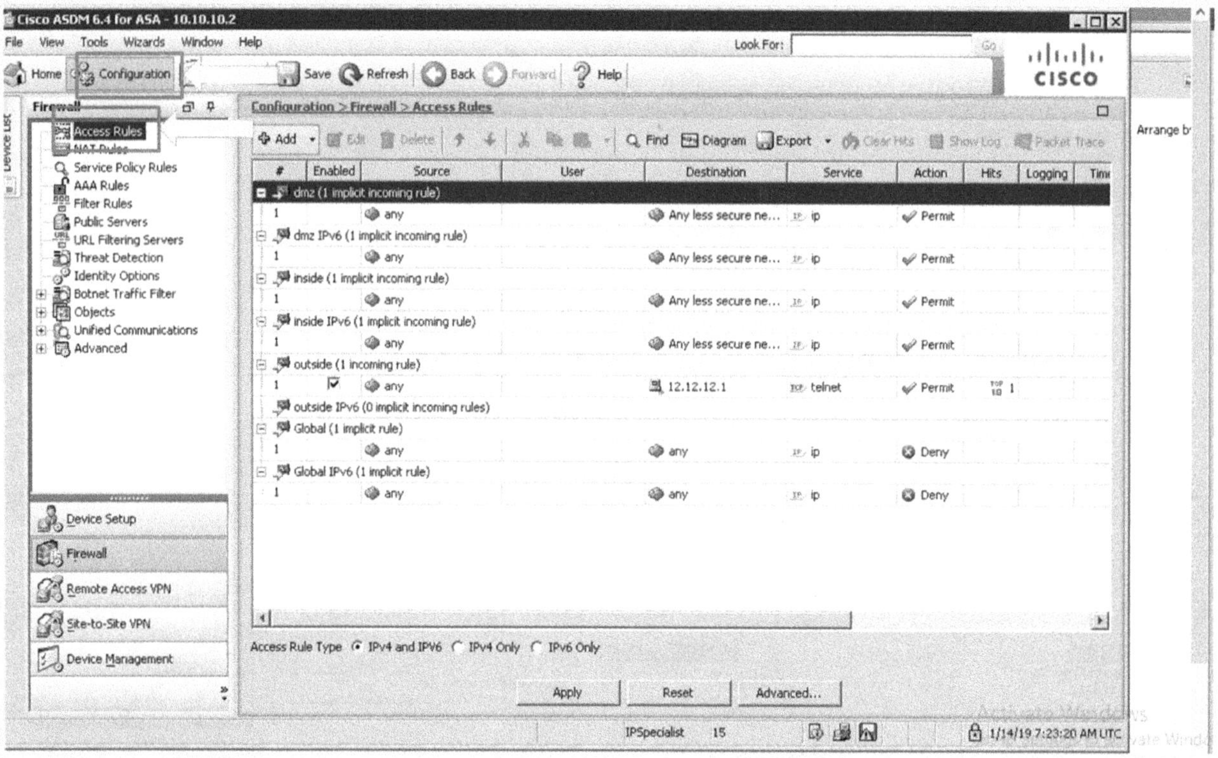

ASDM also provides different tools for troubleshooting the firewall policies and rules. Packet tracer is one of the most favorite tools among the community as it shows the animation of packet passing through different checks while hitting the intended destination address.

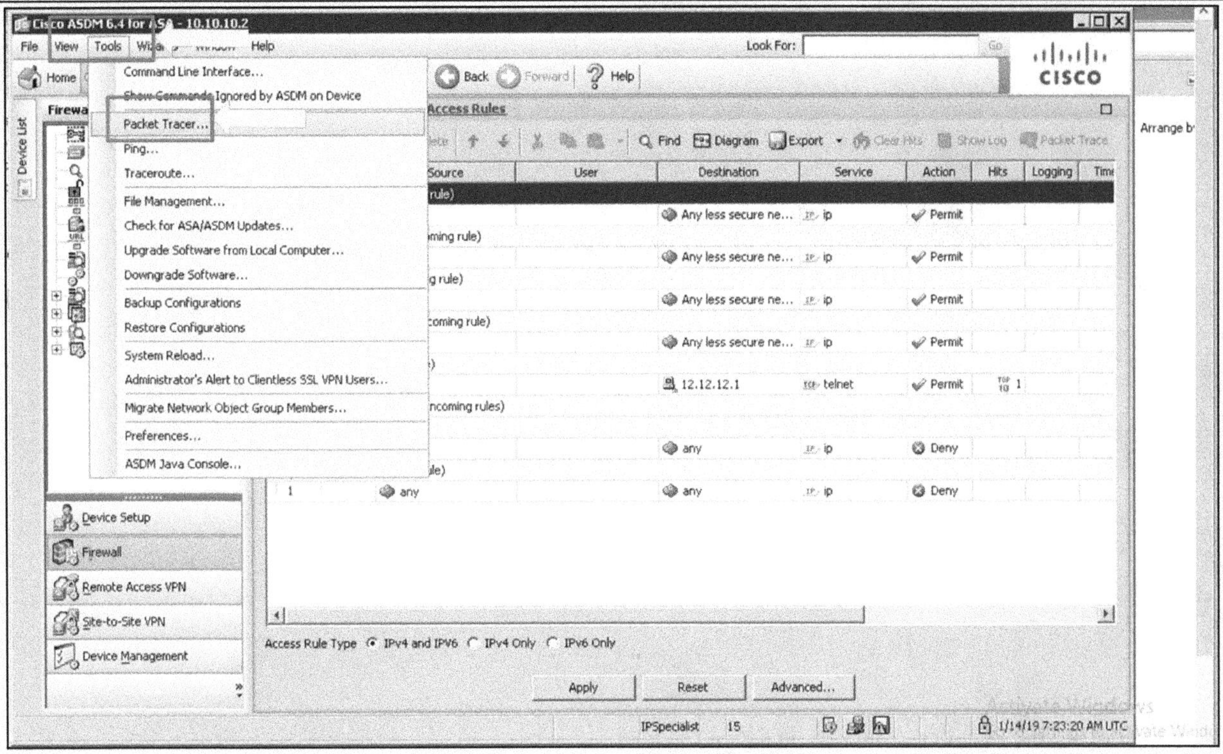

The figure shown below, shows the flow of traffic from source address of 10.0.0.1 towards the destination address of 32.0.0.2. Source and destination port numbers can also be specified in the figure shown below:

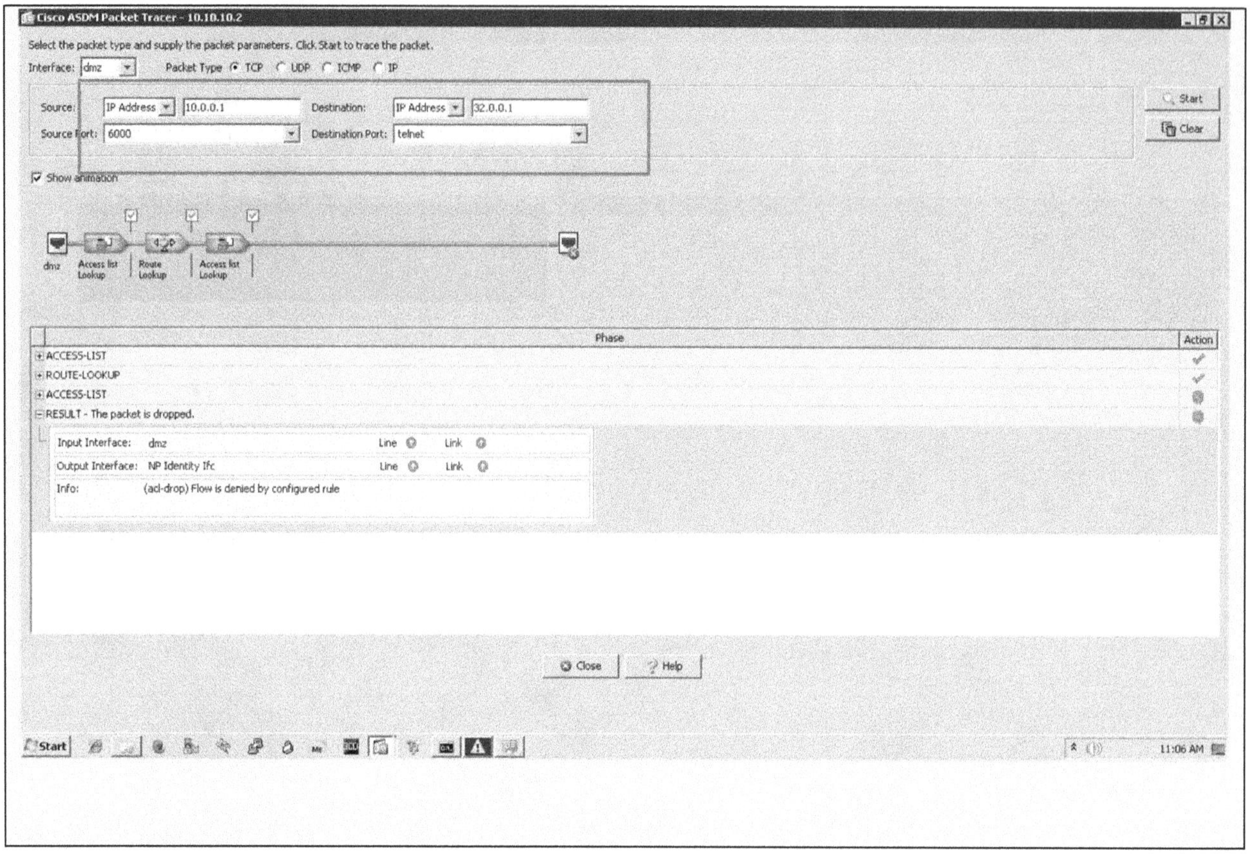

Configuring Dynamic PAT: // to be confirmed

Similarly, in order to implement the dynamic PAT with global address pool for End User's LAN the following commands will be used. A dynamic route for global pool will also be configured on router representing the simulated internet. Configuration of Dynamic PAT is almost same as Dynamic NAT. By adding keyword "overload" at the end of Dynamic NAT statement used above, R2 will implement the Dynamic PAT.

```
Ciscoasa(config)# object network END-USER-LAN
Ciscoasa(config-network-object)# subnet 172.16.0.0 255.255.255.0
Ciscoasa(config-network-object)# nat (inside,outside) dynamic 202.0.0.1
or
Ciscoasa(config-network-object)# nat (inside,outside) dynamic interface
Or
R2(config)# IP NAT inside source list REMOTE-LAN-USERS pool REMOTE-LAN-POOL overload
```

The command above configures the dynamic PAT that hides the network behind the outside interface address.

Verification:

Configuring Policy NAT: // to be confirmed

Policy NAT, also known as conditional NAT, is the combination of network address translations and route maps, to provide much more specific NAT rules. You can specify route maps with access list, so the traffic passed through that specific interface will be first matched with the provided access list.

```
hostname(config)# nat (inside) 1 access-list NET1 tcp 0 2000 udp 10000

hostname(config)# global (outside) 1 209.165.202.129
```

Cisco Adaptive Security Appliance (ASA)

Previously, firewalls were named as PIX (Private Internet eXchange) but PIX was replaced by new series of firewalls known as adaptive security appliance or ASA by 2005. ASA integrates the overall functionality of PIX along with some great new features. The Cisco's ASA Family of security devices provide security to corporate networks and data canters of all sizes. It provides end users with highly secured access to network resources and data anytime, anywhere.

ASA Series: Just as Cisco has created multiple series of routers and switches entertaining small office home office, enterprise networks up to the datacenters category, ASA also comes in different flavors as shown below:

Cisco ASA 5500 series	Ideal for
Cisco ASA 5505-5515 series	Small office Home office environment
Cisco ASA 5520-5545 series	Medium sized offices
Cisco ASA 5550	Large enterprise environment
Cisco ASA 5585-X and services module	Data Center / large enterprise networks
Cisco ASAv	Virtual ASA for virtual networking environment

Table 5-10: Cisco ASA Series

ASA Access Management

Just like routers and switches, both CLI and graphical methods can be used to access and manage the ASA firewall. Following are the official management techniques for accessing ASA firewall:

- **Command Line Interface (CLI):** With a little bit of changes, most features and syntaxes for basic operation are the same as Cisco IOS of routers and switches etc.
- **ASA Security Device Manager (ASDM):** Just like Cisco Configuration Professional (CCP), which is used to manage routers via GUI, ASDM is used to manage ASA in the same way.
- **Cisco Security Manager (CSM):** A GUI based tool, which can be used to manage the network devices like routers, switches and security devices like firewalls.

Here is the lab topology for access management, where we want to access firewall from management station 10.0.0.1:

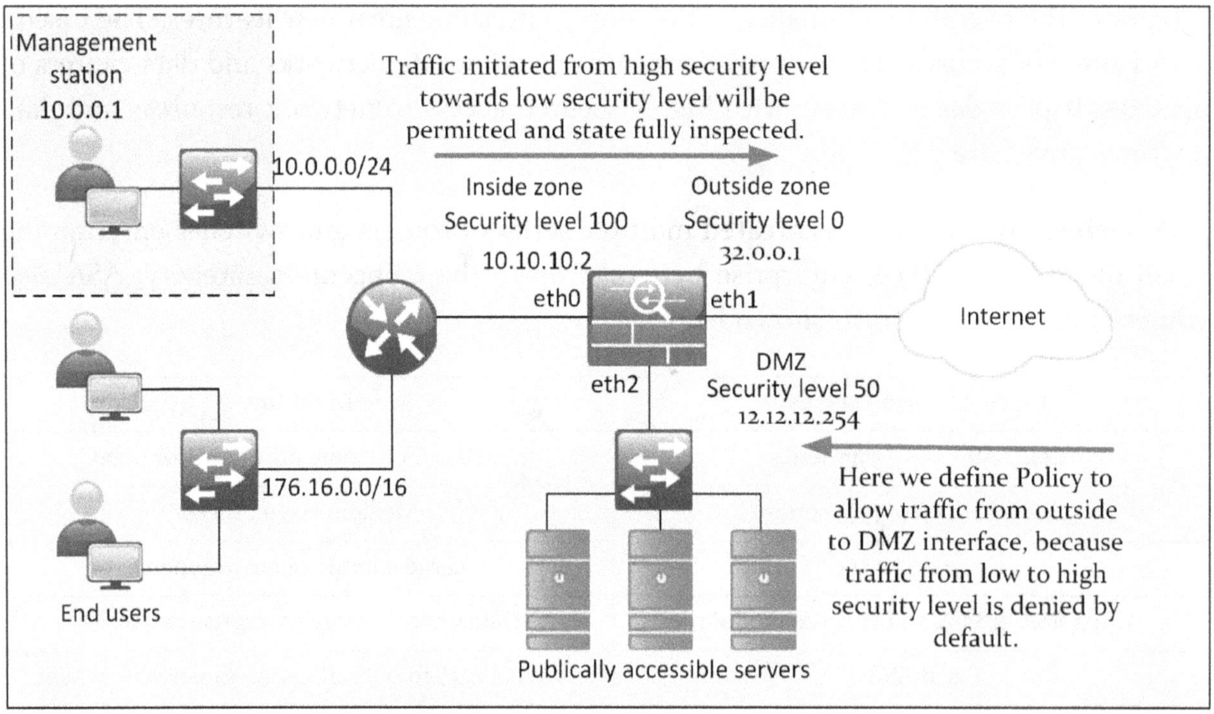

Figure 5-12: ASA Access Management

Access management through command line interface:

Here in this lab, we want to give access rights to the management.

One way to access management of ASA is to get access of its Command line interface. There are two ways to get access of its CLI: Telnet and SSH.

Here are some configuration steps to be done on ASA, which allows a host on the inside interface to telnet ASA:

```
Ciscoasa (config)# telnet 10.0.0.1 255.255.255.255 inside
```

To gain access to the ASA CLI using Telnet, enter the assigned username and login password.

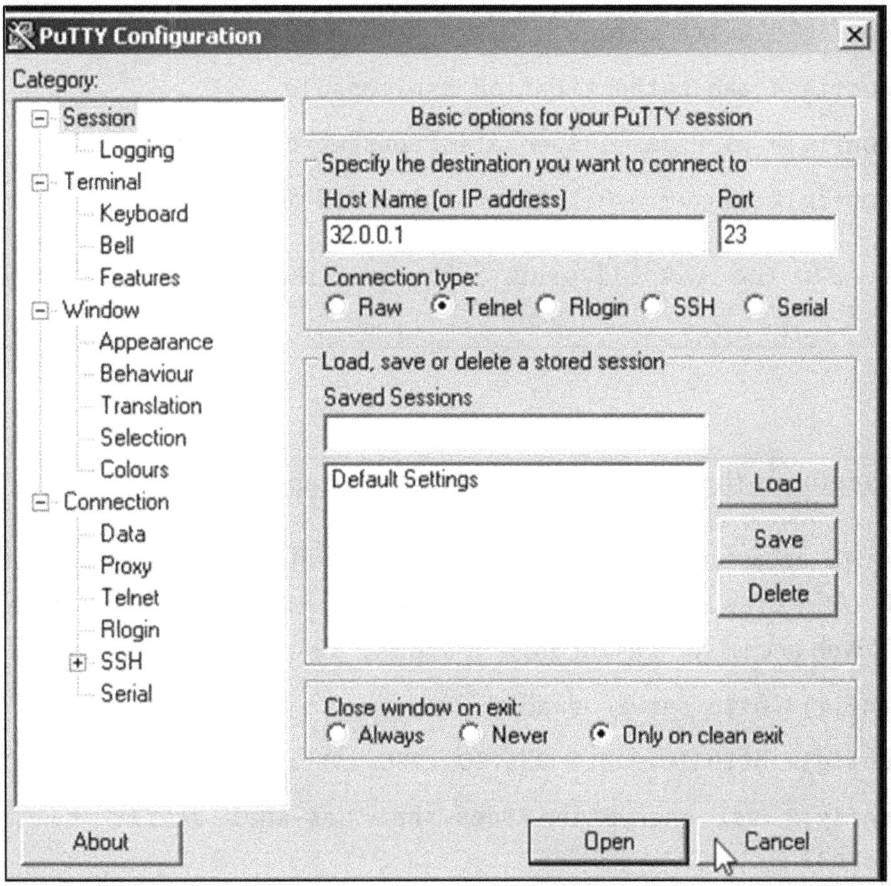

By putting the correct login username and password, you will be able to get access to the CLI of ASA.

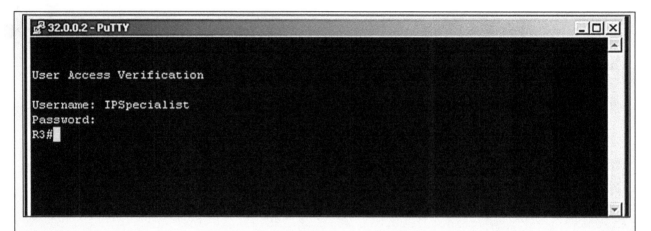

Now, there are some configuration steps to be done on ASA, which allow a host on the inside interface to access ASA through SSH:

```
Ciscoasa (config)# crypto key generate rsa modulus 1024
Ciscoasa (config)# write memory
Ciscoasa (config)# aaa authentication ssh console
Ciscoasa (config)# username IPSpecialist password P@$$word:10
Ciscoasa (config)# ssh 10.0.0.1 255.255.255.255 inside
```

To gain access to the ASA CLI using SSH, enter the assigned username and login password.

Access Management through Security Device Manager (ASDM):

Another way to access management is to use ASDM, which is graphical method of managing the ASA firewall. ASDM comes preloaded with ASA in flash drive. In order to enable HTTP web access for specific host or subnet, following commands will be used:

```
Ciscoasa(config)# http server enable
Ciscoasa(config)# http 10.0.0.1 255.255.255.255 inside
Ciscoasa(config)# ssl encryption 3des-sha1 des-sha1 aes128-sha1 aes256-sha1 rc4-md5 rc4-sha1
```

These first two commands allow http based web access only to management-station from inside interface. The third command configures the supported SSL types to be used between ASDM and management-station web access software like Google Chrome etc.

To access the ASA firewall via webpage, access https://10.10.10.2, which is the inside interface IP of ASA.

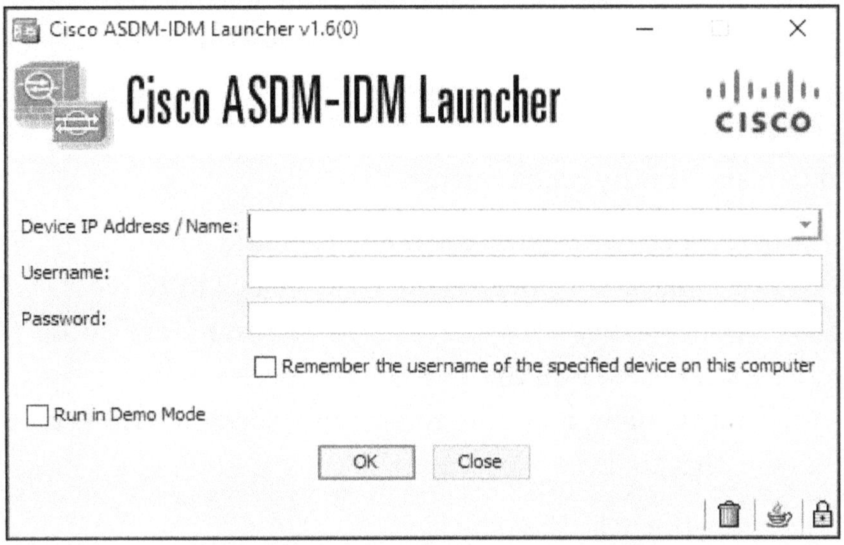

Here is the dashboard of ASDM, from where you can access and configure ASA through GUI.

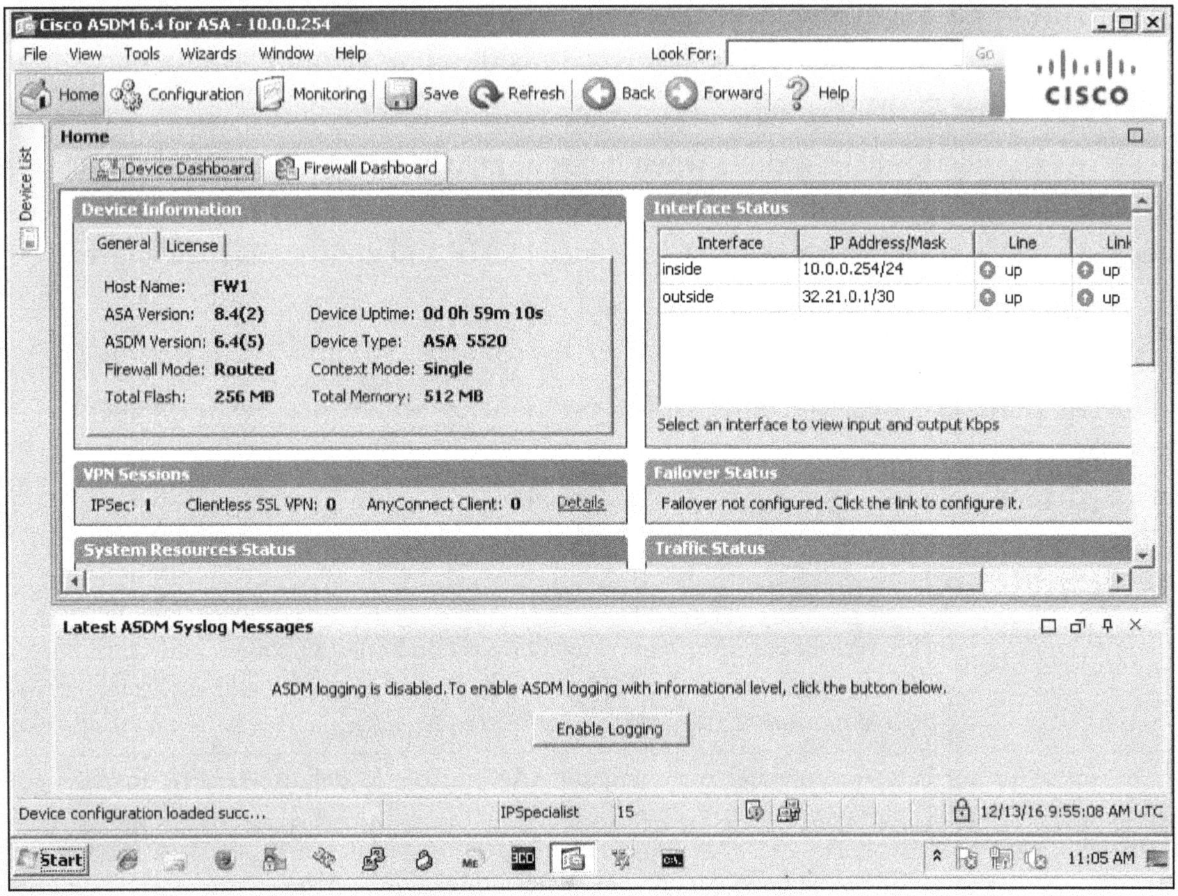

Security Access Policies

A set of system requirements, security objectives of a company and rules of behavior for administrators and users is referred to as Security policy. This policy ensures the security of a network and the data within it. It ensures certainty in system operations, software and hardware's health and use, and maintenance. A security policy also declares the process needed to meet security requirements.

Security access policies specify the rules for the data traffic passing through an interface. These policies will be applied first, before any other policy to the incoming or outgoing traffic. Each packet that hits the interface will be first examined to decide whether to forward or drop the packet based on the criteria you specify in the access policy. In a case where you do not want to allow a specific service to a specific host or network, then use an access rule to deny that traffic.

The ASA supports two types of access policies:

- **Inbound** – Inbound access rules will be applied to the traffic that is entering an interface. Global access rules are always inbound.
- **Outbound** – Outbound access rules will be applied to the traffic exiting an interface. The outbound rule restricts any other hosts from reaching or accessing the outside network

Access list considers real IP address when it has to match against the defined rules for the respective IP. In a case, where NAT is configured, an access rule to allow traffic from outside to inside or vice versa needs to reference real IP and not the mapped address.

Firewall Access Rules:

Following table explains the different access policies which can be implemented on firewalls:

Firewall Rule	Description
Services based access rules	Rules are defined with respect to services, which will be accessed via firewall. An example would be to allow only HTTP/HTTPS traffic while denying everything else
IP Addressing based access rules	This type of rules can permit or deny traffic based on source and destination IP address. An example would be permit statement for IP address from inside or trusted network to the outside or untrusted network while denying everything else.
Set of rules based on user information	This kind of rules can integrate AAA services to define who can access specific services via firewall.

Table 5-11: Firewall Access Rules and their description

In Cisco firewalls, Access-list is the primary tool, which is used to match traffic for performing specific firewall feature. When applied on an interface either inbound or outbound, it is checked for more specific match from top to down fashion. If match is found, then proper action (permit or deny) is performed on packet. Due to presence of explicit deny all statement at the end of ACL, traffic is dropped if no match is found.

Regardless of which firewall access rules, defined above are used, following design considerations should be considered for implementing the access-list for above rules:

- Permit statements defined in access-list should be as specific as possible.
- Users connected to internal or trusted interface should also be considered as part of overall security problem. Sometimes attacker uses backdoors for generating attacks. Corporate user may be unaware of malicious activity being run by his/her computer and may also be allowed by firewall.
- Unwanted network traffic should be filtered. For example, traffic coming from untrusted network with source address being one of the internal networks should be denied at the first place. Similarly, any packet with source address from RFC1918 or loop back address should also be filtered.
- Logging feature should also be enabled and reviewed periodically to make sure of its effectiveness.
- As computer networks are designed to support certain business needs, balanced should be maintained between functionality and security of business objectives.

Similarly, in order to apply any changes on current policies defined on firewall, a procedural document or SOP should be defined which states the changes to be made, the need for it along with the authorized person who approves the changes. Following table summarizes the general rules in this regard:

Rule	Description
Redundant Rules	ACLs are always processed from top to bottom for rules that are more specific. If ACL is too long, a network administrator may accidentally add redundant entries for specific traffic. Although it does not create a security flaw, but makes access list tedious and very difficult to understand.
Shadow Rules	A shadowed rule exists because of incorrect order placement in the access-list, which may or may not have impact on the current operation of infrastructure. If incorrect rule is placed above the correct one, currently working sessions may be dropped because access-lists work from top to bottom fashion.
Orphaned Rules	These rules contain incorrect IP addressing scheme either in source or destination

	address field. For example, if an IP address of 12.12.12.12/24 is never used on the inside network then any statement with source address defined above will never be matched. Such statements only takes the space in configuration.
Incorrectly planned Rules	Such kind of rules exists because of miscommunication between business and technical teams. For example if connection between client and server uses TCP port 4141 and statement allows both TCP/UDP ports 4141 then such statements are considered as incorrectly planned.
Incorrectly implemented rules	Such rules may result because of any kind of misconfiguration by network administrator due lack of technical skills or any other reason. Examples include incorrect binding of port number or address etc.

Table 5-12: ACL Rules and their description

Here is the lab topology for security access policy, where we want to apply policies to the inbound and outbound traffic:

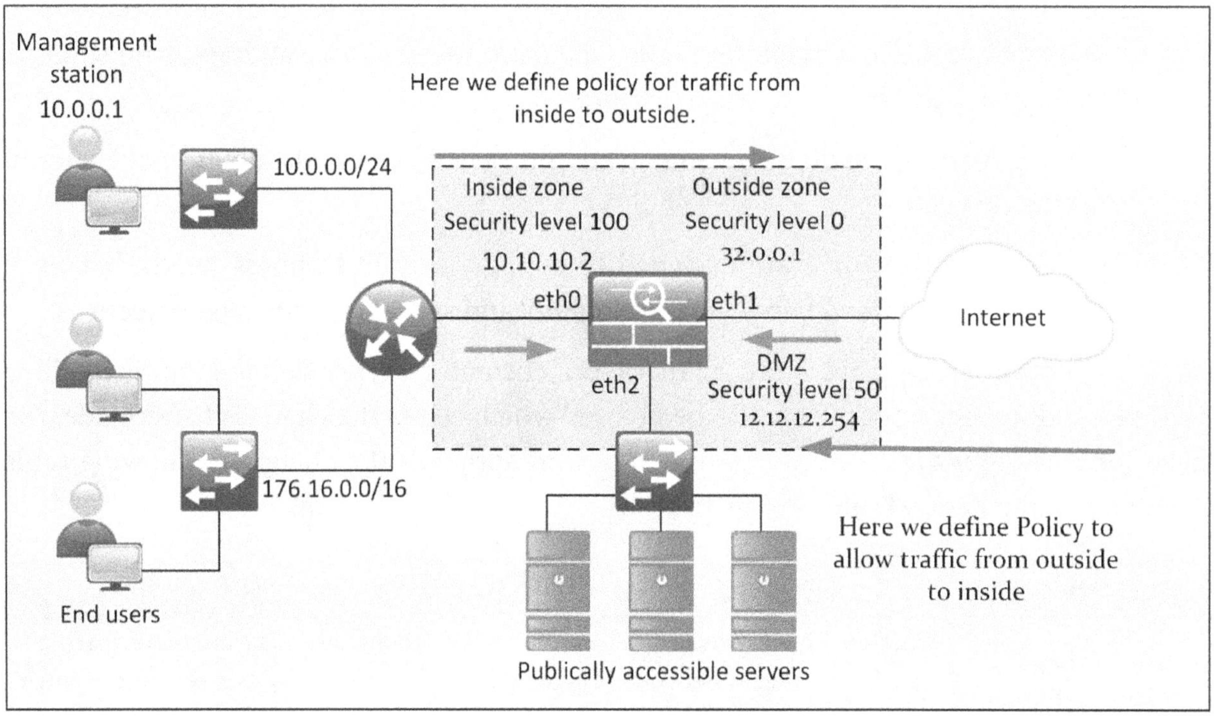

Figure 5-13: Topology Diagram

ASA Security Levels

Just like in ZBFW, where interfaces are placed in different zones and then policy is applied on specific zone pair, ASA assigns different security levels to its interfaces. The basic function of security level is the same as zones in ZBFW i.e. to identify the trustworthiness associated with specific interface and end-devices connected to it. The higher the number assigned to an interface, the more trusted that interface would be considered. In general, Cisco ASA allows only 0-100 different security levels, which seem enough for its operation. A value of 0 indicates the least trusted, and a value of 100 indicates the most trusted.

Consider an example of a medium sized corporate office where internal users must be entertained with a secured internet access. Some of the corporate servers need to be accessed by public internet for business needs. In this case, three different security segments can be easily identified namely the trusted network and its users, which are connected to one of the interface of ASA. Secondly, the untrusted interface, which is the interface of ASA connected to public internet. The third security segment would be the Demilitarized Zone (DMZ) where servers will be placed. With future amendments in mind, three security levels need to be selected in such a way that it would not need to be re-configured in case of any new network changes. As the highest security level that ASA can assign is 100, it would be assigned to the interfaces connected to LAN users. Similarly, the most untrustworthy security level is 0. It will be assigned to interfaces connected to internet. 50 will be assumed as security level of DMZ so that wide range of security levels will still be available for future scenarios.

In ASA, a name can also be assigned to an interface, for example, an interface with security level of 100 can be assigned a name of inside. The same is the case for other networks. The following diagram summarizes the concept of security levels and their assignments.

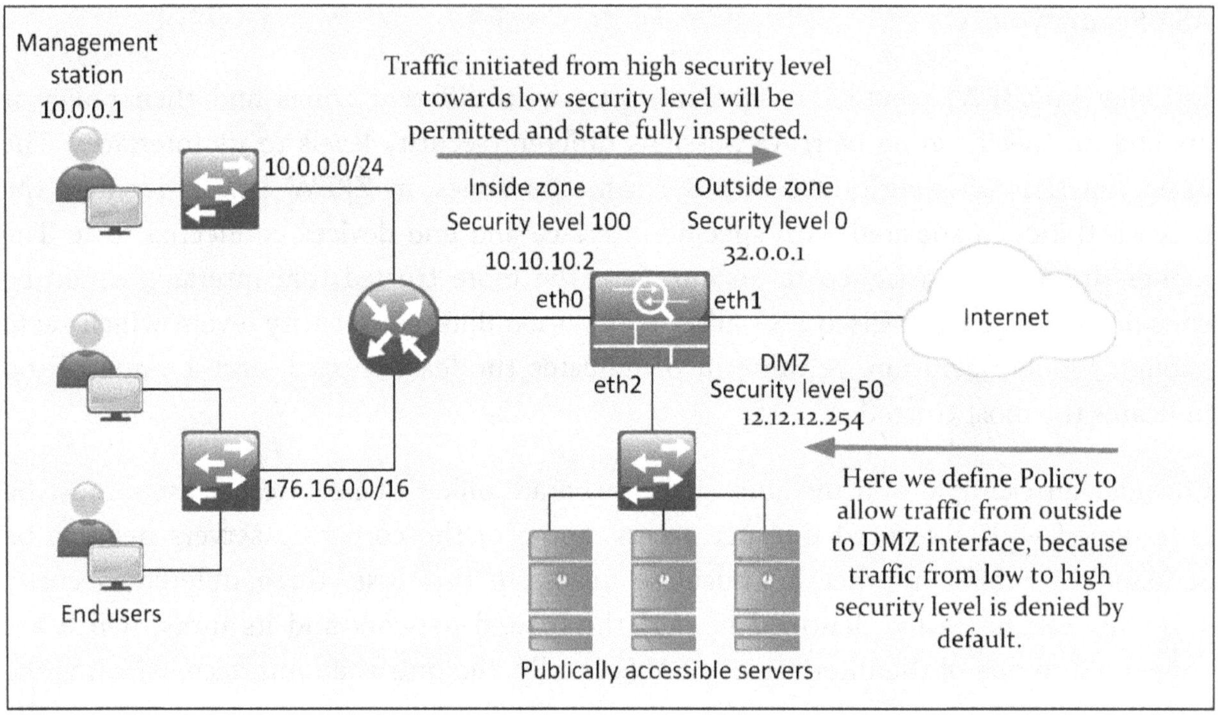

Figure 5-14: ASA Security Levels

- As a default nature, Cisco ASA allows all outbound traffic from a higher security level (i.e etho in the above figure configured as Inside Zone with security level 100) to the lower security level interface (i.e. eth1 configured as an outside interface with security level 0).
- By default, all inbound traffic from a lower security level (i.e. eth1 in the above figure configured as Outside Zone with security level 0) to the higher security level interface (i.e. etho configured as an inside interface with security level 100).
- To allow the particular inbound traffic from lower security level interface to higher security zone, an ACL must be configured in inbound direction on the lower level interface.
- Another important consideration is that the same interface traffic is also denied by default. To allow the communication between the same security level interfaces, enable the command same security-traffic permit inter-interface globally.
- Inbound and outbound traffic through a same interface is known as "U-turn" and is denied by default. To allow this type of traffic, run the command same-security-traffic permit intra-interface globally.

As Stateful inspection is enabled by default on Cisco ASA firewalls, traffic initiated from high security level towards low security level will be permitted. For example, traffic originated from security level 100 and 50 will be permitted towards security level 0 and return traffic, as a result of it would also be allowed. However, traffic initiated from security level, say 50 to security level 100 would not be permitted by default. Access policy would be needed to allow traffic in this regard.

Configuration of ASA security levels:

Here are the following security levels usually created and used on Cisco's ASA:

Security level 100- By default, it is used by the inside interface. It is the highest possible and most trusted level.

Security level 0- By default, it is used by outside interface. It is the lowest possible and most untrusted level.

Security level 1-99- They can be assigned to any interface of ASA. Usually, in a zone-based scenario, the security level of inside zone is typically 100, the security level of outside zone is 0 and the security level of DMZ interface is 50.

Here are the configuration steps for defining security levels on ASA's interfaces:

```
Ciscoasa# configure terminal
Ciscoasa(config)# interface Ethernet1
Ciscoasa(config-if)# ip address 32.0.0.1 255.255.255.252
Ciscoasa(config-if)# nameif outside
Ciscoasa(config-if)# security-level 0
Ciscoasa(config)# interface Ethernet0
Ciscoasa(config-if)# ip address 10.10.10.2 255.255.255.252
Ciscoasa(config-if)# nameif inside
Ciscoasa(config-if)# security-level 100
Ciscoasa(config)# interface Ethernet2
Ciscoasa(config-if)# ip address 12.12.12.254 255.255.255.0
Ciscoasa(config-if)# nameif dmz
Ciscoasa(config-if)# security-level 50
```

Cisco Modular Policy Framework (MPF)

MPF defines the policy of different flows of traffic. There are 3 main components of MPF:

1. **Class MAP**: classifies the traffic.
2. **Policy MAP**: specifies actions for the classified traffic.
3. **Service Policy**: applies the policy map to an interface or to the ASA as a whole.

While implementing the ZBFW in Cisco IOS, class maps are used to filter out the desired traffic, policy maps are used to define the action and then final service policy actually applies the action on the matched traffic.

Same things will be used in ASA; Class map for traffic matching, policy map for defining action on match traffic and service policy for applying the action on one of the interface of ASA or on a whole device globally.

A way is to use this modular policy framework is to let ASA dynamically allow the multiple ports used by single session like in case of FTP. Similarly, another case would be sent the traffic to Intrusion Prevention System (IPS) module, which is installed as hardware module on ASA chassis.

Class Map

A class map can filter out traffic based on layer 3 and layer 4 information primarily. However, it can also be used from layer 5 to layer 7 information can also be used to include application specific information for filtering. For CCNA security objectives, following are the options a class map can use for filtering specific traffic based on layer 3 and layer 4 information:

- Using Access-Lists (ACL)
- Using DSPC/IP precedence fields for prioritizing the traffic
- TCP/UDP port numbers
- VPN Tunnel group

Policy Map

A policy map applies specific action on matched traffic by class-map, which may include:

- Transfer to IPS module
- Stateful inspection
- Prioritizing the traffic
- Limiting the rate of matched traffic

Service Policy

After defining the policy, it will be applied to an interface, which has some security level. If policy is applied globally, it will be applied on all logical as well as physical interfaces of ASA device.

Here is the lab topology for cisco modular policy framework, where we want to apply policies to the inbound and outbound traffic:

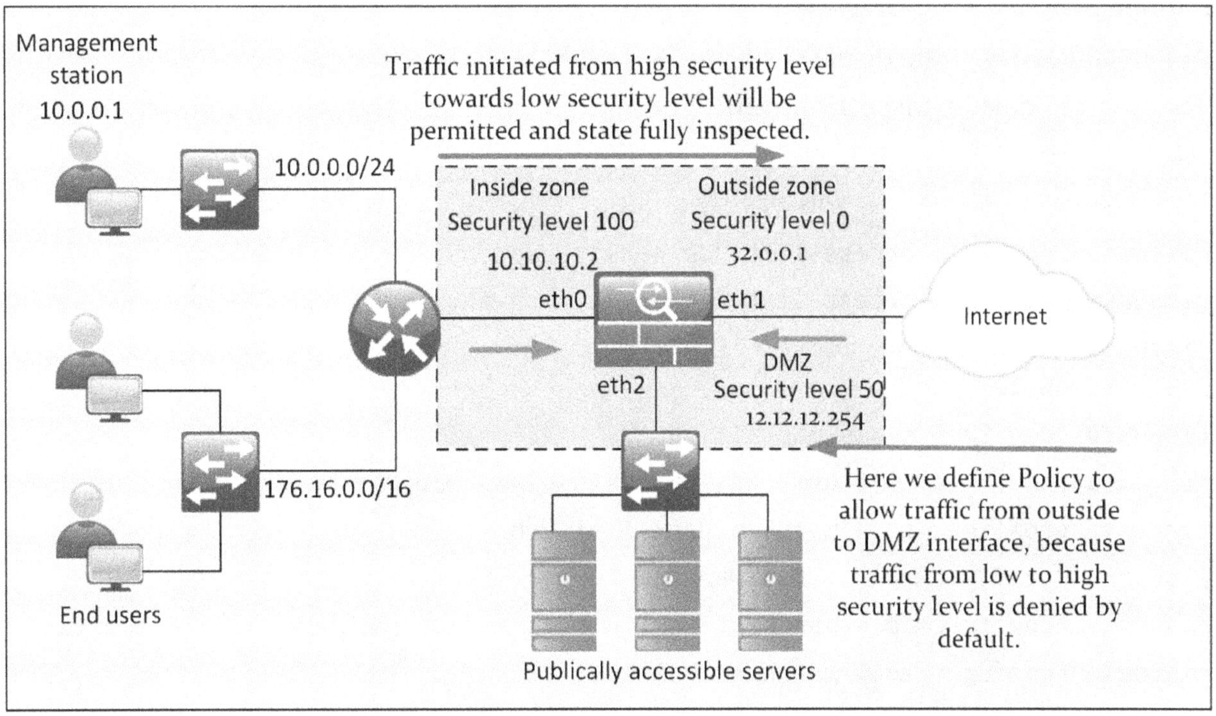

Figure 5-15: Cisco Modular Policy Framework (MPF)

Configuration of Cisco Modular Policy Framework:

Configuration of class map to classify traffic:

As we discussed earlier, class map classifies the traffic hitting an interface. Let us assume that the traffic belongs to layer 3 and 4 i.e. it consists of TCP and UDP packets, then the following steps of configuration will be followed:

```
ciscoasa# config terminal
ciscoasa(config)# class-map all_udp
```

The command "class-map" defines name of the class. You can assign any name of your choice here.

```
ciscoasa(config-cmap)# description ALL UDP TRAFFIC
```

The command "description" adds description to the class map.

```
ciscoasa(config-cmap)# match any
ciscoasa(config-cmap)# match access-list udp
```

Here, the "match access-list" command matches or compares the traffic from extended ACL.

```
ciscoasa(config-cmap)# match port tcp eq 80
```

Here, "match port" command matches the destination port. This destination port can be a single port or a range of ports.

```
ciscoasa(config-cmap)# match default-inspection-traffic
```

The "match default-inspection-traffic" command specifies the ports and protocols to match.

Here is an example of how you classify different types of data traffic using class maps:

```
ciscoasa (config)# access-list udp permit udp any any
ciscoasa (config)# access-list tcp permit tcp any any
ciscoasa (config)# access-list host_foo permit ip any 12.12.12.1
255.255.255.255
ciscoasa (config)# class-map all_udp
ciscoasa (config-cmap)# description "This class-map matches all UDP traffic"
ciscoasa (config-cmap)# match access-list udp
ciscoasa (config-cmap)# class-map all_tcp
ciscoasa (config-cmap)# description "This class-map matches all TCP traffic"
ciscoasa (config-cmap)# match access-list tcp
ciscoasa (config-cmap)# class-map all_http
ciscoasa (config-cmap)# description "This class-map matches all HTTP traffic"
ciscoasa (config-cmap)# match port tcp eq http
ciscoasa (config-cmap)# class-map to_server
ciscoasa (config-cmap)# description "This class-map matches all traffic to
server 12.12.12.1"
ciscoasa (config-cmap)# match access-list host_foo
```

Configuration of Policy Map to Apply Actions on the Classified Traffic:

Here we are assuming that administration wants to limit the number of connections allowed to the web server 12.12.12.1, so we are applying policy over http, tcp and udp class traffic to achieve the required objective. The following is an example of a policy-map command for a connection policy.

```
ciscoasa# config terminal
ciscoasa (config)# policy-map global_policy
ciscoasa (config-pmap)# class all_http
ciscoasa (config)# access-list http-server permit tcp any host 12.12.12.1
ciscoasa (config)# class-map http-server
ciscoasa (config-cmap)# match access-list http-server
ciscoasa (config)# policy-map global-policy
ciscoasa (config-pmap)# description This policy map defines a policy concerning connection to http server.
ciscoasa (config-pmap)# class http-server
ciscoasa (config-pmap-c)# set connection conn-max 256
ciscoasa (config)# class-map tcp_traffic
ciscoasa (config-cmap)# match port tcp range 1 65535
ciscoasa (config)# class-map udp_traffic
ciscoasa (config-cmap)# match port udp range 0 65535
ciscoasa (config)# policy-map global_policy
```

Configuration of Service Policy to Apply Actions on Interfaces:

In order to activate the policy map, create a service policy that applies to one or more interfaces or that applies globally to all the interfaces. Use the following command:

```
ciscoasa (config)# service-policy inbound_policy interface outside
```

The command shown above, will apply service policy on just the outside interface.

```
ciscoasa (config)# service-policy new_global_policy global
```

This command will apply the service policy on all the interfaces globally.

Verification:

To monitor service policies, enter the following command:

```
ciscoasa # show service-policy
```

Describe Modes of Deployment

Usually, Cisco's ASA supports two firewall modes:

- Routed Firewall mode
- Transparent Firewall mode

Routed Mode

By default, Cisco ASA works in layer 3 or routed mode in which an IP address is normally assigned to different interfaces of the device. End-hosts see firewall as a routing hop along with the network path.

Transparent Mode

In transparent mode, ASA works as layer 2 bridge and traffic flows through it without adding itself as routing hop between communicating peers. Consider it as a tap on a network, which is normally used to analyze the network traffic. In transparent mode, no IP address is assigned to an interface. However, name and security level is assigned to an interface to make it operational.

Just like Layer 2 switches and bridges, ASA in transparent mode also saves MAC address associated with an interface in its MAC address table. However, unlike conventional switches and bridges, which tend to broadcast the frame in case of unknown MAC address, ASA firewall drops the traffic if MAC address is unknown to it.

Methods of Implementing High Availability

Just as First Hop Routing Protocols can be used on Cisco routers to provide load balancing and redundancy, two firewalls can be combined to provide similar results. In case one device goes down due to any software or hardware failure, second device will take its place. Two of the most common configurations of implementing high availability are:

Active/Standby failover
Active/Active failover

In Active/Standby failover, one device will act as primary firewall or active firewall while the second one will be in standby mode. Just like HSRP, the standard protocol traffic will be exchanged periodically between firewalls to check the status of active and standby firewalls. In Active/Active failover configuration, both ASAs can pass network traffic. As shown in the figure below, Ge 0/3 link will be used for the transmission of failover information. In case active firewall goes down, standby firewall will immediately take the charge.

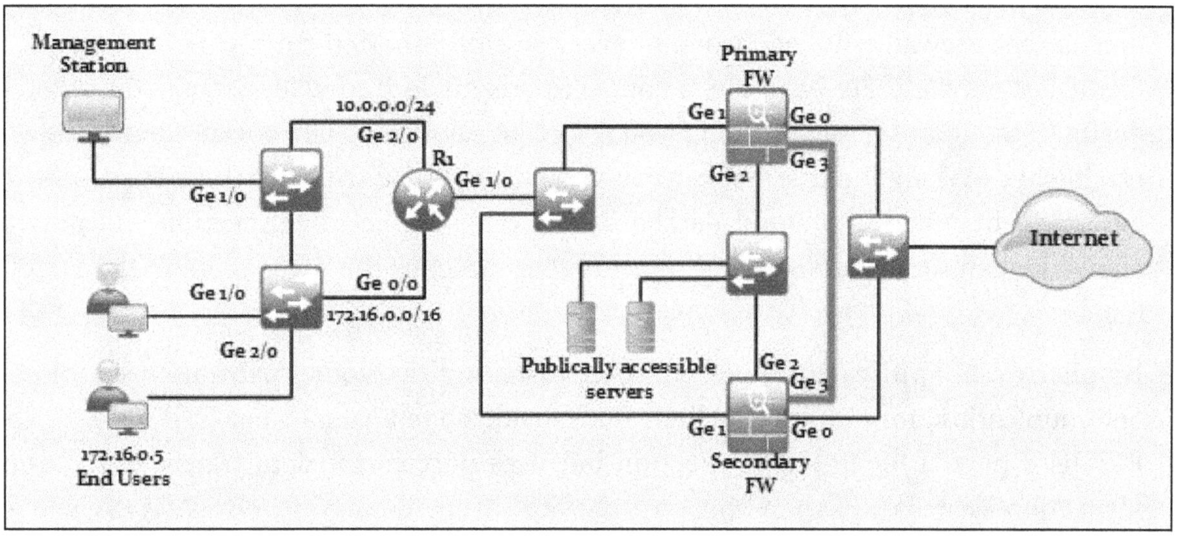

Figure 5-16: Cisco ASA Deployment in High Availability Mode

Security Context:

High-end ASA devices allow you to make multiple virtual firewalls within a single hardware device. These virtual firewalls are known as context. Consider an example of large service provider, which is also providing the security features to its clients. Instead of using single hardware firewall for each client connection, service providers can use one high-end firewall and create multiple contexts in it. In this way, each client will assume to have a separate piece of hardware as his/her next hop as traffic will be isolated virtually within a hardware device. In active/active failover, physical connection may remain same as active/standby failover, instead we make one firewall to act as primary for one context and second firewall to be primary for second context just like HSRP can be tweaked to use multiple routers at the same time by making each router active for one unique VLAN.

Firewall Services

Although ASA as a product provides many security features, it may be very difficult to highlight every single feature in this workbook. Following are the most prominent features of ASA firewalls:

- **Packet filtering:** Simple packet filtering techniques like Access-Lists (ACL) can be used to perform traffic control by using layer 3 and layer 4 information. The main difference between ACL on a routers/switches and on ASA is the firewall uses subnet mask instead of wild card mask as in routers and switches.
- **Stateful filtering:** By default, Stateful packet filtering is enabled on ASA, which means that firewall will keep track of every session initiated from trusted network to untrusted network. For example, a connection is made from client, say 10.0.0.2:800 to destination address, say 12.12.12.1:9090. Let us assume TCP socket connection is established. When the first packet from source hits the trusted interface of ASA, its entry will be made in Stateful database. The reply traffic of connection will only be allowed when source address and port number matches the saved state in the Stateful table.
- **Inspection at application level:** In some cases, multiple ports pairs are used for over communication; for example, a client from inside zone trying to use FTP service. Now FTP uses port 21 for initial connection but uses port 20 for data transfer. If Stateful inspection is working, then the return traffic from data port, which is 20 will be dropped in return. By application inspection, ASA firewall learns dynamically about these ports and allow traffic from extra ports as well.
- **NAT, DHCP and IP Routing:** Cisco ASA firewalls also support multiple features of Layer 3 routing devices like NAT, DHCP and routing protocols like RIP, EIGRP and OSPF.
- **Layer 3 and Layer 2 Operational mode:** One way of ASA deployment is to assign IP addresses to different interfaces and they will appear as an extra hop in end-to-end traffic path. This mode is known as traditional mode. Another case would be to deploy the firewall in transparent mode, in which no IP address is assigned to the interfaces of ASA and it will act as multiport bridge with an ability to inspect the overall traffic just like traditional mode. The advantage of using the transparent mode is that end-users will be unaware of new addition in the network topology.
- **VPN Support:** ASA can also be used to implement the Site-to-Site or SSL VPNs. The number of VPN connections ASA can make may depend on the purchased license

- **Mitigation against BOTNET:** A BOTNET is a group of infected computers that can perform under a centralized command from an attacker. Most of the DDoS attacks are generated by BOTNETs. Cisco ASA can be configured to get regular updates related to BOTNET Traffic Filter Database from Cisco Systems Inc. in order to mitigate latest attacks.
- **Advanced Malware Protection (AMP):** Cisco's Next Generation Firewalls (NGFW) provide the traditional firewall features along with some advanced malware protection features in a single device.
- **AAA Support:** Just like routers and switches, authorization, authentication and accounting features can also be implemented either locally or in integration with some specialized hardware like Access Control Server (ACS).

Cisco Firewall Technologies Mind Map

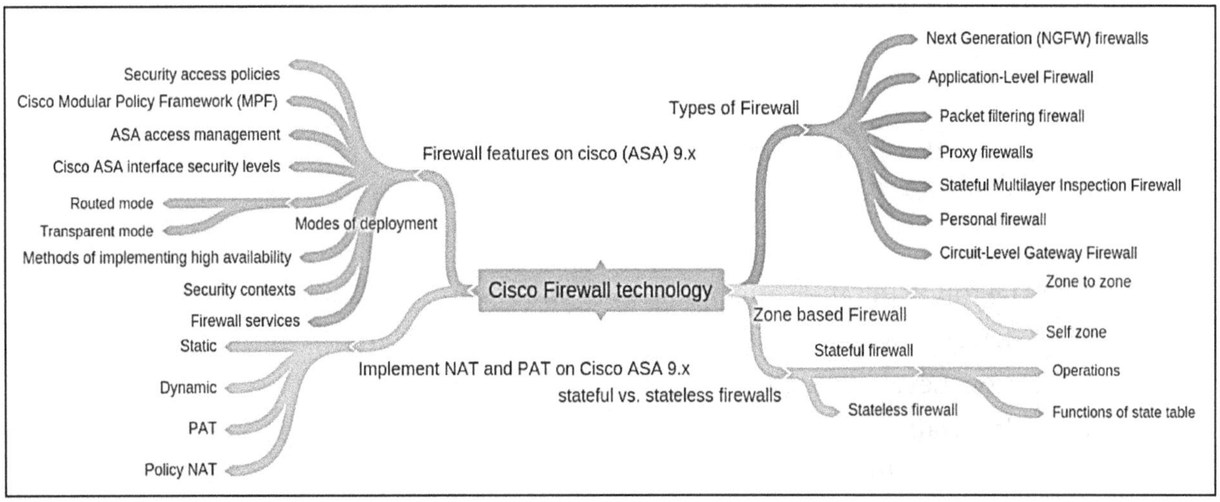

Figure 5-17: Firewall Technologies Mind Map

Practice Questions:

1. Which of the following security features are provided by firewall? (Choose any three)
   A. It does not provide user authentication.
   B. It has the ability to inspect the traffic of more than just IP and port level.
   C. By integrating with AAA, firewall can permit or deny traffic based on AAA policy.
   D. By integrating with IPS/ID, firewall can detect and filter malicious data at the edge of network to protect the end-users.
   E. It does not support encryption and authentication.

2. Which of the firewalls provides granular control over the traffic by using information up to layer 7 of OSI model?
   A. Circuit-Level Firewall
   B. Application-Level Firewall
   C. Stateful firewall
   D. Next generation firewall

3. Which of the following firewalls operates at the session layer of the OSI model?
   A. Circuit-Level Firewall
   B. Application-Level Firewall
   C. Stateful firewall
   D. Next generation firewall

4. What is the advantage of using a Stateful firewall instead of a proxy server?
   A. It performs user authentication.
   B. It provides packet filtering.
   C. It prevents Layer 7 attacks.
   D. It provides better performance.

5. Which of the followings is the limitation of a Stateful firewall?
   A. It is not as effective with UDP- or ICMP-based traffic.
   B. It does not provide user authentication.
   C. It does not filter unnecessary traffic.
   D. It provides poor log information.

6. Which of the following steps must be taken after zones have been created in a Cisco IOS Zone-based firewall?
   A. Assign interfaces to zones.
   B. Apply encryption and authentication to the zones.
   C. Disable the zones.
   D. Establish policies between zones.

7. Which of the following firewalls monitors network traffic and determines whether the packets belong to an existing connection or are from an unauthorized source?
   A. Stateless firewall
   B. Personal firewall
   C. Application proxy
   D. Stateful firewall

8. Which one of the following commands verifies a Zone-Based Policy Firewall configuration?
   A. show interfaces
   B. show zones
   C. show running-config
   D. show protocols

9. Which one of the followings is the function of state or session table?
   A. It saves the best route information for routing.
   B. It saves MAC addresses.
   C. It saves NATing information.
   D. It saves the state of current sessions in a table.

10. The global address either router's interface IP or one from pool, which will represent the client over an internet is termed as ___________.
   A. Inside Local
   B. Inside Global
   C. Outside Local
   D. Outside Global

11. Which class of Cisco Common Classification Policy Language (C3PL) filters out the traffic that needs to be inspected?
    A. Policy map
    B. Class map
    C. Service policies
    D. None

12. Which class of Cisco Common Classification Policy Language (C3PL) inspects (Stateful inspection of traffic), permit (permit the traffic but no Stateful inspection), drop the traffic or generate log of it?
    A. Policy map
    B. Class map
    C. Service policies
    D. None

13. Which of the following two actions can be applied to a traffic class when a Cisco IOS Zone-Based Policy Firewall is being configured? (Choose any three)
    A. Drop
    B. Permit
    C. Forward
    D. Hold
    E. Inspect
    F. Copy

14. Which of the followings are the techniques of accessing firewall for management? (Choose any three)
    A. OPManager
    B. Command Line Interface (CLI)
    C. ASA Security Device Manager (ASDMo)
    D. Cisco security manager (CSM)
    E. Simple network management protocol (SNMP)
    F. None of the above

15. Which of the following actions in a Cisco IOS Zone-Based Policy Firewall is similar to a permit statement in an ACL?
    A. Drop

B. Pass
C. Forward
D. Hold
E. Inspect
F. Copy

16. In a Cisco IOS Zone-Based Policy Firewall, what is the main function of the permit or pass action?
    A. Drops suspected packets.
    B. Forwards traffic from one zone to another.
    C. Performs inspection of traffic between zones for traffic control.
    D. Tracks the state of connections between zones.

17. In which mode of firewall deployment does ASA work as layer 2 bridge and traffic flows through it without adding itself as routing hop between communicating peers?
    A. Routed mode
    B. Transparent mode
    C. Tunnel mode
    D. Transport mode
    E. None of the above

18. Which two of the followings are the modes of ASA deployment?
    A. Routed mode
    B. Transparent mode
    C. Both Routed and Transparent mode
    D. Transport mode
    E. None of the above

19. In which method of High availability does one device act as primary firewall or active firewall while the second stay in standby mode?
    A. Active/Standby failover
    B. Active/Active failover
    C. Both of the above
    D. None of the above

20. The concept of implementing multiple virtual firewalls is known as ____________.
    A. Context
    B. High availability
    C. Security level
    D. None of the above

21. Security level 100- is the highest possible and most trusted level. By default, on which of the following interface it is used?
    A. On inside interface
    B. On outside interface
    C. On DMZ interface
    D. None of the above

22. Which policy specifies the rules for the data traffic inbound or outbound passing through an interface?
    A. Security Access policy
    B. Firewall Management Policy
    C. Network Connection Policy
    D. All of the above

23. Which of the following algorithm can ensure data confidentiality?
    A. AES
    B. MD5
    C. PKI
    D. RSA

24. Why is asymmetric algorithm key management simpler than symmetric algorithm key management?
    A. Two public keys are used for the key exchange.
    B. It uses fewer bits.
    C. Only one key is used.
    D. One of the keys can be made public.

25. Data Encryption Standard (DES) uses ________ bits for data encryption.

A. 42 bits
B. 56 bits
C. 61 bits
D. 78 bits

Chapter 06: Intrusion Prevention System (IPS)

Technology Brief

In the previous chapter, we had discussed about the fundamentals of firewalls, their importance and overall impact of deployment in the network. Awareness about the network security and advance security tools of network is increasing the additional layers of security, which helps the administrator to keep an eye on the network. The techniques of exploiting threats and policy violation are also increasing side by side, so it is very important to make sure that your network is smart enough to detect and prevent such kinds of emerging threats and malicious activities.

In this chapter, we will discuss about the core concepts of one of the security tool, which is Intrusion Detection System (IDS) and Intrusion Prevention System (IPS). IDS and IPS often creates confusion, as the technical concept behind the technology is almost the same. In this chapter, we will discuss how IPS and IDS differ and of their deployment best practices.

Just like other products, Cisco also has developed number of solutions for implementing IDS/IPS for the security of the network. In the first phase of this section, different concepts will be discussed before moving to the different implementation methodologies.

Overview of Intrusion Detection & Prevention Systems (IDS/IPS)

In today's world, malwares like viruses and worms can spread across the network in just a spam of few minutes. A secured network must be smart enough to quickly notice and mitigate such malwares. Firewalls are not enough to protect against such malwares and zero day attacks. A **zero-day attack** or zero-day threat is an attack that exploits the weakness of any software that is unknown even to the software vendor or developer. An attacker discloses this vulnerability before the developer and launches an attack before the vendor releases any patch of this vulnerability. This vulnerability may open a backdoor for attackers and the network can be compromised. In order to defend against these fast-moving attacks, our network needs sophisticated solutions from network security professionals that passively monitor the traffic on a network.

Intrusion Detection System (IDS) is a security solution that provides the real-time detection of such malwares. It analyses the data traffic without affecting the packet flow of the traffic. Here, the traffic is continuously monitored and reported to the management in case of any malicious activity. IDS works passively, as it works on the copied traffic, it cannot stop or respond to an attack actively. IDS works in assistance with other devices like routers and firewalls to react against such attacks.

Intrusion Prevention System (IPS) works somehow similar to IDS, as it provides real-time monitoring and analyzing of data traffic. IPS analyses the content and payloads of layer 3 and layer 4 data traffic to make sure that there is no such malicious content inside. It provides more sophisticated monitoring of data stream, as it does not allow any untrusted packet to enter a network. This sophisticated analysis enables the IPS solution to detect, stop and mitigate attacks that tries to bypass firewall devices. IPS works in inline mode, so it can stop attacks from reaching their target but it also affects the packet flow of the data stream.

The main difference between IDS and IPS is that an IPS responds immediately to an attack and does not allow any malicious traffic to bypass network device, whereas an IDS just does a passive monitoring by scanning the copy of network traffic. IDS detects the malware and notifies the threat detection. This way, malicious traffic may reach to its destination; it does not address the mitigation techniques for such attacks.

The following table summarizes and compares various features of IDS and IPS.

Feature	IPS	IDS
Positioning	In-line with the network. Every packet goes through it.	Not in-line with the network. Gets the copy of every packet.
Mode	In-line/Tap.	Promiscuous
Delay	Introduces delay because every packet is analyzed before being forwarded to destination.	Does not introduce delay because it is not in-line with the network.
Point of failure?	Yes. If sensor is down it may drops good as well as malicious traffic from entering the network, depending on one of the two modes configured on it, namely fail-open or fail-close	Has no impact on traffic, as IDS is not in-line with network.
Ability to mitigate an attack?	Yes. By dropping the malicious traffic, attacks can be readily reduced on the network. If deployed in TAP mode, then it will get a copy of each packet but cannot mitigate the attack	IDS cannot directly stop an attack. However, it assists some in-line devices like IPS to drop certain traffic to stop an attack.
Can do packet manipulation?	Yes. Can modify the IP traffic according to defined set of rules.	No. As IDS receives mirrored traffic, so it can only perform inspection.

Table 6-01: IDS/IPS Comparison

IPS/IDS Integration Options

In order to add IDP/IPS sensor in network infrastructure for enhancing and providing more sophisticated security features, Cisco has provided the following options:

- **A dedicated IPS appliance**: for example, 4200 series appliances
- **Software based support** in Cisco IOS
- **AIM-IPS and NME-IPS** based hardware modules for Cisco Routers.
- **AIP-IPS module** in Cisco ASA series firewall.
- **Cisco FirePOWER** 7000/8000 series appliances.
- **Virtual Next-Generation IPS** for VMware based virtual environment.
- **ASA with FirePOWER services.**

IDS/IPS Deployment Techniques

Depending on the network scenario, IDS/IPS modules are deployed in one of the following configuration:

1. In the host
2. In the network

Host Based IPS

Host based IPS/IDS is normally deployed for the protection of specific host machine and it works closely with the Operating System Kernel of the host machine. It creates a filtering layer and filters out any malicious application occurring at the OS. There are four major types of Host based IDS/IPS:

- **File System Monitoring:** In this configuration, IDS/IPS works by comparing the version of files within some directory with the previous versions of same file and checks for any unauthorized tampering and changings within a file. Hashing algorithms are often used to verify the integrity of files and directories, which gives an indication of possible changes, which are not supposed to be there.
- **Log Files Analysis:** In this configuration, IDS/IPS works by analyzing the log files of host machine and generates warning for system administrators who is responsible for machine security. Several tools and applications are available, which works by analyzing the patterns of behavior and further correlate it with actual events.

- **Connection Analysis:** IDS/IPS works by monitoring the overall network connections being made with the secured machine, it tries to figure out which of them are legitimate and how many of them are unauthorized. Examples of techniques used are open ports scanning, half open and rogue TCP connections and so forth.
- **Kernel Level Detection:** In this configuration, kernel of OS itself detects the changings within the system binaries and anomaly in system calls to detect the intrusion attempts on that machine.

Network Based IPS

The network based IPS solution works as in-line with the perimeter edge device or some specific segment of overall network. A network based solution works by monitoring the overall network traffic (or data packets) so it is as fast as possible in terms of processing power so that latency may not be introduced in a network. Depending on vendor and series of IDS/IPS, it may use one of above technologies in its working.

The following table summarizes the difference between host based and network based IDS/IPS solution:

Feature	Host based IDS/IPS	Network based IDS/IPS
Scalability	Not scalable, as number of secure hosts increases.	Highly scalable. Normally deployed at perimeter gateway.
Cost effectiveness	Low. More systems mean more IDS/IPS modules.	High. One pair can monitor overall network.
Capability	Capable of verifying if an attack succeeded or not	Only capable of generating alert of an attack.
Processing Power	Processing power of host device is used.	Must have high processing power to overcome latency issues.

Table 6-02: Host based vs. Network Based IDS/IPS Solution

Modes of Deployment

Here in this section, we will discuss some of the modes of IDS/IPS deployment:

Promiscuous or Passive Mode

In a promiscuous or passive mode, a copy of every data packet will be sent to the sensor to analyze any malicious activity. A **sensor** is a device that performs the real time monitoring of IP traffic over the network and is based on certain set of rule-set, it determines whether the coming traffic is malicious or trusted. Although the sensor's result is not always 100% accurate, but it helps in mitigating the already detected threats and network attacks.

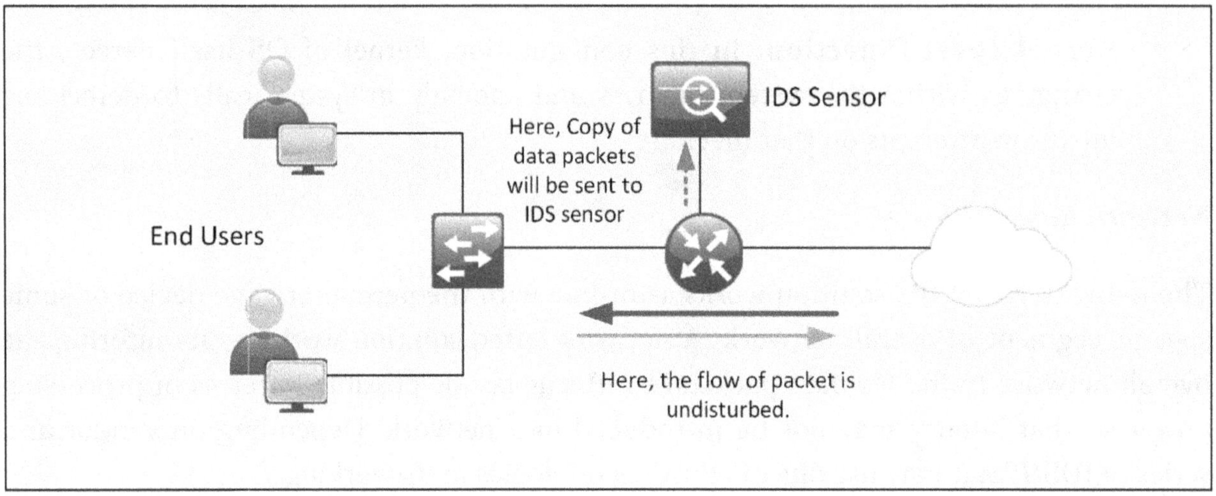

Figure 6-01: Promiscuous Deployment Mode

In other means, the sensor, running in promiscuous mode will perform the detection and generates an alert if required. As normal flow of traffic is not disturbed, no end-to-end delay will occur by implementing IDS. The only downside of this configuration is that, IDS will not be able to stop malicious packets from entering the network because IDS is not controlling the overall path of the traffic.

Inline Mode

When the sensor is placed in line with the network i.e., the common in/out of specific network segment terminates on a hardware or logical interface of a sensor, and goes out from another hardware or logical interface of sensor. Then every single packet will be analyzed and passed through the sensor, only if it does not contain anything malicious. By dropping the malicious traffic, the trusted network or a segment of it can be protected from known threats and attacks. This is the basic working of Intrusion Prevention System (IPS). However, the in line installation and inspection of traffic may result in slighter delay. IPS may also become single point of failure for the whole network. If 'fail-open' mode is used, the good and malicious traffic will be allowed in case of any kind of failure within IPS sensor. Similarly, if 'fail-close' mode is configured, the whole IP traffic will be dropped in case of sensor's failure.

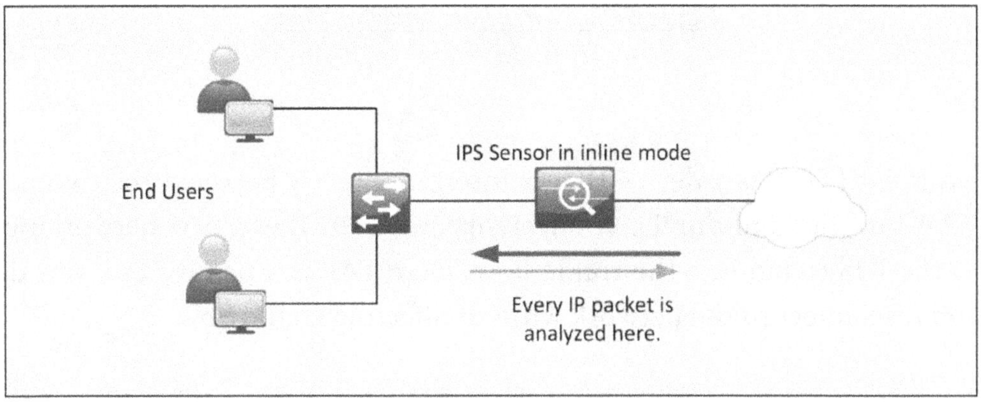

Figure 6-02: In-line Deployment Mode

SPAN Mode

The Switched Port Analyzer (SPAN) or port mirroring is a feature for Cisco switches; its function is to send copies of the frame entering a port to the IDS/IPS sensor. SPAN terminology has two main ports:

- Source (SPAN) port - A port with the SPAN feature enabled on it to send the copies of traffic to the IPS/IDS.

- Destination (SPAN) port - A port where the IDS/IPS or packet analyzer is connected. This port is also called monitor port, as this port monitors source ports.

Source port is monitored for traffic analysis. SPAN mirrors all the ingress or egress traffic on one or more source ports to a destination port for analysis. The relation between source ports and a destination port is called a SPAN session. In each session, one or multiple source ports can be monitored.

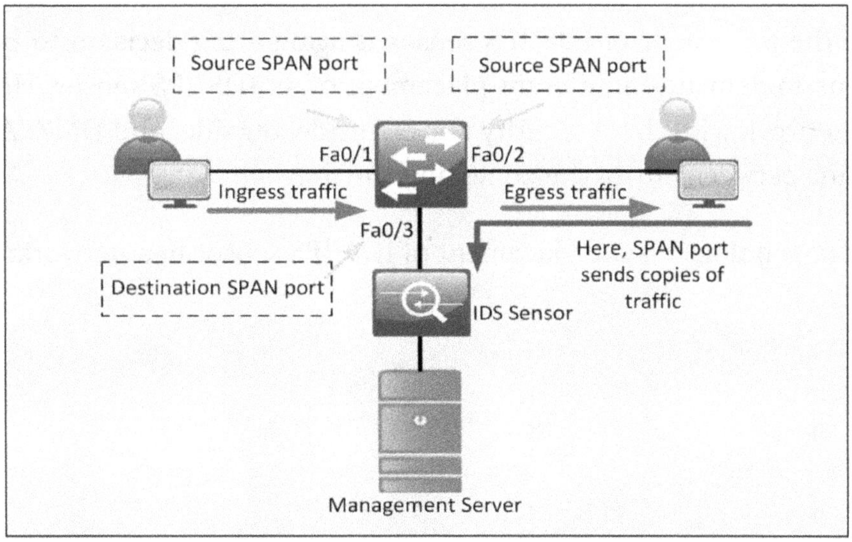

Figure 6-03: Switch Port Analyzer Mode

Tap Mode

Test Access Point (TAP) is a device that is inserted directly between the two networking devices. TAP provides full-duplex connectivity between these two networking devices, and allows the IDS to tap into the traffic flow. Here TAP is a passive tap, this device can connect and disconnect to the network without affecting traffic flow.

The traffic under consideration is referred to as the "pass-through" traffic and the ports used for monitoring and analyzing are called "monitor ports". For a granular visibility and control over the network, a TAP should be placed between the router and the switch.

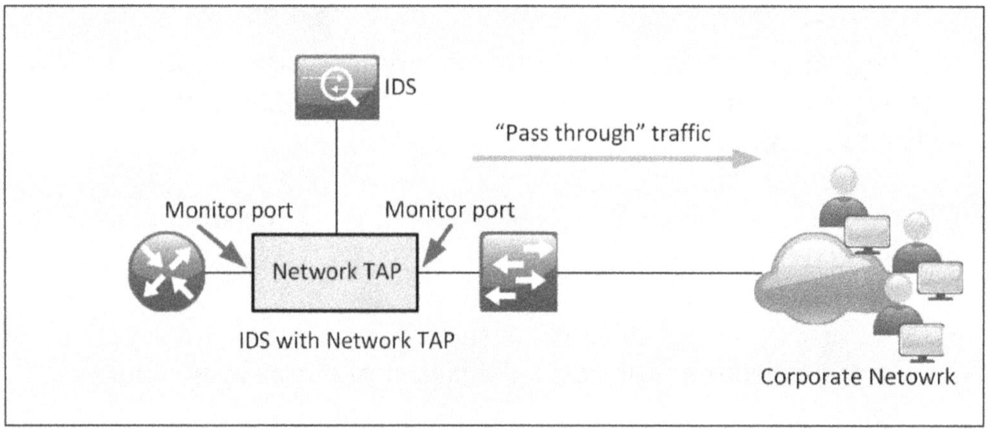

Figure 6-04: Test Access Point Mode

IDS/IPS Device Placement

To determine the placement of IDS/IPS sensor is again a big decision to be made. Each and every scenario demands a different placement of an IDS/IPS sensor. Here, we have a scenario of a network with three security zones: inside, outside, and DMZ. A sensor could be placed in-line between any of the zones and the firewall.

Here is the basic topology for the placement of IDS/IPS sensor in a network:

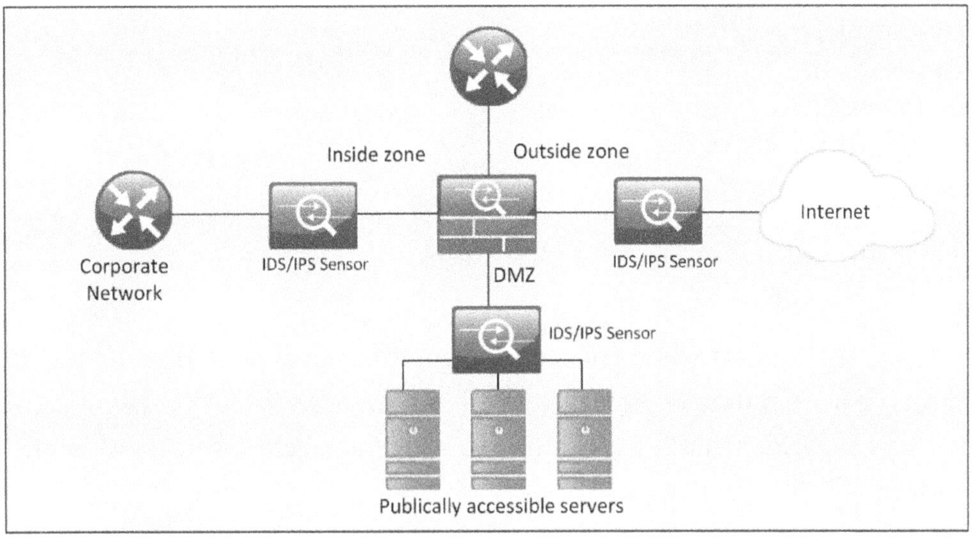

Figure 6-05: Basic Topology for the Placement of IPS/IDS

Inside

If you have just one option of placing an IPS sensor, then placing the sensor just inside the firewall is the best option. Although the inside network is already protected by the firewall, the users can unintentionally introduce malware into the internal network, where the most critical and confidential data is stored and can be compromised.

Outside

The greatest threat can come from the internet, so it sounds the best option to place an IDS/IPS sensor in an outside zone. Placing sensor in the outside network will increase the overall security and the number of alarms; hence, it seems reasonable to use the IPS in the outside zone to protect the network from the Internet.

DMZ

The data stored in DMZ is far more critical than the data stored on internal servers. DMZ servers are exposed to the internet, which leads to the introduction of malwares in a network where any misconfiguration or vulnerability can be exploited. Therefore, the placement of IPS/IDS sensor inside DMZ zone is also a sensible decision.

IPS/IDS Terminologies

When working with IPS/IDS modules, the following terminologies are often used:

1. False Positive
2. False Negative
3. True Positive
4. True Negative

False Positive

A false positive is a situation when the sensor generates an alert about the traffic, which is not malicious, but requires serious attention as long as security is concerned. False positive can be easily identified, as immediate alerts are generated for this and they can be easily viewed.

False Negative

A false negative is a situation when something malicious is introduced in a network and IPS/IDS sensor cannot generate any alert due to some unforeseen reasons. In this case, some extra tools and techniques are required to get updates related to such situations like Syslog messages from routers.

True Positive

A true positive means that a malicious activity is detected by the IPS module or sensor and an alert has been generated for this. Depending on the configuration of IPS, it may be dropped at the first place.

True Negative

A true negative means that general traffic i.e. without having anything malicious has been detected by IPS/IDS sensor and no alert has been generated for this.

Malicious Traffic Detection

When a sensor is analyzing traffic for something that is malicious or suspected, it uses multiple techniques based on the rules and signatures defined on the IPS/IDS sensor. Following tools and techniques can be used in this regard:

- Signature based IDS/IPS
- Policy based IDS/IPS
- Anomaly based IDS/IPS
- Reputation based IDS/IPS

Signature Based IDS/IPS

A signature checks for some specific string or behavior in a single packet or stream of packets to detect the anomaly. Cisco IPS/IDS modules and next generation firewalls come up with the pre-loaded digital signatures, which can be used to mitigate already discovered attacks. Cisco constantly updates the signature sets, which also needs to be updated on a device by the network administrator.

Not all signatures are enabled by default. If some signature is generating an alert for the traffic, which is allowed for some purpose like business needs, then network administrator must tune the IPS/IDS module, so the false positive messages generated for legitimate traffic will not be generated.

Policy Based IDS/IPS

As the name suggests, policy based IDS/IPS module works based on the policy or SOP of an organization. For example, if an organization has security policy that no management session with networking devices as well as end-devices must initiated via TELNET protocol. A custom rule specifying this policy needs to be defined on sensors. If it is configured on IPS, whenever TELNET traffic hits the IPS, an alert will be generated followed by the dropping of telnet packets. If it is implemented on IDS based sensor, then an alert will generate for it but traffic will keep flowing because IDS works in promiscuous mode.

Anomaly Based IDS/IPS

In this type, a baseline is created for the specific kind of traffic. For example, after analyzing the traffic, it is noticed that 30 half open TCP sessions are created every minute. After deciding the baseline, say 35 half open TCP connections in a minute, consider a scenario where, the number of half open TCP connected have increased up to 150 then IPS will drop the extra half open connections and will generate alert for it based on the decided anomaly.

Reputation Based IDS/IPS

If there is some sort of a global attack, for example DDoS attack on servers of Twitter and some other social websites like Facebook, Instagram, etc. The role of Reputation based IDS/IPS is to collect the information from the systems participating in global correlation. Reputation based IDS/IPS includes relative descriptors like known URLs, domain-names etc. Global correlation services are maintained by Cisco Cloud Services. Hence, it would be feasible to filter out the known traffic, which results in propagation of these attacks before it hits the organization's critical infrastructure.

The following table summarizes the different technologies used in IDS/IPS along with some advantages and disadvantages.

IDS/IPS Technology	Advantages	Disadvantages
Signature Based	Easier Implementation and management.	Does not detect the attacks who can bypass the signatures. May require some tweaking to stop generating false positive for legitimate traffic.
Anomaly Based	Can detect malicious traffic based on custom baseline. It can deny any kind of latest attacks as they will not be defined within the scope of baseline policy.	Requires carefully designing the baseline policy. Difficult to baseline large network designs. It may generate false positives due to misconfigured baseline.
Policy Based	Simple implementation with reliable results. Everything else outside the scope of defined policy will be dropped.	Requires manual implementation of policy. Any slighter change within a network will require change in policy configured in IPS/IDS module.
Reputation Based	Uses the information provided by Cisco Could Services in which systems share their experience with network attacks. Someone's experience become protection for the organization.	Requires regular updates and participation in Cisco Could services of global correlation in which systems share their experience with other members.

Table 6-03: Comparison of Techniques Used by IDS/IPS Sensors

Sensors response to the malicious traffic

The following table summarizes different actions performed by IDS/IPS sensors, once the malicious traffic is detected:

Response Action	Description
Deny attacker's source IP traffic	This option is only applicable when sensor is placed inline i.e. in IPS configuration. IPS detects and drops the traffic having source address of an attacker for specific interval of time. After configured time interval, this drop action dynamically is removed.
Drop connection inline	This option is only applicable when sensor is placed inline i.e. in IPS configuration. This action drops the packet, which triggers the attack and

	every other packet of that stream. An attacker can however use another port to make another socket connection, which can be permitted by IPS sensor.
Drop packets inline	This option is only applicable when sensor is placed inline i.e. in IPS configuration. This option removes the packet that triggers the alert.
Logging of attacker's source packets	This option log packet is based on attacker's source address for future use for example, for analyzing the threat. This is done usually for short span of time and after the generation of alert. Log files are stored in format readable by most protocol analyzers like Wireshark, etc.
Logging of packets destined for victim's device	This option log packet is based on destination address of victim device. Being enabled for short span of time, the main purpose of this option is correlation and analysis.
Logging of packets based on source and destination address	The main purpose of this option is same as mentioned in above two points. The main difference here is that both source and destination IP addresses are used to trigger the logging event.
Alert generation	Generating an alert for an event like alert of false positive, which means that something malicious has occurred. This is the default behavior of most IDS/IPS sensors.
Verbose Alert	The basic purpose of this option is the same as the above one. Instead of just generating an alert, this option also attaches a copy of the packet that resulted in the generation of the alert. This option has priority over the above option. It means if both options are enabled, then alert will be generated with attached copy of the IP packet.
Request to block specific connection	If sensor is used in promiscuous mode in which it gets copy of each packet traversing the network, it can generate a request to another networking device within a network to block a session or connection based on source or destination IP address along with TCP/UDP port numbers. The Blocking Device, which actually drops the session, may be a router implementing ACLs, or a switch implementing VLAN ACLs (VACLs) or even an adaptive security appliance (ASA).
Request to block specific host	This option allows the sensor to the send the request to blocking device to drop the traffic based on the source IP address of attacker. This option also deny any traffic if attacker changes the source port number in order to make new socket connection
Generate SNMP Trap	If sensor is also configured for SNMP, which is great for management and monitoring, this option generates SNMP traps and sends it to the configured address of SNMP.

Table 6-04: Sensor Actions on Detecting Malicious Activity

Managing the actions of IDS/IPS sensors

A sensor can take one of the above defined actions if it observes any malicious traffic in a network. As the number of signatures for attacks keeps increasing, it is very difficult to manage and apply action based on every single signature. Cisco came up with a solution to this problem, which allows the IDS/IPS sensor to dynamically consider how significant the risk is, and take appropriate action according to the level of risk.

The maximum risk rating value is 100 and the following three important factors play an important role in calculating the risk value:

Factors defining the risk value	Description
Target Value Rating(TVR)	The random value assigned by network administrators to specific destination address or subnets where the most critical infrastructure lives, when malicious traffic is seen going to these subnets or IP addresses. The final risk value will be high as compared to the situation where attacks happening on IP addresses bind to less critical devices.
Signature Fidelity Rating (SFR)	Based on the accuracy of the signature i.e. the chances of not generating the false positive by given signature. This is the property of signature and it is set by the person who created it.
Attack Severity Rating (ASR)	It is also the part of given signature and it determines the critical level of an attack.
Attack Relevancy (AR)	Sometimes attacks are hardware specific. For example, Microsoft Windows Server based attacks. If an attack is generated on relevant hardware, then its overall risk rating must be high.
Global Correlation	If the sensor is participating in global correlation, a cloud service is ran by Cisco Systems Inc. in which participating systems share their experience against known attacks. If some source IP addresses are known for large-scale attacks, then traffic coming from these source IP addresses must be given a high risk value.

Table 6-05: Components Involved in Calculating Risk Value

Bypassing IDS/IPS Module

Although IDS/IPS module is installed to enhance the overall security posture of network, sometimes, especially in case of sophisticated attacks, an attacker also has some objective in mind. The following techniques may help to bypass IDS/IPS sensor without generating false positive alert.

Bypassing Techniques	Description	Cisco's Solution
Traffic Fragmentation	An attacker may split the intended traffic in to multiple parts and send it to the destination such that IDS/IPS sensors does not generate false positive alert against it.	IDS/IPS sensor completely reassembles the give session to see its entire flow.
Traffic substitution and insertion	An attacker may inject different characters in the legitimate traffic, which may bypass the IDS/IPS sensor but may result in wild actions when interpreted by intended destination machine.	Cisco implements different techniques in like data normalization etc. to look for Unicode, case sensitivity and similar bypassing techniques.
Misinterpretation at protocol level	An attacker may cause sensor to misinterpret the traffic and result in no generation of alert.	Different checksums along with IP time to live (TTL) validation.
Attack variation	An attacker may have some internal support from an organization. Let us say current baseline for specific traffic is set to 1000 packets per second. An attacker may send 800 packets per second to bypass the IDS/IPS sensor.	Uses timely varying policy along with third party correlation.
Sending encrypted data	An attacker may build SSL or IPSec session between itself and victim's device, which will not be interpreted by the IDS/IPS sensor.	Conventional IDS/IPS sensors does not have ability to inspect the encrypted sessions. Latest Sourcefire version of the NGIPS solution has the ability to decrypt and inspect the encrypted session.
Resource utilization	An attacker may be working on hit and trial basis hoping to succeed on launching the intended attack. The sensor may generate an alert for each attempt, which ultimately not only result in resource exhaustion but also become a headache for administration staff who have to address every single generated alert.	Dynamic summarization may generate few alerts for hundreds and thousands of events generated by BOTNET. Sensor may generate alert after regular interval, which may state how many of such attempts have been made since the last alert. It may help in managing the administration work.

Table 6-06: Comparison of Different Techniques to Bypass IDS/IPS

Management and Deployment of Signatures

One of the routine tasks of network security administrators whose job is to tune, deploy and manage the IPS/IDS sensors is to deal with different kinds of signatures. Cisco characterize the signatures in hierarchy based systems. For examples, signatures of same kind will be places in to same group or micro engine. When a packet comes in, all signatures within same micro-engine will be matched simultaneously against the coming packet. The following table summarizes few of the micro-engines, which are relevant to CCNA security exam objectives:

Micro-engine for signatures	Description
Atomic	Signatures designed to analyze single packets instead of stream of packets.
Service	Signatures designed to analyze application layer services.
String or multistring	This category contains signatures, which can compare and match custom patterns inside a single or stream of packets.
Other	Remaining signatures, which may not fit in the above categories.

Table 6-07: Comparison of Signature Micro-Engines

In one of the previous section, risk value and attack severity level (ASR) was defined, which is the property of the signature itself. This value is set by the creator of the signature and it ranges between 0 and 100. The higher value indicates more severity of the attack, represented by the signature.

The Cisco IDS/IPS provides the following four options to tune the initial value of ASR:

- Informational
- Low
- Medium
- High

As the name depicts, *Higher* option weighs selected component more than the remaining options in calculating the overall risk value.

Trigger Actions/Responses

The function or feature, which distinguishes IDS from IPS is whether the sensor deals with the traffic passively (limited to just detection capabilities) or actively (provides protection against threats and attacks).

Here the terms "action" and "response" are used for the reactions of a sensor that can be configured to perform against response to any suspicious activity.

Here are some following terms that define actions or responses that are commonly used in IDS technology:

Alerts

Alert is a generation of log-able message upon every detection of malware or malicious traffic flows. The term "alarm" is also used for this purpose.

Monitor

An IDS can only monitor and analyze traffic, as it cannot prevent an attack from reaching its destination, but it can respond to a suspicious event with the help of other resources like routers and firewalls.

Now here are some following terms, that define actions or responses that are commonly used in IPS technology:

Drop

All those packets that are found to have suspicious payload will be dropped by the sensor. This prevents the suspicious payload from reaching the destination.

Reset

Whenever the sensor detects a suspicious payload with a TCP connection, the sensor will inject TCP resets, which leads to the termination of that particular TCP connection.

Block

The action "reset" is just for the TCP connections, but there are some other protocols as well like UDP and ICMP and attack can be carried out using any other protocol. Therefore, in this situation, IPS uses "block" action to ignore suspicious traffic coming from other protocols rather than TCP.

Shun

If IPS wants the above action of blocking to be performed by some other device like SIEM, then this dynamic action is referred to as Shunning.

Blacklisting

IPS provides network protection by preventing an attack to reach its destination, by enforcing policies, by controlling access to resources and by hardening networking devices. Here in this section, we will discuss about one of the main precautionary features of an IPS sensor, for protecting the network before any attack occurs.

Blacklist or Blacklisting

You can blacklist or deny traffic to and from some particular IP addresses that might cause threat to your network.

Blacklisting can be done in two ways: Statically or Dynamically.

Dynamic Blacklist

IPS helps you to dynamically create a blacklist, with the help of Cisco Collective Security Intelligence Team "Talos" (http://www.talosintel.com/).

It dynamically downloads a collection of IP addresses at regular intervals that have a poor reputation in networking environment.

The feature of Blacklisting in IPS will block matching blacklisted IP address or traffic, in a dynamic blacklist regardless of any other characteristics of the traffic.

Static Blacklist

You can manually define entries of IP addresses in a blacklist or you can manually define a policy, which blacklists an IP, as a response to a rule violation. You can also perform whitelisting. **Whitelisting** is just the opposite of blacklisting, here you allow or permit IP address or traffic of your own choice.

Blacklisting and whitelisting are widely used for security solutions, including IPS, web security, email security, and firewall.

Security Intelligence Operations (SIO) Service

When multiple IPS sensors are used in a network, more granular control and correlation can be performed in case of attacks. In case when information and experience are exchanged with in organizations of same domain, attacks can be correlated in a more defined way. Cisco's Security Intelligence Operations (SIO) is the service used for global correlation in order to have a better protection of networks globally used by Cisco partners.

One of the interesting features of SIO service is the use of dynamic feed (Security Intelligence Feed) from Cisco live servers, which contain list of IPs with poor reputation globally. By blacklisting these IPs, any traffic having one of these IPs either as source or destination address would be rejected even before passing through different policies of IPS/IDS module. Individual IP can also be manually blacklisted with IPS module as per requirements. Similarly, there may be a case when certain IP (being blacklisted by dynamic updates from Security Intelligence Feed) needs to be allowed in current network environment. In such cases, whitelisting capability must be used to allow traffic from certain IP addresses.

IDS/IPS Best Practices

This section explains the industry best practices regarding IDS/IPS deployment and usage:

- IDS/IPS must be implemented so that traffic traversing the critical infrastructure can be analyzed.
- If an organization cannot afford dedicated hardware appliances, then a module or Cisco IOS based feature must be used.
- Global correlation features must be utilized in order to mitigate latest attacks.
- Regular update process must be followed.
- Regular IPS/IDS tuning must be performed.

Cisco Next Generation IPS Solution: With the recent acquisition of *Sourcefire,* Cisco is offering a new series of IPS solutions to its customers under Cisco Next Generation IPS (NGIPS) Solutions. It contains the following products and technologies:

Cisco FirePOWER 8000/7000 series appliances: These products are the foundation members of NGIPS based threat protection solution. Featured with real time context awareness along with intelligent security and automation FirePOWER appliances can also integrates Advanced Malware Protection (AMP) features for enhanced security. The 7000 series is designed for mid-range organizations with limited throughput requirements. The 8000 series is based on modular design with high throughput rate.

Virtual Next Generation IPS (NGIPS v) for VMware: The above defined NGIPS solutions are also available in virtualized format in order to meet the security demands of organizations having virtualized infrastructure.

The ASA with FirePOWER services: The currently available Cisco ASA 5500-X and 5580-X series firewall can also be integrated with FirePOWER NGIPS and AMP technologies in order to have regular security feature like Stateful filtering along with advanced features like full IP stack visibility and control, URL filtering, etc.

FireSIGHT Management Center: The Cisco IPS/IDS sensors can be centrally managed by a number of management solutions. The three main protocols by which IPS sensor can exchange data with management software are *Syslog*, *SNMP* and *Security Device Event Exchange (SDEE).* IPS Manager Express (IME) can be installed on a workstation to monitor up to 10 sensors simultaneously in real time. Similarly, *Cisco Device Manager (CDM)* can also be used to simultaneously monitor 25 sensors in real time. Similarly, the Cisco ASA firewalls with FirePOWER series can be managed by FireSIGHT Management Center. It provides automatic correlation of data gathered from firewalls. This data provides visibility in to end-user's data, (Virtual-Machine) VM-to-VM communication and much more.

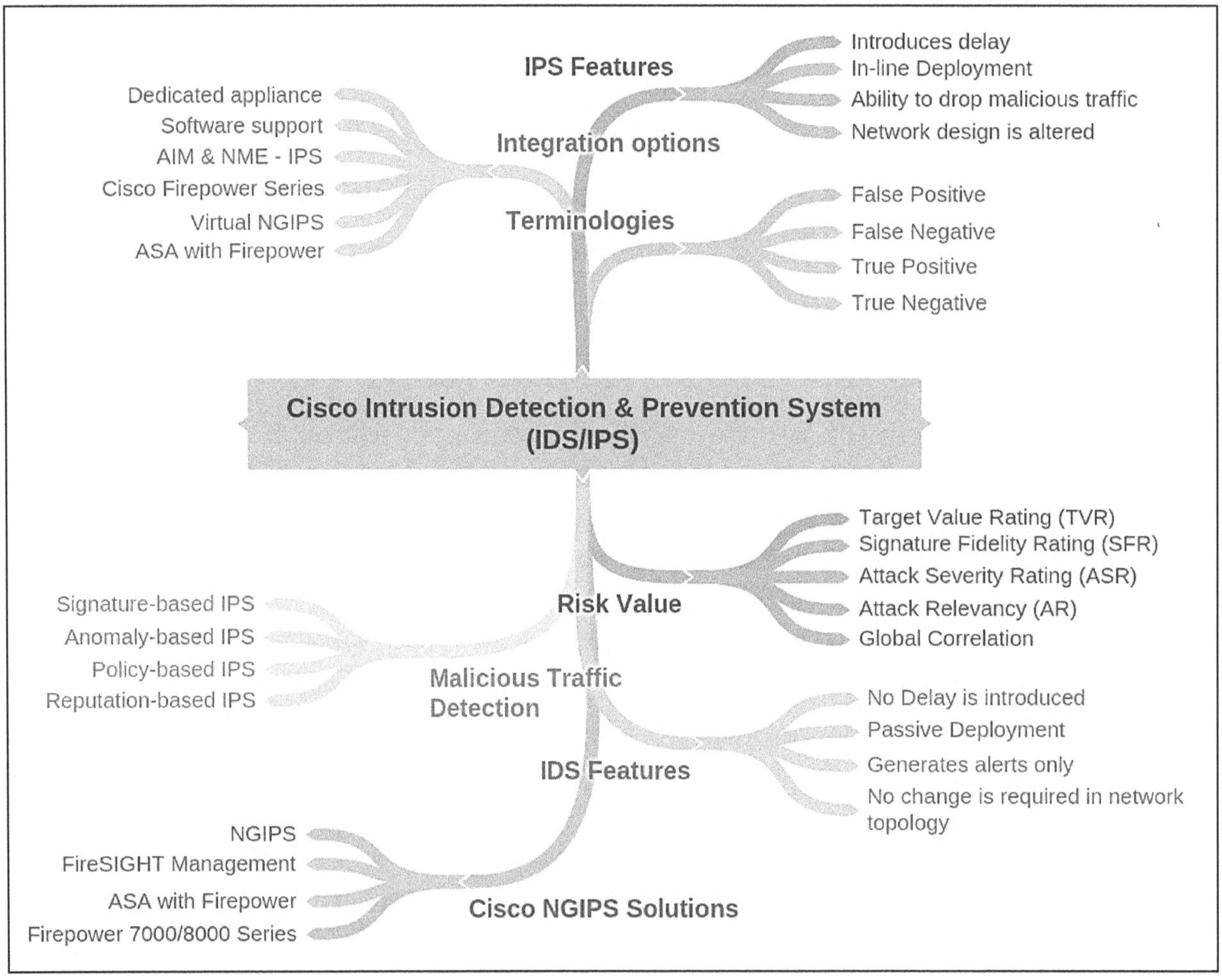

Figure 6-06: IPS/IDS Mind Map

Lab 6-01: Cisco IPS In-line Deployment

Case Study

In order to perform the different concepts learned in theoretical section, the Cisco IDS 4215 will be emulated in virtualized environment. The Cisco IDS 4215 is a 1 RU appliance sensor that delivers 80 Mbps of performance and is suitable for monitoring multiple T1 subnets. The Cisco 4215 IDS Sensor is inline-ready and supports up to five sniffing interfaces in a single 1 RU form factor.

The following topology will be used in this lab:

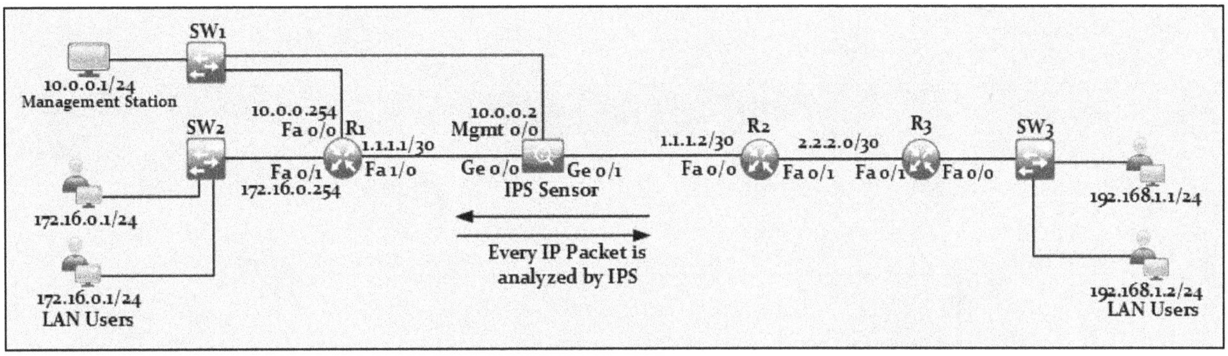

Figure 6-07: Topology Diagram

The scenario above depicts a situation when one segment of LAN within an organization needs more security than other segments. As IPS is configured as inline, no IP address will be configured on its interfaces connected to Router R1 and R2. The only IP address configured on IPS will be for management purposes (GUI access).

IPS Sensor:

In order to configure the management IP address in IPS sensor for GUI access, the following commands will be configured via CLI access. Enter "***cisco***" as username and "***ciscoips123***" as password.

```
IDS-4240# # configure terminal
IDS-4240# (config)# service host
IDS-4240# (config-hos)# network-settings
IDS-4240# (config-hos-net)# host-ip 10.0.0.2/24,10.0.0.254
IDS-4240# (config-hos-net)# access-list 10.0.0.1/32
IDS-4240# (config-hos-net)# exit
```

```
IDS-4240# (config-hos)# exit
Apply Changes?[yes]: yes
```

In the above commands, a management IP address of 10.0.0.2 has been set for IPS GUI access. Note that most of the syntax in IPS module is a little bit different. Complete syntax and features can be explored by consulting the official IPS configuration and deployment guides.

In order to access the IPS GUI, access "https://10.0.0.2" from any available web browser on the management station. The following screen will appear. Select "Run IDM" for web based access.

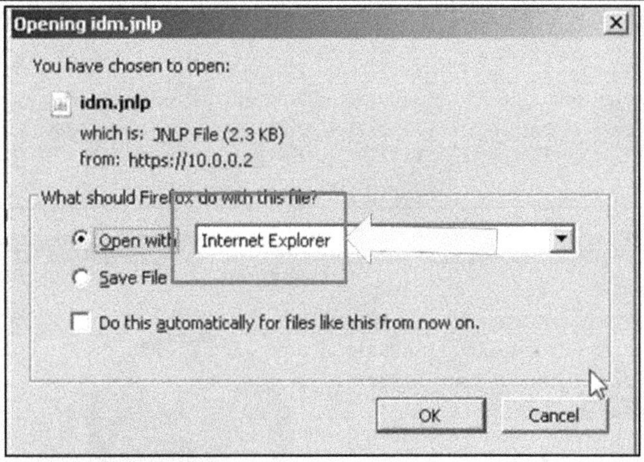

Enter the same credentials used for CLI access for getting GUI via ASDM.

The following dashboard will appear on successful login:

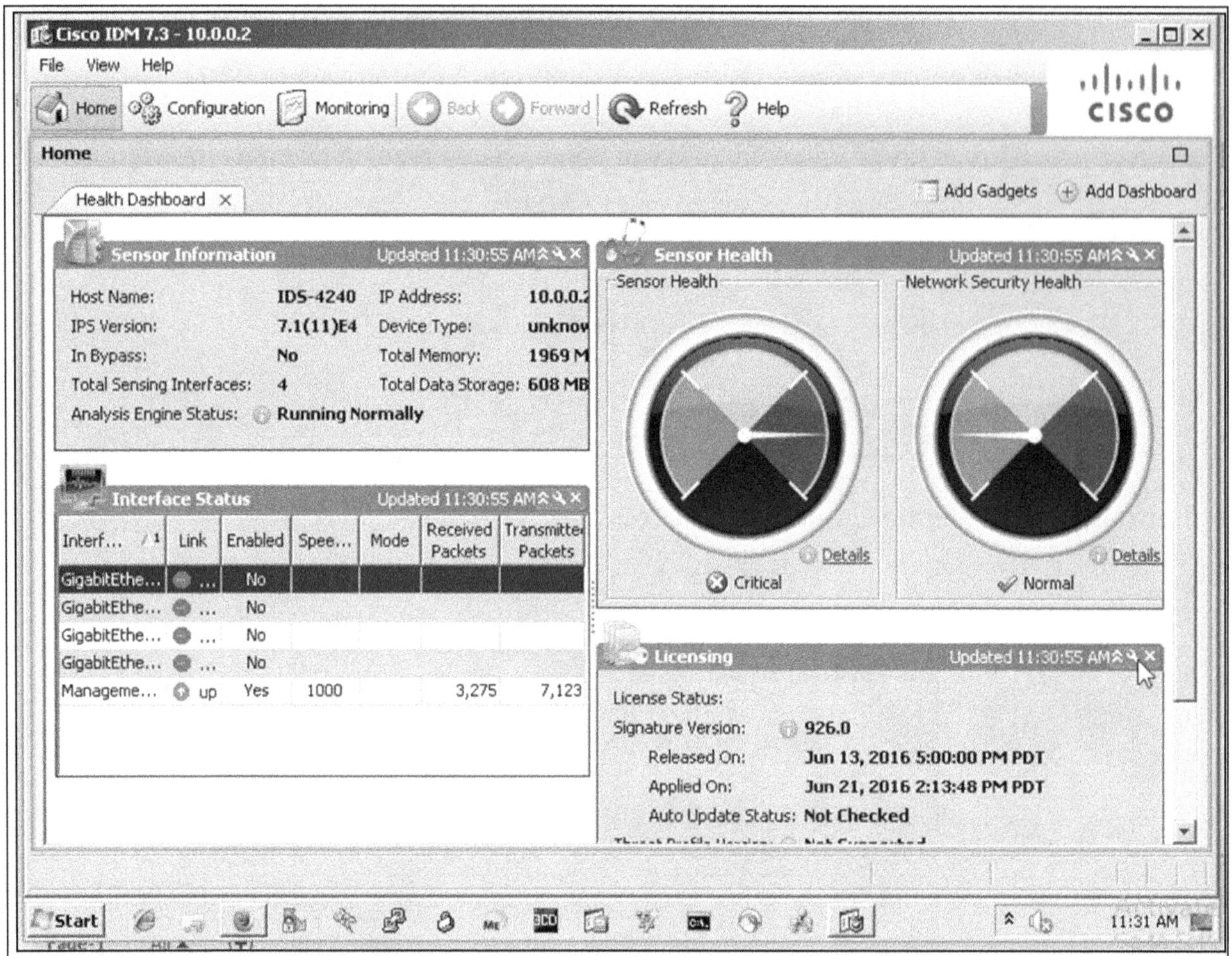

In order to configure the inline configuration for IPS the following CLI commands will be used:

```
IPS4215# config terminal
IPS4215(config)# service interface
IDS-4240(config-int)# physical-interfaces gigabitEthernet0/1
IDS-4240(config-int-phy)# admin-state enabled
IDS-4240(config-int-phy)# exit
IDS-4240(config-int)# physical-interfaces gigabitEthernet0/0
IDS-4240(config-int-phy)# admin-state enabled
IDS-4240(config-int-phy)# exit
```

Above commands make IPS interfaces operational.

```
IPS4215(config-int)# inline-interfaces INLINE
IPS4215(config-int-inl)# interface1 gigabitEthernet0/0
IPS4215(config-int-inl)# interface2 gigabitEthernet0/1
IPS4215(config-int-inl)# exit
IPS4215(config-int)# exit
Apply Changes?[yes]: yes
```

Above commands make a logical pair of interfaces used in current scenario.

```
IPS4215(config)# service analysis-engine
IPS4215(config-ana)# virtual-sensor vs0
IPS4215(config-ana-vir)# logical-interface INLINE
IPS4215(config-ana-vir)# exit
IPS4215(config-ana)# exit
Apply Changes?[yes]: yes
```

Above commands assign the logical pair to virtual sensor "vso".

Now LAN user from both ends should be able to ping each other.

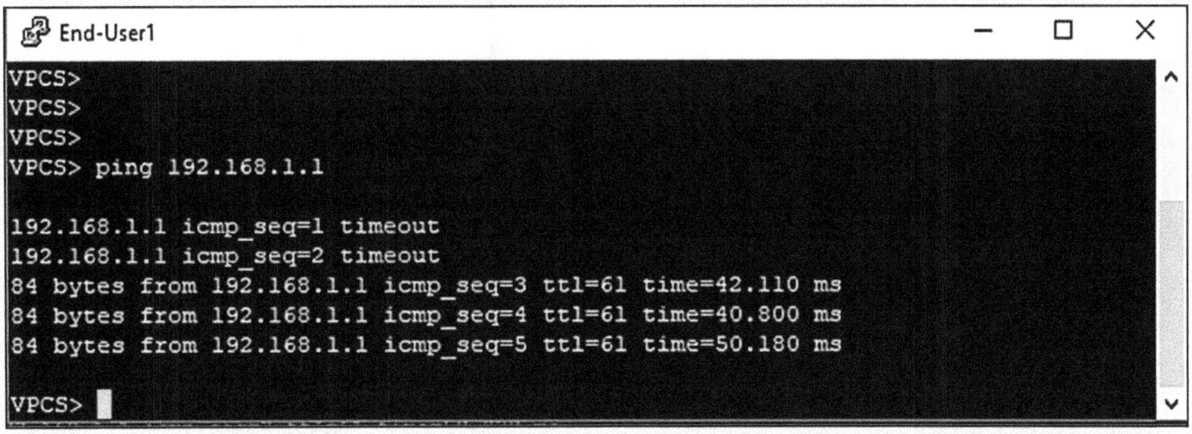
End-User1
VPCS>
VPCS>
VPCS>
VPCS> ping 192.168.1.1
192.168.1.1 icmp_seq=1 timeout
192.168.1.1 icmp_seq=2 timeout
84 bytes from 192.168.1.1 icmp_seq=3 ttl=61 time=42.110 ms
84 bytes from 192.168.1.1 icmp_seq=4 ttl=61 time=40.800 ms
84 bytes from 192.168.1.1 icmp_seq=5 ttl=61 time=50.180 ms
VPCS>

For configuration via GUI, click "Configuration" button to access different configurable options of IPS.

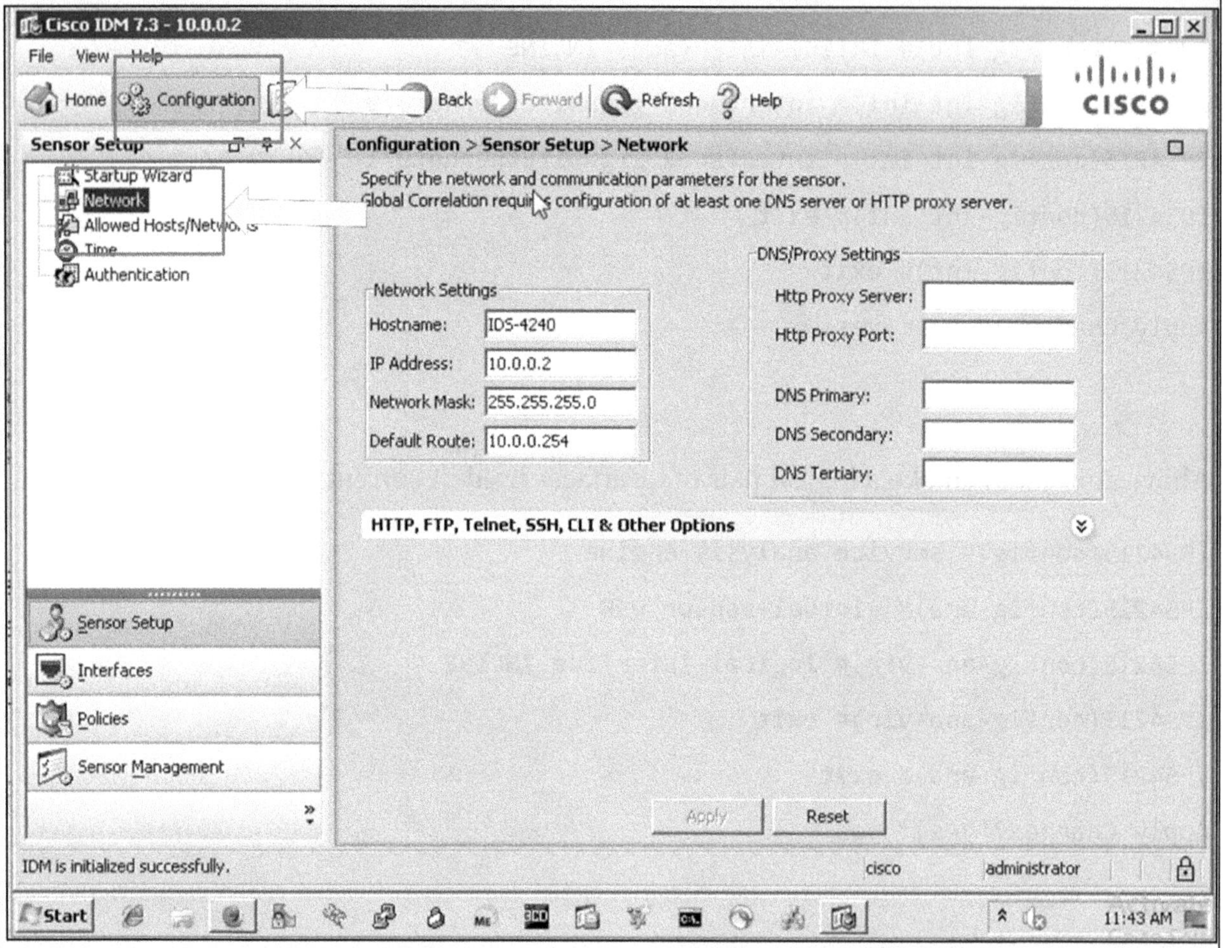

The figure shown above shows the management IP settings of IPS. Similarly, different features of IPS can be accessed and configured from different tables shown on the left side of the above figure.

Practice Questions:

1. Which of the following attacks exploits the weakness of any software that are unknown to the software vendor/developer?
   A. Man-in-the-Middle Attack
   B. Zero-Day Attack
   C. MAC Overflow
   D. ARP Spoofing
   E. STP Attack

2. What are the two common characteristics of the IDS and the IPS? (Choose any two)
   A. Both analyze copies of network traffic.
   B. Both mitigate the network attacks either actively or passively.
   C. Both are deployed as sensors.
   D. Both use signatures to detect malicious traffic.
   E. Both of them are placed in line with the network

3. Which of the followings are two limitations of an IDS? (Choose any two)
   A. The IDS analyzes actual forwarded packets.
   B. The IDS has great impact on traffic.
   C. The IDS works offline using copies of network traffic.
   D. The IDS requires other devices to respond to attacks.
   E. The IDS does not stop malicious traffic.

4. Where can an IDS/IPS be placed?
   A. In Inside Zone
   B. In Outside Zone
   C. In DMZ Zone
   D. All of the above

5. Which of the followings is the limitation of network-based IPS as compared to host-based IPS?
   A. Network-based IPS is less cost-effective.
   B. Network-based IPS should not be used with multiple operating systems.
   C. Network-based IPS does not detect lower level network events.
   D. Network-based IPS cannot analyze encrypted traffic.

6. In which of the following terminologies is a sensor that generates an alert about the traffic, which is not malicious, but requires serious attention as long as security is concerned?
   A. True Negative
   B. False Positive
   C. False Negative
   D. True Positive

7. In which of the following terminologies is a malicious activity that is detected by the IPS module or sensor and for which an alert will be generated?
   A. True Negative
   B. False Positive
   C. False Negative
   D. True Positive

8. Which of the followings is a tool or technique for malicious traffic detection?
   A. Signature based IDS/IPS
   B. Policy based IDS/IPS
   C. Anomaly based IDS/IPS
   D. All of the above

9. Which one of the followings is the characteristic of Reputation Based IDS/IPS?
   A. To detect lower level network events.
   B. To collect the information from the systems participating in global correlation and filter out sites or URLs with bad reputation.
   C. To define security policies on the networking devices.
   D. To analyze specific string or behavior in a single packet or stream of packets to detect the anomaly.

10. Which of the following actions or responses are commonly used in IDS technology? (Choose any two)
   A. Drop
   B. Alert
   C. Reset
   D. Monitor
   E. Block

11. Which of the following actions define actions or responses that are commonly used in IPS technology?
    A. Drop
    B. Reset
    C. Block
    D. Shun
    E. All of the above

12. Which of the following micro-engines designs a signature to analyze a single packet instead of stream of packets?
    A. Atomic
    B. Service
    C. String or multistring
    D. None of the above

13. Which of the followings is a part of digital signature and determines the critical level of an attack?
    A. Attack Relevancy (AR)
    B. Global Correlation
    C. Attack Severity Rating (ASR)
    D. Signature Fidelity Rating (SFR)

14. What is a disadvantage of a pattern-based detection mechanism?
    A. The normal network traffic pattern will be disturbed.
    B. It cannot detect unknown attacks.
    C. It is not scalable.
    D. Its configuration is complex.

15. Which of the following features of an IPS provides regular threat updates from the Cisco Network database?
    A. Simple Network Monitoring Protocol (SNMP)
    B. Event Correlation
    C. Global Correlation
    D. IPS Manager Express

16. In which mode of deployment will a copy of every data packet be sent to the sensor

to analyze if there is any malicious activity?
A. Promiscuous or passive mode
B. Inline mode
C. Tap mode
D. None of the above

17. In which of the following configured modes will the whole IP traffic be dropped, in case of sensor failure?
A. 'fail-close' mode
B. 'fail-open' mode
C. Both of them
D. None of the above

18. Which of the following options helps you to create a blacklist, with the help of Cisco Collective Security Intelligence Team "Talos"?
A. Static Blacklist
B. Dynamic Blacklist
C. Hybrid Blacklist
D. None of the above

19. The technique in which you allow or permit IP address or traffic of your own choice is referred to as ______________.
A. Blacklisting
B. Whitelisting
C. Greylisting
D. None of the above

20. Which of the followings is a limitation of an IPS?
A. It introduces delay because every packet is analyzed before forwarded to destination.
B. IPS does not respond immediately to an attack.
C. It works passively.
D. None of the above.

21. Which of the following techniques does IPS provide for network protection by preventing an attack to reach its destination?

A. By enforcing policies.
B. By controlling access to resources.
C. By hardening networking devices.
D. All of the above.
E. None of the above.

Chapter 07: Content & Endpoint Security

Technology Brief

In the previous chapter, we have discussed about the core concepts of Intrusion Detection System (IDS) and Intrusion Prevention System (IPS), which deal with the detection and prevention of malicious traffic inside your network.

In this evolution of technological world where cyber threat and attacks are evolving side by side, additional security precautions should be taken for the safety of confidential assets of an organization. This chapter deals with the security perspectives and services running on the endpoints. It is really important to enforce security at the endpoint, because all the confidential data resides there and the potential for damage is high there as well. Endpoints can include devices such as laptops, mobile devices, and printers.

Mitigation Technology for E-mail Based Threats

E-mail and web services are used globally. Some applications like *CRM, ERP, SAP,* etc. may depend heavily over the web connectivity. The *E-mail Security Appliance (ESA)* and *Web Security Appliance (WSA)* are the two most used featured Cisco products in this regard. By using cloud based security intelligence along with some advanced features like *Advanced Malware Protection (AMP), ESA* and *WSA* can help the network and system engineers to mitigate and protect against the latest threats and attacks. Many other vendors as MacAfee and Kaspersky are also providing *Data Leakage Prevention (DLP)* and anti-malware filtering software based solutions, which are also popular along with Cisco's products in this domain.

This section starts with identifying different E-mail based threats followed by protection mechanism against them.

Email Based Threats: Some of the common types of E-mail based threats found in today's networks are:

- **Spams:** They are one of the common used methods by which backdoor executable program and malware is injected in local or network based end-points. A spam can be an E-mail with malicious content. It can be categorized based on its subject or files attached to E-mail, etc.

- **Malware Attachments:** Any kind of malware or malicious executed program, attached to an E-mail.
- **Phishing:** As explained in the earlier chapters, phishing tries to get login credentials by manipulating the end-user by presenting different links, which looks legitimate, for example presenting fake social web pages. Sometimes, attackers gather some important information of targeted employees of specific organization and then generate more directed phishing attacks. This is the example of *Spear Phishing*. When phishing attack is directed towards the high-end employees like *Chief Technical Officer (CTO)* etc. then it is called *Whaling*.

Cisco E-mail Security Appliance (ESA)

The Cisco's E-mail Security Appliance (ESA) is a SMTP firewall, which does threat monitoring and protects the E-mail infrastructure by filtering out the malicious and suspected E-mails. ESA is placed as the first server that is directly connected to the internet for the incoming E-mails and placed as the last server for the outgoing E-mails over the internet.

Cisco ESA Series

The following table summarizes different variants of ESA series.

Cisco ESA series	Ideal for
Cisco X1070	Service providers and large-scale enterprise environment
Cisco C680	Service providers and large-scale enterprise environment
Cisco C670	Medium sized enterprise environment
Cisco C380	Medium sized enterprise environment
Cisco C370	Small to medium sized enterprise environment
Cisco C170	Small Office/Home Office (SOHO) environment

Table 7-01: Cisco ESA Series

Just like Cisco, Layer 3 and Layer 2 devices have an IOS providing the different features of routing, switching and security, the Cisco ESA runs *AsyncOS* on them, which provides many features to mitigate E-mail based threats and attacks. Following are the few features provided by AsyncOS running on ESA devices:

- **Access Control:** Just like *Access-List,* Access Control provides inbound control by using either sender's IP address/subnet or domain name.

- **Anti-spam:** Powered by Cisco research group *Talos*, anti-spam is a multilayer protection filter based on Cisco SenderBase Reputation feature.
- **Network Antivirus:** Partnership with Sophos and MacAfee® for integration of their scanning engines allow antivirus scanning capabilities at the edge of network.
- **AMP and DLP features:** Data Loss Prevention (DLP) helps to prevent any critical digital asset from leaving the corporate network by monitoring the outbound traffic. Similarly, AMP feature helps to mitigate against latest threats and attacks.
- **E-mail Encryption:** The network management team can utilize the encryption feature for outbound E-mails. Based on the SOP of an organization, network administrator can implement multiple features related to encryption key on *ESA*.
- **E-mail Authentication:** *ESA* can use multiple authentication mechanism to verify the authenticity of coming E-mails. Some of them are Sender Policy Framework (SPF), Sender ID Framework (SIDF), and Domain Keys Identified Mail (DKIM) for incoming as well as outgoing E-mails.
- **Outbreak Filters:** This feature provides mitigation against latest security outbreaks by using Cisco's threat intelligence information.

The Cisco ESA uses listeners, an E-mail processing/filtering service bind to an interface of ESA, to handle the SMTP connection requests. Listeners can be:

- **Public:** i.e. service to handle E-mails coming from internet.
- **Private:** E-mails generated within the corporate network; for example, E-mails from HR department to employees of other departments within same organization.

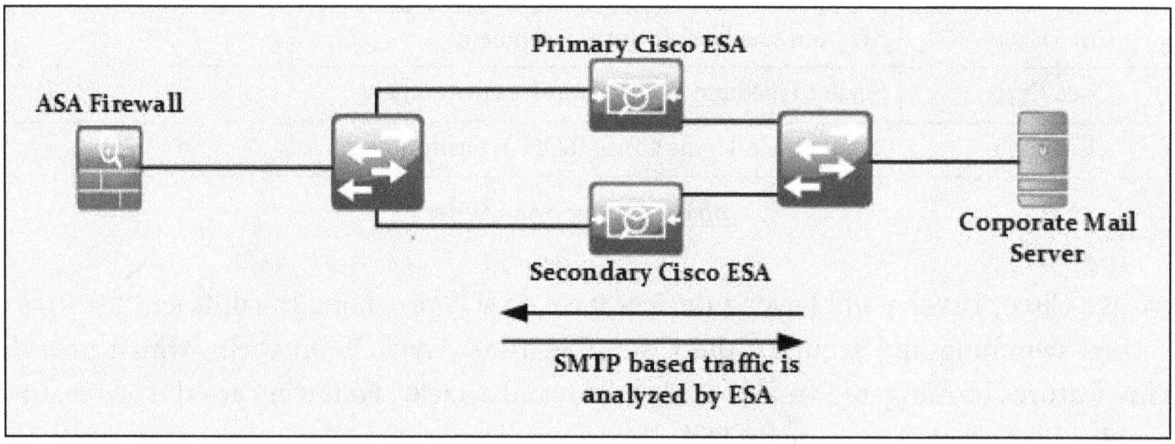

Figure 7-01: ESA Deployment Scenario

As shown in the figure above, we used two ESA devices in order to provide redundancy or failover. To enable listener service on an interface, the following information needs to be provided:

- Specific interface name of ESA along with TCP port number
- Listeners type i.e. either public or private
- By using Access control feature, host filtering is applied to allow limited hosts to be able to connect to the listener
- The local domain name for which listeners can accept requests

Cisco Cloud and Hybrid E-mail Security Solutions

Organizations can outsource the services of E-mail security from Cisco by using either cloud or hybrid based E-mail security solution.

In **cloud security solution**, multiple instances of E-mail security service are provided in Cisco Data Centers. Some organizations have their own regulations, which may require critical digital assets to remain within the premises.

Cisco has also catered this situation by providing **hybrid E-mail security solutions,** which require deployment of multiple ESAs within the premises. Hybrid E-mail security solution also provides advanced malware protection along with some great features like Data Leakage/loss Prevention and encryption

Spam Filtering

There are two ways to avoid spamming E-mails and overcome phishing attacks: reputation-based filtering and context-based filtering.

Reputation-Based Filtering

Reputation based filtering provides the basic level of filtering by comparing the source IP address of the E-mail server and compares it with the reputation data downloaded from Cisco's collective security intelligence team. This type of filtering relies on the reputation of the server, if a server is a known spam sender; it becomes easier to conclude that the E-mail coming from that server is a spam. Similar filters can be implemented to the E-mails carrying viruses and other threats.

Context-Based Filtering

Content based filtering inspects the entire mail, including message contents, analyzing details such as sender identity, its source, its destination, embedded URLs, attachments and E-mails formatting by using algorithms. It identifies spam messages without blocking the legitimate E-mail.

Advanced Malware Protection

Cisco Advanced Malware Protection (AMP) provides control over malware detection and blocking. It provides continuous analysis of data to detect, analyze, track, confirm and mitigate threats before, during and after an attack. The features of Cisco AMP include the followings:

File Reputation

It gets the information from Cisco cloud based intelligence service named as TALOS, for a reputation verdict of an IP or traffic. Here the malicious traffic will automatically be blocked. File reputation service is updated after every 3 to 5 minutes.

File Sandboxing

It analyzes unknown files that are traversing the Cisco E-mail security gateway. It gathers details about a file's behavior to determine the file's threat level and it sends the results to Cisco cloud based intelligence service named as TALOS, which then updates the treat and its mitigations globally.

File Retrospection

It analyzes and solves the problem of malicious files that pass through the E-mail security gateway but might later cause a threat. Sometimes, even the most advanced techniques may fail to identify malware at the perimeter as malicious files simply wait until they are inside the network to start their malicious work.

E-mail Data Loss Prevention (DLP)

In case of E-mail security, Data Loss Prevention (DLP) is a content level scanning of messages and attachments in an email, to detect either the transport for sensitive data is appropriate or not. Sensitive content may include personal identifiers such as credit cards or Social Security numbers or corporate intellectual property like internal or confidential documents etc.

A new category is defined named as **Personally Identifiable Information (PII),** which contains personal and financial account information like personal names, addresses, and telephone numbers, payment card numbers, bank routing numbers, government ID numbers, and healthcare records.

Data encryption provides satisfactory protection in this case but Cisco's DLP features provide a set of rules for identifying different classes of data, or defining your own classes, and taking action on the messages according to the need and demand.

Blacklisting

IPS provides network protection by preventing an attack to reach its destination, by enforcing policies, by controlling access to resources and by hardening networking devices. Here in this section, we will discuss about one of the main pre-cautionary features of an IPS sensor, for protecting the network before any attack occurs.

You can blacklist or deny traffic to and from some particular IP addresses that might cause threat to your network.

Blacklisting can be done in two ways:

1. Statically
2. Dynamically

Dynamic Blacklist

IPS helps you to dynamically create a blacklist, with the help of Cisco Collective Security Intelligence Team "Talos". It dynamically downloads a collection of IP addresses at regular intervals that have a poor reputation in networking environment.

The feature of Blacklisting in IPS will block matching blacklisted IP address or traffic, in a dynamic blacklist regardless of any other characteristics of the traffic.

Static Blacklist

You can manually define entries of IP addresses in a blacklist or you can manually define a policy, which blacklists an IP, as a response to a rule violation. You can also perform whitelisting. **Whitelisting** is just the opposite of blacklisting, here you allow or permit IP address or traffic of your own choice.

Blacklisting and whitelisting are widely used for security solutions, including IPS, web security, E-mail security, and firewall.

E-mail Encryption

E-mail encryption involves the encryption of actual E-mail content so that only receiver has the ability to decrypt and read the message. The following things must be made sure for effective protection of E-mails:

- The connection to E-mail server must use encryption.
- The content of E-mail must be encrypted.
- Stored, cached or archived E-mail messages should also be encrypted.

Here are some techniques to authenticate and encrypt E-mail messages and make them more secure:

Digital Signature

Digital Signature is a technique to evaluate the authenticity of digital documents as signature authenticated the authenticity of a document. Digital Signature ensures the author of the document, date and time of signing. It authenticates the content of the message.

There are two categories of Digital Signatures:

1. Direct Digital Signature
2. Arbitrated Digital Signature

Direct Digital Signature

Direct Digital Signatures involves only sender and receiver of the message assuming that receiver has sender's Public Key. The sender may sign entire message or hash with the private key and send it towards the destination. The receiver decrypts it using the Public Key.

Arbitrated Digital Signature

Arbitrated Digital Signatures involves a third-party called "Trusted Arbiter". The role of this Arbiter is to validate the signed messages, insert date and then send it to the recipient. It requires a suitable level of trust and can implement with either Public or Private Key.

SSL and TLS for Secure Communication

The terms SSL (Secure Socket Layer) and TLS (Transport Layer Security) are often used interchangeably, and provide encryption and authentication of data in motion. These protocols are intended for a scenario where users want secured communication over an unsecured network like the public internet. Most common applications of such protocols are web browsing, Voice over IP (VOIP), and electronic mail.

There are many commercial as well as free E-mail encryption software programs are available. Some of them are:

- Pretty Good Privacy (PGP)
- GNU Privacy Guard (GnuPG)
- Web-based E-mail encryption services

Pretty Good Privacy (PGP)

OpenPGP is the most widely used E-mail encryption standard. It is defined by the OpenPGP Working Group of the Internet Engineering Task Force (IETF) as a Proposed Standard in RFC 4880. OpenPGP is derived from the PGP software, created by Phil Zimmermann. The main purpose of OpenPGP is to ensure an end-to-end encryption over E-mail communication; it also provides message encryption and decryption and password manager, data compression and digital signing.

Mitigation Technology for Web Based Threats

As explained earlier in this chapter, network administrators need to take some additional pre-cautionary steps to protect critical information from being effected by malwares. Cisco's Cloud based Web Security (CWS) along with Cisco Web Security Appliance (WSA) help in this regard by providing continuous monitoring and detection of latest malware and other threats.

Cloud Based Web Security (CWS)

As the name depicts, organizations having Cisco's cloud based web security, gets their web access being monitored and scanned for any kind of threat via Cisco Cloud based web proxy services. Organizations connected to CWS either use *Proxy Auto Configuration (PAC)* installed on user endpoints or through integration with the following Cisco devices:

- Cisco ISR G2 Routers
- Cisco ASA
- Cisco WSA
- Cisco AnyConnect Secure Mobility Client

One of the major advantages of using the CWS is minimum hardware deployment at customer's premises. The following figure explains a scenario in which an organization is utilizing CWS functionality via integration with Cisco ASA:

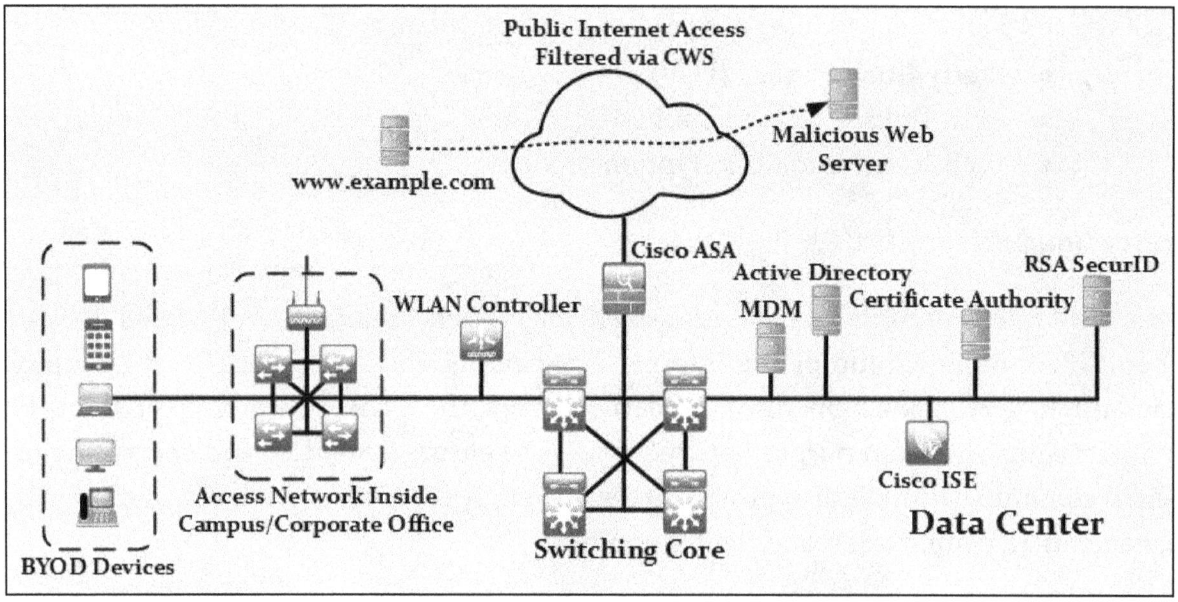

Figure 7-02: CWS Deployment Scenario

Consider a scenario where an internal client makes HTTP request to www.example.com. ASA will send the intended request to Cisco CWS, which acts as proxy for all HTTP traffic. Assume www.example.com has some re-direction to malicious web server as shown in above figure. By inspecting the overall session, the internal client will be kept safe from any malicious traffic being sent towards internal client from *www.example.com*.

Cisco Web Security Appliance (WSA)

Powered by Cisco cloud based intelligence, a service provided by Cisco research group named as *TALOS*, WSA provides protection before, during and after an attack.

The Cisco WSA uses *Web Cache Communication Protocol (WCCP),* a proprietary protocol, to be deployed in the following modes:

Explicit proxy mode: The end-devices are explicitly configured to send HTTP traffic towards WSA. Just like normal web proxy, WSA acts as an intermediary device, makes another connection to intended destination and after inspection, sends the response to end-devices. The following figure shows the WSA deployment in explicit proxy mode:

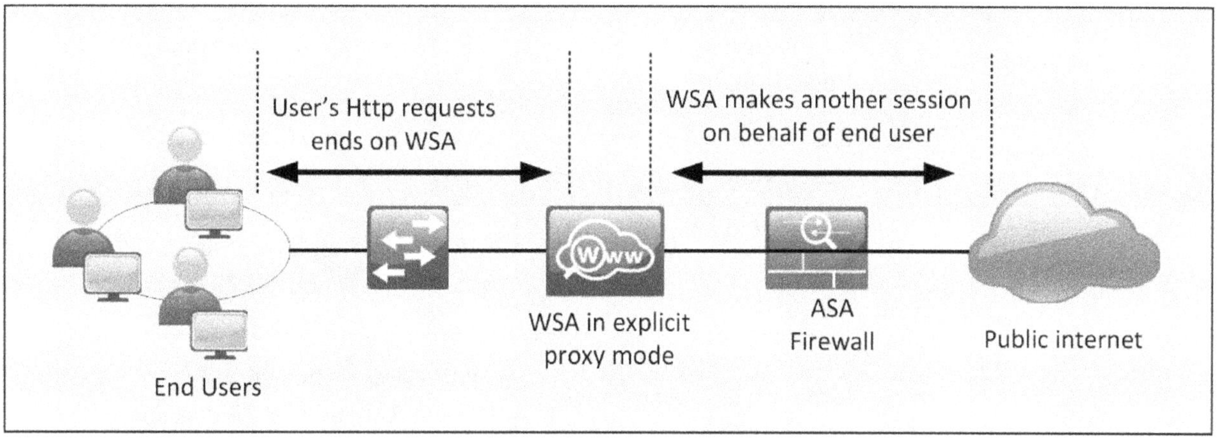

Figure 7-03: WSA Deployment in Explicit Proxy Mode

Transparent Proxy Mode: The end-device becomes unaware of WSA as no configuration will be done on it. The First-Hop is configured to re-direct the HTTP requests towards WSA, which in return makes another connect on end-user's behalf. The following figure shows the WSA deployment in transparent mode:

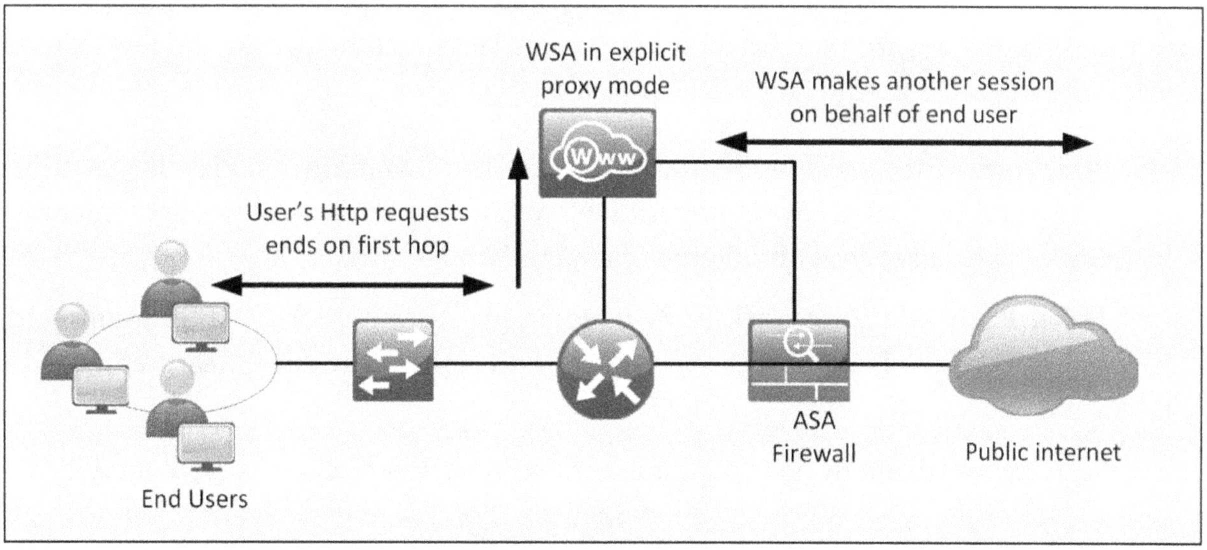

Figure 7-04: WSA Deployment in Transparent Proxy Mode

Cisco Web Security Appliance Series

The following table summarizes different variants of WSA series:

Cisco WSA series	Ideal for	Device Specifications
Cisco WSA S680	Large scale enterprise environment with end-users ranging up to 12000.	2 Rack-Unit appliance with 16 CPUs, 32 GB of RAM and 2.7 TB disk space.
Cisco WSA S670	Large scale enterprise environment with end-users ranging up to 12000.	2 Rack-Unit appliance with 8 CPUs, 8 GB of RAM and 2.7 TB disk space.
Cisco WSA S380	Medium sized enterprise environment with end-users ranging up to 6000.	2 Rack-Unit appliance with 6 CPUs, 16 GB of RAM and 2.4 TB disk space.
Cisco WSA S370	Medium sized enterprise environment with end-users ranging up to 6000.	2 Rack-Unit appliance with 4 CPUs, 4 GB of RAM and 1.8 TB disk space.
Cisco WSA S170	Small to medium sized enterprise environment with end-users ranging up to 1500.	1 Rack-Unit appliance with 2 CPUs, 4 GB of RAM and 500 GB disk space.

Table 7-02: WSA Series

Cisco Layer 2 and Layer 3 devices have an IOS providing the different features of routing, switching and security. Similarly, Cisco WSA runs *AsyncOS* on them, which provides many features to mitigate Web based threats and attacks. Followings are the few features provided by AsyncOS running on WSA devices:

- **Adaptive Anti-Malware Scanning:** WSA uses scanning engines for malware detection in traffic. By configuration, WSA can dynamically select malware scanning engine based on different characteristics of traffic.
- **Third-Party DLP Integration**: By integration, other vendor's DLP solutions with WSA, deep content inspection along with other advanced features can be achieved.
- **File Reputation:** By getting information from Cisco cloud based intelligence service, run by research group named as TALOS, file reputation service gets updated after every 3 to 5 minutes.
- **File Sandboxing:** When certain malware is detected, WSA puts the file in sandbox to inspect its behavior for finalizing its threat level. Powered by Cisco Cognitive Threat Analytics (CTA), which uses machine-learning algorithms, WSA has ability to adapt over the time to provide protection against latest threats and attacks.
- **Continuous Inspection:** When certain malware is detected, WSA continues to examine that file for longer duration to predict its final behavior.

- **Application Level Visibility:** By getting visibility up to application level, network security administrators can block different applications as per organization's SOP. For example, social sites like Facebook® can be allowed but a more granular control allows disabling sub-features like Facebook® games.

Here are some additional techniques to mitigate the level of web-based threats:

URL Filtering

For providing a more granular web security, URL filtering can be performed. URL filtering controls the access of URLs by comparing addresses of sites that users are attempting to visit against a database carrying URL list of either permitted or blocked sites. The purpose of URL filtering is to prevent access of the malicious sites, which may introduce malware or threat in the network.

Here are some actions associated with the URL filtering policy:

- **Blocked**- This action can be applied to the distracting websites like local news, social media, or to the sites known to have various forms of malware.
- **Allowed**- This action can be applied to websites relevant to the organization and its workflow.
- **Blocked or Allowed URL Categories**- When actions are applied by the category not on a site-by-site basis. This might include categories for malware or phishing sites, innocent but distracting sites, or questionable sites.

URL Categorization

URL Categorization controls the user access to specific website category. This feature enables networking device to filter web traffic by using a categorization database. The database contains millions or billions of URLs classified into different categories, such as news media, social networking, gambling, adult content, shopping and entertainment. Further, each URL has a specific reputation score regularly updated and maintained by Cisco Collective Security Intelligence Team "Talos" (http://www.talosintel.com/) in dynamic databases.

In order to filter traffic according to the organization's need, you can configure advanced policies based on categories or category groups. For example, you can restrict access to malicious sites (sites known to be infected with malware), and you can restrict access to content such as adult content, terrorism or content related to violence, illegal drugs or site with low reputation scores, etc.

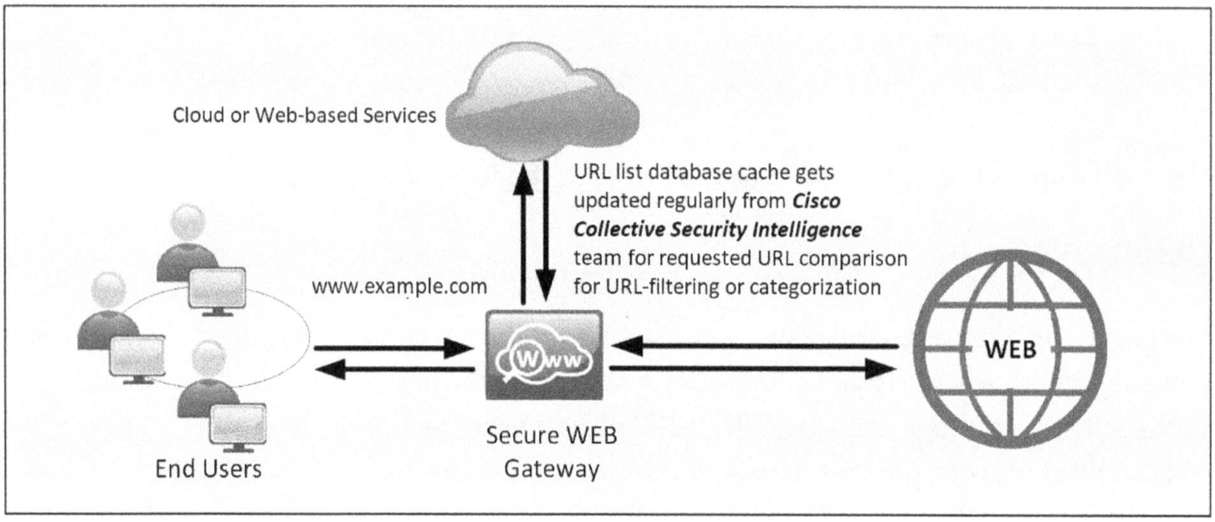

Figure 7-05: URL Filtering or URL Categorization

Web Application Filtering

End-users rely upon different applications every day, that's how they get connected with the company and their job. However, these applications are considered to be one of the threats that could be exploited by an attacker. Web application filtering protects your web or mobile applications from being compromised and prevents data from breaching.

Web application filtering can be done by either defining filtering policy or by using Web Application Firewall (WAF).

Application Filtering Through Access Rules and Policy

Web application filtering can be performed by using Access Control Policy, which identifies and filters the specific application running within the corporate network. Access Control Policy compares the particular application with the defined access control policy; it makes the process of blocking easier, as it only blocks specific applications without disturbing desired applications. Application filtering also offers granular control over some application by blocking features of the application instead of blocking the complete application. For example, Blocking Chat or Upload option in any application.

Web Application Firewall

A Web Application Firewall monitors, filters or blocks data packets as they travel to and from a web application. WAF protects web applications by monitoring and filtering http traffic between the internet and web application. It provides protection against web-based attacks like cross-site scripting (XSS), SQL injection, file inclusion, cross-site forgery etc. WAF provides defense to layer 7, so it does not provide protection against other attacks. WAF works as a shield between web application and the internet.

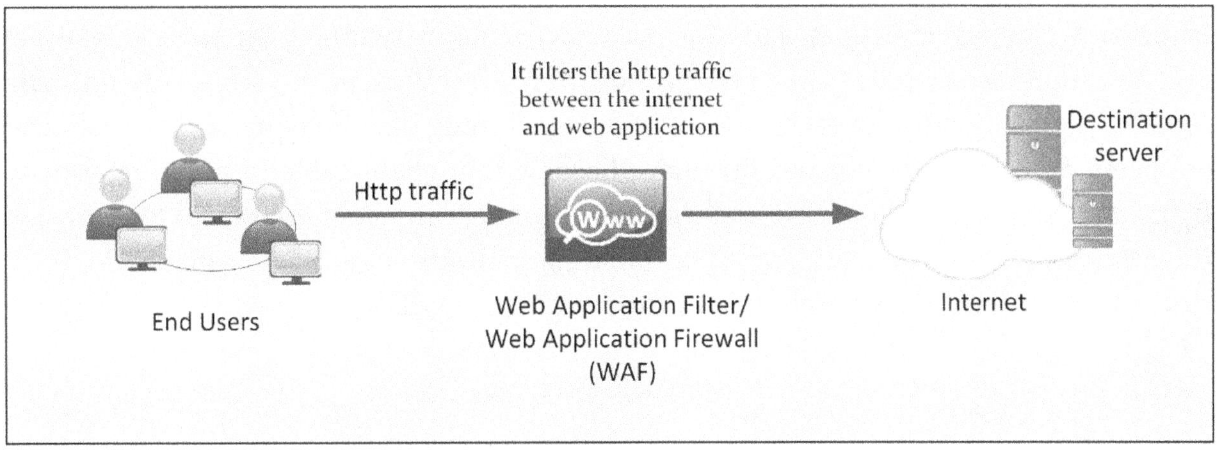

Figure 7-06: Web Application Filtering

Here is the list of some of the vendors proving web application security features in their devices:

- Barracuda Networks – Barracuda Web filter
- Cisco – IronPort Web Security Appliance
- EdgeWave – iPrism Web Security
- Fortinet – FortiWeb Web Application Firewall
- McAfee – WebShield
- McAfee – Web Gateway
- Radware – AppWall
- Sophos – Web Security and Control
- Squid – Squid
- Symantec – Symantec Web Gateway
- Trend Micro – InterScan Web Security Suite
- Trustwave – WebDefend
- Websense – Websense

Malware scanning

Malware scanning is the process of identification of a malware until ensuring that the malware is completely removed. This process includes observing the behavior of the malware, scoping the potential threat to a system, and finding other measures. The major goal of malware scanning and analysis is to gain detailed information and observe the behavior of the malware, to maintain incident response, and take defensive actions to secure the organization.

In order to detect malwares and stay protected from networking threats, a malware scanner shout be installed on every workstation of end-users, it is one of the main security pre-caution for an end-user. With every coming day, millions of new malwares are being detected thus, our websites have become more vulnerable to malware attacks. By using a malware scanner, users and website owners can detect malwares and prevent them from harming their devices. By installing a malware scanner, you may reduce the risk of hackers finding your website and attacking it.

Here is the list of some free anti-malware software:

- Comodo Antivirus
- Malwarebytes Anti-Malware
- BitDefender Antivirus Free Edition
- Emsisoft
- Adaware Antivirus

TLS/SSL Decryption

TSL/SSL decryption is used to convert encrypted traffic into plain text traffic, so that you can then apply policies over it like URL filtering, intrusion and malware control, and other services that require deep packet inspection. The SSL decryption policy cannot be applied to unencrypted traffic; it applies just to the encrypted traffic. The traffic will be re-encrypted before it leaves the device.

Data encryption enables lack of visibility to analyze the type of network traffic. Although it provides data security, but it also increases the risk, as potential attacker can use an encrypted connection to hide his malicious activities just like Man-in-the-Middle attack.

Here the TLS/SSL decryption inspects every encrypted packed and applies security policies to the traffic in order to detect if there is any malicious content. TLS/SSL decryption performs the following actions:

- It blocks hidden malware in encrypted SSL/TLS traffic
- It detects and blocks intrusion attempts from an attacker
- It restricts confidential data from loss, hence provides Data Loss Prevention (DLP)
- It defines the rules and policies to allow or block specific application or data
- It monitors outgoing data

Cisco Content Security Management Appliance

Cisco Security Management Appliance (SMA) is a Cisco product, which can be used for centralized management and reporting of multiple ESA or WSA devices spanning geographically over different regions of the world.

The following table summarizes different variants of SMA series.

Cisco SMA series	Ideal for
Cisco SMA M680	Large scale enterprise environment with end-users up to 10,000.
Cisco SMAV M600v	Service providers and large scale enterprise environment.
Cisco SMA M380	Medium to large scale enterprise environment with end-users ranging from 1000 to 10,000.
Cisco SMAV M300v	Medium to large scale enterprise environment with end-users ranging from 1000 to 5,000.
Cisco SMA M170	Small to medium sized enterprise environment with end-users up to 1000.
Cisco SMAV M100v	Small to medium sized enterprise environment with end-users up to 1000.

Table 7-03: SMA Series

Mitigation Technology for Endpoint Threats

The First Computer Virus

The first computer virus named as "**Brain**" was released in its first form in January 1986 for MS-DOS. The virus Brain was planned and prepared by two brothers, Basit Farooq Alvi and Amjad Farooq Alvi, from Lahore, Punjab, Pakistan. Since its invention in

1986, the sophistication and impact of computer virus or worms has increased with the evolving technology.

Apart from Cisco, various vendors have released their anti-virus and anti-malware solutions. Examples include anti-virus products from Norton®, Kaspersky®, Bitdefender®, etc. Before understanding different mitigation techniques, common types of malicious malwares must be discussed, which are:

- **Computer Viruses:** An executable software program, which may be designed to perform number of possible functions like erasing data, stealing digital assets, etc.
- **Worms:** They are the special type of viruses that spread over the network thus infecting multiple vulnerable systems.
- **Logic Bombs:** An executable malicious code injected into a legitimate application or program. Sometimes a logic bomb has ability to destroy itself after performing the malicious activity.
- **Trojan Horses:** They utilize social engineering tools to fool the end-users to get installed on end-machines and then execute different malicious actions.
- **Backdoors:** When attackers successfully gain access to some system, they want to make future access as easy as possible. A backdoor application will be installed by using different techniques defined above to store confidential information.
- **Spams: They** are one of the common used methods by which backdoor executable program and malware is injected in local or network based end-point. A spam can be an E-mail with malicious content. It can be categorized based on its subject or files attached to the E-mail, etc.
- **Key Loggers:** A type of malware, which logs the keystrokes of already infected computers and then extracts the important information like login credentials, credit card information, etc.
- **Rootkits:** A set of tools used by an attacker to gain the root level access of Linux/Unix based machines.
- **Ransomware:** A type of malware, which demands ransom in order to restore the system to original state. Example would be to encrypt the user's hard drive data and then demanding a ransom from the victim in order to decrypt the data.

Anti-Virus/Snti-Malware

In order to protect workstations from malware types as mentioned above, a number of commercial and free antivirus software are available. Some of them are:

- Kaspersky Anti-Virus
- McAfee Antivirus
- Panda Antivirus
- Sophos Antivirus
- Norton Antivirus
- AVG Internet Security
- Bitdefender Antivirus Free

Personal Firewalls and Host Intrusion Prevention Systems(HIPS)

Host based intrusion prevention system (HIPS) is a software that can be installed on end-user's machine to monitor and analyze malicious activities. It protects operating system and other processes on an end user. It is assumed to be a combination of anti-malware software, anti-virus software and a firewall.

A personal firewall provides protection by using layer 3 and layer 4 information of traffic getting in and out of end-machines. *HIPS* being one-step ahead of personal firewalls, it provides first layer of defense and protection against viruses, worms, Trojans, etc.

Advanced Malware Protection (AMP) for Endpoints

Personal firewalls and *HIPS* are getting obsolete due to more advanced software available in the market today. The Cisco AMP covers the majority of operating systems (Windows, MAC OS X and Android) and uses advanced features like device and file trajectory to help network administrators analyze the complete attack scenario. The following file types are supported by device and file trajectory services in Microsoft Windows® and MAC OS X operating systems:

- MSEXE
- PDF
- MSCAB
- MSOLE2
- ZIP
- ELF
- MACHO
- MACHO_UNIBIN
- SWF
- JAVA

Similarly, android AMP can scan APK files.

Hardware and Software Encryption of End-Point Data

Multiple solutions related to the hardware and software encryption of end-points are available in market today, covering both scenarios of data at rest as well as data in motion. This subsection will describe these solutions:

E-mail encryption: E-mail encryption encrypts the E-mail content so that only the receiver has the ability to decrypt and read the message. The following things must be made sure for effective protection of E-mails:

- The connection to E-mail server must use encryption.
- The content of E-mail must be encrypted.
- Stored, cached or archived E-mail messages should also be encrypted.

There are many commercial as well as free E-mail encryption software programs available. Some of them are:

- Pretty Good Privacy (PGP)
- GNU Privacy Guard (GnuPG)
- Web-based E-mail encryption services

Encrypting Data at Rest: Followings are the few commercial as well as open source software programs, which can be used to encrypt the data at rest, for example, the files and folders of workstation or mobile device, etc.

- **TrueCrypt:** A free data encryption software for Windows, MAC and Linux based operating system.
- **AxCrypt:** Similar in functionality to *TrueCrypt* but only available for Windows based environment.
- **BitLocker:** Latest versions of Microsoft Windows has pre-installed BitLocker software program, which provides full disk encryption and some other features.
- **MAC OS X FileVault:** Just like BitLocker, it provides features of full disk encryption on MAC OS X based systems.

Apart from above mentioned tools, some commercially available tools from companies like MacAfee®, Norton® are also very popular.

Virtual Private Networks (VPN): When Confidentiality, Integrity and availability (CIA) is concerned while minimizing the cost, VPN becomes the obvious choice of most of the organizations. Followings are the different protocols, which can be used in VPN implementation:

- Point-to-Point Tunneling Protocol (PPTP)
- Layer 2 Forwarding (L2F) Protocol
- Layer 2 Tunneling Protocol (L2TP)
- Generic Routing Encapsulation (GRE)
- Multiprotocol Label Switching (MPLS) VPN
- Internet Protocol Security (IPsec)
- Secure Sockets Layer (SSL)

Depending on business needs and current network infrastructure, the following two distinct types of *VPN* are normally implemented to achieve the *CIA:*

1. **Site-to-Site VPNs:** Provide secure connecting between two offices or sites of an organization. End-users remain unaware of VPN deployment as no configuration is done on end-devices.
2. **Remote Access VPNs:** Allow corporate users to connect remotely to enterprise networks via public hotspots or even from home by using third-party software programs or *Cisco AnyConnect Secure Mobility Client.*

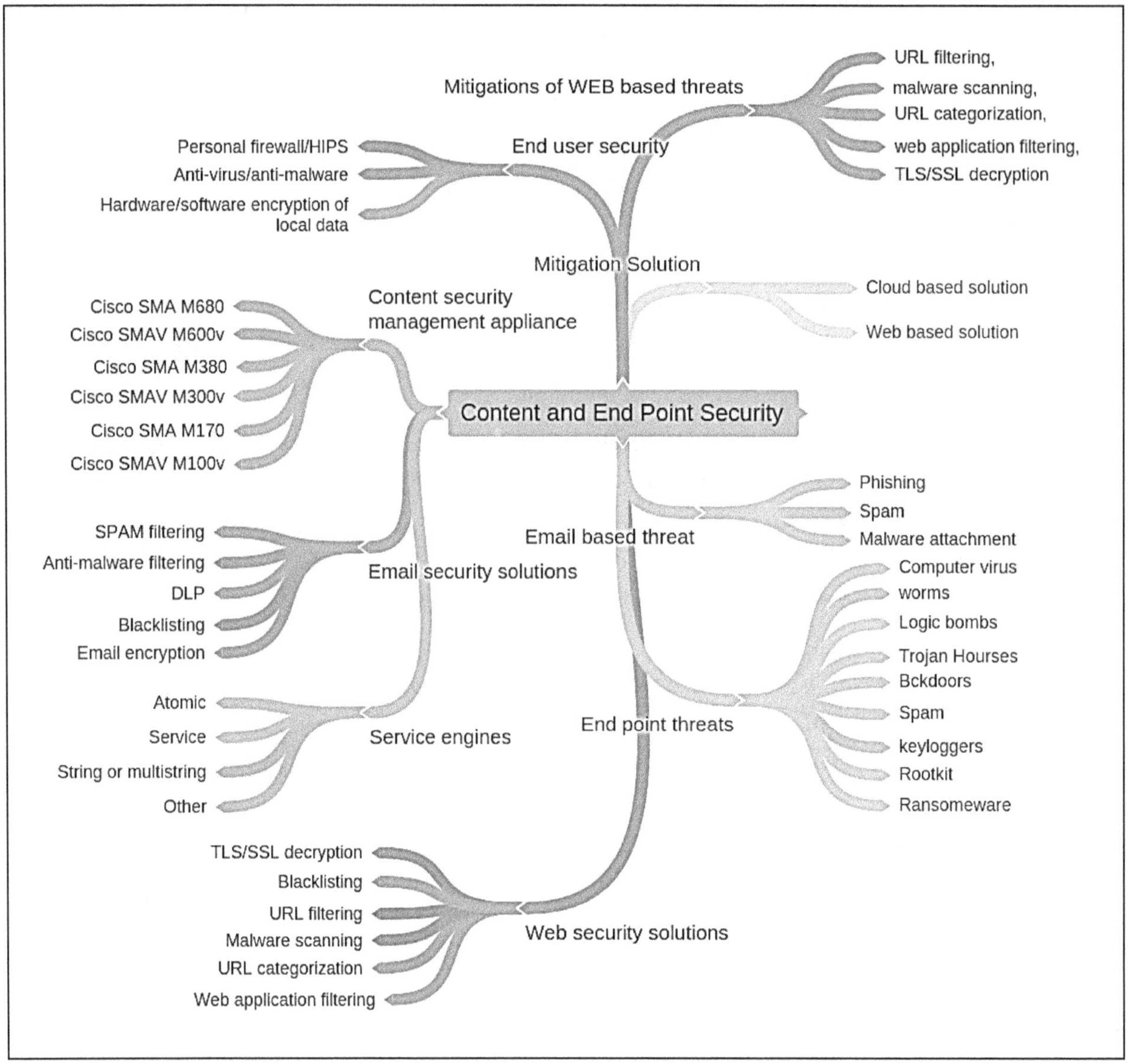

Figure 7-07: Content and Endpoint Security Mind Map

Practice Questions:

1. Which of the followings are E-mail based threats?
   A. Phishing attack
   B. Spam
   C. Malware attachment
   D. All of the above
   E. None of the above

2. Which of the following attacks tries to get login credentials by manipulating the end-user by presenting different links, which look legitimate?
   A. Phishing attack
   B. Spam
   C. Malware attachment
   D. Ransomware attack

3. Which of the followings are the features of Cisco's E-mail Security Appliance (ESA)? (Choose any three)
   A. Network Monitoring
   B. E-mail Encryption
   C. Network Anti-virus
   D. Physical Layer Security
   E. Access Control
   F. Easy VPN Access

4. Which of the followings is a feature of Anti-malware Protection Security Solution?
   A. File retrospection
   B. File sandboxing
   C. File reputation
   D. All of the above
   E. None of the above

5. Which of the following features of Anti-malware protection analyzes file's behavior to determine the threat level and then updates the treat and its mitigations globally?
   A. File retrospection
   B. File sandboxing
   C. File reputation
   D. All of the above
   E. None of the above

6. Which of the followings is a type of spam filtering that identifies spam messages without blocking the legitimate E-mail?
   A. Reputation-Based Filtering
   B. Context-Based Filtering
   C. Both of the above
   D. None of them

7. Which of the followings provides continuous analysis of data to detect, analyze, track, confirm and mitigate threats before, during and after an attack?
   A. Spam Filtering
   B. Data Loss Prevention (DLP)
   C. Anti-Malware Protection(AMP)
   D. E-mail Encryption
   E. None of the above

8. Which of the followings is a characteristic of the Data Loss Prevention (DLP)?
   A. Establishes VPN
   B. Deep content analysis
   C. E-mail integration
   D. Spam Filtering

9. Which of the followings is the most widely used E-mail encryption standard?
   A. Pretty Good Privacy (PGP)
   B. GNU Privacy Guard (GnuPG)
   C. Web-based E-mail encryption services
   D. None of the above

10. Which of the followings controls the user access to specific website category?
    A. URL Filtering
    B. URL Categorization
    C. Spam Filtering
    D. Anti-Malware Protection (AMP)

11. Which of the followings protects your web or mobile applications from being compromised and prevents data from breaching?
    A. Malware Scanning
    B. Spam Filtering
    C. Web Application Filtering
    D. Anti-Malware Protection (AMP)

12. What purposes does SSL/TLS decryption serve? (Choose any three)
    A. It defines the rules and policies to allow or block specific application or data.
    B. It blocks hidden malware in encrypted SSL/TLS traffic.
    C. It detects and blocks intrusion attempts from an attacker.
    D. It establishes SSL VPN.
    E. It provides data encryption and authentication.

13. Which of the followings are the mitigation techniques of Web based threats? (Choose any three)
    A. Web Application Firewall (WAF)
    B. Cloud Based Web Security (CWS)
    C. Cisco Web Security Appliance(WSA)
    D. E-mail Security Appliance (ESA)
    E. Native VLAN
    F. Private VLAN

14. Which of the following ASA series is suitable for small to medium sized enterprise environment?
    A. Cisco C170
    B. Cisco C370
    C. Cisco C380
    D. Cisco C680

15. Which of the followings is a web based attack?
    A. Cross-site scripting (XSS)
    B. SQL injection
    C. File inclusion
    D. Cross-site forgery
    E. All of the above
    F. None of the above

16. Which of the following data state encryptions is provided by the software like TrueCrypt, AxCrypt BitLocker, MAC OS X FileVault?
    A. Data in motion
    B. Data at rest
    C. VPN data
    D. E-mail data

17. Which of the followings are the different protocols, which can be used in VPN

implementation? (Choose any three)

A. Generic Routing Encapsulation (GRE)
B. Multiprotocol Label Switching (MPLS) VPN
C. Internet Protocol Security (IPsec)
D. TCP
E. UDP

18. Host based intrusion prevention system (HIPS) is replaced by?

A. Advanced Malware Protection (AMP)
B. URL Filtering
C. URL Categorization
D. None of the above

Answers

Chapter 01: Security Concepts

1. **B** (A network-scanning technique that indicates the number of live hosts in a range of IP addresses.)

Explanation: A ping sweep is a network-scanning tool to determine the range of IP addresses mapped with live hosts. This utility is popularly used to encounter reconnaissance attack to gather information about live hosts in a network.

2. **C, E, F** (Confidentiality, Integrity & Availability)

Explanation: There are three main components of information security:

a) Confidentiality: makes sure that only authorized users can see and tamper data. It provides encryption to encrypt and hide data.

b) Integrity: makes sure that the data remains un-tampered during transit.

c) Availability: makes sure that the data remains available for authorized users.

3. **A, C, D** (It provides a comprehensive and centralized view of an IT infrastructure, It provides real-time analysis of logs and security alerts generated by network hardware or application, It saves data for the long time, so the organizations can have a detailed report of incident)

Explanation: Security Information Management (SIM) and Security Event Management (SEM) are evolved to form a by-product by the name of Security Information and Event Management (SIEM). In Network security, SIEM technology allows you to get real-time visibility of all activities, threats and risks in your system, network, database and application.

- It provides a comprehensive and centralized view of an IT infrastructure.
- It provides real-time analysis of logs and security alerts generated by network hardware or application.
- It saves data for the long time, so the organizations can have a detailed report of an incident.
- SIEM provides details on the Cause of suspicious activity, which leads you to know "How that event occurred?", "Who is associated with that event?", "Was the user authorized for doing this?", etc.

4. **A** (Common Vulnerabilities and Exposures (CVE))

Explanation: Cisco and other security vendors have created databases known as

The Common Vulnerabilities and Exposures (CVE) that categorizes the threats over the internet. It can be searched via any search engine available today.

5. **A** (Denial-of-Service Attack)

Explanation: Denial-of-Service (DOS) attack is an availability attack intended to downgrade or deny the targeted service or application.

6. **A, C, D** (Social Engineering, Reconnaissance & Pharming)

Explanation: Information gathering is a pre-attack phase, which includes the collection of information about a target using different techniques. An attacker may use different tools, commands for extracting information. Popular methods for gathering information are:

- Social Engineering
- Reconnaissance
- Phishing and Pharming

7. **A** (DoS attack)

Explanation: Denial-of-Service (DoS) is a type of attack in which services offered by a system or a network is denied. Services may either be denied, reduced the functionality or prevent the access to the resources even to the legitimate users. There are several techniques to perform DoS attack such as generating a large number of requests to the target system for service.

8. **B, D** (Intrusion Prevention System & Anti-Spoofing Technologies)

Explanation: The key components to deal with DoS attacks are firewalls and IPSec, but anti-virus software are frequently used to protect a system from viruses and encryption help in mitigating man-in-the-middle attack and reconnaissance.

9. **C** (Man-in-the-Middle)

Explanation: Man-In-The-Middle attack can be explained as a user communicating with another user, or server and attacker inserting himself in between the conversation by sniffing the packets and generating MITM or Replay traffic.

10. **C** (Malicious software, which is designed to disguise itself misleading users of its true intent)

Explanation: Trojan is malicious software, which disguise itself in some legitimate application like free screen saver, free anti-virus cracker, once it is downloaded it will attack end-users.

11. **D** (A worm is a self-replicating malware, which infects system, files or programs)

Explanation: A worm is a self-replicating malware, which infects system, files or programs. They are the special type of viruses that spread over the network thus infecting multiple vulnerable systems

12. **B** (Reconnaissance)

Explanation: Reconnaissance is an initial preparing phase for the attacker to get ready for an attack by gathering the information about the target before launching an attack using different tools and techniques.

13. **A** (Ransomware)

Explanation: Ransomware is malicious software, which is designed to encrypt user's data, then hackers demand ransom payment to decrypt the respective data.

14. **B** (Brute-Force Attack)

Explanation: A brute force attack is a trial-and-error method used to exploit information such as a user password or Personal Identification Number (PIN). In this attack, automated software is used to generate a large number of consecutive guesses as to the value of the desired data. Brute force attacks may be used by criminals to crack encrypted data, or by security analysts to test an organization's network security.

15. **A** (Campus Area Network)

Explanation: Campus Area Network is a type of network topology where multiple LANs are interconnected but it is not expanded as Wide Area Network (WAN) or Metropolitan Area Network (MAN). CAN provides connectivity and services amongst all the branches and end-users of a geographically separated organization like different campuses of a university, multiple offices of an organization etc.

16. **B** (Cryptography)

Explanation: Cryptography is a technique of encrypting the clear text data into a scrambled code. This encrypted data is sent over public or private network towards a destination to ensure the confidentiality.

17. **C** (Symmetric Key Cryptography)

Explanation: Symmetric Key Cryptography is the oldest and most widely used cryptography technique in the domain of cryptography; symmetric ciphers use the same secret key for the encryption and decryption of data. Most widely used symmetric ciphers are AES and DES.

18. **C** (Public Key Infrastructure)

Explanation: PKI is the combination of policies, procedures, hardware, software, and people that are required to create, manage and revoke digital certificates.

19. **D** (When a VM that may have outdated security policies is brought online after a long period of inactivity)

Explanation: The condition Instant ON may create a potential danger to a VM when it is brought online after it has not been used for a long period of time because it may have outdated security policies and can introduce security vulnerabilities.

20. **D** (Identify & Stops Malicious Traffic)

Explanation: SIO uses a monitoring database to differentiate legitimate traffic from malicious traffic to identify and prevent malicious traffic.

21. **B** (Install antivirus scanner or software on all hosts)

Explanation: Anti-virus software is used to provide first layer of defense on end-user devices. It prevents malware from spreading. It generates automatic updates to ensure that hosts are protected from all kind of malwares.

22. **D** (Financial gain)

Explanation:

Cyber criminals or attackers commonly attack or exploit data for money.

Hackers are known to hack for status.

Cyber-terrorists are motivated to commit cybercrimes for religious or political reasons.

23. **B** (It authenticates a website and establishes a secure connection to exchange confidential data)

Explanation: Digital signatures rely on digital certificates to verify the identity of the originator in order to authenticate a vendor website and establish an encrypted connection to exchange confidential data.

24. **D** (Asymmetric)

Explanation: An asymmetric encryption algorithm uses two keys, namely a public key and a private key. A symmetric encryption algorithm uses an identical key for both encryption and decryption. A shared secret is an example of using symmetric algorithm.

25. **B** (Shared Secret)

Explanation: A symmetric encryption algorithm uses an identical key for both encryption and decryption. A shared secret is an example of using symmetric algorithm.

Chapter 02: Secure Access

1. **D** (Restricts unnecessary traffic from overloading the route processor)

Explanation: This plane involves the calculation of best routes in the network for traffic and filtering of data i.e. which packet to be sent to the next level or which packet to be discarded, device discovery and many more.

2. **D** (CLI view, Root view, Super view, Law intercept view)

Explanation: There are following types of role-based CLI access:

CLI view, Root view, Super view, Law intercept view.

3. **B** (1)

Explanation: By default, the Cisco IOS software command-line interface (CLI) has two levels of access to commands: User EXEC mode (level 1) and Privileged EXEC mode (level 15)

4. **C** (2)

Explanation:

To categorize the events, Syslog uses eight severity levels from zero to seven with zero being more critical one when system becomes severely degraded.

Emergencies	0	System is unusable
Alerts	1	Immediate Action needed
Critical	2	Critical Condition
Errors	3	Error Condition
Warnings	4	Warning Condition
Notifications	5	Normal but require attention

5. **C** (SNMP)

Explanation: Simple Network Management Protocol (SNMP) is a protocol that provides the format of messages for communication between managers and agents. SNMP is an application layer protocol, which enables network administer to manage network heath, its performance and its problems.

6. **A** (OIDs are organized in a hierarchical structure)

Explanation: MIB stands for Management Information Base and is a collection of information organized hierarchically in a virtual database.

7. **B** (Authentication)

Explanation: Authentication is the process of proving an identity of a system by login identification and a password. It does the purpose of determining either the user is the same person he claims to be or not.

8. **B** (TACACS)

Explanation: TACACS+ is also used as a communication between networking device and AAA server. Unlike RADIUS, TACACS+ encrypts the entire packet body, and also attaches TACACS+ header to the message body.

9. **B** (SSH protocol has to be configured and a command must be issued to enable the SCP server side functionality)

Explanation: In order to configure Cisco device with SCP server's functionality, we first need to properly configure SSH and a username with proper authorization level for SCP to work properly. For authentication, a user must have a privilege level of 15. The command of "ip scp server enable" has to be issued to enable the SCP server side functionality.

10. **C** (802.1x)

Explanation: The IEEE 802.1X authentication is an IEEE specification that is used to provide Port-based Network access control (PNAC) to the users. This specification is used to restrict unauthorized hosts from connecting to a LAN or WLAN. Each and every host that are intended to connect to the LAN must be authenticated to gain network access.

11. **B** (BYOD)

Explanation: Bring your own device (BYOD) or bring you own technology (BYOT) refers to the network users who bring their own devices - such as smartphones, laptops and tablet PCs – for their work, they use them instead of company's given devices. It provides seamless connectivity between network and end users, while maintaining good security policies for an organization.

12. **C** (MDM)

Explanation: Mobile Device Management (MDM) is a solution that provides a unified management of the entire network (mobile devices, smart phones, tablets, notebooks, Laptops etc.) from a centralized dashboard. The role of Mobile device managers is to manage, monitor and secure mobile devices of end users either they are organization's owned devices or employee-owned devices (BYOD).

13. **A** (Enable Secret Password)

Explanation: AutoSecure executes a script that first makes recommendations for fixing security vulnerabilities and then modifies the security configuration of the router. AutoSecure can lock down the management plane functions and the forwarding plane services and functions of a router, and this includes setting an enable password, and a security banner.

14. **D, E, F** (Create a view using the parser view view-name command, Assign a secret password to the view, Assign commands to the view)

Explanation: Here are the following steps involved in the creation of a view on cisco routers:

a) First of all, enable AAA.
b) Create a specific view.
c) Assign a secret password to that view.
d) Assign command to that view.
e) View configuration mode must be exited.

15. **A, D, F** (Enable inbound vty SSH sessions, Configure IP domain name on the router, Generate SSH keys)

Explanation: Following are the steps to configure SSH on a cisco router:

a) Set the domain name.
b) Generate secret key.
c) Assign username and password.
d) Enable SSH inbound on a VTY lines.

16. **B, C, D** (Specifies the database where captured information is stored, Gathers logging information, Compares the information to be captured and the information to be ignored)

Explanation: Syslog logging service includes, information gathering, evaluating which information to gather and which information to discard and leads the captured information to the storage devices. This information will stay in the storage device for a certain period of time, after that period all information will be vanished and will not be retained when a router is rebooted. It does not authenticate or decrypt messages.

17. **A** (Data Plan)

Explanation: Data plane also known as user plane or forwarding plane. This plane involves the transaction of data packets. We apply policies over this layer to control user's traffic. Packets are sent and received through this part of a network so it takes care of packet flow, it is responsible for forwarding the traffic to the destination using information provided by other planes.

18. **C** (Management Plane)

Explanation: Management plane involves the configuration, management and monitoring of networking devices. It involves accessing the CLI of any device, configuration of IP subnets, configuration of routing protocols and supporting protocols used to access the device. For example, using Telnet, SSH or console port to access router or switch etc. Similarly, when we use SNMP, Syslog, NTP to get information related to different nodes on a network, it is also a part of management plane.

19. **C** (Version 3)

Explanation: SNMP v3 Supports both encryption (DES) and hashing (MD5 or SHA). Implementation of version 3 has three models.

a) NoAuthNoPriv means no encryption and hashing will be used.
b) AuthNoPriv means only MD5 or SHA based hashing will be used.
c) AuthPriv means both encryption and hashing will be used for SNMP traffic.

20. **B** (NTP)

Explanation: Network time protocol (NTP) is a protocol that allows networking devices like routers, switches etc. to synchronize their time with respect to the NTP server, so the devices may have more authenticated time settings and generated syslog messages can be observed more easily, and helps in analyzing problems and attacks during troubleshooting.

21. **B** (Control Plane)

Explanation: Inside the control function/plane lies any kind of traffic which requires some kind of processing usage of networking device. Control plane determines routing Protocols path calculation and their updates. Traffic directed to the IP address of Device itself.

22. **B** (Use the show aaa local user lockout command)

Explanation: The "show aaa local user lockout" command presents an administrator a list of the user accounts that are locked out and unable to be used for authentication. This command also provides the date and timestamp of the lockout occurrence.

23. **C** (Implement Cisco Secure Access Control System (ACS) only)

Explanation: Cisco Secure Access Control System (ACS) supports both RADIUS and TACACS servers. Local databases do not support these servers.

24. **E** (4)

Explanation:

To categorize the events, Syslog uses eight severity levels from zero to seven with zero being more critical one when system becomes severely degraded.

Emergencies	0	System is unusable
Alerts	1	Immediate Action needed
Critical	2	Critical Condition
Errors	3	Error Condition
Warnings	4	Warning Condition
Notifications	5	Normal but require attention

25. **B** (NTP)

Explanation: In order to synchronize the time over, the *Network Time Protocol (NTP)* is used. NTP v3 being latest is used due to its support for encryption.

Chapter 03: Virtual Private Network (VPN)

1. **A** (VPN uses virtual connections to create a secure tunnel over a public network)

Explanation: VPN is a logical network that allows connectivity between two devices. That devices can either belongs to the same network or connected over a wide area network. The term "Virtual" here refers to the logical link between the two devices, as the VPN link does not exist separately, it uses internet as a transport mechanism. The term "Private" here refers to the security VPN provides to the connection between the two devices, as the medium of transport is internet, which is not secure and VPN adds confidentiality and data integrity.

2. **A, C, D, E** (Confidentiality, Data integrity, Authentication, Anti-replay Protection)

Explanation: Following are the key features of VPN technology:

Confidentiality: Data is sent in an encrypted form, data for any other person would be meaningless.

Data integrity: VPN makes sure that the sent data is accurate, secure and remains unaltered end to end.

Authentication: VPN authenticate the peer on both side of the tunnel through pre shared public or private keys or by using user's authentication method.

Anti-replay Protection: VPN technology makes sure that if any VPN packet has sent for transaction and accounted for, then the exact same packet is not valid in the second time of VPN session, so no one can befool VPN peer into believing that the peer trying to connect is the real one.

3. **B** (Remote-access VPN)

Explanation: Types of VPN

a) Remote access VPN makes a networking device to connect outside a corporate office.
b) Site-to-site VPN connects two or more sites that want to connect together over the internet.

4. **A, B, D** (IPsec, SSL & MPLS)

Explanation: The three broad types of VPN technologies used today are:

a) **IPsec:** Used for connecting whole site with another site, IPsec provides security of IP packets at *Network Layer* of TCP/IP stack.
b) **SSL:** Supported by latest web browsers and custom-made software for clients, SSL encrypts TCP traffic by using encrypted SSL tunnels.
c) **MPLS:** *Multi-Protocol Label Switching (MPLS)* and *L3 MPLS VPN* are normally

used by service providers to provide logical connectivity between two sites of an organization. IPsec is then used on top of L3 VPN connectivity to provide encryption.

5. **B** (IPsec)

Explanation: The main objective of IPsec is to provide CIA (confidentiality, integrity and authentication) for virtual networks used in current networking environments. IPsec makes sure the above objectives are in action by the time packet enters a VPN tunnel until it reaches the other end of tunnel.

6. **B, C, E** (AH, ESP & ISAKMP)

Explanation: ESP, AH, and ISAKMP must all be permitted through the perimeter routers and firewalls in order to establish IPsec site-to-site VPNs. NTP and HTTPS are application protocols and are not required for IPsec.

7. **C** (During both Phase 1 and 2)

Explanation: An IPsec VPN connection creates two SAs:

a) First at the completion of the IKE Phase 1 once the peers negotiate the IKE SA policy
b) Second at the end of IKE Phase 2 after the transformed sets are negotiated.

8. **C** (Negotiation of IPsec policy)

Explanation: An IPsec VPN connection creates two SAs:

a) First at the completion of the IKE Phase 1 once the peers negotiate the IKE SA policy
b) Second at the end of IKE Phase 2 after the transformed sets are negotiated.

9. **A, B** (AH provides integrity and authentication, ESP provides encryption, authentication, and integrity)

Explanation: There are two primary protocols used with IPsec are AH and ESP:

a) AH is protocol number 51 and provides data authentication and integrity for IP packets that are exchanged between the peers.
b) ESP, which is protocol number 50, performs packet encryption.

10. **C, E** (MD5 & SHA)

Explanation: IPSec uses SHA, HMAC and MD5 authentication algorithm in tunnel mode for data integrity and authentication.

11. **C, E** (51 & 50)

Explanation: There are two primary protocols used with IPsec are AH and ESP:

a) AH is protocol number 51 and provides data authentication and integrity for IP packets that are exchanged between the peers.

b) ESP, which is protocol number 50, performs packet encryption.

12. **B** (The VPN connection is initiated by the remote user)

Explanation: A remote access VPN makes a networking device to connect outside a corporate office. These devices include smartphones, tablets, laptops etc. commonly known as end devices.

For example, a user wants to build a VPN connection from his individual computer to the corporate headquarters or any other branch of an organization. This is referred to as a remote-access VPN connection.

13. **B** (Transport mode)

Explanation: In transport mode, IPSec VPN secures the data field or payload of originating IP traffic by using encryption, hashing or both. New IPSec headers encapsulate only payload field while the original IP headers remain unchanged. Tunnel mode is used when original IP packets are source and destination address of secure IPSec peers.

14. **C** (MPLS)

Explanation: Multiprotocol Label Switching (MPLS) and MPLS Layer 3 VPNs are the VPN services provided by the internet service provider to allow an organization with two or more branches to have logical connectivity between the sites using the service provider's network for transport. This is also a type of VPN and called MPLS L3VPN, but it does not provide any encryption by default.

15. **B** (Allows NAT to work transparently on one or both ends of the VPN connection)

Explanation: NAT-Traversal encapsulates the datagram with a UDP packet. By doing so, source and destination ports along with source and destination IP addresses will also be included inside a new packet and NATing will work successfully in this case.

16. **C** (Hairpinning)

Explanation: Hair-pinning is a method where a packet goes out from an interface but instead of moving towards the internet it makes a hair pin turn, and returns back to the same interface.

17. **C** (DES)

Explanation:

a) Algorithms that are used to ensure that data is not intercepted and altered (data integrity) are MD5 and SHA.
b) AES and DES are common encryption protocol and provides data confidentiality.
c) DH (Diffie-Hellman) is an algorithm that is used for key exchange.

d) RSA is an algorithm used for authentication.

18. **D** (crypto ipsec transform-set ESP-DES-SHA esp-aes-256 esp-sha-hmac)

Explanation: DES uses 56-bit keys. 3DES uses 56-bit keys and encrypts three times which increases the overall encryption. AES uses 128-bit keys. AES-256 uses 256-bit keys, which is the strongest.

19. **C** (Allows peers to exchange shared keys)

Explanation: DH (Diffie-Hellman) is an algorithm used for key exchange. DH is a public key exchange method that allows two IPsec peers to establish a shared secret key over an insecure channel.

20. **B** (MD5)

Explanation:

a) Algorithms that are used to ensure that data is not intercepted and altered (data integrity) are MD5 and SHA.

b) AES and DES are common encryption protocol and provide data confidentiality.

Chapter 04: Secure Routing

1. **B, C** (area 0 authentication message-digest, ip ospf message-digest-key 1 md5 IPSpecialist)

Explanation: First command shown above defines the authentication type to be message digest. In the second command, authentication password is defined.

2. **A** (To configure OSPF MD5 authentication globally on the router)

Explanation: By using MD5 for hashing, route updates along with other routing information will not be in clear text format and hence enhance the overall security posture of network to some extent.

3. **C** (A snapshot of running configuration of the router can be taken and securely archived in a storage device.)

Explanation: Cisco IOS has a great feature of "*resilient configuration*", which makes a backup copy running IOS image and configuration to mitigate the accidental or malicious attempts of erasing flash and NVRAM of devices.

4. **B** (Shows the list OSPF neighbors)

Explanation: The show "ip ospf neighbor" command observes the neighbor's data structure.

5. **C** (Cisco Express Forwarding (CEF))

Explanation: *Cisco Express Forwarding (CEF)* is the default option selected for the control plane's working mechanism. In CEF, switching cache makes the route for the session in advance even before any packets need to be processed.

6. **A, C** (Forwarding Information Base (FIB) & Adjacency Table)

Explanation: CEF uses two main components to perform its function: The **Forwarding Information Base (FIB)** and the **Adjacency Table**. The FIB makes the forwarding decision for the destination of the packet. It contains information like next hops, prefixes and the outgoing interfaces. The Adjacency Table carries the information about the next directly connected hops.

7. **D** (Restricts unnecessary traffic from overloading the route processor)

Explanation: Control Plane Policing (CoPP) is implemented, which identify specific traffic type and limits its rate that is reaching the control plane of the device.

8. **E** (All)

Explanation: Here is the list of Common Layer 2 attacks discussed in our workbook:

STP attacks, ARP spoofing, MAC spoofing, CAM table (MAC address table) overflows, CDP/LLDP reconnaissance, VLAN hopping and DHCP spoofing.

9. **B** (ARP Spoofing)

Explanation: ARP spoofing is a type of attack in which an attacker actively listens for ARP broadcasts and sends its own MAC address for given IP address. Now, if an attacker provides its MAC address against the IP address of default gateway of LAN, then man-in-the-middle attack will be easily launched without much effort.

10. **B** (MAC Spoofing)

Explanation: MAC Spoofing is a technique of manipulating MAC address to impersonate the legitimate user or launch attack such as Denial-of-Service attack. As we know, MAC address is built-in on Network interface controller, which cannot be changed, but some drivers allow to change the MAC address. This masking process of MAC address is known as MAC Spoofing.

11. **C** (DHCP Snooping)

Explanation: DHCP snooping validates the DHCP messages received from either the legitimate source or from an untrusted source and filters out invalid messages. It is actually very easy for someone to bring accidentally or maliciously a DHCP server in a corporate environment. *DHCP snooping* is all about protecting against it.

12. **D** (All of the above)

Explanation: Here is the list of Mitigation procedures of layer 2 attacks:

DHCP snooping, Dynamic ARP Inspection, port security, BPDU guard, root guard, loop guard.

13. **B** (Loop Guard)

Explanation: Loop Guard feature helps you to prevent loop creation after STP is converged and redundant links are disabled. It prevents root ports or alternate ports from becoming designated ports in case of failure it leads towards unidirectional link. This feature is applicable to all the ports that are or can be non-designated.

14. **A** (It binds the MAC address of known devices to the physical port and associates it with violation action)

Explanation: Port Security is used to bind the MAC address of known devices to the physical ports and violation action is also defined.

15. **D** (Shows clients list with the legitimate IP addresses assigned to them)

Explanation: "*show ip dhcp snooping binding*" command can be used to display client lists with legitimate IP addresses assigned to them.

16. **D** (DHCP Starvation)

Explanation: DHCP Starvation attack is a Denial-of-Service attack on DHCP server. In DHCP Starvation attack, Attacker sends bogus requests for broadcasting to DHCP server with spoofed MAC addresses to lease all IP addresses in DHCP address pool.

Once, all IP addresses are allocated, upcoming users will be unable to obtain an IP address or renew the lease.

17. **A, C, E**

Explanation:

Here are some precautionary measures to overcome VLAN hopping:

a) Disable trunking on all access ports.
b) Disable auto-trunking and enable manual-trunking.
c) Change the native VLAN to a VLAN other than VLAN1.
d) Tag the native VLAN traffic in order to prevent against 802.1Q double-tagging attack to exploit network vulnerability.

18. **B** (If there is an attempt to write more data to a memory location than that location can hold)

Explanation: By sending too much data to a specific area of memory, adjacent memory locations are overwritten, which causes a security issue because the program in the overwritten memory location is affected.

19. **C** (VLAN double-tagging)

Explanation: In a VLAN double tagging attack, an attacker can Spoof DTP messages from the attacking host to cause the switch to enter trunking mode. Here, he applies double tagging the first tag comprises of native VLAN to bypass trunking and other tag is of victim's VLAN to reach the victim. So that, the attacker can send traffic tagged with the target VLAN, and the switch simply delivers the packets to the destination. So it is better to configure any other VLAN as native VLA rather than VLAN 1.

20. **B** (DTP)

Explanation: We can mitigate a VLAN hopping attack by disabling Dynamic Trunking Protocol (DTP) and by setting the native VLAN of trunk links to a VLAN not in use.

21. **B** (On a promiscuous port)

Explanation: Here are the following modes of Private VLAN:

a) **Promiscuous Mode:** Normally connected to a router, this port is allowed to send and receive frames form any other port on the same VLAN.
b) **Isolated Mode:** As name suggests, devices connected to isolated ports will only communicate with Promiscuous ports.
c) **Community Mode:** Community mode is used for group of users who want communication between them. Community ports can communicate with other community port members and with Promiscuous ports.

22. **D** (Port security)

Explanation: Port security feature allows limited number of MAC addresses on a single port. So, if an attacker tries to connect its PC or embedded device to the switch port, then it will shut down or restrict the attacker from even generating an attack.

23. **A** (It prevents rogue switches from being part of a network)

Explanation: BPDU guard feature error-disables a port that receives a BPDU. This prevents rogue switches from being a part of the network.

24. **A** (clientless SSL)

Explanation: When a web browser is used to securely access the corporate network, the browser must use a secure version of HTTP to provide SSL encryption. A VPN client is not required to be installed on the remote host, so a clientless SSL connection is used.

25. **D** (Both SSL and IPsec)

Explanation: Both IPsec and SSL are supported by Cisco AnyConnect.

Chapter 05: Secure Routing & Switching

1. **B, C, D** (It has the ability to inspect the traffic of more than just IP and port level, By integrating with AAA, firewall can permit or deny traffic based on AAA policy, By integrating with IPS/ID, firewall can detect and filter malicious data at the edge of network to protect the end-users.)

Explanation: Firewalls are physical devices and software that defend an internal network or system from unauthorized access by using the traffic-filtering feature.

a) Firewall hides the functionality of network devices, which makes it difficult for an attacker to understand the physical topology of network.
b) It has the ability to inspect the traffic more than just IP and port level.
c) By integrating with AAA, firewall can permit or deny traffic based on AAA policy.
d) By integrating with IPS/ID, firewall can detect and filter malicious data at the edge of network to protect the end-users.

2. **B** (Application-Level Firewall)

Explanation: Application level firewalls can operate up to layer 7 and provides a more granular control of packets moving in and out of network. Similarly, it becomes very difficult for an attacker to get the topology view of inside or trusted network because connection requests terminate on Application/Proxy firewalls.

3. **A** (Circuit-Level Firewall)

Explanation: Circuit Level gateway firewall operates at the session layer of the OSI model. They capture the packet to monitor TCP Handshaking, in order to validate if the sessions are legitimate. Packets forwarded to the remote destination through a circuit-level firewall appear to have originated from the gateway.

4. **D** (It provides better performance.)

Explanation: Both Stateful firewall and a proxy server do packet filtration but a Stateful firewall performs better than a proxy server. A Stateful firewall cannot authenticate users or prevent Layer 7 attacks.

5. **A** (It is not as effective with UDP- or ICMP-based traffic.)

Explanation: Here are some limitations of Stateful firewalls:

- Stateful firewalls cannot prevent application layer attacks.
- Protocols such as UDP and ICMP are not Stateful and do not generate information needed for a state table.
- An entire range of ports must sometimes be opened in order to support specific applications that open multiple ports.
- Stateful firewalls lack user authentication.

6. **D** (Establishes policies between zones.)

Explanation: Here are the following steps to configure zones in a Zone-based policy firewall:

a) Determine the zones.
b) Establish policies between zones.
c) Design the physical infrastructure.
d) Identify subnets with zones and see traffic requirements.

7. **D** (Stateful Firewall)

Explanation: Stateful firewalls analyze the state of connections in data flows during packet filtering. They analyze whether the packet belongs to an existing flow of data or not.

8. **C** (show running-config)

Explanation: The below command can verify zone based policy firewalls:

Show running-config, show zone security and show zone-pair security.

9. **D** (It saves the state of current sessions in a table)

Explanation: When the first packet from source hits the trusted interface of ASA, its entry will be made in Stateful database. As its name depicts, this saves the state of current sessions in a table known as Stateful database. This database is also called state table or session table. The incoming traffic of connection will only be allowed if source address and port number matches the saved state in the Stateful table.

10. **B** (Inside Global)

Explanation: Following table summarizes the different terminologies of NAT/PAT.

Inside Local	The original IP address of host from trusted network. For example 172.16.0.5 has been assigned to end users in diagram above
Inside Global	The global address either router's interface IP or one from pool, which will represent the client out on the internet.
Outside Local	The IP address with which a device is known on the internet. For example, the IP cameras, which are configured to be accessed anywhere from the internet.
Outside Global	The real IP address of host device, which is configured to be accessed over the internet. Like the private IP address of IP camera, which will be accessed via some global IP address.

11. **B** (Class map)

Explanation: Class maps are used to filter out the traffic that needs to be inspected. Traffic can be filtered by using information from Layer 3 up to Layer 7 of OSI model. ACL can also be referred in a class map for the purpose of identifying traffic.

12. **A** (Policy map)

Explanation: Policy maps are used to perform a specific kind of action on traffic matched by class maps. By referring a class-map, policy map can either inspect (Stateful inspection of traffic), permit (permit the traffic but no Stateful inspection), drop the traffic or generate log of it.

13. **A, B, E** (Drop, Permit, Inspect)

Explanation: Policy map can either inspect (Stateful inspection of traffic), permit (permit the traffic but no Stateful inspection), drop the traffic or generate log of it.

14. **B, C, D** (Command Line Interface (CLI), ASA Security Device Manager (ASDMo), Cisco Security Manager (CSM))

Explanation: Following are the official management techniques for accessing ASA firewall:

a) **Command Line Interface (CLI):** With a little bit change, most feature and syntax for basic operation is same as Cisco IOS of routers and switches, etc.
b) **ASA Security Device Manager (ASDM):** Just like Cisco Configuration Professional (CCP), which is used to manage routers via GUI, ASDM is used to manage ASA in the same way.
c) **Cisco Security Manager (CSM):** A GUI based tool, which can be used to manage the network devices like routers, switches and security devices like firewalls.

15. **B** (Pass)

Explanation: The pass action in a Cisco IOS Zone-Based Policy Firewall is similar to a permit statement in an ACL.

16. **B** (Forwards traffic from one zone to another)

Explanation: The pass or permit action performed by Cisco IOS ZPF permits the traffic without Stateful inspection.

17. **B** (Transport Mode)

Explanation: In transparent mode, ASA works as layer 2 bridge and traffic flows through it without adding itself as routing hop between communicating peers. Consider it as a tap on a network, which is normally used to analyze the network traffic.

18. **A** (Routed Mode)

Explanation: Usually, Cisco's ASA supports two firewall modes:

Routed mode

By default, Cisco ASA works in layer 3 or routed mode in which an IP address is normally assigned to different interfaces of the device. End-hosts see firewall as a routing hop along with the network path.

Transparent mode

In transparent mode, ASA works as layer 2 bridge and traffic flows through it without adding itself as routing hop between communicating peers. Consider it as a tap on a network, which is normally used to analyze the network traffic

19. **A** (Active/Standby failover)

Explanation: In Active/Standby failover, one device will act as primary firewall or active firewall while the second one will be in standby mode. Just like HSRP, the standard protocol traffic will be exchanged periodically between firewalls to check the status of active and standby firewalls.

20. **A** (Context)

Explanation: High-end ASA devices allow you to make multiple virtual firewalls within single hardware device. These virtual firewalls are known as context. Instead of using single hardware firewall for each client connection, service providers can use one high-end firewall and create multiple contexts in it.

21. **A** (On inside interface)

Explanation: Security level 100- By default, it is used by the inside interface. It is the highest possible and the most trusted level.

22. **A** (Security Access Policy)

Explanation: Security access policies specify the rules for the data traffic passing through an interface. These policies will be applied first, before any other policy to the incoming or outgoing traffic. Each packet that hits the interface will be first examined to decide whether to forward or drop the packet based on the criteria you specify in the access policy.

23. A (AES)

Explanation: Data confidentiality can be implemented through symmetric encryption algorithms, including DES, 3DES, and AES.

24. A (Two public keys are used for the key exchange.)

Explanation: An asymmetric encryption algorithm uses two keys, namely a Public Key and a Private Key.

25. B (56-bits)

Explanation: DES uses a fixed length of key of 64-bits long, but only 56 bits are used for encryption. Rest of the bits is parity bits.

Chapter 06: Intrusion Prevention System (IPS)

1. **B** (Zero-Day Attack)

Explanation: A **zero-day attack** or zero-day threat is an attack that exploits the weakness of any software that are unknown by the software vendor. An attacker can launch attack before the vendor releases any patch of this vulnerability and the network can be compromised.

2. **B, C** (Both mitigate the network attacks either actively or passively, Both are deployed as sensors)

Explanation: IDS and the IPS are deployed as sensors and use digital signatures to detect malicious traffic. IDS relies on an IPS to stop malicious traffic.

3. **D, E** (The IDS requires other devices to respond to attacks, The IDS does not stop malicious traffic)

Explanation: IDS works passively, as it works on the copied traffic so IDS cannot stop or respond to an attack. IDS works in assistance with other devices like routers and firewalls to react against such attacks.

4. **D** (All of the above)

Explanation: An IDS/IPS sensor could be placed in-line between any of the zones i.e. Inside, Outside or DMZ and the firewall.

5. **D** (Network-based IPS cannot analyze encrypted traffic)

Explanation: Network-based IPS devices are implemented as inline mode to actively monitor the traffic on networks. They can take immediate actions when security policy breaches. One limitation of network based IPS is that they cannot monitor/inspect encrypted packets.

6. **B** (False Positive)

Explanation: A false positive is a situation when sensor generates an alert about the traffic, which is not malicious, but requires serious attention as long as security is concerned. False positive can be easily identified, as immediate alerts are generated for this and they can be easily viewed.

7. **D** (True Positive)

Explanation: A true positive means that a malicious activity is detected by the IPS module or sensor and an alert will be generated for this. Depending on the configuration of IPS, it may be dropped at the first place.

8. **D** (All of the above)

Explanation: The following table summarizes the different technologies used in IDS/IPS along with its uses:

Signature Based	Easier Implementation and management.
Anomaly Based	It can deny any kind of latest attacks, as they will not be defined within the scope of baseline policy.
Policy Based	Everything else outside the scope of defined policy will be dropped.
Reputation Based	Uses the information provided by Cisco Could Services in which systems share their experience with network attacks.

9. **B** (To collect the information from the systems participating in global correlation and filters out sites or URLs with bad reputation)

Explanation: The role of Reputation based IDS/IPS is to collect the information from the systems participating in global correlation. Reputation based IDS/IPS include relative descriptors like known URLs, domain-names etc. Global correlation services are maintained by Cisco Cloud Services. So, it would be feasible to filter out the known traffic, which results in propagation of any attack.

10. **B, D** (Alert, Monitor)

Explanation: Here are some following terms, that define actions or responses that are commonly used in IDS technology:

a) **Alerts:** It is a generation of loggable messages upon every detection of malware or malicious traffic flows. The term "alarm" is also used for this purpose.
b) **Monitor:** An IDS can only monitor and analyze traffic, as it could not prevent an attack from reaching its destination but it can respond to a suspicious event with the help of other resources like routers and firewalls.

11. **E** (All of the above)

Explanation: Now here are some following terms, that define actions or responses that are commonly used in IPS technology:

a) **Drop:** It prevents the suspicious payload from reaching the destination.
b) **Reset:** Whenever the sensor detects a suspicious payload with a TCP connection, the sensor will inject TCP resets, which leads to the termination of that particular TCP connection.
c) **Block:** IPS uses "block" action to ignore suspicious traffic coming from other protocols rather than TCP.
d) **Shun:** If IPS wants the above action of blocking to be performed by some other device like SIEM, then this dynamic action of blocking is referred to as Shunning.

12. **A** (Atomic)

Explanation: Here are some following micro engines for signature:

Atomic	Signatures designed to analyze single packets instead of stream of packets.
Service	Signatures designed to analyze application layer services.
String or multistring	This category contains signatures, which can compare and match custom patterns inside a single or stream of packets.
Other	Remaining signatures, which may not fit in the above categories.

13. **C** (Attack Severity Rating (ASR))

Explanation:

Attack Severity Rating (ASR)	It is also the part of digital signature and it determines the critical level of an attack.

14. **B** (It cannot detect unknown attacks)

Explanation: Signature or pattern based IDS/IPS only mitigates already discovered attacks. It compares the network traffic to a database of known attacks. Hence, this type of intrusion detection cannot detect unknown attacks. It is easy to configure and deploy.

15. **B** (Event correlation)

Explanation: Global correlation services are maintained by Cisco Cloud Services. It makes the network feasible to filter out the known traffic, which results in propagation of any attacks before it hits the organization's critical infrastructure.

16. **A** (Promiscuous or passive mode)

Explanation: In a promiscuous or passive mode, a copy of every data packet will be send to the sensor to analyze any malicious activity. The sensor, running in promiscuous mode will perform the detection and generate an alert if required

17. **B** ('fail-open' mode)

Explanation: If 'fail-open' mode is used, the good and malicious traffic will be allowed in case of any kind of failure within IPS sensor.

If 'fail-close' mode is configured, the whole IP traffic will be dropped in case of sensor's failure.

18. **B** (Dynamic Blacklist)

Explanation: IPS helps you to dynamically create a blacklist, with the help of Cisco Collective Security Intelligence Team "Talos" (http://www.talosintel.com/).

It dynamically downloads a collection of IP addresses at regular intervals that have a poor reputation in a networking environment.

19. **B** (Whitelisting)

Explanation: Whitelisting is just the opposite of blacklisting, here you allow or permit IP address or traffic of your own choice.

Blacklisting and whitelisting are widely used for security solutions, including IPS, web security, E-mail security, and firewall.

20. **A** (IPS does not responds immediately to an attack)

Explanation: IPS responds immediately to an attack and does not allow any malicious traffic to bypass network device, but it introduces delay in a network as it analyzes each and every packet that passes through an interface.

21. **D** (All of the above)

Explanation: IPS provides network protection by preventing an attack to reach its destination, by enforcing policies, by controlling access to resources and by hardening networking devices.

Chapter 07: Content & Endpoint Security

1. **D** (All of the above)

Explanation: Here are some common types of E-mail based threats found in today's networks are:

a) **Spam:** A spam can be an E-mail with malicious content. It can be categorized based on its subject or files attached to the E-mail, etc.
b) **Malware Attachments:** Any kind of malware or malicious executed program, attached to an E-mail.
c) **Phishing:** It tries to get login credentials by manipulating the end-user by presenting different links, which looks legitimate, for example presenting fake social web pages.

2. **A** (Phishing attack)

Explanation: Phishing tries to get login credentials by manipulating the end-user by presenting different links, which looks legitimate, for example presenting fake social web pages.

3. **B, C, E** (E-mail Encryption, Network Anti-virus, Access Control)

Explanation: Following are the few features provided by AsyncOS running on ESA devices:

a) **Access Control:** Just like *Access-List,* access control provides inbound control by using either sender's IP address/subnet or domain name.
b) **Anti-spam:** Powered by Cisco research group *Talos*, anti-spam is a multilayer protection filter based on Cisco SenderBase Reputation feature.
c) **Network Antivirus:** Partnership with Sophos and MacAfee® for integration of their scanning engines allow anti-virus scanning capabilities at the edge of network.
d) **AMP and DLP features:** Data Loss Prevention (DLP) helps to prevent any critical digital asset from leaving the corporate network by monitoring the outbound traffic. Similarly, AMP feature helps to mitigate against latest threats and attacks.
e) **E-mail Encryption:** The network management team can utilize the encryption feature for outbound E-mails.
f) **E-mail Authentication:** *ESA* can use multiple authentication mechanism to verify the authenticity of coming E-mails.
g) **Outbreak Filters:** This feature provides mitigation against latest security outbreaks by using Cisco's threat intelligence information.

4. **D** (All of the above)

Explanation: The features of Cisco AMP include the followings:

a) **File reputation:** Here the malicious traffic will automatically be blocked. File reputation service is updated after every 3 to 5 minutes.
b) **File sandboxing:** It gathers details about a file's behavior to determine the file's threat level and it sends the results to Cisco cloud based intelligence service named as TALOS, which then updates the treat and its mitigations globally.
c) **File retrospection:** It analyzes and solves the problem of malicious files that pass through the email security gateway but might later cause a threat.

5. **B** (File sandboxing)

Explanation: File sandboxing analyzes unknown files that are traversing the Cisco E-mail security gateway. It gathers details about a file's behavior to determine the file's threat level and it sends the results to Cisco cloud based intelligence service named as TALOS, which then updates the treat and its mitigations globally.

6. **B** (Context-Based Filtering)

Explanation: Content based filtering inspects the entire mail, including message contents, analyzing details such as sender identity, its source, its destination, embedded URLs, attachments and E-mail formatting by using algorithms. It identifies spam messages without blocking the legitimate E-mail.

7. **C** (Anti-Malware Protection(AMP))

Explanation: Cisco Advanced Malware Protection (AMP) provides control over malware detection and blocking. It provides continuous analysis of data to detect, analyze, track, confirm and mitigate threats before, during and after an attack.

8. **B** (Deep content analysis)

Explanation: In case of E-mail security, Data Loss Prevention (DLP) is a content level scanning of messages and attachments in an E-mail, to detect whether the transport for sensitive data is appropriate or not.

9. **A** (Pretty Good Privacy (PGP))

Explanation: OpenPGP is the most widely used E-mail encryption standard. The main purpose of OpenPGP is to ensure an end-to-end encryption over E-mail communication; it also provides message encryption and decryption and password manager, data compression and digital signing.

10. **B** (URL Categorization)

Explanation: URL Categorization controls the user access to specific website category. This feature enables networking device to filter web traffic by using a categorization database.

11. **C** (Web Application Filtering)

Explanation: Web application filtering protects your web or mobile applications from being compromised and prevents data from breaching. Web application filtering can be done by either defining filtering policy or by using web application firewall (WAF).

12. **A, B, C** (It defines the rules and policies to allow or block specific application or data, It blocks hidden malware in encrypted SSL/TLS traffic, It detects and blocks intrusion attempts from an attacker)

Explanation: TLS/SSL decryption performs the following actions:

a) It blocks hidden malware in encrypted SSL/TLS traffic
b) It detects and blocks intrusion attempts from an attacker
c) It restricts confidential data from loss, hence provides Data Loss Prevention (DLP)
d) It defines the rules and policies to allow or block specific application or data
e) It monitors outgoing data

13. **A, B, C** (Web Application Firewall (WAF), Cloud Based Web Security (CWS), Cisco Web Security Appliance(WSA))

Explanation:

a) **Cloud based Web Security:** Organizations having Cisco's cloud based web security gets their web access being monitored and scanned for any kind of threat.
b) **Web Security appliance (WSA):** WSA provides protection before, during and after an attack.
c) **Web application filtering:** Web application filtering protects your web or mobile applications from being compromised and prevents data from breaching.

14. **B** (Cisco C370)

Explanation: The following table summarizes different variants of ESA series:

Cisco X1070	Service providers and large scale enterprise environment.
Cisco C680	Service providers and large scale enterprise environment.
Cisco C670	Medium sized enterprise environment.
Cisco C380	Medium sized enterprise environment.
Cisco C370	Small to medium sized enterprise environment.
Cisco C170	Small Office/Home Office (SOHO) environment.

15. **E** (All of the above)

Explanation: Web based attacks includes cross-site scripting (XSS), SQL injection, file inclusion, cross-site forgery etc.

16. **B** (Data at rest)

Explanation:

Following are the few commercial as well as open source software programs, which can be used to encrypt the data at rest, for example the files and folders of workstation or mobile device etc.

a) **TrueCrypt:** A free data encryption software for Windows, MAC and Linux based operating system.
b) **AxCrypt:** Similar in functionality to *TrueCrypt* but only available for Windows based environment.
c) **BitLocker:** Latest versions of Microsoft Windows has pre-installed BitLocker software program, which provides full disk encryption and some other features.
d) **MAC OS X FileVault:** Just like BitLocker, it provides features of full disk encryption on MAC OS X based systems.

17. **A, B, C** (Generic Routing Encapsulation (GRE), Multiprotocol Label Switching (MPLS) VPN, Internet Protocol Security (IPsec))

Explanation: Following are the different protocols, which can be used in VPN implementation:

a) Point-to-Point Tunneling Protocol (PPTP)
b) Layer 2 Forwarding (L2F) Protocol
c) Layer 2 Tunneling Protocol (L2TP)
d) Generic Routing Encapsulation (GRE)
e) Multiprotocol Label Switching (MPLS) VPN
f) Internet Protocol Security (IPsec)
g) Secure Sockets Layer (SSL)

18. A (Advanced Malware Protection (AMP))

Explanation: Personal firewalls and *HIPS* are getting obsolete due to more advanced software available in the market today. The Cisco AMP covers the majority of operating systems (Windows, MAC OS X and android) and uses advanced features like device and file trajectory to help network administrators analyze the complete attack scenario.

Acronyms:

3DES	Triple Digital Encryption Standard
AAA	Authentication, Authorization, and Accounting
ABAC	Attribute-based Access Control
ACL	Access Control List
AES	Advanced Encryption Standard
AES256	Advanced Encryption Standards 256bit
AH	Authentication Header
ALE	Annualized Loss Expectancy
AP	Access Point
API	Application Programming Interface
APT	Advanced Persistent Threat
ARO	Annualized Rate of Occurrence
ARP	Address Resolution Protocol
ASLR	Address Space Layout Randomization
ASP	Application Service Provider
AUP	Acceptable Use Policy
AV	Asset Value
AV	Antivirus
BAC	Business Availability Center
BCP	Business Continuity Planning
BIA	Business Impact Analysis
BIOS	Basic Input/Output System
BPA	Business Partners Agreement
BPDU	Bridge Protocol Data Unit
BYOD	Bring Your Own Device
CA	Certificate Authority
CAC	Common Access Card
CAN	Controller Area Network
CAR	Corrective Action Report
CBC	Cipher Block Chaining
CCMP	Counter-Mode/CBC-Mac Protocol
CCTV	Closed-circuit Television
CER	Cross-over Error Rate
CER	Certificate
CERT	Computer Emergency Response Team
CFB	Cipher Feedback
CHAP	Challenge Handshake Authentication Protocol

CIO	Chief Information Officer
CIRT	Computer Incident Response Team
CMS	Content Management System
COOP	Continuity of Operations Plan
COPE	Corporate Owned, Personally Enabled
CP	Contingency Planning
CRC	Cyclical Redundancy Check
CRL	Certificate Revocation List
CSIRT	Computer Security Incident Response Team
CSO	Chief Security Officer
CSP	Cloud Service Provider
CSR	Certificate Signing Request
CSRF	Cross-site Request Forgery
CSU	Channel Service Unit
CTM	Counter-Mode
CTO	Chief Technology Officer
CTR	Counter
CYOD	Choose Your Own Device
DAC	Discretionary Access Control
DBA	Database Administrator
DDoS	Distributed Denial of Service
DEP	Data Execution Prevention
DER	Distinguished Encoding Rules
DES	Digital Encryption Standard
DFIR	Digital Forensics and Investigation Response
DHCP	Dynamic Host Configuration Protocol
DHE	Data-Handling Electronics
DHE	Diffie-Hellman Ephemeral
DLL	Dynamic Link Library
DLP	Data Loss Prevention
DMZ	Demilitarized Zone
DNAT	Destination Network Address Transaction
DNS	Domain Name Service (Server)
DoS	Denial of Service
DRP	Disaster Recovery Plan
DSA	Digital Signature Algorithm
DSL	Digital Subscriber Line
DSU	Data Service Unit
EAP	Extensible Authentication Protocol
ECB	Electronic Code Book
ECC	Elliptic Curve Cryptography
ECDHE	Elliptic Curve Diffie-Hellman Ephemeral

ECDSA	Elliptic Curve Digital Signature Algorithm
EFS	Encrypted File System
EMI	Electromagnetic Interference
EMP	Electro Magnetic Pulse
ERP	Enterprise Resource Planning
ESN	Electronic Serial Number
ESP	Encapsulated Security Payload
EF	Exposure Factor
FACL	File System Access Control List
FAR	False Acceptance Rate
FDE	Full Disk Encryption
FRR	False Rejection Rate
FTP	File Transfer Protocol
FTPS	Secured File Transfer Protocol
GCM	Galois Counter Mode
GPG	Gnu Privacy Guard
GPO	Group Policy Object
GPS	Global Positioning System
GPU	Graphic Processing Unit
GRE	Generic Routing Encapsulation
HA	High Availability
HDD	Hard Disk Drive
HIDS	Host-based Intrusion Detection System
HIPS	Host-based Intrusion Prevention System
HMAC	Hashed Message Authentication Code
HOTP	HMAC-based One-Time Password
HSM	Hardware Security Module
HTML	Hypertext Mark-up Language
HTTP	Hypertext Transfer Protocol
HTTPS	Hypertext Transfer Protocol over SSL/TLS
HVAC	Heating, Ventilation and Air Conditioning
IaaS	Infrastructure as a Service
ICMP	Internet Control Message Protocol
ICS	Industrial Control Systems
ID	Identification
IDEA	International Data Encryption Algorithm
IDF	Intermediate Distribution Frame
IdP	Identity Provider
IDS	Intrusion Detection System
IEEE	Institute of Electrical and Electronic Engineers
IIS	Internet Information System
IKE	Internet Key Exchange

IM	Instant Messaging
IMAP4	Internet Message Access Protocol v4
IoT	Internet of Things
IP	Internet Protocol
IPSec	Internet Protocol Security
IR	Incident Response
IR	Infrared
IRC	Internet Relay Chat
IRP	Incident Response Plan
ISA	Interconnection Security Agreement
ISP	Internet Service Provider
ISSO	Information Systems Security Officer
ITCP	IT Contingency Plan
IV	Initialization Vector
KDC	Key Distribution Center
L2TP	Layer 2 Tunneling Protocol
LAN	Local Area Network
LDAP	Lightweight Directory Access Protocol
LEAP	Lightweight Extensible Authentication Protocol
MaaS	Monitoring as a Service
MAC	Mandatory Access Control
MAC	Media Access Control
MAC	Message Authentication Code
MAN	Metropolitan Area Network
MBR	Master Boot Record
MD5	Message Digest 5
MDF	Main Distribution Frame
MDM	Mobile Device Management
MFA	Multi-Factor Authentication
MFD	Multi-function Device
MITM	Man-in-the-Middle
MMS	Multimedia Message Service
MOA	Memorandum of Agreement
MOU	Memorandum of Understanding
MPLS	Multi-protocol Label Switching
MSCHAP	Microsoft Challenge Handshake Authentication Protocol
MSP	Managed Service Provider
MTBF	Mean Time Between Failures
MTTF	Mean Time to Failure
MTTR	Mean Time to Recover or Mean Time to Repair
MTU	Maximum Transmission Unit
NAC	Network Access Control

NAT	Network Address Translation
NDA	Non-disclosure Agreement
NFC	Near Field Communication
NGAC	Next Generation Access Control
NIDS	Network-based Intrusion Detection System
NIPS	Network-based Intrusion Prevention System
NIST	National Institute of Standards & Technology
NTFS	New Technology File System
NTLM	New Technology LAN Manager
NTP	Network Time Protocol
OAUTH	Open Authorization
OCSP	Online Certificate Status Protocol
OID	Object Identifier
OS	Operating System
OTA	Over The Air
P12	PKCS #12
P2P	Peer to Peer
PAC	Proxy Auto Configuration
PAM	Pluggable Authentication Modules
PAP	Password Authentication Protocol
PAT	Port Address Translation
PBKDF2	Password-based Key Derivation Function 2
PBX	Private Branch Exchange
PCAP	Packet Capture
PEAP	Protected Extensible Authentication Protocol
PED	Personal Electronic Device
PEM	Privacy-enhanced Electronic Mail
PFS	Perfect Forward Secrecy
PFX	Personal Exchange Format
PGP	Pretty Good Privacy
PHI	Personal Health Information
PII	Personally Identifiable Information
PIV	Personal Identity Verification
PKI	Public Key Infrastructure
POODLE	Padding Oracle on Downgrade Legacy Encryption
POP	Post Office Protocol
POTS	Plain Old Telephone Service
PPP	Point-to-Point Protocol
PPTP	Point-to-Point Tunneling Protocol
PSK	Pre-shared Key
PTZ	Pan-Tilt-Zoom
RA	Recovery Agent

RA	Registration Authority
RAD	Rapid Application Development
RADIUS	Remote Authentication Dial-in User Server
RAID	Redundant Array of Inexpensive Disks
RAS	Remote Access Server
RAT	Remote Access Trojan
RBAC	Role-based Access Control
RBAC	Rule-based Access Control
RC4	Rivest Cipher version 4
RDP	Remote Desktop Protocol
RFID	Radio Frequency Identifier
RMF	Risk Management Framework
ROI	Return on Investment
RPO	Recovery Point Objective
RSA	Rivest, Shamir, & Adleman
RTBH	Remotely Triggered Black Hole
RTO	Recovery Time Objective
RTOS	Real-time Operating System
RTP	Real-time Transport Protocol
S/MIME	Secure/Multipurpose Internet Mail Extensions
SaaS	Software as a Service
SAML	Security Assertions Markup Language
SAN	Storage Area Network
SAN	Subject Alternative Name
SCADA	System Control and Data Acquisition
SCAP	Security Content Automation Protocol
SCEP	Simple Certificate Enrollment Protocol
SCP	Secure Copy
SCSI	Small Computer System Interface
SDK	Software Development Kit
SDLC	Software Development Life Cycle
SDLM	Software Development Life Cycle Methodology
SDN	Software Defined Network
SED	Self-encrypting Drive
SEH	Structured Exception Handler
SFTP	Secured File Transfer Protocol
SHA	Secure Hashing Algorithm
SHTTP	Secure Hypertext Transfer Protocol
SIEM	Security Information and Event Management
SIM	Subscriber Identity Module
SLA	Service Level Agreement
SLE	Single Loss Expectancy

SMB	Server Message Block
SMS	Short Message Service
SMTP	Simple Mail Transfer Protocol
SMTPS	Simple Mail Transfer Protocol Secure
SNMP	Simple Network Management Protocol
SOAP	Simple Object Access Protocol
SoC	System on Chip
SPF	Sender Policy Framework
SPIM	Spam over Internet Messaging
SPoF	Single Point of Failure
SQL	Structured Query Language
SRTP	Secure Real-Time Protocol
SSD	Solid State Drive
SSH	Secure Shell
SSID	Service Set Identifier
SSL	Secure Sockets Layer
SSO	Single Sign-on
STP	Shielded Twisted Pair
TACACS+	Terminal Access Controller Access Control System Plus
TCP/IP	Transmission Control Protocol/Internet Protocol
TGT	Ticket Granting Ticket
TKIP	Temporal Key Integrity Protocol
TLS	Transport Layer Security
TOTP	Time-based One-time Password
TPM	Trusted Platform Module
TSIG	Transaction Signature
UAT	User Acceptance Testing
UAV	Unmanned Aerial Vehicle
UDP	User Datagram Protocol
UEFI	Unified Extensible Firmware Interface
UPS	Uninterruptable Power Supply
URI	Uniform Resource Identifier
URL	Universal Resource Locator
USB	Universal Serial Bus USB
UTP	Unshielded Twisted Pair
VDE	Virtual Desktop Environment
VDI	Virtual Desktop Infrastructure
VLAN	Virtual Local Area Network
VLSM	Variable Length Subnet Masking
VM	Virtual Machine
VoIP	Voice over IP
VPN	Virtual Private Network

VTC	Video Teleconferencing
WAF	Web Application Firewall
WAP	Wireless Access Point
WEP	Wired Equivalent Privacy
WIDS	Wireless Intrusion Detection System
WIPS	Wireless Intrusion Prevention System
WORM	Write Once Read Many
WPA	WiFi Protected Access
WPA2	WiFi Protected Access 2
WPS	WiFi Protected Setup
WTLS	Wireless TLS
XML	Extensible Markup Language
XOR	Exclusive Or
XSRF	Cross-site Request Forgery
XSS	Cross-site Scripting

References:

- http://www.ciscopress.com/store/cisco-firepower-threat-defense-ftd-configuration-and-9781587144806?ranMID=24808
- http://www.ciscopress.com/store/ccna-security-210-260-portable-command-guide-9781587205750?ranMID=24808
- http://www.ciscopress.com/store/ccna-security-210-260-complete-video-course-9780134499314?ranMID=24808
- https://learningnetwork.cisco.com/docs/DOC-3249
- https://learningnetwork.cisco.com/docs/DOC-4144
- http://www.ciscopress.com/store/ccna-security-210-260-official-cert-guide-9781587205668?ranMID=24808
- https://learningnetworkstore.cisco.com/on-demand-e-learning/implementing-cisco-network-security-iins-v3-0-elt-iins-v3-0-019451
- https://learningnetworkstore.cisco.com/on-demand-e-learning/implementing-cisco-network-security-iins-v3-0-elt-iins-v3-0-019451
- http://www.ciscopress.com/store/ccna-security-210-260-complete-video-course-9780134499314?ranMID=24808
- http://www.ciscopress.com/store/ccna-security-210-260-portable-command-guide-9781587205750?ranMID=24808
- http://www.ciscopress.com/store/cisco-firepower-threat-defense-ftd-configuration-and-9781587144806?ranMID=24808
- https://learningnetworkstore.cisco.com/on-demand-e-learning/implementing-cisco-network-security-iins-v3-0-elt-iins-v3-0-019451
- https://learningnetwork.cisco.com/docs/DOC-1566
- https://learningnetwork.cisco.com/docs/DOC-1565
- https://learningnetwork.cisco.com/docs/DOC-4144
- http://www.ciscopress.com/store/ccna-security-210-260-complete-video-course-9780134499314?ranMID=24808
- http://www.ciscopress.com/store/ccna-security-210-260-portable-command-guide-9781587205750?ranMID=24808
- https://learningnetworkstore.cisco.com/on-demand-e-learning/implementing-cisco-network-security-iins-v3-0-elt-iins-v3-0-019451
- https://learningnetwork.cisco.com/docs/DOC-3249
- https://learningnetwork.cisco.com/docs/DOC-3713

About Our Products

Other products from IPSpecialist LTD regarding Cisco technology are:

- CCNA Routing & Switching Technology Workbook
- CCNA Service Provider Technology Workbook
- CCNA CyberOps SECFND Technology Workbook
- CCDA Technology Workbook
- CCDP Technology Workbook
- CCNP Route Technology Workbook
- CCNP Switch Technology Workbook
- CCNP Troubleshoot Technology Workbook
- CCNP Security SENSS Technology Workbook
- CCNP Security SIMOS Technology Workbook
- CCNP Security SITCS Technology Workbook
- CCNP Security SISAS Technology Workbook

Upcoming products from IPSpecialist LTD regarding Cisco technology are:

CCNA CyberOps SECFND Technology Workbook

CCNA Wireless Technology Workbook

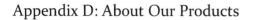

Note from the Author:

Reviews are gold to authors! If you have enjoyed this book and it has helped you along your certification, would you consider rating and reviewing it?

Link to Product Page:

www.ingramcontent.com/pod-product-compliance
Lightning Source LLC
Chambersburg PA
CBHW081456050326
40690CB00015B/2815
* 9 7 8 1 7 9 7 6 0 4 3 2 9 *